# Building Foundations for Communication & Building a Speech

SHELDON METCALFE

SEVENTH EDITION

Timothy Thompson | Andrew Kahl | Jennifer Kafka Smith

CENGAGE Learning™

Australia • Brazil • Japan • Korea • Mexico • Singapore • Spain • United Kingdom • United States

CENGAGE
Learning™

**Building Foundations for Communication &
Building a Speech, SEVENTH EDITION**

SHELDON METCALFE
Timothy Thompson | Andrew Kahl |
Jennifer Kafka Smith

Executive Editors:
 Maureen Staudt
 Michael Stranz

Project Development Manager:
 Linda deStefano

Senior Marketing Coordinators:
 Sara Mercurio

Senior Production / Manufacturing Manager:
 Donna M. Brown

PreMedia Services Supervisor:
 Joel Brennecke

Rights & Permissions Specialist:
 Kalina Hintz
 Todd Osborne

Cover Image:

 Getty Images*

* Unless otherwise noted, all cover images used
by Custom Solutions, a part of Cengage
Learning, have been supplied courtesy of Getty
Images with the exception of the Earthview
cover image, which has been supplied by the
National Aeronautics and Space Administration
(NASA).

For product information and technology assistance, contact us at
**Cengage Learning Customer & Sales Support, 1-800-354-9706**

For permission to use material from this text or product,
submit all requests online at **cengage.com/permissions**
Further permissions questions can be emailed to
**permissionrequest@cengage.com**

ISBN-13: 978-1-4266-5043-7

ISBN-10: 1-4266-5043-4

**Cengage Learning**
5191 Natorp Boulevard
Mason, Ohio 45040
USA

Cengage Learning is a leading provider of customized learning solutions with
office locations around the globe, including Singapore, the United Kingdom,
Australia, Mexico, Brazil, and Japan. Locate your local office at:
**international.cengage.com/region**

Cengage Learning products are represented in Canada by Nelson Education, Ltd.

For your lifelong learning solutions, visit **custom.cengage.com**

Visit our corporate website at **cengage.com**

Printed in the United States of America

# Preface

Human communication is a dynamic field. Evolving technologies and shifting social currents are blurring distinctions among pedagogical approaches to rhetorical communication. At the same time, schools and training programs are responding to demands for learning strategies that support new patterns of human interaction. Courses focusing on specific skills often lack the scope students require in order to learn to communicate effectively in today's complex world.

The purpose of *Building Foundations for Communication* is to provide an overview of the study of human communication and to expand on materials already addressed in the text *Building a Speech*. This companion text employs a wider perspective on the study of human communication while comprehensively addressing issues of perception, interpersonal communication and the mass media appropriate to an introductory course. We hope that this additional resource will allow instructors greater flexibility in course planning without sacrificing the comprehensive approach to speech construction already provided by the *Building a Speech* text. For students, we hope that this supplement will help to provide a resource for broader study in a format that is both readable and accessible.

# Contents

## Chapter 4: Mass Communication    71

CHAPTER

# Defining Patterns of Communication

**Andrew Kahl**

## CHAPTER OBJECTIVES

After reading this chapter you will be able to:

1. Analyze the ways in which communication patterns are chosen and used;

2. Organize communication patterns around a circular communication model;

3. Describe common communication patterns;

4. Recognize the characteristics that make each communication pattern unique.

## Key Terms

| | | |
|---|---|---|
| Content messages | Mass Communication | Relational messages |
| Culture | Motives | Relationships |
| Dyad | Multicultural Communication | Role-playing |
| Gatekeepers | Organizational Communication | Self-concept |
| Interpersonal Communication | Patterns of Communication | Self-disclosure |
| Interview | Perceptions | Self-esteem |
| Intrapersonal Communication | Presentational Communication | Small Group Communication |

Frank calls several friends to invite them over to watch the NCAA basketball finals on his new HD flat screen TV. He mentions to Bill that he could invite anyone else who might want to come along. Bill extends that invitation by posting a note on the activities bulletin board in his fraternity house where John reads about the "party" and creates a Facebook Event Invitation to let all of his friends know. Ricky reads about the event on-line while he is finishing up his retrospective of alternative bands for the college radio station. He mentions in passing that he has just gotten word of a basketball blowout party and gives out Frank's address on the air. Kelly hears about the gathering on the radio, instant messages the address to her boyfriend's mobile phone, and persuades three friends in her biology study group to blow off studying and come with her to the big party. By game time, four hundred people have gathered outside of Frank's apartment building. In a desperate attempt to gain control of the situation, Frank announces to the gathering crowd that there is no party and asks the people to leave. As the disappointed crowd disperses, Frank ponders the appearance of a mob on his doorstep. Finally, he wonders why Bill never showed up to watch the big game.

This example may seem absurd, but it illustrates the complex blend of communication patterns that we use to present, gather and process messages in the world around us. Whenever we pick up a ringing phone, flip on a television, send an e-mail message, or tap a friend on the shoulder we are opening a new pattern of communication. The purpose of this chapter is to strengthen your awareness of the various patterns we all rely on for social communication. We will explore some of the common patterns that emerge, consider the factors that help us to choose a particular pattern, and discuss strategies for using these patterns effectively.

Later in this text, the first chapter of *Building a Speech* will include a detailed discussion of the Circular Communication Model. This model helps us to understand the flow of activity that allows any human communication to take place, and it provides us with terminology that makes this transaction easier to describe. For each of the patterns we will define in this chapter, the

Figure 1-1

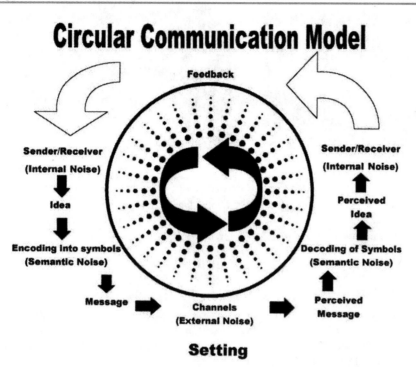

**Circular Communication Model**

Feedback

Sender/Receiver
(Internal Noise)

Sender/Receiver
(Internal Noise)

Idea

Perceived
Idea

Encoding into symbols
(Semantic Noise)

Decoding of Symbols
(Semantic Noise)

Message

Channels
(External Noise)

Perceived
Message

**Setting**

terminology and structure of this communication model can be applied. It is an essential road map for understanding the flow of information. But in much the same way that a roadmap fails to show a disoriented traveler local landmarks and topography, the model does not illustrate the whole story of communication. All the patterns we will explore include critical elements of this model; senders and receivers, symbols, encoding and decoding, messages, channels, feedback, settings, and noise. The ways in which these elements interact help us to define how each pattern works.

## ▊▎ DEFINING PATTERNS OF COMMUNICATION

**Patterns of communication** are the ways in which we choose to organize any exchange of messages. In our daily lives, these patterns often emerge automatically. By turning on a television, we choose to link ourselves to messages generated for mass communication. Greeting an old friend awakens our interpersonal skills, while calling a meeting to order might engage social behaviors appropriate for presentational speaking. Sometimes these patterns are carefully cultivated. For example, Microsoft Corporation develops an advertising campaign, or the President carefully rehearses the State of the Union address, because they both want to control the organization, perception and response to messages they are creating. Regardless of the amount of preparation involved, a decision must be made about how to organize the movement

of information.  This decision requires answering a few key questions.  Who is communicating?  How many people will be involved?  What is the relationship between them?  Why are they communicating?  What messages will be delivered?  And finally, where and when will the messages be exchanged?

## WHO IS COMMUNICATING?

Who are you?  Your answers to this question could be complicated.  You may start with your name, but the question goes much deeper.  **Self-concept** is defined as how we think and feel about ourselves, and it is the first step in human communication.  Our self-awareness is linked to many things, our experiences, the roles we play in our lives, our relationships; all of these factors help us to form a picture of ourselves and our place in the world.  How we perceive ourselves and how we are perceived by others, are critical parts of the communication process because they help us to understand the motives and desires that drive us to communicate.

We view the world through many filters.  Our **perceptions** are the details that we select, organize, and interpret from our surroundings and they have a direct impact on how we understand what we experience.  A young woman with an eating disorder might interpret the question "Have you been working out?" in a very different way than a body builder.  The self-perceptions that filter this question could lead to despair and anxiety from one listener and a sense of pride from the other.  Our self-esteem also guides us to, or away from, different communication situations. For example, how much more difficult would it be for the young woman with body image issues to appear in front of a large audience than for the body builder?  For both of these individuals, self-concept and self-esteem will have a strong influence on the ways in which they choose to communicate with others.

## HOW MANY COMMUNICATORS?

For most of us, telling a funny story to two friends in your living room is much easier than standing in front of a crowd of two hundred strangers to tell the same story as part of a public speech.  Why does this change of audience and circumstance make any difference at all?  To begin with, increasing the size of the group requires a change from an *interpersonal* pattern to a *presentational* pattern of communication.  The message may remain the same, but "stage fright" and the need for effective delivery skills create a variety of new challenges for the speaker.

Shifting the number of communicators also changes how we absorb and respond to *feedback*. For example, two friends talking about current health care issues have little difficulty exchanging ideas and listening to one another. Five people with diverse opinions on the subject might have a more difficult time maintaining a coherent and civil conversation that allows responses from all members of the group. What about fifty people? At a certain point, it becomes impossible for all voices to be heard. If certain individuals do not begin to guide the process, chaos will ensue. An activist promoting universal health care initiatives might be able to address hundreds of people at a public rally, but in that situation the same individual cannot possibly monitor and respond to the individual

feedback of eight hundred listeners. The number of people who are involved in the event restricts the range of communication patterns that can be constructively applied to the situation. Mass media provides the most extreme example of this connection between audience size and feedback. For a television broadcast, one particular viewpoint on health care reform might reach millions of viewers, but only in a pattern that severely restricts—or eliminates entirely—any immediate audience response.

## WHAT IS THE RELATIONSHIP?

We communicate differently with different people. For example, you might speak more casually when having a personal conversation with your brother than you would in a more formal conversation with your boss or when making a presentation to the mayor's advisory council. Social positioning has a direct influence on how we behave and the relationships that we perceive ourselves to have with other people. Arnold Schwarzenegger has been a body builder, an actor, and a powerful Hollywood producer, but he can now add the role of Governor of California to his list of credentials. The actor's screen roles define many of our perceptions of him, and certainly play a role in the kind of media attention he receives. While running for office, Schwarzenegger could rely on constant media coverage because of his celebrity status, but now that he has won the governorship his relationships with the media and his electorate are tempered by the constraints, choices, and responsibilities that define his new role.

Relationships are defined as ongoing interaction patterns that are mutually established and developed between two people. They are habits of interaction based on roles that we agree to play in our lives. Today, you have probably "played" a variety of roles. As a result, perceptions that other people have about you and your relationships to them will vary based on the consistency of your role-playing. For example, in the company of your biology classmates you are likely to be perceived as a student; at least in part, because you are likely to behave like one. When you go to your job, you could be an employer or an employee. Either one of these roles would require you to select a different pattern of appropriate behavior. When you are at home, you may play the role of parent, partner, or child. The relationships that we form and the roles that we play help us to define ourselves and form our

### An Ambiguous Script

A-Hello.
B-Ah, I was hoping you would be here…
A-Really?
B-Of course. Why wouldn't I be?
A-Right.
B- I haven't seen you in ages!
A-Well, ever since last year –
B-Yeah. Yeah, I know…
A-I meant to talk to you about that. Perhaps, when we have more time -
B-Don't worry about it.
(pause)
A-Well.
B-Really. Why don't I give you a call next week?
A-Um-hmm.
B-I've got to go right now.
A-Is your number the same?
B-Um-hmm.
A-Good luck.
B-Thanks.

With a partner, try speaking the dialogue above out loud. If you had to define who they were and what the relationship was between them, how would you describe it? The exercise above is sometimes referred to as an *ambiguous script* and it helps to illustrate the importance of relationships and the messages that unfold underneath our use of spoken language. By manipulating the assignment of roles and relationships in the conversation above it is possible to make the same spoken conversation take on completely different meanings. The relationships we have in our own lives have an equally powerful impact on how our messages are understood.

own self-image. Communication is the tool that we use to develop, reinforce, or change these defining relationships.

As you may have noticed in the ambiguous script exercise, language is a flexible tool of communication. We can bend it to have a range of meanings in a variety of different circumstances. What makes verbal communication specific is the shared sense of meaning created between people who share a set of common experiences and perceptions. When we understand our relationships in a particular context, our use of language can take on deeper and more subtle meanings.

## WHY ARE WE COMMUNICATING?

What do we want? What do we hope to gain? What barriers or advantages do we anticipate? What values guide our actions and fuel our motives?

**Motives** are the goals and desires that drive us to communicate. The conversations that we choose to engage in are directly linked to our motives. We all have goals that we hope to achieve. We may dream of wealth or fame, a celebrity lifestyle, or unattainable romance. More often, we are motivated by immediate needs and desires. We interact with people on a daily basis because we need or want things from them.

Think about the casual interactions that you have had today. Pick any one of them and ask yourself *why* you engaged in that conversation. Did you hope or expect to gain something? It may have been an immediate reward; fries with that order, approval, or advice, directions to the grocery store, or even just a smile of appreciation. Your conversation may also have served a long-term goal: "I want a promotion so I will try to make a good impression on the boss," or "I want this person to be attracted to me." Our motives are not always easy to define, recognize, or understand, but they are always present, and they never fail to make an impact on the ways in which we communicate.

The choice of a pattern for communication is a social contract. It is an agreement within a group or organization, or between two people, or between an audience and a speaker or content provider. The contract is based on mutual rewards. Everyone who chooses to participate has something to gain. We listen to a speaker because she has given us an incentive to listen; we participate in a group discussion or make eye contact with the attractive person across the room because we have an agenda to pursue. We watch *American Idol* or the evening news because we believe we have something to gain from the experience. We also have freedom of choice. We can ignore the speaker and talk to our friend in the audience, disrupt the group discussion, ignore the flirtatious glance, or change the channel on the television if the pattern does not appeal to our motives.

**WHAT IS THE MESSAGE?**

> "You have a piece of spinach stuck in your teeth."
> "The building is on fire!"
> "Could you direct me to the restroom, please?"
> "I would like to make an announcement..."

How does the nature or urgency of each of the messages above change the way in which it will be communicated? The content of a message may have a strong influence on how we choose to express it. What we need to say, or hear, helps us to decide how public or private a conversation needs to be, who needs to hear it, and how urgently it needs to be conveyed. That decision affects our choice of communication patterns. Consider how choosing too public or too private a pattern for each of the examples above would change the situation.

**WHERE AND WHEN WILL MESSAGES BE EXCHANGED?**

The circumstances and environment in which communication takes place also help us to define what patterns we will choose. To consider the circumstances we need to look at the events that have lead us to this moment of communication. What motives and expectations are at work? Do the communicators have a shared sense of the purpose of their interchange or are they responding to conflicting motivations? Has this interchange taken place by accident, or by design? All of these factors affect the ways in which the communicators behave and the role relationships they assume. If you were to meet another student from your class outside of the classroom, the circumstances of that meeting might change how you chose to interact, and the roles that you might assume. If you met while one of you was waiting on the other's table in a restaurant, or on a dance floor at a club, or in a hospital maternity area, the nature of your communication might be very different than when you interact as peers in a classroom. At the same time, the physical environment

8

in which that meeting occurs will also exert an influence on communication. Our physical surroundings have a direct impact on our frame of mind and consequently on our approach to communication.

## Types of Patterns

If we use the number of communicators as a guide and recognize the impact of some of the questions we have just asked, then defining patterns of communication becomes relatively easy. Now we can take a closer look at each of the communication patterns and talk about strategies for using them effectively. These patterns include **intrapersonal communication**, **interpersonal communication**, **small group communication**, **organizational communication**, **presentational communication**, **mass communication**, and **multi-cultural communication**.

### INTRAPERSONAL COMMUNICATION

Have you ever talked to yourself? We all spend time reviewing or anticipating conversations or activities in our lives. While riding in an elevator, a nervous job applicant might imagine or even rehearse the first moments of an interview. As you walk the eight blocks to the gas station, you might rehearse the conversation you plan to have later with your sister who borrows the car and never bothers to fill the tank. As we imagine these conversations we may even fill in the responses we anticipate hearing, or adjust the tone or intensity of what we plan to say.

Intrapersonal communication refers to the communication process that happens within your own thoughts. As the sole communicator involved in this internalized "conversation," you must play the roles of both the sender and the receiver; suggesting and evaluating ideas, constructing messages, and developing feedback in response to your own internal communication. This internal dialogue is an essential element of our ability to reason and to solve problems. It is the first stage in critically analyzing ideas and generating responses. We translate our ideas into symbols; words, numbers, even gestures or facial expressions. While we may not literally "talk to ourselves" as part of this process, we certainly engage in an internal conversation as a way of stimulating and evaluating our own ideas. Brainstorming, keeping lists, writing in a journal or working out a math equation on a piece of paper are all methods for supporting intrapersonal communication. They allow us to reason, problem solve and examine our thinking objectively in ways that reinforce our comprehension and use of information from the world around us.

### INTERPERSONAL COMMUNICATION

Contact with only one other person is a common social interchange for most of us. Generally, we do not spend the majority of our time in a large groups or speaking to crowds. However, we all spend some time in one-on-one conversations. As a result, we tend to have more experience and familiarity with interpersonal contact than with any other social communication pattern. **Interpersonal communication** is the study of interactions between two people used to develop, maintain, or dissolve

In the 2000 film Cast Away, Tom Hanks plays a man trapped on a desert island. In his struggles to survive and overcome his loneliness he creates a companion, a volleyball he names Wilson. His conversations with Wilson, and the internal debates that he shares, are good examples of intrapersonal communication. We all engage in internal debates to consider different perspectives, to solve problems, and to try to make reasonable estimates of the outcomes of our actions. Intrapersonal communication is a critical part of how we reason and gain a clearer understanding of the world around us. It helps us to generate ideas and messages in order to communicate with other people.

10

relationships. The basic building block for this communication pattern is called a **dyad**, a term derived from the Greek term for a pair. A dyad is the interplay between two people that creates a relationship. The Circular Communication Model that begins this chapter provides a graphic illustration of a dyad, with two sender/receivers participating in a communication transaction.

There are times when our contact with someone may seem impersonal. For example, contact with a bank teller or a cashier at the grocery store may involve a polite social exchange but is not automatically the basis of an involved relationship. These surface transactions depend on **content messages,** the surface exchange of information, more than **relational messages,** which reinforce or adjust the rules of interaction between people. In these impersonal interactions, messages are used to complete a necessary social transaction but a personal investment in the relationship is not emphasized.[1]

Most of our casual social contacts do not fully explore the potential of interpersonal communication. They do not require a strong investment in a relationship. By playing the role of customer, or bank teller, we are able to take advantage of a kind of social shorthand. Following the rules of prescribed social behavior allows us to transact business without much *self-disclosure.* In other words, we do not need to express much personal information in order to get what we need. **Self-disclosure** is the sharing of personal information with the people we trust and it is our principle tool for managing relationships. We share personal information in order to reinforce our connections to other people. When we feel the need to distance ourselves from other people, we do this by reducing the flow of shared personal information.

By contrast to our more casual social connections, interpersonal communication within close relationships can be complex and demanding. The intimacy of face to face contact, the adoption of well-established or dynamic roles, the two-way simultaneous exchange of messages, the subtleties of conveyed meaning and intention, and the impact of the process of communication within ongoing relationships are all emphasized in the study of interpersonal communication.[2] Nonverbal cues take on added significance. Eye contact, a smile, nuances of voice inflection, and body language all transmit information about our emotional state and degree of interpersonal involvement.[3] The greater the degree of self-disclosure within an interpersonal relationship the more subtle and dynamic this process becomes. If you think about the people who are closest to you—and in whom you have the most trust—they are likely to be the same people with whom you most readily share personal or intimate details of your life.

We invest in our relationships with other people to varying degrees, but our close personal relationships can have a powerful influence on our behavior. We allow important interpersonal

### Content and Relational Messages

Karin has a very close friendship with Robert, but an extremely uneasy relationship with Robert's girlfriend, Jeannette. When the three of them are together, communication takes place in a variety of ways. On one level, a friendly exchange of content messages takes place as they discuss what movie the three of them would like to see. But woven into that conversation are subtle cues that reinforce and inform the relationships between them. Jeanette reinforces her romantic connection to Robert by flirting with him more openly then usual, particularly since she feels threatened by Karin's friendship with Robert. She latches onto his arm, using body language to assert the nature of her relationship with Robert. Karin's sarcastic rejection of Jeanette's suggestion to see "something romantic," carries relational messages to both Robert and Jeanette. Robert might be put off or embarrassed by Jeanette's forward behavior, or he might resent Karin's disregard for Jeanette's feelings. Either way, his responses are based on his past relationships with both women and will directly affect his relationships with them in the future.

relationships to affect us emotionally and to influence our actions. *Self-disclosure,* that process of entrusting information to the people who are closest to us, can leave us vulnerable. Criticism or praise from your parents, siblings, or close friends can have a deep impact and often stimulates strong reactions. A teenager responds angrily because she feels hurt when her parents speak critically of a new boyfriend. A high school student might adhere closely to the fads and behavior embraced by classmates in order to "blend in." Peer pressure to fit in socially comes from a competitive desire to win approval and establish or strengthen relationships. An older brother's ridicule can be crushing for a young child eager to earn respect or acceptance. When we "take things personally" we are really allowing ourselves to respond to relational messages that we feel are important.

Good interpersonal communicators listen well and are perceptive in recognizing motives and non-verbal cues from other people and in themselves. They use strategies designed to support the communication transaction and to further their own goals when dealing with other people. They also take steps to ensure the cooperation of others and to limit antagonism or hostility that could deflect effective communication or erode constructive relationships.

One specialized form of interpersonal communication is an **interview**. We use this word to describe conversations with a purpose in which one person takes primary responsibility for directing the development of conversation.[4] Interviews take place to accomplish a variety of objectives. They can be used to gather or give out information, provide counseling and personal support, deliver persuasive messages or evaluate factors such as job performance.

Employment interviews are among the most familiar—and most nerve-wracking—interviews most of us will experience. However, careful preparation and a clear understanding of the interviewer's objective can eliminate much uncertainty and anxiety. In order for a job interview to be successful, information gathered by the interviewer needs to match a set of expectations. Anticipating what an interviewer is seeking—from an employee or potential colleague—and disclosing information about you that meets those expectations is useful. Perhaps of greater importance, is the ability to project confidence and present your self without being evasive. Confident, positive self-disclosure with an interviewer creates a strong and memorable impression and may be the best course to a successful job interview.

## SMALL GROUP COMMUNICATION

Small group communication involves interpersonal communication among three or more people who perceive themselves as a group working toward a shared purpose or goal.[5] A group of students from a German class who eat lunch together to practice speaking *auf Deutsch*, a committee assigned to resolve complaints about parking on campus, or a team in an emergency room extracting a bullet from a teenager's spine all depend on small group communication to solve problems and coordinate individual efforts. This pattern of communication can become extremely complicated when a cluster of people attempt to engage and influence one another directly and simultaneously. It might even seem chaotic, but if all members are able to contribute and support the collective work of the group, small group communication can be an extremely efficient and constructive communication environment. Unfortunately, if the size of the group increases to the point where

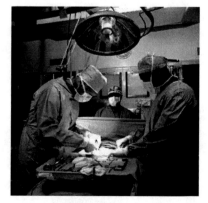

individual contact and feedback are no longer possible among all members of the group, or if the group's unity of purpose is lost, then the constructive dynamics of small group communication begin to unravel.

With the right combination of people, small group communication can be a very efficient way to exchange ideas within a group that is unified by a sense of purpose and still small enough to maintain mutual contact. In much the same way that intrapersonal communication allows us to brainstorm internally, testing ideas and concepts against our own critical voice or bolstering support from our own internal dialogue, small group communication offers a forum for spontaneity, creativity, impulse and immediate critical insight that is difficult to achieve with either a larger or a smaller group of people.

## ORGANIZATIONAL COMMUNICATION

Organizational communication focuses on the dynamics of communication related to structured groups. In any organization, whether it is Apple Corporation, the Internal Revenue Service, or the local community association, structures must be created to allow the exchange and control of messages "into, through, and out of the organization."[6] The form of these structures varies based on the size of the organization, the goals and needs of its members and its established identity, or **culture**.

The size of the organization often dictates the way in which information is managed. Large organizations like the Federal Highway Administration or Wal-Mart Corporation, for example, require complex hierarchies to ensure that all members of the organization receive, generate, and exchange information efficiently. The Red Cross is an international organization that works on the local level to provide disaster relief, coordinate volunteers, sponsor blood drives, and provide educational services. A decision made by the director of the Red Cross must travel through a series of national, regional, and local administrators and managers before it can have an impact on the local activities of Red Cross employees and volunteers. By contrast, a local plumber with only a few employees can pass along a decision simply by providing a set of verbal instructions to his work crew. In both cases, a consistent process of communication indicates how the organization remains connected to all of its members.

When evaluating organizational communication it is sometimes useful to think of an organization as a single person. Like people, organizations engage in internal and external communication; balancing debates and messages within the organization against public communication designed to coherently present a unified image. A person's intrapersonal thoughts can remain internal until there is a conscious choice to articulate them. The same is true of organizations. They use internal communication tools like memos, e-mail, and staff conferences to guide, or limit, the creation of messages for release to the general public. External communication can take the form of advertising, press releases, interviews or publicly accessible records.

Another factor that affects organizational communication is the purpose for which information is being used. For example, the manufacturer of a new computer chip, like AMD or Intel, might need to protect details about a new product in order to turn a profit. In this case, controlling information and keeping it within the organization becomes a priority. Communication among employees working on the chip would need to remain open, but external communication with the general public or other organizations would need to be filtered to protect the profits of the business. Even within the organization, details of the computer chip design might be kept on a "need to know" basis to reduce the security risk. This contrast between private internal communication and public external messages is an important part of understanding organizational communication.

In a professional setting, businesses often use the term culture when defining expectations for social interaction within a company or among employees in a professional field. In December of 2001, Enron Corporation, one of the largest energy companies in the United States, filed for bankruptcy, leaving thousands of employees out of work and tens of thousands of investors holding stock that proceeded to drop from a share price of $85 to a share price of $1 in less than a month. In the aftermath of the Enron scandal, many critics and analysts blamed the corporate culture of Enron for creating an environment with a "survival-of–the-fittest mindset" in which the organization rewarded highly competitive people who were less likely to share power, authority, or information.[7] The corruption of the company's culture helped to create a management atmosphere in which greed and deceit became accepted norms. In the wake of the Enron scandal, investors and corporations alike have begun to look more closely at ways to reinforce ethical behavior in the development of corporate cultures.

By contrast, 3M Corporation has maintained a steady corporate presence for more than a century with innovations in abrasives, adhesives, health, consumer and office products. This global corporation also cultivates an organizational culture centered on innovation and the conscious development of employee and customer loyalty. The company's formula for success owes much to a history of inspired leadership and the inclusion of a shared value system into the day-to-day activities of the organization. [8]

## PRESENTATIONAL COMMUNICATION

The Vice-President delivering a speech to the National Press Club, your aunt presenting a eulogy during a family funeral, or a fellow student welcoming new members to a campus organization, are all examples of public speaking situations. Here are some other examples that you might not have considered: Lewis Black delivering a comedy routine to a live audience, a public performance by Cirque du Soleil, Kanye West in concert, or a bus driver announcing the next stop along the local bus line. Each of these examples creates relationships between presenters and a live audience. As a result, they all qualify as examples of presentational communication.

We are all familiar with speeches, but asked for a definition, most of us would have a hard time explaining the difference between a public speech, based in traditions of oratory, and other forms of presentational communication that owe more to the performing arts of theatre, music and dance. Any performance that connects an individual to a live audience is presentational.

What sets public speaking apart from other presentational forms are the personal exposure of the speaker and the nature of the messages being delivered. To deliver a formal speech requires planning, good research, practice and, above all, nerve. In the performing arts there is typically a shift of perception between yourself and your audience; a pretense of character, or a delivery focused on music or movement. Performing artists creating an artistic event expect the audience to focus attention on "the piece" rather then the artist, even if "the piece" *is* the artist. In public speaking there is no guise, no distraction, and no pretense. There is only you, your message, and an audience.

This direct relationship sets up expectations in the minds of the audience and magnifies anxieties for many speakers. An audience expects a speaker to guide them through a message, to express ideas coherently and to pursue an objective, be it to inform, entertain, persuade or excite the audience.[9] Giving a speech requires being responsible to your audience and asserting your message with clarity and poise. A speaker may fear judgment, failure or ridicule, but these fears are often not rational. The adrenalin response associated with giving a speech—butterflies in the stomach, dry mouth, and sweaty palms—is a physical reaction to danger. You are unlikely to be physically threatened as a result of a public speech, but your body still prepares for that fight or flight moment.

The companion text to this chapter, *Building a Speech,* focuses on the skills and strategies needed to deliver effective public speeches. For now, it is worth noting that public speaking is a unique form of communication. It places greater demands on a single communicator than any other pattern we have discussed and requires more preparation, confidence and acquired skill. Improving public speaking is a constructive way to both measure and develop skills that can be used across the whole range of patterns for communication presented in this chapter.

## MASS COMMUNICATION

The *New York Times*, CNN, *The Star*, DirecTV, 20th Century Fox Motion Pictures, the Cartoon Network, National Public Radio, MTV and even an Internet browser like Yahoo or Google, all share a common structure. As "content providers" in mass communication they all use technology to link a message generated and edited by a complex organization to a scattered and diverse audience.[10] Increasingly, we have come to refer to this conglomeration simply as "the media."

Beginning with the invention of the printing press by Johannes Gutenberg in the middle of the 15th Century, people have invented increasing more efficient ways to rapidly circulate information. From published pamphlets, to dime novels, motion pictures, radio, television, and now digital technology and the Internet, mass communication continues to evolve with remarkable speed. We now take for granted live news reports from Hong Kong, or up-to-the-minute Internet coverage of the Olympic Games. In the process, we often forget the impact exerted by the organizations that provide, control, and profit from the business of mass media.

Mass communication is defined by the presence of a number of characteristics. First, it requires some form of technology to amplify messages. For example, a printing press, a motion picture projector, or your Pentium processor all increase the potential reach of any generated message.

Second, mass communication requires a complex organization. Brian Williams, Oprah Winfrey, Katie Couric, and the latest Survivor Cast aren't broadcasting all by themselves. They are surrounded by production staff and support personnel without whom media companies could not function. What they say—and what we see and hear—has already been filtered by a variety of content watchdogs, often referred to as **gatekeepers**. Gatekeepers control the flow of information, evaluating messages, and either approving them or rejecting them based on quality of content, relevance, accuracy, or entertainment value. They may also promote or reject messages that serve the best interests of the media organization they represent. For example, NBC is a subsidiary of General Electric. In news stories that involve General Electric or its subsidiaries, gatekeepers working for NBC's network news programs must balance the interests of their parent company against issues of free speech and journalistic integrity.

A third factor to consider is that mass communication is big business. Whether it is done through print, television, radio or motion pictures, reaching millions of people with a message is a very expensive process. However, providing access to those millions can also be a very profitable business. During the 1890's the Sears Roebuck Company produced a seven hundred and seventy page mail order catalog and shipped it—free of charge—to millions of homes across the country. The "Consumer's Guide" took advantage of innovations in mass production, printing technology and reliable mail service, to create the world's largest and most profitable mail order company. The Catalog sold everything from tapioca to covered wagons and became required reading in households across America.[11]

A fourth characteristic is that messages cannot be specialized based on immediate feedback from an audience. Any viewer, listener, or reader, will receive the same message. In mass communication, one size fits all. Even on the Internet, where interactivity has allowed for new levels of personal choice, web pages designed for a mass audience deliver consistent content to any user. Websites have allowed mass communication to specialize and serve niche markets. Visitors to Amazon.com or eBay may be able to find just the product that they are looking for, but the same choices are available to any user who visits these sites.

The increasing popularity of the Internet has created new variables in mass communication, bypassing many of the cost and content restrictions found with other media forms. Web sites are relatively cheap to create and maintain. They allow information to reach a potentially massive audience without the same content controls, editorial scrutiny, and profit restrictions that traditional media organizations impose. Whether this freedom and flexibility will always be characteristic of the Internet is anyone's guess, but the creation of the World Wide Web certainly continues to revolutionize the ways in which information can be transmitted to a global audience.

## MULTI-CULTURAL COMMUNICATION

An American businessman fumbles to shake hands with his Japanese host who has greeted him with a courteous bow. A British visitor to Iran is overwhelmed by the sense that people stand too close together when they talk. As a result, he finds himself continuously stepping backwards during conversations. A medical student from Ghana visits a Canadian home for the elderly and is appalled to find family elders living in isolation, apparently abandoned by their disrespectful children. The distinctions that hamper communication between cultures are not limited to languages barriers or geography. They are also intrinsic to the values and perceptions that shape our cultural traditions.

**Multi-cultural communication** focuses on the ways in which mutual understanding of contrasting cultural norms can improve social relationships. Unlike the earlier patterns we have discussed, multi-cultural communication is not dependent on a particular number of participants. It is limited instead by the individual perceptions of the communicators. The willingness of a speaker or listener to look beyond personal, ethnic, or social norms is the only restriction to multicultural communication.

Within the confines of the United States we experience this clash of cultural norms, but we often fail to look beyond socialized stereotypes based on race or ethnicity. Negative attitudes and distrust for unfamiliar traditions leave us isolated from cultural groups with whom we share our schools, neighborhoods, and workplaces. In our ethnically diverse nation, the social values that underpin our identities are never far from the surface. Looking around your classroom, you may be faced with an array of unfamiliar cultural traditions. How is it possible to reach across that divide? Is there any point in trying to do so?

Individuals learn the norms and rules of appropriate interpersonal conduct, and effective interpersonal behavior, within the webs of their culture.[12] In this country, we tend to view culture as inextricably linked to ethnicity, but cultural traditions are far more complicated than skin color or country of origin. One simple definition of **culture** is that it is a reflection of our social loyalties. Some of these may be chosen, such as our professions, friendships, and aesthetic preferences for certain kinds of music or art. Other social loyalties may be involuntary; ethnicity, gender, and age, for example. The combination of these loyalties is what creates our cultural identity.

Street culture is an example of a social group with more links to variables of economic status, social intolerance, and class warfare, then to ethnicity. The defiant values reflected first in rap, and later, in hip-hop music resonate across ethnic lines because they speak to current social experiences as much as to heredity.

Multiculturalism informs all of the other patterns of communication because our social loyalties are a basic part of how we perceive ourselves. Cultural identity is a component of self-concept, and informs both our personal relationships and our public discourse. Social and cultural biases shift with world events and private experiences to reflect the tensions and attitudes of a diverse world. Just as in interpersonal relationships, our cultures shift in and out of conflict with one another based on the ways in which communication is used to strengthen or limit relationships between socially defined groups.

For immediate release --September 14, 2001.
Contact Bob Brammer, 515-281-6699

**ATTORNEY GENERAL TOM MILLER ISSUED THE FOLLOWING STATE-MENT REGARDING THE POSSIBILITY OF REPRISALS AGAINST IO-WANS OF ARAB-AMERICAN AND OTHER RELIGIOUS OR ETHNIC BACKGROUNDS**

The Attorney General advised people to report any harassment or suspicious activities to local police.

Miller's statement: "As shock turns to anger about these horrible acts of terror, we must remain united as Iowans and Americans. We must hold on to our best values. The anger we feel toward the perpetrators of the terror must not be allowed to endanger innocent fellow Iowans. The rights and security of all our citizens must be fully respected, regardless of race, nationality, religion or ethnic background.
"We must bear in mind that these crimes are the responsibility of the individuals who committed them, not of ethnic or religious groups. Americans of every ethnic and religious heritage share intense depths of pain and anger at this attack, but now some feel deep anxiety about becoming the targets of hate and anger themselves. We must not succumb to destructive reactions that diminish us as people. We must channel our strong emotions into constructive paths of embracing one another, helping one another, and offering prayers for victims, their families and our nation."
[END of statement.]

American attitudes toward Arab and Muslim groups in the aftermath of the September 11, 2001 attacks on the Pentagon and the World Trade Center reflect how world events can create dramatic shifts in cultural relationships. For Arabs and Muslims living in the United States, many of whom voiced outrage and horror at the actions of the al Qaeda terrorists, the aftermath of the tragedy was lived under intense suspicion and scrutiny. Even as the US Government was taking aggressive steps to increase national security, local governments and law enforcement braced for the possibility of violent reprisals. The Office of the Attorney General for the State of Iowa felt compelled to issue a statement on September 14th, 2001, cautioning Iowans to respect the rights and freedoms of Arab-Americans and to recognize that the attacks were "the responsibility of the individuals who committed them, not of ethnic or religious groups."

Racism, age-ism, and sexism are driven by conflicting cultural values and by divergent ideas of the roles that cultural groups can and should play in relationship to one another. For example, laws of cultural separation—as in the South African *apartheid* government, or racial segregation in the United States during the century following the Civil War—serve as examples of how restricting multi-cultural communication deepens rifts and resentment between cultural groups. While these social divisions may have served the interests of one cultural group for a period of time, the resulting social inequities created prolonged legacies of pain and misunderstanding.

Rosa Parks, 1955

"I was arrested on December 1ˢᵗ 1955 for refusing to stand up on the order of the bus driver, after the white seats had been occupied in the front. And of course, I was not in the front of the bus. Many people have written that I got on the bus and took the front seat, but I did not. I took a seat that was in back of where the white people were sitting, in fact, the last seat. A man was next to the window, and I took the aisle seat and there were two women across. On about the second or third stop, some white people boarded the bus and there was one man standing. And when the driver noticed him standing, he told us to stand up and let him have our seats. He referred to them as front seats. And when the other three people, after some hesitancy, stood up, he wanted to know if I was going to stand up, and I was not. And he told me that he would have me arrested. And I told him you may do that. And of course, he did. He didn't move the bus any further than where we were and went out of the bus. Other people got off, didn't any white people get off, but several of the black people got off."

"Two policemen came on the bus and one asked me if the driver had told me to stand and I said, yes. And he wanted to know why I didn't stand, and I told him I didn't think I should have to stand up. And then I asked him why did they push us around? And he said and I quote him, "I don't know, but the law is the law and you are under arrest." And with that, I got off the bus, under arrest."[14]

-Rosa Parks, 1995
(Copyright © Academy of Achievement)

The story told by Rosa Parks describes events that have happened within living memory. However, the social norms that help us to interpret the experience of Rosa Parks on that bus have changed significantly. In 1955, life for a black woman in the segregated south included very specific social roles and expectations. The cultural and legal divisions of segregation were rigidly tied to ethnicity. By resisting that social restriction and redefining the role that she was prepared to play; Rosa Parks became a catalyst for the Montgomery bus boycott and the modern Civil Rights movement. In that moment, on that bus, she chose to not accept the cultural restriction of racial segregation. Her defiance helped to foster changes in cultural relationships throughout the United States that continue to evolve to this day. In just over half of a century we have shifted from a history of race-based slavery and segregation to the election of our first President of color. Without a willingness to redefine cultural relationships in our society, such progress would never have been possible.

Cultural loyalties are not always so dramatic. Even an issue as insignificant as loyalty to a sports team can affect the ways in which we communicate, and the relationships that we form with others. Barbara is an ardent fan of the Baltimore Orioles. John is a die-hard Yankees fan. Whenever conversations turn to baseball, arguments develop over the relative merits or weaknesses of the two teams. The conversations may remain cordial, but they reveal a distinctive clash of personal loyalties. Viewed from another standpoint, the cultures with which we align ourselves help to define us. They allow us to give significance and relevance to our actions and meaning to our lives.

Culture acknowledges the relevance of social relationships. We belong to groups and thrive on the acceptance and support of other members of that cultural community. By the same principle, our exclusion from social groupings can create conflict and social isolation. In the wake of the 1999 school shooting in Littleton, Colorado there was much speculation that one of the causes for the tragedy was the social alienation of Dylan Klebold and Eric Harris from their peers, and particularly from student athletes at Columbine High School. In interviews conducted after the shooting, students acknowledged a rigid social environment at the school in which members of a group known as the "Trench Coat Mafia" were targets of derision and harassment. Harris and Klebold were described as outcasts.[15]

In April of 2007, a similar pattern emerged in the history of Seung-Hoi Cho, a twenty-three year old senior who killed thirty-two people before taking his own life at Virginia Tech. Classmates, teachers and university police attested to his social isolation on the VT campus and high school classmates confirmed that he was a subject of ridicule and bullying who "rarely, if ever, managed normal social interactions."[16] While Cho clearly struggled with significant mental health issues, his sense of persecution and social isolation became a focal point for his eventual violence.

There are no simple answers that compensate for all of the misunderstandings that emerge from clashing cultural values. We belong to social groupings based on factors such as our race, sex, religion, political, philosophical or regional loyalties, professions, and social contacts. These cultural loyalties are dynamic, shifting in weight and relevance to accommodate current events and evolving social norms and perceptions. The only certainty is that intercultural contact will continue in our society and that as a multicultural nation we must develop greater tolerance and better strategies for understanding unfamiliar traditions and evolving social values.

## Summary

Human beings are instinctive social communicators. We structure our communication in patterns based on our self-perceptions, relationships, motives, message content, circumstances, and environment. Defining the number of people who are involved helps to draw distinctions between intrapersonal, interpersonal, small group, organizational, presentational, and mass communication. Social loyalties and perceptions have a strong influence on multi-cultural communication. All patterns of communication serve particular goals in human interaction.

Table 1-1

| Pattern of Communication | Number of Communicators | Primary goal of Pattern | For Example |
|---|---|---|---|
| Intrapersonal Communication | 1 | Self concept formation, reasoning, conscious thought | "I think, therefore I am" --Rene Descarte |
| Interpersonal Communication | 2 | Dyadic Communication, forming and maintaining relationships | A date, job interview or telephone conversation |
| Small Group Communication | Typically 3-8 | Free and spontaneous interaction in task or social groups | A family, group of friends, military squad or surgical team |
| Organizational Communication | Any number connected to a structured group | Efficient flow of messages throughout the hierarchy of a structured group | A club, business or school using memoranda or email announcements to inform members, employees or students |
| Presentational Communication | Large groups in the same location | Relates presenter(s) and audience in the same setting | A speech, concert, or performance of a play |
| Mass Communication | Large, remote and scattered audience | Uses technology to spread messages generated by an organization to a large and scattered audience | A television broadcast, Internet web page, newspaper or radio broadcast |
| Multicultural Communication | Any number | Bridges and explores cultural differences to increase mutual understanding | Speaking to someone from a different culture |

## 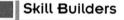 Skill Builders

### 1. Continuous Communication.

Seated adjacent to a partner simply observe this other person. Do not *try* to communicate. In fact, try to avoid sending any deliberate messages. After one minute write down three messages you received non-verbally from your observation. Share them with your partner.

### 2. Ambiguous Script.

In teams, write an imaginary dialogue of a conversation between two imaginary people. Present this conversation to the rest of the class without defining who the speakers are or what circumstances have led to this conversation. Let the class guess at the missing information and discuss the clues that led them to their answers.

### 3. What's My Motivation?

In groups or individually review your activities over the last few hours. Select a moment in your day in which you committed to a particular activity or action and try to reconstruct all of the factors that helped to motivate your choice. Be specific and detailed with your analysis. If you are working in a group, *brainstorm* together to develop a complete list of motivations for each example activity.

**4. Pattern journal.**
Over the course of a single day, keep a journal of all of the patterns of communication in which you participate. Provide examples of the ways in which you use, or avoid using, each of the patterns discussed in this chapter.

**5. Small group jigsaw puzzle.**
In a group with four to six members, spend 15 minutes putting together a complicated jigsaw puzzle. At the end of the time period assess the group's progress and discuss the positive and negative interactions that occurred within the group.

**6. Media analysis.**
Watch or listen to at least three mass media "content providers" and record the ways in which they fulfill the description of mass media provided in this chapter. Indicate what technology is required and what organization is responsible for generating messages. Also speculate on the ways in which the media source is financially profitable and the potential audience that is being targeted.

## Endnotes

1   Adler, Ronald B. and George Rodman. <u>Understanding Human Communication</u>, 7th Ed. Fort Worth: Harcourt College Publishers, 2000. Pgs. 174–175.

2   Adapted from Hartley, Peter. <u>Interpersonal Communication</u>. New York: Routledge, 1993. Pgs. 5–13.

3   Bull, Peter. <u>Body Movement and Interpersonal Communication.</u> Chichester: John Wiley & Sons, 1984. Pgs. 56–57.

4   DeSheinitz, Elizabeth and Karl. <u>Interviewing in the Social Services.</u> London: The National Council of Social Service, 1962. Pg. 9 (As cited by Molyneaux, Dorothy and Vera W. Lane, <u>Effective Interviewing: Techniques and Analysis</u>. Boston: Allyn and Bacon, Inc., 1982, Pgs. 1–2)

5   Redmond, Mark V. <u>Communication: Theories and Applications</u>. Boston: Houghton Mifflin, 2000. Pg. 20.

6   Manning, Peter K. <u>Organizational Communication</u>. New York: Aldine De Gruyter, 1984. Pg. 9.

7   Byrne, John A., Mike France and Wendy Zellner. "At Enron, The Environment Was Ripe for Abuse," Business Week Online, February 25, 2002. <u>http://www.businessweek.com:/print/magazine/content/02_08/b3771092.htm?mz</u>

8   Arndt, Michael. "3M's Seven Pillars of Innovation," Business Week Online, May 10, 2006. <u>http://www.businessweek.com/innovate/content/may2006/id20060510_682823.htm</u>

9   Tierney, Elizabeth P. <u>How to Make Effective Presentations</u>. Thousand Oaks: Sage Publications, 1996.

10  Dominick, Joseph R. <u>The Dynamics of Mass Communication</u>. Boston: McGraw-Hill, 1999. Pg. 28.

11  Israel, Fred L., ed. <u>1897 Sears Roebuck Catalogue</u>. New York: Chelsea House Publishers, 1968. Pg. XVI.

12 Gudykunst, William B. et al., Eds. <u>Communication in Personal Relationships Across Cultures.</u> Thousand Oaks: Sage Publications, 1996.

13 (Press release from the Office of the Iowa Attorney General, Sept 14, 2001.) <u>http://www.iowa.gov/government/ag/latest_news/releases/sept_2001/reprisals2.html</u>

14 From an interview with Rosa Parks. American Academy of Achievement. Interview, June 2, 1995. <u>http://www.achievement.org/autodoc/page/par</u>.

15 "Loners, misfits, 'Trench Coat Mafia' talked openly about blowing up school". *Seattle Times*, 21 April, 1999.

16 "High School Classmates say Gunman was Bullied" (msnbc and new service reports), April 19, 2007. <u>http://www.msnbc.msn.com/id/18169776/</u>

CHAPTER

# Understanding Perception

Sheldon Metcalfe, Ph.D.

## CHAPTER OBJECTIVES

After reading this chapter you will be able to:

1. Identify the stages of the perception process;

2. Recognize the significant influences on perception;

3. Use the Johari Window for self-disclosure;

4. Develop a strategy for evaluating perceptions.

## Key Terms

| | | |
|---|---|---|
| closure | organization | self-concept |
| culture | perception | self-perception |
| figure and ground | physiology | selection |
| interpretation | prejudice | similarity |
| Johari Window | proximity | social expectations |
| motive | repetition | stereotype |

The world is very different for each of us. We perceive our environment, other individuals, and ourselves based upon our knowledge, unique experiences, needs, goals, and values. Our differing viewpoints influence our decisions and actions about whom or what we like, agree with, or accept. Some baby boomers are persuaded to buy "retro" cars such as Chrysler's PT Cruiser or Ford's Mustang because these vehicles make them feel like the "good old days" of the forties and fifties. Other buyers, however, may view the retro appearance as "old fashioned," or as a reminder of unpleasant times such as the Great Depression or World War II. Some listeners think hip hop music is unpleasant jarring noise while others identify strongly with lyrical content that describes experiences of ghetto and street culture. Art critics often see deep symbolism and meaning in the size, shapes, and colors of abstract art while others see only meaningless blobs and sloppy painting techniques. In the 2008 Democratic Presidential Primary, many who supported Senator Hillary Clinton wanted her to continue the race for President while many supporters of Senator Barack Obama wanted her to drop out. You can see that our perceptions of art, music, nature, politics, religion, and each other are affected by our unique personal histories and our individual goals.

In this chapter we will help you to understand the process of perception, recognize some important influences on this process, and develop some strategies for evaluating your points of view.

## The Process of Perception

Perception begins with the information that surrounds us. We choose certain stimuli from our environment and reject other material. Next, we place the information in a particular order or structure that makes sense to us. Finally, we must interpret, translate, and assign meaning to the information we have chosen and structured. We can therefore define **perception** as the process of selecting, organizing, and interpreting stimuli from our environment.

### SELECTION

Since we encounter numerous bits and pieces of information through our five senses each day, we must make decisions about which data we will receive and what we will ignore. **Selection** is the aspect of perception that allows us to pay attention to some information and omit other data. One factor that determines which stimuli we select from our environment is **motive.** A motive is an inner drive that causes us to select certain stimuli that we need from our environment. If you have ever bought a new automobile, you tend to notice cars of the same make on the highway. Or if you are looking through a magazine and you happen to be hungry, recipes or restaurant advertisements seem to jump out at you.

Similarly, an American tourist in Mexico who understands only a little Spanish might recognize familiar expressions like *el cuarto de bano, el banco,* and *la farmacia* when needing to locate items such as the bathroom, bank, or drugstore.

**Repetition** of information can also dictate which data we notice. The irritating sound of a chair squeaking continuously during a final exam or the tick-tick-tick-tick-tick of a grandfather clock disrupting the midnight silence of a room can be so annoying that an individual cannot focus on more important tasks at hand. We easily identify McDonald's Golden Arches, Target's red and white bull's eye, or Wal Mart's yellow smiley face rolling back prices. When we hear advertising slogans such as "It's the Real Thing," "Be all you can be," or "Fly the friendly skies," we immediately know these often repeated phrases refer to Coca-Cola, the United States Army, and United Airlines.

You can see that the information we select is not necessarily based on an objective or unbiased process. Selection can be highly subjective and affected by the power of the message or the individual's needs and interests.

Because we select only some information, we also omit other data, often distorting messages or receiving stimuli partially. It is then possible to generalize or *oversimplify* the message, creating an incomplete summary of a person, event, or object. For example, let's say you have a friend by the name of Jeff whom you have known for a long time. The two of you have been having lunch in a coffee shop and a fellow student from a computer class stops by your table. You briefly introduce Jeff: "This is my friend Jeff. He's majoring in computer programming." Your acquaintance, who notices Jeff's dark, thick glasses, makes the remark, "So you're a computer geek, hey Jeff?" You immediately bristle at the comment because you know that Jeff is a surfer, loves theater, and is on the wrestling team. The individual's insensitive remark linking Jeff's glasses to your brief comment about his computer major oversimplifies and disregards all the other wonderful information you appreciate about Jeff.

In court cases, lawyers often have difficulty gathering concrete evidence because no two witnesses perceive the events of a case in the same way.[1] One witness may focus on an alleged murderer's blue bandana while another will recall facial hair or jogging shoes. One witness who describes a victim as "walking very fast" may be "running" in the words of another. A man who is described as "short and stocky" may be seen by others as "of medium build." Facial hair can refer to anything from a short, well-trimmed or handlebar mustache, (with or without sideburns) to a cropped, full, or "Santa Claus" beard. It is difficult to get a complete, objective, unbiased account because of each individual's unique, subjective perception of events.

We often select or reject data consciously as we would pick and choose appetizers and entrees that we "like" or "dislike" on a restaurant menu. In human relationships we are drawn to certain types of people because of their appearance, abilities, values, and/or intelligence and away from others due to lack of common interests, differing experiences, or conflict in lifestyles. But in the extreme haste of modern life, we must also make choices so quickly that selections and omissions become almost automatic and even subconscious. For instance, imagine that a coworker dashed into your office where you were deeply involved in learning a new computer program and placed a pile of folders on your desk saying, "I've looked over these reports and made some corrections that you'll need to review." Since you were busy, you would probably ignore the coworker's appearance, gestures, posture, or facial expression. You might not even make eye contact with your colleague as you continue working on the computer. The information you would probably select from this encounter would be necessary portions of the message ("looked over..reports...corrections ... you'll need....review."). You might also focus on the tones, inflections or degree of urgency expressed in your coworker's voice.

Selection is a necessary part of the perception process but we must recognize that our choices are highly subjective and serve to alter and distort reality. These selective inclusions and omissions affect our relationships with others and the way we view our world.

## ORGANIZATION

Once we have selected which stimuli we will receive, we must then apply **organization** to group information into units which make sense to us. We organize stimuli through figure and ground, proximity, closure, and similarity.

### Figure and Ground

**Figure and ground** occurs when you focus on some information and place other stimuli in the background. Notice the well known drawing in Figure 2-1. Depending upon which area of the sketch you observe, you will see either a goblet or two identical faces. Now look carefully at the illustration in Figure 2-2. Concentrating on different areas of this drawing will reveal the face of an old lady or a young woman. Are you able to see them easily? On which parts of the illustration must you focus in order to see the different images? If you couldn't find both faces, don't feel defeated. Many viewers have difficulty detecting the images because they do not know which part of the drawing should be the figure and which is the background.

Figure 2-1

Figure 2-2

Figure and ground occurs in communication settings each day. If you hear your name called over the intercom in a crowded department store, your name becomes the figure and all the other noise becomes background. When you see a singing ensemble such as a quartet or rock group and you like or know one of the singers your focus would be the voice, personality, and image of the person you know, with other performers fading into the background. If you are picking up clothing at the dry cleaners and you spot your garments hanging on the rack, you have employed figure and ground. If you are eating vegetable soup at a restaurant and you notice an overpowering pepper flavor, your taste buds have automatically responded to the predominance of the pepper with the other ingredients fading into the mixture. In the numerous stimuli we encounter through our senses, we must place some information in the background, and move other stimuli forward to the object of focus.

### *Closure*

A second way of organizing information is by using **closure** to fill in data that is absent. In Figure 2-3 you can see four lines that are not joined together but your mind quickly connects them to form a square. Similarly, when perceiving people in communication settings, we fill in the meaning from the missing verbal or non-verbal blanks. If we see two people holding hands we assume that they are in a very close or intimate relationship. When we hear a stranger talking on a cell phone we add the missing bits and pieces of conversation to determine who the caller is talking to. If you hear a politician say, "We need to get tougher on criminals," you might assume that the speaker was a law-and-order conservative occupying the right wing of the political spectrum. No doubt you've encountered the maxim, "Where there's smoke, there's fire." This proverb aptly applies to an individual who is using closure to apply meaning to what is seen and heard.

Figure 2-3

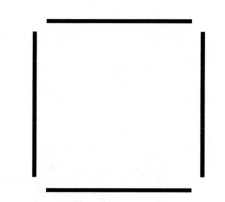

### *Proximity*

Another way to organize data is by the closeness or nearness of stimuli known as **proximity.** We assume objects that are physically near to each other in place, time, or order are part of a group. In Figure 2-4 there are actually six lines, but their closeness makes them appear as if the lines are divided into three groups. When receiving communication we use proximity to connect people, ideas, or objects together. At a party we link people who are chatting in groups around the punch bowl, at the dessert table, or in front of the fireplace. After hearing "Paper or plastic?" several times in a super market line, we quickly blurt out "plastic" because we expect the question again. If all your coworkers have opened their paychecks and found a sizable holiday bonus, chances are you will expect a bonus as well. When the elements in communication are near to each other, the aspect of organization we are employing is proximity.

Figure 2-4

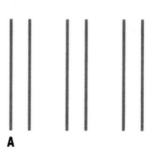

A

### Similarity

One of the easiest ways to organize information is on the basis of **similarity.** Things make sense to us because they simply resemble each other in form, value, color, size, or in other aspects.

When you see law enforcement officers dressed in a similar color and style of uniform you assume they belong to the same police force. If you encounter people of similar ethnicity, you determine that they are from the same region or country.

When you see men wearing a skullcap known as a yarmulke, you associate the head covering with orthodox Judaism. If you observe a rally where people are holding anti-war signs, you are grouping people according to similar political philosophy. If you are a part of a crowd riding a roller coaster at an amusement park, you would conclude that your interests in coasters are alike. We organize stimuli we receive about people, objects, interests, and philosophies based upon properties and appearances that are similar.

## INTERPRETATION

Once we have selected and organized stimuli, we must use **interpretation** to assign meaning to the information we receive. Take a look at the four sets of digits below [2]:

A. 1 713 852 1339
B. 245 96 5180

C. 8742 6500 4418 8821

D. 4523

At first, you may only perceive a jumble of numbers. But upon closer examination you may recall from repeated past experiences that the first item resembles a long distance phone number, the second corresponds to a social security number, the third is identical to a credit card number, and the fourth could be an ATM pin identifier. Now look at the lines in Figure 2-5. Is the top line longer than the bottom? Or is the height of the candle longer than the width in Figure 2-6? You probably have seen drawings like these before and determined that the lines are of equal length. The lengths are often perceived to be different because of the direction of the slanted lines. Now look at the inkblots in Figure 2-7. What do you see? A butterfly? A dog with two ears? A ballerina? Sometimes stimuli such as these are ambiguous and can be interpreted in many different ways. The ambiguity of inkblots allows a psychologist to gain useful information from the various patterns and images a patient perceives.

Figure 2-5

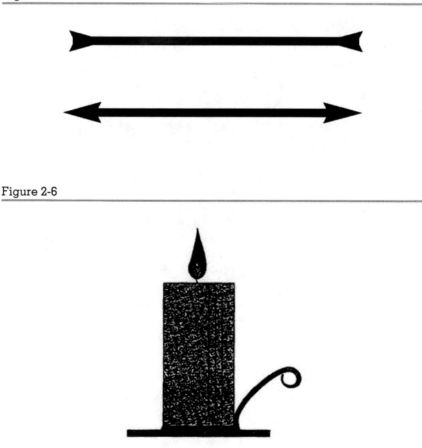

Figure 2-6

Figure 2-7

Interpretation plays a critical role in perceiving human relationships every day of our lives. But since these interpretations are filtered through our subjective needs, values, or past experiences, they can be inaccurate, illogical, or incorrect. For example, if you are presenting a classroom speech and someone in the audience frowns, you could interpret the expression as a negative reaction toward you or as a response to another unrelated event. Does the hug from a new friend convey an act of simple kindness or something more? Is the couple arguing at the next table in the restaurant engaged, married, or ending a relationship? Is the boss who has summoned you in a stern voice upset with your work or stressed from another encounter? You can see that each experience we have can be interpreted in numerous ways. Although our interpretations may be correct according to our subjective perceptions, they can be incomplete or inaccurate when viewed from other points of view.

## Influences on Perception

Our perceptions do not develop in a vacuum. They are subjected to influences that help to shape, alter, and sometime distort the stimuli or messages we receive. The significant influences on our perceptions include our physiology, the self-concept, culture and gender.

### PHYSIOLOGY

**Physiology** refers to how we perceive the world through the physical aspects of our bodies at a given time: the physical senses as well as our physical, psychological and emotional states.

Our perceptions are often altered by the boundaries of the physical senses themselves. Humans, for instance, have a limited range of hearing and smell while many animals such as dogs, have a higher range of hearing and a keener sense of smell.

If you have ever had a bad cold or flu you know that your sense of smell and taste were severely diminished. Our vision is affected by the limits of near or far sighted-

ness and those who are color blind are unable to perceive certain pigments or hues. Individuals with nerve damage report the loss of sensation and feeling in their bodies or extremities.

Couples often argue over the position of the thermostat because one partner feels cold and the other is always warm. Mexican hot sauce is tasty to some while it feels like hot coals to others. The antiseptic odor of a hospital may smell clean and fresh to one person while it may make another individual experience nausea. Although each of us may be blessed with all or most of our senses, we perceive the world quite differently because of the physical limits or differences imposed upon us by those senses.

Physiology affects our perceptions in other ways as well. For example, we view the world very differently depending upon our age. When we are young, time appears to drag very slowly. A child riding in a car might become easily impatient and whine every five minutes, "Are we almost there yet, Mommy?" Or the fourteen-year-old feels it will take forever to reach the age when he can take his driving test and achieve greater independence. Those at middle age, however, complain "how time flies" and are often content spending their leisure time socializing with family and friends, while senior citizens may view time as a precious commodity and appreciate each day as an added gift.

Our emotional states and health can also affect perception. If you have ever experienced a personal crisis such as a death in the family, divorce, or financial difficulty, you know that the crisis becomes the center of your world and you think about little else. Psychologists state that making decisions such as changing jobs or moving to another region in the midst of such altered perceptions could lead to poor choices and actions that are later regretted.[3] A woman who is tired from a long, stressful day at work and returns home to three active children and a husband who wants dinner may not be as positive about communicating or performing household duties as her family would like. The individual who has a degenerative disease views life in terms of a constant battle to survive while the Olympic athlete perceives reality in terms of a competitive struggle to be the best. During the winter when days are shorter many individuals report they sleep longer, burn less energy, and gain weight while the opposite is true in summer. Many women experience different estrogen levels before, during, and after menstrual cycles that can lead to mood swings and emotional changes, affecting communication. Some studies have shown that both men and women can experience different physiological cycles throughout a day that can lead to variations in eating, sleeping, and activity patterns.[4] For example, one spouse may be a "night owl" and enjoy snacking and socializing at late hours while her partner goes to bed just after dinner and arises very early the next morning.

You can see that our physiological states not only affect how we perceive the world, but also how we communicate with one another. If you are fatigued, you might be withdrawn; if you are hungry, you may be grumpy; if you are feeling well, you will probably view the world as a positive place. Knowing that we communicate differently when we are experiencing various physiological conditions helps us to gain insight into communication behaviors and work for greater understanding of ourselves and increased empathy with others.

## SELF-CONCEPT

Another influence on perception is the **self-concept** which determines how we think and feel about ourselves. The self concept represents the totality of what makes up who we are: values, likes, dislikes, roles we play, talents, emotional states, attitudes, beliefs, our culture, and our community. The self- concept can have a dramatic impact upon how we perceive the world around us. Although there are numerous factors that can affect the self-concept, we will consider three influences that we feel are most significant: self-perception, responses from others, and social comparisons.

### *Self-Perception*

**Self-perceptions** represent the way we see ourselves in our minds and the way we feel about ourselves. We arrive at these self perceptions based upon the positive or negative experiences we have had over a period of time. As children, our self-perceptions are based upon how others react to us. A child who is talented in theatre or music and hears repeated applause and bravos during public performances formulates a positive view of his or her artistic capabilities. A high school teenager who has a number of successful dating experiences may see herself as successful in relating to boys. But consider another teenager who is stood-up on a date and is continually rejected by girls throughout his high school experiences. If he encounters enough of these types of situations, he will begin to form negative perceptions about his socialization with the opposite sex.

Fortunately as adults, we form perceptions of ourselves based upon broader experiences. We can often look back on negative situations and draw on more positive experiences which transform how we view ourselves. The little girl who feels ugly attends college and is asked out on numerous dates and begins to see herself as a beautiful woman; the young ex-convict is adopted by a big brother and grows into an exemplary citizen; the alcoholic joins AA and accepts responsibility for his actions and becomes a social worker; the irresponsible preacher's child has life-changing experiences which transform him into a charismatic spiritual leader; the inner city gang member receives nurturing by a religious community and becomes an elected member of congress. Not all such negative self-perceptions have a happy ending of course. But these examples point out the importance of self-perception in helping us to achieve our goals and build confidence.

Self-perceptions not only impact how we view ourselves, but also how we perceive others. If you have a low opinion of yourself, you will tend to view others with greater cynicism, but if you formulate a positive self-image, you perceive others more constructively. Individuals who engage in constant fault-finding may actually be making more definitive statements about themselves than about the people they wish to blame. At the same time, those who continually look for valuable qualities in others often view themselves as more effective and productive people.[5] So how we view ourselves impacts our own level of confidence as well as our perception of others.

34

Maya Angelou is a well-known African American writer of numerous books and poems.

She received the honor of composing and presenting an original poem titled, "The Rock Cries Out To Us Today," in celebration of the First Inauguration of President William Jefferson Clinton. In this inspiring poem, she recalls the upheaval of the American past and urges citizens to embrace the future and "Lift up your eyes upon the day breaking for you. Give birth again to the dream."[6]

In her autobiography, I know Why the Caged Bird Sings, Maya describes a devastating experience that happened when she was an eight-year-old child. Her mother's boyfriend who was living with the family in St. Louis raped Maya and threatened to kill her if she screamed. Afterwards, he coerced her by threatening to kill her brother if she told anyone about the assault.

Maya recalls her turbulent feelings of guilt and helplessness as she struggled to comprehend the violent incident: "Then there was the pain. A breaking and entering when even the senses are torn apart. The act of rape on an eight-year-old body is a matter of the needle giving because the camel can't. The child gives, because the body can, and the mind of the violator cannot. I thought I had died....." "Could I tell her now? The terrible pain assured me that I couldn't. What he did to me, and what I allowed, must have been very bad if already God let me hurt so much."[7]

The rapist moved away and eventually Maya told her mother and brother what had happened. There was a trial where Maya was required to testify against her attacker. After these events, Maya withdrew from the world and did not speak for many months, except to her brother. Today, her writings reflect a deep understanding of human nature. Ms. Angelou's perceptive insights, however, have not occurred as a result of some instant magic, but developed from her painful experiences and agonizing struggles.

Questions for thought: Describe how you think this experience affected Maya's perception of herself as a child. How do you feel this incident influenced her feelings about others? How was Maya able to overcome this traumatic event? What effect did this experience have on Maya as an adult? How do you think Maya's childhood influenced her writings?

### Responses from Others

If you browse through the self-help or psychology sections of most bookstores, you will find authors who write about the need for positive reinforcement of others. We are told that children should be praised when they perform tasks well; employees need recognition when they excel at work; and spouses ought to be reminded in both words and deeds that they are appreciated. A child who receives consistent praise from parents and peers regarding sports activities or school achievements would be likely to form a positive self-concept and view himself with confidence. But imagine if a child were constantly told that she was clumsy and awkward. The child might begin to think of herself as bumbling and spill beverages at the table or stumble while walking. This type of event is known as a "self-fulfilling prophesy"[8] because the goal set by or for the individual has been predicted or expected. Some researchers believe that adolescents are especially vulnerable to negative responses from others[9] As a child, Eleanor Roosevelt was often called "Granny" because her mother thought that her daughter was homely and unattractive. Years later when she was First Lady, Mrs. Roosevelt described her reactions to her mother's harsh comments with these sorrowful words in her autobiography: "I wanted to sink through the floor in shame, and I felt I was apart from the boys [her brothers.]" [10]

What people say to us and about us can have a dramatic effect on the formation of the self-concept. Read the following lines and imagine that you were the receiver of these comments from either a family member or friend:

*"Our family has never done well in science."*

*"You have that ugly Smith nose."*

*"She has buck teeth."*

*"He's not mechanically inclined."*

*"You've never been very good in sports."*

*"She doesn't get many dates."*

*"He walks like a duck."*

*"He's always looked like a string bean."*

*"She can't seem to put two sentences together."*

How did you feel when you read these remarks? Did you find them humorous? Did you feel uncomfortable? Repeated comments such as these can have a devastating impact on a person, especially a child. Now read the following responses:

*"He's an excellent dancer."*

*"She's very sensitive."*

*"You're pretty just like your mother."*

*"You've always been a hard worker."*

*"You're a careful driver."*

*"He's really funny."*

*"She's very active in sports."*

*"He's a good money manager."*

*"She's very professional."*

If you heard these observations repeated often enough, you would think positively about your personality or your behavior. We must remember that each one of us requires constructive responses in order to gain self confidence, excel in our goals, and interact successfully with others. In contrast, blaming, name-calling, and finger-pointing are behaviors that can hurt others and lead to destructive feelings and negative self concepts. When we continually look for the best qualities in our families, friends, and colleagues, we participate in providing reactions that are critical to the development of positive self-concepts.

### Social Expectations

We often compare ourselves against **social expectations** reflected in the media, advertising, and in popular culture. Advertisements tell us that we are too fat, thin, short, tall, unhappy, lazy, or stressed. We are bombarded with measures that we must take to make ourselves better than we are. Television commercials proclaim that for just "$39.99 and ten minutes a day", you can look like the gorgeous model in the ad. Underwear advertisements portray skinny young people showing off their bony figures in revealing poses. News shows feature men and women who have undergone extreme makeovers involving expensive face lifts or other surgery to look younger or painful leg and thigh treatments to remove "ugly" cellulite lumps.

Toy manufacturers promote dolls like thin and shapely Barbie or muscular and handsome G.I. Joe.[11] Tobacco and liquor ads portray attractive men and women smiling and socializing together as they sip cocktails or smoke cigarettes. Numerous authors, dietitians, and doctors advise us how to reduce calories and lose weight to look better. Is it any wonder that people often do not feel they measure up to the ideal person portrayed by our society?

Not only do we measure ourselves by the false standards set by society, we compare ourselves to others. Little Carlos wants expensive gym shoes "just like the other guys" and Patricia "needs" a prom gown that is as elegant as her friend's. Families often go into great debt buying houses, purchasing cars, or joining exclusive country clubs they cannot afford in order to compete with their friends or neighbors. Parents compare their children to others, students compare test scores to classmates, and business people measure their success in sales against other companies.

Unfortunately many of these comparisons can produce deep feelings of inadequacy that can consume our thoughts and dictate our behaviors. The anorexic young girl views herself as overweight even though she is malnourished. The balding man purchases expensive scalp treatments to restore hair follicles. The maturing woman undergoes cosmetic surgery for breast implantation, liposuction, or face lifting. It is important to stress that changes in diet, exercise, and lifestyle can be desirable in improving physical and mental health. But behavior that results from comparisons due to negative self perceptions can be counter productive and discouraging.  Abrupt changes due to clothing, houses, exercise machines, or surgery do not necessarily change self-perceptions of the mind or feelings of the heart.

## CULTURE

Another important factor that influences perception and communication is the culture that  shapes our values, behavior, and language.  **Culture** refers to behavior patterns, arts, beliefs, thoughts, and products that are characteristic of a community or population.  Some researchers believe that cultural differences can be explained by a society's emphasis on individuality or  collectivism.[12]  Western societies are seen as independent cultures in which the value of the individual is stressed and the importance of the group is diminished.  In western countries, we hear social and political leaders speaking about the need for self-determination, personal choice, independence, and individuality.  By contrast, some third world and eastern cultures value the needs of the group and the good of the collective society as opposed to the wishes of the individual.  For many years, China has imposed a one-child-per-family policy as a means of addressing the enormous over-population problem.  Such a remedy would be unthinkable in the United States and considered not only an invasion of privacy, but a violation of our individual rights guaranteed by the Constitution.  In America,  an individual who contemplates marriage makes a personal choice to search for someone who is attractive, has a pleasing personality, and enjoys similar interests or goals.  In India, however, individuals are expected to marry within their same level or class and in the Middle East many marriages are still arranged. In cultures that stress individuality, self concept is measured in terms of achieving independence, individual goals, and personal success.  In societies where collectivism is emphasized, self concept is seen as a function of working interdependently to fulfill the needs and goals of the group. [13]

Culture also affects our non-verbal communication. In Europe, it is common to see individuals of the same gender strolling down the street arm in arm.  This custom is meant to convey personal friendship or close association.  But in America such physical closeness within the same gender would be interpreted as a statement of sexual preference. Americans greet one another by shaking hands while the French kiss each other on both cheeks and Russians say hello with bear hugs. A foreign visitor to a restaurant in Greece is usually startled when the host leads him into the kitchen to inspect the food. Accustomed to twenty-four hour convenience stores, Americans traveling in Italy, Spain, or France often complain when businesses close for a two-hour afternoon siesta.

The concept of personal space also varies depending on the country or culture.  In many Middle Eastern countries individuals engaged in a conversation stand very close together, almost nose-to-nose.  In North America, however, individuals require a personal space of at least one arm's length  for comfortable conversation.

Culture not only affects non-verbal communication, it is also interwoven with the verbal communication and language patterns of a society.  Culture impacts

meaning and grammatical structure as well as the number of letters, words, and tenses needed to convey messages. Anyone who has tried to learn a foreign language understands that phrases often cannot be translated literally from one language to another. For example, an airline company flying Brazilian routes advertised that it had "rendezvous lounges" on its airplanes. Officials didn't understand why business declined until they discovered that "rendezvous" meant a meeting place for sex in Portuguese.[14] When Pepsi introduced its slogan, "Come Alive" in Taiwan, the company unintentionally violated traditional Chinese values by translating the slogan, "Pepsi brings your ancestors back from the grave."[15] In the west, a person who is talkative and assertive is admired but in Asian countries individuals who are quiet and reserved are more highly respected.[16] In China, eastern philosophy is even reflected in written language because the Chinese term for "I" appears very similar to the word for selfish.[17] Culture can also determine the number and configuration of letters, tenses, or words that are needed to describe an object or concept. In Brazil there are numerous words to describe coffee, and the Arabic language includes thousands of terms to identify a camel and the parts of its body. On the other hand, some American Indian languages do not contain past or future tenses[18] and the Hawaiian alphabet has only twelve letters.

You can see that the culture in which we are raised influences our thinking, behavior, and language. Indeed, we view the world through the unique filter provided by our surroundings.

## GENDER

In addition to the physical senses, self concept, and culture, gender is another critical element that affects perception.

We perceive individuals and others respond to us based upon different characteristics associated with gender. In one study, infants who were active, displayed more smiling, and exhibited increased vocalizations were provided with more male toys while babies who smiled less and behaved more passively were given female toys.[19] Little boys are referred to as strong, big, or solid and little girls are described as cute, adorable, and sweet. In preschool, children watch television, play games, or read books where boys and girls are described in distinctly different terminologies. In primary grades, the choice of occupations is influenced by traditional gender perceptions. For example, children often viewed women as ballet dancers, ice skaters, nurses, and cooks, while they more frequently perceived men as baseball players, fire fighters, astronauts, and police officers.[20] As we mature, we view others according to our role as male or female Women often describe others in terms of interpersonal interactions. A woman is more likely to say "She likes to socialize," or "He tends to be shy." Men, however, tend to characterize individuals in terms of their actions or abilities. A man might describe someone as, "He's a great golfer," or "she's very athletic."[21]

Our perceptions of male and female roles also influence our com- munication. Men are likely to discuss topics related to occupations, politics, current events, and sports. Women, however, tend to discuss more personal issues such as weight, relationships, health, food, and repro- duction. Women tend to ask more questions, use personal pronouns, and include justifier phrases in conversation.

Males, however, tend to be more direct, interrupt more frequently, and use more filler expressions at the beginning of sentences. In mixed-gender conversations, women bring up more tentative topics and often adapt to subjects that the more assertive men are more likely to pursue. Women also enjoy talking and commu- nicating in order to maintain relationships, empathize with others, and process feelings. For example, a woman might say, "I can understand what you're saying because I've often had those feelings." Men, however, communicate to accomplish tasks, maintain independence, and engage in competition. A man might dismiss a problem that a friend has disclosed by saying, " You're thinking too much about it. Why don't you just quit worrying." [22]

Just as gender affects individual perceptions, it can also influence cultures. One researcher assessed cultures in terms of their masculine and feminine qualities. Geert Hofstede characterized masculine societies as success-oriented, ambitious, and competitive with an emphasis on conflict and confrontation in problem-solv- ing. By contrast, he portrayed feminine cultures as valuing interpersonal relation- ships, quality of life and modesty, with conflict-resolution occurring through ne- gotiation and compromise. Hofstede even ranked countries according to masculine and feminine characteristics. He determined that the highest masculinity scores came from Japan, Austria, Venezuela, Italy, Switzerland, Mexico, Ireland, Jamaica, Great Britain, and Germany. The United States ranked fifteenth out of the 53 coun- tries studied. Those nations with high femininity scores were Sweden, Norway, the Netherlands, Denmark, Costa Rica, Chile, Finland, Portugal, and Thailand.[23]

Even though there has been significant research into gender and perception, it is vitally important to recognize that there are numerous exceptions to some of the preceding generalizations. Men's and women's roles have changed dramatically in the past few decades. Women can be assertive as well as empathetic . At the same time, men can exhibit emotion and resolve conflicts through common ground. As societies continue to change and gender roles become less distinct, it is important not to view others simply as representatives of a particular gender, but as unique individuals who display a variety of traits, styles, and temperaments throughout a range of engaging personality types.

## Viewing Yourself Through the Johari Window

Now that you know some of the influences on perception as well as the importance of your self concept in determining how you view the world, you can begin to explore some significant areas of your personality in greater depth. The Johari Window is a tool that not only helps us to reveal aspects of our character and personality that are obvious, but also allows us to uncover areas that may be hidden or unknown. The Johari Window gets its name from the first names of its creators, Joseph Luft and Harry Ingham, who studied human personality in the 1950's. It is designed to identify different levels of self disclosure and perception.[24] The diagram in Table 2-1 indicates that the Johari Window is divided into four quadrants or areas of disclosure.

Table 2-1

| | Known to Self | Not Known to Self |
|---|---|---|
| **Known to Others** | 1<br><br>OPEN | 2<br><br>BLIND |
| **Not Known to Others** | 3<br><br>HIDDEN | 4<br><br>UNKNOWN |

The first quadrant is the *open* area that refers to information known to both you and to others. For example, the color of your eyes, the clothes you wear, the kind of car you drive, where you live are pieces of information that are known by others as well as yourself.

The second quadrant or *blind* area, represents information that others perceive about you, but is unknown to you. For instance, an individual with a piercing voice doesn't realize the effect of his voice on a listener who has to hold the telephone a foot from her ear when engaging in conversation. Other behaviors in this area can include a husband who does not recognize that his wife feels that he is overly critical or an employee who is unaware that her coworkers think she is selfish and lazy by failing to perform her share of the work load.

The third quadrant or *hidden* area includes information that is not known by others but only know by you. For example, your monthly car payments, the price of your house, the number of traffic violations, criminal convictions, or the scar from your back surgery are all examples of areas that can be hidden from others and known only by yourself. Writer James Frey's so-called memoirs titled, <u>A Million Little Pieces</u>, was a popular non-fiction book for several months. The book appeared on the <u>New York Times</u> bestseller list and was identified as a book of the month by Oprah Winfrey. Later, however, certain "facts" in the book were found to be made up. Frey recounted that he had spent 87 days in prison but police records indicated that he had spent only a few hours. Such fabrications caused the publisher, Doubleday, to apologize to readers and Oprah to chastise Frey in person on her television show. The misleading information remained hidden and known only to the writer until further fact-checking by the "Smoking Gun" website transformed the knowledge of the event from the hidden to the open quadrant and became known to everyone. Frey was publicly humiliated and one of his publishers dropped him as an author. [25]

The fourth quadrant or *unknown* area represents unexplored aspects of your life that neither you nor others can know about you. We cannot predict, for example, how we will respond when faced with a life-threatening illness such as Severe Acute Respiratory Syndrome (SARS) or a catastrophic event such as a terrorist bombing, unplanned pregnancy, or the sudden loss of a family member. Mountain climber Aron Ralston could never have known, for example, how he would respond when he became trapped on the side of mountain for several days in Canyonlands National Park in eastern Utah. While he was climbing over a boulder, a 1000 pound rock shifted and fell on his arm. After repeated attempts to move the rock, he was unable to dislodge his arm and the rock would not budge. Trapped for five days without food and water, he performed an incredible act of survival. Ralston broke his arm and slowly amputated it below the elbow with a dull pocket knife, freeing him from the boulder. Next, he set up hooks and climbing equipment and rappelled 75 feet down the canyon. He applied a tourniquet to his bloody arm and walked nearly seven miles when rescuers spotted him and airlifted him to a hospital in Colorado.[26] No one could have predicted Ralston's extreme yet life-saving actions in such a traumatic experience.

Table 2-2

|  | Known to Self | Not Known to Self |
|---|---|---|
| **Known to Others** | 1 OPEN<br><br>Your name, eye color, car you drive | 2 BLIND<br><br>Harsh voice, stubbornness, laziness |
| **Not Known to Others** | 2 HIDDEN<br><br>Body scars, convictions, mortgage payment | 3 UNKNOWN<br><br>Reactions to unforeseen or traumatic life events |

Table 2-2 represents a brief summary of the behaviors, feelings, or motivations that describe each quadrant of self disclosure. You can see that the Johari Window is a useful means for achieving greater understanding of yourself and others. Team up with a good friend and use the Johari Window to investigate the four quadrants of your lives.

Write down aspects of your character in the open and hidden areas and ask your friend to write descriptions of you in both the open and blind areas, then exchange the information. This process may seem threatening at first, but it is important to be honest with yourself and your team mate in order to understand each other more completely.

## Evaluating Your Perceptions

Now that you understand the process of perception and recognize several key factors that influence that process, you can develop a strategy to evaluate your perceptions. We suggest the following plan of action: Confirm the accuracy of your perceptions, gather additional data to validate perceptions, avoid the blame game, eliminate prejudices and stereotypes, and be willing to change your perceptions.

### CONFIRM THE ACCURACY OF YOUR PERCEPTIONS

Since perceptions are such individual processes, they are subject to inaccuracies and inconsistencies. One student thinks a professor is "cool" while another perceives the teacher to be biased and unfair. A husband interprets his wife's conversation with a cashier to be flirtatious while his wife perceives the exchange as common courtesy. A smile from the woman in the elevator seems directed toward you but it may actually be aimed at the man on your opposite side. Although the individuals in the preceding examples may feel their assumptions are correct, a strong possibility exists that they may be partially or completely wrong. Be willing to check the accuracy of your perceptions and compare them against others. If you doubt your point of view, don't be afraid to ask questions. Recognize that your perceptions may be limited or incomplete and be ready to compare your perceptions with others if necessary.

## GATHER ADDITIONAL DATA TO VALIDATE PERCEPTIONS

It is easy to make snap judgments about people based upon one or two isolated experiences. The low grade you received on a paper indicates that the teacher is difficult and unreasonable. The girl who abruptly refused your dating invitation is stuck up and conceited. The friend who has stopped calling you is no longer a reliable companion. The failure to seek additional information often compels us to cling to narrow and harmful misconceptions such as these. Gather more data to confirm or reject your perceptions. Are other students in your class receiving equally poor grades on all assignments? Have you spoken with your instructor to determine how and if you can improve? Have you observed your dating interest in different situations or asked others about her? Have you spoken to your friend to determine the reason that phone calls have ceased? Could your friend be experiencing illness, depression, or the sudden loss of a family member? Is it possible that your friend might need *your* support and wonders if you have abandoned *her*? Collect information, ask questions, and talk to individuals in your communication environment. Above all, don't base your perceptions on limited encounters or experiences. Remember that positive perceptions are key to building strong relationships and secure emotional connections with others.

## AVOID THE BLAME GAME

We sometimes inflate our self-perceptions by viewing others as inferior or flawed. When we see others having difficulty, we often blame their misfortune on some personal defect. A friend who had an accident must have been driving recklessly. A colleague who was dismissed from a job must have been incompetent. The in-law who got divorced must have been an irresponsible spouse. Although such perceptions are unfair, they are manufactured to make us feel superior by comparison.

It is equally disconcerting that we often try to blame others when we are the victims of unfortunate circumstances. Consider for example, the following situation. On a trip to Madrid, an American tourist encountered communication situations in a restaurant, a bank, and a hotel where he was treated abruptly by the personnel. After experiencing frustrations ordering food, exchanging money, and securing a hotel room, the tourist remarks to his traveling companion, "You know, people in Spain are just plain rude!" The tourist may have felt that his perceptions were entirely valid, but the others viewed the encounters differently. The waiter perceived an American who couldn't speak Spanish making unreasonable demands about the menu and returning incorrectly ordered food to the kitchen; the busy bank teller was annoyed with a slow American requesting multiple recounts of Spanish pesetas exchanged from dollars; and the hotel clerk was exasperated when the tourist could not make up his mind as to the amenities he wanted with his room.

Avoid blaming others for your difficulties. If you receive a negative evaluation at work, examine what you did wrong before you condemn your boss. When you see other individuals experiencing misfortune, try to develop greater understanding of their circumstances rather than jumping to harsh conclusions. Be sensitive to others and avoid trying to inflate your self-perceptions at the expense of someone else. Above all, be responsible for your actions, mistakes, and feelings, and take ownership of your own perceptions.

## ELIMINATE PREJUDICES AND STEREOTYPES

The root of the word, **prejudice**, means to pass judgment and the prefix, "pre", means "before" or "earlier". If we combine the two meanings, prejudice becomes the act of judging something or someone beforehand without proper evidence. Let's say that Ralph didn't like hazel eyes. In fact, Ralph didn't like any individual who was born with hazel eyes. If you had hazel eyes and met Ralph for the first time, he might smile politely as he greeted you, but his inner voice would remark: "Ok—here's another one of those shifty hazel-eyed people I've got to avoid." The situation sounds ridiculous doesn't it? Unfortunately prejudices are just this ludicrous, yet they are very real and undeserved.

Equally damaging are **stereotypes** which are fixed prejudices or simplistic assumptions about individuals or groups. We are all too familiar with prejudices that stereotype people of a different race, culture, gender, religion, sexual preference, or geographical location.

Stereotypical statements such as "all people from New York.......," or "all people from France......" are especially harmful because they categorize individuals according to group or association through a flawed process known as "hasty generalization" (see "Logos: The Appeal to Reason" in Chapter 16 of <u>Building A Speech</u>). An individual who bases perception of others upon prejudice allows no opportunity for acceptance, growth, or constructive interaction. Prejudice isolates individuals from one another, stifles relationships, and contributes to emotional and sometimes physical injury.

Be honest with yourself and be willing to acknowledge your own prejudices. Examine specific perceptions you hold that can damage others and keep you from constructive interactions. Work to overcome prejudice by beginning a dialogue, exchanging ideas, and building positive relationships with individuals and groups you may mistrust. The motto, "Build bridges, not walls", is an excellent philosophy to follow as we venture to overcome unfounded fears and recognize the value and worthiness of each individual.

## BE WILLING TO CHANGE YOUR PERCEPTIONS

We all form first impressions and make judgments about others based upon limited evidence. Once you have tested your perceptions and gathered additional information, however, don't hang on to original perceptions if they are inaccurate. Imagine that you receive a "D" and an "F" on a quiz and a paper in an English class at the beginning of the semester. Because you are very concerned about your progress, you speak with the instructor who classifies you as a "poor" or "failing student." Determined to improve your performance, you apply extra effort and receive "A's" and "B's" on all assignments throughout the remainder of the course. Since you have greatly improved, you would expect your instructor to change her perceptions of you as well. If the instructor failed to consider the new information about your progress and still persisted in characterizing you as a "failing student", her perception would not only be unfair, but damaging to your college career.

When you form early perceptions based upon limited knowledge of others, keep an open mind. Be willing to accept new information and alter your viewpoint when individuals demonstrate change. The result will be a deeper and more comprehensive understanding of others.

## Summary

Perception is defined as the process of selecting, organizing, and interpreting stimuli from our environment. Selection occurs through motive and repetition, both consciously and subconsciously. Organization takes place through figure and ground, closure, proximity, and similarity. Interpretation is the last step in the perceptual process in which meaning is assigned. Some influences on perception are the physical senses, self-concept, culture, and gender. The Johari Window can be a useful tool to help us reveal aspects of our character that are obvious and uncover areas that may be hidden or unknown. To evaluate perceptions, test for accuracy, gather additional data, avoid the blame game, eliminate prejudice, and be willing to change.[27]

45

### Interpreting e-mail

People often complain that they misinterpret their e mail because it is impossible to decipher emotions and nonverbal expressions in cyberspace. Look at the following lines and try to interpret several possible meanings for each statement:

*Don't you get it?*

*The boss says those reports must be in ASAP!*

*Don't be difficult.*

*Should we meet?*

*Nice putt!*

*Don't ever do that again!*

*I won't tell anyone.*

If you read these lines in your e mail, you might have been offended and angered by some statements and confused or happy about others. As computer users have recognized the limitations of writing in cyberspace, they have developed an entire language or "net lingo" from abbreviations and keyboard symbols. Known as "smileys" and "emoticons", these symbols attempt to make e mail more "human." Notice the same statements with the symbols that have been added to convey some emotion:

| Statement | Meaning |
| --- | --- |
| *Don't you get it? LOL* | *Laughing out loud* |
| *The boss says those reports must be in ASAP. l-o* | *Yawning* |
| *Don't be difficult. :-)* | *Smile (don't take this seriously)* |
| *Should we meet? ( ( (H) ) )* | *Big hug* |
| *Nice putt! : - >* | *Sarcastic* |
| *Don't ever do that again! =: - )* | *Punk* |
| *I won't tell anyone. : - #* | *My lips are sealed* |

Do these cyber symbols really make messages more understandable? Why or why not? What are the limitations of computer messages? What would allow e mail to convey human emotion and nonverbal expressions more comprehensively? After some research on the web, write several lines of e mail and use symbols to express nonverbal emotions in detail. You can do more research into "emoticons" at www.netlingo.com.

## ▓ Skill Builders

**1. Self Perception**

    **A. Self perception list.** Write down a list of "positive" perceptions that you have about yourself. Once this is complete, make a list of your "negative" self perceptions. Now compare the two. Which list is longer: the positive or negative? If the negative self-perceptions are more numerous, try to word each negative perception so that it has a more positive construction.

    **B. Self perceptions compared to perceptions of you from others.** Once you have completed the list of positive and negative perceptions in the first exercise, ask two friends to write their positive and negative perceptions of you. Once you have received their lists, compare them to each other to find what items are similar and different. Then compare their lists with the one you developed. How are they different? What areas are similar? What items appear most frequently on all lists? Are there any areas where you see yourself negatively but your friends do not? As you review these lists, in what areas can you begin to change or improve your self perception?

**2. First impressions**. Describe a situation where you based your perceptions of an individual upon your first impressions. How did the initial impression affect your feelings, interactions, and relationship with that individual? What act or series of experiences with that individual persuaded you that your first impressions were inaccurate?

**3. Culture and perception.** Interview an international student in your class or elsewhere at your campus. Find out as much as possible about the differences in verbal and non-verbal language, social and family customs, and religious practices or rituals. Present a report to the class about this student's culture and highlight the differences with American society.

**4. Stereotypes.** Divide into groups of three and ask group members if they have encountered prejudice or stereotypical behavior at any time during their lives. Have students share their experiences and relate how they felt about the incident (s). Discuss ways to deal with prejudice and strategies for breaking harmful stereotypes.

**5. Perception checking.** Select an interpersonal situation where the meaning of events is uncertain, confusing, or unclear between you and another person. Perform a perception check and list the possible outcomes in each of three steps:
    1. Describe the factual details of the situation.
    2. Assign a preliminary interpretation of the perception.
    3. Seek clarification of the perception.

**6. Perception differences.** Divide into groups of two or three and plan a skit that portrays an emergency situation such as a heart attack, choking, robbery, automobile accident, or argument. Introduce enough detail into the skit to make it multi-dimensional and interesting. Once the skit is concluded ask your classmates to recall significant aspects of the situation in writing:

What were the characters wearing?
What did each person in the skit say?
What were the detailed facts of the situation?
Describe in detail what each person looked like?

When students have completed their written responses have them report their results to the class. Focus on the similarities and differences in the answers.

7. **The Johari Window** Get together with a friend and write down aspects of yourselves in each of the four quadrants of the Johari Window: open, blind, hidden, and unknown. Once you exchange the information and discuss the results answer the following questions:
   1. What were you able to reveal about yourself in the hidden area that the other person didn't know about you?
   2. What did the other person perceive about you in the blind area that you were not aware of?
   3. Did you both agree on those qualities that you considered to be in the open area?
   4. What types of qualities or characteristics did you discuss that could surface in the unknown area?

## Endnotes

1   United States. U.S. Department of Justice, Office of Justice Programs, National Institute of Justice. Eyewitness Evidence: A Guide for Law Enforcement. Washington: US Dept. of Justice , 1999.
2   Verderber, Rudolph. Communicate, 9th ed. Belmont, CA: Wadsworth Publishing Co., 1999.
3   Rice, Phillip L. Stress and Health, 2nd ed. Belmont, CA: Wadsworth Inc., 1992.
4   Groos, G.A. "Circadian Rhythms and the Circadian System." Eds. J. Mendlewicz and H.M. van Praag. Biological Rhythms and Behavior. New York: Karger, 1983.
5   Baron, Penny. "Self-Esteem, Ingratiation, and Evelution of Unknown Other." Journal of Personality and Social Psychology (1974): 104–109.
6   Maya Angelou Page. 1 Jan. 1996. 7 Oct. 2008 <http://www.math.buffalo.edu/sww/angelou/poems-ma.html>.
7   Angelou, Maya. I Know Why the Caged Bird Sings. New York: Bantam Books, Inc., 1970.
8   Verderber: 34.
9   Hattie, J. Self-concept. Hillsdale, NJ: Erlbaum. 1992.
10  Lash, Joseph P. Eleanor and Franklin. New York: W. W. Norton and Company, Inc. 1971.
11  "Boy Toys Too Buff Muscular Figures Skew Picture." Cincinnati Post 21May 1999: 9A.
12  Gudykunst, William B. and Yuko Matsumoto. "Crosscultural Variability of Communication in Personal Relationships." Communication in Personal

Relationships Across Cultures. Eds. William B. Gudykunst, Stella Ting-Toomey, and Tsukasa Nishida. Thousand Oaks, CA: Sage, 1996. 19–24.

13 Adler, Ronald B. and George Rodman. Understanding Human Communication, 7th ed., Ft. Worth, TX: Harcourt College Publishers, 2000.

14 Armao, R. "Worst Blunders; Firms Laugh Through Tears." American Business Jan. 1981: 11.

15 Dodd, Carley H. Dynamics of Intercultural Communication Madison. WI: Wm. C. Brown Publishers, 1991.

16 Adler, Ronald B. and Neil Towne. Looking Out/Looking In, 10th ed. Belmont, CA: Thomson Learning, Inc., 2003.

17 Adler and Rodman, Understanding Human Communication: 46.

18 Dodd: 125.

19 Bell, N.J. and W. Carver, "A Reevaluation of Gender Label Effects: Expectant Mothers' Responses to Infants." Child Development 51 (1980): 925–927.

20 Tibbetts, Sylvia-Lee. "Sex Role Stereotyping in the Lower Grades: Part of a Solution." Journal of Vocational Behavior, 6 (1975): 255–261.

21 Verderber: 39.

22 Adler and Rodman, Understanding Human Communication: 93–95.

23 Hofstede, Geert. Cultures and Organizations: Software of the Mind. New York: McGraw-Hill, 1997.

24 Luft, Joseph. Of Human Interaction . Palo Alto, CA: National Press Books, 1969.

25 Memmott, Carol. "Million Little Problems Follow Writer." USA Today 30 Jan. 2006: 1d, and Neumeister, Larry. "Judge Approves Frey Book Settlement." ABC News 3 Nov. 2007. 6 Oct. 2008 <http://www.abcnews.go.com/entertainment/wireStory?id=3815293> and Barry, Dan, David Barstow, Jonathan D. Glater, Adam Liptak, and Jacques Steinberg. "Times Reporter Who Resigned Leaves Long Trail of Deception." New York Times 11 May, 2003: 1.

26 Sanchez, Rene and Kimberly Edds. "Climber Cuts Off Arm To Free Himself; Boulder Had Mountaineer Pinned for Days in Utah Canyon." Washington Post 3 May, 2003: A01.

27 Images used in this chapter are Copyright © 2003, Sheldon Metcalfe and its licensors. All rights reserved.

# CHAPTER

# Interpersonal Communication and Our Relationships

Timothy D. Thompson, Ph.D.

## CHAPTER OBJECTIVES

After reading this chapter you will be able to:

1. Recognize the impact of language on others and improve your verbal skills;

2. Apply conflict resolution principles to resolve disagreements;

3. Apply effective speaking and listening skills to relationship development;

4. Explain the role of nonverbal communication in relationship development.

## Key Terms

| | | |
|---|---|---|
| interpersonal communication | verbal symbols | conflict resolution |
| dyad | nonverbal symbols | kinesics |
| relationship | denotative meaning | proxemics |
| roles | connotative meaning | information literacy |
| interaction | relational messages | electronic social networks |
| partners | intimacy | mediated social selves |
| power | inferences | |
| status | emotive language | |

People are social beings. Of course, this does not mean that we want to be nestled up under our friends and family members all the time. It does, however, mean that human interaction is the mirror in which we examine our lives in order to mold and shape our sense of self. Without human interaction, we would have no way of measuring how strong, smart, or talented we are. Without human interaction, we would have no way to determine what our mistakes were so that we could set goals for improvement. We do not have to be told to seek others' love and acceptance; we just naturally do it. And when we do interact with others more than once, we begin to form relationships with them. In fact, the process by which we form relationships is our primary training ground for self-awareness. This total process is called interpersonal communication.

In this chapter we will help you to discover ways to make interpersonal communication in your primary relationships more mutually enjoyable. In order to do this, we will explore the nature of interpersonal communication, how we manage our language use, resolve conflicts, and understand the role of nonverbal communication in our relationships.

## What Is Interpersonal Communication?

Before we embark on the main discussion in this chapter, our first order of business is to define the concept called interpersonal communication. In brief, interpersonal communication means communication **between** (symbolized by the prefix "inter") two **persons** (hence, the term personal). In the academic discipline of interpersonal communication, this one-on-one relationship is known as a **dyad**, which means a pair. A dyad is the basic building block for all human relationships because it is the smallest-scale environment for practicing our interaction skills. In order for interpersonal communication to occur, two individuals need a message that includes content and relational information.

## ALL MESSAGES CARRY CONTENT AND RELATIONAL INFORMATION

All messages exchanged in dyads contain information within two main dimensions. We are all familiar with the **content** dimension in communication, which contains information about the meanings of the ideas that form the message. But we may not be aware that messages also are rich in information about the quality of the relationship between the communicators.

Understanding the content of the message (what the words mean according to a dictionary) is crucial, of course, if we are to act on the information we receive. Our ability to accurately comprehend message content depends heavily on the depth of our vocabulary and on our level of familiarity with the setting in which the communication occurs. The larger the vocabulary, the more choices we have of ways to explain our messages clearly to others. If you do not know that a certain part of a mechanical device is called a crankshaft, for instance, you may have to settle for referring to it as a "thingy," which would probably leave your listener uncertain about what you are describing.

The setting or environmental context of the communication is another aspect of the content dimension of messages. Setting includes location, weather, and the nature of the occasion, as well as the communicators' emotional states and motives for interacting with each other. These last two factors play a huge role in our interpretations of content meaning. For instance, if something in my tone of voice leads you to believe that I am being sarcastic when I compliment you about the quality of your choice of music to play on your stereo, you may launch a verbal counterattack. However, if you perceive sincere approval in my tone, you might thank me for my kind words.

Besides providing a rich source of data that informs us about our partners' thoughts and feelings, verbal and nonverbal messages also have a **relational** dimension. That is, we choose our words and our conscious nonverbal responses according to the nature of our relationships with different people in our lives.

One useful way of defining our **relationships** is to think of them as **ongoing interaction patterns that are mutually established and developed between two persons.** This definition assumes that both parties in the relationship are always actively (and equally) involved in deciding on the rules that will govern their interactions.[1] Both parties also determine the roles they each will assume in these interactions.[2] This does not mean that relationships always (or even in most cases) involve equal levels of status or power between the two parties. In fact, power differences are common, and it should be noted that in every relationship, both the lower and higher status participants either actively or passively agree to play a specific role.[3] In other words, a leader cannot lead if no one follows. So no matter whether the participants enjoy equal or unequal status, both contribute equally to the de-

velopment of a pattern of interaction created over time by their responses to each other's personalities.[4]

All of our relationships evolve as they do mainly because of what we contribute to them and what we receive in return. It is an ongoing dance of give and take, ebb and flow. So if you like the way your primary relationships are going, you probably should keep doing what you have been doing already. However, if your relationships with co-workers, friends, or family members are not working for you, you always have the power to influence change by adjusting the contributions that you make to those relationships.[5]

The three primary factors that help us define the nature of our relationships are (1) **roles**, (2) **status** levels, and (3) **intimacy** levels. All of us play a variety of distinct roles in our personal and professional lives.

For instance, at home we may be simultaneously mothers or fathers, daughters or sons, and siblings because we may live with extended family. Meanwhile, at work we may function simultaneously in supervisory roles in relation to those below us and as subordinates to those above us in our workplaces.

Our status levels relative to others also play a key part in how we communicate with those around us. It is not uncommon, for instance, for workplace bosses to call lower level employees by their first names while the lower status workers use "Mr." or "Ms." followed by the boss's last name. The differences between the ways in which the two status groups address each other are barriers designed to show respect for social traditions. Furthermore, the relationship is strictly the product of a social contract based on an exchange of human labor for a monetary reward.

A similar type of exchange operates in your college experience. Most professors maintain at least a minimum level of status barriers between themselves and their students to help uphold the credibility of their institution as an authoritative place of learning. The basic theory behind this is that students who believe a teacher knows more about a particular subject than they do are more likely to seek knowledge from that teacher than from a professor who appears to be no better informed than a typical student. Educators therefore must create and reinforce a perception that they have abundant useful knowledge to offer in exchange for student enrollment and participation. One factor that helps to build such a perception is the establishment of teachers' and administrators' roles as authorities, as those who "know." Within the educational process, students then take on the role of those who are trying to "know." Therefore, in the context of schools, teachers are considered to have higher status than students do.

Most of us have relatively few truly intimate relationships. These relationships are the most demanding in comparison to our relationships with co-workers, casual acquaintances, friends who connect with us solely for specific types of activities, and even blood relatives with whom we do not communicate closely. For instance, let's say that I enjoy hanging out with my buddy Larry when I want to enjoy a basketball or lacrosse match. If I want to get advice from him about how to manage communication problems that I am having with my spouse, I first need to know whether he is capable of providing me with the kind of emotional support I need in that situation. If he cannot give me that kind of support, then our friendship may still be valuable, but it is definitely not intimate.

## CHANGING OUR INTERACTION PATTERNS

### The Saga of Fred and Marian

Fred knows that he can use his girlfriend Marian's desire to please others as a weapon against her to maintain his status as the dominant partner in their relationship. Thus, whenever he feels an urge for an ego-expanding power boost, he criticizes whatever he can think of at the moment about Marian. If Marian accepts his personal attacks each time as if she has done something wrong, then their dominant/submissive pattern of interacting has no chance to change, and it continues indefinitely. However, if she eventually learns that Fred's verbal abuse is actually a product of his own insecurities, and Marian can begin to heal her own insecurities that have driven her to seek approval from an uncooperative source like Fred, then she can stand her ground when necessary. If she refuses consistently enough to submit to Fred's efforts to control her, then eventually he must find another way to get what he wants. In this way, Marian has changed their relationship pattern merely by adjusting her response to Fred's personality expression.

It is important to clarify here that intimacy does not necessarily mean sex. Instead, it means that the relationship partners are connected not only on the surface, but on deeper levels as well. Obviously, your relationship with a sexual partner is intimate. However, our relationships with our parents, with our favorite siblings or other blood relatives, and with our dearest friends are also intimate, because we allow these people to interact with parts of us that we hide from others.

The Indian philosopher Jiddhu Krishnamurti explained, "Life is relationship, which is expressed through contact with things, with people, and with ideas. In understanding relationship we shall have the capacity to meet life fully, adequately." He also said, "Relationship, surely, is the mirror in which you discover yourself. Without relationship you are not; to be is to be related; to be related is existence."[6]

Furthermore, as living beings, we are all receivers and transmitters of electromagnetic energy currents. As such, each of us is surrounded by electrically and magnetically charged energy fields.[7] Electricity is the current that projects energy outward from an object or being, while magnetism is the current that draws energy inside. As they project out from us, these currents link up with compatible currents projected by others. When these energy connections are made, our magnetism draws into our lives the people who are projecting these compatible energies. This ongoing energy exchange process gives us plenty of practice in relating to the things, people, and ideas in our environment.

This constant circular energy flow explains why we are attracted to others in the first place. Additionally, the level of closeness that you share with the other person in a particular dyad helps to determine how you interact with that person. For instance, if you operate like most people, you may be more likely to share certain of your more personal opinions with your best friend or a close sibling than with a casual acquaintance that you have just met at work. In fact, the safer you feel in revealing your innermost self to another person, the more you tend to want to pull that person into your intimate psychological space. This desire, when fulfilled, results in the development of intimate relationships.

## Managing Communication and Resolving Conflict

The "Understanding Perception" chapter of this text[8] thoroughly discusses the crucial role of perception in determining how we relate to the world around us. This role makes our perceptions the foundation of all of our relationships. This section explores how our perceptions get translated into language and listening skills that contribute to creating and resolving conflicts, and help propel the process by which we build, maintain, and dissolve our relationships.

53

All languages are sets of symbols that can be arranged in a wide variety of patterns to enable us to convey our thoughts and feelings to others.[9] Also, all languages share the following characteristics: Language is symbolic, subjective, and rule-governed.

## LANGUAGE IS SYMBOLIC

The statement that language is symbolic simply means that the word is not the thing it points to. Instead, words are symbols or codes that we attach to or associate with ideas, emotions, people, places, and things in order to share our thoughts about the world. To illustrate this point, let us consider how your thoughts get translated into spoken or written dialogues. Thinking involves visualizing or formulating a mental picture.[10] When you want to get another person to see your same mental picture or to feel your same feeling, that desire leads you to search your available vocabulary list for words that will point the other person's thoughts to what you see. For instance, if you want to explain to a friend your opinion about a movie that you have recently seen, you will probably describe scenes or conversations between characters that you liked or disliked, and then use terms that express your approval or disapproval. For instance, depending on who you are, you might say something like:

> *"You should've seen how those people were flying around. The special effects were awesome!"*

> *"Man, that movie was nonstop action. It was definitely 'tight!'"*

You have learned these terms by growing up in a particular cultural environment, and therefore you have attached word symbols (labels) to mental images according to your culturally influenced desire to understand the world around you. Yet, you may have also noticed that the meaning you assign to a particular word may not be the same way the other person is defining your words. Meanwhile, the object is still the object, but you have now labeled it. No matter what happens, your label does nothing to transform the object into something else. The label is nothing but a symbol to be used as a way to stimulate thought pictures so that we can share meanings with each other.

## LANGUAGE IS SUBJECTIVE

Besides being symbolic, language is also subjective. We basically attach two kinds of meaning to word symbols. The formal kind of meaning is called **denotative**— the dictionary meaning—while the informal kind of meaning is **connotative**. Connotative meaning is each individual's personal meaning for a particular word. Unless you consult a dictionary before you say anything, you rely instead on your own connotative meanings for each word and phrase you speak in every conversation you have.

One reason that you use language so personally, and therefore subjectively, is that the feelings you associate with your own unique experiences belong to you alone. When you speak a word, you not only convey information value, but you also transmit your feelings about the object that you associate with the word. For instance, if your experience of mother has been gratifying, the imagery that you link to the word "mother" will probably be more favorable when you say or hear the word than it would be for a person who has suffered through a series of abusive encounters with mother.

Groups can use language subjectively as well. Slang words or expressions such as, "That's tight," may convey meanings within one group that do not apply to other groups. In this way, such expressions act as group membership identifiers or boundaries.

## LANGUAGE IS RULE-GOVERNED

The final characteristic of language to be covered here is the fact that it is governed by rules. In order for anyone to understand what anyone else is saying, structural patterns and the rules that guide them must form the foundation of all language systems. For example, every language system uses action words (verbs); attaches labels to persons, places, and things (nouns); and uses modifiers (adverbs and adjectives) to further describe these verbs and nouns. The rules of semantics (word meanings) and syntax (sentence structure) are passed on from generation to generation through the formal educational process and through daily language use. Consider the following simple sentence in the English language: Johnny went home. The word "Johnny" is used here as a proper noun indicating the subject who will act upon something. The transitive verb "to go" is conjugated or used in the past tense, indicating that Johnny has already made his trip. Of course, the word "home" is the object or destination of Johnny's trip, which helps us to determine where Johnny went if we know his address.

If we had no structural patterns or rules like those in the simple example above to help us organize a group of letters or words into a recognizable pattern, we would have no basis for determining what any set of symbols means. Obviously, such a hopeless state of affairs would render these symbols completely useless as communication tools, and would leave us all with no effective tools for resolving conflicts that inevitably happen in all of our relationships.

## WHAT ARE CONFLICTS?

Unlike effective language use, conflicts are one of the least understood aspects of human interaction. They arouse anger. They stimulate frustration. And they transport us into places within ourselves to which we perhaps would rather not go. Most of us find conflict highly unpleasant, so we often act and speak as if we desperately want to eliminate all conflict from our lives forever.[11] We do not like to feel angry, frustrated, and out of control the way we do when we face conflict with another person outside the context of an organized competitive activity. In interpersonal relationships, which are generally meant to be cooperative arrangements rather than contests, there are no predetermined rules of engagement to guide us when conflicts arise. Furthermore, too many of us do not know how to develop and negotiate rules to govern our conflict solving behaviors in relationships. Due to this lack of knowledge, we naturally feel uncomfortable about awakening powerful negative emotions that could potentially escalate into extreme forms of abusive, destructive actions.

Our distaste for the discomfort that usually accompanies conflict tends to blind us to the true nature of conflict. Conflict is not necessarily a bad or harmful thing. In fact, it is fair to say that conflict is as natural a part of human relationships as smiling at each other. Furthermore, conflict provides us all with a wide variety of learning opportunities to help us grow in our understanding of the world around us.

This does not become obvious until we have a clear, practical definition of conflict, like the one offered by Joyce Hocker and William Wilmot below:[12]

> *"Conflict is an expressed struggle between at least two interdependent parties who perceive incompatible goals, scarce rewards, and interference from the other party in achieving their goals."*

### How Do Conflicts Occur?

By breaking down the terms in our definition above, we can see how all kinds of everyday situations present us with conflict, which in turn forces us to choose actions that either bind us to our relationship partners or separate us from them. Let us isolate the terms and discuss them one by one.

The idea of an *expressed struggle* refers to both parties' awareness that the total fulfillment of their personal desire at the moment will automatically restrict the other's fulfillment.

If you are in any type of relationship with another person, then you are *interdependent*. This simply means that your personal growth and development is influenced in some way by the nature of the energy that you exchange with that person.

The issue of *perceived incompatible goals* boils down to one of two kinds of scenarios. (1) You and your partner want the same item and you both believe that if one gets it, the other will not. (2) You and your partner are moving in different directions, and each of you wants the other to go where you are headed. In either case, you both perceive that someone will win and someone will lose.

*Perceived scarce rewards* means that neither of you believes that both of you can completely get what you want from the situation. For instance, if there is only one muffin on the table, and you both want a whole muffin, then splitting it may at first feel inadequate for each of you.

*Interference* in the context of natural conflicts does not mean sabotage. Rather, it refers to how your complete fulfillment may interfere with your partner's total fulfillment in the conflict situation.

Sometimes our mistaken beliefs about how to use language effectively actually may create conflicts. This can happen when we "buy into" any of the three communication misconceptions discussed below.

**(1) Misconception: More communication is always better.** In many of our conflicts with dyad partners, we may mistakenly assume that that more talking is the key to clearing up the problem. It is certainly true that effective, honest communication helps to build strong bonds among people. It is also true, however, that the quality of communication is a much better indicator of the strength of a relationship than quantity. So it is wise to choose your words carefully, or to think before you speak. When we fail to think before speaking, and we just blurt out the first unedited thought that enters our minds, we create barriers of distrust and resentment that sometimes cannot be overcome.

One of the basic ideas behind the "more communication is better" misconception is that honesty in any form is better than lying. Unfortunately, for some people honesty equals saying whatever we think without bothering to adjust the wording of the message according to the listener's temperament. The problem with doing this in our relationships is that saying what we think without sensitivity to our partner's feelings is hurtful and sometimes brutal. When it crosses over into brutality, our so-called honesty tends to cause more problems than it can resolve. Consider, for instance, the following hypothetical conversation between newlyweds Caleb and Rashida as they prepare to enjoy an evening of dinner and dancing on the first night of their honeymoon cruise:

> **Rashida:** *"Honey, what do you think about the combination of colors in my outfit?"*
> **Caleb** (*with disgust in his voice*): *"I think it looks horrible. What were you thinking when you bought that? How much did you pay for that, anyway?"*
> **Rashida:** *"You're so mean! Where do you get off talking to me like that? You aren't exactly Mr. GQ yourself!"*

In the above case, Caleb believes he is simply expressing how he really feels because he wants to "keep it real" and to avoid pulling any punches. After all, he reasons, a solid marriage is built on honesty. However, in addition to showing no sensitivity to the likelihood of hurting Rashida's feelings by failing to carefully choose his words, Caleb also has added more information than was necessary to answer his wife's question. He probably would have been much better off if he had softened his evaluation and avoided attacking her thinking. His two biggest mistakes were stating his opinion too harshly and then further complicating the situation by adding a personal attack.

Sometimes talking is not even the best way to connect with the important people in our lives in certain situations. For instance, if you are angry about something that has happened to you at work and you just want to vent to a friend or to a loved one, you might find yourself responding more receptively to a hug than to some words of advice. That may not mean that you have no interest in hearing what your partner has to say, but instead you might be looking for an affectionate nurturing show of support that may come across most powerfully through a physical embrace.

The bottom line in all of this is that we cannot and should not try to verbalize every thought and feeling that we experience. When barriers exist between our significant others and us, conversations about those relationships need to occur at times when both partners are receptive and willing to cooperate with each other.

(2) **Misconception: Communication will solve all problems.** When a conflict arises in one of your relationships, it is a good practice to ask yourself whether communication is even the key to resolving it. Don't fall into the trap of believing that poor communication is always responsible for your inability to achieve a mutual understanding with a dyad partner. Sometimes people are so different in fundamental areas of their lives, such as their spiritual and career goals, that no amount of communication will make them compatible with each other. Of course, incompatibility does not necessarily start out as a problem in all relationships, because the partners may at first enjoy the challenge of expanding their horizons by becoming close to someone very different from themselves. But what if they both have strong desires to fulfill radically different dreams over time? Even if the partners demonstrate respect for each other's dreams, the dynamic tension of pulling in different life directions cannot be ignored indefinitely.

It is important to realize that communication will not solve all of our problems. Understanding this helps us to place the true value of developing communication skills in its proper perspective. As screwdrivers, wrenches, hammers, and saws are useful tools for building a cabinet in your home, so effective communication skills can help us to solve the problems that arise because we fail to understand each other. However, communication skills are not particularly useful for changing someone else's motives. When we understand clearly what communication can accomplish and what it cannot, then we can more effectively minimize our frustrations in our relationships.

(3) **Misconception: Communication is a natural ability.** Finally, as with anything else, we must work on developing communication skills in order for us to consistently build mutually satisfying relationships. We cannot afford to assume that our communication skills will improve simply because time passes.

While it is true that we all practice communicating throughout our lives, it is equally true that many of our ideas about communication and our interaction patterns leave us clueless about how to handle certain situations. Additionally, our preferences, prejudices, beliefs, feelings, and experiences may interfere with our awareness of how much influence we have over the human interaction process. When we do not recognize that our own poor communication skills are primarily responsible for much of the pain in our relationships, we hold onto habits that do not work for us. So we hold onto these habits because we have no idea of the power that we have to create and recreate our life circumstances. Therefore, instead of increasing our skills, we master ineffective habits, which do nothing but make us better at communicating badly.

Practicing effective communication techniques is therefore a must for anyone who truly wants to build and maintain lasting, cooperative relationships. Even if you are a people-oriented person, you still need to face a wide variety of situations

over time in order to become more comfortable with responding appropriately to unfamiliar encounters. For instance, how would you respond if you were Miguel, a retail customer service employee, and an irate customer started abusing you unfairly about some defective merchandise?

> **Customer:** *You'd better give me my @#$%^&\* money back or I'll sue every last one of you in this stupid store! And don't bother trying to give me the run-around, either. I know about your tricks, and I'm not in the mood to listen to any of your fake, patronizing crap!*
>
> **Miguel:** *I'm sorry you've had such a hard time resolving this issue, sir. May I have your receipt so I can straighten this out for you right away?*

If Miguel's employer had neglected to train him to effectively handle different types of irate customers' complaints, he would have had no choice but to resort to the highly valued response options from his home or community foundation. In other words, if Miguel had been brought up to fight back aggressively whenever he was attacked, a heated argument with the customer would be inevitable. On the other hand, if he had been raised to negotiate compromises, a different interaction pattern would probably emerge. In any case, leaving the choices totally up to Miguel would be a risky move for his company. The simplest way to reduce this risk is for the company to train Miguel and the other customer service representatives to build goodwill with customers who may be caught up in a variety of emotional states.

The same principle holds true in our personal relationships, where our careless statements can inflict tremendous emotional damage on the young and old alike. Relationships require constant, careful nurturing, or else they can crumble into dust. The strongest bonding agent that can safeguard our relationships against disintegration is getting training in and practice with effective communication techniques by both partners. Without such training and practice, our risk of exposure to severe misunderstandings increases dramatically.

## HOW DO WE RESOLVE CONFLICTS?

By now it should be a little clearer that conflicts occur regularly in each day of our lives. Therefore, the key to functioning effectively in our relationships is to use our language and listening skills effectively to resolve these conflicts. Effective listening and speaking enable us to accurately assess the central issues within our conflicts and then to negotiate fairly, with **win/win** solutions in mind.

Win/win solutions are those that honor the underlying desires and needs of both parties. In <u>Getting to Yes: Negotiating Agreement Without Giving In</u>, authors Roger Fisher and William Ury[13] suggest that negotiators should not hold onto positions, but should instead should work toward discovering what both parties really want. From there, the negotiators can work out an arrangement based on the common ground of a mutually held vision. To successfully accomplish this, we need to develop our active listening skills so that withholding judgment about others becomes a habit. By starting conversations without judgments, we position ourselves to more easily understand our partner's underlying desires. This understanding opens the door to achieving results that can leave both parties mutually satisfied and improve the health of our relationships. Therefore, as chapter four in your main text explains, active listening is a practical and useful tool for resolving most kinds of conflicts because angry people are more likely to calm down when they feel that we care about what they have to say.

Effective language use is an equally important tool for creating win-win solutions to our conflicts. The next section explores effective ways to use language in this way.

## UNDERSTANDING HOW TO USE LANGUAGE EFFECTIVELY

Knowing how to "get our point across" does not guarantee that we understand how to use language effectively, which means getting our dyad partners to respond in ways that we want.[14] The question is whether some people are just born with a high degree of charm while others are just naturally abrasive. Or are there skills and techniques for developing them that we can all use to improve our effectiveness as communicators? The counseling profession has answered these questions by providing non-counselors with some helpful relationship management tools in the form of three basic principles of language use. Understanding these principles, which are discussed briefly below, can help you to smoothly handle all kinds of potentially volatile emotional exchanges.

## BE PRECISE INSTEAD OF VAGUE

What if you are a supervisor at your workplace and you have to evaluate the work of an employee who has failed to meet his performance goals and objectives? In a situation like that, you could be facing a firestorm of bitterness and frustration in your evaluation meeting with that person. Interpersonal communication scholars Adler and Towne[15] recommend that you try to be as precise and clear as possible in a situation like this so that the employee knows exactly what he needs to work on. You could accomplish this precision and clarity by focusing the discussion on a comparison between the employee's written goals and objectives and his actual performance, as well as using and encouraging results-oriented statements about the reasons why he did not accomplish his goals.

On the other hand, in some situations ambiguity and vagueness (defined as using terms that can be interpreted in many ways) are more appropriate and practical. This might apply, for instance, if you are discussing religious beliefs with a person from a different background and you wish to avoid getting into an unproductive argument. If you and/or the other person are expecting to encounter angry disagreements about some aspect of the religion issue, then you may be better served by talking in more general terms and staying away from making too heavy an emotional investment in each other's salvation. Precision in this case would probably only emphasize differences, and thus create more divisions between you.

## UNDERSTAND THE LANGUAGE OF RESPONSIBILITY

It is very hard for most of us to take all of the responsibility that we really should when problems arise in our interactions with others. By taking responsibility, we come face to face with both the positive and negative contributions that we make to our communication experiences. By facing our contributions honestly, we may expose ourselves to feelings of guilt. Such guilty feelings could be consciously or unconsciously associated with the results of our interactions. Since most of us do not look forward to experiencing guilty feelings, we may try to avoid them by creating all sorts of rationalizations to justify blaming our relationship problems on anything or anyone besides ourselves.[16]

One of those rationalizations is the assumption that we react in certain ways *because* of a relationship partner's words or actions. The main idea behind this assumption is that a verbal message or action can automatically cause one specific response, and no other. The problem with this assumption is that automatically choosing a response without first assessing whether other options may be more appropriate automatically locks us into certain patterns of communication. And these patterns may or may not help us achieve the kinds of results that we want our interactions to produce. Of course, even when we do not get what we really want from a negative encounter, identifying the other person as the cause of our own response choice enables us to avoid taking responsibility for the pain that we feel because we have mindlessly fallen into an old response habit. Blaming the other person also allows us to disassociate ourselves from the impact that our choice has on our relationship partner.

When we blame others for our response choices, we create listening barriers that prevent us from seeing clearly what our interactions are trying to show us about ourselves and our dyad partners. In other words, blaming others kills mutual understanding and does little to connect us to others' hearts. When you intentionally (either consciously or unconsciously) blame others for your communication errors, nothing can be done to correct your problem at that point.

When you accept the responsibility of truly understanding how your personal communication habits affect others' emotional and action responses toward you, you can more easily open doors to higher levels of emotional and intellectual harmony. In fact, as soon as you take responsibility for the psychological contributions that you make to your relationships, you begin to realize that repairing the cracks in some of those relationships can be as easy as changing the language you use to express your feelings. Some of the simplest steps that you can take are to minimize your "it," "but," and "you" statements and include more "I" and "we" statements in your messages in order to sound less like an attacker and more like a supporter of your partner.

"It" statements make some unidentified force responsible for our experiences. This shifting of responsibility, in turn, allows us to falsely objectify our experiences as if the rest of the world either does or should feel the way we do about what is happening in our lives. "Owning" our feelings by describing them as precisely as possible and connecting them to our partners' behaviors, however, can do a lot to help us get positive results without stimulating defensiveness.

For instance, instead of complaining that "It's not fair for you to treat me this way," try something like "I feel disrespected when you agree to do household chores and then leave me to complete your part." Or if you are used to saying "It's too warm in here," give "I'm too warm and uncomfortable in here" a try. These alternative statements focus our attention on how we are responding to stimuli in our environment, and therefore promote a greater understanding of where each relationship partner's responsibility for misunderstandings and conflicts begins and ends. They also empower us to either adapt ourselves to the situation or to adjust elements of the environment to suit our needs.

Like "it" statements, "you" statements also help to create barriers between others and ourselves because they do not provide a clear enough picture of the underlying nature of the issues we are discussing. However, "you" language often sounds much more threatening than "it" language because it focuses all of our attention on our value judgments about our partner's behavior. Because of this focus, saying something like "You never pick up after yourself" is almost guaranteed to prompt the target of this accusation to feel attacked.

"I" language will generally help you overcome the '"You" Language Blues' better than anything else because it accomplishes three goals: It describes (1) the other person's behavior, (2) your feelings, and (3) the consequences the other's behavior has for you. Once again, being specific focuses attention on the issues that can be addressed by the interacting parties. Therefore, instead of accusing the other of never cleaning, you can increase your chances of gaining a mutual understanding by saying something like "When you leave clothes and papers lying around the house (Behavior), I have to spend a lot longer time clearing up clutter (Consequences). I feel uncomfortable and frustrated (Feeling) living in a messy space."

Using "I" language in these ways will not guarantee that your relationship partners will automatically cooperate with your attempts to influence their behaviors. What this tool will do, however, is give you a new way to talk about difficult issues without arousing the degree of defensiveness that almost always accompanies perceived verbal attacks. When you minimize defensiveness, you enable yourself to direct all of your energy toward resolving the conflict at hand.

A second language tool that can sometimes help us to minimize the other's defensiveness is "we" language. "I" language is most useful when you are only trying to get your partner to assume a share of the responsibility for achieving an outcome. "We" language, on the other hand, may work better than "I" language when you both need to participate in a mutual effort in order for a problem to be solved. If we apply "we" language to our cleaning conflict, it might sound like; "We aren't doing a good job of keeping our place clean, are we?" This approach conveys a clear message that both partners are in the mess together, and a joint effort will help you both solve the problem.

## ELIMINATE LANGUAGE HABITS THAT WORSEN CONFLICT

As we have seen, we can prevent some of the conflicts in our lives by using language that shows we accept responsibility for our actions. Now let us look at how we can prevent or resolve even more conflicts by not blurting out emotionally charged comments before we have thought through what we want to say.

**Emotive language** is probably the worst offender of the language habits that cause misunderstandings. This type of language seems descriptive, but it really just announces the speaker's attitude toward what is being described. Emotive language refers specifically to the adjectives or descriptive terms we use when we tell stories or comment on life situations. Using emotive language amounts to trying to pass editorial comments off as factual statements. Here are some examples:

| If you approve of something, you say | If you disapprove of something, you say |
|---|---|
| persistent | pushy |
| confident | arrogant |
| quick-witted | obnoxious |
| sale | rip-off |
| bold | careless |
| humorous person | clown |
| cordial | phony |
| energetic | hyperactive |
| reserved | Boring |

Emotive language is full of judgments. Because of this, using emotive terms tends to arouse barriers or defensiveness in those who disagree with our judgments. Generally, it is better to avoid emotive terms and to describe the person, thing, or idea that you are discussing in neutral terms. For instance, instead of saying "I wish you wouldn't be so greedy," try saying something like "I would probably be willing to share the last piece of chicken with you if you would first check to see if anyone wants it." In addition to keeping discussions between relationship partners more focused on the relevant issues in a given interaction episode, descriptive neutral or non-emotive language also helps us to express our interpretations and beliefs without arousing as much defensiveness as emotive language does.

Confusing facts with opinions is the other conflict-creating habit that we will cover here. This language habit called **fact-opinion confusion** is usually not as harmful as emotive language. However, too often it still leads us to a false sense of agreement and togetherness. Facts are pieces of information that can be verified as true or false. Opinions are our personal emotional belief responses to either facts or

personal preferences. Distinguishing between facts and opinions is one of the most valuable and practical qualities of a skillful communicator. This is true because being able to detach ourselves from others' beliefs helps us to develop our own internal responses to the world around us. This skill opens us up to personal growth opportunities beyond what others may envision for us and to which they may try to limit us. Yet despite the importance of recognizing statements as expressions of fact or opinion, many of us often use fact and opinion statement interchangeably. Below are some examples of typical fact and opinion statements:

| Fact | Opinion |
|---|---|
| "Rain has been falling all day today." | "This has been a miserable day." |
| "I closed three sales today." | "I love my job today." |
| "I have momentarily exhausted the hot water supply in my home." | "My water heating system is terrible." |

It is easy to see the difference between these two kinds of statements when they appear together in contrast like this. Unfortunately, however, in many of our everyday conversations, we may not carefully consider differences between facts and opinions, and therefore, we may yield to a habit of stating our opinions as facts. This is especially likely when we want others to feel the same way that we do about an issue or experience. The bottom line is, when we use language carelessly in this way, we rob ourselves of a true appreciation for how our dyad partner really does feel about an issue.

## UNDERSTANDING NONVERBAL COMMUNICATION

In this so-called information age, it is easy for us to get caught up in thinking of communication as merely a matter of exchanging words or information content with each other. However, this is not even close to being an accurate view of what relationship partners exchange when we interact together. Everything about us, including how we adorn our living and work spaces, how we dress and move our bodies, and how we manage the space around us as we interact with others, sends messages about who we are and how we view the world around us. That is why it is important for us to understand what nonverbal communication is, in addition to learning the basic characteristics of this powerful aspect of our communication. Verbal communication is communication via (by way of) language symbols or words. Nonverbal communication, therefore, is the variety of things we do that provide the context for interpreting the meanings of our words. The following characteristics apply to all forms of nonverbal communication:[17]

1) Nonverbal communication exists within all communication.
2) All nonverbal behavior has communicative value.
3) Nonverbal communication is culture-bound.
4) Nonverbal communication is primarily relational.
5) Nonverbal communication serves multiple functions.
6) Nonverbal communication is ambiguous.

## NONVERBAL COMMUNICATION EXISTS WITHIN ALL INTERACTIONS

It is impossible to not communicate. Furthermore, because we express our thoughts and feelings in such a wide variety of nonverbal ways, these nonverbal forms of expression supply most of the meaning behind what we say to others. For instance, if your dyad partner asks you "What are you doing here?" with an angry voice and a frown, you will probably interpret that differently than you would if your partner uses the same words with a smile and a vocal inflection (tone) that sounds pleased. In other words, the "way" we say things to people always plays a major role in how others interpret our messages.

This fact goes beyond our vocal tone as well. In fact, we also receive messages from facial expressions; eye contact; body posture, movements, and positioning; proximity; and artifacts.

Facial expressions are also important, as shown in the above example, because frowns convey vastly different feelings from smiles. Eye contact also makes a huge difference, as you will see in the discussion of nonverbal communication and culture. Artifacts refer to things like the way you dress, the kind of jewelry you wear, the type of car you drive and how clean you keep it, as well as the way your living space is decorated and maintained.

Probably the most complex area of nonverbal communication focuses on body movement. This branch of nonverbal communication, also known as **kinesics**, examines the roles of posture, movement styles and speed, and body positioning in how we create and perceive meanings. The area of kinesics that might be most familiar to you is gesturing, or hand movements.

Another area of nonverbal communication that is closely related to kinesics is **proxemics**. This specialized area focuses on how we claim space (territoriality) and how we use the space around our bodies as a way to show how intimate a relationship is (personal space). For instance, you are much more likely to feel comfortable talking to your lover with your faces only inches apart than you would if the other person is a casual acquaintance. The general rule in personal space is that the more intimate the relationship is, the smaller the personal distance you need to keep in order to feel comfortable while talking to that person.

Ultimately, the more accurate you and your dyad partners can learn to become in observing and interpreting nonverbal communication characteristics, the more thoroughly you can understand each other without lengthy explanations of everything.

## ALL NONVERBAL BEHAVIOR HAS COMMUNICATIVE VALUE

Many of us work very hard to hide our true feelings from others. And while we may succeed in hiding our feelings from most others, those who know us best may still recognize when something is wrong with us without us saying anything about our condition. There is good reason for this. Consider the following scenario. If someone tries to talk to you and you refuse to talk to them, you are still sending nonverbal messages. The most obvious message that you are sending is that you are either angry with them or you simply do not want to connect with them in any way. If you send this message by obviously blocking out communication or ignoring the other person, then that person may feel disrespected, and may react negatively, even though you have not verbally attacked them. Every one of us wants to feel as though our lives matter to others. Being treated as if we have no importance can devastate our self-esteem, among other things.

## NONVERBAL COMMUNICATION IS CULTURE-BOUND

Just as all people do not speak the same verbal language, the same nonverbal symbols do not necessarily convey the same meanings within different cultures. For instance, in some cultures, eye contact is a sign of one's status in the society. In an environment like that, the higher status person can look into a lower status person's eyes, but the lower status person is considered rude for returning the gaze. In the United States, we all are encouraged to make eye contact with the person to whom we are speaking. In fact, many Americans get suspicious when a dyad partner refuses to make eye contact while conversing.

The meanings of gestures can also differ greatly from culture to culture. A U.S. college student raised in Thailand related the story in the box to the left about a nonverbal encounter that he had with an American teacher:

## NONVERBAL COMMUNICATION IS PRIMARILY RELATIONAL

If you closely observe skillful communicators as they interact with a variety of others, you will notice that they vary their body movements and facial expressions according to the kinds of relationships that they share with each of those people. Likewise, the way we move and dress at a rap or rock concert, which is usually a peer activity, shows respect for that occasion, but the same body language shows disregard for behavioral rules in a conservative business environment. In short, skillful communicators generally do not lose sight of "who they are dealing with," and they behave in ways that help them achieve their communication goals.

## NONVERBAL COMMUNICATION SERVES MULTIPLE FUNCTIONS

The proverb, "A picture is worth a thousand words," applies heavily to nonverbal behaviors, which help to provide context to our speaking in a variety of ways. Just

*Communicating*
*Nonverbally across Cultures*

"We were just finishing the class and my teacher, a woman, dismissed us. As I was about to walk through the door out of the room, I looked back at my teacher and saw her gesturing at me (Her palm was turned outward and she wagged her fingers in what is considered a goodbye motion in U.S. culture). Not wanting to be rude, I stopped and walked back over to her, and asked her what she wanted. She said she was just waving goodbye. I said I was confused about why she was calling me to her. When she insisted she didn't, I explained to her that her gesture means 'come here' in my country. We both had a good laugh and learned something we did not expect to learn that day."

as nonverbal communication has many elements to it, it can also convey many meanings. For instance, standing with your arms crossed in front of you could mean that you are deep in thought, cold, or angry. In order for me to accurately decipher the meaning of your gesture, I would need to receive a variety of other signs from you as well.

### NONVERBAL COMMUNICATION IS AMBIGUOUS

The meanings behind the words we use are not always clear, and are often mis-understood, but nonverbal symbols tend to be even less clear and more likely to be misunderstood. This is true because much of our nonverbal communication consists of unconscious forms of expression such as those mentioned throughout this discussion. When we speak, at least we are trying to point others toward a particular meaning. However, this is often not the case with nonverbal messages. For instance, if you scratch your head, does that mean you are confused or that your head is itching? Unless I am a skillful nonverbal symbol decoder, I may not be able to draw accurate conclusions from your behavior to interpret it correctly. My best course of action in a case like this is to test my hunch verbally by asking about your condition or state.

Table 1 illustrates the main differences between the information conveyed by words and by nonverbal symbols. Practicing effective techniques in both areas will make your of your relationships more satisfying for both partners.

### Table 1: Differences Between Verbal And Nonverbal Communication

| Verbal | Nonverbal |
|---|---|
| Travels along single channels | Travels along multiple channels |
| Discrete or clustered messages | Continuous streams of messages |
| Relatively clear meanings | Relatively ambiguous meanings |
| Verbal impact relatively weak | Nonverbal impact relatively strong |
| Deliberate communication purpose | Unconscious communication purpose |

## The Evolving Face of Interpersonal Relationships in Electronic Times

The interpersonal communication knowledge contained in this chapter up to this section is based on the fundamental premise that we human beings are wired to continually seek to expand the scope of our awareness. This means that the more accurate information we can gather about whatever is happening in our lives, the more effectively we can respond to the experiences that we have. Furthermore, the more we expose ourselves to face-to-face interactions in which we transmit

and receive messages using all of our senses to maximize the amount of information we have available to process, the more practice we will get at navigating the peaks and valleys of our intimate relationships. And of course, the more we practice applying the relationship management tips contained in this chapter, the more skillful we will become at making our relationships as satisfying as possible.

These statements point to a basic irony that simultaneously holds great promise for the evolution of a true global community and threatens to retard the development of our current generation's **information literacy** skills. Information literacy refers to the ability to gather, select, and use information in effective ways to accomplish strategic communication goals and objectives. The irony referred to here is the emergence of **electronic social networks**. Electronic social networks are communities composed of individuals who are creating "**mediated social selves**" that serve as identities crafted for, presented on, and "known" through such personally controlled media forms[19] as MySpace.com, Facebook.com, and texting, to name a few.

The generation of people who were born and raised in the United States after 1980 have grown up in a social and educational environment dominated by rapidly expanding access to ways of plugging into a global computer-mediated communication network. Largely because of this fact, the possibilities for building international and cross-cultural coalitions and mass movements are growing exponentially, as demonstrated by the election of Barack Obama as our 44th President. Individuals can now reach more people faster, and with any message, than ever before. High speed wireless communication devices are easy to find, easy to buy, and getting easier to use all the time.

When used as tools to support our need to stay connected to growing numbers of people, these networks give us the potential ability to control our destinies to an unparalleled extent. On the other hand, using media devices as a substitute for face-to-face interaction can act as an avoidance mechanism, severely restricting the relationship partners' opportunities to practice the conflict management and team building skills introduced in this chapter. Writer Antonio Larosa observed in an August 2007 Contract magazine article[20] that "We are losing basic interpersonal communication skills. People are so busy gabbing on their cells, texting, or popping into Web chat rooms that we are losing the ability or desire to say a few words to the person standing next to us. Many are fine with talking to strangers over the Internet, yet the thought of speaking to someone in person turns them mute."

In the final analysis, regardless of what we think of the impact of electronic social networking on our interpersonal communication skills, this growing phenomenon is here to stay. Therefore, all students of effective communication would do well to strike a proper balance between in-person and electronically mediated contact.

## Summary

Interpersonal communication is interaction within a dyad, or (generally) between two persons, which forms a relationship between the participants. All communication begins with the self and expands outward into our environment. All of your messages indicate something about how you view the world and about the kinds of relationships you have with the recipients of those messages.

Understanding the role and proper uses of language is vital to your success as a member of the world community. Developing positive habits of thinking and speaking will help you to build healthy relationships, and eliminating bad language habits will enable you to resolve conflicts with relative ease. A major key to building and maintaining harmonious relationships is developing a deeper understanding of how to derive accurate meanings from the mysterious world of nonverbal communication. Finally, nonverbal communication provides symbols that enable us to understand others' messages accurately. Therefore, the more attentive you are to the various components of nonverbal communication behavior, the more satisfying your relationships are likely to be.

## Skill Builders: Establishing Mutually Satisfying Communication Patterns

### Exercise #1 (Empathic Listening)

The next time you are in a discussion that someone else tries to turn into a debate, try observing your own internal reaction to the other person's attempts to rope you into an argument. If you feel yourself getting anxious to win a contest, fight the urge and force yourself to just listen attentively to what the other person is saying. Try to determine whether he or she is confusing facts with opinions or inferences and using emotive language. Use the active listening steps outlined in the main text. Instead of directly confronting the other person about any fallacies, ask questions that require him or her to focus on facts. Make a note of how the other person responds and contrast those responses to the ones you get when you debate.

### Exercise #2 (Good Will – Bad Will Scoreboard)

Recall and list as many instances as you can during the last week or two in which you said the nastiest thing you could think when you were angry. Then recall and list the times when you said something kind to another person. Compare these two lists to each other. Which one is the longest? If the nasty comments list is longer, try looking for more opportunities to add to the kind comments list.

### Exercise #3 (Improving Your Descriptive Ability)

Do you really know the difference between facts and opinions? The next time someone asks for your opinion about a food or a movie, try focusing almost your entire response on describing what you liked or did not like about it. Minimize the discussion of your opinion and see how that affects the conversation.

### Exercise #4 (Using the Language of Responsibility Wisely)

Role-play a dispute with a classmate to gain practice in the art of using "I" and "we" statements to remove some of the sting from your relationship negotiations. Have the class members report orally about their reactions to this way of fighting defensive communication.

## ▌ Endnotes

1   Infante, Dominic A., Andrew S. Rancer, and Deanna F. Womack.  <u>Building Communication Theory</u>.  Prospect Heights, IL: Waveland Press, Inc., 1990: 187–189.

2   Wells, Jr., Leroy. "The Group-as-a-whole Perspective and Its Theoretical Roots." In A.D. Coleman and M.H.Geller (eds.), <u>Group Relations Reader 2.</u> Baltimore, MD: A.K. Rice Institute, 1985: 109–126.

3   Burgoon, Judee K and Norah E. Dunbar. "An Interactionist Perspective on Dominance-Submission: Interpersonal Dominance as a Dynamic, Situationally Contingent Social Skill." <u>Communication Monographs</u> . March 2000: 96–121.

4   Brennan, Barbara A.. <u>Light Emerging: The Journey of Personal Healing.</u> New York: Bantam Books, Inc., 1993: 161–176.

5   Brennan, p. 168.

6   Krishnamurti, Jiddhu. <u>The First and Last Freedom.</u> San Francisco, CA: Harper-Collins Publishers, 1975: 104.

7   Brennan, p. 21.

8   Metcalfe, Sheldon. "Understanding Perception." In <u>Building Foundations for Communications.</u> Fort Worth, TX: Cengage Custom Publishing, 2001.

9   Adler, Ronald B. and Neil Towne. <u>Looking Out/Looking In: Interpersonal Communication</u>. 8th ed. Fort Worth, TX: Harcourt Brace College Publishers, 1996: 172.

10  Krishnamurti, Jiddhu. <u>The Network of Thought.</u> San Francisco, CA: Harper & Row Publishers, 1982: 8.

11  Hocker, Joyce L. and William W. Wilmot, <u>Interpersonal Conflict</u>. 3rd ed. Dubuque, IA: W.C. Brown, 1991: 21–30.

12  Hocker and Wilmot, pp. 11–20.

13  Fisher, Roger and William Ury, <u>Getting To Yes: Negotiating Agreement Without Giving In</u>. New York: Penguin Books Ltd., 1983: 3.

14  Guerrero, Laura K., Susanne M. Jones, and Judee K. Burgoon, "Responses to Nonverbal Intimacy Change in Romantic Dyads: Effects of Behavioral Valence and Degree of Behavioral Change on Nonverbal and Verbal Reactions." <u>Communication Monographs</u>. (December 2000):325–346.

15  Adler and Towne, p. 186.

16  Brennan, pp. 162–165.

17  Adler and Towne, pp. 228–238.

18  All images in this chapter are copyright © 2001 Microsoft Corporation, One Microsoft Way, Redmond, Washington 98052-6399 U.S.A. All rights reserved.

19  Anonymous. "Reality TV Begets "Promiscuous Friending." USA Today (Farmingdale) 137.2759 (Aug. 2008): 10, 11.

20  Larosa, Antonio. "Designers Against the iPodization of Society." Contract 49.8 (Aug., 2007): 168.

CHAPTER

# Mass Communication

Jennifer Kafka Smith

### CHAPTER OBJECTIVES

After reading this chapter you will be able to:

1. Understand how mass communication differs from other patterns of communication both in function and in relation to the Communication Model;

2. Appreciate the significant innovations that have brought mass communication from the early days of print to today's highly changeable electronic media;

3. Become aware of the responsibility the audience has to evaluate messages of mass communication;

4. Recognize how mass communication serves the public to deliver information and entertainment and how business and industry drives this pattern of communication.

*ARPANET*

*Communication model*

*context*

*critical thinking*

*demographics*

*feedback*

*gatekeeping*

*innovation*

*Internet*

*mass communication*

*mass media*

*propaganda*

*psychographics*

*target audience*

You might be surprised how much you already know about mass communication. It's nearly impossible these days to find someone who doesn't own a television, hasn't listened to a radio, or hasn't seen a billboard advertisement on the highway. As a college student, you've had ample opportunity to become familiar with the Internet and with over 70 percent of the U.S. population using the web[1], you are not alone. There are people who read a daily newspaper—although many of us now prefer to read our news online. There's a good chance that you discuss television programs with your friends and family. You are probably able to recognize a product just by its mascot, jingle, slogan, or just the style of the television commercial itself. All of these ways that we receive information and entertainment fall under the topic of **Mass Communication**—or communication that occurs when "one person or a group of persons send a message to a large group through a transmitting device to large audiences".[2]

From a very early age, you've had preferences for different forms of media and different programming within that media. Without realizing it, you are already something of an expert on the topic of mass communication; at least from the consumer's perspective. But do you really know the purpose that mass communication serves in our society? Do you know how it all began?

This chapter will provide information about the evolution of mass communication; the various ways that mass communication serves businesses and the public; and the evolving technology that supports mass communication via the Internet.

## WHAT IS MASS COMMUNICATION?

Mass communication distinguishes itself from other patterns of communication because the intended audience is too large to reach otherwise. Most of your day-to-day communication takes place between a relatively small number of people. In mass communication, the sender may be reaching out to hundreds or even millions of people.

Another way that mass communication is different from the other patterns of communication is its dependence on assorted mass media in order to carry the message to the public. **Mass media** refers to any method of getting the message to the public. You've probably heard the term mass media referring mostly to electronic media—television and cable TV, for example. Commonly, the media format used for mass communication relies on print, audio, or video.

### Mass Media in Print

Newspapers are one type of printed mass media. Can you think of others?
Books—Magazines—Billboards—eBooks—Online Blogs

### Mass Media in an Audio Format

The radio is a popular way to receive audio messages. Radio programs include more than just music; news, weather, humor, politics, and personal opinion. How do you receive audio messages?
CDs—MP3s—Satellite Radio—Internet Radio— Streaming Audio Online

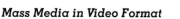

### Mass Media in Video Format

Movies, DVDs, and television are popular ways to receive messages created for video. The Internet carries a tremendous quantity of video content—YouTube is a popular location online to find video content —but video is available on many web sites.

## THE COMMUNICATION MODEL AND MASS COMMUNICATION

One of the best ways to understand mass communication is to look at it through the organization of the Circular Communication Model described in Chapter 1 of this text:

In mass communication the **sender** is an individual, a business or an organization that has a specific message that they want to share with the public. In many cases, the process of **encoding** requires research and the contribution of experts to find the most effective way to craft the **message**. The sender selects the **channel** that best fits both the message and the audience making the effort to minimize **barriers** (of course, it's not possible to eliminate all barriers). The **receiver** is the public or a segment of the public that the sender wants to reach. The receiver **decodes** the message as in all other patterns of communication.

When the President of the United States gives a speech that is broadcast over radio and television, that is an example of mass communication. As the sender, the President delivers the message but we all know that he has a staff of speechwriters and advisors who have input on the content of the message. For The White House speechwriters, the process of encoding requires time and careful planning to ensure that the President's words fit the occasion perfectly. While he may be in front of an audience made up of members of the Senate and the House of Representatives, his speech is being transmitted across multiple channels to millions of listeners and viewers. The audience of a presidential address may not just be American. In this age of satellite transmissions, an international audience is likely. Imagine the millions of listeners and viewers of just one speech and how each person will hear the speech differently depending on their knowledge and experience. It's easy to understand why so much effort is put into the crafting of the original message—because once the message is sent using a channel of mass communication, the sender no longer has any control over it.

### Feedback

It's in the *feedback* step that mass communication is dramatically different from other patterns of communication. Logically, the sender cannot possibly receive or process feedback from thousands to millions of receivers. The President of the United States does receive public feedback following a speech. Feedback to the President comes in several forms: public opinion expressed in polls, call-in programs on television and radio, political debate, newspaper editorials and even in public demonstrations. The advent of the Internet has created a more immediate way for feedback to be offered. The American public is free to write editorial comments or they may blog their support or concern for the President's actions. Regardless of the accessibility of feedback channels, it is just not possible for the President (or his advisors)to manage all the feedback that might be offered—even with a team of Communication professionals working to collect as much feedback as possible.

Feedback in mass communication requires the audience to take some action since the sender and receiver are not face-to-face. When communicating in small groups or in an interpersonal setting, the feedback is immediate and we are highly dependent on both verbal and non-verbal feedback to guide our responses. In mass communication, those visual qualities of feedback are not present. It's not likely that the President would take your telephone call offering him your feedback on his 9 o'clock State of the Union address. Internet polls, online voting, and telephone voting systems (including text votes with cellular telephones) have offered more expedient feedback to mass communication in recent years, but it still lacks the personal details that we receive as feedback in other communication patterns. These tools for feedback are effective when collecting quantitative feedback (as in counting votes for American Idol) and less effective when tracking qualitative feedback (as in the opinions presented in web blogs and other editorial content).

### GATEKEEPING

An important aspect of mass communication is gatekeeping. **Gatekeeping** is the process of controlling the content that the intended audience receives. Consider the example of a newspaper. There are several people who, in the role of gatekeeper, pick and choose the news stories that are in the paper. The Assignment Editor determines which stories the reporters will cover. The Copy Editor decides how the stories will fit into the layout of the paper. A gatekeeper also determines which stories are on the front page and how much column space each story is allotted. Have you ever reached for the newspaper anxious to see a specific story of interest to you only to find an inch of copy on one of the back pages? Think of all the newsworthy events that happen every day that never make it to your local newspaper. Gatekeeping is a necessary part of controlling communication in settings where either time or space for messages is limited.

Gatekeeping can be used to control messages in a way that could be interpreted as a deliberate attempt to keep information from the public. If you live in a large metropolitan area, there is probably more than one daily newspaper printed locally. *USA Today* is a national newspaper. Have you ever examined the content differences between your local papers and *USA Today*? What differences would you expect to find? In your community newspaper, you'll find stories that pertain to your neighborhood—the people and the places that impact your daily life. In a national newspaper, the content features stories of interest to a broader audience both in terms of geography and subject matter.

Some newspapers or magazines have a very specific audience. Publications like *The Wall Street Journal* or *Rolling Stone* magazine are specifically written to meet the content needs and interests of their readership. Gatekeeping is not always a negative aspect of mass communication; it is often a necessary and desirable filter that helps manage and focus the information.

Gatekeepers are not only found in the newspaper industry but in any setting where the goal is to deliver information to the public. As a consumer of information, you should keep your eyes (and ears) open for the information or point of view that is not presented and realize in some cases, you aren't getting the whole story.

**CONTEXT**

To define context, we'll borrow an organizational tool that's used in Journalism—the Five W's: Who, What, When, Where, & Why:

- "*Who*" details the people (the communicators) that are involved and their relationship to each other
- "*What*" provides the detail about the communication
- "*When*" refers to time of day or situation as the communication takes place
- "*Where*" describes the physical location for the communication ; and
- "*Why*" reveals the purpose of the communication

Utilizing these five words may help you understand the whole idea of context specifically as it applies to the Communication Model. To put it simply, context gives communication meaning, but as you now understand—the meaning comes from many factors. **Context** provides the information the participants need to make sense of the communication event.

We regularly adjust our communication to fit the circumstances of our situation. Do you communicate differently in the classroom than you do at home or with your friends? Would you speak to a manager during a job interview the same way you'd chat with a friend over the phone? Our relationships and the purpose of each communication event causes us to adjust our own style of communication —our verbal, non-verbal, and listening habits change to fit the situation. To fully grasp context, ask yourself what a job interviewer would think about you if you sent a text message to a friend during your interview. A friend might be tolerant of this behavior—a prospective employer would view your behavior as disrespectful. Context gives meaning to the communication and it changes how we both send and receive messages. This is equally true in mass communication. We expect to hear certain types of communication on the radio and view specific types of messages on television. When communication occurs that does not fit the expected context of the moment, it creates confusion or grabs our attention.

***The "War of the Worlds" Radio Broadcast***—In any communication situation, it is important that the message reaches the intended audience and it's equally important that the audience understands the purpose or context of the message. To illustrate the idea of how important context is in mass communication, consider this:

A radio broadcast in 1938 struck fear in its listeners—simply because of context.

On the front page of *The New York Times* the next day (October 31, 1938) the headline read: "Radio Listeners in Panic, Taking War Drama as Fact Many Flee Homes to Escape 'Gas Raid From Mars'—Phone Calls Swamp Police at Broadcast of Wells Fantasy".[4] The article described the public's panic in detail including reports that people fled their homes in fear of the Martian attack. The terror created by the broadcast caused traffic jams as people filled the streets trying to escape the city.

Real news and radio drama are not easily confused unless the context of the message is not clear to the receiver. It frequently happens in our daily contact with people that our messages are misinterpreted. When we have face-to-face contact with the receiver, we can determine with relative ease when our message has been misunderstood and make the corrections on the spot. When the audience is as vast as in mass communication, it's much more difficult to set the record straight when a mistake or misunderstanding has occurred. This illustration helps support the idea that, especially in mass communication, the sender has an enormous responsibility to the audience to keep the message and its purpose as clear and accurate as possible.

## Mass Communication's History

Historically, mass communication was in many forms such as ancient hieroglyphics, smoke signals, and even drums. In each case, these methods of communication accomplished the desired outcome—reaching a limited public audience. Whether these forms of communication were too cumbersome to duplicate or distribute or just too dependent on nature to carry the smoke or the sound of the drum, man endeavored to find a better way to share information with large groups of people. Inventions spanning hundreds of years have led us to the most common tools of mass communication used today—the printed document (newspapers, books, and magazines), radio, television, and the Internet.

### PRINT

The first form of mass communication, as we know it today, was the printed document. Today, it's hard to imagine a world without books, newspapers, pamphlets, and even junk mail. It wasn't until the invention of the printing press by Johannes

**76**

On the eve of Halloween in 1938, Orson Welles, a well-known radio personality delivered a theatrical radio program based on the science fiction novel *War of the Worlds*[3] by H.G. Wells (1898). [While their names are similar—Wells and Welles—there is no other connection between these two men.] Rather than present the story in the traditional play format that was popular at that time on the radio, Welles decided to tell the story in the style of a news broadcast. Throughout the program, seemingly real news bulletins were inserted into the play reporting an invasion of Martians including "a huge flaming object" falling on a community in New Jersey and sightings of monsters. Unless the listener heard the very beginning of the broadcast and the disclaimer that the program was for entertainment only, the broadcast sounded very real. The hysteria that broke out over that program is legendary.

Gutenberg in 1455 that mass communication became recognized as a tool for sharing information.[5] It's important to recognize the contribution made by the Chinese who developed a process for making paper dating back to A.D. 105. The Chinese used a block printing method resembling today's rubber stamps. The Chinese alphabet consists of many more characters than the western alphabet probably helping explain why it was the western Europeans who were able to advance the technology of the printing press. Until Gutenberg's printing press was invented, multiple copies of a document were prepared by copying them over by hand—one at a time.

From studying American history, you may be familiar with communication innovations like the Town Crier and the Pony Express. You may remember people in history who distinguished themselves by the documents they printed. Benjamin Franklin's *Poor Richard's Almanac* and Thomas Paine's *Common Sense* are examples of early American documents dispersed via mass communication. When you think about the impact of these documents on a young nation, it helps illustrate the significant role the printing press has played in our history alone.

## RADIO

Another form of mass communication is the radio. The invention of radio is attributed to Guglielmo Marconi, a 20 year old Italian who discovered wireless transmission of sound after studying the work of three names that should be familiar to you: Samuel Morse (inventor of the telegraph and the Morse Code), Alexander Graham Bell (inventor of the telephone), and Heinrich Hertz (who proved that electricity can be transmitted in electromagnetic waves). Marconi's first broadcast took place in 1899 to a very limited audience. Beyond Marconi, several men advanced the development of radio. In 1916, David Sarnoff, a 25-year-old Russian immigrant to America working for the Marconi Company, predicted that radio would someday become a household utility. Sarnoff's career is legendary as he was involved in the evolution of broadcasting from the early days of radio and eventually the birth of television in 1939.

Before television, families gathered around their radio the same way people watch television today. The Programs that were broadcast on radio have become the foundation of today's television staples: game shows, drama series, comedies, news programs, sports, variety shows, and talent showcases. Today, our taste in radio programming has changed as has our listening habits. Despite the popularity of television, radio—regardless of the delivery method—maintains a strong listening audience. Nearly every household in the U.S. has a radio and almost every automobile on the road does too.

Radios have changed considerably throughout the years increasing the portability and quality of sound with each new generation of radio. In recent years, our options for radio listening have expanded to include Internet radio broadcasts and satellite radio. Satellite radio is rapidly gaining popularity—despite the need for a monthly subscription. Just as traditional radio permeated the marketplace in new cars post World War II, satellite radio is duplicating that effort and can be found as a feature in most new cars. Installing satellite radio in new cars and offering a temporary free subscription to the service, helps grow the audience for satellite radio.

Satellite radio provides the same rich and diverse programming options to the listener as cable television brought to viewers in the 1980s. The audience for satellite radio has grown to nearly 18 million subscriptions in 2008[6]—but since subscriptions do not necessarily count listeners, it's difficult to determine the actual number of people listening to satellite radio.

With the surge of interest in new radio technologies and the popularity of mp3 players, traditional radio (often called terrestrial radio referring to land-based radio) has experienced a series of setbacks. Advertising revenue on terrestrial radio dropped every month throughout 2008[7]. Broadcasters insist that the audience is not leaving terrestrial radio, but the push to provide 'high definition' radio or digital radio suggests that there's a desire to compete more aggressively with satellite radio. Obviously, the radio marketplace is in a state of change driven by the numerous options available to the audience.

## TELEVISION

Considering most of the inventions that touch our daily lives, TV is a relatively new innovation. Television, as a common household appliance, is just over 50 years old but the first invention leading to television dates back over a hundred years. In 1884, a German inventor, Paul Nipkow, invented a mechanical rotating disc that would transmit images over a wire.[8] During the next 30 years  and throughout the world, different inventors worked on their ideas to transmit images first mechanically and later electronically. Each inventor made a contribution that advanced the technology of television. In 1927, American Philo T. Farnsworth transmitted the first experimental television images[9]. Finally, in 1932, the National Broadcasting Company (NBC) opened the first experimental television station in New York's Empire State Building.

It wasn't until 1939 at the New York World's Fair that commercial television was presented to the public as an emerging technology. That same year, RCA began selling television sets priced from $199.50 to $600.00. These sets were very expensive in terms of the economy of the time and too costly for many families. Still, there were people who could afford to buy a television. By 1947, only 4,000 televisions had been sold and nine years later, nearly 10 million televisions are reported to have been sold—establishing TV as a staple of the American home by 1950.[10] Today, you can find a television in nearly every home and it is commonplace for a home to have televisions in several rooms throughout the house. New technology continues to expand the programming and services available through local, cable, satellite, and Internet transmission.

Television has changed our perceptions of the world. In our homes we've watched world-changing news events. You're likely to never forget watching the images of September 11, 2001 as the World Trade Towers collapsed; in 2003, the beginning of the War in Iraq; in August 2005,the devastating impact of Hurricane Katrina; and in April 2007, the shootings at Virginia Tech. Generations before you remember the first televised presidential debate in 1960 between Richard Nixon and John F. Kennedy and just a few years later the assassination of President Kennedy in Dallas, Texas. In your future, you will tell your children and grandchildren about events you witnessed on television.

While television has helped document major news events and disasters, television has also captured major milestones—the amazing Moon Walk in 1969, the grand international fireworks celebrations as cities around the world reached the Year 2000, the Winter and Summer Olympic Games, and all presidential elections—most recently the historic election of Barack Obama. We have all been influenced by what we've seen on TV. Think about the things you've seen on television that have changed how you think, feel, or behave. These televised images shape our view of our community, our country, our culture, and ourselves.

## Evolving Technology and Mass Communication

In today's world, the technology that drives mass communication is changing at a rapid pace. Most college students cannot remember a time without video games, MTV, and the Internet. Your parents remember the dilemma consumers experienced between purchasing cassettes versus 8-track tapes and Beta versus VHS and the Video Disc. Your grandparents remember bringing their first black and white television into the house. What relics of mass communication still linger in your home? Consumers are understandably frustrated because as soon as they purchase the new electronic device, it has been replaced by something else that has more features for less money.

In the 1980s, the personal computer became small enough and sufficiently affordable to be brought into offices and homes. The first desktop computers transitioned slowly into the marketplace. The United States Bureau of Census has kept track of the percentage of homes with personal computers since 1984 when they reported that 8 percent of American homes had computers. By 1989, that number had doubled and they reported an increase to 15 percent.[11] In just 10 more years, the 2000 Census determined that 51 percent of American homes had at least one personal computer.[12] Since that time, a private research group has released their findings in their Technology User Profile for 2007 stating that 70 percent of American homes now have personal computers and 80% of Americans use computers.[13] Not since the American public began watching television in 1950 has a device had as great an impact on the nation. We're seeing that just as today's youth favors the Internet and other contemporary technology over newspapers and radio for information and entertainment, television audiences are also shrinking as the Internet becomes the preferred method for obtaining news, information, socialization, and entertainment.

Technology has become increasingly affordable permitting many of us to carry pagers and cell phones—many of which have Internet access and the ability to send and receive email and photos. It seems as though cell phones are in everyone's hands and gradually people are replacing their landline phones with cell phones. Maybe there will be a time when all our phones are cell phones—or maybe cell phones will be replaced with other new technology that's yet to be invented.

You may not think of your pager and cell phone as a tool for mass communication. However, if your phone or pager receives news, weather, or the Internet, you are already connected to outlets for mass communication through that device.

Maybe someday your cell phone, or another similar portable device, will receive advertising that is sent out to large groups of people. It is possible that one day special news reports will be broadcast on our cell phones just as we see television programming interrupted today. The potential of these portable communication devices has yet to be uncovered. One thing holds true, as these new devices are introduced—each of them provides a new way to access messages of mass communication.

**Innovation** is the constant development and introduction of new technology. Innovation is what drives today's mass media marketplace. It seems that as soon as you buy a new cell phone or media player, a new one with more features and greater storage is introduced. Last year's new computer can be replaced by one that costs less and has more features. It wasn't that long ago that the Internet was just being introduced to the public. Personal computers have only been found in homes in the last twenty years. Technology changes quickly. We can be certain that new technology will be announced within the next five years that doesn't even exist today. There is one thing we can count on—we cannot keep up with the evolving technology.

## THE INTERNET

The Internet is a network of computers that send and receive information in a standardized software format called TCP/IP, which stands for "Transmission Control Protocol over Internet Protocol". Some of us may not be able to remember what the world was like without the Internet. We can find movie schedules, shop, send email, attend classes, do online research for school projects, and receive radio and television programming—all online. Nearly every business has as web site and they want to make sure you know how to find them when you are online. You can't see or hear an advertisement today without there being a web address included. The Internet has even introduced terminology that didn't exist a mere fifteen years ago. Words like Homepage, Dot Com, Email, blog, and YouTube are now commonly used in our daily language.

The Internet had its early roots in the late 1960's as the US Department of Defense devised a communication system to support the military in the event of a national emergency.[14] The first communications network was launched at UCLA (the University of California at Los Angeles) and called **ARPANET** for the Pentagon's Advanced Research Projects Agency. The ARPANET users began using the user-to-user messaging function (now email) and it gained popularity very quickly in that group. Before long, they began creating group mailing lists to send the same message to multiple users at the same time.

As computers became more affordable to businesses, the network of computers interested in the services provided on the Internet increased. The software technology permitting the electronic exchange of information was public domain meaning that any organization could use it creating a small network of computers that ultimately wanted to link into the larger computer-networking universe … the Internet. That's how the Internet began but as you well know, the Internet changes at a very rapid pace.

The hardware technology that permits access to the Internet began with the desktop and laptop computer but now people can access email and some websites with their PDA (Personal Digital Assistant—a handheld computer), Cell phone, or other current generation interface device. To access the Internet, we purchase subscriptions from Internet Service Providers (ISPs) and they provide access to the Internet via their computers. If we don't have a computer at home, we may have access to the Internet at work, at school, or at the local library. Internet access is also becoming widely available at Wi-Fi hotspots—a wireless local area network (LAN). Wi-Fi accessibility is offered—often free of charge—at restaurants, hotels, and airports. An attempt to provide Wi-Fi service for entire cities proved to be too costly—but as technology develops and costs come down, the idea of a wireless community is very possible. In the meantime, the increased availability of Wi-Fi service from individual hotspots will keep those of us who thrive for a connection online.

Still, the Internet is a tool of mass communication and a unique tool as well since it has no true owner or censor. As consumers of information on the Internet, you should be aware that content on the Internet is not controlled or verified for accuracy. You should always check the source of information and determine whether the website is accurately presenting information.

How do you see yourself utilizing the technology of the Internet? Will you order your groceries online? Will you view your child at day care on a camera that transmits images to you across the Internet? Will you turn on appliances in your home while you are still at work? All of these things are already available and we can only imagine what the future may hold for us through the Internet.

## CRITICAL EVALUATION OF MESSAGES

Whatever the content of the message, it's up to the receiver to interpret the meaning of the message and understand why the sender sent the message. If your little brother offers to wash your car—what's in it for him? Will the infomercial's exercise machine help you lose 25 pounds overnight? Probably not—but whether the celebrity's claim is true or not, he will be paid for his endorsement of the product. It's up to you to consider the content of each advertisement, each speech, each message, and determine for yourself what is likely to be true.

In order to evaluate a message, you'll need to utilize your critical thinking skills. Generally speaking, **critical thinking** is "the ability to analyze facts, generate and organize ideas, defend opinions, make comparisons, draw inferences, evaluate arguments, and solve problems."[15] As you develop your skills as a critical thinker, you'll become a detective seeking to understand the truth and motives behind mass communication messages.

As a member of the mass communication audience, you will constantly be challenged to make sense of the information being delivered to you. Your awareness of the goal of each message will certainly help you make sense out of the mass communication messages you receive.

## PROPAGANDA

All messages require us to evaluate their meaning but in mass communication, the intent is not always clear. Propaganda is the "spreading of viewpoints or doctrines by government authority through the use of media."[16] During the 2003 War in Iraq there were broadcasts from the Iraqi Information Minister, Muhammed Saeed al-Sahaf to the people of Iraq giving them updates on the status of the military advances on Baghdad and surrounding areas in Iraq. Despite the fact that television cameras were broadcasting images of US tanks moving through the streets of Baghdad, the Iraqi Information Minister broadcast messages insisting that the city had not been taken. In other broadcasts, he would report that the city was quiet of bombings and other military activity while guns could be heard in the background. The morale of the Iraqi military certainly was impacted by the reports from Al-Sahaf. Even though his reports were false, do you see the potential benefit of his message? Was he wrong to report false information?

Propaganda doesn't always have a negative purpose—or at least a perceived negative purpose. There are times when a message can be delivered in such a way to gain support and help the public cope with a difficult situation. During World War II, the American film industry produced a large number of films helping families understand the plight of their loved ones both in battle and at home. This type of film had the specific goal of providing information and guiding Americans to support the military initiatives of the country and to be prepared for the special needs of the soldiers as they returned home from war. These films helped inform the public as well as entertain them. On the other hand, these same films introduced ideas of bias and stereotypes of our wartime enemies. Unfortunately, these messages of international prejudice lingered in the minds and actions of Americans for generations beyond the war and long after animosity between our countries had been erased.

A message that has the purpose of being propaganda does not follow a specific formula other than its intent is to be persuasive often tapping into the emotions of the audience. While persuasion should be driven by logical arguments and research, propaganda may include dishonesty or omission of information that keeps the receiver from getting the complete picture. It's up to you, the receiver of the message, to ask yourself who could benefit from this information or whose point of view is represented by the message. Be aware that some quotes may be taken out of context robbing the audience of the information that is needed to get the entire story. Asking questions and seeking more information is key to understanding the purpose of the message and applying the elements of critical evaluation to mass communication messages.

## ▋ The Impact of Mass Communication

In our society we look to newspapers, radio, television, the Internet, and other electronic media for information and entertainment. They represent our most frequently utilized sources of mass communication. Messages from these sources shape how we dress, what we eat, the language we use and what we talk about. Before we can truly understand the power of mass communication we need to take a step back and look at the primary purpose this type of communication serves.

### THE PURPOSE OF MASS MEDIA

Now that we've looked at several elements of mass communication, you may think you understand why this assortment of media is available. You may think that your radio exists to play your favorite music, the television's purpose is to broadcast your favorite programs, and that newspapers are for the distribution of news. If so, think again. Each of these forms of media exists for the purpose of advertising and selling goods and services. Yes, the programming elements of mass communication are important to those of us who love to listen to the radio, watch TV, or read the daily newspaper. But without the advertising, the cost of the programming would be too high for the regular consumer to afford. Advertising pays the bills that make the programming possible.

In the early days of newspapers, people wanted more than just the ads. Articles about the community kept people coming back to read the latest news—and the ads were there too. The same held true for radio and television. Programming is there to hold your interest from commercial to commercial. Manufacturers sponsor programs to put their name in front of the audience.

Mass communication serves the public by providing information and mass communication serves commerce by providing businesses a means to reach the public. Advertisers pay for the ad space they use whether in print or in broadcast airtime. The more people that are expected to view a broadcast, the more the airtime costs the advertiser. The cost for ads in the 2003 Super Bowl were at an all time high of $2,7 million dollars for a 30 second spot[17]. The 2009 Super Bowl is projected to yield $3 million for that same 30 seconds of advertising[18]. How can businesses afford to pay that much for advertising? When television ratings tell you that 97.5 million Americans[19] (more than any previous Super Bowl game) is watching the same program and your commercials along with that program, advertising rates climb. The Super Bowl is typically one of the most-watched programs every year and as a result it commands the highest advertising rates.

## DEFINING THE AUDIENCE

Advertising is expensive even when the commercial is not being shown during the Super Bowl. Ad space in newspapers and magazines costs more than you'd imagine. For example, to purchase just one column inch (just one inch of one column) in *The Washington Post* costs between $856 weekdays to $1,198 on Sundays.[20] These rates are based on one-time-only ad placement with *The Washington Post*. Their rate sheet describes adjusted fees if a commitment is made for additional advertising. With *The Washington Post* reaching a daily readership of 1,599,900 and a Sunday readership of 2,171,200, there is no easier way for a local merchant in the District of Columbia to reach as many potential customers at one time.

To make sure that an advertisement or commercial reaches the greatest number of potential customers, the audience is put into categories depending on several factors. The **target audience** is the segment of the population that fits the criteria for a particular product or service. The advertiser defines their product in terms of who might buy it—their age, gender, and marital status might be considered. Then the advertiser creates a commercial that might appeal to that specific group. Finally, the commercial is placed in print, radio, or television (or a combination) at a time of day, during specific programming, or in a specific publication to reach the intended target audience.

The process of identifying a target audience applies to any group or organization that is planning a message for mass communication. They want to reach their desired audience. When the audience is being defined one of the considerations is to look at the demographics and psychographics of the audience. **Demographics** are the traits of the audience—age, gender, race, religion, education, and marital status. **Psychographics** are the lifestyle characteristics of the audience revealing their beliefs and attitudes. Psychographics might include prior purchasing behavior, hobbies, and the preferences that guide a person's standard of living.[21] Understanding the ability to categorize audiences using demographics and psychographics may help you look at advertising a new way. Pay attention to products that you see advertised in an assortment of media and media channels—soft drinks and fast food are good examples of products that are presented differently depending on the demographics and psychographics of the audience.

### MEASURING IMPACT

When it comes to evaluating the success of a commercial for a new brand of soap or new flavor of Doritos™, the manufacturer pays attention to sales—the more he sells, the more successful the ad must have been. There are other ways that organizations can determine the effectiveness of their communication. The public may phone the organization, visit their stores, or go to their website.

Have you ever filled out a questionnaire that asked—How did you hear about our services? When you answer that you found them in the *Yellow Pages*, the business knows that the advertising they bought in the *Yellow Pages* is worthwhile. Questionnaires and surveys are another way that organizations measure the successfulness of their communication. This is the same idea behind the cashier asking you your Zip Code. The data can be used to evaluate which parts of the community are visiting the store and which are not. Once a weak area is identified, advertising can be focused to that particular part of the community with special mailers or by placing ads in newspapers that reach that geographic area.

It's important to the people who create mass communication to know who their audiences are. Cereal and toy commercials are aired on TV during times of the day when the audience is primarily children. Products typically used in the home and for childcare are aired during the weekday when homemakers and parents of young children are likely to be tuned in. You've seen advertising on MTV that you probably wouldn't see on any other channel. Advertisers want to reach their audience—the people who are most likely to purchase their product or services. Television and radio ratings provide important information that guides the placement of advertising by time of day and channel. By paying attention to these details of the mass communication audience, advertisers get the most for the money they spend creating their commercials.

## ▌ Summary

Mass Communication provides an endless source of entertainment and information through print, radio, television, and the advanced technology of today—the Internet. The media that deliver mass communication into our lives is changing rapidly—so rapidly in fact, that it's challenging for many of us to keep up with the changing technologies.

The creators of mass communication messages make the effort to ensure that their message reaches their ideal audience. Gatekeeping limits the information presented to the audience and the persuasive technique of propaganda can deliberately present messages in a one-sided way. The audiences of these messages in mass communication bear the responsibility of having to pay attention to the motives of the sender. The audience must be aware that the information being presented to them may not be the entire story or even the truth.

Lastly, mass communication may bring information and entertainment to the public, but it serves businesses by providing a forum for them to advertise their goods and services. By identifying the target audience, an organization has the ability to direct their message to a specific portion of the public.

## Skill Builders:

### Exercise #1: Comparing the News

Select a newspaper, radio program, and television program and on the same day, compare the top news stories. Are they the same? How do they differ?

### Exercise #2: Propaganda Detective

Rent a video or DVD of a World War II movie and see if you can create a list of the messages that are presented in the film. Are there pro-American messages? Is there propaganda about the political climate in the US or other countries?

### Exercise #3: Categorizing Advertising

Watch 30 minutes of television at three different times of day and log the commercials that are broadcast. Think like an advertising executive and attempt to determine the specific audience that the commercials are trying to reach. Or, select a product or service and look for advertising on different media. Is the message the same on TV, radio, the Internet, and in print?

### Exercise #4: Mass Communication Relics

With rapidly changing technology, we tend to bring new tools of mass communication into our homes and shove the outdated ones aside. What relics of mass communication can you find in your home? Ask your friends and family, which tools were the hardest to let go?

## Endnotes

1   Miniwatts Marketing Group. Internet World Stats. 2001–2008. 30 November 2008 <www.internetworldstats.com>.

2   Biagi, Shirley. Media/Impact: An Introduction to Mass Media, 6th ed. Belmont, CA: Wadsworth, 2003.

3   Wells, H.G., Seven Science Fiction Novels of H.G. Wells. New York: Dover Publications, 1950 [c1934].

4  "Radio Listeners in Panic, Taking War Drama as Fact." The New York Times 31 October 1938: A1.

5  Staubhaar, Joseph and Robert LaRose. Media Now: Communications Media in the Information Age, 3rd ed. Belmont, CA: Wadsworth Group 2002: 72.

6  "Sirius and XM Complete Merger." Sirius.com. 29 July 2008. 29 November 2008 http://investor.sirius.com/releasedetail.cfm?ReleaseID=324858

7  Clifford, Stephanie. "Radio's Revenue Falls Even as Audience Grows." NYTimes.com. 26 November 2008. 29 November 2008.

8  Dominick, Joseph R., Fritz Messere, and Barry L. Sherman. Broadcasting, Cable, the Internet, and Beyond: An Introduction to Modern Electronic Media, 6th ed. Boston: McGraw-Hill: 2008.

9  Biagi, Shirley. Media/Impact: An Introduction to Mass Media, 6th ed. Belmont, CA: Wadsworth, 2003.

10 Television History—The First 75 Years. 2001–2006. 4 December 2008 <www.tvhistory.tv/facts-stats.htm>.

11 U.S. Department of Commerce—Bureau of the Census. Statistical Brief: "The Growing Use of Computers." SB/91-11, April 1991: 1.

12 U.S. Department of Commerce—Bureau of the Census. Special Studies: "Home Computers and Internet Use in the United States: August 2000." P23-207, September 2001: 1.

13 Pew Research Center. World Publics Welcome Global Trade—But Not Immigration. Press Release. Washington, DC: The Pew Global Project Attitudes, 4 October 2007: 75.

14 Leiner, Barry M., Vinton G. Cerf, David D. Clark, Robert E. Kahn, Leonard Kleinrock, Daniel C. Lynch, Jon Postel, Larry G. Roberts, and Stephen Wolff. A Brief History of the Internet. 4 August 2000. 4 December 2008 <http://www.isoc.org/internet/history/brief.shtml>

15 Chance, P. Thinking in the Classroom: A Survey of Programs. New York: Teachers College, Columbia University, 1986: 6.

16 Davie, William R. and James R. Upshaw, Principles of Electronic Media. Boston, MA: Allyn and Bacon, 2003: 277.

17 Thomasch, Paul. 4 February 2008 "Giants and Patriots draw record Super Bowl audience. Reuters. 29 November 2008 <http://www.reuters.com/articlePrint?articleId=USN0420266320080204>

18 Sivaraman, Aarthi. 6 May 2008 "Super Bowl 30-second ads to cost $3 mln in 2009: report. 29 November 2008 <http://www.reuters.com/articlePrint?articleId=USN0644484220080506>

19 Guthrie, Marisa. 'Super-Sized Super Bowl" **Broadcasting & Cable.** New York: Jan 28, 2008: Vol. 138, Iss. 4: 18.

20 The Washington Post. 2009 General Ad Rates January 1, 2009: 3.

21 Gross, Lynne Schafer. Telecommunications: Radio, Television, and Movies in the Digital Age. 8th ed. New York, NY: McGraw-Hill, 2003: 387.

# BUILDING
# A SPEECH

seventh edition

## Sheldon Metcalfe
Community College of Baltimore County

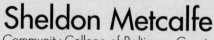

WADSWORTH
CENGAGE Learning

Australia • Brazil • Japan • Korea • Mexico • Singapore • Spain • United Kingdom • United States

**WADSWORTH**
CENGAGE Learning™

**Building a Speech, Seventh Edition**
**Sheldon Metcalfe**

Senior Publisher: Lyn Uhl

Executive Editor: Monica Eckman

Development Editor: Larry Goldberg

Assistant Editor: Rebekah Matthews

Editorial Assistant: Colin Solan

Media Editor: Jessica Badiner

Marketing Manager: Erin Mitchell

Marketing Coordinator: Darlene Macanan

Marketing Communications Manager:
Christine Dobberpuhl

Production Manager: Pre-PressPMG

Art Director: Linda Helcher

Print Buyer: Justin Palmiero

Permissions Editor: Roberta Broyer

Production Service & Compositor:
Pre-Press PMG

Photo Researcher: Bill Smith Group

Cover Designer: Red Hangar Design

Cover Image: © Construction
Photography/Corbis

For product information and technology assistance, contact us at
**Cengage Learning Customer & Sales Support, 1-800-354-9706**

For permission to use material from this text or product, submit all requests online at **cengage.com/permissions**
Further permissions questions can be emailed to
**permissionrequest@cengage.com**

Library of Congress Control Number: 2009920072

ISBN-13: 978-0-495-56757-8

ISBN-10: 0-495-56757-4

**Wadsworth**
20 Channel Center Street
Boston, MA 02210
USA

Cengage Learning products are represented in Canada by
Nelson Education, Ltd.

For your course and learning solutions, visit **www.cengage.com**

Purchase any of our products at your local college store or at our preferred online store **www.ichapters.com**

Printed in the United States of America
1 2 3 4 5 6 7 13 12 11 10 09

*To my mother, who gave me the values,*
*and my father, who gave me the vision,*
*to write this book.*

# brief contents

## unit five CONSIDERING DIFFERENT TYPES OF STRUCTURES

# contents

## Chapter 5  Understanding and Reducing Your Apprehension  64

## Chapter 6  Considering the Ethics of Public Speaking  75

## unit two PREPARING THE FOUNDATION

## Chapter 7  Selecting the Topic and Purpose 94

## Chapter 11  Selecting the Introduction and Conclusion  168

# unit four REFINING THE APPEARANCE

## Chapter 12  Using Audiovisual Aids  194

## Chapter 13 Considering Language 216

## unit five  CONSIDERING DIFFERENT TYPES OF STRUCTURES


## Chapter 15  Speaking to Inform  254

# preface

Public speaking is a building process, wherein students gradually acquire skills in speech research, organization, and delivery. Students learn these skills step-by-step from their own experiences, by observing the presentations of others, through peer criticism, and from the guidance of effective instructors. This book establishes a caring environment for the learning process, using a conversational style that aims to both interest and motivate students while conveying encouragement through topics such as apprehension and listening that will help students to realize that they are not alone in their struggles. It is grounded in the philosophy that students can master the steps of speech construction if provided with a caring environment, clear blueprints, and creative examples.

## PLAN OF THE BOOK

The five units in this book organize skills in a sequence that is meaningful and understandable to students.

Unit One, "Surveying the Landscape," presents the classical origins of public speaking and modern theories of communication and introduces students to their first speaking experience. In addition, it considers audience analysis, listening, ethics, and apprehension.

Unit Two, "Preparing the Foundation," describes how to select topics, write purpose statements, conduct research, and choose supporting materials for speeches.

Unit Three, "Creating the Structure," discusses outlining and speech introductions and conclusions.

Unit Four, "Refining the Appearance," describes the refinements necessary to complete speech construction. It helps students build skills in delivery and language, explains the use of visual aids, and includes a sample demonstration speech.

Unit Five, "Considering Different Types of Structures," discusses descriptive and process speeches and includes a sample descriptive speech; examines persuasive speaking, with sample convincing and actuating speeches; considers presentations for special occasions, including the after-dinner speech; and explores the dynamics of speaking in group situations.

## FEATURES OF THE SEVENTH EDITION

The Seventh Edition retains all of the popular features of previous editions, including a conversational style, vivid examples, and guidelines for speeches. It retains essential chapters on apprehension, listening, ethics, and discussion of diversity. In addition, *Building a Speech*, Seventh Edition, includes the following new and revised features.

### *New Section on the Career Speech*

A study released by the Bureau of Labor Statistics in 2002 found that workers held an average of 9.6 jobs from age 18 to age 36. These statistics mean that most current college graduates will probably change jobs several times in their lives. Because of the variability in the working environment this text introduces a new section on careers in Chapter 2, "Building Your First Speech," to help students research various professions and develop a speech on a specific career topic. Also included in the chapter is a new sample career speech titled "Careers in Anthropology," by an honors student in the basic speech course.

### New Speeches

In addition to the career speech, a new speech on ethics, "Practice, Practice, Practice: Knowing Is Not The Same Thing As Doing," by Thomas C. Stewart, is presented in Chapter 6, "Considering the Ethics of Public Speaking." Another new student speech titled "The Flag Raisings on Iwo Jima" appears in Chapter 9, "Choosing Supporting Materials." Finally, the appendix includes President Barack Obama's inaugural address.

### Revised Research Chapter

Since technology is so important in accessing library resources, Chapter 8, "Conducting Research," includes a comprehensive discussion of library databases, including a grid that describes some of the most common databases students may encounter when using library resources at their own institutions. In addition, the chapter provides useful Web addresses for credible resources such as statistics, quotations, encyclopedias, and dictionaries. The chapter suggests using the Modern Language Association style for documenting student bibliographies and includes comprehensive citations showing online library databases, the Internet, and traditional resources. The chapter also includes an updated example of plagiarism to help students understand the serious nature of this intellectual infringement.

### Chapter Exercises

Two exercises are included at the end of every chapter. Some exercises direct students to databases such as InfoTrac® College Edition or their library databases to research articles and/or speeches that support the content of chapters.

### Suggested Topics

A list of eleven topic areas is included at the end of the book. Used successfully in basic speech courses, these topics have helped students gather ideas for informative and persuasive speeches.

### Revised Introductions and Updated Examples

Most chapter introductions have been changed or altered to be more student-friendly. In addition, examples have been updated throughout the text incorporating current events such as the presidential campaign of 2008 (Chapters 3 and 13), the tragic massacre at Virginia Tech (Chapter 18), and illegal immigration (Chapter 16).

### Appendix of President Obama's Inaugural Address

Because the historic contest of 2008 resulted in the election of the first African American to the presidency, President Barack Obama's Inaugural Address is included in the Appendix for analysis and discussion.

## STUDENT RESOURCES

*Building a Speech*, Seventh Edition, features an outstanding array of supplements to assist in making this course as meaningful and effective as possible. Available student resources include:

- **Resource Center.** This useful site offers a variety of rich learning assets designed to enhance the student experience. Organized by tasks as well as by chapter, these assets include self-assessments, Web activities, chapter outlines, and review questions. The Resource Center also features course resources such as Speech Builder Express™ 3.0, InfoTrac College Edition, and more.

- **Speech Builder Express™ 3.0.** This online program coaches students through the entire process of preparing speeches and provides the additional support of built-in video speech models, a tutor feature for concept review, direct links to InfoTrac College Edition, an online dictionary and thesaurus, and leading professional organizations' online documentation style guidelines and sample models. Equipped with their speech type or purpose, a general topic, and preliminary research, students respond to the program's customized prompts to complete interactive activities that require critical thinking about all aspects of creating an effective speech. Students are able to specify a speech purpose, identify an organizational pattern, write a thesis statement or central idea, establish main points, integrate support material, craft transitions, plan visual aids, compose their speech introduction and conclusion, and prepare their bibliography. Students are also able to stop and start work whenever they choose and to complete, save online, export to Microsoft Word®, or e-mail up to five outlines.

- **InfoTrac College Edition with InfoMarks™.** This online library provides access to more than 18 million reliable, full-length articles from over 5,000 academic and popular periodicals. Students also have access to InfoMarks—stable URLs that can be linked to articles, journals, and searches to save valuable time when doing research—and to the InfoWrite online resource center, where students can access grammar help, critical thinking guidelines, guides to writing research papers, and much more. For more information about InfoTrac College Edition and the Info-Marks linking tool, visit www.infotrac-college.com and click on "User Demo."

- **Book Companion Website.** The website features study aids such as chapter outlines, flash cards and other resources for mastering glossary terms, and chapter quizzes that help students check their understanding of key concepts.

- **iChapters.com.** This online store provides students with exactly what they've been asking for: choice, convenience, and savings. A 2005 research study by the National Association of College Stores indicates that as many as 60 percent of students do not purchase all required course material; however, those who do are more likely to succeed. This research also tells us that students want the ability to purchase "a la carte" course material in the format that suits them best. Accordingly, iChapters.com is the only online store that offers eBooks at up to 50 percent off, eChapters for as low as $1.99 each, and new textbooks at up to 25 percent off, plus up to 25 percent off print and digital supplements that can help improve student performance.

- **A Guide to the Basic Course for ESL Students.** Written specifically for communicators whose first language is not English, this guide features FAQs, helpful URLs, and strategies for managing communication anxiety.

- **Conquer Your Speech Anxiety.** Learn How to Overcome Your Nervousness About Public Speaking by Karen Kangas Dwyer. Drawing from the latest research, this innovative resource helps students understand and develop a plan to overcome their fear of public speaking. The CD-ROM includes both audio relaxation exercises and techniques for overcoming anxiety.

## RESOURCES FOR INSTRUCTORS

*Building a Speech*, Seventh Edition, also features a full suite of resources for instructors. To evaluate any of these instructor or student resources, please contact your local Cengage Learning representative for an examination copy, contact our Academic Resource Center at 800-354-9706, or visit us at www.cengage.com/. **Instructor resources include:**

- **Instructor's Resource Manual.** Written by the author, the Instructor's Resource Manual provides a comprehensive teaching system. Included in the manual are a syllabus, criteria for evaluation, chapter objectives, in-class activities, handouts, and transparency masters. All of the Skill Builder and InfoTrac College Edition exercises included on the Resource Center and companion website are included in the Instructor's Resource Manual in case online access is unavailable or inconvenient. The Instructor's Resource Manual includes a printed test bank that features class-tested and reliability-rated multiple-choice, true-false, short-answer, essay, and fill-in-the-blank test questions. Print and electronic versions are available.

- **Instructor's Website.** The password-protected instructor's website includes electronic access to the Instructor's Resource Manual and other tools for teaching. To gain access to the website, simply request a course key by opening the site's home page.

- **PowerLecture.** This CD-ROM contains an electronic version of the Instructor's Resource Manual, ExamView computerized testing, and videos associated with *Building a Speech*. This all-in-one tool makes it easy for you to assemble, edit, and present materials for your course.

- **Turn-It-In®.** This proven online plagiarism-prevention software promotes fairness in the classroom by helping students learn to correctly cite sources and allowing instructors to check for originality before reading and grading papers and speeches. Turn-It-In quickly checks student work against billions of pages of Internet content, millions of published works, and millions of student papers and speeches and within seconds generates a comprehensive originality report.

- **Wadsworth Communication Video and DVD Library.** Wadsworth's video and DVD series for speech communication includes communication scenarios for critique and analysis, student speeches for critique and analysis, and ABC News videos and DVDs for human communication, public speaking, interpersonal communication, and mass communication.

- **The Teaching Assistant's Guide to the Basic Course.** Written by Katherine G. Hendrix of the University of Memphis, this resource was prepared specifically for new instructors. Based on leading communication teacher-training programs, this guide discusses some of the general issues that accompany a teaching role and offers specific strategies for managing the first week of classes, leading productive discussions, managing sensitive topics in the classroom, and grading students' written and oral work.

- **The Art and Strategy of Service-Learning Presentations, Second Edition.** Written by Rick Isaacson and Jeff Saperstein of San Francisco State University, this handbook provides guidelines for connecting service-learning work with classroom concepts and advice for working effectively with agencies and organizations.

- **TLC Technology Training and Support.** Get trained, get connected, and get the support you need for seamless integration of technology resources into your course with Technology Learning Connected (TLC). This unparalleled technology service and training program provides robust online resources, peer-to-peer instruction, personalized training, and a customizable program you can count on. Visit www.cengage.com/tlc to sign up for online seminars, first days of class services, technical support, or personalized, face-to-face training. Our online or on-site training is frequently led by one of our Lead Teachers, faculty members who are experts in using Cengage Learning technology and can provide best practices and teaching tips.

- **Custom Chapters.** Create a text as unique as your course—quickly, simply, and affordably. As part of our flex-text program you can add your personal touch to *Building a Speech* with a course-specific cover and up to 32 pages of your own content, at no additional cost. Bonus chapters available now include expanded discussions of group speaking and mediated speaking.

## ACKNOWLEDGMENTS

A writing project of this scope cannot be accomplished without the assistance of many individuals. My thanks goes to the reviewers whose comments helped in the revision of the Seventh Edition: Jonathan Amsbary, University of Alabama at Birmingham; Patricia Cutspec, East Tennessee State University; Michael Demson, Broome Community College, SUNY; Paula Haug, Folsom Lake College; Butch Owens, Navarro College; Gayle Pesavento, John A. Logan College; and Diana Sims, Brown College.

I also wish to thank the Wadsworth team who provided advice and assistance for this new edition: Monica Eckman, acquisitions editor, Larry Goldberg, development editor, Greer Lleuad, senior development editor, Katy Gabel, production manager.

I am indebted to my outstanding colleagues in the Speech Communication Department at the Community College of Baltimore County. Jennifer Kafka Smith graciously offered the speech "How Airplane Wings Produce Lift" in the visual aids chapter as well as suggestions for Chapters 17 and 19. Tim Thompson and Drew Kahl provided helpful perspectives and suggestions as they used the text in their basic speech communication classes. And my wonderful basic speech students deserve special praise for their continued help, creative examples, and energetic suggestions.

*Sheldon Metcalfe*

# unit one

# SURVEYING THE LANDSCAPE

© Ariana productions inc/Getty Images

# chapter 1

# INTRODUCING THE STUDY OF PUBLIC SPEAKING

## chapter objectives »

After reading and studying this chapter, you should be able to

1. Recognize the importance of communication in the modern world
2. Describe the communication process
3. Understand the classical origins of public speaking
4. Apply the communication process
5. Describe three overall objectives for studying public speaking

> 66 *Talking and eloquence are not the same; to speak, and to speak well are two things. A fool may talk, but a wise man speaks.* 99
>
> —Ben Jonson

- His high school commencement speaker was so boring that Blake unzipped his academic gown and slumped down in his seat to get some extra zzzz's.
- Teneka never took public speakers seriously. She thought they were all scam artists and lumped them together with politicians and used car salespeople.
- After Brooke walked away from a disagreement with her Dad about the contributions of the hip-hop music industry, she thought of more things she wished she had said to support her side of the argument.
- Otis is so nervous before he has to give a departmental report at work that he sometimes calls in sick to avoid the presentation.

- Every time he listened to his favorite politician deliver a speech, Chavez always wanted to hear more.
- Tasha's physics professor ended the lecture by asking, "Do you have any questions?" Even though Tasha didn't understand the instructor's concepts, she didn't speak up because she thought she would look stupid in front of other students.

If you identified with any of the people in these situations, you are not alone. Many individuals express a variety of these feelings when it comes to presenting or listening to public speeches. This text is designed to help you handle some of these issues. This text also gives you some strategies that can help you to succeed when building your own presentations.

We'll introduce the study of public speaking in Chapter 1 by considering the importance of communication in today's world and exploring a contemporary communication model. Finally, we will look at some historical perspectives about communication and briefly discuss how to apply communication today.

We wish you success. Welcome!

## communication in the modern world

A JOB INTERVIEW is one of many speaking situations requiring effective communication skills.

© Jupiter Images

Think of the numerous circumstances in your life that require some form of communication activity. You use your iPhone to e-mail a friend. You take notes in an economics class where the instructor supports her lecture with PowerPoint slides. You argue with an officer at an airport security checkpoint about a bottle of lotion in your carry-on luggage. You follow the assertive commands from a GPS navigation system to get to a party. You watch a CNN newscast about imported toys contaminated with lead paint. You prepare for a job interview you've located on http://www.monster.com. Each of these situations requires some form of communication skill. The airport encounter and job interview require a knowledge of persuasion. The economics lecture requires you to know how information is organized. And in all of these communication examples, active listening skills are critical.

Communication is vital to each of us, whether in our own worlds or in the world community.

**key terms »**

ARISTOTLE
BODY
CHANNEL
CICERO
COMMUNICATION MODEL
CONCLUSION
CORAX
DECODING
ENCODING
ETHOS
FEEDBACK
GORGIAS
INTRODUCTION
ISOCRATES
LOGOS
MESSAGE
NOISE
PATHOS
PLATO
QUINTILIAN
RECEIVER
RHETORIC
SENDER
SETTING
SHANNON AND WEAVER
SOPHISTRY
SOPHISTS
SOURCE
SYMBOL

Think of the 2008 primary election campaign where the number of pledged delegates for the top two Democratic candidates was so close that a few votes in several states could have tilted the nomination to Hillary Clinton instead of Barack Obama. Or consider the popular evangelist Joel Osteen who has a congregation of thousands and is highly influential with his messages of inspiration to millions of viewers on television. When we see graphic images of sick cows being prodded into slaughter houses we worry about buying steaks at the grocery store. When we see the price of oil exceeding $100 a barrel, we begin to think about purchasing the most fuel-efficient vehicle available. We send food, clothing, and medical supplies when we see hundreds of Americans who have suffered a loss because of hurricanes, raging forest fires, floods, or terrorist attacks. We donate food when we hear the pleas of starving families in Somalia or the Sudan. We experience horror when we see suicide bombers taking innocent lives in Baghdad or extinguishing the life of a presidential candidate in Pakistan. We examine our living standard when home foreclosures reach record levels, food prices soar, and the stock market plummets. We laugh when we hear a comedian do an impression of a famous politician or actor. We become silent when we see the flag-draped caskets of deceased soldiers being carried to their final resting places.

Every day of our lives, we apply principles of communication. We inform, we shape, and we move others; we are equally informed, molded, and moved by others. Our success in these everyday situations often depends upon how effectively we speak and how carefully we listen.

Success will take some energy on your part. But if you are willing to spend the time, you can improve your speaking skills and be more successful in each situation you encounter. Remember that your goal is not to be Maya Angelou, Will Smith, Jennifer Lopez, Brad Pitt, Oprah Winfrey, or George Clooney. Your goal is to be you: a more confident and effective you.

## the communication process

When we speak or listen in any given situation, most of us take communication for granted; sometimes we succeed and sometimes we fail. But communication is not just a haphazard, trial-and-error occurrence. Often there are very good reasons for our success or failure. The more we understand how communication works, the more we can improve our skills.

A great many experts have written about communication and have developed theories called **communication models**. In the 1940s, Claude Shannon, an engineer at the Bell Telephone Company, and Warren Weaver, a mathematician, wrote *The Mathematical Theory of Communication*,[1] which became a classic in the field. **Shannon and Weaver** stated that in order for communication to take place, there must be a **source**, a **message**, a **channel**, and a **receiver** (Figure 1.1).

FIGURE 1.1 Shannon and Weaver's Mathematical Theory of Communication *Source:* Claude E. Shannon and Warren Weaver, *The Mathematical Theory of Communication*, copyright 1949 by the University of Illinois Press. Used by permission.

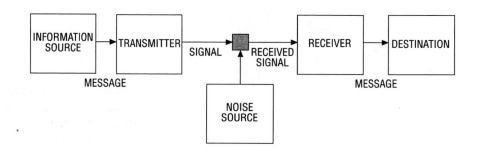

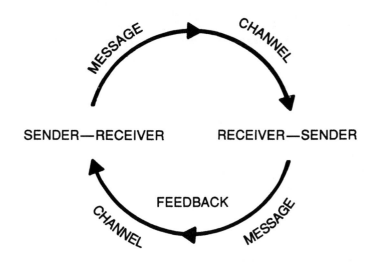

FIGURE 1.2 Example of Communication Model

Although this model was helpful in understanding communication, it was later criticized for its lack of flexibility. The communication model was often illustrated as a flat line with a source at one end, the message and channel in the middle, and the receiver at the other end. The model tended to give the inaccurate impression that communication is a static activity that does not change or develop. The model may accurately simulate mechanical transmission of signals over a telephone line, but it does not describe the fluid interaction of human beings.

More recent theories have emphasized the idea that communication is dynamic: It is always changing, growing, and developing.[2] These communication models can be illustrated by a circle rather than a line (Figure 1.2). Senders can receive messages as they are sending them; receivers can likewise send and receive at the same time. Human communication can be adjusted to new feedback and influenced by the environment. Communication changes and unfolds on the basis of ever-changing human experiences.

## A COMMUNICATION MODEL

The fact that you've made it to this point in your life means that you probably communicate well. But we take all kinds of things for granted when we communicate. It's helpful to break down communication into its individual components in order to understand the process: That's the purpose of a communication model. We'll consider seven aspects: sender, message, channel, receiver, feedback, setting, and noise. To understand each part of the model, we will look at a simple example that happens whenever you or your classmates deliver a speech.

### The Sender: Encoding Ideas into Symbols

The **sender** originates communication. Within the sender are the ideas, thoughts, feelings, and intentions that begin the process of communication. Suppose that your speech instructor has assigned you to prepare an informative descriptive speech about a person, place, object, or event. The idea-thought-feeling "place" and "Hawaii" have just popped into your brain since you recently returned from a family trip to the Big Island. You think about the idea for a while until you encode it. **Encoding** is simply the thought process and motor skill of the sender that changes an idea-thought-feeling into an understandable symbol. **Symbols** are verbal and nonverbal expressions or actions that have meaning. In this case, words such as *Big Island, volcano, snorkeling,* and *luau* symbolize the verbal meanings, and visuals such as a photo and a flowered lei could symbolize nonverbal meanings.

### The Message

Even though symbols have meanings, they must be arranged in some kind of logical structure. If you simply jumbled all your words together and threw them out randomly at your listeners, your ideas would make very little sense. You need a **message**, that is, a set of structured symbols. This is where you begin the process of organizing your thoughts. You might start by writing a thesis to explain what aspects of Hawaii you want to cover. For instance you might encode your thoughts into the following sentence: "A trip to the Big Island includes viewing the volcano, snorkeling through lava tubes, and experiencing a luau." You have now arranged your word symbols into an organized message. Your message is clear, precise, and understandable: It has meaning to you and potentially to someone else. But even though you have organized the appropriate message, you have not yet been able to communicate to your audience.

### The Channel

The next step in the communication process is the selection of a channel. A **channel** is the means of transporting the message. The channels we use to transmit messages are sensory: We convey our messages through the five senses of sight, sound, smell, taste, and touch. To communicate, you now choose one or more of these sensory channels to convey the message of your speech. The most obvious channel is verbal. You start with an introduction that catches your listeners' attention and follow it up by your thesis statement. But there are other channels as well that can make your speech really interesting to your listeners. You could show PowerPoint photos or a Google Earth image of Kilauea Crater. You could display objects such as macadamia nuts or let the audience smell the aroma of Kona coffee beans. You might even have a volunteer from the audience feel a sample from a black sand beach. Each decision presents you with a different combination of sensory channels. You therefore make the decision to use all the techniques in order to employ as many senses as possible to communicate to your audience.

### The Receiver: Decoding Symbols into Ideas

At this point in the process, there is a sender (encoding the ideas into symbols), a message, and several channels. However, communication is still incomplete, because no connection has been made to the receiver. The **receiver** is the destination, the goal of communication. When you are standing in front of your class, you now have the potential for communication because you have a destination for the message: your listeners. You deliver your speech using all five channels of communication.

Immediately, the process that occurred to generate communication within the sender now takes place in reverse within the receiver. The receiver **decodes** or changes the symbols in your organized message or speech into ideas-thoughts-feelings that the receiver can use to give meaning to the message. Although we now have a receiver and decoding to add to the communication model, we still need a response to complete the communication circle (Figure 1.3).

### Feedback

**Feedback** is a verbal or nonverbal response. Feedback can tell you whether communication has occurred, how it has been received, and whether it has been understood. Feedback is a reaction from the receiver to the sender: It can be positive and negative, verbal and nonverbal. The wonderful thing about feedback is that it transforms senders into receivers and receivers into senders; in other words, we can send and receive messages simultaneously and alter our messages based upon the responses that occur.

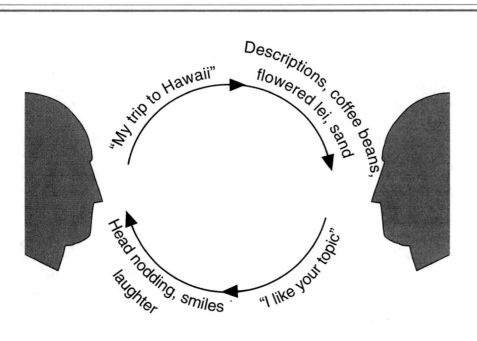

FIGURE 1.3 Completing the Communication Circle

Feedback provides dimension and transforms communication from a one-way process into at least a two-way experience. If there are numerous senders and receivers, as in your speech class, the communication is multidimensional.

The most obvious feedback to your speech is from your classmates, the receivers. Having gone to all the trouble you just did to send your multichannel message about Hawaii, you would hope for positive feedback from your audience such as nodding heads of agreement or even some laughter if you tell a humorous story. We hate to mention this, but negative feedback can occur as well. You might see someone frowning, a couple of listeners whispering to each other, or even someone rudely text messaging during your speech. If you see a listener frowning, you might alter your message by more clearly defining an unfamiliar term. You might increase your volume to drown out or stop the listeners who are whispering and ignore the text messager. Messages continue to change on the basis of new information sent and received. Feedback circularizes communication, provides dimension, and allows us to adapt to new circumstances.

### Setting

The communication process does not exist in a vacuum. Instead, it occurs in a **setting**, which includes occasion, environment, space, and time. A speaker must consider how the occasion influences the message. The physical and psychological conditions differ for a business meeting, an anniversary, a marriage proposal, a birthday, or a Christmas party. When the occasion is clearly understood beforehand, the speaker adapts the message to the environment of the speech.

Think of your classroom as the setting for your speech. It might be a conference room where students are seated around a rectangle with a lectern at one end. Your speaking area might be a so-called "smart classroom" that contains a computer with internet access, a document camera (see Chapter 12), and a projector for enlarging visuals onto a screen. Or you might be presenting your speech in a large lecture hall in an amphitheatre with a lectern set on a stage. Your class might meet first thing in the morning, after lunch, or late at night. The room might be lit by traditional fluorescent lighting or have floodlights that can be adjusted with dimmers.

You can see how important it is to understand the setting in supporting the communication process. You need to adapt to the speech setting by making adjustments. In a small, intimate room with just a few students you could speak in a moderate volume and make eye contact with everyone. But in a large lecture hall you might have to increase your volume if there is no microphone and look at areas rather than each individual. The time of day might affect the level of audience alertness and you might need to make adjustments in speaking length as well as employ visuals or other channels to maintain your listeners' attention. When thinking through any speaking situation, consider the aspects of occasion, environment, space, and time so that the setting will support your communication successfully.

### Noise

It is clear that in order for communication to take place there must be a sender, message, channel, receiver, feedback, and setting. Noise, however, is a factor that can cause disruption or disturb the flow of communication. **Noise** is a distortion or a distraction to communication; it interferes with any part of the communication process and reduces the effectiveness of communication (Figure 1.4). There are three types of noise: external, internal, and semantic.

FIGURE 1.4 How does this cartoon demonstrate the problem of noise in the setting? Can you relate the point of this illustration to any speaking situations that you've encountered?

**External Noise.** External noise is any interference that can be perceived by the senses in the speech setting. It is important to emphasize that the word *noise* can, but does not always, refer to sound.

Any number of external distractions can occur while you are delivering a speech. The classroom may be too hot or cold, leaving the audience perspiring or shivering. A jazzy ring tone may go off on a listener's cell phone. There may be an odor of melting tar as workmen are repairing the roof. Or you as a speaker could cause external noise by wearing something distracting, like long dangling earrings or a T-shirt with a bizarre graphic.

If the external noise is too great, listeners will stop paying attention and communication will be lost. For communication to occur, either the interference must be eliminated or the sender must adapt to the situation. If you can control the environment, try to change it. Don't wear clothing that causes external distractions and turn the heat up if it's too cold. Sometimes, however, you may not have control over the environment of your speech, but you can change how you relate to the situation. If the temperature is a problem, make a comment about it and condense your speech so your listeners (and you) don't have to suffer. If the odor is offensive, make a joke about it. What is important is that you adapt to the external noise so that the audience sees that you are sensitive to it.

**Internal Noise.** Although you can usually sense the source of external noise, you may or may not always perceive the cause of internal noise. Internal noise is any interference or disruption to communication that occurs within the sender or receiver. You may be nervous as you are giving the speech and you feel your heartbeat racing, your knees knocking, and your palms sweating. Your audience may have no idea what is going on inside you and in their minds you appear visibly calm and relaxed. As you are presenting the speech you may think that the scowling student in the back row is offended by something you said. But the frown may not be directed to you at all. He may have had a bad day, received a poor grade in a previous class, or simply be feeling sick.

Finding and resolving the source of the negative feedback is sometimes a way to understand the disruption and restore communication. If you are the sender and nervous about a speaking event, try some deep breathing or relaxation exercises to take your mind off the occasion. If you are a receiver who is having personal conflicts, try to reduce or resolve them as best you can so they do not take your focus away from paying attention to the speaker's message.

**Semantic Noise.** One other disruption to communication is semantic noise. Semantic noise is any barrier to word or symbol meanings because of differences in environment, culture, language, pronunciation, values, or experiences. If one of your listeners is Japanese and speaks little English, there is an obvious language barrier to communication. If one of the speakers in your class is a Boston native and tells the instructor "I'm sorry I'm late for class—I had to 'paahk' the 'caah,'" the accent might create a semantic barrier. If a speaker uses the word *soda*, she could mean anything from a soft drink to an ice-cream-and-syrup concoction. If you are presenting your speech about Hawaii and use a huge word like humuhumunukunukuapua'a (really, it's a word), you would need to explain to listeners that you are describing the Hawaiian state fish. If you gesture using the Hawaiian "shocka," you would need to tell your audience that to Hawaiians, its meaning is similar to the thumbs-up motion. Whether verbal, nonverbal, cultural, or geographical, semantic noise interferes with communication. To be a more effective communicator, you must become aware of these disruptions and begin to adapt to the semantic noise that exists between sender and receiver.

## SEMANTICS: The Power of Words

After the horrendous terrorist attacks of September 11, America began to prepare a military response to the Taliban regime in Afghanistan. President George W. Bush referred to America's military retaliation as a "crusade" and used this term to rally Americans and gain the support of America's allies. But when many of the world's Islamic people heard this remark, they reacted with hostility because they remembered the Crusades of the eleventh to the fourteenth centuries when Christians murdered thousands of Muslims in the effort to stop the spread of Islam and retake the Holy Land. Aware of the negative reaction, the president changed the name of the war to "Operation Infinite Justice." This phrase was no more successful, because it appeared to many Muslims as if America was equating its military might with God's divine justice. The president finally settled on the inoffensive term "Operation Enduring Freedom" to describe the military campaign in Afghanistan.[3]

## classical origins of speaking

Now that you understand the process of communication in modern society, discover its origins in the ancient world. In the time of the Greeks, communication was equated with public speaking and was called **rhetoric**, which meant "the art of the orator."[4] Classical rhetoric specifically dealt with skill in persuasive oratory, or the ability to convince and to move an audience to a specific point of view.

**Corax** is considered to be one of the founders of rhetoric. In the fifth century B.C., a tyrant subjugated the citizens of Sicily and confiscated their property. When the dictator was overthrown and democracy was restored to the island, the courts were jammed with people trying to reclaim their lands. Corax influenced judicial oratory by developing a method of speaking that helped the common people argue their court cases more successfully.

**Gorgias** (483–376 B.C.) was a brilliant speechmaker and a highly influential teacher in Athens. He tended to emphasize an ornate style, figures of speech, and emotionalism in his speaking. Those, like Gorgias, who taught oratory and charged a fee to their students were called **sophists**. At first sophists were respected teachers, but later a number of con artists took over the schools and exploited students for financial profit. The word **sophistry** came to have a negative connotation, implying the use of deceitful methods and faulty reasoning.

**Isocrates** (436–338 B.C.) was a more influential rhetorician in Athenian society than Gorgias. In addition to teaching many Greek orators, Isocrates wrote several manuscripts and an autobiography describing his ideas. He believed that a speaker should be well educated in the liberal arts and of good moral character, and he emphasized that a speaker must possess freedom and independence, yet demonstrate self-control. He adapted the ornate style of Gorgias into a more fluid prose style of writing and speaking.

**Plato** (428–348 B.C.) had little regard for rhetoricians such as Gorgias and Isocrates. He described his concepts in "dialogues," which were actually stories written in play form. In his dialogue entitled *Gorgias*, Plato attacked the methods of the sophists and claimed that rhetoric is not a useful pursuit. In his dialogue *Phaedrus*, Plato charged that sophists corrupt young people and that rhetoricians are more interested in dishonesty, style, and opinion than in truth. While conceding that rhetoric could deal with truth, he continued to insist that rhetoric was "not a true art."

Plato's famous student **Aristotle** (384–322 B.C.) wrote *The Rhetoric* and challenged many of Plato's negative opinions about oratory. To Plato's charge that rhetoric lacks truth, Aristotle responded that objective truth exists only in science and math. Plato wrote that rhetoric is flawed because men base their reasoning on opinions and beliefs. Aristotle replied that belief is the highest degree of certainty in the world of human beings. Aristotle introduced what he called three methods of proofs: **ethos**, the ethical appeal; **pathos**, the emotional appeal; and **logos**, the appeal to logic and reason. Aristotle's work helped to elevate public speaking to a respected place and has influenced thinkers and speakers to the present day.

Among those influenced by Aristotle were Cicero and Quintilian, two Roman orators who also added to the literature of rhetoric. **Cicero** (106–43 B.C.) was a skillful orator and a respected teacher who thought that the speaker should be educated in the liberal arts.[5] In his book *De Oratore*, he discusses topics such as writing, audience analysis, anxiety, evidence, and argument. **Quintilian** (A.D. 35–95) was a famous Roman lawyer who stressed that the "true orator must be, above all, a good man . . . skilled in speaking."[6] In his book *The Institutes of Oratory*, he describes the speaker's purpose when he writes, "There are also three objects which an orator must accomplish: to inform, to move, to please."[7]

Classical rhetoric involved real human beings who persuaded, who moved, and who influenced nations and civilizations. The writings of Aristotle, Cicero, and Quintilian were read by thinkers during the Renaissance, by reformers in England, and by revolutionaries in America. Men such as Patrick Henry, Tom Paine, Thomas Jefferson, and James Madison applied many of Aristotle's speaking techniques and energized the spirit of a new nation. Throughout our history, speakers like Abraham Lincoln, Sojourner Truth, Susan B. Anthony, Theodore Roosevelt, Franklin D. Roosevelt, John F. Kennedy, Martin Luther King, Jr., and Ronald Reagan have applied the ancient speaking principles to move an often reluctant nation into a more ethical or progressive course of action.

The classical Greeks and Romans influence *our* communication as well. When you arrange a speech into an **introduction**, **body**, and **conclusion**, you are applying Aristotle. When you research your topic, Cicero smiles. When you practice the delivery, Quintilian nods knowingly. When you apply moral principles, Isocrates sheds a joyful tear. We are indebted to these individuals for their contributions, and we continue to employ their speaking principles in our contemporary lives.

## applying the communication process

Think back to the situations we presented at the beginning of the chapter. Blake is bored with his commencement speaker. Is it Blake's problem or is it the speaker's? Maybe it's both. Blake has shut off all communication and has decided to go to sleep instead of listening. There is no possibility that he will receive any communication from the speaker by turning off. But commencement speakers are too often insensitive to their listeners. Graduations frequently take place in non-air-conditioned auditoriums during the month of June, and graduates, dressed in hot academic gowns, are in no mood to hear a long-winded speech full of trite phrases. The most successful commencement speakers are those who connect to their audiences and recognize that the occasion is about the graduates— not the speech. Remember the discussion of external noise earlier in this chapter? In this circumstance the effective commencement speaker would acknowledge the distractions of the setting, attempt to make audience members more comfortable, and emphasize her intention to be brief.

Then there is Teneka who thinks that public speaking is performed by scam artists. Just as classical history had its share of unscrupulous speakers, so too has modern society produced many ruthless leaders, such as Adolf Hitler, Stalin, Osama bin Laden, and Jim Jones, who have misused their speaking gifts to victimize people. But as we've seen in this chapter, there are just as many others, such as Martin Luther King, Jr., Nelson Mandela, Princess Diana, and Mother Teresa, who have used their speaking power and actions to improve the lives of millions. We will explore more about the ethical considerations of public speaking in Chapter 6.

Otis and Tasha have similar problems: They are both very anxious about speaking in public. Tasha lacks confidence in her ability and Otis is so afraid of delivering a speech that he'd rather take his sick leave than give a report to his coworkers. As we'll discover in Chapter 5, fear of speaking in public ranks among the top two fears of most Americans. But there is good news! Taking a basic speech course as you are doing can actually help to reduce your anxiety.

Brooke wanted to stand her ground when arguing about hip-hop with her Dad. But she went away feeling that she didn't make the strongest case to support her ideas. In Chapter 16, you can learn how to build credible persuasive arguments so you can be more confident in the strength of your positions.

Finally, there is Chavez, who absorbs every word of a politician he admires. But when listening to a speaker, it is critical to weigh variables such as emotion, ethics, and charisma to determine what part they play in persuasion. In Chapters 4, 6, and 16, we'll discuss how these factors can interact positively or negatively to influence an audience.

## designing a plan for success

You now find yourself in a course where you will be required to present speeches to an audience. This experience is important to your growth and development as a communicator. Learning from your classroom successes and failures should help you in communication situations beyond the course. We will discuss many concepts and principles, but there are three overall objectives for you to achieve:

1. *You should be able to critically evaluate speaking situations.* Be able to understand and evaluate the speaking situation. What makes a "good" speaker? What constitutes a "good" speech? What are some aspects of the audience you need to consider when preparing a speech? What are some factors about the occasion you should know before making a presentation? When you can survey the landscape and answer some of these questions about the speaking situation, you are well on your way to delivering successful speeches.

2. *You should be able to plan, prepare, and organize speeches.* To speak effectively, you must prepare effectively. An architect draws a set of blueprints with clear specifications before a builder can erect a house. And although it may seem time-consuming, a speaker must structure ideas into a coherent plan before presenting a speech to an audience. Effective planning takes effort, but the process is not necessarily difficult. In fact, if you have put sufficient time into researching and outlining your speech, you may find that speechmaking is a lot easier than you expected.

3. *You should be able to deliver speeches in front of an audience with ease.* How well do you communicate your ideas in public? Do you appear confident, knowledgeable, and enthusiastic about your topic? Are you able to deliver different types of speeches in different speaking situations? Are you able to progress logically from one idea to another? When you look at members of the audience, do you actually "see" them? Do you concentrate on what you are speaking about at a

given moment, or does your mind wander? Do you employ gestures and facial expressions, or do you have nervous mannerisms? Do you rehearse the speech before presenting it to the audience?

Build your speaking ability block by block. Survey the landscape, prepare the foundation, create a skeletal structure, refine the appearance, and, finally, develop different types of structures. Learn from your mistakes, profit from your achievements, and effectively communicate to benefit yourself and others. When you develop the speech step by step, block by block, you will build a functional, pleasing structure.

## summary »

Communication, so important in our society, includes modern theories like the Shannon and Weaver communication model as well as a more recent communication model comprised of seven components: sender, message, channel, receiver, feedback, setting, and noise. Communication is grounded in the rhetoric and oratory of ancient times. Develop the ability to apply the communication process to your daily speaking situations. Three objectives of this course will help you to (1) evaluate speech situations; (2) plan, prepare, and organize speeches; and (3) effectively deliver speeches in front of an audience.

## SKILL BUILDERS »

1. Name an example of a good speaker you have heard in the past several weeks. Describe the qualities that you feel made this person effective as a communicator.
2. Keep track of the communication process in your classroom, listing all the different senders and receivers during one class period. What types of noise can you detect as you are recording this exercise?

## @ BUILDING A SPEECH ONLINE »

Now that you've read Chapter 1, use your online Resource Center for Building a Speech for quick access to the electronic study resources that accompany this text. You can access the Resource Center at http://academic.cengage.com/login using the access code that came with your book or that you bought online at http://www. iChapters.com. Your Resource Center gives you access to Interactive Video Activities, the book's companion website, Speech Builder Express 3.0, InfoTrac College Edition, and study aids, including a digital glossary and review quizzes.

# BUILDING YOUR FIRST SPEECH

## chapter objectives »

After reading and studying this chapter, you should be able to

1. Understand extemporaneous speaking and styles of delivery
2. Create a blueprint of 10 building blocks for constructing a speech
3. Understand how to research and develop a career speech

Candita Chapman was an international student from the Island of St. Kitts in the Caribbean. Candita's classmates in the basic speech course always enjoyed hearing her outstanding presentations, which ranged from preparing authentic Caribbean potato pancakes to warning listeners about the evils of fast food. When asked why she was successful in developing her speeches, Candita offered this blueprint:

*When I get the assignment I read over it and then I start brainstorming. Sometimes the topic just hits me. When I'm sitting on the bus, vacuuming, or watching TV, a key word pops up. After I get the topic, I Google. I go to the library and look for information in the catalog and in books. Research is very important because you want to be credible. I look for statistics and I look for other supporting materials like stories. I look for a cute picture that I'd like to use. I call my parents in St. Kitts. For instance, when I did the Caribbean potato pancake speech, I called my mother and she e-mailed me the recipe.*

*When I actually write the speech, I dedicate a whole day, a Saturday. I sit at the computer and I write a thesis and an outline and then I add a couple of sentences to develop each point. Then I write the introduction and the conclusion—you want to start strong and end strong. After I've written the speech, I practice it, and then I develop a PowerPoint presentation. I go through the speech paragraph by paragraph and*

> " *Speech is like any other class. You have to spend the time.* "
>
> —Candita Chapman

*I say to myself, OK, I can add a picture here, a picture there, or I can add a statistic here. Then I put it all together. Then I practice the speech with the PowerPoint program.*

*When I practice, first I just read it to myself. Then I read it and time it. If it's too long, I go back over the speech and take out the least relevant information. If it's too short, I'll find a point that can be elaborated on. Usually it ends up with good timing. Then I practice it two times the night before. Then in the morning when I'm coming to school, I read it through and practice it on the bus so I can use good eye contact. I don't want to read it word for word from the note cards, but I want to use different words. You have to put it across so that it's interesting, exciting, and people want to listen to you. The gestures, the facial expression, the eye contact, are all very important. In our culture we're very emotional, and I guess the delivery part of the speech just comes naturally for me. Putting the speech together takes time and dedication. I try to put into the effort exactly what I want to get out.*[1]

Candita was a hard worker who followed the basic steps of speech preparation.

In this chapter, we look at the importance of extemporaneous speaking and examine 10 general guidelines to help you build your first speech. We also present a career speech to help you research and develop a speech on a specific profession. If you are willing to work and spend the time, you can be just as successful as Candita.

## extemporaneous delivery and speaking styles

Whenever you make a speech, you will need to choose a style of delivery that is appropriate to the speech setting. The style of **delivery** refers to your method of presenting the material—that is, whether the speech is extemporaneous, manuscript, impromptu, or memorized.

As you build your first presentation, you will find that **extemporaneous** delivery is the most helpful to you. As Candita Chapman's story indicates, an individual using this style researches a topic, prepares an outline, and employs speaking notes—the method we suggest in this chapter and describe throughout the text. Extemporaneous delivery allows the speaker to develop eye contact with the audience, adapt to feedback, and concentrate on the sequence of ideas rather than on word or sentence order. Speakers in business and industry select this approach to help them project confidence and credibility to their listeners. An accountant presenting a quarterly report to corporate executives or an office manager training new employees wants the freedom to look at listeners, yet the security of a clear, well-organized outline. With an extemporaneous delivery, these speakers can be relaxed, spontaneous, and well prepared and yet maintain eye contact with their listeners.

In addition to extemporaneous delivery, there are other styles of delivery that speakers use for various purposes. In situations where precision and detail are extremely important, speakers often choose to read word-for-word **manuscripts** to audiences. A scientist reporting on the results of fusion research at a convention, or a physician describing a new vaccine for Alzheimer sufferers to medical professionals, would write out the entire speech in advance. President Obama employs manuscript delivery because his words are analyzed and interpreted by millions of people around the world.

You may already have had to present an **impromptu** or "surprise" speech without any notes or prior preparation. If your supervisor requested you to "say a few words" about your current work project at a department meeting, or a friend asked you to propose a toast at a birthday party, you were required to organize your thoughts and ideas on the spur of

## key terms »

BODY
CONCLUSION
DELIVERY
ENTERTAINING SPEECH
ETHICAL RESPONSIBILITY
EXTEMPORANEOUS
GENERAL PURPOSE
IMPROMPTU
INFORMATIVE SPEECH
INTRODUCTION
MANUSCRIPT
MEMORIZED
PERSUASIVE SPEECH
SPECIFIC PURPOSE
THESIS STATEMENT
TOPIC
TRANSITION

the moment. An impromptu speech is good to experience occasionally and helps you to develop the ability to think on your feet.

In situations where constant eye contact and accurate timing are necessary, speakers frequently use **memorized** delivery. Tour guides, stand-up comics, after-dinner speakers, and individuals presenting or receiving awards are often more effective if they memorize their material. In a David Letterman–style monologue, for instance, the speaker wants to convey the punch line smoothly, without distractions from notes. In this setting, memorization can help a speaker to respond quickly to audience feedback and to judge the right moment to deliver the humorous line.

Although these approaches can be effective in various speaking situations, they have some clear disadvantages. In manuscript delivery, speakers often use their notes as a crutch and forget to look at the audience. These speakers may also tend to sound mechanical, forced, or monotone when reading material that is written out word for word. Audiences rarely like speakers to read to them; they enjoy being acknowledged with eye contact in a spontaneous and conversational manner. Speakers often use memorized delivery to promote the secure feeling that they have it all down in their heads. In practice, however, memorization causes speakers to spend large amounts of time concentrating on word, phrase, and sentence order rather than on ideas. This style of delivery can even contribute to fear and insecurity about forgetting some crucial portion of the speech. An impromptu speech works in a surprise setting, but it is not advisable to create this type of speech when the situation requires a carefully researched and structured presentation. You can't make up a speech as you go along when you must show research and preparation.

An extemporaneous style of delivery is the best approach to public speaking in a college classroom. This style allows you to be more spontaneous and spend more time looking at your listeners and connecting with them visually.

## creating a blueprint

To assist you in your first assignment, this section provides a blueprint for building a speech. Although these 10 guidelines are presented in a suggested sequence, not all speeches will follow this arrangement. In some presentations, the steps may overlap or even reverse. You might select and narrow a topic while you are conducting library research, or you might analyze the audience before writing the specific purpose. The process is similar to constructing a building: Some steps—such as preparing the foundation and erecting the walls—occur in a prescribed order; other steps, however, are more flexible. The guidelines are presented as a suggested sequence for you to follow.

## STEP 1: CHOOSE AN INTERESTING, WELL-DEFINED TOPIC

The first step in building your speech is to choose a **topic** that is interesting to you, has potential interest to your audience, and is limited in scope. As you think about the topic, examine some of your past experiences and present concerns—areas that challenge you and stimulate your enthusiasm. Review your background and life experiences, places you've traveled, professional expertise, career goals, practical knowledge, or unique interests and hobbies. Your chosen topic should also challenge your listeners and relate to their needs or curiosities. Audience members tend to be motivated by issues that involve their personal survival or their physical and emotional well-being. Finally, narrow the topic to a specific area, which you can develop in some detail within your allotted time limit. See Chapter 7, "Selecting the Topic and Purpose," for a more complete discussion.

## STEP 2: UNDERSTAND THE GENERAL PURPOSE

Once you have chosen your topic, you must clearly understand the general purpose of the speech. A **general purpose** represents the direction of the material presented: General purposes can be *informative*, *persuasive*, or *entertaining*.

**Informative speeches** enlighten and educate audiences. Informative speeches can define concepts, demonstrate procedures, or describe people, places, events, and experiences. For example, a speech about the Big Island of Hawaii would be informative because it would be describing a place. **Persuasive speeches** influence and alter the beliefs, feelings, or behavior of listeners. In persuasive presentations, speakers seek to convince audiences to change beliefs, actuate people to perform an action that solves a problem, or stimulate and intensify listeners' feelings. For instance, a speaker advocating the legalization of gay marriage would be presenting a persuasive convincing speech on a controversial issue. The goal of the **entertaining speech** is to gain a humorous response by poking fun at people, places, or events. A "roast" at a fiftieth birthday party or a Steve Colbert–style stand-up routine would be examples of entertaining presentations. Entertaining speeches may contain biting satire or convey serious underlying messages, but the material itself should be lighthearted and enjoyable rather than persuasive or seriously informative. See Chapter 7 for more discussion about the general purpose of a speech.

## STEP 3: CONDUCT EXTENSIVE RESEARCH

Your next step is to find interesting factual materials to support the topic and to establish your credibility as a speaker. Thorough research involves using resources such as the library catalog or library databases like Proquest or Academic Search Premier to find books and periodicals that contain testimonies, examples, and statistics relating to the topic. Your research may also require you to conduct interviews with experts on the topic or to gather information from institutions, businesses, or specialized organizations. The research process helps you to gain the respect and trust of your listeners; audiences tend to believe speakers who are knowledgeable about their topics and back up their ideas with facts or documented evidence. For more information, see Chapter 8, "Conducting Research."

MATTHEW (MATTIE) STEPANEK was a peace advocate and poet whose books sold over one-half million copies. Before his death in June of 2004, Mattie was a goodwill ambassador for the Muscular Dystrophy Association. Through his poems and appearances on the Oprah Winfrey and Larry King shows, Mattie focused national attention on the disease and inspired millions of viewers.
*Source:* Photo courtesy of the Muscular Dystrophy Association

## STEP 4: WRITE SPECIFIC PURPOSE AND THESIS STATEMENTS

When you have researched the topic, you need to determine the specific purpose and thesis statements of the speech. The **specific purpose** represents the main objective, which joins all ideas to one common theme and enables the speaker to keep on target. The specific purpose statement includes the general purpose (or its paraphrase) and one topic idea stated in clear and concise language.

> **Specific purpose:** To inform listeners about my interest in skateboarding

The **thesis statement**, often called the *central idea* or the *central objective*, expands the specific purpose and tells the audience exactly which main points the speech will develop.

> **Thesis statement:** I want you to know how I became interested, my experience in tournament competition, and some of my most challenging stunts.

This thesis clearly indicates that the speech is organized around three major headings. For more examples of specific purpose and thesis statements, read Chapter 7, "Selecting the Topic and Purpose."

## STEP 5: WRITE A COMPREHENSIVE OUTLINE

Once you have determined your purpose and thesis, structure your thoughts by writing a logical outline. The outline will help to keep you on track throughout the presentation and still allow you to maintain contact with the audience. A speech has three basic parts: an introduction, a body, and a conclusion.

Since the **body** is the longest portion of the speech, it should be developed first before either the introduction or conclusion. The body contains the main headings that were identified in the thesis statement. For example, the speech about skateboarding identifies the following three headings:

BODY

    I.  How I became interested
   II.  My experience in tournament competition
 III.  My most challenging stunts

Each numeral is then reinforced by subordinate points containing the examples, testimonies, and/or statistics you collected in your research. Your time limit often dictates the number of main points the body should develop. Generally, the shorter the speech, the fewer the main points. A 1- to 2-minute speech would probably contain no more than two or three main points, while a speech of 6 to 7 minutes could expand upon as many as four headings. In order to provide clarity between each main point of the body, it is helpful to state a **transition** that acts as a listening cue to tell listeners that one main point is ending and the next point is beginning.

Although the introduction and conclusion are much shorter than the body, they must also be carefully organized. The **introduction** should get attention and promote curiosity as well as prepare the audience for the topic and thesis statement. You can generate listener curiosity by beginning with a catchy quotation, shocking statement, thoughtful case study, or stimulating question that relates to the issue. The **conclusion** resolves the ideas you have presented in the speech. You can summarize the main points, appeal to the emotions, cite a quotation, or use an illustration. The important thing is for your audience to sense a finality and a resolution of the topic. For more complete information about outlining, read Chapter 10, "Organizing the Body of the Speech," and Chapter 11, "Selecting the Introduction and Conclusion."

## STEP 6: BE SENSITIVE TO AUDIENCE MEMBERS

As you organize the speech, consider carefully the needs and feelings of your audience. Present the topic at their intellectual level without talking over their heads or beneath them. Use language that they understand, and define any terms that may be unfamiliar. Be sensitive to the diverse backgrounds and experiences of your listeners. Does your audience include individuals from different countries or geographical regions? Will men or women view your topic with contrasting attitudes? Could age differences or marital status affect listeners' perceptions? Are your listeners' values and ideals shaped by their cultural, ethnic, or religious heritage? Be aware of the values and ideals that motivate the members of your audience. Avoid statements or examples that stereotype individuals, and stay away from offensive language. Let the audience know that you are genuinely interested in them, responsive to their differences, and concerned about their welfare. For additional information, read Chapter 3, "Analyzing Your Audience."

## STEP 7: UNDERSTAND YOUR ETHICAL RESPONSIBILITIES

Whenever you present a speech, you are claiming to have knowledge about a topic that could benefit the audience. At the same time, you have an **ethical responsibility** to convey this knowledge fairly and accurately without misleading your listeners.

Speakers who plagiarize or steal information without giving proper credit, withhold or distort facts, engage in name-calling, or advocate harm are employing unethical practices designed to deceive or manipulate their audiences. These tactics demonstrate a lack of respect for individuals and will eventually destroy the speaker's credibility.

As an ethical speaker, you want to gain your listeners' confidence; be reliable and fair when you report information, and avoid deceptive practices. You will earn the respect and trust of your audience if you are honest and respectful. To read more information about ethics, see Chapter 6, "Considering the Ethics of Public Speaking."

## STEP 8: CHOOSE EXTEMPORANEOUS DELIVERY

Remember that the extemporaneous style is the most helpful type of delivery for both speaker and listener in a basic speech course. The topic is researched, structured, and delivered from speaking notes that are written in outline form. The speech is not written out or memorized word for word. Extemporaneous delivery allows you to make greater eye contact with your listeners and respond more effectively to audience feedback. For more information, read Chapter 14, "Developing the Delivery."

## STEP 9: PRACTICE THE SPEECH

Success in presenting a speech requires practice. Transfer your outline to speaking notes, and double- or triple-space between lines for easy scanning. Good notes will allow you to maintain eye contact with your audience and still proceed logically through your material. As Candita Chapman suggests at the beginning of this chapter, go over the speech several times so you are confident with the order and placement of ideas. If you can, rehearse your speech in the setting where you will deliver it. Work to eliminate distractions such as fidgety mannerisms, standing on one foot, or vocalized pauses like "uh, uh, um." Convey words and sentences so listeners can hear and understand you easily. Be accurate and descriptive

# Building Your First Speech »

To assist you in building your first assignment, the ten guidelines presented in this chapter are summarized here as a blueprint for speech construction.

1. Choose an interesting, well-defined topic.
   a. Examine past, present, personal, and professional experiences.
   b. Narrow the topic to a specific area within the time limit.
2. Understand the general purpose.
   a. The general purpose is the direction of material presented in a speech.
   b. General purposes are informative, persuasive, and entertaining.
      (1) *Informative speeches* enlighten and educate; they can describe, demonstrate, or define.
      (2) *Persuasive speeches* seek to influence; they can convince listeners to change beliefs, move people to action, or stimulate and intensify feelings.
      (3) *Entertaining speeches* poke fun at people, places, or events to gain a humorous response.
3. Conduct extensive research.
   a. Establish credibility by conducting thorough research; use library search engines to investigate books and periodicals, interview experts, and gather information from institutions.
   b. Gather factual supporting materials such as examples, quotations, statistics, and audiovisual aids.
   c. Be certain that your supporting materials are verifiably clear, correct, and complete.
4. Write specific purpose and thesis statements.
   a. The specific purpose includes the general purpose and one topic idea, stated clearly.
   b. The thesis statement is a one-sentence preview of the main points that are developed in the body of the speech.
5. Write a comprehensive outline.
   a. Write a logical outline that includes three basic parts: introduction, body, and conclusion.
      (1) Since the *body* is the longest part and includes the main headings identified in the thesis, it should be developed before either the introduction or conclusion.
      (2) The *introduction* gets attention, promotes curiosity, and introduces the thesis.
      (3) The *conclusion* resolves ideas in the speech by summarizing, appealing to emotions, and reinforcing the ideas in the speech.
   b. The outline keeps you on track and helps you to maintain contact with the audience.
6. Be sensitive to the audience.
   a. Consider diversity of background: culture, ethnicity, geographical region, gender, age, religion, politics, interests, attitudes, values, ideals.
   b. Connect to listeners at their level.
   c. Avoid offensive language or stereotypes.

7. Understand your ethical responsibilities.
   a. Gain credibility by conducting thorough research and reporting information fairly and accurately.
   b. Avoid deceptive practices such as plagiarizing, withholding or distorting facts, or name-calling.
   c. Earn the confidence and trust of listeners by being honest and respectful.
8. Use extemporaneous delivery.
   a. When using extemporaneous delivery, a speaker researches, structures and delivers the speech from notes that are written in outline form.
   b. Extemporaneous delivery allows the speaker to show more spontaneity, enthusiasm, and eye contact without reading or memorizing a manuscript word for word.
   c. The extemporaneous style helps the speaker to view and adapt to feedback from listeners during the speech.
9. Practice the speech.
   a. Transfer your outline to double-spaced speaking notes for easy scanning.
   b. If possible, rehearse in the setting of the speech or have several verbal and mental run-throughs of your presentation.
   c. Work to maintain eye contact with listeners, and avoid distractions such as vocalized pauses ("um," "ah") and fidgety mannerisms.
   d. Pronounce words clearly, use descriptive language, and let gestures and facial expressions flow spontaneously.
10. Be confident and prepared.
   a. Arrive at the speech setting on time, prepared, and in control, avoiding any last-minute rush or scramble.
   b. Review speaking notes, take deep breaths, and walk calmly to the speaker's stand, placing notes securely in front of you.
   c. Look at the audience, state the first line of the speech with conviction, and take your time.
   d. Project confidence, speak clearly, stand up straight, and avoid making excuses or apologies.

in your use of language, and know how to pronounce difficult terminology. Let gestures and facial expressions flow spontaneously from your natural enthusiasm. If circumstances do not allow you to rehearse in the speech setting, look over your speaking outline and conduct a mental review of your presentation. Remember that your goal in speech rehearsal is to unite all of your research and organization into a coherent, unified construction. For more information about speech practice and delivery, read Chapter 14, "Developing the Delivery."

## STEP 10: BE CONFIDENT AND PREPARED

On the day of the presentation, arrive at the speech location early enough to avoid any last-minute scramble. Look through your notes to see if they are in the proper order. Relax, and take a few deep breaths as you wait for your turn. When it is time for your speech, walk calmly to the speaker's stand, placing your notes securely in front of you. Don't start the speech while you are still on the way to the lectern or while you are arranging your material. Take your time, and don't rush. Make certain that you are ready to begin. Look at the audience, and then state the first line of your speech with conviction. Project confidence when you speak. Avoid making excuses or apologizing for mistakes. Speak clearly and distinctly. Try to make eye contact with all segments of your audience between brief glances at your notes. Stand up straight, and show the audience that you are prepared and ready to make the presentation. When you finish, don't pack up your notes while you are still talking or walk off in the middle of a concluding line. Wait until you have completed every part of the conclusion. When the last line of the speech is over, collect your notes, and walk calmly to your seat. To help you establish more confidence, read Chapter 5, "Understanding and Reducing Your Apprehension."

## the career speech

A study released by the Bureau of Labor Statistics in 2002 found that workers held an average of 9.6 jobs from age 18 to age 36.[2] These statistics indicate that you may change jobs and even careers several times during your life. This startling information means that you need to be knowledgeable about different fields of study and the future prospects for employment in specific professions. The career speech gives you the opportunity to research different fields and investigate one profession in depth for a classroom presentation. A sample career speech is also provided later in this chapter to help you organize and deliver this type of presentation.

### RESEARCHING THE CAREER SPEECH

As a student in a college or university, you may still be undecided about a field of study or you might be well along in your selected major. No matter what your phase of career planning, you can begin your speech research into areas of interest at your institution's career center. An appointment with a career specialist can provide testing about your skills and interests, inform you about types of careers, and give you information about training needed in specific fields. A good career counselor can also help you narrow your interests, focus on a specific career topic, and provide additional resources for further investigation.

In addition to your career center, you can research a number of credible online sites. The U.S. Department of Labor publishes an *Occupational Outlook Handbook* at its website, http://www.bls.gov/oco. This valuable resource is revised every two years and offers a wealth of information about hundreds of occupations, training and education required, potential earnings, working conditions, and expected job prospects. In addition, there are links to related sites that provide information about the job market in each state, jobs in industries, and career publications.

Another useful site is http://www.online.onetcenter.org/. This web address is a national occupational information network that provides comprehensive information about employees and occupations. It matches your skills and interests with related occupations. This site is also helpful if you need to identify occupations requiring skills that are difficult for people with health issues or disabilities.

Career information at http://www.aacinet.org/acinet helps you build a profile combining employment, wages, and skills. It also assists you in finding industries with the largest employment and the fastest projected growth. You can find state labor market information and link to educational, cultural, and recreational resources.

An interesting and creative site is the University of Missouri Career Center at http://www.career.missouri.edu. This website provides a Career Interests Game that matches your abilities and interests with a variety of corresponding careers. (The game is located in a drop-down menu at the bottom corner.)

As you are conducting research for your speech, look for information that can be grouped into categories. For example, the first area you might want to describe is the nature of the work—for example, the areas of opportunity, the responsibilities, and/or the skills required for the career. The next category could be the requirements for the career, such as the education, training, and/or experience needed. Finally, you might talk about the outlook for the occupation, such as job growth, salary potential, and trends in the field.

Remember that the better your research, the more credible, interesting, and clear your speech will be to your listeners.

## DEVELOPING THE CAREER SPEECH

Once you have completed your research, you are ready to develop the rest of the speech. Remember that the general purpose of a career speech would most probably be informative since you are not necessarily trying to persuade listeners to choose a particular occupation. Next, you want to write your thesis statement, which previews the main points of the body of your speech. The following sentence presents a clear, three-point thesis for a career in law:

**Thesis statement:** The law profession is a rewarding career that requires extensive education but provides unlimited potential.

As you remember from the 10 guidelines, you write the outline once you have completed the thesis. The three categories in the thesis makes developing the outline easy:

I. Nature of a law career
II. Education required
III. Unlimited potential

When you have written your main and supporting points, think of an introduction, such as a quotation, example, or startling statement that gets your listeners' attention and arouses their curiosity about the career. Also end the speech with a conclusion that summarizes your main points and reinforces the ideas stated during your presentation.

Once you have finished the outline, you are then ready to complete the process of building your speech. Consider the audience by relating your topic to their diverse needs or interests and define any difficult terms that may be unfamiliar. Report your information ethically by citing your resources clearly and stating facts fairly and completely. Finally, as we've described in this chapter, speak extemporaneously from brief notecards and practice the speech thoroughly to develop your confidence.

## SAMPLE CAREER SPEECH: careers in anthropology

*As an honors student in a basic speech communication course, Jamie Garonzik was interested in a career in anthropology and the variety of occupations related to that field. His speech was well organized, with an introduction, a clear thesis, main points of the body separated by transitions, and a brief conclusion. As you read the speech, notice how Jamie uses examples, statistics, and visual aids with credible sources to keep listeners interested in his topic.[3]*

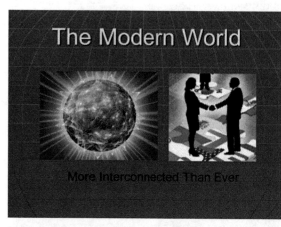

SLIDE 1

Fields of Anthropology

**Biological Anthropology**
•Paleontologists
•Primatologists

**Cultural Anthropology**
•Ethnographers
•Archaeologists

SLIDE 2

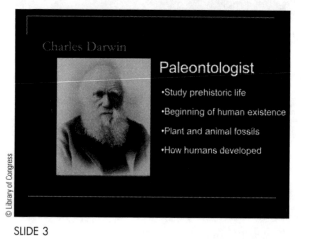

Charles Darwin

Paleontologist

•Study prehistoric life

•Beginning of human existence

•Plant and animal fossils

•How humans developed

© Library of Congress

SLIDE 3

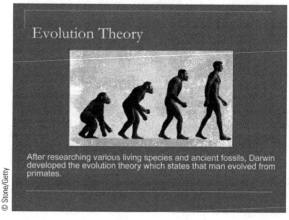

Evolution Theory

After researching various living species and ancient fossils, Darwin developed the evolution theory which states that man evolved from primates.

© Stone/Getty

SLIDE 4

### AN INFORMATIVE DESCRIPTIVE SPEECH
*Jamie Garonzik*

**1. The speaker begins the introduction.**

Jamie uses a PowerPoint slide to create audience interest in the topic.

The speaker uses suspense as a strategy to generate curiosity.

1.  It is impossible to deny that the modern world is more interconnected than ever due to the advancement of computers and technology. (slide 1) Innovations such as the Internet have allowed each of us to actively communicate with and learn about other countries and cultures. American businesses of today have branches half-way around the world and rely on other foreign companies for essential goods and services. They've erased many boundaries over the past two decades. You may think that I'm leading into a career in business or technology but instead, I'd like to talk about the field of work that has helped us to confront our own ignorance and shed light on those cultures unlike our own, both past and present—the intention to come to a greater understanding of our fellow man. I'm speaking of the field of anthropology, which, simply put, is the study of humans and primates.

**2. The speaker states a three-point thesis.**

2.  I will discuss various forms and functions of anthropology, the skills and education required, and the level of pay that one may receive.

**3. Jamie uses a slide to introduce his point.**

3.  There are two major fields (slide 2) of anthropology—biological and cultural—and there are many subfields, but I'd like to discuss only a few today. Paleontologists study prehistoric life, the beginning of human existence, and how humans developed, and

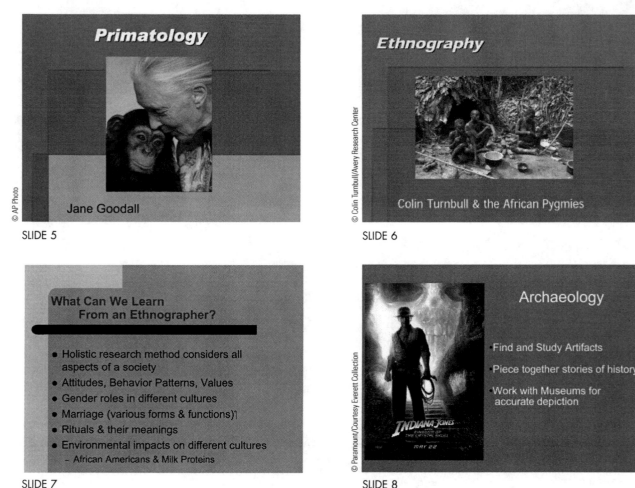

SLIDE 5 — Primatology — Jane Goodall (© AP Photo)

SLIDE 6 — Ethnography — Colin Turnbull & the African Pygmies (© Colin Turnbull/Avery Research Center)

SLIDE 7 — What Can We Learn From an Ethnographer?
- Holistic research method considers all aspects of a society
- Attitudes, Behavior Patterns, Values
- Gender roles in different cultures
- Marriage (various forms & functions)
- Rituals & their meanings
- Environmental impacts on different cultures
  - African Americans & Milk Proteins

SLIDE 8 — Archaeology
- Find and Study Artifacts
- Piece together stories of history
- Work with Museums for accurate depiction

(© Paramount/Courtesy Everett Collection)

they also study plant and animal fossils. (slide 3) I'm sure you're familiar with Charles Darwin, the famous naturalist and paleontologist who founded the evolution theory. (slide 4) This theory states that humans evolved from primates such as chimpanzees, and we now know that chimpanzee DNA differs by only 1 percent from that of humans. Evolutionary theory leads directly into the study of primates, known as primatology. (slide 5) Jane Goodall, the most famous primatologist of all, studied chimpanzees for over 30 years. She focused on behavioral and social aspects, which confirmed many similarities to humans, according to the Minnesota State University website.

4.  We'll now move from biological to cultural anthropology. (slide 6)

5.  Ethnographers have the job of living with, observing, and recording the many aspects of foreign culture. They provide detailed, unbiased research to determine the similarities and differences in the cultures they study. One example of a famous ethnographer is Colin Turnbull. He lived with and studied the African Pygmies in the Congo for many years—the Bambuti and the Ilk. He wrote books called *The Rain Forest People* and *The Mountain People* which opened our eyes to the ways of indigenous peoples. (slide 7) And what can we learn from ethnographers? We learn that they use holistic research methods that include gender roles, marriage, the forms and functions of rituals and their meanings, and the environmental impacts on different cultures.

The speaker cites the names of Darwin and Goodall as examples of different kinds of anthropologists.

The visuals and the cited source add interest and credibility to the ideas.

4. The transition moves from main point I to II.

5. Jamie cites an example of a famous ethnographer and names the books he authored about the Pygmies. The PowerPoint slides again add interest to the speech.

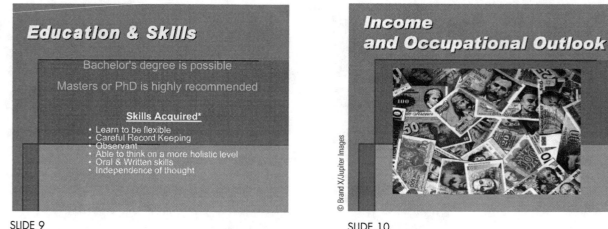

SLIDE 9

SLIDE 10

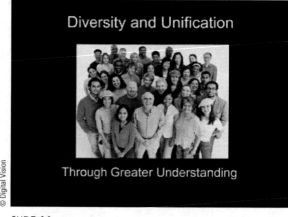

SLIDE 11

**6. The speaker's reference to the fictitious movie character keeps listeners interested.**

6. Next we move on to archeologists, and for lack of a famous, (slide 8) identifiable archeologist, we're all familiar with Indiana Jones, who taught us that they find and study artifacts to piece together history, understand the changes that took place, and provide a greater understanding of the rise and fall of civilization. Archeologists also work with museums to piece together historical representations.

**7. A transitional sentence ends the first main point and introduces the second.**

7. In order to accomplish these goals, anthropologists must receive the proper education and training to develop certain skills.

**8. Jamie begins the second main point by citing a source.**

**The speaker describes the degrees required and reinforces the information with a visual.**

8. According to the American Anthropology Association (slide 9) you can get away with a Bachelor's degree, but you have to sell yourself. You usually have to work with businesses and product marketing and you learn to think holistically and appreciate diversity. It is more advisable, though, to earn a Master's or a Ph.D. in order to accomplish things such as Colin Turnbull's achievements. The skills you acquire from your education help you to be flexible and observant. You learn to think independently, become analytical, and think on a deeper, more holistic level. You are trained to keep careful records and develop good oral and written communication skills.

**9. The transition introduces the third main point of the body.**

9. After your education has been completed, the goal is to find a self-satisfying job that pays money.

10. (slide 10) Anthropologists and archeologists will experience the majority of job growth in the management, scientific, and technical consulting services industry. As construction projects increase, more archeologists will be needed to monitor the work and ensure that historical sites and artifacts are preserved, according to the Bureau of Labor Statistics website. As for income, a Bachelor's degree will earn you about $30,000, a Master's could start at about $43,000, and a Ph.D could start at about $50 to 60,000, and if you move on to become a professor you could earn up to $100,000 per year.

10. Jamie uses a slide to reinforce salary information he cited from the Bureau of Labor Statistics.

11. (slide 11) Well hopefully, you now have an idea of the requirements and rewards of being an anthropologist. The variety of jobs and skills make this career very appealing and you will gain many useful skills and the pay can be good. Anthropologists not only research, analyze, and recover details from the past so we can have a better understanding of history but they also help us to understand each other so that we may move together towards a more unified future.

11. The speaker ends with a brief concluding summary and a stimulating last sentence.

## summary »

Recognize that there are four styles of delivery: extemporaneous, manuscript, impromptu, and memorized. One of the most effective styles is extemporaneous delivery, which requires research and organization but enables the speaker to use a brief outline and maintain eye contact and spontaneity.

Ten general guidelines may assist you in constructing your first speech:

1. Select a topic that is interesting to you and to your audience and is sufficiently limited in scope.
2. Be aware of the three general purposes or directions of a speech.
3. Conduct research into your topic to obtain appropriate testimonies, statistics, and examples to support your ideas.
4. Write a clear, specific purpose or speech objective followed by a thesis statement that states the two, three, or four main points the speech will include.
5. Write a comprehensive outline of the introduction, body, and conclusion to develop your ideas in a logical sequence.
6. As you construct the speech, be sensitive to the needs and motivations of your audience.
7. Be ethical and credible when speaking.
8. Use the extemporaneous style of speaking to maintain eye contact with your audience.
9. Transfer your outline to speaking notes, and practice the speech to develop a conversational, spontaneous delivery.
10. Project confidence in yourself and in the material when you deliver the speech.

When developing a career speech, conduct research by consulting your campus career center as well as several Internet sources. Follow the 10 building blocks for constructing the speech.

## SKILL BUILDERS»

1. Develop and present a short 2- to 3-minute speech introducing yourself to your class. Topic suggestions might include a unique interest, experience, place you've traveled, or an embarrassing incident.

2. Develop and present a 4- to 6-minute informative descriptive speech about a possible career choice you may have selected following the 10 guidelines presented in this chapter. Make an appointment with your campus career center to gather information about possible career topics. For additional research, you may use your library's databases, and Internet sources such as www.acinet.org/acinet, www.bls.gov/oco, www.onetcenter.org, or www.career.missouri.edu, and/or an expert in the career you've chosen. Organize the thesis and body of your speech around the following three key points: I. Nature of the career, II. Requirements or training, and III. Occupational outlook.

## @ BUILDING A SPEECH ONLINE »

Now that you've read Chapter 2, use your online Resource Center for Building a Speech for quick access to the electronic study resources that accompany this text. You can access your Resource Center at http://academic.cengage.com/login, using the access code that came with your book or that you bought online at http://www.iChapters.com. Your Resource Center gives you access to Interactive Video Activities, the book's companion website, Speech Builder Express 3.0, InfoTrac College Edition, and study aids, including a digital glossary and review quizzes.

# chapter 3

# ANALYZING YOUR AUDIENCE

© Masterfile (Royalty-Free Div.)

## chapter objectives »

After reading and studying this chapter, you should be able to

1. Recognize the importance of audience analysis

2. Describe five factors that can influence audience reactions to a speech

3. Conduct an audience analysis

- Radio shock host Don Imus referred to the Rutgers University women's basketball team as "nappy-headed hos." He later apologized for the remark but was forced out of his job at CBS radio.
- Actor Isaiah Washington referred to a fellow cast member on the TV show *Grey's Anatomy* as a "faggot." Washington later apologized but was fired from the show.
- Comedian Michael Richards used racial slurs against African Americans in a comedy routine. Even though he apologized for saying the "n" word, he was publicly scorned and his career spiraled downward.
- After being detained for driving while intoxicated, actor and director Mel Gibson made defamatory remarks, saying that "Jews are responsible for all the wars in the world." He apologized, blamed the comments on alcoholism, and checked himself into a rehab facility.[1]

Unfortunately each one of these celebrities violated an important principle of audience analysis repeated by Abraham Lincoln more than 100 years ago:

> It is an old and a true maxim that a "drop of honey catches more flies than a gallon of gall." So with men. If you would win

> « *The public is like a piano. You have to know what keys to poke.* »
>
> —Al Capp

*a man to your cause, first convince him that you are his sincere friend. Therein is a drop of honey that catches his heart."[2]*

Our objective in this chapter is to help you analyze your audience in a speech setting. We will explore several ways for you to build strategies that encourage listeners to receive your messages favorably.

## the importance of audience analysis

When individuals or companies decide to invest millions of dollars in developing new products or services, they conduct a market analysis to determine consumers' needs, their characteristics, their buying habits and motives, and their receptivity to new products.[3]

A developer, for instance, who intends to build a high-rise condominium must determine the nature of potential buyers and what they want in housing. Will homeowners be older individuals who can afford spacious living environments with cathedral ceilings, Jacuzzis, and wraparound balconies? Or will prospective buyers be young professionals who want housing that is inexpensive, convenient, and practical?

We see the results of successful market research all around us. Automakers introduce new hybrid and "green" vehicles or reinstate vintage "retro" models. Food companies produce dietetic and low-cholesterol products for health-conscious consumers. Political campaigns sway voting blocs such as senior citizens, women, recreational hunters, farmers, or minorities with special-interest advertising.

Like the investor, you must analyze your particular "market"—your audience. Audience analysis refers to the speaker's examination of audience characteristics to determine

This famous photograph depicts Lincoln delivering his second inaugural address in which he extended compassion even to his enemies, in the phrase "with malice toward none, with charity for all."

the most appropriate means of motivating them to share or participate in the speaker's concerns.[4] You need to understand your listeners' needs, their environment, and their perceptions of you as a speaker. If you understand at least some of these characteristics, you will be able to adapt your speech to gain the most favorable hearing. Knowledge of the audience helps you to choose topics that are interesting, connect to listeners' needs, select supporting evidence that contributes to clarity and vividness, and use language that is appropriate. Audience analysis does not mean that you must compromise your values or tell your listeners what they want to hear. The point is to adapt and adjust your presentation. The audience is your most valuable asset in the speech setting—it is the listeners whom you ultimately want to inform, persuade, or entertain.

Audience analysis involves understanding five principal factors that can significantly influence listeners' reactions to a speech (Figure 3.1):

1. Their perception of the speaker
2. Their perception of the topic
3. Their needs and motivations
4. Social groups to which they belong
5. The occasion

## AUDIENCE PERCEPTION OF THE SPEAKER

Audiences develop very clear perceptions of speakers. They like or dislike speakers based on the content of their presentations or reputations created through past speeches or actions. We return to the same doctor, hairdresser, insurance agent, or accountant because of favorable perceptions and positive relationships we have built with them over a period of time.

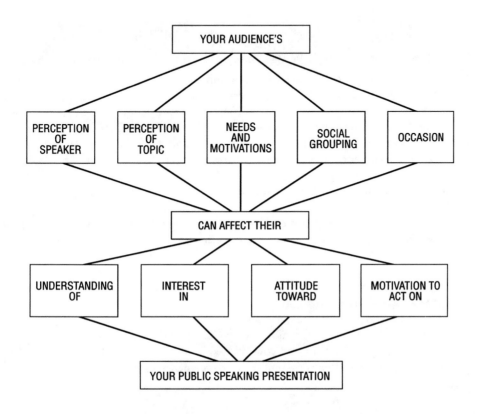

FIGURE 3.1 Five Principal Factors Influencing Listeners' Reactions

Your audience will likewise develop a perception of you as a speaker. They will evaluate what they hear in your presentations, and they will form attitudes about your choice of topics and your manner of delivery. If your speeches are usually interesting and well prepared, the audience will anticipate those qualities even before you speak—they will be receptive unless you prove them wrong. At the same time, speakers who are poorly prepared, who make illogical arguments, or who use unethical methods will create negative expectations that will be hard to overcome.

A student presented a speech demonstrating shoplifting. He wore a long trench coat with large inside pockets and proceeded to tell his audience in great detail how to stuff various sizes of merchandise into the garment. He explained how to avoid discovery by store detectives and by mechanical devices. Some members of the class giggled nervously during the speech; others sat in frozen silence. After his conclusion, the speaker added, "Oh, this was only a joke; I didn't really mean it. I don't believe in shoplifting." But it was too late; the speaker had severely damaged his reputation. When he delivered his next classroom speech, his negative image still influenced listeners. It took several presentations for the speaker to earn back his credibility with the audience.

Audience perceptions are not necessarily etched in stone; they can be changed or even reversed over time. In the race for the Republican presidential nomination in 2008, former New York City Mayor Rudolph Giuliani was the front-runner. His extraordinary leadership and compassion during and after the attacks of 9/11 on the World Trade Center earned him the title of "America's Mayor." Many voters saw him as a leader who could stand up to terrorists and keep America safe. During the campaign, however, information surfaced about his personal life, including two divorces and three marriages as well as some estranged children. In addition, Giuliani had submitted the name of his former police commissioner to President Bush as a nominee for Secretary of the Department of Homeland Security. The commissioner's name, however, was later withdrawn by the Bush

## OBAMA AND CLINTON: how do perceptions of candidates change over time?

At the start of the presidential primary campaign of 2008, many Americans celebrated the history-making contest between an African American and a woman. As the protracted campaign wore on, however, information surfaced that troubled voters about both candidates. Rev. Jeremiah Wright, Jr., Senator Obama's pastor of twenty years, made inflammatory statements blaming America for 9/11 and developing the AIDS virus to exterminate African Americans. The senator denounced the remarks and said that Wright's "ridiculous statements offend me." Obama also had to modify his stated views that Americans ". . . cling to guns or religion . . . as a way to explain their frustrations."

Senator Clinton had her troubling moments as well. Several times during the campaign she recalled an experience traveling to Bosnia as First Lady in 1996: "I remember landing under sniper fire. There was supposed to be some kind of greeting ceremony at the airport, but instead we just ran with our heads down to get into the vehicles to get to our base." Video coverage of the event showed, however, that her story wasn't true. Saying she was tired from the campaign and didn't remember details, she apologized for misstating the facts.[6]

How seriously do you think these events affected voters' perceptions of Senators Obama and Clinton? From your observation of the remainder of the presidential campaign, was either senator able to overcome these negative issues?

THE IMPORTANCE OF AUDIENCE ANALYSIS    33

administration due to a scandal. Primary election voters became disenchanted with the former mayor, and Giuliani lost his front-runner position, never winning a single primary election.[5]

An audience may be unfamiliar with a speaker and feel hesitant about accepting the speaker's ideas or viewpoints. An expert in fire safety who informs listeners how to protect their homes may project interest and concern, but if the audience has never heard of the "expert," the speaker may need to increase believability by describing his or her professional qualifications and experience.

Positive audience attitudes work to your advantage in a speech. If you have developed a favorable reputation, listeners won't be resistant to your influence. If listeners believe your ideas are supported by solid evidence and sound reasoning, they will be more open to you. If you appear confident and relaxed in your delivery, the audience will relax and listen to you. The attitudes the audience forms about you play an important role in your ability to educate and influence them.

## AUDIENCE PERCEPTION OF THE TOPIC

If a large company hired a computer consultant to lecture on "Innovations in Informational Technologies" to a hundred administrative assistants and clerks, the speaker might assume the entire audience was knowledgeable about computer technology. That assumption might be erroneous, however. Administrative assistants, like people in many skilled occupations, have become highly specialized professionals. In many companies, certain employees, known as *information specialists*, have received advanced computer training and supervise the computer and data area of an office. Other personnel, such as receptionists or clerks, may perform only data entry and possess limited technical knowledge. The consultant who assumes that every administrative assistant is literate in every type of software or computer hardware may present a speech that is far too complex for a significant segment of the audience.

As you build your speech, don't make assumptions about the audience until you ask questions. If you understand the level of awareness about a topic, you can gear the speech toward more listeners by not isolating or losing any audience segment.

You also need to consider the attitudes of listeners toward your topic. **Attitudes** are prior inclinations people have about issues, and **opinions** are verbal expressions of these attitudes.[7] When you deliver a persuasive speech, for instance, you may have listeners who agree, disagree, or have no opinion concerning your point of view.

Suppose that you want to present a speech favoring the death penalty for drug dealers. You conduct judicious research. You obtain statistical evidence from the U.S. Justice Department regarding the amount of illegal drugs entering the country every year. You also include some examples of specific drug dealers who have profiteered from the broken lives of dependent addicts. You even use some emotional appeals—"Would you want these drug dealers making profits from your son or daughter, brother or sister?" But when you deliver the speech, you find yourself facing listeners with tight lips and unfriendly frowns. Once the speech ends, you discover too late that most of your evidence and emotional appeals were irrelevant—your audience is strongly opposed to the death penalty, period. The one piece of research that is missing for this topic is audience analysis. If you don't know how your audience feels about an issue, you are less likely to use your supporting data to the best advantage.

It is crucial for a speaker to ask questions about listeners, either verbally or through surveys, before delivering a speech; the information helps the speaker to determine audience attitudes in order to adjust the approach of the presentation. Generally speaking, the stronger their attitudes against an issue or idea, the harder it is to influence the audience.[8]

Before her death from lung cancer in March of 2006, Dana Reeve, wife of actor Christopher Reeve, was a strong advocate for spinal cord research. After she was diagnosed with lung cancer, she became an advocate on behalf of cancer research and early detection.

© Stephen J. Boitano/Getty Images

It is unreasonable to expect individuals to move from extreme opposition to approval after a 5- or 10-minute speech. With hostile audiences, the best you can do is to establish common ground and focus on areas of agreement as well as the need for change. If people are mildly against your topic, you have a good chance of changing their minds—provided that the evidence is forceful. If your listeners are neutral, you are in the best position. Neutrality often means that the audience may not know enough about the issue or simply has not yet formed clear opinions. You have a good chance of exerting influence through strong evidence and sound reasoning. And if the audience completely supports your viewpoint, you can change the focus of your speech to motivate them to act—to contact their legislators, form political action committees, or educate the greater public about the problem.

With many issues, you will find audience attitudes ranging from strong agreement to equally strong disagreement. If you found a variety of audience perceptions about capital punishment, for example, you would focus most of your persuasive appeals on the neutral group, including those who mildly agree and disagree. You would want to maintain contact with those who favor your position strongly and, at the same time, indicate that you respectfully disagree with your extreme opposition.

## MOTIVATIONS OF THE AUDIENCE

As they are listening to your speech, the audience will ask some mental questions: "Can I use this? Will this help me? Does the topic relate to my interests?" Your answer is to appeal to the needs that are most important to your listeners. Needs and goals provide incentives to your audience to become interested and involved in your information. When you focus on significant needs, audience members realize that they can benefit from the speech, that they have something to gain by allowing the speaker to influence them.

One way to discover your listeners' strongest needs is to understand their beliefs and values. **Beliefs** are conclusions people have about the world based on observations, knowledge, and experiences.[9] The following statements would qualify as individual beliefs:

"An exercise program prolongs life."
"God answers prayers."

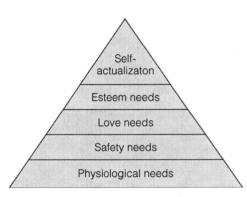

FIGURE 3.2 **Maslow's Hierarchy of Needs**

"Abstinence prevents STDs."
"Democrats are more sympathetic toward social problems."
"Censorship of the Internet violates the Constitution."

Collections of beliefs, called **values**, cause us to behave in certain ways and to achieve goals or states of mind.[10] Most people have general values in common—physical, social, love, ego, security, and moral needs. All of us have basic physical needs—such as food, water, shelter, rest, sex, and security—which include safety and social order. Abraham H. Maslow, a psychology professor at Brandeis University, recognized that needs are strong motivating forces in human beings. Figure 3.2 identifies the five levels of basic drives, called a **hierarchy of needs**, that Maslow believed influence our thinking and behavior. Maslow suggested that people must satisfy the lowest order of needs (physiological) before they are able to progress to the next level (safety, then love, then esteem, and finally, self-actualization).[11]

Even though all of us have similar needs, our values cause us to give these drives different priorities. Some who put a high emphasis on family-type love needs will change jobs and move long distances to be near better schools or help sick relatives. Others who value ego needs will uproot families and change jobs to increase status and responsibility. Those who place strong emphasis on physical needs may spend a great deal of time exercising, choosing well-balanced foods, and getting the appropriate amount of rest. Individuals who place a high priority on moral or spiritual values may cherish religious services, daily meditation, and participation in religion-centered activities. When you analyze your audience, try to determine their values so that you can connect your topic to their most significant goals.[12]

The following list identifies the five principal needs in Maslow's hierarchy and provides a sample appeal designed to motivate listeners within each step. Notice how speakers phrased appeals to link topics to specific audience values.[13]

### Physiological Needs

*Imagine. It's midnight, and you still have four chapters of sociology to study. You decide to take a break. You turn on the TV and all you see is food commercials. And what does your mind go to? Cheeseburgers? Naw. Chicken? Naw. PIZZA! Just a phone call away is a sauce-filled, cheese-covered, crisp-crusted pizza pie.*
—EVAN FEINBERG, STUDENT SPEAKER

### Safety Needs

*Imagine your doctor shooting up drugs before your major surgery.*
—HEATHER HAY, STUDENT SPEAKER

### Love Needs

*Without the volunteer coaches, officials, and huggers, the Special Olympics would not be able to operate. These Special Olympians would not be gaining the physical exercise and emotional support that is crucial to their self-esteem. As I've listened to your speeches over the last two months, I know that many of you are interested in athletics. Volunteering would be a great way for you to continue your love of athletics, and in turn you'd be helping others.*

—COLLEEN V. DEITRICH, STUDENT SPEAKER

### Esteem Needs

*Not only will you feel better if you exercise, how would you like to look better?*

—KRISTINE OZGAR, STUDENT SPEAKER

### Self-Actualization Needs

*How many people in this room can say that they love their jobs—I mean truly love their jobs? I am here to tell you that there is a career field that you can go into and actually enjoy your job. It is the aviation industry. In the May 2000 issue of* Private Pilot *magazine, professional pilot Chris Baker makes this statement: "There is one thing for certain, a job in aviation is a dream career for many. I mean, think about it. How many industries out there can say that they actually have employees serving lawsuits [that have reached as far as the Superior Court] in order to prevent their retirement?"*

—J. LUKE SNOW, STUDENT SPEAKER

The preceding quotations present positive and negative appeals as well as one that is psychologically threatening. Each approach, however, seeks to connect the topic to a specific audience need. Listeners' attention is aroused because speakers have motivated them to care by telling them that they are directly or indirectly involved with their topics. Be certain that you really understand the beliefs and values of your audience without making false assumptions or stereotypes about them. **Stereotypes** are fixed notions or simplistic preconceptions applied to individuals or groups. Not all Democrats are equally interested in funding social programs. Not all people emphasizing moral values are responsive to quotations and examples from the Bible. Not all people who value health want an exercise program. To develop appropriate appeals to values, analyze your audience thoroughly and know the differences in their beliefs.

## IMPACT OF SOCIAL GROUPS ON LISTENERS

Audience members belong to a wide variety of groups that can influence their perception of ideas. When you build a speech, you must understand the composition of the audience and the impact of specific social groupings on listeners. Consider the following areas when you analyze the audience: age, gender, religion, cultural and ethnic origin, educational level, occupation, interests, income level, geographical location, and group affiliation.

### Age

When preparing a speech, you will discover that your approach to a topic will change depending on the age of the audience. If you were speaking about Social Security to individuals in their early 20s, you would likely find listeners concerned about high Social

Security taxes and how the president's proposed Social Security reforms will affect the reliability of the system in the distant future. If, however, the audience were retirees in their 60s, they would be more concerned about the high cost of prescription drugs and whether reforms of the system will affect their current benefits. When selecting examples, use those within the knowledge or experience of your listeners. If a speaker mentioned Watergate, the Vietnam War, or *Howdy Doody,* and the audience consisted of people under the age of 25, listeners would have little appreciation for the examples unless they were experts in history or whizzes at the game of Trivial Pursuit. Similarly, an audience over 65 might have little understanding of an iPod, Xbox, or m-pact. A speaker should either clearly define the examples or use other illustrations from their listeners' contemporary experience:

> *Because of their experience not only on the job but in real life, older workers tend to have fewer accidents. According to a 1988 Bureau of Labor Statistics study, older workers account for 9.7 percent of work-related accidents while workers in your age group of twenty to twenty-four account for 50 percent of such accidents. You can see that there's no replacing life-long experience.*
>
> *People also age at different rates. There are neither biological nor psychological reasons to connect a number, such as sixty-five, to the onset of old age. Every one of you in this room is aging at this very moment and will face retirement sooner or later. When you face that time, retirement should be a decision that you make for yourself.*[14]

Colleen Deitrich knew that her speech against mandatory retirement could be potentially uninteresting to her younger listeners in their early 20s. But she connected the topic to them by comparing accident rates of older workers to those of younger wage earners. Colleen also confronted her listeners with the issue by saying that they were aging "at this very moment."

Avoid alienating members of your audience by ridiculing their age or insulting their intelligence. Put-downs of any age group create animosity. A young speaker who referred to an audience of senior citizens as "you old people" would be met with anger and resentment. At the same time, if an older speaker were to describe a person under 25 as "just a 22-year-old kid," listeners in their 20s would probably react with equal hostility.

Eliminate false assumptions and stereotypes about age. Older people are not necessarily wiser, and younger people do not necessarily lack experience with many issues. As an effective speaker, you want to influence rather than alienate listeners. You can acknowledge generational differences yet bring people together and appeal to the audience by establishing a common ground.

### Gender

The gender of your audience is an important factor to consider when you prepare a speech. With the changes in roles that men and women have experienced in the past decades, it has become increasingly difficult to identify "women's" or "men's" topics. Women may be doctors, Army captains, truck drivers, airline pilots, or devoted homemakers. Men may be chefs, florists, kindergarten teachers, or nurses. You can no longer assume that male and female audiences will be interested only in certain subjects.

An effective speaker should be sensitive to the subtle differences in women's and men's perceptions and communication patterns. Although much research concerning gender appears to be inconclusive, the following chart presents a few generalities that provide some interesting implications for speakers.

## Differences in Communication Between Men and Women

| CHARACTERISTIC | WOMEN | MEN |
| --- | --- | --- |
| Talk | Use talk to build rapport with others | Use talk to assert ideas and oneself |
| Self-disclosure | A way to share yourself with others | Sharing makes you too vulnerable |
| Empathy | Express understanding of others' feelings | Give advice and tell others how to solve problems |
| Sharing experiences | Matching experiences shows understanding | Matching experiences is a competitive exercise[15] |

Although the preceding statements are based on research, it must be emphasized that many studies into gender differences are contradictory or uncertain at best and generalities have numerous exceptions. Simply stated, speakers need to be aware of the unique qualities of gender in every audience situation.

One classroom speaker defended the persuasive proposition that mothers who kill their babies as a result of postpartum depression should be given more lenient sentences. The audience listened carefully as the speaker provided evidence that postpartum psychosis is a psychological imbalance requiring treatment and understanding. During the discussion, listeners were polarized based on gender. Men generally felt that a woman who killed her own baby should be severely punished to the limit of the law. Women, however, were much more sympathetic and agreed that the offender should be given a program of treatment and rehabilitation.[16]

Another speaker described date rape, informing listeners what it is, how it happens, and what to do about it. Audience members appeared to listen intently to the horrifying examples, expert opinion, and statistics, but their reactions were mixed. Women felt that the topic was helpful and caused them to be more aware and enlightened. But men in the audience argued that they were left out of the speech and treated as if they were being implicitly linked to the criminal behavior. Both examples indicate the need for speaker sensitivity. In the first, the speaker needs to examine audience perception of the topic before the speech to understand potential polarization according to gender. In the second, the speaker should take a more inclusive and less hostile approach to connect to men as well as to women in the audience.

When presenting a speech, avoid stating prejudicial generalities or false stereotypes that anger your listeners. To make sexist remarks such as "a woman's place is in the home" or "all men are potential rapists" would arouse hostility in any audience. Carefully consider the sensitivities of your listeners and demonstrate that you care about them.

### Religion

Even in an audience of twenty people, there may be adherents of several religious attitudes and beliefs—Christians, Jews, agnostics, atheists, Buddhists, Muslims, Hindus. Religious beliefs are a matter of deep personal conviction and must be taken into account if a speaker is going to touch upon religious subject matter:

*The book of Genesis advocates a vegetarian diet of fruits, grains, and nuts. Buddha commands, "Do not indulge a voracity that includes the slaughter of animals." The Hindu Mahabharata reads, "Those who desire to possess good memory, beauty, long life with perfect health, and physical, moral and spiritual strength should abstain* *from animal foods." The Islamic Koran prohibits the eating of "dead animals, blood and flesh." The ancient Greeks, led by Pythagoras and supported by Socrates and Plato, believed vegetarianism was natural and hygienic and necessary for healthy living. The Romans conquered the world with an army fed on vegetables, porridge, bread, and wine. These examples were gleaned from Gary Null's <u>The Vegetarian Handbook</u> and they illustrate how history has attempted to teach the philosophy and practice of vegetarianism in order to have a long, prosperous, and healthful life.*[17]

After researching his audience, Jim Kilduff decided to identify a variety of religious philosophies to build an argument for a vegetarian lifestyle. Unlike the offensive remarks of the celebrities mentioned in the introduction to this chapter, Jim's inclusive approach helped to win enthusiasm for his topic by bringing philosophically diverse listeners together.

In any audience, avoid religious slurs that reflect prejudicial attitudes. These statements will arouse hostility and promote dissension among your listeners. It is important to unite the members of your audience and establish a sense of community.

### Cultural and Ethnic Origin

We live in a racially charged society where thoughtless words or actions not only injure feelings but can arouse animosity serious enough to ignite violence. Inappropriate ethnic humor, questionable examples, or a hostile delivery can alienate listeners and ultimately backfire on a speaker. Unfortunately, individuals sometimes convey ideas and exhibit behavior that are considered to be **ethnocentric**, that is, the belief that one culture or environment is superior to another. A speaker with this attitude usually feels "my culture is better than yours."[18] Such arrogant attitudes may be openly expressed or implied. A speaker from one culture who repeatedly refers to listeners of another culture as "you people" may be exhibiting ethnocentric attitudes that will alienate the audience. Speakers who engage in constant put-downs about the superiority of city dwellers over rural residents, Greeks over Turks, blacks over whites, whites over blacks, American citizens over immigrants, and so forth are expressing ethnocentric attitudes that offend audiences. To gain an effective hearing, speakers must avoid such ideas and expressions and exercise extreme sensitivity to listeners from diverse backgrounds and cultures.

One of the strengths of our society is its cultural diversity. The traditional Anglo-Saxon domination of America is rapidly changing, and it is predicted that the white majority will continue to decline and African American, Hispanic, and Asian populations will steadily increase in numbers. Demographers predict that by the year 2060, these three minority groups combined could become the majority.[19]

Because of this increasing diversity, speakers face interesting challenges when presenting messages. An effective speaker must not simply acknowledge, but must really understand the cultural and ethnic background of the audience. Speakers must recognize that culture and ethnic background influence language patterns, vocabulary, word meanings, dialect, accent, nonverbal delivery, and even the listening behavior of an audience. An American speaker making a presentation to an Asian audience might interpret a lack of eye contact from listeners as evasive or disrespectful. But because of their cultural background, many Asians would consider such indirectness more polite and considerate than straightforward stares. Some American slang expressions or regional dialects are difficult to understand and translate. Imagine a Scandinavian hearing the slang term *Jeet*, a Mexican encountering the Pennsylvania Dutch expression "it makes down," or an Australian trying to understand the Cajun phrase "gumbo z'herbes" for the first time. Unless these listeners hired the services of a good American guide or linguist, they might not realize that they are being asked "Did you eat?," told that "it is raining," or being offered a bowl of "green gumbo." Similarly, some English words do not have equivalent terms in other languages. For example, the manufacturers of Pet milk advertised their product in French-speaking countries and didn't realize that the word *pet* is a French term that means "to break wind."[20]

Don't take your audience for granted, and don't assume too much or too little. Analyze your listeners and their background, experiences, and knowledge, and know how they are different and alike. At the same time, recognize your cultural differences as a speaker and be able to acknowledge or interpret these differences when it is necessary to help listeners understand you, your topic, or your speech more completely. In addition, it is important to avoid conclusions and opinions that stereotype your listeners. Just as there are many similarities within cultures or groups, there are also tremendous differences. Not all Asians are polite and bow when greeting one another. Not all Southerners are friendly, not all Italians are extroverts, and not all Californians are laid back. Recognize that your audience is comprised of individuals who have unique life experiences, cultures, and knowledge. Choose your words, illustrations, and concepts carefully. Exercise good judgment when you refer to unknown events or unfamiliar places to involve people of diverse backgrounds and help them connect as fully as possible to your speaking message.

Addressing an audience of public school science teachers in Hughesville, Maryland, Benjamin H. Alexander used the outmoded phrase "colored people," and then said:

*Shocked? No, because you are scientists and you know you are not white—but people of color. Were you the color of this white sheet of paper that I am holding up, you would be void of melanin, and the ultraviolet rays from the sun would burn you up. Nor am I or any other so-called black person in the world, black. Again, you are scientists and know that were we black, we would have an abundance of melanin—and be perfect receptors of the ultraviolet rays from the sun; our body temperature would quickly rise to over 108 degrees and into a fever so severe, we too would burn up. Because you have melanin in your skin—and so do I—it is factual that all people on God's green earth are people of color. God knows what He is doing when He makes no black or white people to inhabit the earth. He knows that if He had, some of them would always be fighting on this planet and disagreeing with the other. So He made a beautiful flower garden of people of all colors ranging from a pleasing cream to an exquisite sable.[21]*

Alexander, a research chemistry professor at the American University, succeeded in shocking audience members by employing the term *colored*. But having carefully analyzed the audience, the speaker quickly translated his message into scientific terminology that listeners could easily understand. He not only connected to his audience, he gave them a feeling of togetherness and pride by referring to them as "people of color" whom God made into a "beautiful flower garden."

### *Educational Level, Occupation, and Interests*

When selecting a topic, a speaker must analyze the educational level, occupation, and interests of the audience. Imagine a doctor using the following language in a speech describing the pancreas to an audience of businesspeople and musicians:

*The pancreas, an elongated gland situated between the spleen and the duodenum, secretes an external juice which passes through the pancreatic duct into the duodenum. It also creates an internal secretion, called insulin, which is produced in the beta cells and regulates carbohydrate metabolism.[22]*

The speaker has talked over the heads of the lay audience and used terms that would be appropriate only if listeners were medical professionals. Many speakers create this kind of communication problem. But the topic has potential interest because it involves information about good health maintenance. In this situation, however, it is advisable for the speaker to use language that is easier to understand:

> *The pancreas is a rather large gland located behind the stomach. It has two very important functions that are essential to the stability of our bodies. First of all, it secretes a fluid, called an enzyme, which helps in the digestion of food. Second, it produces insulin, which helps to reduce the amount of sugar in the blood and urine.*

This example is superior because the speaker has used terms appropriate to the audience's level of knowledge on the topic.

The key idea in understanding audience education, occupation, and interests is speaker adaptability. A good speaker who talks about the treatment of childhood illness must interest young nonparents as well as parents in the audience. Referring to the nonparents' future role in child-rearing will probably help to gain their attention. If an accountant speaks to a mixed audience of medical people and air transportation workers on how to manage money, the speaker knows that there is potential for success because almost everyone is interested in personal finances. A good speaker makes topics come alive for the audience by adapting to their education, occupation, and interests.

### Income Level

A married student decided to tell his audience how to obtain a home mortgage. He talked about the preliminary steps of filling out application and credit forms as well as obtaining income verification. He discussed the property survey, insurance policy, and the termite inspection. Finally he described settlement costs, such as points, stamps, and recording fees. He told the audience that he was especially excited about the topic because he and his wife had just purchased their first home. But when his speech was over, audience members responded negatively. One student complained, "He seemed enthusiastic about his topic, but I couldn't get into it. I'm a commuter student and I live at home with my parents. Someday I'll need to know all of this, but right now I don't have a prayer of buying my own place—I just want to graduate so I can get a decent-paying job." That critique described almost everyone's economic situation in the class.

This example graphically portrays the problems that occur when a speaker does not consider the income level of the audience. In this instance, even the speaker's enthusiasm could not motivate the class. He would have been more successful if he had chosen a topic such as taking out a car loan, which would have enabled him to adapt to the needs of his audience.

Another key idea for a speaker to remember is audience sensitivity. If you talk about joining a country club or about gourmet cooking to low-income people who can hardly afford to pay their rent, your feedback might be anything from indifference to hostility. Similarly, if you speak to a group of doctors or bankers and ridicule rich people's fancy cars and expensive tastes, you will also find your audience switching you off quickly.

### Geographic Location

Effective speakers take time to research the geographic location of an audience. When a speaker demonstrates knowledge about the audience's community, the speaker gains the admiration and respect of the listeners:

> *It's an honor to address the Executives' Club of Chicago. Over a half century ago, the English writer G. K. Chesterton visited Chicago and recommended that everyone interested in the future should do the same. As Chesterton put it, "Although I won't*

*venture a guess about the shape of things to come, if you wish to feel the pulse of things to come, go to Chicago." Chesterton's observation is still true. Despite the delays getting in and out of O'Hare [Airport], Chicago has the pulse of tomorrow.*

*New Yorkers, of course, like to make a similar claim for their city. And while I'm a loyal resident of the metropolis, who cheered when the Giants took on the Bears and will cheer again when the Mets beat the Cubs, I refuse to let civic loyalty get in the way of truth.*[23]

The speaker, N. J. Nicholas, Jr. (co-chief executive officer of Time-Warner, Inc.), demonstrated respect for his hosts by using a complimentary quotation that put his Chicago audience in a receptive mood. A listener who is approached in this manner tends to think, "He's really interested in me," or "I'll listen to him because he's really gone out of his way to refer to my community."

### Social Organizations

Audiences appreciate speakers who take the time to research some of the characteristics of their organizations. Notice how former Chrysler Corporation Chairman Lee Iacocca refers to attorneys at a convention of the American Bar Association:

*Let me just say that it's an honor to be asked to be here. And a little bit of a surprise, to tell you the truth. When I got the letter from Mr. Thomas last December, it said "It is my privilege to invite you . . ." and ended by wishing me "Happy New Year." Most of the letters I usually get from lawyers start out with "You are hereby summoned," and wind up with "Ignore at your peril." So this is a treat. And I'm glad to be here. I'm also a little curious because I've often wondered just what lawyers do when they have a convention. I know what car dealers do! I noticed, for example, that as soon as I sit down you're scheduled to get into something called "The Statement of the Assembly Resolutions Committee." Now, that sounds like serious business: Last year at our convention, my speech was the warm-up act for Willie Nelson!*[24]

Iacocca's remarks were carefully designed to make good-natured fun of the legal profession as well as of his own automotive industry. You can be sure that the attorneys appreciated his personal references to them.

Whenever you speak to a group or organization, there are certain identifiable catchwords and customs that will gain positive feedback from your audience. Knowing something about the PTA, the Longshoremen's Union, the Future Farmers of America, the Sierra Club, or the Bowling League will help you use terms and phrases that will get the attention of your listeners.

### Targeting Specific Groups

One way you can arouse interest is to target segments of your audience. **Targeting** is the process of identifying selected groups of listeners and designing specific appeals to motivate them. In the Democratic primary elections of 2008, Barack Obama appealed to young voters, upscale, educated Americans, and African Americans to persuade them that "change" is needed in the White House. By contrast, Hillary Clinton's campaign created ads to persuade blue-collar workers, older Americans, and white women that experience is essential for the presidency.

You can also employ targeting in your speeches by using examples, statistics, or quotations that appeal to specific interests of listeners. If your topic is about proper nutrition and there are joggers in your audience, you can specifically refer to them as you explain the benefits of a healthy diet. You can formulate appeals to specific interest groups such as businesspeople, young parents, part-time wage earners, church members, suburbanites, or inner-city residents. Targeting helps you to motivate listeners in very personal ways to become involved with a topic. Notice how this speaker targeted listeners and related their topics to his speech:

> *Several class periods ago, each of us had the opportunity to share something personal about ourselves. I'd like to take a moment to revisit that night and review some of the topics we spoke about. Karen, you described your passion for art. Jennifer talked about sailing and Tom spoke about scuba diving, the final frontier. Madalen presented a speech about insurance rates and George explained what it's like to be a member of the state police SWAT team. Donna, you shared your feelings about returning to school—the pursuit of your dreams. Kelly described her passion for jigsaw puzzles, and George discussed roller skating for exercise. Bob presented his thoughts about friendship and Elizabeth described her feelings about coming to the USA, and we're glad you did. Jean, you talked about Girl Scouts, truly an American tradition. Jagdish introduced medicine. Shannon, you described your college roommates, giving new meaning to the term "private property." Beth introduced skiing and Michelle talked about playing the guitar. Lastly, and appropriately so, Rustin spoke about procrastination.*
>
> *Is there a common link to these passions? I would say yes. Actually, there are three: a man, a date, and a piece of paper. The man's name is Thomas Jefferson, the date was the Fourth of July 1776, and the piece of paper was the Declaration of Independence. This document laid the foundation for the Constitution of the United States, allowing each of us the freedom to follow our dreams and pursue our passions.[25]*

Dan Callahan listened closely to the topics presented by other classroom speakers and used this personal approach to motivate the audience. After the speech, listeners commented that Dan's strategy of identifying their names and topics encouraged them to become involved with his topic.

## IMPACT OF THE OCCASION ON LISTENERS

The **occasion** is a major influence on the audience, and a speaker must know how the environment will affect the speech. An audience subject to the antiseptic odors of a hospital will perceive a speech differently from that of an audience at a spring flower festival. Listeners on Christmas Eve display a contrasting mood from that of an audience on New Year's Eve. People have certain expectations of speakers; they want a judge to convey wisdom, a doctor to project confidence. No analysis of the audience is complete unless you understand the impact of the speaking occasion on listeners: the purpose, location, and expectations of the speaker.

### *The Purpose of the Occasion*

People exhibit a variety of moods and feelings depending on the purpose of the occasion. Listeners are festive at a ball game or a Fourth of July celebration and more serious at a professional convention or a lecture. Jokes and humorous sketches would be entirely appropriate at a retirement banquet but (usually) out of place at a funeral or memorial service. Listeners are also influenced by upcoming holidays or by events of local and national significance. A reference to a tragedy in the community or to a special occasion such as Christmas, Veteran's Day, or the Great American Smokeout can help to make your speech more timely and meaningful to the audience. Notice how John M. Scheb, judge of the Second District Court of Appeals in Lakeland, Florida, referred to the occasion in a speech commemorating Presidents' Day:

*As we reflect on the meaning of this Presidents' Day, our individual thoughts may focus on a particular president of the past. We all remember our history lessons about our early presidents—Washington, Jefferson, Lincoln, and the others who led our country up to the twentieth century. And then we have our own personal memories of more recent leaders. I can remember my parents speaking of President Hoover, and I have vivid memories of serving in the military under Presidents Roosevelt and Truman during World War II. Most of us recall Presidents Eisenhower, Kennedy, Johnson, Nixon, Ford, and Carter. And of course we have fresh memories of Ronald Reagan and George Bush.*

*Our presidents over the years have differed philosophically, emotionally, and culturally. But each wove a thread of love of country into his leadership. And although those threads have been different in strength and design, together they have formed a tapestry displaying cherished values of country and a willingness to serve. This tapestry is patriotism.*[26]

Judge Scheb's references to past presidents helped listeners to reflect on the significance of Presidents' Day and prepared them for the theme of patriotism.

## The Physical Location of the Event

The physical location of a speech can affect both the audience and speaker. An audience shivering in a drafty auditorium in the middle of winter will not listen effectively. A speech presented in the New Orleans Superdome requires a huge TV screen to project visual aids. A craft demonstration at a senior citizens center might require close proximity to listeners rather than a remote speaker's lectern. A speech given outside, at the local county fair, may be subject to a sudden downpour.

An effective speaker carefully examines the physical location of the speech to anticipate and adapt to as many problems as possible. Here are some questions to ask when you are investigating a speaking site:

1. Is the event inside or outside?
2. What is the size of the room?
3. How many people will be present?
4. Is there a stage or raised platform for the speaker?
5. Will there be a speaker's stand or lectern?
6. Does the room have adequate heat, air-conditioning, or ventilation?
7. Does the room have good acoustics?
8. Will there be a microphone, or will the speaker need to rely on strong vocal projection?
9. Could any possible external noise in or near the speaking area cause a distraction?
10. Will props or visual aids need to be set up before the speech?
11. Are adequate electrical outlets, thumbtacks, extension cords, chalk, erasers, easels, tables, or other devices needed for the speech, available?

## The Expectations of the Speaker

Audiences attending events have certain expectations of speakers. They expect a graduation speaker to be warm and congratulatory. They expect a minister or priest to reinforce beliefs and include references to moral and spiritual values. They expect politicians to be responsive to social and governmental concerns.

Audiences even have expectations regarding the speaker's appearance. During a televised speech on energy early in his presidency, Jimmy Carter wore a sweater as he told Americans to turn down their thermostats to reduce dependency on foreign oil. In this "honeymoon" period, public and press reaction appeared favorable to the speech. Over time, however, the public returned to more traditional expectations regarding presidential appearance. Most Americans expect that the president of the United States will deliver an official speech "in proper attire"—meaning a conservative suit and tie.[27] President Carter never wore his cardigan again for a major address.

Whenever you present a speech, you need to know the expectations of your audience. To avoid "speaking surprises," ask questions. Here are points to cover when determining your speaking role on a particular occasion:

1. Do your topic and general purpose suit the occasion?
2. What is the order of speaking, and where is your speech in that order?
3. What time of day do you speak—morning, afternoon, or evening?
4. What is the time limit of the speech?
5. Who is the featured speaker?
6. Will you be introduced to the audience, or must you introduce yourself?
7. How is the ceremony organized?
8. Is someone clearly in charge of the event?
9. Are there any customs or traditions associated with the event that you will be expected to know or to perform?

Once you have gained as much information as possible about the purpose, location, and expectations regarding the event, you will be more confident that your speech will be appropriate to the occasion.

## conducting an audience analysis

As a speaker you should conduct an analysis of your audience in order to develop strategies that will help your speech to receive a favorable hearing. In this section, we look at some strategies to assist you in gathering information about your listeners.

## COLLECTING DEMOGRAPHIC DATA ABOUT THE AUDIENCE

**Demographic analysis** refers to the science of gathering social and statistical information about any group of people. You can collect demographic data by informal assessments, surveying audience opinion or knowledge, circulating questionnaires, or conducting personal interviews.

### Informal Assessments

In a fast-paced society where information is exchanged rapidly and speaking engagements are arranged quickly, it is often difficult for speakers to do a comprehensive, written, or computer analysis of the audience. If you find yourself in this situation, you can still get information from individuals who know your listeners well. E-mail or telephone the host or organizers of the event to ask questions about the composition of your audience.

- What are the gender and ethnicity of your listeners?
- What are their age ranges?
- What are some of their principal interests and concerns?
- What do they know about you as the speaker?
- What special characteristics of the audience should you be aware of?

Although a complete analysis may not be possible, a brief investigation that obtains the answers to some of these critical questions may provide information that is extremely beneficial as you develop your speech.

When you are more familiar with your audience, you may not have to ask as many questions. For example, if you are asked to speak at your church, you probably already know the answers to many questions about your listeners. In your speech communication class, your instructor may already have asked you to do a written demographic analysis of your audience. If not, you can simply observe the gender, ethnicity, age, and marital status of your classmates. If you have heard some preliminary speeches in class, you have already had the opportunity to observe and listen to many of their interests. These quick observations can help you develop topics and strategies that connect your speeches to your listeners, as long as you do not make false assumptions.

### Surveys

One way to determine the attitudes of your listeners is to survey the relative strength and weakness of their opinions. You can accomplish this by constructing a scale like the one shown here.

### Audience Attitude Survey

**Proposition:**    The practice of cloning cells to reproduce exact copies of humans and animals should be stopped.

Do you agree, disagree, or are you neutral? Please place a check mark at the appropriate place on the scale that describes your attitude about the above specific purpose:

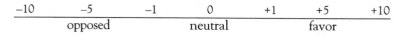

| −10 | −5 | −1 | 0 | +1 | +5 | +10 |
|---|---|---|---|---|---|---|
| | opposed | | neutral | | favor | |

This survey helps you to determine audience attitudes about controversial issues prior to a presentation. Circulate the survey to audience members while you are preparing a speech. When you get the results, carefully analyze how many in the audience favor, oppose, or are neutral. The range of audience attitudes will help you decide the types of supporting materials to use and even influence your persuasive approach.

Another type of survey can help you determine the degree of knowledge your listeners possess concerning your topic.

### Audience Information Scale

**Topic:**    The Patriot Act

How knowledgeable are you about the topic listed above?

| 1 | 2 | 3 | 4 |
|---|---|---|---|
| I know a lot about it | I have some information about it | I've only heard about it | I've never heard of it |

This scale is especially useful with informative speech topics. When you add and then average the score, you will have a good indication of how to gear your speech. A low audience average of 1.6 would indicate that listeners are quite knowledgeable about the topic. Your speech could then include examples and terms with a degree of depth and sophistication. On the other hand, a higher score of 3.4 would imply that your audience lacks knowledge, and your speech should include definitions of unfamiliar terms and examples that are easy for listeners to absorb.

### Questionnaires

Another way to get demographic information is to circulate a questionnaire. You can develop a list of open-ended questions about age, gender, religion, income range, nationality or ethnic origin, education, occupation, social groupings, experiences, and interests. You can then have the questions distributed to audience members well before your speech to collect the needed information. Data obtained through questionnaires can help you to determine the significant values, beliefs, and interests of your listeners and assist you in preparing motivational appeals that stimulate audience receptiveness.

*Interviews*

Personal interviews with audience members provide more flexibility than surveys or questionnaires and allow you to ask in-depth and follow-up questions.[28] In a personal interview you also have the advantage of one-to-one observation: You can watch an individual's reactions to questions, evaluate the person's use of language, and observe the audience member's appearance. One disadvantage is that a personal interview can be time-consuming. If you have more than a hundred people in the audience, you may have difficulty interviewing each one. It might be more efficient to interview a cross section or sample of the group.

## PROCESSING THE DATA WITH A COMPUTER

One effective way to process and organize demographic information about an audience is by using a computer program called SPSS (Statistical Package for the Social Sciences). Speakers in government, business, and industry use this program to assess demographic information and to develop profiles of audiences. This powerful program can process data according to keywords or command names such as age, sex, occupation, or interest area. You can determine if there are relationships between audience interests and geographical region or correlations among race, age, income, education, and social grouping.[29] If you have access to a personal computer and a statistical program, you can also enter demographic data and develop profiles using specific commands or keywords. For more information about computer programs that include demographic profiles, you may want to contact your college or university sociology, mathematics, social sciences, or computer programming department.

## EVALUATING THE AUDIENCE PROFILE

When you have a printout of your data, analyze and evaluate the information. Make some assessments about the audience and try to identify some of the most significant qualities that could affect their perceptions of your speech. Develop specific appeals that relate to the most important interests and needs of your listeners.

## summary »

When building a speech, you need to understand some of the major influences on your listeners and how these factors will affect your presentation:

1. Be aware of listener perceptions toward you as a speaker.
2. Assess audience perceptions of the topic.
3. Understand audience beliefs, values, and value systems. When you know the motivations of your listeners, you can develop specific appeals that link your topic to their needs.
4. Determine the composition of your audience according to age, gender, religion, ethnic origin, educational level, occupation, interests, income level, geographical location, and group affiliation. You can target specific groups of listeners by creating appeals that relate to their concerns.
5. Know how the occasion of the speech influences the audience and speaker. Analyze the purpose of the occasion, the physical location of the event, and audience expectations of the speaker.

You can conduct an audience analysis by gathering demographic information, processing the data with a computer, and evaluating the audience profile.

## SKILL BUILDERS »

1. Conduct a demographic analysis of the social groups in your classroom audience. What appeals could you include in your speech that would effectively connect to the needs and motivations of your listeners?
2. Describe the elements of the occasion relative to your class, and explain how these elements can affect your speech.

## BUILDING A
## SPEECH ONLINE »

Now that you've read Chapter 3, use your online Resource Center for Building a Speech for quick access to the electronic study resources that accompany this text. You can access your Resource Center at http://academic.cengage.com/login, using the access code that came with your book or that you bought online at http://www.iChapters.com. Your Resource Center gives you access to Interactive Video Activities, the book's companion website, Speech Builder Express 3.0, InfoTrac College Edition, and study aids, including a digital glossary and review quizzes.

© Reuters/Landov

# chapter 4

# IMPROVING YOUR LISTENING SKILLS

## chapter objectives »

After reading and studying this chapter, you should be able to

1. Recognize the significance of listening

2. Understand the process of listening

3. Identify five types of listening behavior

4. Recognize six barriers to listening

5. Describe how to become an active listener and speaker

In February 2008, passengers on Go! Airlines Flight 1002 boarded their plane in Honolulu expecting a short 30-minute interisland flight to the Big Island. As the airplane approached its destination of Hilo, it didn't land; it just kept flying. Passenger Derrick Lining commented, "When I noticed we weren't descending I told my wife, 'I think something's kind of weird in this flight pattern.'" Air traffic controllers tried to reach the pilots but there was no answer for 25 minutes. In fact, the airplane flew 15 miles out to sea beyond its destination before it turned around and landed safely. Why didn't the pilots respond? Were they taking a coffee break? Eating lunch? Or were they—asleep?[1] The Federal Aviation Administration immediately began an investigation into the incident.

Examples such as this indicate the importance of effective listening in the communication process. Often

> " *To listen is an effort, and just to hear is no merit. A duck hears also.* "
>
> —*Igor Stravinsky*

our success and sometimes our safety depend upon how effectively we listen to directions and data, how carefully we evaluate and weigh information. Lives depend upon a pilot's ability to pay attention to flight instructions from the control tower or upon a surgeon's ability to listen to nurses or patients.

This chapter presents four kinds of listening, introduces the concept of active and passive listening, identifies six behaviors that create barriers to effective listening, and discusses a four-point program to build better listening skills.

## the significance of listening

The International Listening Association has gathered some interesting facts regarding listening behavior.[2] You might find some of them surprising. Eighty-five percent of what we know we learn by listening. We spend 75 percent of our time distracted, preoccupied, or forgetting something. We spend 45 percent of our time actually listening, but we remember only 20 percent of what we hear. After hearing someone speak to us, we can immediately recall about 50 percent of the information. Finally, fewer than 2 percent of us have ever had formal education or training in any aspect of listening.

A 1977 study was conducted at Auburn University to determine how various communication activities were divided during a typical college student's day. Researchers surveyed 645 students and found that listening occurred 52.5 percent of the time, speaking took place 16.3 percent of the communication day, reading occurred 17.3 percent of the time, and writing occupied 13.9 percent of the communication day.[3]

As you can see, each of these surveys indicates that we spend most of our communication time engaged in some type of listening behavior. Often, however, we don't listen very well. Christine De Chello, a vice president of Ron Weber and Associates, a telemarketing and database development organization, writes about the direct relationship of listening to the use of successful telemarketing techniques:

> *Think of all the conversations that take place around you, and you'll realize how few of us take the time to listen to the person who is speaking. Extend that scenario to the call center environment, and you're talking missed sales opportunities and lost revenues. After all, no one makes a purchase based on a monolog anymore. The days of the fast-talking salesperson with the hard-sell approach are long over. Today, effective selling evolves from constructing solid customer bonds through excellent listening skills. Indeed, effective listening is the catalyst to building results-driven, interactive conversations with customers and establishing rapport rooted in trust.*[4]

Unfortunately, poor listening is a fact of life in all professions and at every level of our society. Examples abound of problems created because individuals or groups refused to listen, didn't listen carefully, or listened only to information they wanted to hear. A few concrete examples will illustrate the magnitude of the listening problem.

The independent commission investigating the attacks of September 11 played a tape of a telephone call from Betty Ong, a crew member on American Airlines Flight 11, which crashed into the north tower of the World Trade Center. In the call, Ms. Ong told supervisors that the airplane had been hijacked. She also described the weapons that were used and the seat locations of the hijackers. Betty Ong's phone call was received skeptically, however, when her supervisors responded, "Are you sure?" and requested her to verify that the incident wasn't simply a matter of air rage. The 9/11 commission went on to find that before September 11 U.S. intelligence agencies had circulated secret memos titled, "Bin Laden Determined to Strike in U.S." and "Islamic Extremist Learns to Fly," that received little response or action from officials at every level of government.[5]

## POOR LISTENERS IN THE MEDICAL PROFESSION

*Why did a recent article in the Journal of the American Medical Association indicate high dissatisfaction in traditional doctor-patient appointments? Why is it The Wall Street Journal claims that perception of physical concern and not physician expertise is the deciding factor in the rising number of malpractice suits? Why did The New England Journal of Medicine report that the care and attention quotient is causing "alternative" medical practices to grow by leaps and bound? Given this litany of events, what does it really mean to listen? And why, in the name of science don't we produce better listeners in the medical profession?[7]*

David Koresh, leader of the Branch Davidians, charmed followers with his charisma and twisted interpretation of the Bible. He passed out business cards inscribed with the word *Messiah* to potential converts who were looking for direction in life or had no place to live. Although he exhumed a body from a gravesite and failed at an attempt to raise the corpse from the dead, his followers seemed persuaded that Koresh was more than just a man. At their Waco, Texas, compound the Branch Davidians built up an arsenal of more than 300 weapons that included semiautomatic rifles, grenades, and explosives. Unfortunately, Koresh's charismatic power led to a 51-day standoff between his followers and the U.S. government that ended in a fiery raid, killing 80 of the cult members on April 19, 1993.[6]

Research shows that many doctors don't allow their patients to fully complete a description of their ailments during office visits. A study reported in the *British Medical Journal* found that on the average, doctors wait only 20 seconds before interrupting a patient.[8] Another study surveying 74 office visits reported that only 23 percent of the patients were allowed to complete an opening statement of their medical issues because doctors interrupted patients in 69 percent of the visits.[9] In a survey of approximately 800 pediatric visits to a hospital outpatient facility, 25 percent of the mothers reported that they had not been able to discuss the most important issues on their minds, 20 percent felt that they were not given clear explanations as to what was wrong with their children, and about half weren't sure what had caused the illness.[10]

Even though some of these examples are extreme, they are real. They remind us of what can happen to a nation, a group, or an individual if people block out essential communication, avoid listening critically, or listen selectively.

## the process of listening

In Chapter 1 we discussed the fact that communication is a dynamic, ever-changing process that can be understood through a communication model that includes a sender, message, channel, receiver, and feedback. But listening, a critical component in communication, is also complex and involves its own dynamic process of receiving stimuli, assigning meaning, and formulating responses. Listening is so interesting to human beings that entire books have been written, numerous definitions have been proposed, and special college courses and curricula have been developed to help us understand this often elusive subject more completely. In this text, we will explore the definition and model developed by Andrew Wolvin and Carolyn Gwynn Coakley[11] to help you gain a deeper insight into the exciting process of listening.

Wolvin and Coakley define listening as "the process of receiving, attending to, and assigning meaning to aural and visual stimuli."[12] The **listening model** in Figure 4.1 indicates that the receiver decodes the stimulus through the aural (hearing) and visual senses. The listener first receives a stimulus—let's say, "Do you want some ice cream?" The upper funnel is called the listening cone and is wider at the top, indicating that receivers can interpret a stimulus in many different ways. But the bottom of the cone is narrower to indicate that an individual makes choices to limit meaning and interpret stimuli according to the receiver's own personal criteria. Between the wide and narrow portions of the cone are three overlapping elements that are critical to listening: receiving, attending, and assigning meaning. The long oval cylinder linking the three components refers to the process of remembering and responding covertly as the listener uses the three elements to decode the stimulus and make limited choices against the backdrop of remembered experience, perception, and many other variables.

So the listener receives the stimulus, "Do you want some ice cream?" and pays attention to it, beginning to interpret the question and assign meaning. The receiver may covertly think, "Ah, ice cream: soft serve, hand dipped, store bought, home made—mmmmmmm." The listener continues to make selections. "Butter pecan, death by chocolate, mint chocolate chip, rocky road." The receiver makes further choices. "Some ice cream. Could that be a small scoop? Three scoops? A quart?" The listener then provides additional limits to the meaning of the stimulus based on her own remembered criteria: "I'm on a diet. Can't do three scoops. Maybe I'll be good and order just one teeny dish." The receiver has now begun to finalize her choices and assign meaning as the process nears the narrower bottom of the listening cone. She thinks, "I'll probably get three scoops of chocolate chip cookie dough ice cream. I'll worry about the diet tomorrow!"

The lower funnel in Figure 4.1 is known as the feedback cone. Unlike the upper listening cone, it is narrower at the top and wider at the bottom. The lower cone and the stimulus are surrounded by dotted lines to indicate that a listener may or may not

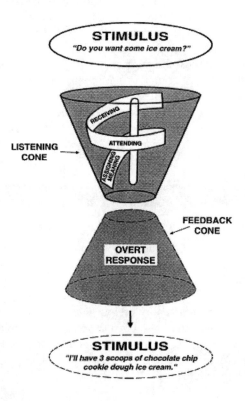

FIGURE 4.1 Wolvin-Coakley Model of the Listening Process *Source:* From *Listening*, by A. Wolvin et al., p. 75. Reprinted by permission of the McGraw-Hill Companies.

choose to make an overt response to a received stimulus. The narrow top indicates that a receiver limits the meaning of a stimulus according to personal criteria. The wider bottom demonstrates that the feedback message or stimulus formulated by the listener can be interpreted in many different ways by receivers. And thus the listening process repeats the cycle through different perceptions and choices made by various receivers. So our listener has decided that she wants some ice cream and has decided to make an overt response: "I'll have three scoops of chocolate chip cookie dough ice cream." And the ice cream store attendant responds, "Will that be in a cup, or in a cake or waffle cone?" Now the process must be repeated, because the listener didn't narrow her choices quite enough. Notice that throughout both the upper and lower funnels are diagonal lines representing perceptual filters that receivers use to decode stimuli and feedback senders use to encode messages when they respond covertly or overtly to stimuli.

You can see that the process of listening is complicated. Many other variables are involved, such as the efficiency of the visual and hearing mechanisms, numerous stimuli competing for attention, and the dynamics of memory. Listening scholars are still theorizing and conducting experiments to determine if the process can be more precisely defined and the elements of listening more clearly identified. Although the process is complex and could require many pages of discussion, the Wolvin-Coakley model serves merely as an outline to give you a brief introduction to the interactive process of listening.

## kinds of listening

Just as speakers have general speech purposes for sending messages, listeners also have goals for receiving them. We will examine four kinds of listening: discriminative, evaluative, appreciative, and empathic.[13] In addition, we will briefly consider the concept of active and passive listening.

## DISCRIMINATIVE LISTENING

When we listen discriminatively, we listen to learn, to be instructed, and to test theories. **Discriminative listening** can occur in formal settings such as in class, at work, or in a business

Discriminative listening often occurs in formal settings such as in class or at work where we listen to learn, to be informed, or to test theories.

meeting. If you are taking notes at a history class lecture, receiving instructions on how to operate a new computer program, or hearing a committee report, you are acquiring instructional information for future use. Discriminative listening also occurs informally in the process of daily conversation. When you hear your lunch friends describing a new restaurant, the service manager explaining what is wrong with your car, or an insurance agent providing details of a policy, you have applied discriminative listening. Whether formal or informal, discriminative listening helps us to make distinctions and to differentiate in order to be enlightened, informed, or educated.

## EVALUATIVE LISTENING

**Evaluative listening** is our response to a persuasive message. We listen to convincing, actuating, or stimulating messages and formulate reactions based upon our needs and the strength of the persuasion. We are bombarded with persuasive messages daily. Advertisers on television, on the Internet, and in magazines actuate us to buy products; family members persuade us to run errands, purchase gifts, or plan vacations; supervisors encourage us to use new strategies to enhance the company image or to improve sales; a colleague urges us to buy candy to help her daughter raise money for a class trip. Persuasion is often difficult because listeners have built up resistance due to the constant barrage of competing stimuli. Listeners ultimately evaluate persuasive messages and decide to agree or disagree based upon the credibility of the speaker and the material, the logic of the speaker's reasoning, the extent of the commitment exhibited by the speaker, and the need of listeners to buy into the speaker's goal.

## APPRECIATIVE LISTENING

If you have ever been to a movie, listened to a favorite recording, taken a long walk in the woods, or just enjoyed hearing the sounds of the ocean at the beach, you have participated in **appreciative listening**. We listen appreciatively to hear the power and beauty of words, images, music, or environmental sounds. We may enjoy hearing the variety of instruments in an orchestral symphony; we might respond with strong emotion to the vivid language of an eloquent speaker; we may listen in passive contentment to the delicate trickle of a waterfall or to the patter of rain on a roof. We might hear the call of an owl at night or the hiss of an alley cat springing off a garbage can. We learn appreciative listening as we become sensitized to new sounds and experiences. When we learn to listen appreciatively, we establish an emotional bond by responding to the works of others and enhance our sensory enjoyment of life.

## EMPATHIC LISTENING

The primary goal of discriminative, evaluative, and appreciative listening is to benefit ourselves and contribute to our understanding, decision making, and personal fulfillment. The goal of **empathic listening** differs, however, in that the objective is to understand and facilitate the needs and feelings of someone else.

We use empathic or therapeutic listening when we are responding to the needs of a close friend, work associate, or family member who is sharing personal joy, anxiety, or concern. We could be hearing a friend describing a failed marriage, a family member sharing pride about a successful promotion, or a relative discussing a struggle with alcoholism.

Numerous businesses, professions, and volunteer organizations require their employees to possess skills in effective therapeutic listening. Lawyers assist clients in developing the best defense or offense after hearing the nature of the charges against them. Educators are required to plan strategies for growth after listening to the needs of students. Psychiatrists must provide therapeutic progress toward mental health when responding to the anxieties of patients. Volunteers often spend hours on hotlines listening to distraught individuals who describe suicidal feelings, spouse abuse, or rape. Hospice workers listen with love and devotion to the last cries and wishes of the dying. Empathic listeners must pay attention completely, without giving in to distractions, without making irrelevant comments, and without ignoring the sender's message.

## ACTIVE AND PASSIVE LISTENING

Most listening behavior is either active or passive. **Active listening** is attentive and involved behavior. Active listening is the kind of listening we should be using at work, in a meeting, or in class. Active listening is hard work—it represents complete mental commitment on the part of the hearer. **Passive listening** is relaxed or "easy" listening. Often when you listen to your stereo or watch a movie, you are listening passively. Passive listening helps us escape from the pressures of everyday life. Most of us, however, are already accomplished in passive listening and probably not attentive enough to the demands of active listening. If you have ever received a poor grade on a test because you didn't take good notes in class, you have experienced the results of passive listening.

## BARRIERS TO LISTENING

We all need to become better active listeners. But in order to improve our listening, we need to understand **listening barriers** and analyze some of the poor listening behaviors we often practice. Six barriers to effective listening are

1. Yielding to distractions
2. Blocking out communication
3. Listening selectively
4. Overcriticizing the speaker
5. Faking attention
6. Avoiding difficult listening situations[14]

## YIELDING TO DISTRACTIONS

We've already discussed "noise" as a barrier to the communication process in Chapter 1. As a listener, you are constantly battling distractions that result from external, internal, or semantic noise. If a speaker has a broken pair of glasses held together at the nose by tape, you are going to have difficulty listening to the speaker's remarks because of the external distraction. Equally distracting are your own internal "noises," such as anger at a person or situation; fatigue from staying up all night; or anxiety about an upcoming conflict, court appearance, or final exam. You also might not understand several of the terms that the speaker is using, or you might react negatively to an outdated word or phrase the speaker employs.

Not only are we plagued by the distractions within or immediately around us but our society puts great emphasis on messages that tempt us to escape. Ads tell us to get away from it all by going on vacation, taking a coffee break, eating a candy bar, buying a flat screen TV, or going to a movie. We are not condemning the practice of listening to relax. Listening to a good recording or watching a comedy can do wonders for your mental health. But many of us are very good at passive television listening and not very good at active listening that requires energy and work. Often, the more time we spend in passive listening, the lazier we become in our active listening patterns.[15] It becomes easier and more fun to daydream and let our minds wander than to concentrate on more difficult information.

## BLOCKING OUT COMMUNICATION

Sooner or later, most of us are accused of "blocking out" information and of not listening. One of the most common stereotypes of blocking behavior is the husband who reads the newspaper and mutters "uh-huh" while his wife is trying to talk to him. We have probably all watched an exciting TV program and blocked out the phone talk or other conversation around us.

Sometimes blocking behaviors are purposeful, and sometimes they are habits acquired as a result of pressure, stress, and overstimulation of the senses. Even conscientious, active listeners can be so bombarded by competing stimuli that they are forced to adopt blocking behavior as a survival mechanism. For example, you wake up in the morning and hear on the radio about a bomb that exploded in a crowded subway, causing numerous injuries. At noon you hear about a fellow office worker's sudden heart attack; coming home you hear of another suicide bombing in the Middle East; and the evening news reports that violent crimes in your community have doubled in the past two years. At home you discover that your little sister has broken her finger and your aunt has cancer. In these circumstances, you might well choose to block out information for a while.

The problem occurs, however, when normally active listeners become so saturated by what they hear and see that blocking out stimuli becomes habitual, and they can no longer pay the necessary attention to *real* crises. When a husband and wife begin to block each other out in their marriage, or children cannot get through to their parents, serious communication barriers can be created.

Blocking can also result when a listener who disagrees turns off immediately when the topic of the speech is announced or when certain catchwords are stated. Instead of giving the speech a fair hearing, a listener with an extreme bias will have a mental fight with the speaker about each point. A biased individual might not be able to get around the mere mention of the names Barack Obama, Hillary Clinton, or John McCain; the terms *tax cuts, immigration reform, universal health insurance;* or the labels *Republican, Libertarian, or Democrat.*

Active listening is hard work and requires complete mental commitment on the part of the hearer.

© Stone/Getty Images

Sometimes an individual will block out the opposing speaker so that mental time can be spent storing up all of the verbal ammunition to fire back. The listener is not hearing the speaker, but is blocking out any opposing views so that he does not have to examine the speaker's position.

## LISTENING SELECTIVELY

Often we create a listening barrier when we try to listen for all of the details, and we don't catch the overall point of the information. An equal problem is the desire within all of us to hear what we want to hear or to listen only to information that supports our own thinking.

Consider this example. In September of 2002 a woman at a Shoney's restaurant in Calhoun, Georgia, overheard what she thought were three terrorists plotting a violent attack in Miami. The woman reported to police that she heard three Muslim men saying, "Do you think we have enough to bring it down?" and "If we don't have enough to bring it down, I have contacts and we can get enough to bring it down." Police tracked down the three men—who were medical students—closed Interstate 75 in Florida, and searched the men's two vehicles. Authorities reported that they found no explosives and that the men had no connections to any terrorist organizations. The students were released and were not charged with any crime. A lawyer for the students explained that they were talking about a car that one of the men owned and was going to ship down for his use in Florida. The students were U.S. citizens and on their way to attend an internship program at a Florida hospital.

Unfortunately, the woman who overheard the conversation caught only a few key words that she pieced together to draw a faulty conclusion. Thinking she was being patriotic in reporting a potential threat against the United States in the wake of the September 11 attacks, this woman, through selective listening, caused three innocent students to be detained for questioning for 17 hours. In addition, the Florida hospital where the students were interning received threatening e-mails and racial slurs, causing the hospital to ask the three students to intern at some other institution. The students told the media, "We're medical students. We are not terrorists. Our primary concern in life is to become doctors. We want to help people. We don't want to hurt." It is understandable that Americans are on edge as a result of terrorism, but the three students' medical careers were said to be "in limbo" because of selective listening.[16]

## OVERCRITICIZING THE SPEAKER

We can criticize a speaker to such an extent that we destroy any possibility of hearing the speaker's intentions or purposes. The speaker's appearance may be wrong, the speaker may lean too much on the lectern, or the speaker's tie may be the wrong color. Maybe we think the speaker shouldn't wear a tie, or the speaker's voice is too soft or too loud, or the speaker is too emotional or too logical.

Many listeners feel that communication is solely the responsibility of the speaker. If the speaker isn't exciting enough, attractive enough, funny enough, emotional enough, or logical enough, these listeners switch mental channels and perform their own mental activities.

The responsibility for effective communication must be *shared* between the speaker and listener. The speaker is responsible for encoding the feelings into symbols, structuring the message, and selecting the channels of communication. But the listener is responsible for decoding the message and for providing clear feedback, which signals to the speaker if communication is taking place and how effective the communication has been.

An individual who overcriticizes a speaker often assumes that it is solely the speaker's responsibility to convey a message. Often these listeners develop the attitude "Okay—here I am sitting in front of you. Do something to me. Interest me. Get my attention. Humor me."

Not only is this poor listening behavior, it keeps the individual from shouldering his or her part of the communication transaction—to listen.

## FAKING ATTENTION

Many of us are good at faking attention. When we're involved in a boring conversation, we can smile, look interested, and nod our head as if we are giving our complete attention. But in our mind we are performing some other activity, such as planning our weekend or finalizing the grocery list.

Students are very good at faking attention. A student can look straight at the instructor, smile and frown at all the appropriate times, lean forward and take notes (doodles on the paper), and generally appear to be involved in the class. The problem occurs, of course, when a question demands a specific response or a pop quiz is given on material just discussed. The faked response can quickly turn into embarrassment, with an inattentive listener feeling angry at being taken by surprise. Faking attention is a bad habit that creates a barrier to communication.

## AVOIDING DIFFICULT LISTENING SITUATIONS

Sometimes we avoid listening situations that we feel are too demanding. We feel insecure, and our lack of experience makes us dread the situation.

A poster in a college math department reads: "Mathophobia can cost you a career."[17] Underneath the caption is a list of careers such as commercial flying, dental technology, and engineering, all of which are inaccessible to individuals without skills in mathematics.

We could expand the caption in the poster to state, "Avoiding difficult listening situations can cost you enlightenment, growth, and fulfillment." Imagine someone canceling a trip to the Greek Islands or the Spanish Riviera due to insecurity about foreign languages. Think of individuals passing up free tickets to a symphony concert because they don't "understand" classical music. Imagine an individual not learning how to use a computer program because it appears too complicated. Unfortunately, these situations can and do occur when individuals fear difficult listening circumstances.

Sometimes listening is a matter of rethinking and overcoming inner fears. Whatever you do, don't avoid situations that you think may be difficult. Overcome the difficulty by facing it directly. Open your mind to the situation and allow yourself to receive communication. Take on the listening circumstance as a challenge: Gain perspective by exploring an unfamiliar culture, develop sophistication from an aesthetic experience, and gain satisfaction by acquiring a new skill. You will be surprised at your growth and achievement in a constructive environment.

## how to become an active listener and speaker

We have already pointed out that being an active listener is hard work. But this hard work helps you to become not only a better listener but an improved speaker as well. Here is a simple four-point program to help you increase your awareness of the way you listen:

1. Withhold judgment.
2. Provide honest, attentive feedback.
3. Eliminate distractions.
4. Evaluate the speech when it is finished.

# WITHHOLD JUDGMENT

Keep an open mind. As a listener, don't turn off when you hear the speaker's name, the statement of the topic, or the purpose of the speech. Wait until the speaker has finished before you begin to evaluate the speaker or any portion of the speech. As a speaker, don't make judgments about the demographics of your listeners or the setting and occasion of the speech. When you withhold judgment, it is important to consider the following:

1. Avoid the appearance trap.
2. Don't be easily swayed by delivery and style.
3. Give all topics a fair hearing.
4. Avoid extraneous mental activity during the speech.

## *Avoid the Appearance Trap*

We are easily influenced by the physical appearance of a speaker or listener. It is easy to misjudge a sloppily dressed person or to feel that someone who is neatly dressed in the latest fashion is more worthy of our time.

Although it is important for a speaker to do everything possible to support the speech nonverbally as well as verbally, we must recognize that not all speakers share the same ideas about what constitutes effective speaking. "Dressing for success" may be important to some speakers, but others might care very little about appearance. Recognize your own attitudes and standards about appearance, and try not to impose these attitudes on the speaker.

It is also important for you to avoid making judgments about your listeners' appearance when you are speaking to an audience. Any instructor who has taught in a college or university classroom knows that it is impossible to evaluate student performance on the basis of how students dress when they come to class. Avoiding misjudgments will help you speak more openly to your audience and keep you from stereotyping your listeners.

## *Don't Be Easily Swayed by Delivery and Style*

Don't allow yourself to become seduced or alienated by delivery and style when you are either a speaker or a listener. A speaker who has a soothing voice could be advocating ideas that are harmful to the audience; a speaker with an irritating voice could be well organized and coherent in logic and ideas. Work hard not to let a speaker's hesitations, vocalized pauses, or monotonous delivery affect your judgment unfairly. Don't be too easily impressed by a speaker's ability to use big words and flamboyant phrases that send you on a hunt through the dictionary. Recognize that every speaker has limitations in delivery. Try to accept the speaker and learn as much as you can without mentally trying to change the speaker.

If you are speaking to an audience, don't allow yourself to be taken in by listeners who may seem to appear "friendly" or alienated by those who you may feel look hostile. Speakers often tend to gravitate toward listeners whose smiles, head nods, and facial expressions seem more favorable to them. Such a practice is not helpful if you are trying to communicate to everyone in your audience. Look at the skeptics as well as the allies. Your task as a speaker is to connect to as many listeners as possible.

## *Give All Topics a Fair Hearing*

We all like some topics more than others. Don't let your own attitude for or against an issue prejudice your receptivity to a speech. You have nothing to lose if you keep your mind open to an issue. If you still disagree with the topic at the conclusion of the speech, you will have learned something—even if it is just the speaker's organization or research.

As both a speaker and listener, force yourself to listen to ideas you oppose. Listening to different beliefs develops your active listening capacities and helps you grow as a communicator. When developing topics, you will be more willing to look at all sides of issues and more honestly examine the strength or weaknesses of your arguments.

### Avoid Extraneous Mental Activity During the Speech

Some books and articles on listening advise people to take mental notes, make mental summaries, or write mental outlines while listening. Such mental activity is said to help the listener concentrate on what is being discussed and more effectively retain the main points of the presentation. One author rejects these ideas and feels that such advice causes listeners to become distracted.[18] Some research indicates that when people are still thinking about a speaker's previous point (or making mental summaries), they are usually not listening to what the speaker is currently saying.[19]

It is important for speakers and listeners to concentrate on what is being said and not think behind or ahead of communication. When you give the speaker a complete hearing, all of your mental activity will be focused on the speaker, and you will postpone all other evaluation, summarizing, or inference making until the speech is over. As a speaker you should be focused on your communication and not on distractions such as your nervousness or your mistakes. Being in the moment helps the speaker to reduce fear and communicate the speech more effectively. (For more discussion about reducing nervousness, see Chapter 5, "Understanding and Reducing Your Apprehension.")

## GIVE HONEST, ATTENTIVE FEEDBACK

Work hard to listen actively. As a listener, provide clear signals that show the speaker you are paying attention. Sit up straight. Make eye contact with the speaker. Nod your head to let the speaker know you understand what is being said. Show interest in the speaker and in the speaker's topic. Give the speaker a smile or laugh when the speaker tells a joke. Try to support the speaker as much as you can. If you don't understand a part of the speech, give the speaker a puzzled expression to indicate that you don't follow what is being discussed.[20]

When you are a member of an audience, don't fake attention. Don't pretend to listen when you really aren't. In Chapter 3, we talked about credibility and the necessity of trusting a speaker. It is equally important that a speaker be able to trust an audience. The speaker needs to know that the speech is being actively heard and that the listener is providing clear, accurate, and sincere feedback to the speech.

As a speaker, be willing to be attentive and respond to honest feedback. If you see listeners with puzzled expressions, try to adjust your speaking to draw them into the speech. Stand up straight, show enthusiasm for your topic, and use eye contact with as many listeners or areas of the audience as possible. Show that you care about the audience and want them to gain a clear understanding of your communication.

In your speech class, you could conceivably deliver speeches exclusively to your instructor without class members present. In such a situation, your only concern would be to direct your speech to an audience of one (your instructor) and to get a good grade on each presentation. You could also conceivably deliver speeches to an audience

FIGURE 4.2  What listening problems are illustrated in this cartoon that have implications for both speakers and audiences?
*Source:* GUMDROP reprinted by permission of United Features Syndicate, Inc.

commanded to fake pleasant facial expressions, giving you the false impression that whatever you said was positively received. But your speech instructor does not want a one-person audience or a fake audience: Your instructor wants every speaker to communicate to a "live" audience that is sincere, receptive, and attentive. Your positions as a speaker and listener in your classroom are equally important. How well you listen as a member of the audience can affect the learning atmosphere of the class as well as the success of each individual speaker.

## ELIMINATE DISTRACTIONS

Be conscious of the disruptions caused by external, internal, and semantic noise, and work hard to overcome them. You must continually remind yourself that your roles as both a speaker and listener require you to share in the communication process and to be active in relation to the communication process.

As a listener, don't allow yourself the luxury of daydreaming, studying for an exam, or rudely text-messaging during a speech. Avoid the pitfalls created by these distractions. Remind yourself that, as a listener, you have the same responsibility of keeping to your task as does the speaker. Learn to block out the distractions—not the speaker.

Eliminating distractions when you are a speaker requires you to do everything possible to keep the communication process on track. Define difficult terms that may be unfamiliar to listeners. Concentrate on your communication at hand, and don't wish that you were somewhere else. If the room is too cold or noisy, try to change the conditions if possible, or at least make a comment to relieve tension. One speaker who asked the audience to turn off their cell phones and iPods found his phone ringing "The Star-Spangled Banner" as he was delivering his presentation. Be courteous to listeners and give them the same respect that you expect of them.

# EVALUATE THE COMMUNICATION WHEN IT IS FINISHED

When the speech is completed, evaluate the presentation. Begin to ask questions, make mental summaries, and try to recall the main points of the speech. After you deliver or listen to a speech, analyze both the content and the delivery. Speech **content** refers to the research, organization, and logical development of the topic. The **delivery** refers to the style or presentation of the speech. Here are some questions about content and delivery to use when you analyze speeches presented in your course:

## Content

1. Was the speech well organized?
2. Did the speech reflect the existence and development of an outline?
3. Was there a clear, specific purpose and/or a thesis statement in the speech?
4. Were there an introduction, body, and conclusion in the speech?
5. Were the main points in the body of the speech easy to follow?
6. Was the introduction interesting? Was the introduction designed to gain the attention of the audience?
7. Did the speaker use credible sources to support the main points of the speech?
8. Did the speaker use examples, case studies, illustrations, or other supportive materials to explain some of the major points in the speech?
9. Did the speaker use statistics? Were these clear and easy to understand? Were the statistics logical, and did they support the main points in the speech?
10. Was the speaker's information accurate and up-to-date?
11. Was the topic appropriate to the audience?
12. Did the speaker attempt to adapt the topic to audience interests and needs?
13. Did the speaker define any unfamiliar terms?
14. Was the content of the speech generally well prepared?
15. Was the conclusion interesting? Was the conclusion designed to wrap up the speech effectively?

## Delivery

1. Did the speaker use eye contact?
2. Did the speaker use supportive facial expressions?
3. Did the speaker use gestures for emphasis and clarity?
4. Were the speaker's posture and body position appropriate?
5. Did the speaker use note cards effectively?
6. Was the speaker spontaneous and conversational?
7. Was the speaker's voice easy to hear?
8. Did the speaker make use of vocal inflections?
9. Did the speaker appear to be enthusiastic and energetic about the subject?
10. Did the speaker's vocal tone, vocal inflections, and verbal emphasis indicate a commitment or belief in the topic? Was the speaker's articulation effective? Did the speaker have an understanding of English usage?
11. Was the language appropriate to the topic and the audience?
12. Did the speaker use external transitions to mark the main points of the body? Did the speaker make use of internal transitions within main headings?
13. If visual aids were used, did the speaker use the visuals effectively? Were the visuals easy to see, neat, and clear, and were they an asset to the speech?
14. Did the speaker have any mannerisms that created external noise?

## summary »

Research indicates that people spend the majority of their communication time in listening-related activities. Problems occur when people do not listen effectively.

Listening can be identified as discriminative or instructional, evaluative or persuasive, appreciative or emotional, and empathic or therapeutic. Active listening is an attentive and involved activity, while passive listening is a relaxed behavior.

Barriers to listening include yielding to distractions, blocking out communication, listening selectively, overcriticizing the speaker, faking attention, and avoiding difficult listening situations.

To become a more active listener and speaker, withhold judgment, provide honest, attentive feedback, eliminate distractions, and evaluate the speech when it is over.

Content deals with the research, organization, and logical development of the ideas in the speech; delivery represents the style or manner used to present the content.

## SKILL BUILDERS »

1. Using InfoTrac or one of your library's databases, search for a recent article on the topic of effective listening in *Vital Speeches of the Day*. Present a short 2- to 3-minute speech describing the major points the speaker recommends for effective listening.
2. Go to the International Listening Association's website at http://www. listen.org and search on "resources" in order to find recent information and examples about listening that can apply to you and your audience. Report the results of your findings in a brief presentation to your class.

## BUILDING A SPEECH ONLINE »

Now that you've read Chapter 4, use your online Resource Center for Building a Speech for quick access to the electronic study resources that accompany this text. You can access your Resource Center at http://academic.cengage.com/login, using the access code that came with your book or that you bought online at http://www. iChapters.com. Your Resource Center gives you access to Interactive Video Activities, the book's companion website, Speech Builder Express 3.0, InfoTrac College Edition, and study aids, including a digital glossary and review quizzes.

# chapter 5

# UNDERSTANDING AND REDUCING YOUR APPREHENSION

## chapter objectives »

After reading and studying this chapter, you should be able to

1. Recognize that speech anxiety is common

2. Be aware of research into stress and communication apprehension

3. Adopt an eight-point plan for reducing speech apprehension

A student came to the speech instructor at the beginning of the semester with these worried comments: "I am so nervous when I get up in front of people that I freeze up—I can't remember what I am going to say, and I start to fumble with my words. I live in fear that I will try to open my mouth and nothing will come out. I'm really good speaking in one-to-one situations, and I would do fine if I could just give my speeches to you in an empty classroom or in your office."

This student's fear of speaking in public is shared by many Americans, as you will see in this chapter. The good news is that if you understand speech apprehension, you can begin to develop a program that helps to reduce its effect on your speaking presentations. In this chapter we survey the territory of speech anxiety: public speaking fears, research about anxiety, and ways to reduce your nervousness as you build your speeches.

> " Courage is resistance to fear, mastery of fear—not absence of fear. "
>
> —Mark Twain

key terms »
AWFULLIZING
COMMUNICATION
 APPREHENSION
GENERAL ADAPTATION
 SYNDROME
NEGATIVE SELF-TALK
POSITIVE SELF-TALK
SYSTEMATIC
 DESENSITIZATION

# speech anxiety is common

A student began his first classroom speech. His voice trembled, his mouth seemed parched, and his hands visibly shook as he presented the introduction. At one point, he tried to control his quivering hands by placing them in his pockets; but he started to rattle his change, calling even further attention to his stage fright. When he decided to make a gesture, he suddenly withdrew his hand from his pocket, spilling change all over the floor.

If you have ever felt this kind of anxiety, or if you have ever lost sleep because you had to give a report in class or in front of an organization—you are normal. Several researchers have conducted studies to determine some of the greatest social fears among Americans. In a 1986 study of about a thousand individuals, researchers discovered that people identified public speaking as their number-one fear.[1] Public speaking anxiety even outranked such fears as going to the dentist, heights, mice, and flying.[2] In a study conducted in 1984, investigators asked 3,000 people to list situations that caused the most anxiety.[3] Individuals ranked fear of public speaking as their second greatest anxiety and attending a party with strangers as their greatest social fear. Table 5.1 summarizes the fears identified in the survey.

Almost everyone experiences some type of anxiety about public speaking. Many famous performers, such as Barbra Streisand, or well-known speakers, such as former First Lady Barbara Bush, have also experienced anxiety about public speaking.[4] John F. Kennedy was considered to be one of the most effective presidential speakers in the twentieth century. Yet even President Kennedy could be nervous when delivering a speech. Biographer William Manchester cites a specific incident:

*The president [Kennedy] laughed, apparently relaxing. But he wasn't relaxed. In press conferences he could be at ease, despite the size of the television audience. Question-and-answer sessions were a challenge, a test of intellect. He had never learned to enjoy formal speeches, however, and his casual appearance was a triumph of the will. Unlike Lyndon [Johnson, then vice president], he was not an extrovert. To his audiences his easy air seemed unstudied. Very few knew how hard he had toiled to achieve it. On a rostrum, the illusion of spontaneity was almost perfect; only his hands would have betrayed him, and he was careful to keep them out of sight . . . they were . . . vibrating so violently at times that they seemed palsied. Now and then the right hand would shoot up and out, the index finger stabbing the limelit air to make a point. The moment it dropped the trembling would begin again. Several times he nearly dropped his five by seven cards. Why, the President's nervous.[5]*

| Situation | Percent |
|---|---|
| A party with strangers | 74 |
| Giving a speech | 70 |
| Being asked personal questions in public | 65 |
| Meeting a date's parents | 59 |
| First day on a new job | 59 |
| Victim of a practical joke | 56 |
| Talking with someone in authority | 53 |
| Job interview | 46 |
| Formal dinner party | 44 |
| Blind date | 42 |

TABLE 5.1 Ten Social Situations Causing Greatest Anxiety

## research into stress and communication apprehension

As you begin to deal with your anxiety about public speaking, it is helpful for you to understand some of the research that has been done in the field. In 1936, Hans Selye conducted research that has become classic in the field of stress reduction. From his laboratory experiments, Selye concluded that the human body reacts to stress in stages known as the **general adaptation syndrome**.[6]

The initial *alarm reaction* is a physical "call to arms" for the body to release various chemicals in response to the fight-or-flight situation. When you deliver your first speech, you will probably experience some of these physiological alarms:

**Physical Symptoms of Nervousness**

1. Increased heart rate
2. Thickening speech due to decreased flow of saliva
3. "Butterflies" in the stomach
4. Increased sweating
5. Tiredness or yawning
6. Jumpiness or jitteriness

FIGURE 5.1  How does this illustration relate to apprehension in your basic speech classroom?
*Source:* Reprinted with special permission of North American Syndicate.

7. Tightening of muscles
8. Shaky hands and legs, twitching in some muscles

The body's alarm reaction is often the extra shot of adrenaline that enables you to face your audience or allows you to perform superhuman feats of strength in times of emergency.

During the *resistance stage*, the body reduces the general physiological alarms and channels energy to those organs that are most capable of handling the tension. The body stabilizes, maintains itself, and begins to adapt to the stress. For instance, once you have been speaking for a minute or two, you may notice that your physical symptoms begin to decrease.

In the final *phase of exhaustion*, the body systems that were summoned to cope with the stress are depleted. The body can endure tension for only so long; when tension is chronic and continues for a period of days or years, serious damage can result. People who are under severe chronic pressure can develop ulcers, hypertension, and heart disease. Your public speaking class will not create any prolonged anxiety—only relaxation and mild fatigue after you have finished your speeches.

Although Selye's conclusions represent a classic contribution to understanding tension, there is more recent research related to public speaking. In the 1970s, James C. McCroskey, a university speech instructor, coined the term **communication apprehension** to describe an individual's anxiety about speaking to another person or a group.[7] McCroskey found that most college students experience some level of apprehension about public speaking, and he determined that at least 20 percent of these students experience high levels of anxiety.

McCroskey also found that apprehension can be reduced. Many people who experience normal levels of anxiety can actually decrease apprehension and build self-confidence by taking and successfully completing a public speaking course. For instance, the anxious students mentioned in the opening examples were able to overcome many of their fears as they progressed through speech classes and other public speaking experiences. McCroskey also discovered that individuals who experienced high apprehension levels could lower anxiety through behavior modification techniques known as **systematic desensitization**. In systematic desensitization, a trainer administers a test to determine individuals with high levels of communication anxiety. Subjects chosen for treatment are seated comfortably in a quiet room, where they are told to close their eyes while a relaxation tape is played. When the tape is finished and individuals are relaxed, the trainer reads the first item on a list of anxiety-producing situations (such as presenting a speech, being interviewed for a job, conducting a meeting). There is a 15-second silence while subjects mentally visualize the stressful situation. If no anxiety is reported, the trainer reads the next item from the list. If trainees report anxiety, they are asked to put the situation out of their minds while the trainer conducts additional relaxation exercises. The trainer then returns to the situation producing stress, repeating the process until no tension is indicated. McCroskey found that after five to seven 50-minute sessions, almost all subjects had responded favorably to the process and reduced or overcome their apprehension.[8]

## reducing communication apprehension

Although you may not have severe apprehension, you will probably experience normal levels of speech anxiety. Here are eight suggestions that, if practiced, will help you to reduce your fear and build your self-confidence.

# ACCEPT ANXIETY HONESTLY AND FACE IT

Try to understand your apprehension and determine your specific fears. Write down a list of things you fear about speaking in public. Here are some examples of common performance anxieties that students often express in speech classes:

> I'm afraid I'll fall flat on my face.
> I'm afraid I'll babble like an idiot.
> I'm afraid that people will see my knees knocking together.
> I'm afraid that people won't like me.
> I'm afraid I'll make a mistake.
> I'm afraid I'll forget everything I'm trying to say.
> I'm afraid I'll make people angry.
> I'm afraid I'll get sick.

When you've completed your list, take a good long look at each statement and analyze it carefully. You will probably discover that you are creating irrational fears and that most of your anxieties have no basis in fact. Anxieties are often worst-case scenarios. You will never literally fall flat on your face; and yes, you will probably make a mistake every once in a while. But who told you that you have to be perfect? A standard of achievement that is perfectionistic is unrealistic, irrational, and will probably cause you a lot of unhappiness. Although you are very aware of your own nervous symptoms, many people in your audience will not detect your apprehension. So if your knees knock, you are probably the only one who knows it.

In a setting such as a speech class, where you have a supportive group of people with a common purpose, the fear of people disliking you is also irrational. There will always be someone who disagrees with you and a few who may not like the speech. No one can, or should, try to please everyone. And you probably won't become sick unless you eat something that upsets your stomach.

Two well-known psychotherapists, Albert Ellis and Robert Harper, refer to the dread of the future as the concept of **awfullizing**.[9] The future is *awfullized* when people worry that something terrible will happen to them. These fears about tomorrow usually have no basis in fact. Awfullizing causes people to paralyze themselves with anxiety, to avoid situations thought to be unpleasant, and to stop performing constructive activities important to their growth.

Whatever you do in this speech class, don't run away from your fear or from your speaking experiences. Don't use some of these lines employed by students who try to avoid giving speeches:

> I've lost my note cards, so I can't give my speech today.
> I didn't have time to prepare my speech last week, so I just can't go through with it.
> I've developed a severe headache—may I be excused from the speech?
> I've been having car trouble all week and I'm terribly upset so I don't think I'm in
>     any condition to present a speech.
> I have an awful case of laryngitis, and there is no way I can talk today.

While we do not want to ridicule legitimate problems that people may experience, it is human nature for people to create excuses to avoid fearful and unpleasant situations. If you run away from apprehension, you are simply creating a greater problem for yourself. In addition to postponing your performance, you will turn anxiety into a monster that will be more difficult for you to conquer the next time. Don't run away—face your fear. Stare down anxiety; you will discover that you can control the monster so that it won't control you.

## SUCCESS IN A CAREER REQUIRES EFFECTIVE PUBLIC SPEAKING SKILLS

"Everyone needs to be able to get his or her ideas across, but try moving up in management without being able to speak out at meetings," says Wicke Chambers, co-owner of the Atlanta speech-training firm, Speechworks.

Or if you're a salesman, it's one thing to make a one-on-one pitch, but don't expect to close hot deals if you freeze up in front of executive committees. It's effective speakers, the experts say, who are perceived as leaders—and perceptions can be more important than reality. Put another way, you may be an Einstein, but you're not going to get anywhere unless you can get your ideas across with ease.

The fear of public speaking, Ms. Chambers points out, has killed many a promising career. And many a manager has ended up answering to the trusted subordinate he delegated to attend a meeting or make a speech, says David Greenberg, owner of another training firm, Simply Speaking.

## DEVELOP A POSITIVE ATTITUDE

When you begin to face your fear, you may also need to examine the attitudes you have about public speaking. Psychologists and speech instructors alike have discovered that many people fail at public performance simply because they think negatively and develop **negative self-talk**.[10]

> I'm really not smart enough to speak in front of people.
> I don't do well speaking in groups.
> I seem to have bad luck.
> I can't finish a coherent sentence in public.
> I say some really ridiculous things at times.

Researchers have discovered that if people can transform their negative self-talk into **positive self-talk**, anxious people can unlearn old patterns and reeducate themselves into thinking more constructively.[11] Monitor the way you talk about yourself. Keep a journal or diary of the feelings you experience before every speech in your course. When you find yourself talking negatively about yourself, consciously begin to change your attitudes by writing down positive statements to replace the old negatives. The previous negative attitudes can become positive self-talk:

> I'm intelligent, and I usually have something to contribute to people.
> I can do well speaking in groups if I try.
> Good things happen to me all the time if I look for them.
> I can finish my thoughts and my sentences if I'm patient with myself.
> While I know I'll make mistakes at times, I know I'll also say some important things in my speeches.

In addition to thinking positively about yourself, begin to develop positive attitudes about your speech course. Look at this course as a challenge—an opportunity for you to grow from other people's experiences as well as from your own. You can even develop a positive attitude about the opportunity to make mistakes in a helpful, constructive climate. When your communication is critiqued in a supportive environment, there is much less anxiety than in a competitive atmosphere such as your job. In your class, communication

Thorough preparation, listening to constructive criticism, and a positive attitude can reduce apprehension and help you become a successful public speaker.

© Comstock/PictureQuest

mistakes mean simply that you try to improve when you speak again. In your job, communication mistakes may mean that you lose your livelihood.

Begin now to replace negative self-talk with positive self-talk. By reeducating yourself in this fashion, you can start to think more rationally about yourself, and you can open yourself up to good experiences that will help you to grow.

One student placed these words of encouragement at the beginning of his speaking notes:

Calm yourself.
Look at them.
They are not vicious!
Take deep breath.
You can always do better next time.
Begin.[12]

## ADOPT CONSTRUCTIVE BEHAVIORS

Once you begin to think more positively about yourself, start doing something constructive related to your speaking assignment. Jot down speech topics when they pop into your mind. Think about some of your interests and abilities and ask yourself a few questions: What ideas would I like to share with an audience? At what activities am I successful? What do I feel confident about? What subject areas would I like to know more about? Go to the library and leaf through some magazines that interest you. Write down some ideas under a few different subject headings. Look at these rough outlines and decide which areas you want to pursue.

But whatever you do, *do something.*[13] Distract yourself from apprehension by performing constructive activities. Even if you do something that you may think is insignificant, sketching a rough list of ideas or doing a few deep-breathing exercises to relax, you will help yourself. Remember that apprehension is circular; it feeds on itself and defeats your growth. Develop an active program that helps you to make progress toward your goal.

When you adopt constructive behavior, you will begin to forget your worries and start advancing toward your objective of successful speechmaking.

## MAINTAIN A HEALTHY BODY

Exercise can help us to relax and reduce stress. If you jog, lift weights, do aerobics, participate in team sports, or have a consistent exercise program, you are already aware of the tremendous physical and mental benefits you gain from these activities. The night before giving a speech, exercise so that you can relax, feel tired, and get some sleep rather than drink five cups of coffee to stay up all night cramming for the presentation.

Occasionally in speech classes a student will say, "I think I need a couple of tranquilizers to relax before the speech" or "I think I'll fix a good stiff drink to loosen me up." The worst thing you could possibly do is to cloud your head with artificial remedies before you perform in public. You can learn to relax naturally rather than chemically. Remember that the body has its own unique chemicals that will give you the shot of energy you need.

To speak clearly, you need a clear head. There are even a few exercises you can do to help control your breathing and to relax. Singer Barbra Streisand listens to relaxation tapes before a performance in order to calm down and "think about positive things."[14] If you don't have an exercise program, this is your excuse to start one. Physical activity can relieve tension and help you to maintain a healthy body.[15]

## BE THOROUGHLY PREPARED

One of the best ways to reduce anxiety is to be completely prepared for a speech. Being prepared means that you have worked on every aspect of the speech as much as you possibly can: the research, the outline, and the delivery. When you have selected a subject, you need to thoroughly investigate it. The more research you put into your topic, the more confident you will be when you speak about it. You must also prepare a clear and well-organized outline. When your thoughts are structured into a coherent and logical format, you can relax because you know where you're headed in the speech. It is also important that you practice the speech several times before you deliver it to an audience. Practice doesn't always mean you'll be perfect, but it does mean that you will feel more comfortable with the wording of the speech when you're in front of an audience.

Many bright and capable college students do poorly in public speaking simply because they don't take the course seriously enough. The student who rushes into class late, or scribbles an outline down on paper 5 minutes before the speech, is not respecting the audience or his or her own abilities. If you fail to research your topic, the audience will detect that you are delivering an impromptu rather than a prepared speech. If you don't outline your thoughts, you will be disorganized and rambling. If you don't practice the delivery, you will create unnecessary external noise, such as vocalized pauses (and ahs), stumbling over words or sentences, and mannerisms. There is no substitute for preparation; one thing you can control in a speech is the amount of time you are willing to invest. The more time you spend, the more confidence you will gain; the less time you spend, the more insecurity you'll experience. Careful research, clear organization, and a prepared delivery will help you to build confidence and security in each speaking assignment.

## REWARD YOURSELF

One public speaking student was a chronic worrier. She always sat in the front row, taking furious notes on every detail of classroom discussions. After presenting a speech, she would focus on her negative points and never give herself credit for doing anything well. During the critique, as the instructor began to point out some of the positive improvements in her speaking, she reacted by saying, "Yes, but I know I did poorly—I just know it! My eye contact was rotten, I had all kinds of mannerisms, and I didn't state my purpose—how much worse can you get? Now I'm really going to have to work doubly hard to improve on the next speech."

It is important to take your public speaking course seriously, but not so seriously that you destroy the educational value of learning. This student was trying so hard that she was actually defeating herself and causing more anxiety.

When you have finally arrived at the night before the speaking assignment and you have done everything you possibly can to prepare, don't create more apprehension by dreading the assignment. Do something nice for yourself. Go out to a movie, go to dinner, or treat yourself to a hot fudge sundae. If it makes sense to prepare thoroughly for a speech, it also makes sense to relax so that you can take your mind off the event. Speaking shouldn't be drudgery; it should be enjoyable and positive.

But you should reward yourself only if you've worked hard and deserve it. If you have neglected some aspect of preparation or if you have waited until the last minute to cram for the speech, don't reward your negligence. If you have been successful, reward the success, and you'll look forward to the next speaking event.

## LET GO OF MISTAKES

You must face the fact that sometimes you will make mistakes when you speak in public. When you make a mistake, analyze it, understand it, and then let go of it. Life goes on. You'll have another chance to improve.

Even presidents make speaking mistakes that they'd like to forget. In a 1976 televised debate with Governor Jimmy Carter, President Ford mistakenly stated that there is "no Soviet domination of eastern Europe." Four years later, President Carter said in a debate with Governor Ronald Reagan, "I had a discussion with my daughter Amy the other day [to ask her about] the most important [governing] issue. . . . She said she thought it was nuclear weaponry and the control of nuclear arms." Even President Reagan, the Great Communicator, made his share of speaking errors. While campaigning in the northwest United States, Reagan made the mistake of saying, "Trees cause more pollution than people." And in the 1988 presidential campaign, Vice President Bush misstated the date when he said: "On this day, September 7, 1941, the Japanese attacked Pearl Harbor." (It was in fact December, unfortunately.) The son of the 41st President, former President George W. Bush, often made numerous speaking mistakes with vocalized pauses and a halting delivery.

Presidential speakers often pay a price for their verbal mistakes. Ford's and Carter's gaffes contributed to their election losses. Reagan's error caused his political support in northwestern states to falter for a while, and political cartoonists enjoyed ridiculing former Vice President Bush's brief lapse. The verbal flaws of former President Bush were often mimicked and impersonated by comedians in TV monologues or skits.

If seasoned professionals can make speaking errors, remember that you are no different. Don't dwell on the past or on your failures—just try not to repeat them. Whenever you prepare for a new speaking situation, try to profit from both the positive and negative aspects of your past efforts. Don't place too much importance on any one speaking event; each will benefit you in some way if you let it. Life will not end if you make an error—pick yourself up and keep going. Letting go of mistakes helps you to keep your mind on improvement and makes room for success.

## ACCEPT CONSTRUCTIVE CRITICISM

You are in a classroom situation where you will probably be asked to evaluate other people. In these evaluations, you will critique both positive and negative elements you have found in the speeches. You will be expected to be honest in your critiques but not personal or vindictive. Your classroom instructor wants to build a supportive atmosphere where every student can feel comfortable. You can help in this process if you accept constructive criticism from others. It is important that you listen to each critique as objectively as possible so that you can improve.

Sometimes people block out criticism by being defensive or by exhibiting hostile behavior. Here are a few common statements that block out criticism, create tension, and inhibit growth:

Criticism in this class is destroying me.
I don't have poor eye contact—I don't care what anybody says.
I've seen good speakers slouch in public, and it doesn't bother me at all.
Politicians read their speeches word for word, so why can't I?
I already know enough about public speaking and I'm not going to learn much of
    anything in this class.
Speaking is a snap—all you have to do is throw a few things together.
People in this class don't know anything anyway, so why should I pay any attention
    to them?
Who do these people think they are, telling me what's wrong with my speeches?
I'll just sit here and let everybody say what they please. It doesn't really matter anyway.

These types of comments can cause tension in a classroom and can be harmful to the individual who states them. Individuals who cannot accept constructive criticism cannot look at themselves honestly and cannot grow—they are held captive by their fear.

Help yourself and your class by allowing yourself to hear and absorb constructive criticism. Remember that criticism is meant to promote success and to help you overcome failure. Criticism might be hard to take at first, but you'll learn to develop the ability to bounce back and improve after hearing critiques of your speeches. If you accept constructive criticism, you will help to create a positive classroom environment, and you will also help to reduce tension within yourself.

## taking responsibility to reduce apprehension

Begin to adopt the eight-point plan (summarized below) to reduce apprehension as you prepare to build your first speech. This approach can help you to overcome your anxiety by getting your mind on other issues related to the speech. When you use this plan actively, you'll begin to feel more confident. Recognize that reading theory is easy, but making theory work is totally up to you.

## summary »

Most people fear public speaking, as several studies and McCroskey's research into communication apprehension have concluded. You must understand your fear and utilize the eight-point plan to help control and reduce your apprehension:

1. Accept your anxiety and face it.
2. Develop a positive attitude.
3. Adopt constructive behaviors.
4. Maintain a healthy body.
5. Be thoroughly prepared.
6. Reward yourself.
7. Let go of mistakes.
8. Accept constructive criticism.

It is important that you take responsibility for yourself and your own growth in public speaking by putting this program into effect.

## SKILL BUILDERS »

1. Write down all the negative self-talk you experience in your mind before you give a speech. Then, next to each negative item, write an opposite positive statement that you can achieve. After you have presented your speech, write down all the things that actually happened. Which positive statements were you able to accomplish? Which ones still need work?
2. Using InfoTrac College Edition or another library database, locate an article on speech apprehension, stage fright, or speech anxiety that can help you understand and manage your fear of public speaking.

## BUILDING A SPEECH ONLINE »

Now that you've read Chapter 5, use your online Resource Center for Building a Speech for quick access to the electronic study resources that accompany this text. You can access your Resource Center at http://academic.cengage.com/login, using the access code that came with your book or that you bought online at http://www.iChapters.com. Your Resource Center gives you access to Interactive Video Activities, the book's companion website, Speech Builder Express 3.0, InfoTrac College Edition, and study aids, including a digital glossary and review quizzes.

© JOHN ANGELILLO/UPI/Landov

## chapter 6

# CONSIDERING THE ETHICS OF PUBLIC SPEAKING

## chapter objectives »

After reading and studying this chapter, you should be able to

1. Understand the relationship of ethics to a career
2. Recognize the need for ethics in society
3. Evaluate a speaker's ethics
4. Develop and apply ethical standards in speech analysis

Jake was a busy premed student. With a part-time job at a local bookstore, a full academic schedule, and a place on the wrestling team, Jake was just barely maintaining the B average he needed in order to get into medical school. This week was especially stressful. He had an anatomy test on Monday, a persuasive speech due on Tuesday, and a semifinal wrestling match on Wednesday. Jake had spent much of the weekend studying for his anatomy exam and he had pulled an all-nighter on Sunday. Once the test was over on Monday, he realized he hadn't done anything to prepare for his speech. Since he was specializing in medicine, he had thought about the topic of universal health care, but he hadn't gotten any farther than just the idea. After he finished work at 9 p.m., he went to the library to start his research for tomorrow's speech. His search in Proquest yielded dozens of magazine articles and he quickly realized that merely reading them would take hours. Jake was running out of time. Unexpectedly he

> *"Honesty is the first chapter of the book of wisdom."*
>
> —*Thomas Jefferson*

## key terms »

CODE OF ETHICS
ELEMENTS OF
  VIRTUE
ETHOS
HIDDEN AGENDA

came across an excellent article opposing universal health insurance on the editorial page of a well-known news magazine. Jake wrestled with his thoughts. "This might be the perfect answer to my problem. I could create an introduction and conclusion that fit the content of the article and then just add some transitions." And then he thought, "But it wouldn't be the right thing to do. The professor is strict about plagiarism, credible bibliographies, and outlines. But I'm in a jam. I should have started on the speech over a week ago when the assignment was given."

The next day Jake arrived in class and handed his outline to the professor. Jake presented his speech with seven other students and waited for the audience critique. Some of his fellow students seemed impressed with the speech and thought he had an effective delivery. The professor, however, commented that there were no sources stated in the speech to generate credibility and influence listeners. At the end of class, the professor asked to see Jake in his office. What do you think the professor said?

Trust is a value that people seek in political leaders, clergy, sports heroes, and each other. But people feel betrayed when their valued role models or relationships do not measure up to standards of honesty and integrity. As Jake's dilemma indicates, it is critical for speakers and listeners to consider the ethics of public speaking. Unethical speaking practices not only affect your listeners but can also damage your college career, your job, and your relationships. In this chapter we will look at ethics and your career, the need for ethics, ways to evaluate a speaker's ethics, and some recommendations for developing your own speaking standards.

## ETHICS AND YOUR CAREER

Jake may be headed for real trouble. A decision to plagiarize just one speech could not only affect the grade in a speech course but could lead to other consequences as well. Colleges and universities can impose stiff penalties for plagiarism, resulting in either course failure or more drastic consequences, such as suspension or dismissal. Jake could have put his entire medical career in jeopardy because of a serious error in judgment in one course. Consider the following examples.

Marion Jones was a star athlete at the 2000 Summer Olympics in Sydney, Australia, winning three gold medals and two bronze in track and field events. As a result of her inspiring victories, she received lucrative product endorsements, made appearances on numerous talk shows, and posed as a model on the cover of national magazines. She had become a respected, exemplary figure to many Americans. However, in subsequent years, federal officials began investigating Ms. Jones for using performance-enhancing drugs, a practice that she repeatedly denied to federal investigators and in the media. But on Friday, October 5, 2007, the former celebrity pled guilty in federal court to lying about her use of steroids. In a tearful, tragic courtroom appearance she said: "It's with a great amount of shame that I stand before you and tell you that I have betrayed your trust. I have been dishonest and you have the right to be angry with me. I have let [my family] down. I have let my country down, and I have let myself down."[1] Not only was Ms. Jones disgraced in public, she was forced to return her five medals, make restitution of over $100,000 in bonus money she received from the U.S. Olympic Committee, and face a possible jail sentence. Marion Jones lost her reputation, her fortune, and her career.

After a 20-month inquiry regarding the use of steroids in baseball, former Senator George Mitchell issued a report that named numerous top players who were alleged to have taken illegal steroids. Among them were Cy Young Award pitcher Roger

Clemens, home run champion Barry Bonds, and New York Mets teammates Todd Hundley and David Segui. Mr. Segui admitted taking anabolic steroids, but Clemens strongly denied ever using the drug and Barry Bonds denied "knowingly" taking steroids. The cloud that hangs over these players may not go away. The report may affect Clemens's consideration for the Baseball Hall of Fame, and Barry Bonds's all-time home run record may be tainted. As for other players, Baseball Commissioner Bud Selig said that he may decide to punish the players named in Mitchell's report.[2]

Brian McCoy, CEO of a construction company that has been featured rehabilitating homes on the ABC-TV program *Extreme Makeover Home Edition*, delivered a commencement speech to graduates at Texas State University. Notice how he sums up the importance of ethics:

"You need to become a person of integrity. It's a word that's tossed around all the time, but I still want to talk about it. There is such a lack of integrity in our workplaces, that unless you commit to having it, you will certainly be pulled from demonstrating it. Integrity is telling the truth. Sounds easy, but it isn't. Sure, it's reporting financial statements accurately and citing references in papers honestly, but don't miss that it is much more than the obvious. It is telling the truth even when it's embarrassing, awkward, inconvenient, or even when it may impact your job promotion."[3]

These examples show the consequences of cheating and not telling the truth. A lack of integrity can derail a promising career and put an individual on the wrong path.

## the need for ethics in society

Ethics and ethical codes have been matters of concern for a long time. Centuries ago, Aristotle referred to character, which he called **ethos**, as "the most potent means of persuasion."[4] He also identified **elements of virtue** as "justice, courage, temperance, magnificence, magnanimity, liberality, gentleness, prudence, and wisdom."[5] These elements defined a clear code of ethical conduct for speakers in Greek society. Centuries before the Greeks, according to the Bible, God gave Moses the Ten Commandments on Mount Sinai. They were not, as former TV commentator Ted Koppel once humorously observed, "the Ten Suggestions"; they were, in fact, a guide for living.[6] In Roman times, the emperor Justinian revised the law for his empire. He was the first to incorporate ethics into the legal system and to establish schools to educate lawyers concerning ethics, morality, and law. Medieval Germanic tribes, recognizing the need for ethical conduct, enacted the Salic laws to codify common law and guide relationships. Following Justinian's example, Napoleon simplified French law and established a code of thirty-six statutes based on the concept that all citizens, regardless of circumstances of birth or social stature, should be treated fairly and equally. And one of the most famous and widely respected documents is the American Bill of Rights, which identifies and guarantees our basic democratic freedoms. Indeed, every civilization has recognized the need for establishing laws and codes to guide human relationships and behavior.[7]

As we look at contemporary American life, however, it is often difficult to perceive our ethical heritage in it. Scandals and questions about trust and integrity seem to surround numerous individuals entrusted with leadership in almost every aspect of society. Consider these examples:

- Allegations, charges, and convictions were enacted against hundreds of priests who abused their sacred vows and engaged in improper behavior with underage parishioners.[8]

- Floyd Landis won the 2006 Tour de France but was stripped of his title by the United States Anti-Doping Agency, which charged that he used performance-enhancing drugs during the bicycle race.[9]
- In testimony before a congressional committee in October 2008, former Lehman Brothers CEO Richard S. Fuld, Jr. defended his $500 million in salary and bonuses as he led the once prosperous company into bankruptcy.
- Even talk show queen Oprah Winfrey had to apologize for defending a writer, James Frey, who fabricated parts of his "true" memoirs in a book she recommended. When the deception was first discovered, Winfrey told Larry King that "no matter what, the book still retained its 'underlying message of redemption.'" Later, after newspaper columnists observed that her remarks insinuated that "the truth does not matter," she apologized and said she was "really embarrassed."[11]

Whether it is a high-profile leader or a private individual claiming to be something he or she is not, unethical behavior ultimately hurts everyone. Michael Josephson, founder of a Los Angeles institute studying ethical issues, says that leaders in positions of authority often avoid asking two crucial questions: "Is what I'm doing deceptive?" and "Am I resolving dilemmas in a self-interested way?"[12]

## evaluating a speaker's ethics

It is apparent that the speaker and the audience each have special responsibilities regarding ethics in public speaking. It is the speaker's responsibility to practice ethics in every aspect of speech development, and it is the listener's obligation to determine whether the speaker lives up to ethical standards. Our purpose is not to prescribe rules or behavior, but to raise important issues pertaining to ethics and suggest areas for your consideration. We begin by analyzing a speaker's honesty, reliability, motivation, and policies.

## HONESTY AND THE SPEAKER

Our society places strong emphasis on honesty at all levels. The Constitution requires that the president swear to a thirty-six-word oath of office to "preserve, protect, and defend the laws and Constitution of the United States." Courtroom witnesses must swear to tell "all the truth and nothing but the truth." Contractual agreements are signed and sealed before notaries to reinforce the truthfulness of statements contained in the documents. Similarly, wedding ceremonies include vows of mutual love, loyalty, and fidelity, which couples pledge for a lifetime.

Too often, however, speakers violate these standards and this can set in motion potentially devastating consequences. Speakers who mislead or lie to the public not only undermine their own credibility but also contribute to the erosion of public confidence in national offices and institutions. President Nixon, for example, denied any knowledge of the break-in at Democratic Party headquarters in Washington, D.C. The investigation into the scandal known as "Watergate" concluded that the president was aware of the burglary and engaged in a conspiracy with his advisors to cover up the crime. The House Judiciary Committee approved articles of impeachment, and Nixon was forced to resign from office. Upon assuming the presidency, Gerald Ford observed, "Truth is the glue that holds governments together . . . . Our Constitution works."[13] Unfortunately, the Watergate scandal seriously eroded public confidence in government, and it was years before this trust could be repaired.

In late fall of 2001, Enron Corporation, the once-prosperous energy giant, declared bankruptcy, causing hundreds of employees to lose billions of dollars in stock and retirement

If listeners detect a difference between a speaker's words and actions, they are unwilling to allow the speaker to influence them significantly.

© A. Ramey/PhotoEdit

accounts. In the months before the bankruptcy occurred, Chairman Kenneth Lay and CEO Jeffrey Skilling earned millions by selling shares of Enron stock. Among the witnesses who testified at the Senate Commerce Committee hearings to investigate charges of accounting manipulation was Sherron Watkins, Enron vice president and whistle-blower, who had previously warned top executives about hidden partnerships that allowed Enron to cover up losses and exaggerate profits. Watkins, criticizing Enron executive Kenneth Lay, reported that the corporation might have been saved had he acted quickly after she warned him about the dubious accounting procedures. Had Enron executives been willing to listen to an uncomfortable message delivered by a straightforward whistle-blower, they might have been able to save the giant energy company from ruining the future retirements of hundreds of employees and defaulting on billions in loans to creditors. For her honesty and courage in exposing the unethical practices at Enron, Sherron Watkins appeared with two other corporate whistle-blowers on *Time* magazine's cover for the 2002 Persons-of-the-Year award.[14]

## THE RESULTS OF DISHONESTY

"A Washington man, whose claims to have slaughtered civilians as a U.S. Army Ranger in Iraq were seen by millions on YouTube, admitted in federal court in Seattle today that he was a fake and a liar. Jesse Adam Macbeth, 23, pleaded guilty to charges he faked his war record. 'He was in the Army for 40 days before he was kicked out of boot camp for being unfit,' said U.S. Attorney Jeffrey C. Sullivan. 'He was never in Iraq.' Macbeth's story of killing men and women as they left a Baghdad mosque included claims that he was a U.S. Army Ranger and had received the Purple Heart for injuries suffered in combat in Iraq. His interview was translated into Arabic and distributed in the Middle East, said the U.S. attorney. 'Macbeth's lies fueled hostility to our servicemen in Iraq and here at home,' Sullivan said."[15]

Tania Head was president of the World Trade Center Survivors' Network. She claimed to be a survivor of September 11, 2001, and for six years volunteered as a tour guide at the site of the World Trade Center attacks. She would tell hundreds of tourists stories about being burned in the South Tower and her heroic rescue on the 78th floor. She explained that her determination to survive was motivated by her love for her fiancé, who she later discovered had died in the North Tower. Survivors of 9/11 and family members who had lost loved ones often listened to Ms. Head's tales and tried to comfort her. None of her story was true, however. Merrill Lynch, where Ms. Head claimed she was employed, reported that she never worked for their company and the family of her so-called fiancé said they never heard of her. Individuals who had been involved with her volunteer work since 9/11 felt betrayed. "I've been there anytime she needed someone to listen. . . . she has stolen my time and my soul," said a fellow board member of the Survivors' Network. She concluded by saying, "We have members who thought Tania's trauma was so extreme they did not want to discuss their own. They gave their time to help her, and she didn't even need it."[16]

Whether the fabrication is made by a president, a corporation, or a private citizen, the consequences can still be enormous. In a USA Today article, Joe Saltzman summarized the destructive effect of dishonesty on society: "The problem is that private behavior and public policy built on deception corrupt the heart and soul of a country and its people, leaving both morally bankrupt and untrustworthy. The news media should be worried about this, reminding readers and viewers about this epidemic of deceit that goes from the highest office in the land to the average person on the street. They should be telling us on a daily basis that a lying tongue not only is an abomination to God, but one that is intolerable to any conscientious citizen." [17]

## THE SPEAKER'S RELIABILITY

One important standard in ethical evaluation is the reliability of the speaker. Audiences make judgments about speakers by measuring actions against words. What is the speaker's record? Does the speaker keep promises? Is the speaker committed to the ideas presented and willing to practice the deeds advocated?

Unfortunately, our political leaders are not always models of reliability. Former President Bill Clinton, for example, flatly denied having an affair with a White House intern. "I did not have sexual relations with that woman, Miss Lewinsky," he declared. "I never told anybody to lie, not a single time—never. These allegations are false." Unfortunately, these words, as well as accusations that the president had lied under oath, led to the approval of articles of impeachment in the House and an impeachment trial in the Senate.[18] When Republican Senator George Allen of Virginia was running for reelection, he used the word macaca to describe one of his opponent's campaign workers. It is a derogatory term, which means a type of monkey, and is sometimes used as an obscure racial slur. Allen was forced to apologize and the remark is credited as one of the reasons the senator was defeated. The Democrats took control of the U.S. Senate in 2006 by a one-vote majority.[19]

These two political leaders are fine Americans who have served in government with distinction. But these examples and their consequences reflect the high ethical standards that are expected of many public figures. We have already mentioned the use of steroids in sports, the priest abuse scandals, and convictions of prominent corporate executives. When an audience sees that a speaker does not abide by his or her own standards, many listeners are no longer willing to allow the speaker to have a significant influence over them. Reliability once destroyed is difficult to rebuild.

Even in a public speaking class, a speaker's words are measured by actions. One student presented an informative speech about the dangers of secondhand smoke. Although the material was enlightening, audience members had difficulty taking the topic seriously, because sticking out of the speaker's shirt pocket was a pack of cigarettes. Another student delivered an impassioned plea for the homeless. The speaker urged listeners to bring donations of food and clothing to a subsequent class period and assured them that she would distribute the goods at a local shelter. Class members faithfully brought their donations at the appointed time, but the speaker never came to pick them up. Commenting that they felt betrayed by the speaker's lack of commitment, listeners returned home with their gifts.

When assuming the role of speaker, you have the opportunity to show your commitment to an idea. While you are spending time and energy presenting your speech, remember that your audience is devoting considerable effort to this experience as well. You can build trust and generate reliability if you are willing to live by your words.

## THE SPEAKER'S MOTIVATIONS

One aspect of ethics that is sometimes more difficult to assess is the speaker's motivation. While the speaker's stated purpose may be obvious to an audience, there may also be an unstated objective, often called a **hidden agenda**. We all have these internal agendas, and they can be positive motivators. We take notes, study for exams, and maintain constructive relationships with faculty in order to pass courses and obtain degrees. We work hard, form helpful relationships with supervisors, and present a positive appearance in order to advance in a company so as to provide greater psychological and financial benefits for ourselves and our families.

Problems occur, however, when the intent is to deceive and the agenda would significantly alter audience attitudes if stated openly. Consider these examples: After Hurricanes Katrina and Rita devastated the Gulf Coast of the United States in 2005, unscrupulous scam artists tried to sell reconditioned cars that had been flooded to unsuspecting buyers. In addition to these scams, dozens of fraudulent websites promised to circulate immediate food and money to hurricane victims if donors would make contributions by using credit or debit cards. Here, the hidden agendas led to the exploitation and manipulation of consumers and hurricane victims.

But agendas are not always so hidden, and often members of an audience can easily assess an individual's motivation.

In early 2006, a female escort accused three members of the Duke University lacrosse team of raping her at a party. The incident immediately became headline news as the police and Durham County District Attorney Mike Nifong became involved. Nifong was in the midst of a hotly contested reelection campaign in a heavily African American district and he quickly sided with the accuser, who was black, against the three white defendants. Even though the accuser's story changed several times and Nifong failed to read police reports or wait for DNA test results, the prosecutor proceeded with his case against the three students. Months later, however, a state panel was convened to investigate the prosecutor's case. The state commission exonerated the three lacrosse players and found that Nifong, who had "repeatedly lied and cheated," should step down from his job as district attorney and be disbarred from practicing law. The panel also concluded that "at the root of it [the district attorney's case] is self-deception arising out of self-interest."[20]

Analyze a speaker carefully. Listen actively to the stated objectives, and read between the lines. Go beyond verbal pronouncements, and evaluate the speaker's reasons for making a presentation. Examine the relationship between a speaker's public declarations and personal activities. Are the public and private actions the same, or is there a difference between what the speaker says and what the speaker does? Know the speaker's background, and proceed with caution before trusting information or submitting to persuasion.

## THE SPEAKER'S POLICIES

Good indicators of a speaker's ethical standards are the policies and actions the individual recommends. Consider:

- Does the speaker exhibit concern for the welfare of the audience?
- Does the speaker advocate choices that are helpful to listeners?
- Does the speaker propose solutions that benefit society?

The language of terrorists is an extreme example of how appalling rhetoric can influence horrendous actions against humanity. Speaking about the bombing of the Federal Building in Oklahoma City, convicted murderer Timothy McVeigh said, "I understand what they felt in Oklahoma City . . . . I have no sympathy for them." McVeigh also referred to the nineteen children who died in the day-care center as "collateral damage."[21] Another terrorist, Osama bin Laden, appeared animated, chuckling, and smiling in a homemade video as he described the terrorist attacks of September 11: "I was thinking that the fire from the gas in the plane would melt the iron structure of the building and collapse the area where the plane hit and all the floors above it only. This is all that we had hoped for . . . . They were overjoyed when the first plane hit the building, so I said to them: be patient."[22] The controversial leader Mahmoud Ahmadinejad, president of Iran, has denied the existence of the Holocaust as well as the events of 9/11, proposed the obliteration of the state of Israel, and claimed there are no homosexuals in Iran. During a guest appearance at Columbia University, Ahmadinejad was described by the university president as exhibiting "all the signs of a petty and cruel dictator."[23]

Individual terrorists, dictators, or extremist groups such as the neo-Nazis, skinheads, antigovernment militias, Klansmen, and street gangs who openly preach and practice hatred, fear, and violence pose obvious threats to our society. But an equally dangerous problem is posed by groups who claim to be fighting for justice but encourage prejudice and engage in damaging behavior. Some extreme antiabortionists condone the bombing or burning of abortion clinics "to save the lives of the unborn." Some speakers who believe homosexuality is a sin engage in gay bashing and advocate discrimination in housing and employment. Racial violence is sometimes viewed by minorities as a justifiable remedy for past wrongdoing or present injustice. Speakers who advocate prejudice, hatred, stereotypes, lawbreaking, or violence are not promoting ethical solutions to problems and show little compassion for the welfare of human beings.

A student presented a persuasive speech encouraging audience members to smoke marijuana. He reasoned that "marijuana is no worse that drinking alcohol and it makes you feel just as good or better." Another speaker demonstrated how to make fake identity cards. The student explained how to copy false information, forge signatures, and laminate the phony document, making it appear realistic. She concluded her speech with the lines, "So remember, if you're under age and you want to get into that really neat club, you've got a solution—a fake I.D. You'll be able to drink as much as you want because nobody will be able to throw you out!" Another speaker, who opposed the increased airport security measures taken after September 11, attempted to persuade listeners to undermine airport security systems by setting off X-ray machines and holding up lines of disgruntled passengers. To accomplish his purpose, he distributed T-shirts with numerous metal staples attached that he asked listeners to wear as they passed through security checkpoints.

These speeches are extremely unethical because the speakers are asking the audience to violate laws or procedures. In the first example, the speaker failed to mention that smoking marijuana is illegal and that listeners could be arrested and even jailed for possessing the substance. The second speaker displayed similar disregard for her audience. Not only did she advocate making a counterfeit identification card but she also avoided

Mahmoud Ahmadinejad is the controversial Iranian president who has delivered speeches denying the facts of the Holocaust and the events of 9/11. He has proposed the destruction of Israel and claims there are no gay citizens in his country.

describing the possibility of fines or jail sentences as penalties for possessing such a document. In addition, she seemed unconcerned about the physical consequences of drinking "as much as you want." The last speaker did not bother to explain what might happen to passengers who wore T-shirts full of staples. In an era of increased anxiety and heightened security at the nation's airports, passengers setting off metal detectors would not only invite a more comprehensive inspection but also might be detained for questioning, refused a boarding pass, placed under surveillance, or worse. These three speakers lacked a sense of social responsibility and were indifferent to the potentially damaging results of their recommendations.

Examine the policies that a speaker promotes. Think about the results of ideas or actions that a speaker recommends. Observe whether the speaker is interested in the well-being of the audience, and analyze the extent to which the speaker demonstrates concern for the well-being of society.

## applying ethical standards

We have explored several ethical issues and examined some examples of unethical practice. It is now up to you as a speaker to formulate your own ethical standards. We suggest that you consider the following areas: honesty, concern for the audience, your motivations for speaking, and a personal **code of ethics**.

## BE HONEST

When you are building a presentation, be straightforward in every phase of speech development. Research information thoroughly, making sure that your material is accurate. Be sure that your research is complete and that you have taken the necessary time and energy to examine all the relevant sources. As you outline, be fair in reporting the data. Don't withhold portions of examples, statistics, or quotations if they are unfavorable to your ideas or viewpoints, but present these supporting materials in context. Stay away from twisting, distorting, or fabricating evidence if you cannot find information to back up your issues. When you deliver the speech, give proper credit for direct quotations, and paraphrase information in your own words to avoid plagiarism. Here are some examples of quoted, paraphrased, and plagiarized material.

### Direct Quotation

> According to a February 2008, ABCNews website (quote) "A congressional committee believes the creator of the first artificial heart may have misled viewers by using a body double in advertisements for a popular cholesterol drug he endorses. Dr. Robert Jarvik has worked as a spokesperson for the top-selling anti-cholesterol drug Lipitor."[24]

### Paraphrased Passage

> A February 2008, ABCNews website reported that some members of Congress have accused Dr. Robert Jarvik, inventor of the artificial heart, of using an actor as a double in advertisements that promote the cholesterol-lowering drug Lipitor. Members of a congressional committee believe that the ads where Dr. Jarvik endorses the popular drug are misleading the public.

### Plagiarized Passage

> Members of Congress believe that the creator of the first artificial heart may have misled viewers by using a body double in advertisements for a popular cholesterol drug he endorses. Dr. Robert Jarvik has worked as a spokesman for the top-selling anti-cholesterol drug Lipitor.

In the direct quotation, the speaker gives credit to the source and restates the exact words by setting up the passage with the word quote. In the paraphrase, the speaker uses different words to convey the intention of the author and also cites the source of the information. The plagiarized passage merely eliminates or alters a few words but retains the original wording of the author. Notice also that the speaker provides no reference to the source of the material. The audience is led to believe that the words originated with the speaker. However, the passage would still be considered plagiarism even if the speaker added the specific reference to the last example. The important point here is that a passage is plagiarized when the original wording is not changed or altered enough to recap the ideas in the speaker's own language.

Be willing to take the necessary time to develop your speech. Avoid cutting corners or taking shortcuts that are unethical and dishonest. Give credit to the appropriate sources or individuals for materials, handouts, and audiovisuals used in the speech. At all times, provide honest information and present information honestly.

## ADVOCATE IDEAS THAT BENEFIT OTHERS

Numerous topics and many points of view are appropriate for speeches. Many controversial issues will generate a variety of opinions among listeners and often strong disagreement. We would expect such diversity of ideas in a free and open democracy. But we have already examined how public speaking can be used as a weapon to promote hatred, injustice, and lawbreaking. As you approach topics and strategies for speeches, ask yourself some questions:

- Do you have any hidden agendas or ulterior motives for speaking?
- How would you feel if a particular strategy or topic was used on you as a member of the audience?
- Do your ideas and recommendations benefit society?
- Do the actions you promote help people to work together toward solutions?
- Are you careful to avoid stereotyping groups, individuals, or cultures?
- Do you stay away from tactics that include name-calling or offensive language?
- Do you respect the needs and values of your audience?
- Do you care about people, and do you demonstrate that concern in your speech?

## EVALUATE YOUR MOTIVES FOR SPEAKING

All of us need to present positive images in order to gain acceptance from others. But as a speaker, you have more encompassing needs to meet than simply your own ego fulfillment. Before developing your speech, carefully examine your motives for making the presentation. Determine whether your principal objectives are entirely self-serving, or if your motivations include interest in others.

Speakers are often tempted to exploit difficult situations for profit. Convicted felons who have been prominent politicians, religious leaders, sports figures, or entertainers often earn huge salaries on the lecture or talk-show circuit discussing their latest books or escapades. Such behavior is questionable and demeaning to the speaker-audience relationship unless the speaker can demonstrate that the objective is to educate others to avoid similar criminal activity.

Be willing to stand for principle rather than compromise your values to gain quick audience approval. Recognize that resisting opposition is often difficult and uses a great deal of a speaker's energy. But when you are in the right, there are benefits to both speaker and listeners. In spring 1992, Los Angeles exploded into a riot after a jury found four white police officers "not guilty" in the beating of an intoxicated, speeding driver named Rodney King. During this riot, Reginald Denny, a white truck driver, was stopped while hauling a load of sand and gravel through an intersection in south-central Los Angeles. He was pulled from his truck by several black males and severely kicked and beaten. Other black citizens who had been watching the incident on television came to Denny's assistance and rushed him to the hospital.[25] These heroic individuals looked beyond color to risk their lives for a fellow human being. Their actions took great courage, yet became a reassuring symbol to millions of Americans who anguished over racial tensions. Such individuals suffer initial setbacks but often reap psychological rewards and satisfaction because of their bravery.

Take responsibility and be true to yourself. Avoid the hypocrisy of disguising questionable motives with superficial appeals. Make sure that your stated objectives and internal goals are in harmony. Constantly ask yourself, "What have I to give?" rather than "What have I to gain?"

## DEVELOP A SPEAKING CODE OF ETHICS

According to a study by the Conference Board, more than 75 percent of the companies surveyed have now enacted codes of ethics for their employees.[26] Although these codes are not necessarily the Ten Commandments, they are standards that act as guides for ethical behavior and practice.

In a speech to a conference on business ethics, Richard R. Capen, Jr., vice chairman of Knight-Ridder, Inc., a publishing company, related his recommendations for an ethical code in business.[27] They are reproduced here in condensed form:

*1. Build trust. Getting along in today's pluralistic world starts with trust. Trust is an ultimate value that protects an orderly, civilized society from chaos and anarchy. Trust in marriage. Trust at work. Trust among friends. Trust in public life. Trust is never guaranteed. It must be constructed carefully, nurtured vigorously, and reinforced daily.*

*2. Be optimistic. Attitude in the process of serving others is important. Often what happens in our lives comes down to the way we look at life. If we believe it will be a lousy day, it will be. If we believe there is no hope, the chances are there will be no hope . . . . On the other hand, if we believe we can win, the chances are we will. If we think we can make a difference in life, we will. The difference between such success—and failure—is usually a matter of attitude.*

*3. Be an encourager. Each week, dozens cross our paths crying out for help, for love, for encouragement. For them, it's a challenging, lonely world, and such people desperately need our love. In my business, I'm surrounded by special opportunities—big and small—to be a thoughtful listener, an enthusiastic encourager, a caring advisor, a special friend.*

*4. Lead by personal example. To be the best, leaders must be truthful and candid. They must be decisive and courageous. They must keep promises and be loyal to their family, friends, employees, clients, and country.*

We present these ideas only as suggestions to think about when developing your speaking code. Whether you adopt Capen's model, the Golden Rule, or another viewpoint, begin to develop an ethical framework to guide you through the process of building your presentations. Remember that it is up to you as a speaker to set a responsible standard as you convey ideas and recommend actions to the members of your audience. Good speaking means good ethics.

## SAMPLE SPEECH: practice, practice, practice: knowing is not the same thing as doing

*At the time of this speech, Mr. Stewart was a managing principal for Andrew Thomas and Company, a biotech investment and business development firm headquartered in Oregon. Stewart has been an executive director for Morgan Stanley and Company, was a commanding officer in the United States Navy, flying the A-6E jet aircraft, and served in the Persian Gulf War. He delivered this address to the National Collegiate Athletic Association (NCAA) Leadership*

*Conference in Orlando, Florida, on May 26, 2006. At a time when there have been numerous controversies surrounding professional sports figures in the past few years, Mr. Stewart presented this speech on values and ethics to an audience of NCAA officials, members, and students. Notice the examples he uses to support his point about the need to practice ethical behavior in everyday life.*[28]

## A PERSUASIVE SPEECH
*Thomas C. Stewart*

1. There are a lot of young people in this section, so maybe I can get away with telling a very old joke. A first-time visitor to New York City stops a passer-by and says, "Excuse me: How do you get to Carnegie Hall?" And the passer-by replies, "Practice, practice, practice."

   Well, maybe that's not a joke after all. You young people here are athletes—how do you win competitions? You practice, practice, practice? You're outstanding students—how do you get straight A's? You practice, practice, practice? You are all, I hope, young people of high moral character. How do you build character? You practice, practice, practice? You practice all these things—athletics, academics and character—so you'll be ready for the time when you're tested. And it's in the nature of the test that character differs from athletics and academics.

   > 1. He begins the introduction with a joke. Was it really humorous or did it have a more serious point?

2. Let me explain. You know when some tests are coming, and you're prepared for them when they arrive. You know the date and time of that big athletic competition you've trained for. You know the date and time of that final exam in calculus or history. But you never know for sure when your character will be tested. You only know that someday—perhaps in circumstances that you can't even imagine right now—your character is going to be put to a real test and you're going to find out what kind of a person you really are. That's why it's so important to practice ethical and responsible behavior in your daily life. So you'll be ready to make those big character tests when they take you by surprise. And when they do, the moral choices you've made in the small things leading up to that time will either help keep you afloat—or they'll sink you.

   > 2. The speaker uses a hypothetical example.
   >
   > The speaker states his thesis about the need "to practice ethical and responsible behavior" in order to meet "those big character tests ...."

3. They say that "honesty is the best policy." It isn't. What I mean is, honesty isn't a policy. You don't come face-to-face with a moral decision and ask yourself, "What is the best policy in this situation?" As if honesty were just one of a series of options to choose from. You're honest not because it's the best policy, but because it's right. If you've read my bio, you know that I was a combat flight officer in the Navy. Combat is one of the toughest tests of character a person can face. It's one situation where you can't cheat and you can't fake your response. OK, people who volunteer for the military—or to be firefighters or police officers or some other dangerous occupation—are expected to be brave. They are also expected to hold themselves to a higher ethical standard. But that doesn't mean you're off the hook because you choose a career in business or in one of the professions. Do you think accountants don't have to worry about their character being tested? Ask someone who used to work for Arthur Andersen.

   > 3. The speaker refers to his own character tests as a Navy combat flight officer.
   >
   > Stewart mentions the example of Arthur Andersen, a large accounting firm, that was convicted of trying to destroy evidence related to its customer, Enron.

4. I assume that many of you are planning careers in business or the professions, so I'm going to give you fair warning of the kinds of tests you're going to face.

   > 4. His transition leads to the next main point.

5. You've seen movies and TV shows that have depicted dishonest businessmen. I've seen them too, and I'm not very impressed. Because when you see a dishonest businessman

portrayed in the popular media, he's usually portrayed as a one-dimensional character. He has no depth, no nuance. He's a crook, pure and simple. And you look at such a repulsive character and you think, "I could never stoop that low." But the real world is a lot more complicated than the world you see on TV and in the movies. In the real world, the moral choices are not always clear-cut, or black and white.

**6. He uses another hypothetical example, putting the audience in a setting where they must make an ethical decision.**

6. Imagine that you're a CEO. Consider the fact that every quarter—every three months—you will be confronted with a balance sheet, telling you what your company has made or lost—during that three-month period. Consider further that it's not enough just to show a profit. You have to show a profit that is competitive with the profit margins of all the other companies on the stock market that are bidding for investors' money. What do you do when the numbers for one quarter aren't quite good enough? That's one of those unexpected character-testing moments I warned you about. Suddenly, the moral situation isn't as black and white as it so often is on TV or in the movies. You may think, "If I release these figures, a lot of investors are liable to pull their money out of my company and invest it somewhere else." And that's true. The stock market is ruthless. People do switch investments simply because of a bad quarter. So the heat is on.

**7. The speaker develops the hypothetical example in greater detail.**

7. Now, let's assume that you're not some one-dimensional character. Let's assume that you have integrity. Let's assume that you're willing to take the responsibility for the company's poor showing in that quarter. But then, you have others besides yourself to think of. You've got a family. You've got employees who could lose their jobs if you lose money and have to cut back. There are charities, educational institutions, and civic organizations that depend on your company's generosity. People may suffer real pain if you have to cut back. Or what if your company is working to find a cure for cancer? Or a solution for the energy crisis? Or an answer for the global warming problem? What if people may die if you publish that negative report and have to slash your research?

**8. Stewart develops the example to show how a person of integrity can rationalize an unethical decision.**

8. And now suppose—just suppose—that if you tinkered just a little bit with those numbers on the balance sheet, that everything will be all right. You know it will be all right, because if you fiddle with the numbers, you'll reassure your investors. They will keep their money in your company and, because they do that, the company will do so well in the next quarter that you'll justify the doctored figures you've given out to the public. Nobody will ever know.

**9. Stewart uses examples to illustrate the destructive power of moral compromises. Enron, a large energy company, was held accountable for hiding billions of dollars in debt, and Pete Rose, who was destined for the Hall of Fame, lied about betting on baseball.**

9. This is the kind of character test you'll be facing in your own careers, ladies and gentlemen. It's a very slippery slope once you start making moral compromises. Look at Enron. Or look at ballplayer Pete Rose, who finally admitted in 2004 that he had lied for fourteen years about betting on baseball games. Rose was a star player who had more hits that Ty Cobb. He was a sure candidate for baseball's Hall of Fame. But he let himself become addicted to gambling, and took to betting on games as a way out. When he admitted he had lied all those years, he claimed that he never bet on inside information or let his bets influence his decisions as a player or manager. "So in my mind," he said, "I wasn't corrupt."

**10. The speaker draws the conclusion from his examples that poor moral choices are a result of a "slippery slope" of progressive rationalizations.**

10. Well, whatever Mr. Rose thinks in his mind, the fact is that the rule against betting on games is posted prominently in every baseball clubhouse in the country. Pete Rose agreed to be bound by that rule and he broke it. He didn't wake up one fine morning and decide he was going to break a rule that stared him in the face every single day in the clubhouse. It was probably a gradual process—a slippery slope that started

with gambling. Then gambling more than he could afford to lose. Then falling into debt. And then inventing a rationalization that let him tell himself he wasn't doing anything wrong when he broke one of the cardinal rules of baseball.

11. That's why it's important to practice, practice, practice in your moral lives as well as in the classroom and on the playing field. Because if you resist the small temptations, you'll develop the moral muscle you'll need to resist the big ones. You probably know that, or else you wouldn't be here today. You know it isn't easy to lead a disciplined life. But I think you're all going to be glad, as you get older, that you made the effort.

11. Stewart returns to his theme of the need to "practice" in order to develop "moral muscle."

12. One of the shrewdest observations I ever heard on the importance of setting and meeting high standards for yourself was made by Winston Churchill.

12. The speaker states the transition to his next main point.

13. In 1900, when he was just 26, Churchill published his only work of fiction. It was a novel called *Savrola*. It's not a great novel. In fact, later in life, Churchill was embarrassed to have written it. He actually begged his friends not to read it. But it's of interest today because of the insights it reveals into the development of Churchill's greatness. For example, in the novel, the hero asks: "Would you rise in the world? You must work while others amuse themselves. Are you desirous of a reputation for courage? You must risk your life. Would you be strong morally or physically? You must resist temptations."

13. Stewart uses the example of Churchill.

The speaker cites a quotation from Churchill's novel, *Savrola*.

14. Does that sound familiar? It's a fancy way of saying, "practice, practice, practice." And then Churchill's hero delivers the punch line. He says: "All this is paying in advance . . . . Observe the other side of the picture; the bad things are paid for afterwards." And that should sound familiar too—look at Enron and Pete Rose—the bad things were paid for afterwards, because they didn't do the hard things, the morally right things, in advance.

14. He cites another quotation from the same source to compare to the examples of Enron and Pete Rose.

15. If you know anything about the life of Churchill, you know that Churchill's hero in this novel is speaking for Churchill himself.

16. Churchill paid in advance. Some of you might be surprised to hear that Churchill never had a university education. He attended an exclusive prep school in England called Harrow, but he graduated at the bottom of his class. From there, he went to Sandhurst, Britain's equivalent of West Point, where he learned things like tactics, fortifications, and map-reading. He knew that this sort of education was not enough if he wanted a career in politics. So, as a young officer posted in India, he set about to plug the gaps in his education. He established what he called his "university of one." While his brother officers drank, played cards, and did the other things that young officers did and still do, Churchill immersed himself in economics, philosophy, and other tough subjects. On weekends, he administered examinations to himself to test himself on what he had learned. "Would you rise in the world? You must work while others amuse themselves."

16. The speaker explains how Churchill was self-made and instead of attending college, he received a military education and created a "university of one."

He repeats the earlier quotation.

17. During his military career, Churchill also risked his life. Not once, but many times. You probably know that Churchill wrote some very thick books. But he also wrote some shorter works that are quite easy to read and very entertaining. In particular, he wrote an account of his formative years called *My Early Life*.

17. Stewart cites Churchill's auto-biography as the source for this section.

The speaker cites another quotation.

In this book, he tells how he was taken prisoner in South Africa during the Boer War. He made a sensational escape, and a reward was offered for his capture, "dead or alive." If you read the story of his escape—even today, when we know the outcome—I guarantee that it will have you on the edge of your chair. "Are you desirous of a reputation for courage? You must risk your life."

**18. The speaker cites examples of discouragement and depression from Churchill's life.**

18. Churchill returned to England a national hero, and was elected to Parliament. But again, if you know anything about his life, you know that his career in politics included heart-breaking setbacks as well as phenomenal successes. Many people don't know this, but when Churchill suffered these setbacks, he was frequently plunged into severe depressions. In fact, there were times in his life when the people closest to him feared that he might commit suicide. But here again, he paid in advance. He learned how to cope with adversity and depression. He came to call them his "Black Dog" moods. A noted British psychiatrist once wrote a penetrating study of Churchill's character. He concluded that it was through Churchill's struggles with the Black Dog that he acquired the iron will he needed to stand against Hitler when all seemed lost. The psychiatrist put it this way: He said that only a man who had conquered despair in himself could have led a nation through its darkest hours.

19. We learn moral lessons from studying the lives of towering individuals like Churchill. We learn from our respective faiths, from our families, from our friends, and from our own experiences how to be ethical and responsible human beings.

**20. The speaker begins his conclusion and returns to his theme of "practice."**

**The speaker uses a reference to Aristotle towards the end of the conclusion.**

20. We learn. But it isn't enough to just learn. We have to put that knowledge to work in our everyday lives. We have to practice, practice, practice. There's nothing new or startling in that. Over two thousand years ago, the Greek philosopher Aristotle said everything I've just told you—and he said it in fewer words. Aristotle said that character was a matter of habit. We do not do the right thing, said Aristotle, because we have virtue or excellence. Rather, he said, we have virtue or excellence because we do the right thing.

**21. He repeats his theme as an ending.**

21. We are, in short, the sum of what we do. We know that. People have known that for thousands of years. But knowing is not the same as doing. That's why we must practice, practice, practice! If we do that, we can be confident that when the great tests of our lives come, we will be ready for them.

Thank you.

## summary »

The study of ethics has been important through the centuries and is vital to the modern speaker. When evaluating a speaker's ethics, consider the speaker's honesty, reliability, motivations, and policies. When applying your own ethical standard, be honest, convey concern about others, assess your personal motives for speaking, and develop a speaking code.

## SKILL BUILDERS»

1. Select an example from current events of a person who has made a poor ethical decision. Present a short speech about the individual and describe the nature of the ethical choice, how the ethical problem affected the individual, other people, and the public's reaction to the person.
2. Develop a personal code of ethics for public speaking. How realistic or workable are your ideas? Present a 2- to 3-minute speech describing your code.

# BUILDING A
# SPEECH ONLINE »

Now that you've read Chapter 6, use your online Resource Center for Building a Speech for quick access to the electronic study resources that accompany this text. You can access your Resource Center at http://academic.cengage.com/login, using the access code that came with your book or that you bought online at http://www.iChapters.com. Your Resource Center gives you access to Interactive Video Activities, the book's companion website, Speech Builder Express 3.0, InfoTrac College Edition, and study aids, including a digital glossary and review quizzes.

# unit two

# PREPARING THE FOUNDATION

© Thomson Learning

# chapter 7

# SELECTING THE TOPIC AND PURPOSE

## chapter objectives »

After reading and studying this chapter, you should be able to

1. Describe how to generate ideas for a speech
2. Identify five guidelines for selecting speech topics
3. Describe three guidelines for developing the specific purpose
4. Recognize the function of the thesis statement
5. Develop a specific purpose and thesis statement on a given topic

> ❝ If you have an important point to make, don't try to be subtle or clever. Use a pile driver. Hit the point once. Then come back and hit it again. Then hit it a third time—a tremendous whack. ❞
>
> —Winston Churchill

*I've listened to everything you've said in class, and I've read the book. But I just can't think of what to give my speech about. I'm not really a very unique person—I don't sky dive or bake ethnic foods, I haven't traveled much, and I don't have hobbies or keep exotic pets. I'm just your average college student trying to get a degree. Please, PLEASE give me some ideas for a speech.*

The inability to think of a **subject** is one of the most common complaints heard in speech classes. The same people talking with other students in the lounge, the cafeteria, or after class seem to have no problem coming up with ideas for conversation. But in a situation requiring public speaking and evaluation of abilities, ideas seem to dry up.

In this chapter we will describe some resources that can help you get ideas for your speech. In addition to speech subjects and topics, this chapter explains the general purpose, the specific purpose, and the thesis statement.

## getting ideas

There are a number of ways to search for speech topics. Here are some resources and techniques that can stimulate your thinking and help you get started.

### YOUR OWN KNOWLEDGE AND EXPERIENCE

One of the best resources for speech ideas is your own knowledge and experience. When trying to think of subjects for a speech, people often overlook their backgrounds. After thinking and worrying for several days, a student still had no subject for her informative speech. When asked about her interests, she responded, "Well, I really like to square dance. As a matter of fact, every week I go square dancing, and my partner and I usually try to attend a square dancing contest once a month. I'm pretty good at it, but I can't talk about anything like that, can I?" When she finally realized that she could use some of her own experiences, she recognized that public speaking could actually be interesting.

Students have delivered speeches about traveling to India, climbing mountains, shearing sheep, extracting venom from poisonous snakes, studying fossils, training dogs, collecting coins, hang gliding, making theatrical masks, excavating ancient ruins, recovering from alcoholism, military duty in dangerous war zones, stomach stapling, and tattooing. These subjects were drawn from students' personal knowledge or experiences. Don't

When you choose a topic from your own interests or experiences, you are more likely to project vitality and enthusiasm to listeners.

take your background for granted. Examine your unique experiences; you will often find something to expand into a topic that fits a particular assignment.

## BRAINSTORMING

One technique to help generate many subjects in a short period of time is **brainstorming**— the rapid and unrestrained listing of ideas. Take a pencil and paper and jot down anything that comes into your mind. Don't try to judge or evaluate the ideas when you list them; the goal of this exercise is to stimulate your thoughts and imagination. After a few minutes, you will have a long list of subjects on a wide variety of issues. Naturally, some of the subjects will seem ridiculous; but the purpose of the exercise is to generate a lot of ideas quickly. You can easily eliminate the irrelevancies later.

## LIBRARY DATABASES, INFOTRAC COLLEGE EDITION, THE INTERNET

Additional places to look for subject matter are library databases such as ProQuest Research Library, Academic Search Premier, ProQuest Newspapers, or the InfoTrac College Edition which was included with your textbook. Many databases such as ProQuest Direct and Academic Search Premier contain lists of magazine titles and summaries, called abstracts, describing the content of the articles. These computerized indexes may include full texts of articles as well. (See Chapter 8 for a more extensive discussion.) In addition, many libraries have databases of major national newspapers such as the *New York Times* and *Wall Street Journal* and your college library may provide access to your local newspapers through a specific database as well.

Another method of researching a topic is to do a simple search on the Internet using a search engine such as Yahoo! or Google. These indexes allow you to search for people, places, and objects or use keywords in a more generalized topic search. If you are unsure what index or computerized source to use, ask your librarian to help you get started.

The appendix at the back of this text contains a comprehensive list of topics. These topics are grouped by eleven general categories and can help you get ideas for your informative and persuasive speeches.

## ASK FOR HELP

If you are having difficulty selecting a topic, ask for help from other individuals. Solicit suggestions from friends and family or talk to your associates at work. Ask your instructor to react to several ideas or seek advice from fellow students. Talking to others helps you to verbalize feelings and restore your perspective on significant interests, abilities, and motivations.

You'll find that plenty of subjects are available if you actively look for them. Get busy and do something—don't wait for inspiration. Examine your own experiences, try some brainstorming techniques, go to the library, or ask for suggestions from others.

## selecting the topic

Once you have chosen the subject, you must narrow it down to a **topic**—the specific, limited issue that you can effectively develop into a 5- to 8-minute speech. Here are five guidelines to consider as you build the speech.

# IT SHOULD BE SUFFICIENTLY NARROW AND CONFORM TO THE TIME LIMIT

If you took almost any general list of subjects, you would probably find that most are too general for a 5-minute classroom presentation. For example, you could sign up for entire courses on barrier reefs, baseball, or Buddha. These subjects must be narrowed down to more specific topics:

- The types of plant life existing in a barrier reef
- Solving the problem of steroids in professional baseball
- Some of the basic beliefs of Buddhism

Each of these three topics can be supported by several main points, and each can be made to conform to the time limit.

A speech on the problem of mental health in the United States, for example, would be too broad and could be narrowed down, as the following list shows:

**Subject:** Mental health in the United States
**Topics:** Causes, effects, and treatments of impotence
Common phobias experienced by "average" people
Hyperactivity in children
Mental illness and the homeless
Myths about mental illness
Personal injury claims resulting from job stress
Problems of mental health insurance
Pros and cons of mainstreaming the mentally retarded
The destructive effects of perfectionism
Treatments for Alzheimer's disease
Unethical practices in psychiatry

Eleven major speech topics have been generated from the one general subject, and many more are possible. Your topic must be limited so that you can develop it in sufficient detail within your allotted time.

# IT SHOULD INTEREST YOU, THE SPEAKER

You must be certain that the topic interests you. A speech is not like a book report on an assigned issue; the topic you select reflects your interests, your personality, and your motivations. You cannot go to the dictionary, close your eyes, pick out a random topic, and expect to feel positive about communicating it. You need to feel confident and challenged by your choice; you must be able to use appropriate aspects of delivery—vocal inflection, gestures, facial expression—to communicate your enthusiasm to the audience.

A student in the air transportation curriculum asked his audience to play the role of passengers on a domestic flight. A few seconds into the presentation, the speaker, who played the pilot, stated that the aircraft was experiencing mechanical difficulty and that he would need to make an emergency landing. The "passengers" listened carefully as the "pilot" reviewed the safety precautions and the emergency exit procedures to carry out when the plane landed. The audience was fascinated because the speaker was interested in his topic and creative in his delivery.

You may be interested in a topic, but you may not be very knowledgeable about it. Don't throw out the idea simply because you will have to do some additional investigation. One student who had presented three very creative speeches during the semester was having difficulty finding a dynamic topic for her final speech to inform. She had always been curious about ants but didn't know very much about them. At first she thought her idea might be too trivial, but as she began to do research, she found the subject compelling. She became so involved that she even created some visual aids to support her narrowed topic, "Life in an ant colony." During the speech she was enthusiastic, animated, and extremely knowledgeable because of her extensive research. But her success started with her interest in the topic.

## IT SHOULD PROVIDE NEW INFORMATION

Successful speakers can make almost any topic interesting. With proper research and audience analysis, few topics are boring. But some topics can be classified as overworked or trivial and should be avoided or altered:

- Toxic pollution is dangerous
- How to make a cake by following the microwave directions on the back of the box
- Drinking a beer
- Registering for a course at this university
- Technology is helpful in medicine

To involve your audience, alter these topics and provide new or more sophisticated information:

- Home carpeting can contain toxic pollution
- Secrets of making a perfect German chocolate cake
- How beer is manufactured
- Some of the most popular elective courses at the university
- Innovations in heart implant technology

These topics are not simplistic; they don't rehash information that is common knowledge, and they have the potential of providing additional knowledge.

A speaker began a presentation by identifying a process that was familiar to most audience members—decorating Easter eggs. But as the speech progressed, listeners soon realized that the speaker was not describing the ordinary Easter-time activity. The speaker's purpose was to demonstrate "How to make Ukrainian Easter eggs"—a centuries-old process requiring skill and dedication. The speaker briefly described Ukrainian traditions and demonstrated the application of intricate designs symbolizing Easter themes. The audience was completely involved: The speaker handled an overworked topic creatively and provided her listeners with new information.[1]

## IT SHOULD BE APPROPRIATE

While setting up visual aids for a process speech, a nursing student asked the audience for a volunteer, and a male student eagerly came forward. As the speaker proceeded with her introduction, it became clear that the purpose of her speech was to demonstrate how to give a bath to a hospital patient. The audience began to giggle nervously as the male volunteer turned red in the face. Undismayed, the nursing student instructed her volunteer to lie down on the table as she proceeded to demonstrate in great detail how a patient is bathed. The speaker's topic was appropriate in a nursing classroom, but it was extremely inappropriate in a speech class.

Appropriateness is highly subjective; what is appropriate to one person is not appropriate to another. An individual speaking about personal religious convictions might be on target in a church group, but the topic would be completely out of place at a secular meeting. Use common sense when you think about a topic, and select an issue that is appropriate for as many of your listeners as possible.

Ideas for speeches are often generated through brainstorming, thinking about personal interests, going to the library, or asking for help from friends.

## IT SHOULD CONFORM TO THE GENERAL PURPOSE

Once you have chosen a topic, you must then consider the **general purpose** or the direction of the material presented in the speech. You need to know whether your speech assignment is to **inform**, to **persuade**, or to **entertain** your audience.

### Speeches to Inform

Informative speeches are presentations that enlighten and educate audiences. Speeches to inform can be **definitions** of concepts, **demonstrations** of procedures, **descriptions** of people, places, objects, or personal experiences, or *business reports* or *lectures* on issues in which you have expertise.

If you were to define jazz, describe life in the Marines, convey the experience of sky diving, demonstrate how to make clay pottery, speak about the life of Ray Charles, recount principal historical sites in Boston, describe the effects of pancreatic cancer, report on stock-market projections for the year 2012, or lecture about the political and military struggle in Iraq, you would be contributing to audience awareness and understanding.

### Speeches to Persuade

Unlike informative presentations, your goal in persuasive speeches is to influence the beliefs, feelings, or behavior of listeners. Although you must present accurate and well-researched material, you must also take a clear position regarding the information. There are three principal types of persuasive speeches: the speech to **convince**, which changes belief; the speech to **actuate**, which moves to action; and the speech to **stimulate**, which intensifies feelings.

Persuasive speaking is similar to taking one side in a debate. You tell your audience to do something ("plant a tree"), to believe something ("require federally funded national health insurance"), or to feel something strongly ("support our firefighters and police officers"). Your goal is to build a case using logic and emotion to persuade the audience that your point of view is the correct one.

### Speeches to Entertain

The purpose of the speech to entertain is to promote enjoyment and to amuse and divert the audience. Entertaining speeches could include an after-dinner speech, a roast of a boss or friend, or a monologue satirizing a person, place, or event. But entertainment does not mean a lack of research and preparation; often, speeches to entertain are some of the most difficult to prepare and present. The speech to entertain requires creativity, skill in writing and organization, and accomplished delivery.

College speech instructors tend to emphasize informative and persuasive speeches over speeches to entertain. But developing an entertaining speech is good experience; most people have an occasion sometime in their careers or personal lives to present a humorous speech—a friend's fortieth birthday, a toast at an anniversary party, an office-party spoof.

## writing the specific purpose

The **specific purpose** is the reason for the speech. This statement communicates the speaker's goal to the audience; that is, it represents where you are going. Unlike the thesis, it does not always need to be stated in the introduction, but it is included on the speaker's outline to keep the speaker focused on the overall objective. Spend time developing your specific purpose, so that it clearly defines and conveys your objective. Here are three guidelines to follow as you prepare the specific purpose statement.

## BE CLEAR, CONCISE, AND UNAMBIGUOUS

The specific purpose should be phrased in simple and concrete language. Avoid wordy descriptions and vague terminology. The specific purpose should be easy to read and easy to verbalize. Most important, your audience must clearly understand your specific purpose.[2] For example:

- To inform you about the potential for life on Mars
- To explain how you can help children afflicted with the disease called spina bifida
- To convince you that cosmetic surgeries are dangerous

The first specific purpose tells the audience that they will receive information about the topic, the second urges listeners to become actively involved with the issue, and the third asks them to agree with the speaker. The first promotes curiosity, the second introduces terminology that may be unfamiliar (but spina bifida is clearly defined as a disease), and the third takes a strong position on a persuasive issue. Each statement is clearly worded and communicates the speaker's specific intention. Now look at the following specific purpose:

**Poor:** To tell you of the serious implications of central and obstructive sleep apnea and explain how these conditions impact the psyche and the physiology

This specific purpose is weak because it is too long, imprecise, and wordy. The sentence also introduces terminology—"central and obstructive sleep apnea"—unfamiliar to many listeners. The objective of the speech is not clearly communicated; we have the impression that the speech is about some type of sleeping disorder, but we are not exactly certain about the topic, and we are not told whom it affects. This statement confuses audience members and discourages them from listening. Here's how the specific purpose can be improved:

**Better:** To inform about the major causes and effects of a common sleeping disorder

Here the wording is clear, and the phrase moves logically and quickly to the point. The statement eliminates technical terms and ambiguous references to "psyche" and "physiology." The specific medical terminology can be identified and explained later in the speech.

**Poor:** To talk about M. C. Escher
To tell you about airport security
To inform you about spying on Americans

In each of these phrases, the subjects are not yet narrowed. A speaker who fails to make changes in these statements will probably speak overtime or jump from one topic to another. These are better:

**Better:** To inform about the stylistic influences on M. C. Escher, the pop artist
To inform about measures that have been taken since 9/11 to tighten airport security
To convince the audience that government wiretapping without a court order
    threatens Americans' constitutional rights

These statements are improvements because the subjects have been narrowed and the wording is more precise.

## INCLUDE ONLY ONE MAJOR IDEA

A specific purpose should contain only one principal topic. If it contains more than one topic, the speaker will be developing at least two speeches.

**Poor:** To describe the effects of criminal behavior on the victim and explain the
    merits of crime compensation plans
To demonstrate how a dentist fills a tooth, performs a root canal, and cleans your
    teeth
To describe the conflict between Israel and the Palestinians and explain efforts to
    bring peace to the region
To describe computer viruses and to convince you that these viruses threaten us

Often beginning speakers are afraid they will not have enough material for a 5- to 7-minute speech so they include too many topics in their specific purpose statements. The first specific purpose example contains at least two topic ideas. "The effects of criminal behavior on a victim" is at least one topic, and "the merits of crime compensation plans" is another. The second example contains three separate demonstration speeches. A speaker cannot possibly demonstrate three dental procedures in 6 or 7 minutes. In the third sentence, there are numerous topics: the history of the conflict between Israel and Palestine, which includes many regional bombings and wars as well as several peace plans. In the fourth statement, there are two distinct purposes: The first part of the statement is a speech to inform, and the last half is a speech to convince. Your specific purpose sentence should clearly indicate whether the speech is informative or persuasive; it should not include both types. Here is how each statement can be altered to incorporate only one main topic:

> **Better:** To inform about the merits of victim compensation plans
> To demonstrate how a dentist performs a root canal
> To describe the current U.S. plan to end the conflict between the Israelis and the Palestinians
> To convince the audience that computer viruses threaten our national security

Each specific purpose statement includes only one major topic, which can be developed adequately in a 5- to 7-minute speech.

## USE A DECLARATIVE STATEMENT

The specific purpose should include a declarative statement that contains an infinitive phrase and the general purpose—such as "to inform," "to demonstrate," "to persuade," "to convince," or "to actuate"—combined with the topic. The following examples are poor:

> **Poor:** Skin disease
> Lead fishing sinkers
> African tribal body painting and how it is done
> The words "under God" in the Pledge of Allegiance—pro or con?
> Should the United States engage in preemptive invasions of sovereign nations?

In each of the statements above, the speaker has not clearly identified the goal of the speech. The first example merely names a broad subject; there is no topic, purpose, or declarative statement. Although the second example could be an adequate topic for a speech, it is not phrased in the form of a statement with a general purpose; it has no direction or goal. The third example still is not complete, because it lacks an infinitive phrase. The fourth and fifth examples raise questions when they should make clear statements as to the intention of the speech; we are not sure if the speeches are informative or persuasive. Here are better examples:

> **Better:** To inform the audience about a disfiguring skin disease known as vitiligo
> To demonstrate how to make lead fishing sinkers
> To demonstrate an African tribal ritual of body painting
> To actuate the audience to support legislation that permits the words "under God" in the Pledge of Allegiance
> To convince the audience that the United States should not engage in preemptive invasions of sovereign nations

These five examples have the following points in common: (1) Each contains an infinitive phrase that clearly describes the intent and general purpose of the speech; (2) each includes a precise statement of the topic; (3) each specific purpose is phrased as a declarative statement; and (4) no specific purpose is stated as a question. Each specific purpose statement will provide the audience with a clear understanding of the speaker's goal.

## wording the thesis statement

The **thesis statement**, often called the "central idea" or the "central objective," is the phrase that tells the audience the main points the speech will include. If a member of your audience walked in late but just in time to hear your thesis statement, the listener would know exactly what your speech was going to cover. This sentence tells the audience how you are going to accomplish your goal, and it should be clearly stated at the end of your introduction. The wording of the thesis statement is important because it acts as the organizational hub of your speech; all of the main points of the body of the speech carry out the thesis statement. Here are two effective examples:

> **Topic:** Communication of dolphins
> **General purpose:** To inform
> **Specific purpose:** To inform the audience about how dolphins communicate
> **Thesis statement:** Dolphins communicate through their sense of vision and through their sense of sound.

> **Topic:** Meat "analogues" or substitutes
> **General purpose:** To inform
> **Specific purpose:** To inform you about the benefits of meat "analogues" or substitutes
> **Thesis statement:** Meat substitutes can be high in protein, low in cholesterol, and contain less fat.

In each instance, the thesis statement expands and clarifies the specific purpose; it describes what will actually be covered in the speech. In the first example, the thesis tells the audience that the speech will include two main points: (1) communication of dolphins through vision, and (2) communication of dolphins through sound. In the second example, the thesis tells listeners that the speaker will describe three benefits of meat substitutes: (1) high protein, (2) low cholesterol, and (3) less fat.

A speech is confusing or hard for an audience to follow when the speaker does not have a clear thesis statement in mind.

> **Topic:** The insanity plea as a defense
> **General purpose:** To convince
> **Specific purpose:** To convince the audience that postpartum depression should not be allowed as a legal defense when mothers kill their children
> **Poor thesis statement:** Postpartum depression shouldn't be permitted as a legal defense because women who kill their own children shouldn't be allowed to get away with murder.

This thesis statement is a prescription for speaking disaster. The statement is merely a run-on sentence that does not include the main points of the body of the speech. The speaker will probably ramble on without much logic or organization, and the confused audience will probably stop listening. Here's how to correct the problem:

> **Better thesis statement:** Postpartum depression can be faked, inaccurately diagnosed, and used to undermine the legal system.

This thesis clearly introduces three areas that will be covered in the body of the speech. The audience will be able to follow the speaker's organization with ease.

## PROBLEMS WITH THE THESIS STATEMENT

If you have difficulties when writing your thesis statement, it is possible that problems exist elsewhere in your speech.

> **Poor thesis statement:** I want to describe the religious rituals of the North, Central, and South American Indians.

This thesis contains a topic that is too broad. The numerous Indian tribes with their many religious practices would require an entire series of speeches. Here is a better thesis statement:

**Better thesis statement:** Living in the area of the Dakotas, the Sioux Indians practiced several unique religious rituals.

This thesis is much improved because it incorporates a narrow topic and clearly indicates that the speech will contain two central points.

Here is another difficulty often detected in student speeches:

**Poor thesis statement:** I want to demonstrate how the Cape Hatteras Light Station was moved.

This is not a thesis statement; it is still the specific purpose sentence. If a speaker were to use this as the thesis, there would be at least ten main points in the speech—too many for a 5- to 7-minute presentation. The speaker needs to write a thesis statement that expands the specific purpose and includes only a few main points.

**Better thesis statement:** Moving the lighthouse required lifting it from its 131-year-old foundation, rolling the lighthouse on tracks and with hydraulics, and resetting it at its new location.

Here is another frequent difficulty in student speeches:

**Poor thesis statement:** I want to describe the board game of backgammon.

This thesis indicates that the topic is much too limited. The statement contains only one point—not enough for a 5- to 7-minute speech. A speech given on this topic would only take about 1 minute. Here is how to correct the problem:

**Better thesis statement:** When learning backgammon, it is helpful to know the history, rules, and steps to playing the game.

This thesis is better because it broadens the topic and includes three main points in the speech. If you are having trouble writing your thesis statement, you may not have enough information and need to do more research.

## putting it together

To help you build your own speeches, here are some examples of topics, specific purposes, and thesis statements other students have used in their classroom presentations.[3] The brief commentary explains why each sample speech was successful.

Collecting comics was Dan Urton's hobby, and the audience could sense his enthusiasm for the topic. During the speech, Dan used some of his own comic books as visual aids to support key ideas. Listeners commented that the topic was "different"—many were surprised to learn how valuable old comic books can be. The specific purpose and thesis statement made Dan's speech objectives completely clear to the audience.

**Topic:** Collecting comic books
**General purpose:** To inform
**Specific purpose:** To inform you about the value of collecting comic books
**Thesis statement:** Collecting comic books requires some basic knowledge of the art in order to protect and increase your investment.

Professional chef John Fields showed his audience how to make a cheesecake. John went to the trouble of preparing three cheesecakes in various stages of completion. His audience watched with fascination as he skillfully used his visuals to demonstrate the details of the general process he identified in the thesis. When he finished the speech, John revealed an elegant gourmet cheesecake, which he divided among his delighted listeners.

**Topic:** Making a cheesecake
**General purpose:** To demonstrate
**Specific purpose:** To demonstrate how to make a cheesecake
**Thesis statement:** Making a cheesecake requires understanding a recipe and using a step-by-step method to create a beautiful finished product.

Jelilat Salako was extremely concerned about drilling for oil in Alaska. She connected to her listeners when she said, "Imagine that you lived out in the wilderness with your family and all of a sudden some strange being came along and spread some dark, sticky substance all over the place, killing your loved ones and friends. Well this is what the animals in Alaska will have to put up with if we start to drill for oil." To reinforce her point, she wore a T-shirt picturing a globe of the world with polar animals standing together at the top.

**Topic:** Drilling for oil in Alaska
**General purpose:** To convince
**Specific purpose:** To convince the audience that the United States should not drill for oil in Alaska.
**Thesis statement:** Drilling for Alaskan oil hurts the wildlife, could speed the process of global warming, and cause us to be less energy independent.

What impressed the audience about this speech was that Kelly Burns was committed to her topic. Kelly wore a T-shirt declaring "Human Rights Now" as she described her involvement with Amnesty International. Kelly evoked the feelings of love and commitment in listeners when she spoke of children who were stolen from their families and illegally adopted in other countries. "Think of your own children, or brothers and sisters," she said, "and be glad this can't happen to them." Audience members were genuinely moved, and many offered to help Kelly with her cause.

**Topic:** Amnesty International/human rights
**General purpose:** To actuate
**Specific purpose:** To actuate the audience to write letters to human rights violators
**Thesis statement:** I want to define human rights, explain how Amnesty International works, and tell you what you can do to help those whose rights are being violated.

## summary »

In your search for speech topics, explore various areas. Select a topic that is narrow in scope and will conform to the time limit, appeals to your own interests as a speaker, is appropriate to your listeners, and conforms to your assigned purpose—to inform, to persuade, or to entertain. The specific purpose is the overall objective of the speech. The thesis statement amplifies the specific purpose and tells the audience exactly what your speech will cover.

## SKILL BUILDERS »

1. Following the guidelines presented in this chapter, write informative and persuasive specific purposes and thesis statements for the following topics:
   a. The 2008 battle for the White House
   b. Wind, solar, and hydrogen power as a solution to the nation's energy problem
   c. The cloning of human cells
   d. The philosophy of Feng Shui in architectural design
2. Use the brainstorming technique to jot down ideas for an informative speech. When you have completed your list, apply the criteria presented in this chapter for selecting your final topic.

## @ BUILDING A SPEECH ONLINE »

Now that you've read Chapter 7, use your online Resource Center for Building a Speech for quick access to the electronic study resources that accompany this text. You can access your Resource Center at http://academic.cengage.com/login, using the access code that came with your book or that you bought online at http://www.iChapters.com. Your Resource Center gives you access to Interactive Video Activities, the book's companion website, Speech Builder Express 3.0, InfoTrac College Edition, and study aids, including a digital glossary and review quizzes.

© Thomson Learning

# chapter 8

# CONDUCTING RESEARCH

## chapter objectives »

After reading and studying this chapter, you should be able to

1. Understand the difference between credible and noncredible sources
2. Access and research library resources
3. Understand important guidelines for using the Internet
4. Know how to cite sources in your speech effectively
5. Develop an effective system for keeping accurate notes
6. Write a bibliography accurately
7. Understand what plagiarism is, its potential consequences, and how to avoid it
8. Know how to conduct an interview
9. Think critically about speech research and construction

*" Knowledge is of two kinds; we know a subject ourselves, or we know where we can find information upon it. "*

—Dr. Samuel Johnson

Alicia was enthusiastic about her speech. Her professor had assigned her communication class to research, outline, and present an informative descriptive speech about a person, place, object, or event. Alicia decided to speak about a person and she chose the topic of Mother Teresa because she had always admired the late nun's humanitarian work in Calcutta, India. Alicia got busy at the computer and went to a Wikipedia web source and found some biographical information that she quickly printed. Hoping to find some newspaper or magazine articles, she Googled "Mother Teresa" and was overwhelmed that her investigation yielded more than two million websites, which included blogs, discussion groups, and personal testimonies. Since it would take her days to conduct an investigation, she took notes from some of the first few sites and printed out items that she could paraphrase in her speech. She then used Google Earth to pinpoint the exact location of the hospital and orphanage founded by Mother Teresa and the Missionaries of Charity, her religious order. Alicia was pleased with her Internet research, which took only about 35 minutes, and she began to develop her outline and notecards in preparation for the speech.

How did Alicia do? Was her research accurate and complete? How do you think Alicia's communication professor and audience reacted to her speech based on her sources? Was her speech successful?

This chapter is designed to help you avoid the problems that Alicia experienced. Our focus is on explaining how to access the library through the catalog and databases and search the principal sources that you will need for your topic. In addition, the chapter includes discussion of credibility, primary and secondary sources, the Internet, citing sources in a speech, keeping accurate notes, interviewing, writing a bibliography, and thinking critically about research.

## preparing for research

Alicia was headed for significant problems with her speech because she didn't use the proper tools that would allow her to conduct comprehensive and reliable research. Unlike Alicia, if you know what you are doing, you can accomplish a great deal quickly and efficiently. Although it may take a bit more time than Alicia was initially willing to spend, the key to conducting good research is knowing where to look and what to look for on a particular topic. There may also be times when doing research means not using the library, but finding experts on issues or looking for information in more specialized sources. But even in these cases, you must know the correct process to use in order to make progress toward your goal of presenting an effective speech.

## establishing credibility

Your audience must be able to trust you as a speaker and to believe what you are telling them is accurate. This confidence, known as **credibility**, is developed when you support ideas with evidence that is verified by research utilizing sources that are respected, reliable, accurate, and relevant to the topic.

Sources exhibit varying degrees of credibility. Some—like reputable newspapers, newsmagazines, books, experts, trade journals, and encyclopedias—are extremely authoritative and reliable. Others—like some autobiographies, TV programs, self-help books, well-meaning friends, or condensed publications containing only excerpts of articles—have far less credibility. Even these are not all created equal. Quoting from a BBC, PBS, or CNN documentary may be much more credible than using the opinions of a well-meaning "friend."

Noncredible sources are easily detected by audiences. A student who presented an informative speech on the positive existence of UFOs made the statement: "There have been numerous sightings of UFOs according to a recent issue of the *National Enquirer*." Listeners tried to be polite and conceal their smiles. However, they eventually exploded into laughter because the speaker, who was entirely serious, did not perceive the credibility problem that the mention of his source had caused.

Here are some examples of other types of noncredible, hearsay, or "phantom" sources often cited in speeches:

"I got some information on diet from a website that said . . . ."
"I was talking to this guy and he said . . . ."
"Everybody knows that this is true . . . ."
"Studies have proven it to be a fact . . . ."
"Doctors recommend that . . . ."
"According to many web sources . . . ."
"I was standing in line at the supermarket and read in a movie magazine that . . . ."
"There is some clinic in France, or Spain, or somewhere, that has developed a cure for Alzheimers."
"I was watching this TV show and it was real interesting and it said that . . . ."
"I saw this movie and it talked about . . . ."
"The astrology magazine predicts a major earthquake in California by the year 2015."
"I read this book written by a lawyer who has been born eleven different times over the past 1,000 years."

If you want to establish credibility with the audience, cite reputable sources in your speech. Check the reliability of authors and the authenticity of publications or so-called experts. Make sure that the sources you are using have been composed by authors who have the necessary credentials. Don't rely on hearsay, gossip columns, or fabrication for evidence. If you need a complete source, consult the original article rather than an abstract, summary, or a condensed version. Be willing to spend the time researching ideas from sources that are credible and trustworthy. Cite specific sources, specific studies, and specific authorities to build confidence and believability with your listeners.

## primary and secondary sources

Sources can be either primary or secondary. **Primary evidence** is original, firsthand fact or experience. For instance, if your topic were "Driving the Winning Racecar," a primary source would be an article written by champion NASCAR driver Jeff Gordon, who won seventy-seven career victories and surpassed Dale Earnhardt, Sr.'s NASCAR record. Primary sources are also those pieces that were written or created at the time of the event and not months or years later. For example, a primary source could be an interview with Jeff Gordon that you read in a newspaper or magazine article published at the time of the event. Primary sources, however, are often difficult to obtain or unavailable and an article by Jeff Gordon may not exist and a personal interview is probably unrealistic.

For many topics, secondary research may be more accessible. **Secondary evidence** is information reported secondhand by an intermediary standing between you and the original source. You may find an article in *Sports Illustrated* written by a sportswriter who witnessed the NASCAR race at Talladega, Alabama, where Jeff Gordon surpassed Earnhardt's all-time record, or you may read a description of the race in the *New York Times*. These sources would be extremely helpful to your speech, and they could be obtained quickly through the library. You will probably use secondary evidence frequently as you research speech topics.

## accessing the library

The home page of your college or university library is a good starting place for finding what resources are available to you. The library **home page** will provide menus to help you search for books, periodicals, or other sources that contain the information you need for your speech. The principal search tools to access these materials are the online catalog and the databases that are also available online.

## THE ONLINE CATALOG

The online library catalog was once known as the "card catalog" because it contained drawers of index cards that listed all the books in the library. Today, however, college and university libraries have computerized catalog systems that provide faster and more efficient access to the library collection. In most libraries, the online catalog includes CDs as well as audiovisual materials. Books are located in the catalog according to author, title, subject, and keyword. If you know the author or title, it is easy to find your specific source. If, however, you are looking for a number of books in a general subject area, you will probably find a wide variety of sources from which to choose by simply conducting a keyword search.

## ONLINE DATABASES

The advent of the computer has made libraries efficient and easy to use. College, university, and public libraries have online databases that allow students to find periodical

Speakers must know how to use computerized library references to locate credible sources for presentations.

articles quickly and reduce or eliminate lengthy manual searches. The computer also facilitates finding resources by allowing a variety of keyword entry points. A **keyword** is a term or group of words that is used to search for documents in an electronic database or a library catalog. In an online database system, you can use more keyword access points, such as publisher, date of publication, or a word within a title or abstract.

Your college or university library pays for **databases**, which are collections of articles from periodicals, newspapers, or journals that can be searched by a computer with Internet access. These databases are often grouped together according to subject areas—current events, business, humanities, art, or other fields. Articles in these databases are often full-text and are available via the World Wide Web, although they are *not* Internet sources. In other words, you can't find them through a Google search, as Alicia attempted in the introductory example. Fortunately for students, these sources are available through library Internet home pages and can be accessed easily through a university, dorm, home, or office computer. These databases are made available through student tuition or technology fees and are accessed through college ID or public library cards. (Most public libraries have databases but they are often not as comprehensive as university online databases.)

We recommend your library's online databases as some of the first and best approaches to begin researching your topic. Many of these databases provide full texts of articles in magazines and journals as well as **abstracts**, or brief summaries of articles. Keep in mind, however, that some databases will provide only abstracts without full text access; in that case, you will need to do further research by contacting your interlibrary loan specialist in the reference section of the library. The following chart lists some of the databases that

| Database | Company | Information Included |
|---|---|---|
| Academic Search Premier | EbscoHost | Articles from research-oriented materials and general-interest magazines. |
| CQ Researcher | Congressional Quarterly | Explores a single "hot" issue in the news each week. Topics include social, teen issues, the environment, health, education, science, and technology. Includes charts, graphs, and bibliographies. |
| ERIC (Educational Resources Information Center) | U.S. Department of Education | Full-text database of education research and information that includes over 1.2 million items since 1966. |
| InfoTrac College Edition (See "Building Your Speech" at the end of this chapter.) | Gale | Full texts of more than 5,000 academic journals, magazines, and newspapers. |
| Opposing Viewpoints | Gale | Full-text periodicals, newspapers, journals, pamphlets, and primary-source documents on controversial topics. |
| National Newspapers | ProQuest | Major newspapers such as the New York Times, Wall Street Journal, Christian Science Monitor, and Washington Post. |
| ProQuest Research Library | ProQuest | A full collection of journals, magazines, and newspapers for information on a broad range of general reference subjects. |
| UnCover | CARL (Colorado Alliance of Research Laboratory) | Information taken from over 17,000 journals in numerous disciplines. |

you may encounter at your library. It is important to note, however, that you may not find these search engines in your library, since each college or university may have multiple databases with different titles in specialized fields, such as medicine, archeology, or law. If you are unsure of which database to use or where to find the full text of an article, ask your librarian, who will be glad to assist you.

Examine your library home page and explore the various online databases available to you. Talk to your reference librarians to determine which resources would be best suited to your topic.

## guidelines for searching the internet

Although the World Wide Web can help a speaker find materials for a speech, it is usually not the best starting point, as Alicia's experience clearly demonstrates. Millions of people throughout the world can access billions of information sources from home or office computers using the Web, or, the **Internet**, as it is frequently called. At the same time, any individual, institution, government agency, or business can develop and publish a computerized **home page** describing interests, jobs, objectives, or products. Individuals can also publish or access **blogs**, a type of online personal journal in which an individual or group describes daily activities, experiences, or opinions. Consumers can search the World Wide Web for goods and services; download or upload photographs, music, and videos; and gain access to unlimited sources of reliable (and unreliable) data. Users can also communicate by sending e-mail via the Internet or participate in interactive communication known as "live chat."

Even though the Internet can be valuable, like any research tool, it has great strengths, limitations, and weaknesses. If you use some of the major **search engines**, such as Google, Yahoo!, Hotbot, or Altavista, you may spend many hours trying to locate what you need, often sifting through irrelevant junk pages and advertisements that can lead to blind alleys or dead ends. Alicia's Google search yielded literally hundreds of thousands of websites about Mother Teresa. Imagine the time it would take to plow through two million .com and .net web pages trying to find something credible for your topic. In such cases, a brief visit to the library home page or a short discussion with your librarian could yield far more credible information and save you considerable amounts of time. To help you become more critical in your investigation, we suggest that you consider these guidelines when using the Internet to research supporting materials for a speech.[1]

1. **Examine the authorship or source of the website.** It is important to determine the authorship of a website and examine the qualifications and credibility of the source. Ask these questions about authorship:
   - Is the source an institution, governmental agency, commercial enterprise, network, or individual (.edu, .gov, .com, .net, .org, etc.)?
   - Are the authors, researchers, scholars, groups, or organizations reliable?
   - Are the authors' qualifications provided?
   - Can the authors' expertise on the subject area be verified?
   - Do the authors have an e-mail or other address where you can contact them for further information?
   - Who sponsors the web page? A governmental agency or institution? An unofficial sponsor, unfamiliar alliance, or counterculture organization?

Check the URL to see if the address includes ".gov" for a governmental site, ".edu" for an educational address, ".org" for an organization, or ".com" for a commercial enterprise.

Governmental and educational sites are often far more reliable but still require scrutiny to determine if the affiliation is legitimate, facetious, or even subversive. Commercial and organizational groups require special investigation for credibility because they are often attempting to sell products, render services, win converts, or solicit donations. Remember that anyone from a legitimate organization to an ex-convict can publish a web page. Don't be afraid to verify, ask questions, and think critically. If you still have unanswered questions about the authenticity of the site, search for another, more reliable source.

2. **Identify the purpose of the website.** Another area that requires close examination is the purpose of the site. Here are some areas to consider:
   - Does the web page propose to educate the public or to sell products and/or services?
   - Is there a concise and specific goal and/or mission statement included by the maker of the website?
   - Is the purpose of the site clearly stated, or are there hidden agendas?
   - What is said, what is implied, and what is unstated on the web page?

A group or organization with a bias can often distort its conclusions or findings to fit its narrow motives. A glowing movie review appearing on the web page of the Hollywood studio producing the film should be questioned for its objectivity. A student once delivered a persuasive speech about the problem of police brutality in many police departments. To demonstrate his point, he played a video he found on the YouTube website. The 20-second video showed a policeman using his nightstick to hit a screaming woman during an arrest. The scene was very troubling and emotional for the audience to witness. The problem with the visual was that the student could not explain any of the circumstances surrounding the incident, such as where and when the event occurred, the alleged crime of the offender, the outcome of the incident, or if the video was taken out of context. When asked about the visual during the question-and-answer period, the speaker replied: "I don't know anything about it other than what you saw. I just found the video on YouTube." Further investigation of the reliability of the source could have spared the student the embarrassment and loss of credibility that resulted. In this case, a better, more reliable example from a reputable newspaper or magazine could have made his point more clearly. Examine your Internet sites carefully, and do all you can to investigate the purpose and intention of a web page.

3. **Evaluate the content of the site.** When you have identified the authorship and purpose of the site, your next task is to make a thorough assessment of the content:
   - What type of language, sentence structure, grammar, and spelling is used on the web page? (A scholarly site should have few, if any, grammatical mistakes or misspellings, whereas a nonacademic or individually sponsored site might have numerous errors.)
   - What are the claims and conclusions made by the authors?
   - Does the site offer explanations that describe how claims were developed or how the conclusions expressed were reached?
   - Does the web page include links to other Internet sites, do these links actually work effectively, and are these linked sites credible?
   - Is the site trying to advertise and sell products?
   - Does commercialization of the site distort the content or conclusions of the document or findings?
   - Is the content of the website accurate and up-to-date or is a date even clearly available?
   - Is there an annotated bibliography that includes library sources such as books, as well as other non-Internet sources, for verification?
   - What is the overall design and layout of the site?

Often a web page of a major institution or corporation will help you assess how recent it is by clearly indicating the month and year it was last updated. It is also important to evaluate the overall design and layout of a site. A slick web page with lavish graphics might gain significant attention but offer little substance beyond selling a product or spreading propaganda. For example, if you were to Google "Bigfoot," you would find some dazzling websites with impressive graphics, blogs describing eyewitness accounts, and even videos proclaiming the existence of the huge hairy creature. But careful investigation reveals "testimonials" that are merely opinions and grainy videos that show nothing but shadows. Attractive design, sketches, subjective theories, and opinions are no substitute for hardcore facts and data. Sites that promote myths as fact, engage in inflammatory propaganda, advocate violence, or use hate speech are obviously not worth your time or attention. Examine the validity of Internet sources as carefully as you would verify any library or nonliterary source. Recognize that there are virtually no regulations governing the Internet: It can be used by anyone for any purpose. Don't be afraid to question a web page for authorship, purpose, and content. Remember that the inclusion of an Internet source is your decision, and like any source, it can help you achieve your speaking goal or cause needless damage to your credibility.

## researching reference sources

Reference sources located in the library are bibliographies, biographical collections, directories, dictionaries, government documents, and encyclopedias, as well as almanacs, collections of quotations, and many books. Often these resources are available online, either as free sites such as government documents (.gov) or through subscriptions that a local library purchases. Recognize that browsing a .gov or other online site may be more difficult than obtaining a print copy of the source from your library. Browsing capabilities are often not easy to use, and a simple keyword search may turn up hundreds of hits that require time-consuming review to find the appropriate information. As always, ask a librarian for help if you are having difficulty finding the necessary materials to support your topic. Reference sources outside the library include interviews with experts as well as the resources of large institutions or specialized organizations. We will examine the interview in more depth later in this chapter.

### BIOGRAPHIES

Biographical collections are frequently good places to search for topics. For example, a speech about a little-known American like John Hanson, who was technically the first president of the United States under the Articles of Confederation, would be interesting. Biographies can also be helpful in providing background information about a person you intend to use as an authoritative source in your speech. Collections such as *Current Biography*, *Dictionary of American Biography*, or *Who's Who in America* can assist you.

### DIRECTORIES AND HANDBOOKS

Directories can be helpful if you need information about specific agencies or institutions. These directories provide names, addresses, and the services provided by all types of groups. The government also publishes an index called the *Monthly Catalog of Government Publications*, listing the numerous booklets and pamphlets put out by the U.S. Government Printing Office. You could use this source to find the names of pamphlets on such subjects as stem cell research, fire safety, or CPR. This resource is also available online at **http://www.catalog.gpo.gov**. There are numerous directories and handbooks, and a search of the library or a librarian can help you locate the directory or handbook you may need.

## THE DICTIONARY AND THESAURUS

In Chapter 1 we talked about misunderstandings in the speaker-audience relationship because of differing interpretations of a word's meaning. A good way for you as a speaker to overcome semantic noise is to be very clear about the meanings of the words you employ. Consult a good dictionary like *The American Heritage Dictionary* or *Webster's New International Dictionary*. Webster's can be accessed online at **http://www.websters-online-dictionary .org**. If you need to understand technical terms in a specific field, consult a specialized dictionary. *Black's Law Dictionary*, *Dorland's Illustrated Medical Dictionary*, or the *Scientific Encyclopedia* are all examples of sources that can provide technical definitions in specialized areas.

If you need to find a synonym to avoid using the same word repeatedly in a speech, consult a thesaurus such as *Roget's International Thesaurus*. An online version is also available at **http://www.thesaurus.com**.

## ENCYCLOPEDIAS

Encyclopedias are often good places to start when you are researching a topic because they provide you with an overview of a general subject very quickly. However, their information is not always comprehensive, and, in many cases, the material is not up-to-date. Be careful not to base your entire presentation on information taken from encyclopedias, or your speech might be superficial or very dated.

There are encyclopedias on literally every subject. Two good general subject encyclopedias are *Collier's Encyclopedia* and *World Book*. The *Encyclopaedia Britannica* is also excellent if you need a more scholarly source; it can be accessed online at **http://www .britannica.com**. Numerous specialized encyclopedias are also available on subjects such as aviation, music, photography, religion, and automotive repair; they can be helpful for demonstration or process speeches. Browse the collections in your library to determine which sources will be most useful in your research.

A *note of caution:* Avoid popular sites such as Wikipedia, which Alicia used in the opening example to find information about Mother Teresa. Although it claims to be an electronic "encyclopedia," Wikipedia's own home page states: "Visitors do not need specialized qualifications to contribute, since their primary role is to cover existing knowledge."[2] In other words, anyone, young or old, from any background can write or edit anything on the site regardless of their expertise or credibility on a subject.

Use credible resources. Know where you are searching and what you are searching for. Spend your valuable time investigating reliable resources and avoid those that are untrustworthy.

## ALMANACS, YEARBOOKS, AND STATISTICAL PUBLICATIONS

Often you will need to find statistical information to give your speech credibility. Almanacs, yearbooks, and statistical abstracts contain numerical data on subjects such as crime, deaths, births, accidents, disease, incomes, agriculture, and budgets.

When you do statistical research, it is important to exercise care in your interpretation of the material. Be certain that you clearly understand the information as it is presented.

Statistics can be presented in decimals, in percentages, in total numbers of cases, in means (averages), in medians (middle number), or in modes (number occurring with greatest frequency). Know what the statistics measure, and be able to draw clear and accurate conclusions from the data before you decide to include the information.

Some of the most useful sources for statistics are *Statistical Abstract of the United States*, *Vital Statistics of the United States*, *World Almanac and Book of Facts*, and *Information Please Almanac*. Many of these are available online as well as in the more standard written form. For example, you can find *Statistical Abstract* at **http://www.census.gov**. Consult your library to obtain the **URLs** (uniform resource locators) for these resources if you want to access them on the Web.

## COLLECTIONS OF QUOTATIONS

Many sources can provide you with the right quotation to introduce or conclude your speech. Quotations can often synthesize ideas that might take several lines for you to paraphrase. You might want to consult *Bartlett's Familiar Quotations*, *Morrow's International Dictionary of Contemporary Quotations*, and *The Macmillan Book of Proverbs, Maxims, and Famous Phrases*. A less comprehensive but helpful resource can be found online at **http://www.bartleby.com**.

## BOOKS

One of the most obvious sources for a speech is an authoritative book written on your topic. Frequently you will find a collection of readings compiled by one editor or author that will be useful in your research. Be sure to notice the date the book was published. If you were researching the latest computer technologies in a book published in 1985, you would not find much current information. If your topic were the history of computer technology, the 1985 source might be excellent as a beginning point. For some topics, however, using a rare book or a classic study might be more significant than a more recent source. In a speech about the *Titanic*, for example, a speaker could quote an eyewitness from a book written in 1912 by one of *Titanic's* survivors. In this case, the speech would contain material from an excellent primary source.

Some books, like the huge selection of self-help publications in bookstores, are popular with the general public, but frequently authors of these publications are not experts: They are merely lay individuals writing from their own personal experiences about divorce, jogging, or making millions in real estate. The fact that people have been enterprising enough to put their thoughts into print does not mean their words should be regarded with reverence and considered to be credible. Analyze carefully what you read; examine how writers document and reference their material; and above all, feel free to question and even to discard information if other evidence proves the data questionable or false.

## MAGAZINES, JOURNALS, AND NEWSPAPERS

Newsmagazines, such as *Time*, *Newsweek*, or *U.S. News & World Report*, are excellent sources and will provide much of the information you need on current events and recent trends. As you investigate these sources, however, be able to distinguish between fact and opinion. Many newsmagazines contain articles that report facts in a fairly objective manner. But these periodicals also include material, such as editorials, columns, or features, that provide opinions and interpretations of facts. Also be aware of any political or social bias of the publications, and double-check articles with other news sources for accuracy.

Quarterlies and journals contain articles relevant to specific disciplines. Periodicals such as *The Automobile Quarterly*, *The American Journal of Psychology*, or *The Criminal Law Quarterly* can be helpful in your research, even though they are written in the technical jargon of the discipline. Be certain that you understand journal articles clearly enough to be able to communicate the information easily to the audience. This is especially important because most of these scholarly publications assume a high level of expertise and/or knowledge on the part of the reader.

Newspapers will give you some of the most up-to-date published information available in print on current events and social issues. Check the political bias of the newspaper you use for research. The *Washington Post* and the *New York Times*, for instance, are considered liberal publications, while the *Wall Street Journal* and the *Christian Science Monitor* are more conservative. Be careful about using newspapers as comprehensive sources for any issue. Because current events are constantly unfolding, one news story or article will rarely be complete. It is wise to cross-reference newspaper articles with other sources for accuracy.

Most national magazines and newspapers have websites that you can access free of charge. Recognize, however, that these .com websites frequently provide incomplete information and omit numerous portions of the publication, which are available only if you pay a fee. Remember that these companies make money by selling their publications and so will not allow full access to their resources free of charge. The best way to retrieve the full texts of many periodicals is through a database at your library.

## LEGAL RESEARCH

You may need to cite a number of court cases in order to prove a point in a persuasive speech or describe the details of litigation for an informative presentation. If so, don't be intimidated by the number of official-looking legal volumes in your library. You simply have to learn how to use these resources. If you know what information you need, a good librarian should get you to the right source.

## AUDIOVISUAL AIDS

In addition to books and periodicals, libraries have maps, atlases, and extensive media collections that you can research to support ideas. The Internet is also a resource for materials such as clip art, photographs, and illustrations that you can download to use as a visual in a portion of a speech. In the opening example, Alicia did a useful Google Earth search to pinpoint a location of one of Mother Teresa's orphanages. A visual aid, such as a map, can quickly display a physical location and make a topic more understandable to listeners. Including a brief excerpt from a *National Geographic* video or playing a portion of a symphony may also add interest to particular speech topics. Audiovisual aids are effective because they help you communicate with listeners through additional channels. Just remember to cite these sources as well. Plagiarizing images, lyrics, and music frequently carries the same consequences if a student is found guilty of using them without giving proper credit. (Chapter 12 provides a complete discussion of the types and uses of audiovisuals in a presentation.)

## INTERVIEWS WITH AUTHORITIES

For certain topics, your research will take you away from the library. **Interviews** with professionals, such as physicians, lawyers, police officers, or teachers, will yield invaluable primary source material—as long as the experts are authorities in their fields. If you are doing research about victims of rape, speak to an official in a community rape crisis center. Your professional may be able to provide you with a wealth of supporting materials, even in a brief telephone interview. Don't be content to include just a single interview; use several so that your speech will contain a number of authoritative viewpoints.

You can also include personal testimonies from individuals who have actually experienced some aspect of the topic. A testimonial from someone injured by a drunk driver, or a brief quote from a person afflicted with AIDS, can vividly convey the impact of an issue.

# citing sources in a speech »

In this chapter we have discussed the importance of using credible resources when you research a topic. It is equally important to cite your sources to confirm your credibility with listeners as you present your speech. Some speakers are unsure how to cite sources and so avoid referring to them altogether. But you can refer to sources in a conversational way that helps your speech to flow naturally while still providing believability.

First, you need to decide which portions of your resources are important to state in your speech to establish your credibility with listeners. If your facts are taken from a periodical, the name of the newspaper or magazine and the date of publication are the most essential items to cite verbally. Citing the title of the article can be helpful if it is not too lengthy, but mentioning the writer's name is unnecessary unless he or she is an expert in the field. Avoid stating page numbers: This specific information will be located in your bibliography if listeners want to look up an article. When referring to a book, cite the title, and author's name and give a brief explanation of the author's expertise in the field. It is not necessary to state the publisher or copyright date of a book recently published. If you use the Internet, give the title of the website and the person or group that publishes it. It is unnecessary to provide the URL unless you want listeners to go to the site to find more information about your issue. If you have interviewed a person, give the name and title of the individual and state why he or she is an expert or authority on your topic. Whenever you say "studies show . . . ," "doctors recommend . . . ," or "it's a fact that . . . ," you are telling your listeners that you are about to cite verifiable information with a clear reference. Failure to provide such data can erode your listeners' confidence in you as a speaker.

Cite your sources clearly. Build the trust of your audience members and gain their confidence. Demonstrate that you know what you're talking about and that your information is reliable. Here are a few examples of ineffective and more effective ways to verbally cite sources in a presentation.

### Newspaper

**Ineffective:** "According to the *Washington Post*, more than 97 million people watched the New York Giants defeat the undefeated New England Patriots." (The newspaper reference is too general; no date is offered.)

**Better:** "More than 97 million people watched the New York Giants defeat the undefeated New England Patriots according to a February 5th, 2008 article in the *Washington Post*." (A specific date is provided.)

### Book

**Ineffective:** "Margaret Brownell writes in her book *Dieting Sensibly* that fad diets telling you to 'eat all you want' are dangerous and misguided." (Although the speaker provides a specific quote and cites an author and book title, who is Margaret Brownell? No information is presented to establish her authority on the topic.)

**Better:** "Margaret Brownell, a professor of nutrition at the University of New Mexico, writes in her book, *Dieting Sensibly*, that . . . ." (The author's credentials are clearly described.)

### Interview

**Ineffective:** "One of the high school principals in this county says, 'I believe that uniforms would improve the academic and social atmosphere of our school and reduce incidents of violence and harassment on our campus.'" (The speaker presents a quotation but offers no names or other documentation for the material.)

**Better:** "Last week I interviewed Dr. James L. Hunt, who is the principal of Elkhorn Senior High School. He said that . . . ." (The data of the interview is specified, and the name and job title are documented.)

### Library Databases

**Ineffective:** "An article in ProQuest quotes Jeff Godon's observations when he won his 77th NASCAR victory at Talladega, Alabama: '. . . hopefully nobody got injured with what happened. But I wanted to break the record, and it's pretty awesome to do it here today.'" (Although ProQuest is a library database that includes numerous periodicals, it is not a newspaper or a magazine and should not be cited as the source.)

**Better:** "A *Baltimore Sun* article on April 30, 2007, quotes Jeff Godon's observations when he won his 77th NASCAR victory at Talladega, Alabama: '. . . hopefully nobody got injured with what happened. But I wanted to break the record, and it's pretty awesome to do it here today.'" (The name and date of the newspaper are cited and not the ProQuest library database. The same holds true for other databases with multiple periodicals.)

**Ineffective:** "A September 29, 2006, article titled 'Biofuels Boom' notes that midwestern energy companies are building new factories to convert corn into ethanol." (The citation states the date and article title, but there is no periodical or database name to identify the information source.)

**Better:** "An article titled, 'Biofuels Boom' in a September 2006 issue of CQ Researcher notes that midwestern energy companies are building new factories to convert corn into ethanol." (Because the item is from CQ Researcher, which gathers articles supporting a single "hot" issue each week, it is appropriate to cite the database in addition to the article title and date for credibility. Articles from Opposing Viewpoints should be cited in the same manner.)

### The Internet

**Ineffective:** "According to the World Wide Web, researchers are discovering that strong evidence exists that the spinal cord can regenerate." (The vague reference to the Web is not credible because no specific site is identified.)

**Better:** "The website of the Reeve-Irvine Research Center, named for Christopher Reeve, indicates that scientists are discovering . . . ." (A specific, credible site is mentioned as well as the founder and advocate of the site.)

## LEGISLATIVE AND GOVERNMENTAL RESEARCH

You may have a topic that requires you to investigate specific legislation enacted by the state legislature or by the U.S. Congress. A quick phone call to the office of one of your representatives can help you to gather valuable information on a local or national legislative issue.

*The Congressional Index* is an excellent source if you want to know about legislation currently pending in Congress. This index gives you the current status of legislation, that is, whether the bill is in committee, if it has passed one or both houses of Congress, if it was signed into law or vetoed by the president, or if a presidential veto was overridden by the Congress.

If you want to investigate the daily proceedings of Congress, consult *The Congressional Record*, which transcribes the floor debates and votes of the members of the Senate and the House of Representatives. (In addition, both houses of Congress televise their daily proceedings, making a video record.)

A source that can help you obtain information from the three branches of the federal government is the U.S. Government Printing Office, which has a website at **http://www .gpoaccess.gov.** This resource has links to numerous government data, including the *Congressional Record*, legislation enacted by Congress, public and private laws, presidential materials, and the Supreme Court website.

When you need to understand how Congress and the government spend our tax money, you can obtain a copy of *The Budget of the United States Government*, which can tell you how the federal government allocates the multi-trillion-dollar budget in the current fiscal year. The budget is typically available in the library or through the U.S. Government Printing Office.

## INSTITUTIONAL AND ORGANIZATIONAL RESEARCH

Many institutions and organizations have public relations or information offices that can provide you with material on specific subjects. In addition, most institutions and organizations have websites where you can find information. If you need data on an eye bank, for example, contact a hospital specializing in this field. For information related to institutions of higher learning, get in touch with your college or university's public relations office. If you are doing research on a foreign country, call or e-mail the embassy or the consulate office nearest you. Ask your state's department of motor vehicles for data regarding accident rates, insurance guidelines, or driving tests. To collect examples and statistical evidence concerning specific crimes in your community or state, consult the information office of the police department. If you need to know what people are doing to prevent drinking and driving, contact Mothers Against Drunk Driving (MADD). If you want to gather differing viewpoints about the policy known as "No Child Left Behind," contact the Department of Education, the National Education Association (NEA), and your local public school board. Information from these institutions and organizations can provide more depth and substance for a speech topic.

## SPECIALIZED LIBRARIES AND MUSEUMS

Many cities and communities have specialized libraries for law, medicine, literature, science, astronomy, or agriculture. The Library of Congress is a comprehensive source that includes material from these libraries, as well as anything that has ever been published in the United States. The Library of Congress and many other libraries have interlibrary loan services that allow you to obtain materials from other libraries at your local institution. The only disadvantage of interlibrary loan systems is that you may have to order information in advance. Check with your librarian for specific information regarding the interlibrary loan system nearest you.

Museums can be fascinating resources for information on a variety of subjects. Although you may not be able to visit many of these places in person, accessing the website can give you some useful background material. For example, if you want to find information about the National Cryptologic Museum in Washington, D.C., or the Baseball Hall of Fame in Cooperstown, New York, you can explore their websites at **http://www.spymuseum.org** and **http://www.baseballhalloffame.org**. But remember that most websites won't show much of the displays located in the museums; you may need to conduct more comprehensive research if you are looking for specific materials.

## keeping accurate notes

When you are doing research, it is important that you have a well-organized system of note taking so that you will use your time efficiently. Often people will use a resource tool, jot down or print out a list of sources, and then obtain articles and forget to write down the statistics or examples they wanted to use in their speeches. They have to return to their sources a second or third time and plod through the material all over again to recall their information. A good method of taking notes can help you avoid such a time-wasting process and assist you in making substantial progress toward getting your speech organized. If you have a laptop computer, you can jot down notes in the library, at personal interviews, or wherever you conduct your research. If you don't have a portable computer, get some 3-by-5 or 4-by-6 notecards. When you find a source you want to use, write a topic heading at the upper right-hand corner of the card. Then, at the upper-left corner, add the type of supporting information you are listing on the card, such as statistics, quotation, comparison or contrast, and so forth. Then place a bibliographic entry on the next line so that you will be able to identify the exact reference for later use in your speech or in case you ever need to investigate it again. Finally, jot down the specific details of the information. Include all the necessary statistical data, illustrations, or other material you want for the speech. When you follow this system, you will be able to build a file of supporting materials that will be easy to use and can be arranged in any order.

The following notes demonstrate how to identify the topic, the specific type of supporting data, the bibliographic reference, and pertinent details of the researched material.

| Statistics          The New York City Freedom Tower ————— | Topic heading |
| --- | --- |
| | Type of support / Source |

"The New York City Freedom Tower Design." U.S. Times 3 July 2006. ————— Source
    23 Jan. 2008 http://www.ustimes5.com/the_new_york_city_freedom_tower_
    design.htm

1. Tower to be 1,776 feet tall—echoing date of Declaration ————— Statistical data
   of Independence

2. 2.6 million square feet in building's interior

3. Base of tower to be 200-by-200 feet square

4. 187 feet of base will be enclosed with glass prisms

5. Tower tapers from a square to octagon to smaller square of
   145-by-145 square feet

**Conclusion: Freedom Tower scheduled for completion in 2011 at a cost** ————— Conclusion
**of over $2 billion!**

Quotations        **Tribute to Sean Taylor, Washington Redskins** — Topic heading
                  **football player, who died when burglars shot him**
                  **in his home**
                                                                — Type of support

Shipley, Amy, and Peter Whoriskey. "Hail, and Final Farewell; Teammates, Friends
   Join Family in Paying Tribute." *Washington Post* 4 Dec. 2007: A1+ ——— Source

"There are not enough adjectives in the dictionary to describe how special he ——— Quotations
   was."

                                              —Michael Outar, Uncle

"Gibbs said he had imagined God watching Taylor on the field and
   marveling, 'Man, I made a great football player.'"

                                              —Joe Gibbs, Redskins Coach

"Sean was at peace in his life. It showed in everything he did. He was always smiling in the locker room. He came to work with the right attitude."

                              —Clinton Portis, Redskins Running Back ——— Qualifications of
                                                                          quoted person

"For those who took the liberty of restlessly speculating that this young man's death
   was caused by the way he lived, I would like to say that they should be ashamed."

                                              —Otis Wallace, Florida City Mayor

---

Example         **Amazing feats in advertising—Bungee** ——— Topic heading
                **jumping—GMC truck**
                                                            — Type of support
Bromer, Cliff. "Jumpin' Jimmy." *Popular Mechanics*, March 1998: 56–57. ——— Source

1. Bungee cord was attached to tail hook of GMC sport truck. ——— Details of
2. Bungee cord also fastened to new river Gorge Bridge, Beckley, West Virginia.    example
   a. Bridge is 876 ft. high and has largest steel arch span in continental U.S.
   b. Engineers determined that bridge could sustain stresses of truck bungee jump.
3. Bungee cord specially designed with 9 individual cords.
4. Launch platform from bridge required stunt engineering.
5. Jump was a success for a brief 30- to 60-sec. commercial.
6. Truck had to be "reeled in" like a fish.

## interviewing

Many of your speech topics will require you to interview people who are experts or authorities in their fields. You can conduct interviews by telephone, webcam, e-mail, or in person.

Most organizations and institutions have websites that tell users how to contact their representatives by toll-free phone numbers or via e-mail. A benefit of

the telephone call is that you are provided with quick access to an individual at a remote location. A disadvantage of telephoning is that you are not able to see an individual's nonverbal reactions, and the time of the interview may be more limited, making it difficult to ask follow-up questions. Although a webcam allows you to interact visually with your interviewee, not everyone has access to this technology. E-mailing is another way to interview a busy individual whom you may not be able to telephone or meet face-to-face.

Although you may be able to collect valuable information by e-mail, you may be frustrated if it takes several days to gain responses and disappointed if the answers are too brief due to the busy schedule of your interviewee. Perhaps the most effective means of interviewing is the face-to-face meeting. The live, one-on-one interview allows you to observe nonverbal reactions, ask immediate follow-up questions, and raise additional issues generated in the meeting if necessary.

Whether you gather material by telephone, webcam, e-mail, or in person, you should know how to conduct an interview to get the information that you need from an individual.

## PREPARING FOR THE INTERVIEW

When you interview an expert on your topic, you must be completely prepared by conducting preliminary research into the topic and developing a list of questions to ask. This kind of preparation will help you to focus on your task and keep you from wasting valuable time.

When you have done your research and prepared your questions, call or e-mail the interviewee to make an appointment. Be sure that the individual understands your topic and knows the reason for the interview. You might even tell the person one or two of the questions you are going to ask so that he or she can be adequately prepared with answers. When you set up the interview, you may want to double-check the interviewee's qualifications to be certain that you are talking to the appropriate expert. When the individual

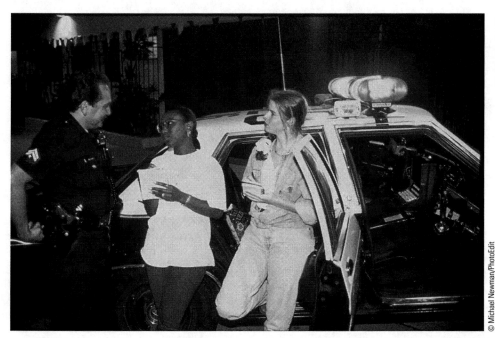

A speaker should know how to conduct a successful interview with an expert to gather the most appropriate information.

© Michael Newman/PhotoEdit

agrees to the interview, set a date and a time that accommodate his or her schedule and yet allows you to obtain all the information you need.

## CONDUCTING THE INTERVIEW

Be sure that you are on time for the interview. Establish good rapport with your interviewee by being friendly, courteous, and conversational. Demonstrate active listening skills: Nod your head, sit forward, and show interest in the person you are interviewing. Let the individual know that you are easy to talk to, receptive, and noncombative.

Next, introduce your topic and state the purpose of the interview. Start by asking questions from your prepared list. As the interviewee introduces new or relevant information, think of other follow-up questions to ask. If the individual brings up ideas that are irrelevant to your topic, gently bring the person back on track by saying, "Let's go back to what you were saying before," or "Now, if you don't mind, I'd like to ask you another question." Remember that you do have a time limit, and you must gather the information you need.

Be sure that your interviewee adequately clarifies and explains material. One-word answers like "yes" or "no" will not really help when you need detailed information. Ask your interviewee to expand on the issue by posing open-ended questions, such as "Can you give me an example of what you're saying?" or "How do you handle that type of situation?"

During the interview, make verbal summaries to help you understand the material clearly and to allow the interviewee to correct any misinformation or misconceptions you may have. Keep the interview moving; if it gets bogged down, ask more questions or make additional comments to get the discussion going again. Don't monopolize the conversation; give the person adequate time to formulate a response. And don't interrupt an interviewee unless it is absolutely necessary. This practice is not only rude, it also interrupts the individual's thought process.

Conclude the interview on time. Don't stay longer unless you are specifically asked to continue. The person has set aside a specific time for you in a busy schedule—don't impose any further.

## TAKING NOTES DURING THE INTERVIEW

During the interview, be sure to take notes that are accurate and complete. But remember that your writing should usually be notation—not a verbatim transcript of the entire conversation. If your interview covers detailed information that requires more careful transcription, ask for permission to bring a tape recorder or a laptop; but never bring one to an interview unless you have asked for prior permission. There will be times when taping will not be acceptable to an interviewee. For example, if you were talking with a rape crisis counselor about specific case histories, the counselor might not allow you to tape or transcribe the interview because of the need to protect client confidentiality.

If you use a direct quote from the individual, make certain that everything you jot down is completely correct. Double-check the accuracy of the statement with the interviewee. Don't be afraid to ask questions to clarify an issue if you are not certain about the information.

When the interview is over, immediately review your notes while the ideas are still fresh in your mind. Expand your notes by writing summaries and additional comments. At a later time, you may want to make a follow-up call to clear up any unanswered questions or points of confusion.

# the bibliography: how to record an entry

When you write your outline, list the sources you have used to research the topic. When you enter a book, magazine article, or Internet source in your bibliography, you need to use a style that is uniform and consistent. There are many styles and methods of documenting sources in a bibliography: the Modern Language Association (**MLA**), American Psychological Association (**APA**), and *Chicago Manual* (CM). Colleges and universities also have their own style booklets that contain their required bibliographic procedures. Your instructor may want you to use your college or departmental style system or even another approach.[3]

Because you will probably be using books, magazines, newspapers, interviews, and Internet sources frequently, study these sample entries based upon the MLA style. Be sure to alphabetize the bibliography as you write each reference item.

## BOOKS: ONE AUTHOR

Obama, Barack. The Audacity of Hope: Thoughts on Reclaiming the American Dream.
    New York: Crown Publishers, 2006.
Author (last name first). Book title underlined. Place of publication: name of publisher
    and date.

## BOOKS: TWO AUTHORS

Shirk, Martha, and Gary Stangler. On Their Own. Boulder, CO: Westview Press, 2004.
Authors (as written above). Book title underlined. Place of publication: name of publisher
    and date.

## MAGAZINES: ARTICLE WITHOUT AUTHOR PROVIDED

"Front-Loading the Presidential Primaries." Time 7 Jan. 2008: 30–31.
Article title in quotes. Name of magazine underlined. Date of publication: page
    number(s).

## MAGAZINES: ARTICLE WITH AUTHOR PROVIDED

Stuhlman, Jonathan. "Georgia O'Keeffe: Circling Around Abstraction." American Art
    Review Dec. 2007: 124–133.
Author (last name first). Article title in quotes. Name of magazine underlined. Date of
    publication: page number(s).

## NEWSPAPERS: ARTICLE WITHOUT AUTHOR PROVIDED

"Legg Mason Makes Deal With Equity Firm." New York Times 15 Jan. 2008: C2.
Article title in quotes. Name of newspaper underlined. Date of article with section and/
    or page number.

## NEWSPAPERS: ARTICLE WITH AUTHOR PROVIDED

King, Laura. "Pakistan Lays Blame on Taliban." Baltimore Sun 29 Dec. 2007: 1A+.
Author (last name first). Article title in quotes. Name of newspaper underlined. Date
    of article with section and/or page number. (Use a + sign if article is not printed on
    consecutive pages.)

## ONLINE LIBRARY DATABASES

Bedard, Paul, Kenneth T. Walsh, and Suzi Parker. "Washington Whispers." U.S. News &
    World Report 140. 20 29 May, 2006: 8–10. Academic Search Premier. EBSCOhost.
    *Your library's name, city, and state. 5 Feb. 2008 <http://web.ebscohost.com>
Bettelheim, Adriel. "Biofuels Boom." CQ Researcher 16.34 29 Sept. 2006: 1–33. CQ
    Researcher Online. *Your library's name, city, and state. 31 Jan. 2008 <http://0-library.
    cqpress.com.library.ccbcmd.edu/cqresearcher/document.php?id=cqresrre200. . .>

Boot, Max. "Illegal Immigrants in the U.S. Military Should Be Granted Citizenship." At Issue: What Rights Should Illegal Immigrants Have? Ed. Lori Newman. Detroit: Greenhaven Press, 2006: 1–4. Opposing Viewpoints Resource Center. *Your library's name, city, and state. 4 Feb. 2008 <http://0-find.galegroup.com.library.ccbcmd.edu:80/>

Hamm, Steve. "The Electric Car Acid Test." Business Week 4069 4 Feb. 2008:42-47. InfoTrac College Edition. Gale Group and Thomson Learning. *Your library's name, city, and state. 15 Feb. 2008 <http://infotrac-college.thomsonlearning.com//itw/infomark/650/672/21278893w16purl-rc1_. . .>

Author's last name first. Article title in quotes. Periodical title underlined, volume and issue numbers. Date of publication: inclusive pages. Name of database. Name of subscription service. *Name of library where you retrieved the source, city, state. Date of access and URL of site in angle brackets.

### THE INTERNET: ORGANIZATION (NO AUTHOR)

Hopkins Team Identifies Autism Susceptibility Gene. 22 Jan. 2008. Johns Hopkins Medicine. 23 Jan. 2008 <http://www.hopkinsmedicine.org/press_releases/2008/01_22_08.html.>

Title of site underlined. Date of publication. Name of organization responsible for site. Date you accessed site. URL of site in angle brackets.

### THE INTERNET: MAGAZINE (WITH AUTHOR)

Marsh, Altonk. "NASA Releases Controversial Survey." AOPA Online 3 Jan. 2008. 23 Jan. 2008. <http://www.aopa.org>.

Author (last name first). Article title in quotes. Periodical title underlined. Date of publication. Date you accessed the periodical. URL in angle brackets.

### INTERVIEWS

Lowrey, Joan. Personal interview. 12 Mar. 2008.

Name of person interviewed (last name first). Personal interview. Interview date.

### TV PROGRAM

"Justice Scalia On The Record." Interviewed by Lesley Stahl. Sixty Minutes. CBS. WCBS, New York. 27 Apr. 2008.

Title of program and name of interviewer or narrator. Title of program, name of network, broadcasting station, place and date.

## avoiding plagiarism

*Plagiarism* is the act of stealing the writings or ideas of another and using them as your own. It can involve taking word-for-word passages from articles, Internet sources, or verbal lectures or conversation and failing to give proper credit and/or quotations as to the original source of the information. Likewise, paraphrasing without giving credit to the author or source is still considered plagiarism. Plagiarism is unethical and it is against the law. Colleges and universities have very clear policies against this offense, and many college instructors specify unpleasant consequences including dismissal from the institution if students plagiarize research papers or classroom presentations.

It is important to understand the difference between plagiarized material and a paraphrase. Notice the box on page 127 showing an original passage that is taken word for word from the January 2008 issue of *Consumer Reports*. Both plagiarized passages use almost the exact wording of the original with only slight alteration. The first example provides no source and only changes the pronouns in a further attempt at deception. The

## ORIGINAL PASSAGE:

"For the fourth straight year, the Toyota Prius hybrid is the top car for owner satisfaction. Ninety-two percent of Prius owners who responded to our survey said they would definitely buy or lease one again. . . . The Prius is clearly benefiting from today's wave of enthusiasm for fuel-sipping hybrid cars. Boasting the best gas mileage of any five-passenger vehicle we've tested—44 mpg overall—the Prius has generated an almost cult-like following among many environmentally conscious consumers."[4]

### plagiarized passage 1:

For the fourth straight year, the Toyota Prius hybrid is the top car for owner satisfaction. Ninety-two percent of Prius owners who responded to a survey said they would definitely buy or lease one again. . . . The Prius is clearly benefiting from today's wave of enthusiasm for fuel-sipping hybrid cars. Boasting the best gas mileage of any five-passenger vehicle tested—44 mpg overall—the Prius has generated an almost cult-like following among many environmentally conscious consumers.

The passage does not state where the information came from, does not use the word *quote*, and restates the passage word for word. Notice that the plagiarist has left out "our" in front of "survey" and "we've" before "tested," in an attempt to hide his plagiarism.

### plagiarized passage 2:

For the fourth straight year, the Toyota Prius hybrid is the top car for owner satisfaction according to a 2008 issue of *Consumer Reports*. Ninety-two percent of Prius owners who responded to their survey said they would definitely buy or lease one again. . . . The Prius is clearly benefiting from today's wave of enthusiasm for fuel-sipping hybrid cars. Boasting the best gas mileage of any five-passenger vehicle they tested—44 mpg overall—the Prius has generated an almost cult-like following among many environmentally conscious consumers.

Even though the source is initially cited, the passage is still plagiarized because it uses the original words of the printed article with no attempt at paraphrasing or using the word "quote." The plagiarist has only changed "our survey" and "we tested" to "their survey" and "they tested."

### paraphrased passage

A January 2008 issue of *Consumer Reports* said that the Toyota Prius is the number-one car in buyer satisfaction for the fourth year in a row. Many of today's consumers are environmentally conscious and want fuel-efficient cars like the Prius, which gets about 44 mpg in *Consumer Reports'* testing and gives the best mileage compared to any other similar car. Over ninety percent of Prius owners surveyed by the magazine said they would buy one again. In fact, *Consumer Reports* calls the Prius buying phenomenon a "cult."

Here the passage is paraphrased in the speaker's own words. The speaker clearly cites the source and also quotes a descriptive word that was taken directly from the article.

second example cites the source, but the material is still worded the same as the original. The paraphrased passage is not plagiarized. It states the source, but uses the speaker's own wording and clearly indicates that a specific word characterizing the popularity of the Prius is a direct quotation from the article.

Avoid plagiarism at all costs. Cutting corners will only hurt the speaker and raise serious questions about the speaker's integrity. When you cite your research honestly and openly, you have nothing to fear and everything to gain from your speaking experience.

# thinking critically about speech research and construction

Unfortunately, when we hear the word *criticism*, we often think of it in negative terms, such as tearing down the ideas or arguments of others. **Critical thinking** should not be destructive; rather, it should be a constructive process in which we examine and evaluate the facts and ideas in order to make more rational decisions and improve our understanding.[5] As you go through the process of research and speech construction, you can think critically by testing information, being organized, listening to different perspectives, and thinking for yourself.

## BE WILLING TO TEST INFORMATION

Critical thinking implies asking relevant questions. When you are researching a topic or choosing supporting materials, evaluate the information carefully. If you find a shocking statement or startling statistic, cross-check the material with other sources for reliability. If you are conducting an interview, don't be afraid to ask questions or ask for concrete verification of information. If you are listening to a speaker describing a new cure for a disease, examine the evidence presented and analyze the quality of the research. One speaker presented "constructive thought therapy" as a cure for cancer. Although the topic was interesting, listeners were skeptical as the speaker expressed her opinions on the issue. One audience member commented, "I've heard of this kind of therapy, but I mistrusted the speech—there seemed to be no evidence." The speaker did not test the information by verifying it and was too willing to rely on her own opinions and upon the hearsay of others. You can avoid this kind of difficulty by conducting a thorough analysis of your data and research materials. Do a keyword search using a library database.-Examine periodical articles for credibility and determine which sources will support your ideas with reliable information. As always, ask a librarian if you are having difficulty finding credible research sources for your topic.

## BE ORGANIZED

Critical thinking is organized thinking. When you encounter difficulties in the process of building a speech, view them as challenges to be overcome rather than obstacles to be avoided. Think of logical strategies for attacking the problems your speech creates. Define and understand the problem, seek solutions to the challenge, and then select a clear plan of action. Know your audience. If you discover that your audience disagrees with your controversial persuasive topic, find creative methods of appealing to their interests and needs. If you can't find material on your topic in the library, develop alternative resources by asking individuals, experts, or other institutions for information. If you have difficulty presenting the speech in front of an audience, analyze your problems and make changes by being more prepared, engaging in additional speech rehearsal, or requesting extra feedback from your class and instructor. Identify problems, develop strategies, and be systematic in your approach to the speech process.

# VIEW IDEAS FROM DIFFERENT PERSPECTIVES

When we think critically, we learn from our own experiences, as well as the experiences of others. As an informed speaker, remember that your point of view is not the only perspective on an issue. Be open to other ideas, and be willing to learn from different viewpoints. If you find that the facts do not support your idea, don't hang onto that idea, stubbornly refusing to give in. One student enjoyed rap artist Tupac Shakur and had a collection of his CDs and videos. For his informative speech, the student wanted to describe Tupac's life and violent death and play samples of his rap music for the audience—older part-time students with families. The instructor suggested that he more carefully consider his choice of topic in relation to his audience. Feeling insulted, the student rigidly insisted that he could make the topic interesting to anyone. Unfortunately, the student learned the hard way. After listening to the music and hearing little evidence, listeners repeated the earlier suggestions of the instructor.

In a speaking situation, the composition of the audience requires that a speaker listen carefully to others. A speaker making a presentation to an audience of different races, religions, genders, or ages needs to demonstrate sensitivity and skill in responding to diverse perspectives and opinions. One student presented an informative speech about the dangers of skin cancer. The speaker had researched the disease and had developed some helpful information and advice for many of her listeners. Difficulties occurred, however, when the speaker suggested that skin cancer causes problems for "people with light skin." Members of the audience, which included Asians, Middle Easterners, and African Americans, did not agree with the speaker's assumption and reported contrasting information once the speech

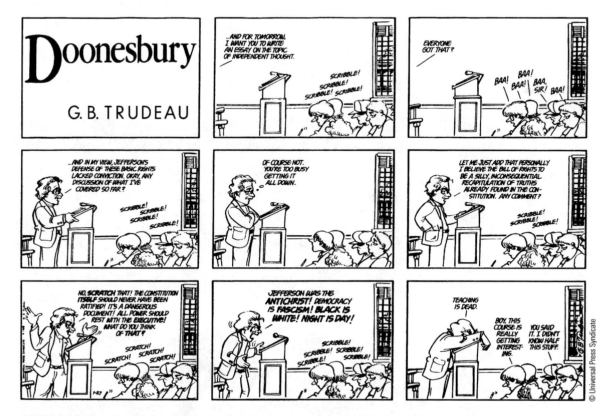

FIGURE 8.1  How does this cartoon demonstrate the importance of critical thinking when listening to a speech? What kind of listening should the audience be doing in this situation? (See Chapter 4.)

*Source:* DOONESBURY copyright 1988 G. B. Trudeau. Reprinted with permission of Universal Press Syndicate. All rights reserved.

was finished. Audience members argued that facts and experience suggest that almost everyone is susceptible to skin cancer regardless of color and that individuals must take different precautions depending upon skin pigmentation. Listeners concluded that the speaker needed to do further research and more extensive analysis of her audience and should discard the erroneous information she presented. Had this speaker been able to view her topic from her listeners' perspectives, she would have understood the need for more analysis and could have eliminated the false assumption that troubled her audience. A sign of maturity is profiting from the experiences of others and growing as a result of different perceptions.

## THINK FOR YOURSELF

Thinking critically means coming to your own conclusions after weighing the evidence. It does not mean believing everything that is handed to you. It is easy for us to point accusing fingers at those Germans who blindly accepted government propaganda and helped to perpetuate state-sponsored crimes in World War II. But ask yourself how many times you have accepted and believed someone else's opinion without question as the Doonesbury cartoon humorously demonstrates in Figure 8.1. For instance, imagine that you are on your way to class the first day of the new term, and a friend sees you going into the lecture hall. She stops you at the door and insists, "Don't take that class because the professor never gives A's or B's." Do you immediately drop the class, do you ignore the comment, or do you proceed with extreme caution? This situation calls for critical thinking. Perhaps your friend is a chronic alarmist or is having difficulty in some of her courses. Possibly your fellow student had some kind of conflict with the instructor and holds a biased viewpoint about the situation. It is also possible that your friend is entirely credible and is giving you helpful advice. Whatever the case, the situation probably calls for more investigation and more information before you make a decision.[6]

Although it is necessary to ask for help, it is equally important to arrive at your own decisions. Don't let advertisers, salespeople, or biased parties tell you what to think by quoting ambiguous "facts" or subjective opinions. Examine the evidence yourself, and arrive at a sound, verifiable conclusion.

## summary »

Sources should be credible and reliable; they may be primary or secondary.

Library sources for locating information are found in the catalog, the online databases, and the World Wide Web. Library reference sources are biographical collections, bibliographies, directories, and encyclopedias, as well as almanacs, collections of quotations, books, and periodical articles.[7] Nonliterary sources are interviews with experts and research from large institutions or specialized organizations. An accurate system of note taking should be used to collect research materials, and a credible system of source citation should be used in the delivery of a speech.

Clearly understand what plagiarism is, and avoid it at all costs. The consequences can be severe.

When interviewing experts, be prepared, conduct the interview skillfully, and take notes.

Learn how to create a bibliography by consulting your institution's style guide or by asking your speech instructor which style is preferred.

As you build your speech, think critically about speech research and construction by testing information, being organized, listening to different perspectives, and thinking for yourself.

## SKILL BUILDERS»

1. Select a topic for an informative speech using two different databases in your library. Find four periodical articles that could support your speech and discuss the credibility of each article and periodical. List the databases you used to find these resources. Using these periodicals, write a bibliography according to the form recommended by your instructor.
2. In the introductory example to this chapter, Alicia used several ineffective means to collect information. What would you suggest to improve her search? Are there any credible primary sources available to support the topic of Mother Teresa? What are they?

## BUILDING A SPEECH ONLINE »

Now that you've read Chapter 8, use your online Resource Center for Building a Speech for quick access to the electronic study resources that accompany this text. You can access your Resource Center at **http://academic.cengage.com/login**, using the access code that came with your book or that you bought online at **http://www .iChapters.com**. Your Resource Center gives you access to Interactive Video Activities, the book's companion website, Speech Builder Express 3.0, InfoTrac College Edition, and study aids, including a digital glossary and review quizzes.

# chapter 9

# CHOOSING SUPPORTING MATERIALS

## chapter objectives »

After reading and studying this chapter, you should be able to

1. Identify the principal types of supporting materials

2. Describe how to use each type of supporting material effectively in a speech

Charles Francis is president of Idea Bank, an online research service that is used by many professional speakers. In a speech titled "How to Stop Boring Your Audience to Death," presented to the New York Chapter of the International Association of Business Communicators, Francis tells how a speaker can hold the interest of an audience.

> I know you all grapple daily with that implacable foe—audience boredom. . . . It isn't that people aren't interested. It's just that, from the time we open our eyes in the morning to when we go to bed at night, all of us are assailed by messages of every kind and description. . . . I read recently that no less than 70 percent of what one hears is forgotten an hour after hearing it. There is a catchy acronym for this lack of memorability. It's called MYGLO for "My Eyes Glaze Over," a physical phenomenon that takes over the minute you lose the audience's attention. . . .
>
> There are three magic talismans that can greatly increase your ability to hold people's attention. They are known to every professional writer and speaker, but even professionals don't call on their occult powers as often as they should. These three powerful Genies are, simply: quotations, anecdotes, and humor.[1]

Quotations, anecdotes, and humor are among the various types of supporting materials we explore in this

> " *A quotation in a speech, article, or book is like a rifle in the hands of an infantryman. It speaks with authority.* "
>
> —Brendan Francis

final chapter on preparing the speech foundation. We include examples from student and professional speakers and consider suggestions that you can apply to your own presentations. We want you to use supporting materials accurately and appropriately to build strong connections with your audience.

key terms »

ANECDOTE
CASE STUDY
COMPARISONS
CONTRASTS
EXAMPLE
HUMOR
HYPOTHETICAL
    EXAMPLE
ILLUSTRATION
NARRATIVE
OBSERVATION
PERSONAL
    EXPERIENCE
POLLS
QUOTATION
ROLE-PLAYING
STATISTICS
SURVEYS
TESTIMONY

## making the appropriate selection

When you research a speech, you must look for supporting materials. If you are talking about heart disease, a quotation from a prominent heart surgeon such as Dr. Mehmet Oz builds credibility. If you are asking listeners to favor bicycle helmet laws, you would use statistics from the Bicycle Helmet Safety Institute to show that wearing helmets decreases fatalities. If you are educating the audience about lupus disease, a disturbing story of a child's chronic illness obtained from an interview with a mother would paint a vivid picture. Whether your speech is informative or persuasive, you need information and credible examples to support your topic.

When you use supporting materials, it is advisable to mention the source for your information. Although you certainly don't need to pepper your speech with "according to's," you do need to make it clear to your audience that your topic is based upon concrete evidence. If you use several facts or examples from the same source, you can make one reference that does not interfere with the flow of the speech. If you say, "Some of my information today is taken from an article I read in a February 2009 issue of *Newsweek*," you have shown your audience that your evidence is grounded in credible research.

Some of the most authoritative supporting materials are statistics, polls, and surveys; examples, stories, illustrations, and case studies; quotations and testimonies; and comparisons and contrasts. A speaker can use these materials to build a credible case for a persuasive speech or to provide verifiable support in an informative presentation.

Less verifiable, yet stimulating, forms of support are personal experience and observation, humor, anecdotes, and role-playing. Speakers use these materials to enliven speeches and to maintain audience interest and attention. It is often difficult to validate experiences, humor, or skits with sources. But a speaker can enhance a speech if these forms of support are based upon realistic circumstances and are combined with more authoritative statistics, testimony, or examples.

In the following sections, we will examine each type of supporting material and describe its potential use in a speech.

## statistics, polls, and surveys

One way to support a topic is by using statistical data. **Statistics** are a collection of facts in numerical form, **polls** are samplings of opinion on selected issues, and **surveys** are studies that draw conclusions from research.

Statistics can provide data about population, income, death, crime, and birth. You can determine the increase in the number of deaths due to heart disease by looking at statistics over a 15-year period. If you need to know how many people favor or oppose a specific political candidate, you can consult the Gallup Opinion Poll or the CBS/*New York Times* Poll. If you need to know how student performance compares in different racial or economic groups, you can investigate the conclusions provided in a specific study.

## USING STATISTICS

You must be careful when deciding to use statistics, polls, or surveys as your supporting evidence. If you use too many complicated numbers, you'll bore your audience. Just stating that the federal budget for 2007 was approximately $2,730,192,712,001.29 is a mouthful. The audience will probably forget most of it by the time they hear the twenty-nine cents!

It is often advisable to round off your statistics to the nearest whole number so the audience can grasp the overall concept. Be sure that you draw conclusions from the data and relate the conclusion to your point. It is helpful to relate complicated statistics to a simpler concept. Although few people could comprehend the staggering budget figure just mentioned, anyone could understand the number if it were compared to thousand-dollar bills stacked several miles high. If you need to be more precise with statistics, you can develop a PowerPoint visual aid or chart to display the data so that the audience can draw conclusions at a glance.

When you cite statistics, polls, or surveys, it establishes credibility to state who conducted the research as well as when and where the research was done. When presenting a survey, you might want to mention the purpose of the research in addition to the conclusions of the study.

In an April 2008 hearing before the House Select Committee on Energy Independence, oil company executives were questioned about the constant increase in the price of oil and the soaring gas prices at the pump. Shell Oil Company President John Hofmeister told committee members that the increase was partly due to the accelerated global demand in recent years and he used these startling statistics to describe American's dependence on oil:

> The United States has 5 percent of the world's population but uses nearly 25 percent of the world's oil. Americans use 10,000 gallons of oil—enough to fill a backyard swimming pool—every second of every day. Consumers—and that means all of us—must think more about our own energy footprints: when and how we drive, what we buy, how we work, and the kind of world we want to create for coming generations.[2]

Hofmeister knew that raw data is not interesting unless the audience can relate to the numbers easily. The speaker made the statistics come alive by stating a familiar example such as a swimming pool and using small numbers that his listeners could quickly understand.

In a speech about recycling materials, David Zebraski used a survey to demonstrate the problem of wastefulness:

> Dr. William L. Rathje, an anthropologist at the University of Arizona, conducted a long-term study of the residents of Tucson. In research funded by the Environmental Protection Agency and the National Science Foundation, Dr. Rathje and his students actually collected samples of garbage from different economic neighborhoods in the city. He found that, overall, Tucson's residents throw away 15 percent of their food, wasting $11 to $13 million per year. He also discovered that middle-income people throw away more food, tools, and appliances than do low- or high-income people. This study found that middle-class people—individuals like you and me—are the most wasteful.[3]

In addition to stating the findings of the study, the speaker mentions the name of the researcher, the place where the study was conducted, two funding agencies, and even the process used for research. The study results credibly support the speaker's point about the average person's wastefulness.

# examples, illustrations, case studies, and narratives

When conducting research, you should look for examples, illustrations, case studies, or narratives to support your topic. An **example** is a brief factual instance that demonstrates a point; a **hypothetical example** is a fictitious situation that has a realistic application; an **illustration** is a long example that clarifies and amplifies an idea; a **case study** is an in-depth account of a situation or a set of circumstances; and a **narrative** is an experience or story told by the speaker.

A brief example or case can often demonstrate a point more dramatically than a long description of facts. People love a good story, and they appreciate research that stimulates curiosity. By combining a balance of theoretical facts with illustrations and examples, you keep your audience involved.

## USING EXAMPLES

In a speech on drunk driving, a speaker might use one or two brief examples combined with a minute-long personal narrative about driving while intoxicated. In a 5- to 7-minute speech, two brief instances and one long illustration would probably be sufficient. A speaker could also cite many brief examples of drunk driving. This type of rapid-fire approach is effective in communicating a great deal of information in a short time.

You build credibility in your speech if you cite references. Let your audience know if the narrative is from your own knowledge and experience or from someone else's. State your sources for case studies, examples, and illustrations. Use a variety of sources, and use a variety of instances. Don't base your speech on one personal narrative or on one brief example. Provide examples and cases that develop your topic in depth.

In the following speech, Stanley Eitzen, professor emeritus at Colorado State University's sociology department, cites a series of brief examples to support his point:

> Many popular sports encourage player aggression. These sports demand body checking, blocking, and tackling. But the culture of these sports sometimes goes beyond what is needed. Players are taught to deliver a blow to the opponent, not just to block or tackle him.
>
> Coaches often reward athletes for extra hard hits. In this regard, let me cite several examples from a few years ago:
>
> - At the University of Florida a football player received a "dead roach" decal for his helmet when he hit an opponent so hard that he lay prone with his legs and arms up in the air.
> - Similarly, University of Miami football players were awarded a "slobber knocker" decal for their helmets if they hit an opposing player so hard that it knocked the slobber out of his mouth.
> - The Denver Broncos coaching staff, similar to other NFL teams yet contrary to league rules, gave monetary awards each week to the players who hit their opponents the hardest.[4]

This rapid-fire technique builds a strong argument, bombarding the audience with specific instances to show that many American sports teams reinforce and support the use of physical violence.

The following illustration is an example of the use of a hypothetical situation. It is a powerful tool to use in a speech because it briefly allows listeners to experience blindness.

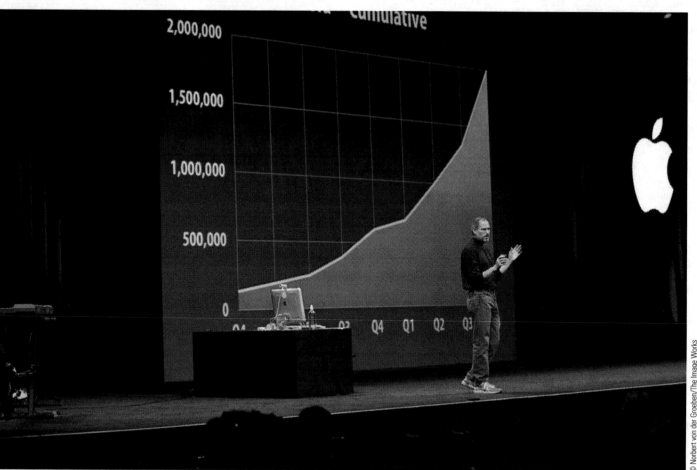

A speaker provides concrete support for ideas and concepts by using examples, statistics, quotations, and visual aids.

*I'd like you all to close your eyes for a minute. Imagine that it is early morning. The alarm rings, but you must feel for it to turn it off. You get up and search for your clothes. You go downstairs to make breakfast, but you touch the food to find out what there is to eat. After breakfast, you carefully go to the door, step outside, and listen for the sound of oncoming traffic. Hearing none, you gingerly cross the street to the bus stop on the other side. You wait for the sound of the creaking brakes to stop in front of you. When the doors squeak open, you carefully make your way up the steps. You give what you hope is the correct change to the bus driver. You then feel for an empty seat. You've made it one more day! This is what it feels like to be blind. And that's what we're talking about here—a real problem that happens to human beings just like you and me. You can open your eyes now.*[5]

This illustration is more effective than simply describing the difficulties of blindness because the speaker simulates the experience by cutting off the visual channel. The speaker provides clear directions to audience members as to when they are to close or open their eyes. The "you" approach has effectively placed listeners in the sightless world of the blind: The speaker has successfully communicated his point through the use of a hypothetical illustration.

The next illustration comes from the real-life experience of the speaker's family:

*Three months ago, I went to my cousin's wedding, which lasted an entire weekend—Friday through Sunday. You'd be surprised though—I don't know where the time went. In India, a wedding is usually a two-day occasion, and everyone in the bride and groom's family plays a role in the wedding ceremony. The ceremony begins with the bride's and groom's parents in prayer. Heinrick Zimmer, in the book* Philosophies of India, *explains how the priest generally begins with an explanation of the union of two families with the groom present. The priest then calls to the bride, giving her one last chance to run away. Next the bride is given away by her uncle. The ceremony continues as the bride and groom walk around a fire in seven circles. During the first six turns, the groom is in the lead and the priest explains the significance: The wife will follow her husband in all the trials they go through in life, she will respect his decisions, and she will follow whatever he decides to do with the family. Then in the last turn, the bride leads, and undoes almost everything that was said during the first six circles. The groom vows to respect his wife, to love and cherish her, and always to include her as an equal in this partnership.[6]*

Neha Badshah used an illustration to describe a portion of the wedding ceremony in her native India. The personal experience combined with a credible reference provided the audience with an interesting portrait of a different culture.

In the next example, Andrea Hoguet selected a case study from a local newspaper to support a persuasive speech:

*It is one thing for children to have learned aggressive behavior at a young age, but it is quite another for a parent or a relative to contribute to this aggressive behavior. I read about a case in the November 13th issue of our local* Carroll County Times *newspaper. Mrs. Luella Wilson, a 91-year-old woman of Bennington, Vermont, was sued for $950,000. Here's what happened. Mrs. Wilson gave her nephew a large sum of money to buy a new car for his 18th birthday, knowing that he had a drug problem and that he did not even possess a license. After drinking heavily and smoking marijuana one evening, the nephew drove the car off a bridge. The passenger riding with him was paralyzed and finally had to have his leg amputated. The passenger sued Mrs. Wilson for negligence. She apparently knew about her nephew's problem with drugs, yet she still gave him $6,300 for a car. Should she be liable? Yes, she should! And apparently the jury agreed and awarded the victim almost $1 million in damages. The case is currently under appeal.[7]*

Andrea used this case to support the persuasive proposition that parents and guardians should be held accountable for the criminal actions of their children. The topic was controversial, and some listeners disagreed with the speaker's viewpoint. But Andrea strengthened the evidence by describing the details of the case and by citing a credible source. The speaker used gestures, vocal inflections, and emphasis to stress her conclusion to the case: "Should she be liable? Yes, she should!"

The following narrative was related by Richard D. Lamm, former governor of Colorado:

*Let me begin with a metaphor. The United States fleet was on the high seas. All of a sudden a blip appeared on the radar screen. "Tell that ship to change its course fifteen degrees!" said the Admiral. The radio man did, and the word came back on the radio, "YOU change YOUR course fifteen degrees." "Tell that ship that we're the United States Navy and to change its course fifteen degrees," said the Admiral. The radio man did and the word came back again, "YOU change YOUR course fifteen degrees." This time the Admiral himself got on the radio and said, "I am an Admiral in the United States Navy. Change your course fifteen degrees." The word came back over the radio, "You change your course fifteen degrees. I am a lighthouse!" We often expect the world to adjust to our course, but alas, we find we must adjust to the realities around us. I would go further—I believe it is the duty and the obligation of each generation to perceive the realities of their times.[8]*

This kind of story makes the audience sit back, relax, and listen. The narrative is interesting and has a humorous punch line. But Governor Lamm draws a conclusion from the story and relates it to his overall theme: the need to change course. If you choose to relate a narrative such as this one, you must be certain to deliver the story smoothly so that the details and punch line retain their vigor.

## quotations and testimonies from authorities

You can also build credibility by using quotations and testimonies from experts or authorities. A **quotation** is the exact restatement of a person's words, and a **testimony** is a statement or endorsement given by an expert or an individual with a logical connection to the topic. Quotations can be used to evoke emotion, synthesize feelings, and establish the authenticity of ideas. In his inaugural address, President Obama quoted the words of George Washington, who rallied Americans during the darkest hours of the Revolutionary War. Baseball announcers are fond of quoting baseball heroes in a tense situation. During a tie game in the bottom of the ninth inning, you might hear the announcer say, "Yogi Berra once said, 'It ain't over 'til it's over.' That sure applies here." If, for example, you are giving an informative speech on brain surgery in newborns, a brief quotation from Dr. Benjamin Carson, a pioneer physician in pediatric neurosurgery, could provide you with sufficient expert testimony.

### USING QUOTATIONS AND TESTIMONIES

You need to be careful not to use too many quotes, or you may sound like a name-dropper. Select quotations with significance to your topic, and use them where they will have maximum emphasis. Often, a brief quote is more effective than a long, involved one that has to be unraveled with a lengthy explanation.

When using testimonies, be sure that the individuals you cite are qualified through experience or expertise to comment or represent your topic. Though Tiger Woods is a golfing superstar, he is not professionally qualified to tell you which aspirin to take or which breakfast cereal has more vitamins and nutrients. You should briefly tell the audience what qualifies the expert you have chosen to provide testimony on your topic.

When you use a quotation from someone who is not widely known, it is important to identify that person for your audience. If you are using that individual's exact words, it is a good idea to use the words *quote* and *end quote* before and after the quoted material. A paraphrase is a general summary of the material in your own words. In that case, you would not use quotes. Be certain your quotation or paraphrase is accurate. If you use only a portion of the quotation, don't change the author's meaning or intention by taking it out of context.

In this persuasive speech about buying American products, Kathy Birckhead paraphrased two experts to support her topic:

> *Foreign imports are taking over a larger share in almost all markets. What is the effect on our economy? I interviewed Eddie Bartee, vice-president of the United Steelworkers of America, Local 2609, who told me that imported steel has virtually crippled the steel industry. I also spoke with Ted Baldwin, the public relations representative for Bethlehem Steel at Sparrows Point, who told me that in 1970 Bethlehem Steel employed 26,500 people. At the present time they employ only 9,000.*[9]

Because her listeners were unfamiliar with Eddie Bartee and Ted Baldwin, the speaker supplied the necessary information to build credibility. If you provide a brief phrase identifying your authority, you can quickly establish reliability.

In the following example, the quotations from the "amazing young man" are meant to arouse emotional feelings and inspire listeners.

*When you talk about winners, consider Dustin Carter, who is an amazing young man. He was a perfectly normal kid until the age of 5 when he developed a rare blood disease that required amputating both his arms and legs. From that point on, his life seemed to spiral downhill. "I was a trouble maker. I got bad grades, didn't care, didn't turn in my work, didn't do much." Then something unbelievable happened in the eighth grade: Dustin got interested in wrestling. In his first match, he says, "I got beat pretty bad." In his high school freshman year he won only 5 matches and lost 15. But Dustin was determined and incredibly, he started to succeed. "After that first win," he said, "I loved it. I was out to win when I started wrestling. I'm a pretty determined person. I'll sit at something and sit at it for hours until I get it." He got it all right. By his senior year, this 18-year-old paraplegic had 41 wins and only 4 losses. He sums it up by saying: "I didn't know if I'd make it out there. I never dreamed I'd be 41 and 4 in my senior year. But I ended up making it myself. I'm a winner—and winners like to win."[10]*

Notice that the speaker sets the stage by briefly describing the pertinent details of the story; then he used Dustin's own words to stir feelings of admiration and pride within listeners.

## comparisons and contrasts

There will be times in your speeches when you will need to show similarities or differences between two or more things. **Comparisons** point out similarities in situations or events, and **contrasts** show differences.

Suppose you were giving a persuasive speech on the enforcement of drunk-driving laws. You could contrast the enforcement of drunk-driving laws in the United States with the enforcement of such laws in Scandinavian countries. In your research, you would probably find that American and Scandinavian laws are very similar, although they are applied in very different ways by the two countries.

If you were persuading listeners to legalize gambling in your state, you could contrast the higher revenues in gambling states with lower revenues from non-gambling states. On the other hand, if you wanted to persuade the audience not to legalize gambling, you could focus on contrasting crime rates if they were higher in gambling states.

## USING COMPARISONS AND CONTRASTS

Using comparisons and contrasts can be tricky. You must be careful that what you are comparing or contrasting has similar principles or characteristics. Imagine that a speaker tried to contrast gun control in the United States with gun control in England by making the following statement:

*The murder rate in the United States is five times greater than the murder rate in England. The reason for this is that England has a strict gun control law and we have a very weak one.*

Although we will examine logical reasoning more extensively in Chapter 16, it is necessary to point out here that the information provided in this contrast is faulty and misleading in several areas. The United States does have a gun control law known as the Brady Law. Since the law went into effect in 1994, it has been effective in stopping more than 1.3 million felons from purchasing firearms from federally licensed firearm dealers. But the Brady Law does not apply to private or unlicensed sellers, who are still able to sell guns without conducting background checks.[11] Also, the statement does not account for the numerous cities and states that have some form of gun control. It is true that in the United States the murder rate is about 10 for every 100,000, and in England the rate is 2.5 murders per 100,000.[12] However, the lower rate of murder in England could be due to other factors besides gun control. England has a homogeneous population with a lengthy common history. The British operate under different cultural rules than do Americans. British police do not wear guns, and it is rare for British police to be murdered in the line of duty. There appears to be an unwritten "agreement" between British criminals and British police that neither side will use violence when conducting "business."

In this excerpt, the speaker uses contrast to highlight the differences between Americans and Russians:

> I'd like to tell you about some of the specific differences between the American and Russian people. The statistics and examples are from Almanac of the American People, a Russian newspaper, which, translated, is entitled Arguments and Facts, and my own personal experience.
>
> In America there were 6.2 strict vegetarians [for every hundred people] in 1989. This is a practice that would be just unbelievable to the Russian people. In Russia, we eat many internal organs of a cow or pig such as the tongue, tail, and brains. But according to the Almanac, Americans hate this type of food. In Russia, vodka is very popular and Russians drink on every occasion. But in America, only 19 percent of men older than 40 prefer vodka. Seventy percent of the American people get drunk once a year but in Russia, 70 percent of the people get drunk every day. There are also differences in exercise habits. Sixty-nine percent of Americans exercise, and 50 percent enjoy walking for pleasure. Russians don't walk for pleasure—they just walk to buy things from shops. Russian people tend to be ashamed of exercise. They think bicycling, diving, and swimming are for children. You'll never see an elderly woman in tight pants on a bicycle riding through town. In my Moscow neighborhood, there was only one guy who went jogging every morning, and we all thought he was crazy![13]

Olga Norko was a recent immigrant from Russia to the United States. She combined personal experience with statistics and examples to create a fascinating series of contrasts for her classroom audience. By identifying her sources at the beginning of the contrasting examples, the speaker was able to strengthen her credibility with the audience.

In the next example, the speaker compares and contrasts horrific images with hopeful symbols:

> Nothing so dramatizes living between two ages as does the image of the fireball engulfing the World Trade Center, an image burned into the world's psyche September 11th. . . . The image of the imploding World Trade Center must be seen as part of a panorama of images for its full significance to best be understood. The image, for instance, of death camps and crematoriums in central Europe. The image of a mushroom cloud rising over the Pacific. Of Neil Armstrong stepping onto the moon. Of Louise Brown, the first human to be conceived outside

*of the human body. Of a man standing near the summit of Mt. Everest talking on his cell phone to his wife in Australia. Of the first human embryo to be cloned. Of a computer performing billions of calculations that could not have been performed by all the mathematicians who ever lived, even in their combined lifetimes. These are some of the images, representing both human greatness and depravity, that mark the end of one age and the approach of a new time in human experience.*[14]

Willam Van Dusen Wishard, president of World Trends Research, compared the sickening site of the crumbling World Trade Center towers to other horrifying images representing human depravity. He then contrasted these appalling examples with illustrations signifying hope and "human greatness."

## personal experience and observation

Personal experience and observation can help to make your speech interesting. If you are giving a speech demonstrating how a volcano is formed, you create interest if you have an experience to relate. If you are informing your audience about poverty, you make your topic personal if you describe some of the impoverished conditions you have observed. **Personal experience** is direct, firsthand knowledge of a situation. **Observation** is a judgment based upon what an individual has seen.

## USING EXPERIENCE AND OBSERVATION

Be sure that the experience you use is appropriate to your topic. Don't use too many personal experiences, and don't base an entire speech on one elongated experience. Sometimes speakers with an abundance of personal experiences don't use enough research to support their topics, hoping their observations and experiences will make up for their lack of hard evidence.

Don't try to improvise a speech by stringing together a multitude of observations. One effective personal experience combined with some factual research can make the topic interesting and give you authority on your issue.

*What are the long-range consequences? Denying same-sex couples their civil unions leaves our country vulnerable to government-sanctioned discrimination. And where will it stop? Well, hopefully with you.*

*Since it's 2005, chances are that the majority of you know someone who is gay, lesbian, or even bisexual. And if you didn't before this semester, you do now: Me. But answer me this: If murderers and rapists can get married any day of the week in this country, why am I, a decent, law-abiding, citizen denied the right to marry, or even enter into a civil union with the man I love? The answer is, there is no answer. It's wrong. It's unconstitutional, and it needs to change.*[15]

Robert Kammerzell delivered this effective persuasive speech to actuate listeners to support same-sex civil unions. Even though not all members of the audience agreed with him on this controversial topic, they listened intently to the courageous personal example that Robert used to influence their thinking.

Pat Sajak used his experience as host of the TV show *Wheel of Fortune* to relate the following observation to listeners at Hillsdale College:

*And I can tell you, based on my day-to-day work as a television host, this country needs all the educated citizens it can find. I am frequently appalled when a player struggles with a puzzle, not because he's nervous, nor because it's particularly difficult, but because he has absolutely no clue as to what the puzzle means. For example, we once had a puzzle, which was "Former President John F. Kennedy." Most of the letters were filled in . . . a well-informed chipmunk could have solved it. Yet, our player was stumped. When we went to commercial, this young, seemingly bright, man complained that he couldn't have known it, because, as he said, "That was before my time." It is not an uncommon complaint by players on our show. That's why "The Ural Mountains" was once solved as " The Urak Mountains" and "Amarillo, Texas" became "Armadillo, Texas."*[16]

Sajak's experiences helped him remind his college audience of the great value of an education and describe the "disconnect between Hollywood and America."

## humor and anecdotes

**Humor** is the use of lighthearted, entertaining material in a speech to generate a reaction from the audience. An **anecdote** is a brief, humorous story used to demonstrate a point. Humor can be very effective in a speech. Telling a joke or a humorous anecdote can create a positive climate in a speaking situation. If your audience smiles and nods at your wit, you have them in a receptive mood. A humorous anecdote can frequently make a point more successfully than can a long, theoretical statement.

### USING HUMOR AND ANECDOTES

Employing humor has some risks. There is always the possibility that the joke you tell will not get the response you might have expected. When practicing your speech, think about being prepared for a variety of audience reactions. If listeners fail to laugh at your humor or groan at your attempts, you can joke about their response, relate safer humor that has worked previously, or acknowledge the response and move on. Don't let negative audience reactions destroy your confidence. You can still overcome momentary difficulties if you maintain your composure and keep to your stated objective. Your audience might also respond by breaking up into laughter. Don't let a positive response catch you off-guard. Pause after the joke or story and wait for your listeners to enjoy the moment. Don't try to resume the speech until the laughter subsides.

It is best to use humor that can be related to your topic. Using irrelevant jokes simply to gain attention can often disappoint and even anger an audience. If you've ever inquired about a brand-new car for $14,999 described in a newspaper ad, remember how you felt when you discovered that the car was a stripped-down model without tires! Audiences also don't appreciate the bait-and-switch tactic.

Despite the risks, don't be afraid to use humor. If you're good at humor, use it to your advantage and develop it as a part of your style. Even if you do not feel comfortable with humor, try a few anecdotes. You might surprise yourself. A speech is not a stand-up comic routine, but you can look for ways to use humor appropriately.

Retired General Norman Schwarzkopf used humor effectively in this commencement address, delivered at the University of Richmond:

*Now, first of all for those of you who don't recognize me, I am the General Schwarzkopf. I said that because for some reason people expect me to be wearing camouflage. If I am not wearing camouflage, I'm not General Schwarzkopf. It's amazing the perceptions people have about you.*

*I work out every other day as you can tell from this magnificent body that stands before you, and at the end of my workout I always go into the steam bath. True story—last summer I walked into the steam bath. I was not wearing camouflage at the time, and there was a man in there, and he turned and looked at me and said, "Did anybody ever tell you that from a distance you look exactly like General Schwarzkopf?" And I thought I'd play along, and I said, "Yes, I hear that a lot." He said, "Yes, it's only when you get up close you realize you're not General Schwarzkopf." I never told him—he does not know to this day.* [17]

A large, imposing figure who was almost legendary for his success in leading allied troops in the first Iraq war, known as Operation Desert Storm, General Schwarzkopf was willing to poke good-natured fun at himself, making him more human to members of his audience.

In the following excerpt from another graduation speech, *Doonesbury* cartoonist Garry Trudeau used an anecdote to his advantage:

*I first learned about pertinent questions from my father, a retired physician . . . [whose] own practical experience frequently contradicted his worthiest intentions. A man once turned up in my father's office complaining of an ulcer. My father asked the pertinent question. Was there some undue stress, he inquired, that might be causing the man to digest his stomach? The patient, who was married . . . . allowed that he had a girlfriend in Syracuse, and that twice a week he'd been driving an old pick-up down to see her. Since the pick-up frequently broke down, he was often late in getting home, and he had to devise fabulous stories to tell his wife. My father, compassionately but sternly, told the man he had to make a hard decision about his personal priorities if he was ever to get well. The patient nodded and went away, and six months later came back completely cured, a new man. My father congratulated him and then delicately inquired if he'd made some change in his life. The man replied, "Yup. Got me a new pick-up."* [18]

Trudeau presents his humor effectively and smoothly, logically developing the details of the story. The last sentence of the anecdote served as the punch line to stimulate a response from the audience. Trudeau used this anecdote to illustrate the point that an "unexpected or inconvenient truth is often the price of honest inquiry." [19]

## role-playing

**Role-playing** is a technique that uses an individual to act out a brief skit, assume a character, or simulate a conflict. Role-playing can be a creative way of motivating listeners to become more personally involved with a speaker's topic. A skit portraying the effect of divorce on a young child might have more impact on an audience than a verbal description would. One student, playing the role of a waiter in a restaurant, used two "customers" from the audience to demonstrate the proper and improper methods of taking orders and serving food.

## USING ROLE-PLAYING TECHNIQUES

Speakers can use skits they have researched, or they can create their own dramas. If the situation is taken from one of your sources, give the author proper recognition. If you write a brief dramatic piece, be sure that the skit is true to life and based on factual information. It is helpful if the situation is brief and to the point. Long, drawn-out dramas can bore listeners with unnecessary material and detract from the speech. If you need volunteers, rehearse with them in advance, making sure that they are familiar with the script and know how to respond appropriately in the roles. Remember that role-playing is one of the less factual ways of supporting ideas; it should not be used as a substitute for cases, statistics, or verifiable sources. Role-playing is most effective when combined with other types of supporting materials.

Speaker Gina Alexander created a skit to demonstrate the proper and improper techniques of interviewing for a job. The speaker portrayed the applicant while a member of the audience played the role of the interviewer.

**Interviewer:** Can you tell me why you're leaving your present employer?
**Applicant:** Well, it's like, I'm so bored there, ya know? It's like I hate to go to work there every day—I can't stand it. Ya ever felt like that?
**Interviewer:** Is it the work itself, or is it your environment?
**Applicant:** Yeeeah, both I guess, kinda, ya know?

*What can I say? You do that, and you've probably lost the job right there. No matter what college you've gone to or what fancy degree you have, it's not showing. There's a better way to display the exact same message.*

**Interviewer:** Can you tell me why you're leaving your present employer?
**Applicant:** Well, I'm considering leaving my present employer to seek new opportunities that they don't offer.
**Interviewer:** Is it the work itself, or is it your environment?
**Applicant:** Actually, it's a combination of both factors that are contributing to my desire to leave.

*In the first example, I was sprawling all over the chair, I didn't appear interested, and it looked as if I wasn't paying attention. I used street jargon, and it appeared as if I had few language skills. Notice that I was running my fingers through my hair. This is an action that is very distracting. In some jobs, such as a food-service position, picking your face or touching your hair could lose you the job.*

*In the second situation, I said the exact same thing, but I displayed some intelligence. My posture was effective. I didn't sit like a soldier, but I sat up straight, appearing as an interested, active communicator who is open to new ideas. My vocabulary was precise, thoughtful, and I spoke in complete sentences. While I didn't stare, I maintained eye contact with my prospective employer.*[20]

The skit was successful because the speaker conducted several rehearsals prior to the classroom presentation. Although the skit was entertaining and humorous, it successfully demonstrated the speaker's point that language, organization, and poise make a powerful persuasive impression on an interviewer.

## SAMPLE SPEECH: the flag raisings on Iwo Jima

*The majority of Peter Hollands' family served in the Marines and as a recruit himself, Peter was interested in continuing his family's tradition. He was also interested in military history, especially the events surrounding the flag raising at Iwo Jima in World War II. As he delivered this speech to his classmates, he used many types of supporting materials to verify his ideas and interest his listeners.*[21]

SLIDE 1

SLIDE 2

SLIDE 3

SLIDE 4

## INFORMATIVE DESCRIPTIVE SPEECH
*Peter Hollands*

1. (slide 1) At some point in time, you've probably all seen this photograph whether it be in a history book, on television, or even in monument form. This is the flag raising at Iwo Jima, and it has become a symbol as patriotic as the Statue of Liberty. (slide 2) Today I'm going to inform you of the Iwo Jima flag raisings by elaborating on the battle, the flag raisings, and the legacy.

   1. The speaker creates interest and attention with the PowerPoint slide.

   Peter states his three-point thesis statement.

2. First let me talk about the battle. (slide 3) After Pearl Harbor, the United States began to attack Japan. According to a website created by John H. Bradley, a grandson of one of the flag raisers, Iwo Jima was a key Japanese air strip in the Southern Pacific and it was also a volcanic island. When the U.S. arrived at Iwo Jima they brought with them a force of 110,000 Marines and 880 Naval ships. The Japanese only had a force of 22,000 but they had dug in and were heavily fortified. The United States focused their attack on the southern part of the island at Mt. Suribachi. For thirty-five days a heavy battle waged and at the end of the battle 6,825 Americans were

   2. For his narrative and statistical information about the battle, the speaker cites a credible website created by the grandson of one of the flag raisers.

   He quotes the famous Navy admiral who honored the men.

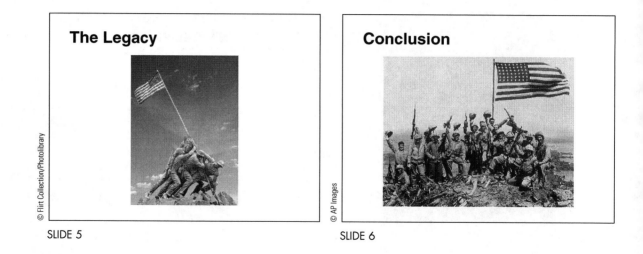

**The Legacy**

SLIDE 5

**Conclusion**

SLIDE 6

killed in action and nearly 20,000 were wounded. Of the 22,000 Japanese, virtually all of them passed. At the end of the battle, Navy Admiral Chester W. Nimitz was quoted as saying, "Among the men who fought at Iwo Jima, uncommon valor was a common virtue."

3. Now that I have talked about the battle, let me talk about the flag raisings. (slide 4)

**3. The transition connects main points I and II of the body.**

4. On the fifth day of combat two flags would be raised that would raise morale for soldiers on the island and people at home. The first flag was raised when Commander Chandler Johnson sent First Lieutenant Harold G. Schrier up Mt. Suribachi with a platoon of men. He instructed them if they met no resistance when they got to the top of the mountain to raise the flag. Harold G. Schrier took the platoon up and they met no resistance. The flag was raised and men all over the island began to cheer. At the same time, the Secretary of the Navy, James Forrestal, was landing ashore. He saw the flag being raised and asked that it be a souvenir for the Navy. Commander Chandler Johnson did not like this because he believed that the flag should belong to the Marine Corps and the men who fought on the island. So he sent a new group of Marines up the mountain with a larger flag. On the way up the mountain they met up with a photographer by the name of Joe Rosenthal. (slide 4) When they got to the top of the mountain, they switched flags, as you can see in this photo, and Joe Rosenthal snapped a picture of six men—John Bradley, Rene Gagnon, Ira Hayes, Frank Sousley, Michael Strank, and Harlon Block. In an article by the Associated Press entitled "Fifty Years Later, Iwo Jima Photographer Fights His Own Battle," Rosenthal explains how he captured the photo. He says, "Out of the corner of my eye I saw a flag raised, and I turned and snapped." Although this was not the picture of the original flag raising, the brilliance of six Marines hoisting a flag atop Mt. Suribachi proved to be a very powerful image.

**4. The speaker continues with the narrative of the flag raisings.**

**Peter cites his source for the information and uses a quotation from the photographer who captured the famous event.**

5. Now that I have talked about the flag raisings, let me talk about the legacy. (slide 5)

**5. The transition leads from point II to III of the body.**

6. This photograph was a great morale boost for soldiers and civilians all over America. It was also a great help to the country's war effort. As soon as the photo was released,

it became hugely popular and for a lot of people it summed up the war in the Pacific. In 1945 Joe Rosenthal won the Pulitzer Prize for photography. When President Roosevelt saw the photo, he decided they would use it in the upcoming Seventh War Bond Drive. Again the photo was successful as the drive raised 26.3 billion, which was nearly double of what was expected. Of the six men photographed, only three of them survived the island. They would be brought back immediately after the battle and paraded during the Seventh War Bond drive. The three men were Ira Hayes, Rene Gagnon, and John Bradley. Originally the military had released the names of the six at the flag raisings, however they misidentified Harlon Block as Hank Hansen. One-and-a-half years later, Ira Hayes decided he could not live with the lie anymore and went to tell Harlon Block's family the truth. Block's family wrote the Marine Corps Commandant and several congressman and had it officially changed. This image is also used as a Marine Memorial in Arlington, Virginia, and it has become a national symbol of patriotism to this day.

6. The PowerPoint slides throughout the speech are effective supportive materials to describe the significance of the battle and the flag raisings.

Peter cites an impressive statistic indicating the success of the photo and the men who helped raise the flags.

7. Now that I have talked about the legacy, let me conclude. (slide 6) This image is probably one of the most memorable images of all time. Only if we understand the battle can we understand the triumph that these men went through. Although two flags were raised, only one image drew enough power to capture the attention of millions. The legacy the photo carries has transcended generations and it is a resounding proof that a picture truly is worth a thousand words.

7. It is not necessary to mention the word *conclude* or *in conclusion* when a speaker ends the speech.

The speaker ends with a well-known maxim.

## summary »

Gather supporting materials to create interest and to provide evidence for your ideas. Some of the most authoritative materials are statistics, polls, and surveys; examples, illustrations, case studies, and narratives; and quotations and testimonies from authorities. Less verifiable, yet interesting materials are comparisons and contrasts; personal experiences and observations; and humor, anecdotes, and role-playing.

## SKILL BUILDERS»

1. Read through Peter Hollands' speech titled "The Flag Raisings at Iwo Jima," and list all the supporting materials he uses in his informative presentation. Which materials are most effective and what information is less effective? Explain your answer and suggest ways to improve the areas that you feel are less effective.
2. For your next speech topic, select at least one in each of the following categories to support your speech: an example, a statistic, a quotation. In addition, include one of the following where appropriate: personal experience, anecdote, comparison and contrast, or role-playing.

# BUILDING A SPEECH ONLINE »

Now that you've read Chapter 9, use your online Resource Center for Building a Speech for quick access to the electronic study resources that accompany this text. You can access your Resource Center at http://academic.cengage.com/login, using the access code that came with your book or that you bought online at http://www .iChapters.com. Your Resource Center gives you access to Interactive Video Activities, the book's companion website, Speech Builder Express 3.0, InfoTrac College Edition, and study aids, including a digital glossary and review quizzes.

# unit three
## CREATING THE STRUCTURE

# chapter 10

# ORGANIZING THE BODY OF THE SPEECH

## chapter objectives »

After reading and studying this chapter, you should be able to

1. Recognize how to approach speech organization logically
2. Describe the ten building blocks of outlining
3. Organize the body of a speech outline
4. Construct effective speaking notes from an outline

As president of the Humphrey Group, Judith Humphrey coaches leaders of corporations and businesses throughout the United States and Canada. She reports that a mainstay of her company is the Executive Speechwriting Program, which helps CEOs and business executives to build effective presentations "through learning and practice." In a speech to the Board of Trade in Toronto, Canada, Humphrey had this to say about speech organization:

*To begin with, the structure must support the message. Too many executive presentations or speeches simply ramble on, from topic to topic. When a structure elaborates an idea, it takes on an excitement, an energy. It has a pulse to it.*

*. . . Most speeches can be structured by one of five common patterns. First is the one we call the "Four Reasons" speech—although it might be the three reasons or nine reasons speech. It's a clear, powerful format. Second is the "Ways" speech, which demonstrates the ways or areas in which the main idea can be shown to be true. Next is "Problem and Solution." It's a good way of first addressing a problem and then showing how you'll solve it. It's great for customer*

" *Good order is the foundation of all good things.* "

—Edmund Burke

*presentations. There's also the "Process" or "Chronological" model. You discuss a sequence of steps. This talk with its seven-fold path to eloquence follows that model. Last is the "Present Situation/Future Outlook" talk. Annual meeting speeches often take this approach. You tell your audience that while this year's results were good, we will restructure to make the future still brighter for the company.*[1]

Humphrey recognized the vital importance of logical structure and clear organization in public speaking. She also stressed the importance of using the structure of a speech to elaborate an *idea* or *message*, giving "excitement" and "energy" to a topic.

An outline is just as important to you as it is to a professional speaker like Judith Humphrey. An outline is a structured plan of your ideas: It acts as a visual guide to the main and supporting elements in your presentation. You can think of the outline as the framework of your speech: It holds the speech together, keeps you within the boundaries, and clarifies the layout for the audience.

A speech has three parts: the introduction, the body, and the conclusion. It is the middle part, or body, that represents the major portion or framework of the speech and will comprise about two-thirds of your speaking time. Once you have researched the topic, written your specific purpose, and worded your thesis, you should first spend your energies outlining the body of the speech. You can develop the introduction and conclusion after organizing the meat of your presentation. In this chapter we consider ten building blocks that will help you to outline the body of your presentation.

## approaching organization logically

The thought of outlining a speech might seem difficult at first, but if you think logically about the topic, sorting through your research will be less complicated. Some topics almost organize themselves. For example, if you were to give an informative speech on a historical issue such as the history of the cell phone, your research would fall into several categories according to years or time periods. By contrast, a travelogue about Alaska could be organized using location or geography such as the arctic, western, southern, and interior areas as structural points. Research can also cluster around logical categories such as three types of clowns—straight man, joker, and character clown. Your research could also be outlined according to several major causes or effects.

What is important is that you begin thinking in an organized manner. Look for key ideas, patterns, and trends in your research that are supported by examples, quotations, or testimony. Think in terms of the overall plan of your speech, and don't try to fill in all details at the beginning of the process. After wording your thesis statement, begin by developing the body of the speech. To do this, separate your main points (taken from the thesis) and begin adding supporting material. Don't be afraid to adjust the main points, or the thesis, to make your plan more clear and consistent. Try not to be intimidated or enslaved by the process. Remember that the outline is simply a tool for structure and clarity, and it should help speech construction to be more enjoyable and less complicated.

## principles of outlining

If you carefully apply each of these ten principles, your clarity of organization and speaking effectiveness will be greatly enhanced. In this text we use the term **formal outline** when referring to the body of the speech. We use the term **informal outline** when referring to the introduction, conclusion, bibliography, and other outline preliminaries.

## key terms »

CAUSE-EFFECT
SEQUENCE
CHRONOLOGICAL
SEQUENCE
COMPARATIVE
ADVANTAGES
COORDINATION
EXTERNAL
TRANSITIONS
FORMAL OUTLINE
INDENTATION
INFORMAL OUTLINE
INTERNAL
TRANSITIONS
LINGUISTICALLY
PARALLEL
MOTIVATED
SEQUENCE
ORGANIZATIONAL
SEQUENCE
PROBLEM-SOLUTION
REASONS
SENTENCE OUTLINE
SPATIAL SEQUENCE
SPEAKING NOTES
SUBDIVISION
SUBORDINATION
SUBTOPIC
TOPIC OUTLINE
TOPICAL
SEQUENCE

## BUILDING BLOCK ONE: THE BODY SHOULD CONTAIN BETWEEN TWO AND FOUR MAIN POINTS OR NUMERALS IN A 5- TO 7-MINUTE SPEECH

The thesis statement identifies how many main points or numerals you will have in the body of a speech. In a classroom speech with a 5- to 7-minute time limit, the best guideline to use is to have no fewer than two and no more than four main points. If you have only one main point, your speech will be too short, because you will not have enough supporting material to develop your topic. If you have six or seven points, you have the opposite problem—a lengthy speech with too much information to cover in the allotted time. Notice that the following thesis statement incorporates three elements:

> **Specific purpose:** The purpose of the speech is to inform the audience about three funeral customs of the ancient Egyptians.
> **Thesis statement:** Egyptian funeral customs included embalming, the use of coffins, and a process called "dry burial."

BODY

   I. Explanation of Egyptian embalming practices
  II. Description of Egyptian coffins
 III. Explanation of "dry burial" techniques

The thesis statement tells you that there will be three numerals (the main points) in the body: (1) explanation of embalming, (2) description of coffins, and (3) explanation of burial techniques. The organization is tight, and there will be enough time to develop the main points in sufficient detail.[2]

## BUILDING BLOCK TWO: MAIN POINTS IN THE BODY SHOULD BE STRUCTURED IN AN ORGANIZATIONAL SEQUENCE THAT IS LOGICAL, INTERESTING, AND APPROPRIATE TO THE TOPIC

When structuring your main points or numerals, you can select an **organizational sequence** that is appropriate to the topic and that stimulates audience interest. Organize main points according to chronology, space, cause-effect, topical or natural sequence, or other sequence.

### Chronological Sequence

When you use **chronological sequence**, you arrange the main points according to time or order of events. For example, topics such as "Human life from fertilization to birth" or "How to make yeast bread" or historical topics such as "American exploration of space" or the "Life of Salvador Dali" would be organized according to chronology. Consider this example:

> **Specific purpose:** To inform you about the rise and fall of the American muscle car
> **Thesis statement:** American muscle cars were introduced in 1964, increased in popularity during the latter 60s, reached a "high-water" mark in 1970, and began to decline in the early 1970s.

BODY

   I. The early years—1964 to 1966
  II. The rising popularity—1967 to 1969
 III. The "high-water" mark—1970
 IV. The decline—1971 to 1972

The topic is arranged according to chronology by the historical events occurring over a period of years.

## Spatial Sequence

Space is the structuring of main points according to geography or location. Topics relating to the description of a building, a city, or a physical object are organized using **spatial sequence**.

> **Specific purpose:** To inform you about four principal areas in the White House
> **Thesis statement:** The interior of the White House includes executive offices, formal reception rooms, First Family living quarters, and a kitchen complex.

BODY

    I. Executive offices
   II. Formal reception rooms
 III. First Family living quarters
 IV. Kitchen complex

To build a successful presentation, a speaker must be willing to spend time developing ideas, structuring thoughts, and writing a clear, logical outline.
*Source:* Photo by Bill Dennison/© Thomson Learning

© Bruce Laurance/Getty Images

In this example, you can see that each main point describes a different spatial area in the White House.

### Cause-Effect Sequence

Another way to structure the main points of your speech is by **cause-effect sequence**. This sequence simply arranges the main points according to cause and effect. You could inform your audience about several causes of drug dependency and then talk about the effects on the family and the individual. Here's another example:

> **Specific purpose:** To inform the audience about the causes and effects of colon cancer
> **Thesis statement:** While there are several known causes of colon cancer, there are advanced treatments that have significant effects on the patient.

BODY

   I. Known causes of colon cancer
  II. Advanced treatments for the disease
 III. Effects of treatments on the patient

Here the first and last main points present causes and effects. Notice that numeral II is not a cause or effect, but identifies a topic area necessary for the logical development of the speech.

You could also structure the main points entirely by causes or by effects. A speech about child abuse, for instance, could expand upon three principal causes of child abuse or describe three tragic effects of abuse on the victim.

### Topical Sequence

Another method of structuring the main points is by logical or natural sequence. This pattern can also be called **topical sequence**. On some issues, you will find that your research clusters around natural divisions that can be earmarked as categories for your outline.

> **Specific purpose:** To inform the audience what it is like living in Dunoon, Scotland
> **Thesis statement:** During the year I lived in Dunoon, Scotland, I got to know the town, learned how to negotiate the transportation system, became acclimated to a Scottish home, and enjoyed leisure activities.

BODY

   I. Brief description of the town
  II. Transportation in the town
 III. Life in a Scottish house
 IV. Activities for leisure enjoyment

In this example, the speaker has created four logical categories that accurately describe her experiences and observations.

You can also create a natural sequence by identifying trends in your information. For instance, you could structure your main points from least to most important, simple to complex, or familiar to unfamiliar. These types of arrangements not only create interest in the topic but they also help your audience to remember your main points. Consider these examples:

LEAST TO MOST IMPORTANT

> **Specific purpose:** To convince the audience that there are four reasons why HMOs do not provide quality health care

**Thesis statement:** Waiting rooms are impersonal, open enrollment is limited, getting immediate appointments with specialists is often difficult, and patients frequently experience inaccurate diagnoses and treatments.

## BODY

I. Clinical, impersonal waiting rooms
II. Limited open enrollment, requiring high premiums
III. Immediate appointments with specialists difficult
IV. Frequent inaccurate diagnosis and treatment

### SIMPLE TO COMPLEX

**Specific purpose:** To inform the audience about some troubleshooting techniques they can use when their car doesn't start
**Thesis statement:** Be able to read and understand the instrument panel, identify possible difficulties with the starter mechanism, and know what to look for under the hood.

## BODY

I. Understanding instrument panel
II. Identifying problems with starter mechanism
III. Looking under hood

### FAMILIAR TO UNFAMILIAR

**Specific purpose:** To inform the audience about five different types of stars in the universe
**Thesis statement:** Stars are grouped into five categories: stars, black holes, novas, binary stars, and neutron stars.

## BODY

I. Stars—glowing gas in the sky
II. Black holes—collapsed, former stars
III. Novas—exploding bright and diminished stars
IV. Binary stars—revolving and eclipsed stars
V. Neutron stars—gaseous, atomic stars

In the first example, the speaker has arranged main points from the least to the most important reason. Numeral I, "Clinical . . . waiting rooms," states a good reason why HMOs don't provide quality health care, but it is the least important of the four statements. Numeral IV, "Frequent inaccurate diagnosis . . .," deals with human life and is therefore the most important item. In the second example, numeral I, "Understanding instrument panel," is the least complicated troubleshooting procedure; numeral III, "Looking under hood," is the most complex. In the last example, the speaker assumes that the audience is most familiar with stars and may have some limited familiarity with black holes as well as novas. But the speaker has assumed that binary and neutron stars are the least familiar to the audience, and she has arranged them as the last two points.

### Other Sequences

There are a number of other ways to arrange the main points or numerals of the body. Many of these organizational patterns relate specifically to persuasive speeches, which we will discuss in Chapter 16, but we want to briefly mention them now.

**Problem-solution** order is the arrangement of main points by identifying a problem and moving to a solution. The **motivated sequence** pattern is a five-stage system—attention, need, solution, visualization, action—in order to motivate the audience to act on an issue. The **reasons** organizational pattern simply arranges main points in the body according to reasons. There is also a **comparative advantages** sequence that develops each main point by stressing the advantages of a desired plan or idea.

## BUILDING BLOCK THREE: A SYSTEM OF ROMAN NUMERALS, LETTERS, AND ARABIC NUMBERS SHOULD BE COMBINED WITH INDENTATION TO IDENTIFY MAIN AND SUBORDINATE LEVELS

Begin by using Roman numerals to outline the main points (numerals) of the speech body. Remember that the Roman numerals signify your main points, which carry out all the components of the thesis statement. Then introduce the next level of subordinate points with capital letters A, B, C, and so forth. Supporting points under the capital letters should be indicated with numbers 1, 2, 3, and so on. And if you need more levels, indicate those items with small letters *a* and *b* and an even lower level of detail with (1) and (2).

Each level of supporting points is *indented* so that the outline clearly indicates the relationship between the main point and the **subdivision**. An **indentation** is one tab space on the computer. Just by glancing at this outline, you can easily see how to attach subordinate points to their appropriate main point. You will notice that similar symbols are lined up underneath each other. The body of a speech is the only portion of the outline that includes this many levels of supporting items. Good organization in the form of a tightly structured outline helps to trigger your thoughts so that you can maintain eye contact with your audience. The pattern shown is just a guide to general outlining procedure. The shape of every outline depends upon the topic and varies according to the number of main points and the amount of supporting items.

# BUILDING BLOCK FOUR: THE OUTLINE SHOULD INCLUDE SUPPORTING MATERIALS THAT ARE COORDINATED AND SUBORDINATED IN A LOGICAL MANNER

Once you have written two, three, or four main points of the body, your outline still represents only claims or assertions but no factual evidence or proof. You need supporting materials—that is, examples, quotations, statistics, and/or audiovisuals to provide detailed verification of each main point or numeral. When you place supporting materials beneath the main points of the body, your outline presents the details that are necessary to inform or influence your listeners.

> **Specific purpose:** To demonstrate how an ointment is made
>
> **Thesis statement:** In order to make an ointment you need to know its history, the basic tools needed, and the process required for preparation.

BODY

I. Man found ways to treat skin irritations/infections in ancient times
   A. Primitive cave dwellers used available materials
      1. Cool water
      2. Leaves
      3. Dirt
      4. Mud
   B. Galen invented cold cream
      1. Roman physician-pharmacist
      2. First century A.D.
      3. Very first formula
   C. Pharmacists now customize ointments
      1. Due to advances in research/technology
      2. Required to meet individual needs
II. Basic tools needed for ointment (visual aids)
   A. Ointment board
   B. Plastic spatulas
   C. Mortar and pestle
III. Process required to make ointment (visual aids)
   A. Measure ingredients
   B. "Triturate" ingredients
      1. Procedure means grinding
      2. Particles made smaller
   C. Incorporate into glycerin
   D. Dilute geometrically
      1. Add equal parts to equal parts
      2. Ensures thorough mixing
   E. Package ointment
   F. Label ointment immediately
      1. To ensure correct identification
      2. To avoid forgetting

In this speech Olivia Ellis wanted to show listeners how to make a pharmaceutical ointment. In numeral I of the body, she used four examples of how primitive people used materials that were available to them. She also used another example of a first-century Roman who was the inventor of cold cream. Then in numerals II and III, she uses visual aids to describe the tools needed and demonstrate the process of making the ointment.

Remember that an outline is not a word-for-word account of all supporting materials, but a framework that provides an overall blueprint of the areas included in the speech.

When writing the statements in your outline, you must be sure that ideas are of equal importance at each level, that subordinate ideas logically support each heading, and that statements do not duplicate each other. **Coordination** refers to the placement of equal ideas within the same level of an outline, and **subordination** refers to the placement of secondary or lower-ranking ideas beneath higher-order items. Look at the following incorrect outline:

> **Specific purpose:** To provide information that helps the audience to define and understand mental retardation
>
> **Thesis statement:** I will define mental retardation, explain how it is classified, and identify some common misconceptions about it.

INCORRECT

I. What it is
   A. A definition of mental retardation
   B. Public myths about the mentally retarded
   C. Public fears of the mentally retarded
   D. Mental retardation vs. mental illness
      1. Mental illness conditions
      2. Mental retardation conditions
II. Classifications of mental retardation
   A. Factors determining mental retardation
      1. Mental ability
      2. Adaptive behavior
      3. Physical development
   B. Degrees of mental retardation
      1. Mild to moderate
      2. Severe to profound
III. Common misconceptions about mental retardation

This outline is incorrect for the following reasons: Under Roman numeral I, item A ("definition") is not equal to other items at the same level: It is identical to the heading's main point and should be eliminated. Items IB ("myths") and IC ("fears") are overlapping points that should be combined. And if you take an overall look at the outline, it appears that numeral I contains points that are not supportive. "Fears" really belongs under numeral III ("Common misconceptions"), and ID1 ("mental illness conditions"), which does not define retardation, can also be categorized under numeral III. Here is a more effective outline:

CORRECT

I. Definition of mental retardation
   A. Subaverage intellectual functioning
   B. Arrested or incomplete development
   C. Limitations in present functioning
   D. Abnormal brain function
II. Classification of mental retardation
   A. Factors determining mental retardation
      1. Mental ability
      2. Adaptive behavior
      3. Physical development

B. Degrees classifying mental retardation
    1. Mild to moderate
    2. Severe to profound
III. Common misconceptions about mental retardation
  A. Confusion with mental illness
  B. Fear of "different" behavior
  C. Inability to function in society
    1. Failure to have relationships
    2. Failure to be employed
    3. Failure to perform survival tasks

This outline now contains main and subordinate points that are arranged in their appropriate relationships.

## BUILDING BLOCK FIVE: EVERY SUBDIVISION MUST CONTAIN AT LEAST TWO ITEMS

In the concept of division, it is assumed that elements have been divided into two separate but equal categories. If there is only one item, there has obviously been no division. At each level of your outline, there should be a minimum of two **subtopics** (subdivisions); for example, point A will have at least subtopics 1 and 2. If you find that a topic area can be supported by only one point, don't try to force another element, but simply incorporate the single point into the heading above.

  **Specific purpose:** To demonstrate how to juggle three objects
  **Thesis statement:** I will explain the selection of objects, the process of juggling, and provide a brief demonstration.

INCORRECT

  I. Selecting the objects
    A. Between four to six ounces
      1. Must not be too heavy
  II. Explaining the process
    A. Display visual aid describing steps
      1. Pick imaginary points
      2. Toss ball to points and catch
      3. Use opposite hand to throw ball
      4. Use steps B and C together
      5. Repeat the process
  III. Demonstrating the art of juggling

Under Roman numeral I of this example, there is a point A but no B, and there is only one subtopic under the A. In numeral II there is again only one point, A, but there are five subtopics under the A. Here's how to correct these problems:

CORRECT

  I. Choosing the objects
    A. Should weigh four to six ounces
    B. Should not be slick
    C. Should be able to bounce
  II. Explaining the process (using visual aid)
    A. Pick imaginary points
    B. Toss ball to points and catch

      C. Use opposite hand to throw ball
      D. Use steps B and C together
      E. Repeat the process
    III. Demonstrating the art of juggling

Under numeral I, subtopic 1 from the incorrect version ("Must not be too heavy") has been eliminated because it can be included with point A, "Between four to six ounces." An additional B and a C have also been created to further complete the subdivision. Under numeral II, the original point A ("Display visual aid") was eliminated because it can be incorporated with the numeral. That change eliminates the need for subtopics 1 through 5, which have been upgraded to the next level—A through E. The main and subordinate points are now correct.

## BUILDING BLOCK SIX: EACH POINT SHOULD INCLUDE ONLY ONE TOPIC OR IDEA

Here is an outline that violates the principle of building block six:

> **Specific purpose:** To inform the audience about preventing teenage suicide
> **Thesis statement:** I will identify the warning signs of teenage suicide and explain how to help the individual.

**INCORRECT**

    I. Warning signs of teenage suicide
      A. Direct suicide threats
      B. Indirect statements revealing desire to die
      C. Previous suicide attempts and sudden changes in behavior
        1. Social withdrawal
        2. Variable moods
        3. Severe depression and impulsive behavior
   II. Getting help to the individual
      A. Talk to the teen
      B. Show interest in the person
      C.  Be certain teen can reach adult
      D. Solicit help from professional

Under numeral I, point C ("Previous suicide attempts and sudden changes in behavior") is clearly two ideas. The subtopics for point C seem to support "changes in behavior," but they do not clearly support "previous attempts." Subtopic 3 also includes two separate thoughts—"depression and impulsiveness." When ideas are mistakenly clumped together like this, the audience briefly tries to put the pieces together but often stops listening in confusion. The outline should be revised as follows:

**CORRECT**

    I. Warning signs of teenage suicide
      A. Direct suicide threats
      B. Indirect statements revealing desire to die
      C. Previous suicide attempts
      D. Sudden changes in behavior
        1. Social withdrawal
        2. Variable moods
        3. Severe depression
        4. Impulsive behavior

II. Getting help to the individual
   A. Talk to the teen
   B. Show interest in the person
   C. Be certain teen can reach adult
   D. Solicit help from professional

Notice that a new point D ("Sudden changes in behavior") has been added, as well as a new subtopic 4 ("Impulsive behavior") to separate the ideas. The outline is now accurate. The audience will be more capable of sorting out one idea at a time.

## BUILDING BLOCK SEVEN: MAIN POINTS (NUMERALS) AND SUPPORTING ITEMS SHOULD BE LINGUISTICALLY PARALLEL

The sentence construction and wording used in each level of your outline should be structurally similar. Your outline represents your speaking notes; the more uniformly items are structured, the easier it will be for you to follow as you are delivering your speech. For example, if your first main point (numeral I) begins with a noun plus a prepositional phrase (causes of pollution, effects on streams) or an infinitive phrase (to enjoy freedom, to participate in democracy), then other main points should begin in a similar manner. Subordinate points should also have a **linguistically parallel** language structure: for instance, points A, B, and C should be comparable, and subtopics 1, 2, and 3 should show similarity.

**Specific purpose:** To understand and demonstrate the art of tattooing
**Thesis statement:** To truly appreciate the art of tattooing you must first understand the history of tattoos, the machine used, and the actual process of applying a tattoo.

INCORRECT

I. History is interesting
   A. Origin
   B. Brought to western world
II. Machine
   A. About Samuel O'Reilly and his invention of the modern tattoo machine
   B. Operates on a simple principle
III. Tattooing process
   A. To pick out a piece
   B. Waiver
   C. Follow health and safety procedures
      1. Autoclave
      2. Handle needles properly
      3. Gloving techniques
   D. Shave area
      1. Wash area thoroughly
      2. Disinfecting
   E. Placing stencil on area
   F. The machine needs to be applied and controlled
      1. Use of pigments
      2. Use needle with steady hand

CORRECT

I. History of tattooing
   A. Where tattoos originated
   B. How tattoos came to western world
II. Invention of tattoo machine
   A. Invented by Samuel O'Reilly
   B. How the tattoo machine works
III. Process of tattooing
   A. Pick out a piece
   B. Sign a waiver
   C. Follow health and safety procedures
      1. Autoclave process
      2. Needle-handling procedures
      3. Gloving techniques
   D. Shave area
      1. Wash
      2. Disinfect
   E. Place stencil on area
   F. Apply and control machine
      1. Selecting pigments
      2. Using needle
   G. Take care of new tattoo
      1. Wash area

G. Care of tattoo
   1. You need to wash area
   2. Sterile dressing
   3. Discussion of care and cleaning

   2. Apply sterile dressing
   3. Discuss care and cleaning

In the incorrect example, the main numerals I–III and their supporting points are not parallel. Notice the different wording and structure of the two main points: Numeral I is a brief phrase, II is only a one-word noun, and III is a noun ending in –*ing*. Notice also that subordinate items are not linguistically parallel. The incorrect example then demonstrates improper outline form. These mistakes may actually impede the speaker's progress. The speaker is forced to read and decipher each item in detail while delivering the speech. This improper outline can then reduce eye contact and hinder the flow of ideas.

Now look at the correct example. Each main point begins with a noun followed by a prepositional phrase. Subordinate items are also linguistically parallel to one another. Notice that not all levels have to be identical in sentence structure; for example, points IA and IB are grammatically different from the topics that support IIA and IIB. In addition, the subtopics beneath points IIIC, D, F, and G are linguistically different from each other. Each level, however, maintains internal structural consistency. This parallel outline will be easier for the speaker to read and will facilitate the speaker's eye contact and thought process.

## BUILDING BLOCK EIGHT: THE OUTLINE SHOULD BE EXPRESSED IN EITHER SENTENCES OR TOPICS

When writing the formal outline of the body, you should use either complete sentences or topics—never mix the two forms. If you begin using complete sentences for numeral I in the body, you must continue employing sentences throughout all main and subordinate levels to keep the outline consistent. If you begin with topics or phrases, employ topics throughout the outline. Some speakers use a **topic outline** because they feel it keeps them from reading their outline word for word. Others use a **sentence outline** form because they can get a more precise idea of the wording in the speech. Use either sentences or topics—whichever you find most helpful.

Here are examples of the two types of outlines:

**Specific purpose:** To inform the audience about the increasing emphasis on sex in advertising
**Thesis statement:** Sex is increasingly used in advertising because of the economic benefits to advertisers.

SENTENCE OUTLINE

I. Sex has invaded contemporary advertising.
   A. More men are shown as sexual objects.
   B. Women are now shown to be aggressors in sexual encounters.
   C. More nudity of both sexes is shown.
II. Provocative advertising benefits the advertiser.
   A. They receive positive feedback from consumers.
   B. Advertisers experience increases in their sales.

TOPIC OUTLINE

I. The use of sex in advertising

   A. Men as sex objects

   B. Women as sexual aggressors

   C. Increased nudity of both sexes
II. Benefits of provocative ads to advertiser

   A. Positive feedback from consumers

   B. Increases in sales revenues

Even though one is a sentence outline and another is a topic outline, each form is consistent throughout. The topic outline uses phrases—not just one or two words—to make each topic and subtopic as clear as possible. Either form would be a useful tool in helping the speaker successfully communicate to the audience.

## BUILDING BLOCK NINE: THE OUTLINE SHOULD IDENTIFY SOURCES FOR MAJOR SUPPORTING MATERIALS

Portions of the outline that include significant examples, statistics, or testimonies drawn from your research should clearly identify the sources of the information. Indicating references on the outline reminds you of where you obtained the information and helps you to integrate sources more easily when delivering the presentation.

Source notations can be abbreviated in the body of the outline because you will be including a more comprehensive bibliography at the end. Here is a suggested system you can follow when annotating your sources:

**Specific purpose:** To examine and explain the uses of four types of masks
**Thesis statement:** For thousands of years man has used masks for religious/ceremonial, theatrical, festive, and practical reasons.

BODY

    I. Religious/ceremonial
    A. American Indians
        1. Hopi tribe
            a. Katchina masks (Underhill, *Red Man's Religion*, pp. 90, 208)
            b. Use of masks
        2. Northwest Indians
            a. Half-man, half-animal mask
            b. Use of masks (Kondeatis, *Masks*, p. 11)
    B. Central African
        1. Northern Ba Kete mask
        2. Construction of masks (Segy, *Masks of Black Africa*, pp. 33–37)
        3. Function of masks

This outline clearly identifies sources. In subtopic 2b under point IA, the parentheses indicate that the material was researched in the book *Masks*. The abbreviated form lists only the last name of the author, the title of the book, and the page numbers. You will notice that you don't need to annotate every item in an outline—only those topics and subtopics that include specific quotations or provide extensive data necessary to the development of the speech.

## BUILDING BLOCK TEN: THE OUTLINE SHOULD INCLUDE EXTERNAL TRANSITIONS BETWEEN MAIN NUMERALS

External transitions are phrases that connect the major numerals of your speech. These carefully crafted statements should tell listeners that one main idea is ending and another is beginning. When you build the outline, write out the complete transitional phrase or sentence, placing it between the appropriate numerals.

**Specific purpose:** To inform the audience about one of America's passions—chocolate
**Thesis statement:** Chocolate, a sweet substance we all take for granted, has an interesting background, affects our health, and is the object of a love affair with the American consumer.

**BODY**

    I. General background about chocolate
       A. Brief history of cocoa bean
       B. Location of groves
       C. Manufacture of chocolate

      **Transition:** Now that you've heard about the history and background of chocolate, you need to know about chocolate and your health.

    II. Health issues related to chocolate
       A. Effect on teeth
       B. Effect on skin
       C. Problem with addiction
       D. Calories in chocolate
       E. Aphrodisiac in chocolate

      **Transition:** In spite of the health issues, American consumers have an ongoing love affair with chocolate.

   III. American consumers' love of chocolate
       A. U.S. largest importer of cacao beans
       B. 90 percent of U.S. sales from milk chocolate
       C. Protection by federal standards
       D. Novelty items of interest

Remember to make a clear distinction between external and internal transitions. **External transitions** are one-sentence phrases occurring *between* the major numerals of the speech and are placed in the body of the outline. These "listening cues" are a guide to help audiences determine the speaker's progress through the presentation. By contrast, **internal transitions** are brief words such as *also, then, next, in addition to,* or *finally* that link the supporting materials *within* a subtopic. Although internal transitions are also important to the delivery of the speech, these brief connectives are not needed in the outline. (To see examples of external transitions in a completed outline, turn to pages 188–189 in Chapter 11 for the speech titled, "Raising the *Monitor*.")

## your speaking notes

This emphasis on outlining is important, not only for building a coherent, logical structure for the speech but also for its delivery. This text emphasizes the importance of extemporaneous delivery, in which you speak spontaneously from notecards that include the elements of your outline (in Chapter 2, see "Extemporaneous Delivery and Speaking Styles"). Brief notecards that contain words and phrases will help you speak with more spontaneity and eye contact than when reading word-for-word from a manuscript.

    Your **speaking notes** will include the introduction, the body, and the conclusion. Construct your notes so that you can see where you're headed in one brief glance. Select either 4-by-6-inch or 6-by-9-inch notecards, and number them at the upper right-hand corner. Write legibly, use large lettering, and double-space between some of the lines. You may want to underline or occasionally use all caps for emphasis. You may even want to use different colors to highlight specific examples, statistics, or quotations. Use a reasonable number of notecards; don't cram too many phrases on two or three cards, and don't use too many notes. You don't want to squint as you read, and you also don't want to flip a card every few seconds. When transferring your outline to notecards, remember that your objective is ease of communication; you want notes that help you communicate quickly and effectively.

To help you understand how to connect outlined speaking notes to the complete wording of a speech, we have included several sample notecards and the corresponding manuscript from the body of the informative speech "Raising the *Monitor*." These sample notecards do not include all of the bibliographic references that are listed in the formal written outline. The speaker can include only those sources that are necessary to provide credibility during the speech. (See the box in Chapter 8 titled "Citing Sources in a Speech.") Notice that the notecards are numbered at the upper right, beginning with 3. Keep in mind that these notecards are incomplete and demonstrate only the first main point of the body of a three-point speech; they do not include the several notecards for the introduction or the conclusion. In Chapter 11 we will discuss how to outline the introduction and conclusion and provide you with sample notes that coincide with the notecards presented here. You can see the entire outline of this speech at the end of Chapter 11, and you can read the entire speech at the end of Chapter 15.

**Specific purpose:** To describe the historical significance of raising the *Monitor's* turret

**Thesis statement:** The historical significance of the *Monitor* led scientists and nautical engineers to overcome extreme challenges that resulted in the successful recovery of the vessel's turret.

## NOTECARDS

(3)

I. History and importance of the *Monitor*
  A. BUILDING AND LAUNCHING OF MONITOR (slide 3)
    1. Built in Greenpoint, Brooklyn, and launched into East River, January 30, 1862
    2. Rotating turret, distinguishing feature, now standard on modern war ships
  B. SPECIFICATIONS
    1. 8-inch-thick iron-plated walls, 9 ft high, 21 ft across, 150 tons
    2. Dahlgren-manufactured guns, firing shells/cannonballs 2 miles

(4)

  C. IMPACT AND EFFECTS (*New York Times,* Jul 30, '02, 1)
    1. Union started building a new class of *Monitor*-type vessels
    2. British Royal Navy canceled construction of wooden warships

## SPEECH

The *Monitor* was built in Greenpoint, Brooklyn, (*slide 3*) and launched into the East River on January 30, 1862. The distinguishing feature of the ship was her rotating turret, a technological first that is now standard on all modern warships. With 8-inch-thick walls of iron plating, the turret measured 9 feet high, 21 feet across, and weighed 150 tons. It housed two 9-foot, Dahlgren-manufactured guns that were capable of firing shells or cannonballs farther than 2 miles.

After the historical battle, the Union began building a whole new class of *Monitor*-type vessels. According to a July 2002 *New York Times* article, when the British Royal Navy heard about the clash of the two ironclads, the world's preeminent naval force canceled all construction of wooden warships.

| NOTECARDS | SPEECH |
|---|---|

**(5)**

D. SINKING IN A STORM (*Slides 4–5*)
1. Encountered violent storm off Cape Hatteras New Year's Eve
2. 10:30 p.m. commander sent lantern distress signal to tow vessel
3. Some men saved; after midnight, lantern disappeared
4. Turret sunk to seafloor, 240 ft upside down
5. Missing were 12 crewmen, 4 officers, ship's mascot, black cat

Nine months after the battle, (*slide 4*) the *Monitor* encountered a violent storm off the coast of Cape Hatteras on New Year's Eve. At 10:30 p.m., the commander sent a distress signal, via lantern, to a tow vessel. Some of the men were saved, but shortly after midnight the lantern disappeared. The famous turret came to rest upside down on the seafloor at a depth of 240 feet (*slide 5*). Among the missing were twelve crew members, four officers, and the ship's mascot, a black cat.

**(6)**

E. DISCOVERY OF WRECK
1. Duke University expedition found remains 16 miles from Hatteras in 1973
2. Named nation's first marine sanctuary for protection from treasure hunters in 1975
3. Hull plate and signal lantern recovered in 1977
4. Anchor recovered in 1983

The ship was lost until 1973 when a Duke University expedition found the scattered remains 16 miles off Cape Hatteras. In 1975, it was named the nation's first marine sanctuary to protect the wreck from treasure hunters. A hull plate and the signal lantern came up in 1977, and the anchor was recovered in 1983.

**(7)**

F. TURRET WAS PRIZE, CONTAINING ANSWERS TO 140-YEAR-OLD QUESTIONS
1. Turret only way crew could exit ship
2. Turret contained answers to 140-year-old questions
3. Human (and feline) remains, artifacts expected
4. Federal officials made plans made for extensive retrievals in 1997

The turret, however, was the prize they were aiming for. Aside from its historical significance, the turret may contain the answers to 140-year-old questions. The turret was the only way out of the ship, so scientists expected to find human (or even feline) remains as well as important artifacts that may have been dropped by crew members trying to escape. Federal officials laid plans in 1997 for more extensive retrievals.

## summary »

Approach the organization process in a logical manner, and follow these ten principles for outlining the body of your speech:

1. Include between two and four main points in the body of a 5- to 7-minute speech.
2. Structure the main points in an organizational sequence that is logical, interesting, and appropriate to the topic.
3. To identify main and subordinate levels of the outline, use a system of Roman numerals, letters, and Arabic numbers combined with indentation.

4. Include supporting materials that are coordinated and subordinated in a logical manner.
5. Be sure to provide at least two items in every subdivision.
6. Include only one topic or idea in each statement.
7. Make the main points (numerals) and supporting items linguistically parallel.
8. Express the main points and supporting items of your outline as either sentences or topics.
9. In the outline, identify sources for major supporting materials.
10. Include external transitions between main numerals of your outline.

Your speaking notes should include elements of your outline so that you can see where you're headed in one brief glance, allowing you to speak extemporaneously.

## SKILL BUILDERS »

1. Carefully read one of the speeches included in your text (Chapters 2, 6, 9, 12, 15, 16, or 17). Outline the introduction, body, and conclusion of the speech following the guidelines presented in this chapter.
2. Conduct an InfoTrac search of *Vital Speeches of the Day* to find a speech that you feel is well organized with a clear thesis and a body that follows the main points previewed in the thesis. Report your findings to your class. (For access to InfoTrac, see the following section.)

## BUILDING A SPEECH ONLINE »

Now that you've read Chapter 10, use your online Resource Center for Building a Speech for quick access to the electronic study resources that accompany this text. You can access your Resource Center at http://academic.cengage.com/login, using the access code that came with your book or that you bought online at http://www.iChapters.com. Your Resource Center gives you access to Interactive Video Activities, the book's companion website, Speech Builder Express 3.0, InfoTrac College Edition, and study aids, including a digital glossary and review quizzes.

© Patricia Crocker/The Image Works

# chapter 11

# SELECTING THE INTRODUCTION AND CONCLUSION

## chapter objectives »

After reading and studying this chapter, you should be able to

1. Discuss the objectives of an introduction
2. Describe strategies for beginning a speech
3. Discuss the objectives of a conclusion
4. Describe strategies for ending a speech
5. Describe how to outline the introduction and conclusion
6. Construct speaking notes for the introduction and conclusion
7. Develop a comprehensive speech outline

A student began his speech by clearing his throat. "My name is Joe," he said, "and my topic is snowboarding. So I guess I'll start now." This type of beginning is certainly direct and to the point, but it is abrupt and uninteresting. Many students who have adequately prepared the body of their speeches have difficulty thinking of ways to begin and end.

In an article titled "How to Be an Effective Public Speaker," two faculty members at California State University describe the importance of the introduction and conclusion:

*Start your presentation with a bang. The first few moments of a talk influence the audience's reception*

> " *Don't let it end like this. Tell them I said something.* "
>
> —Pancho Villa

*of the rest of it. Try to convey an air of dignity, authority (on the topic, not over the people), confidence, and trust. Raising your voice for the first few sentences can help grab and hold audience members. They will be less inclined to think that another drab speech is under way. A rhetorical question is a good way to spark the interest of an audience. Such questions generally begin with "What if . . .?" or "What do you think about . . . ?" The question should lead into the topic at hand, and should get audience members to think, "Why am I being asked this?" . . .*

*Make your finish a strong one. A great quote or a plea for action can inspire listeners and help them remember your message. A feeble "thank you" can leave the audience hanging. If you've done a good job on stage, the "thank you" should come from the audience.*[1]

These professors are right on target. The audience forms its first impressions of your speech while listening to your introduction. If you are going to be successful throughout your presentation, you must get your listeners' attention and stimulate their curiosity at the very beginning. In addition, the ending must indicate that you are well prepared, thoughtful, and memorable. The essential message is: Start with a bang and finish strongly!

Speech introductions and conclusions are the focus of this chapter. It is important to know the purpose and structure of the opening and closing, as well as the various ways you can begin and end. Included here are suggestions to help you construct your **speaking notes** and an informative speech outline as a model for your own presentations.

## planning the introduction

The purpose of the introduction is to provide an entry point into your topic. You want to capture the attention of the audience, arouse their curiosity about your topic and link the topic to their needs, and introduce your specific purpose and thesis statements.

The introduction is the place where the audience decides to listen or tune you out. How well you understand your listeners and how effectively you develop an introduction to connect to their unique characteristics often determine whether the audience will give you a hearing. Imagine a woman who presents a speech about breast cancer to an audience of mostly men, a Muslim from Saudi Arabia speaking about the religious fast of Ramadan to an audience of mostly Americans, or a speaker with strong views favoring gay marriage to listeners who are strongly opposed. It is doubtful that these speakers would be successful unless they understood the differences within their audiences and developed introductory strategies that connected the topic to their listeners' background and interests. For example, the woman speaking to male listeners could develop an introduction indicating that breast cancer also afflicts men and is not just a women's issue. The Saudi Arabian speaker could begin by relating Ramadan to Western religious holidays such as Passover and Christmas. And the gay marriage proponent could develop an introduction that established areas of agreement with listeners about the Constitution and Bill of Rights.

As you face the diverse members of your audience, use the introduction as a strategy to show how your topic relates to your listeners' interests and motivations. Understand differences in culture, ethnic background, gender, and age. Know how social affiliations or groups, educational background, occupational goals, and geographic location influence your audience and affect their perception of your topic. If you are speaking about the U.S. budget to listeners from other countries, indicate why your topic is important to them. If you are demonstrating the Heimlich maneuver to an audience of business majors, describe how the topic can assist employees in a restaurant or save a company

**key terms »**

APPEAL
CHALLENGE
COMPLIMENT
EXAMPLE
HUMOR
ILLUSTRATION
OPEN-ENDED
   QUESTIONS
PERSONAL
   REFERENCE
QUOTATION
REFERENCE TO THE
   INTRODUCTION
REFERENCE TO THE
   OCCASION
RHETORICAL
   QUESTIONS
SHOCKING
   STATEMENT
SPEAKING NOTES
STATISTICS
STORY
SUMMARY
SUSPENSE

from lawsuits. If you are talking about exchanging Social Security for personal retirement accounts to listeners under age 30, describe how this program can benefit their own futures. Use the introduction to prepare listeners to hear and receive your ideas. Acknowledge the audience, and help them to understand that your topic can be important to their needs.

The introduction must be well thought out and very carefully prepared. A boring, insensitive, poorly worded, or poorly delivered introduction can quickly destroy a speaker's credibility with listeners; on the other hand, a meaningful, curiosity-provoking introduction can motivate listeners and bring your topic to life. Recognize that an introduction isn't just one or two sentences placed together; it incorporates a carefully devised technique or variety of techniques to gain your listeners' interest and goodwill. Generally, a good introduction is at least a paragraph in length.

In this section we consider some examples of effective introductions and explore why they are successful. Some of these examples are taken directly from students' presentations in beginning speech classes, and some are excerpts from individuals who are experienced in delivering public speeches.

## EXAMPLES, STORIES, AND ILLUSTRATIONS

You can always begin your speech with an **example**, **story**, or **illustration**. Examples make your introduction vivid and help your audience to quickly understand the reality of a person, experience, or circumstance. Notice how the following story creates interest and generates horror as it moves forward:

> *Juliana McCourt was a beautiful, happy little girl who . . . boarded U.S. Airlines flight 175 from Boston to Los Angeles. It was early morning, September 11, 2001. A beautiful sunny and cloudless morning—a day to match her little life. To be sure, the flight attendants smiled at her and her mother; perhaps she received a toy or a set of little plastic wings, the way that kids do. In stark contrast to this little bundle of joy and innocence, a handful of men, intent on neither joy nor innocence, overwhelmed the crew and terrified the passengers. Without question, Juliana was afraid . . . . Who were these grownups? Why were they doing these mean things? . . . Try to think of a 4-year-old baby, terrified with fright, reaching to its mother for comfort. Try to imagine a mother, crying, praying to God to save her little child . . . . Mother and child died that day in the vaporization of U.S. Airlines flight 175—and so did the joy, innocence, hope, and faith of a nation . . . . The men who murdered little Juliana McCourt on September 11 were neither "real men" nor martyrs—they were cowards. It's just as simple as that.[2]*

Professor Gary Anderson at Maryland University College in Germany could have started his address by stating that "the events of September 11 were ghastly," a fact that most of his listeners already believed. Instead, he began by describing the happy innocence of a little child. As he continued, the chilling events of this unfolding story became familiar, vivid, and devastating. This introduction dramatically creates and holds attention as it prepares listeners to hear the thesis and body of the speech.

In the next introduction, Gina Alexander uses a series of brief examples as her strategy:

- Susan's boss told her that her dress was too tight and too loud in color.
- Beth's supervisor pinched her every time she walked near him.
- Michelle was the object of many dirty jokes by her coworkers.
- John knew that making love to Norma, the vice-president of the company, was the only way to get that essential promotion.
- And Ralph had to endure hugs from his professor in order to get an A.

*Degrading, counterproductive, and criminal—these words describe sexual harass-*
*ment in the workplace. This is the cancer of our workplace. Sexual harassment is*
*a problem for both men and women. These harassers want power over us, and*
*victims are unaware of how to cut off this power.*[3]

Gina Alexander understood that her listeners had probably heard a lot about this
topic. Some listeners had participated in job-related seminars educating them about
sexual harassment, and others had heard general news reports about the issue. But this
speaker decided to present a series of brief examples to gain her listeners' attention.
When developing her introduction, Gina analyzed the gender and age differences within
her audience. In her speech, she presented instances drawn from the experiences of both
men and women to indicate that sexual harassment can victimize either gender. She
also used examples such as the student-professor situation that could connect to younger
listeners as well as instances that were more typical of older listeners who were already
pursuing their full-time careers. As audience members listened, they were able to connect the examples to their own environments and realize that the issue affects everyone. This rapid-fire technique is effective because the speaker conveys several examples
quickly in order to motivate listeners. An example, story, or illustration helps to create
immediate interest, because an audience can empathize with a vivid situation or specific
experience.

## SHOCKING STATEMENT OR SITUATION

A **shocking statement** or situation that shocks the audience is also an effective method of
creating interest. In the following introduction to a speech on tornados, Michael Gerber
used the first line to startle his audience:

*It's raining toads and frogs. This may seem impossible, but it is only one of the many*
*astonishing feats of a tornado. Yes, toads and frogs have been sucked up by a tor-*
*nado and poured out by a cloud. A railroad coach with 117 passengers aboard was*
*carried aloft by a tornado and dumped into a ditch 25 meters away. A schoolhouse*
*was demolished and eighty-five students were transported 100 meters. Amazingly,*
*none of these students was killed. Chickens have lost their feathers and straw has*
*been driven into metal pipes. These are only a few examples of the meanest and*
*deadliest wind of all—the tornado.*[4]

Mike could have started by saying, "My topic today is tornados. They are very dangerous, and I'm sure you've heard stories and maybe seen movies about them." But he realized
that a more creative way of getting the attention of listeners was by referring to the unexpected. Audiences tend to be more involved and responsive when they are surprised or
startled by an idea. The one-liner combined with the brief examples effectively set up the
entire speech: Listeners were completely receptive and anxious to hear other pertinent
information about the tornado.

Here is another way to use a shock technique in the introduction. Before his speech
began, student Stephen King got the attention of his listeners by distributing a small white
cup to each of his classmates. He then held up a "memo," which he began reading to his
audience:

*I'd like to read you this memo from the dean of the university. "It has come to the*
*attention of the administration and faculty that an increasing number of students*
*have been abusing alcohol and illegal drugs on campus. In response, the university*
*has adopted a policy of mandatory drug testing for all full- and part-time students.*
*Moreover, since this serious problem could cause the university to lose its state*

*funding, students must submit to a witnessed urinalysis by the medical staff of the university by November 30. Should any student fail to comply or fail this test, he or she will be immediately dropped from class rosters and dismissed from the university."*

*Now I've passed around some paper cups and labels and I'd like you to fill out your name, Social Security number, and any prescription drugs you are taking. In the hall are members of the medical department to witness your test. Now, I'd like to start at the rear of the room. One at a time please.*

*This memo is not real. But how would you feel if it were? Would you be insulted, embarrassed, outraged? Would you say "Who the hell do you think I am?" Well get prepared, because it's happening all across America. Sooner or later, don't be surprised if someone wants you to urinate in a cup like this. These drug tests violate our Constitutional rights and invade our privacy.*[5]

Steve understood his student audience extremely well. He recognized that they would listen carefully to the contrived memo from the "dean" of their university. When developing the document, the speaker used words such as *moreover, comply,* and *class rosters* as well as bureaucratic sentence structure that sounded authentic and appeared to have been issued by a university official. This beginning strategy of a startling situation was overwhelmingly successful. One student said, "I thought this was all true. The memo that he read sounded official, and I was going to take my little cup to the restroom for the sample." Another listener commented, "I was incensed that anyone would try something like this. It really drove the point home." Steve used this method to get to the heart of the issue. He quickly communicated that although the situation was hypothetical, the problem was real, and he placed his audience in a situation that forced them to examine the issues involved. He had his audience sitting on the edge of their seats. Notice that the end of the introduction identifies a two-point thesis statement: "These drug tests violate our Constitutional rights and invade our privacy."

## STATISTICS

You can begin your speech by citing **statistics** to involve the audience.

*Of the eighteen people in this classroom, nine were sexually molested as children—that's one out of every two, men as well as women, according to figures from Family and Children's Services of Central Maryland. Actually, there are only eight in the audience, because I'm the ninth person. And I kept that secret for thirty-six years.*

*I've been a rape crisis counselor for two years, and I've put in one hundred hours working with sexually abused child victims. Victims of child abuse have no control over what happened to them. It is the secrecy surrounding the incident that causes significant damage. As parents and future parents, you need to know what sexual child abuse is, who the offenders are, how the victims are affected, and some preventative measures you can take to protect your children.*[6]

Kathy Birckhead could have started this introduction with a simple statement of the statistic and a general comment about the unfortunate implications revealed by the numbers. Instead, she related the statistics to the audience and got immediate attention by using the numbers to appeal to the physical and emotional well-being of her listeners. Because the statistics indicated that half of them were abused as children, audience members listened intently to learn more about the topic. Concern intensified when the speaker acknowledged her own abuse and established credibility as a counselor. Notice that Kathy involves the audience by connecting to parents as well as "future parents" when she states the thesis that includes four points at the end of her introduction.

# QUESTIONS

Another way to introduce a topic is by asking a question. *Questions* can be either rhetorical or open-ended. **Rhetorical questions** are self-answered: Listeners respond silently. In a speech titled "The Changed World," George P. Shultz, director of the Bechtel Group and former secretary of state in the Reagan administration, begins a speech with two rhetorical questions:

> *I want to ask two questions. What, from a security standpoint, is going on in the world? When we answer that, that's the key to answering the second question: Where do we go from here?*
>
> *We are at war.*
>
> *We have struggled with what we have called terrorism for a long time, without quite realizing the nature of the threat. In the Reagan administration, I was a hawk on the subject. I said terrorism was a big problem, a different problem, and we have to take forceful action against it. Fortunately, Ronald Reagan agreed with me, but not many others did.*[7]

Mr. Shultz uses the two questions in the introduction to focus the audience on the two key points of his thesis. He then divides the body of his speech into two sections to develop specific answers.

Questions can also be of the open-ended type, which stimulate a direct response from the audience. Asking **open-ended questions** can be effective, but you need to be careful with this method. Don't ask the audience for more than a show of hands or one-word answers. If you request more complicated information, you may find them taking control of your speech. In this example, the speaker asks for a simple show of hands to gain a response:

> *By a show of hands, how many people in this room are Baptists? Okay, there are a few of you. I want you to listen closely, because what I'm about to read concerns you. By order of the governor, all Baptists have been proclaimed enemies of the state and must be exterminated, or driven from the state, if necessary, for the public good.*
>
> *This sounds crazy doesn't it? It's the 1990s and we live in the United States and things like this just don't happen. Well, you're kinda right, they don't happen in the 90s, but they did happen in 1838. In the state of Missouri in 1838, Governor Lillburn W. Boggs issued an order of extermination for all Mormons. Today I want to talk about the three events leading up to that extermination order, namely, the existing anti-Mormon sentiment, the election day riot, and the Crooked River incident.*[8]

Michelle Allred decided to ask a question that seemed to invade her listeners' privacy. But the question combined with the hypothetical example helped the audience to understand the results of discrimination and religious persecution. When you seek an open-ended response, you must be clear that you want an answer from your listeners. In this instance, Michelle asked the question and told her audience the type of response she wanted. She also paused a moment to let the audience know she was waiting for their answer. The introduction then proceeded in a logical manner from the example to the 1838 extermination order, which the speaker used to introduce her three-point thesis statement. The strategy was extremely effective and helped the audience to connect to Michelle's historical topic.

# QUOTATION

Another good way to introduce your speech is by using a **quotation** appropriate to your topic. In a nationally televised campaign speech, 1992 presidential candidate H. Ross Perot used a quotation to introduce a speech on the economy:

*"The budget should be balanced. The treasury should be refilled. Public debts should be reduced. The arrogance of public officials should be controlled." These are not new words. Cicero said these words over 2,000 years ago, but certainly they apply to our country today.*

*Anytime we do anything, we try to learn from experience. We learned a lot from the first program from your comments. First, you wanted better charts that you can see the fine print on, and you'll have those tonight. Secondly, we had one news announcer that criticized the pointer that I used before. So, since we're dealing with voodoo economics, a great young lady from Louisiana sent me this voodoo stick and I will use it as my pointer tonight. Certainly, it's appropriate, because, as you and I know, we're in deep voodoo!*[9]

Perot began with the quotation from Cicero to stress the seriousness of the issue. But the speaker demonstrated that he could "learn from experience" about the needs and interests of millions of viewers. Perot interjected humor with the visual aid to motivate listeners and to connect them to a difficult subject. He also used humor as a political weapon. In the presidential primaries of the early 1980s, candidate George Bush had commented that candidate Ronald Reagan's economic plan for the country was "voodoo economics." By reminding voters about Bush's earlier comment and using the voodoo stick, Perot mocked President Bush, who was presiding over an economic recession at the time. The combination of strategies was successful: Millions of Americans listened intently to the 30-minute speech.

You can also include a longer quotation in the introduction, such as a poem, song, or other work that is appropriate to your topic:

*I'd like to quote a poem entitled "To Santa Claus and Little Sisters."*

*Once . . . he wrote a poem.*
*And called it "Chops,"*
*Because that was the name of*
*his dog, and that's what it was*
*all about.*

*And the teacher gave him an "A"*
*And a gold star.*
*And his mother hung it on the*
*kitchen door and read it to*
*all his aunts . . .*

*Once . . . he wrote another*
*poem.*
*And he called it "Question Marked*
*Innocence."*
*Because that was the name of*
*His grief, and that's what it*
*was all about.*
*And the professor gave him an*
*"A"*
*And a strange and steady look.*
*And his mother never hung it*
*on the kitchen door, because*
*he never let her see it . . .*

*Once, at 3 A.M. . . . he tried*
*another poem . . .*
*And he called it absolutely*
*nothing, because that's what it*
*was all about.*
*And he gave himself an "A"*
*And a slash on each damp wrist,*
*And hung it on the bathroom*
*door because he couldn't reach*
*the kitchen.*[10]

*This poem was written by a 15-year-old boy two years before he committed suicide.*
*The National Institute of Mental Health recently reported that every 90 minutes a*
*teenager commits suicide. We must know the warning signs of teenage suicide so*
*that we can recognize them and intervene the next time a child cries out for help.*[11]

In this introduction, Tina Cerrato immediately aroused the attention of her audience. They were completely involved as they listened to the poem, and they were curious to find out the underlying meaning. Tina made them wait in suspense until the final sentences of her introduction, when the point of the poem became entirely clear. If parents, teachers, or friends cannot recognize the obvious warning signs of teenage suicide, they will be powerless to stop an often preventable tragedy. The poem and statistical evidence, validated by a credible source, demonstrated that the issue was real, important, and required the full attention of the audience.

## SUSPENSE

In addition to using quotations or poems to stimulate interest, you can make listeners curious about a topic by using **suspense**.

*A harness locks you into place. You move slowly forward and then upward, climbing*
*to a height of fifteen stories. Next you drop 55 degrees, making you feel as if you just*
*drove off a cliff at more than 60 miles per hour. You zoom through two 60-foot-high*
*loops, you are turned upside down, you gyrate through a 200-foot corkscrew, and*
*you are thrown like a boomerang into a final loop. You've been turned upside down*
*and around six times, and pressed against your seat by the force—of gravity, that is,*
*which is nearly four times your body weight.*

*Is this some kind of masochistic exercise or strange ceremony? No, not really.*
*You've just experienced the Vortex, the roller coaster ride at King's Island Amuse-*
*ment Park in Ohio as described by Kerry Hannon in an August 1987 issue of* Forbes
*magazine. Today I'd like to give you some information that you may not know about*
*the design and safety of these wonderful, whirling thrills.*[12]

Karen Leonard realized that students in a speech class would respond favorably to the element of suspense. Without identifying her topic at the beginning, Karen described a series of events designed to sustain the curiosity of audience members. The speaker painted concrete images that allowed listeners to picture the experience in their minds. The audience could "feel" the pressure of the locking harness; they could experience the sensation of the fifteen-story climb and the 55-degree drop; and they could endure the gravitational forces of the corkscrew and the slinging shot of the final loop. Karen's strategy was successful even though most listeners had guessed the topic before she revealed it. After identifying the source of her descriptive statements, the speaker stated a clear two-point thesis at the end of the introduction.

## PERSONAL REFERENCE, COMPLIMENT, OR REFERENCE TO THE OCCASION

Another way to begin an introduction is by making a **personal reference** or by giving a **compliment** to the audience. Speakers sometimes face audiences they do not know and speak in places they've never been. In this kind of situation, it is important for a speaker to establish a common ground. Effective audience analysis will help the speaker mention the appropriate catchwords that will build a relationship with listeners. Notice how David Archambault, president of the American Indian College Fund, used a personal reference in the following introduction:

> *Thank you and good afternoon. Hau Kola. That is how we Lakota say "Greeting, Friends." I am happy to be here today to represent Native American people. I am a Ikoeya Wicaska—an ordinary man. We think of an ordinary man as not superior to anyone else or for that matter to anything else. We—all people and all things—are related to each other.*
>
> *We begin our spiritual ceremonies with the phrase "Oni takuya Oyasi," which means all my relations. We believe that all people are ultimately part of one nation— the nation of mankind—but that this nation is only one of many nations that inhabit the Mother Earth. To us all living things are nations—the deer, the horses, things that crawl, things that fly, things that grow in and on the ground. All of these nations were created by the same Power, and none is superior to another. All are necessary for life. We are expected to live and work in harmony.*[13]

Because he presented his remarks to an audience with few Native Americans, Archambault acquainted listeners with his culture by expressing warm greetings in his native language and by describing the spiritual philosophies of his tribe. The speaker's key to this effective personal reference was good audience analysis. He understood his audience members and knew the appropriate references needed to help listeners understand his background and culture.

In a speech class where you get to know everyone during the semester, you might not need to begin by complimenting the audience. But it is possible that circumstances could require you to make a personal reference. If you are from an environment or culture that is different from that of your listeners, you might find it beneficial to acknowledge this diversity and use it as a device for stimulating interest and curiosity. Like Archambault, a Turkish student once referred to his native country by its language and customs. A speaker from Zimbabwe began by presenting verbal descriptions of wild animals roaming freely over the countryside. And a speaker from the Philippines asked the audience to study her facial features and attempt to guess her country of origin. These speakers used personal references as a strategy to connect to the curiosities of their listeners.

You can also begin your introduction by making a **reference to the occasion** of the speech. In a speech presented at the Smithsonian Institution, Senator Hillary Rodham Clinton made the following reference at the opening of a new exhibit honoring the victims and the heroes of September 11:

> *Thank you, Secretary Powell, for those kind words. I know that our country is so grateful for your dedicated service, and we welcome your leadership and guidance.*
>
> *. . . It is an honor to be here with Mrs. Bush to open this deeply moving exhibit. On behalf of all New Yorkers, I want to thank her for her service that she has performed in so many ways. But particularly with respect to the words that she has spoken and the example she has set so that all of us have a better idea of how to comfort and help our children . . . .*

*In this audience today are people who were there at the Pentagon. People who were there at the World Trade Center. People who lost loved ones in those terrible attacks, when the airplanes hit our cherished places of commerce and government and crashed because of our heroes' efforts in the fields of Pennsylvania. And to each of you, I thank you for being willing to share your memories and to look forward because this is not just an exhibit about the past—it does honor the past but it calls on each of us to think deeply about what it means to be an American at the beginning of the 21st century.[14]*

Senator Clinton acknowledged Secretary of State Colin Powell and then thanked First Lady Laura Bush for her service to the nation. Finally, the senator made reference to audience members who lost loved ones in the attacks of September 11 and who were willing to share their memories by donating objects of sentimental value for the exhibit.

In your speech class, you could refer to a serious event such as September 11, Memorial Day, or Veterans' Day. You could also acknowledge an upcoming holiday like Christmas, Passover, Easter, Independence Day, or Thanksgiving, or a special event like Valentine's Day, Mother's Day, or even April Fool's Day. An opening reference to the occasion can be related to the topic and simultaneously gain the attention and interest of your audience.

## HUMOR

**Humor** is an excellent way to introduce a speech. Humor can establish goodwill between the speaker and the audience, and a joke or humorous anecdote can relax the audience and put the speaker at ease. Read this short introduction from a speech that Benjamin Alexander, president of Drew Dawn Enterprises, presented to the American Association of Retired Persons:

*It was twelve months ago that Mrs. Brown invited me to address this distinguished group of retired Americans. My role is to speak to you; your job is to listen. If you should finish your assignment before mine is completed, and you wish to leave— please do so. But if too many of you begin to depart at the same time, let me know where you are going and if it sounds better than here, I will join you.[15]*

The remarks are genuinely funny, yet they have a serious point. Alexander demonstrates his sensitivity to the speaker-audience relationship and through the use of humor, tells the listeners that he intends to interest them.

When you think about using humor for an introduction, remember that it can be a two-edged sword. Never start an introduction with humor that can offend, insult, or hurt members of your audience. Beginning with inappropriate sexist jokes, insulting religious stories, or cultural put-downs can seriously backfire and drive listeners away. Once turned off by offensive humor, listeners will be difficult to win back.

Be certain that your humor is appropriate and gets the response you want from your audience. Recognize that humor can be tricky: A joke that flops or an anecdote that is poorly presented will defeat the purpose of the introduction. Be relatively sure that your humor will work by trying it out on friends or classmates in advance.

## THE FLEXIBLE INTRODUCTION

There will be times when your prepared introduction may not be appropriate. Unexpected events sometimes create difficult situations, making an audience unreceptive to a presentation. A humorous introduction would not be appropriate if an audience had just heard a wrenching testimonial about drug addiction; a sad story about adoption might not be effective after rollicking humor; an introduction presented to listeners who are freezing might generate very little positive response. You may need to alter your prepared beginning by presenting another introduction that puts listeners in a more receptive mood.

One student, who was among several scheduled to present a classroom speech, had planned a statistical introduction for a speech about recycling. By coincidence, however, another speaker presented almost identical factual materials on the same topic. The student with the second recycling speech adapted to the unwelcome situation with the following impromptu introduction:

> My topic is recycling as well. I was glad to see that someone else had an interest in the waste problem. (I was also shocked to see this!) That speech informed us about developments in recycling in different companies today, it showed that recycling is not developed as much here as in other places in the country, and it described the problems with dumping in the sea. I'll try not to reiterate the main points, but rather, I'll try to reinforce the urgency and the need for recycling.[16]

Naming the topic is not the most effective way of beginning an introduction, but the situation that Rick Trader encountered demanded quick thinking. The speaker did not let circumstances destroy his confidence. He transformed a negative situation by acknowledging the difficulty, by joking about the coincidence, and even by restating the previous speaker's thesis. He then reassured listeners that he would provide new information in addition to material already presented. The impromptu introduction worked. Rick's listeners were positive and supportive and appreciated his different perspective on the same topic.

## COMBINATION OF STRATEGIES

You will often find that it is useful to combine a variety of strategies in your introduction. Chris Koeppen used a combination of approaches to stimulate his listeners' interest:

> When you were a kid, did you ever play with building blocks like this? Well, I used to enjoy them as I'm sure you did. I found blocks to be fun and educational, and I used to create all kinds of structures, like the one I've made here. Building these objects helped me to imagine larger structures. Consider, for example, that there are only six little blocks in my pyramid. Imagine that you had to put together 21.2 million of these blocks. Furthermore, instead of small blocks, imagine that each one of them weighed about 5,000 pounds. That's the type of project that the ancient Egyptians undertook when building the Great Pyramid. What is equally amazing is that the exact reason for its existence remains a mystery. Thus the intrigue of the Great Pyramid stems from the facts about its construction and the theories on why it was built.[17]

The speaker asks the audience a rhetorical question and uses a visual aid to remind audience members of their childhood. The opening statements create suspense, and the small pyramid is an effective visual aid that provides a comparison to the Great Pyramid of Egypt. Finally, Chris mentions some startling statistics and ends with his two-point thesis statement.

If you combine a question with a quote, or a statistic with a startling statement or visual aid, you can develop an introduction both interesting and meaningful to your audience.

## outlining the introduction

The introduction is part of the informal outline of a speech. Remember that the purpose of the outline is to help you communicate the content of your introduction. Although it is never advisable to mix sentences and topics in the formal outline of the speech body, it may actually be helpful to adopt this practice in your introduction. Here are two different sample outlines you can choose from for your introduction.

The first example demonstrates a one-level outline.

| ONE-LEVEL OUTLINE: | INTRODUCTION |
|---|---|
| (First sentence) | I. "A harness locks you into place." |
| (Strategy) | II. Suspenseful example |
| (Specific purpose) | III. To provide information about roller coasters |
| (Thesis statement) | IV. "Today I'd like to give you some information that you may not know about the design and safety of these wonderful, whirling thrills." |

Numeral I identifies the very first sentence that you will actually state in your introduction. Numeral II simply describes the overall strategy (or strategies) you will be using for the entire introduction, that is, whether the introduction uses an example, quotation, statistics, humor, suspense, personal reference or combination of strategies. In this instance, the speaker is using a suspenseful example for her introduction. Numeral III is the specific purpose that may or may not be stated in the introduction itself. The specific purpose may be so obvious by the end of the introduction that it does not require a formal statement. Numeral IV is the thesis, which should always be clearly stated at the end of the introduction. A one-level outline is uncomplicated and easy to transfer to speaking notes. The disadvantage of this approach is that it requires the speaker to be completely familiar with all the details of the introduction from memory.

Here is a two-level outline that includes all of the important details of the introduction:

| TWO-LEVEL OUTLINE | INTRODUCTION |
|---|---|
| (First sentence) | I. "A harness locks you into place." |
| (Strategy) | II. Suspenseful example |
| |    A. You move forward and upward to 15 stories |
| |    B. You drop 55 degrees as if dropping from a cliff at 60 mph |
| |    C. You zoom through 2 loops, turn upside down, gyrate through 200-ft corkscrew, and are thrown like boomerang into final loop |
| |    D. You've been turned up, down, around 6 times and pressed by gravity 4 times body weight |
| |    E. You've experienced Vortex—coaster at King's Island Amusement Park, Ohio (described in *Forbes*, by Kerry Hannon) |
| (Specific purpose) | III. To provide information about roller coasters |
| (Thesis statement) | IV. "Today I'd like to give you some information that you may not know about the design and safety of these wonderful, whirling thrills." |

You can see that the two-level outline has the same number of points as used in the first example, but it includes more details. The detail obviously helps to keep you on track if you feel you need more information to guide you through your introduction. Use whichever approach your instructor recommends to suit your particular needs.

## planning the conclusion

Just as a speech requires an introduction, a speech also needs a conclusion. We've often heard endings like this:

*Well, uh, I guess, uh, that's about it!*

*And now in conclusion I'd just like to say that I hope you've learned something about holograms.*

*And now for my conclusion, I'll leave you with a quote: all's well that ends well.*

*And so finally, in conclusion, I'd like to end by telling you that my last point is that you might want to pick up a kit to test radon gas the next time you're in the home improvement store.*

*Thank you.*

These are not successful ways to end speeches. The "techniques" are abrupt, trite, awkward, or repetitious. Sloppy conclusions increase the speaker's apprehension and make the audience equally uncomfortable.

An effective conclusion gives finality to a speech. The speaker must choose a clear method or device that tells the audience that the topic has been resolved. A speaker must also clearly demonstrate in his or her delivery (voice tone, slower rate of speech) that the speech has ended.

You should not introduce new material in the conclusion; rather, you should choose a method that reinforces the information and ideas you have already presented. We will provide brief explanations and examples of a conclusion—summary, quotation, reference to the introduction, challenge and appeal, humor, question, story, and statistics.

## SUMMARY OF MAIN POINTS

A **summary** of the main points can be an effective way to end a speech on complicated or difficult subject matter. Summaries help to remind your audience of the major points and leave them with a sense of order. Meredith Kreczmer summarized her demonstration on creative photography and used a visual aid as reinforcement:

*The key to a good picture is not the number of lights or the quality of your camera and lens, but it is your ability to "see" and "think" in terms of pictures. Remember the simple steps on this poster:*

> *First, get to know your camera—*
> *the viewfinder*
> *shutter release*
> *aperture shutter*
>
> *Second, remember the key techniques—*
> *less is more*
> *move around your subject*
> *look at your background*
> *close in on the subject*
> *simplicity is never wrong*
>
> *So snap away, and maybe someday you'll see your picture in* National Geographic![18]

The speaker used several visuals and described a number of techniques during the body of the speech. An ordinary verbal summary would have been adequate; instead,

Meredith used words and cartoon sketches on a visual aid to remind her audience of important ideas stressed in the speech. The summary included both main and supporting points, because the body of this presentation included only two numerals. In longer, more complex speeches, however, speakers might tend to recap only the main points.

Don't use a summary conclusion simply because you can't think of any other approach. Remember that a successful speaker has a good reason for the type of conclusion he or she selects. Summaries are good with complex material in informative speeches, but they are not effective when you need to be persuasive and appeal to the audience or challenge their thinking in another way.

## QUOTATION

A quotation is often an excellent way to end a speech. A quote can express feelings eloquently and reinforce the speaker's ideas. Kim Jones combined an example with a quotation to end a speech commemorating Sojourner Truth, a famous African American orator and reformer:

> Sojourner Truth fought for increased education, Negro rights, world peace, and women's rights. But some did not give her the respect that she deserved. According to William Jacobs' Great Lives, the newspapers started a rumor. Because she was six feet tall, they said that she was probably a man disguised as a woman. In order to prove her womanhood, they asked her to show her breasts. With quiet dignity, she opened her blouse before the stunned crowd and declared softly: "It is not my shame, but yours, that I must do this."
>
> Sojourner Truth died in 1883. A quotation in the Jacobs book presents a fitting tribute to the life of this great African American. "With her arms outstretched, and her eyes aflame, she argued in a deep voice about women's rights: 'If the first woman God ever made was strong enough to turn the world upside down, all alone, then together we ought to be able to turn it back and get it right side up again and now they are asking us to do it, the men better let them.'"[19]

Kim cited this vivid example to demonstrate the courage and regal dignity that Sojourner displayed in the midst of degrading and humiliating circumstances. The end quotation resolved the speech effectively by painting an elegant portrait of a strong, compassionate, yet determined woman. Listeners experienced feelings of rage, empathy, and pride as Kim delivered the quotation slowly, with strength and emotion.

Quotations can also be used to provide emotional support in a conclusion. Gary Anderson, whose speech, "In Memory of Juliana McCourt," was mentioned earlier in this chapter, ended with a moving tribute to those who fell on September 11:

> Don't forget Juliana McCourt and the other little children, parents, brothers, and sisters who died on September 11, taken so unexpectedly from this world. Don't forget the hundreds of firefighters and policemen who ran into the buildings as the others were running out. To them I dedicate this poem, written by an unknown American poet. It is entitled "The Last Time."
>
> > "If I knew it would be the last time that I'd see you fall asleep, I would tuck you in more tightly and pray the Lord your soul to keep.
> > If I knew it would be the last time that I see you walk out the door,
> > I would give you a hug and kiss and call you back for one more. . . .
> > If I knew it would be the last time I could spare an extra minute or two, I'd stop and say 'I love you,' instead of assuming 'you know I do.' . . .
> > So hold your loved ones close today, and whisper in their ear, tell them how much you love them, and that you'll always hold them dear.

> *Take time to say 'I'm sorry,' 'please forgive,' 'thank you,' or 'it's o.k. . . .' And if*
> *tomorrow never comes, you'll have no regrets about today."*
> *God bless little Juliana McCourt.*[20]

The speaker, who began with the story of 4-year-old Juliana McCourt engulfed in the terrorist attacks, ended with a moving tribute expressed in a poem. The poem and final blessing for Juliana honored the victims and conveyed a moral to his listeners and readers. Nothing more needed to be said.

## REFERENCE TO THE INTRODUCTION

One good way of concluding a speech is a **reference to the introduction**. This strategy can be used successfully with any type of introduction to promote unity within a presentation. Earlier we mentioned an introduction in which Stephen King shocked his audience by reading a memo from "the dean of the university" requiring drug tests for all students (see page 171–172). Steve ended that speech with this conclusion:

> *I want you to think about the urine cups you have in front of you. How does it feel to be looked upon as a drug user until you can prove your innocence? Suppose that your test came back positive, and you were dismissed from college because of an inexperienced lab technician. Let's stop treating people as if they're being spied upon. Let's keep our Constitution strong and never relinquish our right to privacy. Let's stop drug testing—now!*[21]

Steve effectively referred to the shocking situation he had presented in his introduction, in which he passed out urine cups and read a fictitious administrative "memo" forcing students to take mandatory drug tests. The reference drew his listeners' attention back to the injustice of the opening situation. He ended by challenging the audience to uphold the right of privacy granted by the Constitution. This strategy is effective because it uses similar details in the beginning and ending of the speech.

## CHALLENGE OR APPEAL

In some speeches, especially persuasive speeches, you may need to conclude by issuing a general challenge or a specific appeal to the audience. A **challenge** is usually a broad, generalized summons to the audience to make some kind of effort to support the topic. A speaker telling the audience "We need to preserve liberty" or "We must protect our children" is using a general challenge in the conclusion.

Notice how Jacquelyn Shields ended her persuasive speech about increasing the length of the school year:

> *Last week I received notification of my eligibility to become a member of Phi Theta Kappa, the national honor society for community colleges. It's extremely ironic that I received this announcement while I was researching this speech. If I could walk into a Japanese classroom with my Japanese counterpart, a college sophomore, and be tested on my pool of knowledge, I would come up short. Each one of you must also consider how you would compare to your counterpart in Japan. And if you feel that you also would come up short, then you must remember that you are a product of the American educational system.*
>
> *If you don't want your children to suffer in the future, I urge you to think about changing the system. Let's improve our educational process by lengthening the school year. Let's regain our economic and technological leadership by helping our children to compete with other nations on an equal footing.*[22]

Jackie's reference to her membership in Phi Theta Kappa gave her credibility as an honor student. But the comparison of American and Japanese educational systems motivated listeners to think. In the final paragraph, she directly challenged the audience to improve American education. The challenge is general rather than specific; she allowed listeners to decide for themselves how to carry it out.

You can also end a speech by using a specific **appeal** to the audience. Unlike challenges, appeals are usually well defined for the audience. When a speaker asks you to vote for someone, give to a specific cause, or support a philosophy or issue, he or she is using a direct appeal.

Notice how Shelley Snyder used appeals to conclude a persuasive speech on racism:

*I hope all of you can admit that there still remains a problem of racism and that you can commit to taking a stand against it; that you evaluate yourselves, your preconceptions, your prejudices, and yes, your racist views. I really never thought of myself as a racist. I abhor violence. I abhor blatant discrimination and all the inequities I see. But in researching for this speech, I found that, in too many instances, I am racist. But my personal appeal, and the appeal I put before you, is to understand where our attitudes come from and to ask ourselves for a change of heart—to defend the victims of racism, to work to improve legislation for equal justice for all. I am going to hand out a test from a book entitled The Day America Told the Truth. I want you to take it in the privacy of your own home and assess yourself—honestly. Again, I ask you: Take a stand against racism. For in the words of Martin Luther King, Jr., "To ignore evil is to become an accomplice to it."[23]*

The speaker employed several appeals in this conclusion. Shelley asked listeners to stop racism by honestly evaluating their own views. But she did not simply accuse the audience: The speaker was able to refer to her own racism, making the persuasion even more powerful.

In his famous speech, "I Have a Dream," Martin Luther King, Jr. made skillful use of his conclusion, which included the ringing words, "Free at last! Free at last! Thank God almighty, we are free at last!"

© Bob Adelman/Magnum Photos, Inc.

Shelley urged listeners to take action by answering questions about racism, and she combined her final appeal with a forceful quotation from Martin Luther King, Jr. The appeals were highly successful with audience members. One listener commented: "Shelley really persuaded me to take a look at my own attitudes." Another observed: "I'm going to take the test, and if I don't like what I see, I'm going to do all I can to change. I guess we can't solve racism until we solve it within ourselves."

## HUMOR

*Humor* that is appropriate to your audience and the topic can be a good way to end a speech. Telling a joke or brief anecdote can leave your audience in a good mood and can stimulate a spontaneous positive response at the end.

Kimberly Kittle informed listeners how to use substitute remedies for household problems when the appropriate products were too expensive or unavailable. She advocated using hairspray to remove ink stains, mayonnaise as a cure for brittle hair, and vegetable oil to keep car doors from freezing in winter. She ended the speech on a light, but cautionary note:

> *Even though these alternative remedies can work wonders, remember that nothing is 100 percent foolproof, and one always has to be moderate and cautious. While some products can be used to solve common household problems, they can create even worse nightmares. For example, a man who thought he'd found the perfect way to absorb unsightly motor oil in his driveway spread kitty litter on every inch of concrete outside his house. The remedy worked and the oil disappeared, but the poor man ended up creating a monstrous cat litter box that attracted every happy feline in town!*[24]

The audience was enlightened by Kim's helpful hints and enjoyed laughing at the humorous punch line.

Your humor must be entertaining; stories from joke books or worn-out anecdotes tend to backfire. Be certain that your humor is fresh, spontaneous, and appropriate.

## QUESTION

You can also conclude by asking the audience a *rhetorical question*. This approach encourages the audience to "think about it" for a while. Ernestine Cooper presented a convincing speech about the dangers of aerobic exercise. After providing statistics, examples, and a personal experience to support her point of view, the speaker delivered this conclusion:

> *If you are thinking about getting into aerobics, listen to your body's signals. Check out your health clubs. Check out the floors. Wear the appropriate shoes. And most important, check out the instructors. Ask to see those credentials. Where did they receive their training? Will they address your needs on an individual basis? Remember, it is your body, your limbs that need to be protected. You have a right to know. Ask yourself, are the health benefits from aerobic exercise worth the pain? Do you want to wind up as a statistic in the next survey of aerobic injuries?*[25]

Because of Ernestine's impressive evidence and the questions posed in her conclusion, the audience was persuaded to think seriously about the potential harm of aerobic exercise. The final question stimulated a silent "no" response within her listeners.

## STORY, ILLUSTRATION, AND EXAMPLE

Once you have provided your audience with extensive information about a topic, you can end with a *story*, an *illustration*, or a brief *example* to keep the audience interested and at the same time drive home your point.

Notice how Norma Ferris concluded her speech about the Meals on Wheels program:

*But we often think, "Well there're so many problems in the world, and I'm just one person, what could I do?" With the Meals on Wheels program, there's no question that you can do something. You—just one person—can make a difference in someone's life—someone who would otherwise be forgotten.*

*Let me tell you about one woman on my route who was a childless widow. It was Eastertime, and while I was delivering her meal I saw someone selling flowers. So I picked up just a small hyacinth and brought it to her. She was so taken with it, she said, "No one but the Meals on Wheels people have treated me kindly in so long—I'm so grateful—I just wish there was something I could do for you." She thought for a minute, and she went back into her bedroom, and she came out with an old mink stole—it must have been thirty years old. She said, "My husband gave this to me. Would you take it? Because I appreciate what you've done so much—I'm very grateful." Well, I couldn't take it. But it just goes to show you how important you can be to someone. With the Meals on Wheels program, you can make a difference.*[26]

This brief story was drawn from the speaker's personal experience and gave the topic a powerful sense of credibility. The emotional quality of the story maintained audience interest and attention to the very end of the speech. Norma communicated the idea that the Meals on Wheels program was not just another charity begging for money. Listeners could see that their involvement would benefit the elderly and would give those volunteering personal satisfaction and reward.

## STATISTICS

A speaker can state or reemphasize an alarming *statistic* to get the audience to think seriously about an issue. Statistics are often effective when combined with other types of conclusions.

In a speech about battered women, a speaker combined two approaches:

*We need to help these battered women. Often we overlook the problem just because it's not happening to us. Sometimes we overlook the problem because we don't want to get involved. Twenty women were beaten as I was giving this speech. I hope you all understand the importance of getting involved by hearing, seeing, or assisting someone in need of help. It's not okay. Don't let it happen. Help—please.*[27]

Tresse Bailey asked her audience to provide volunteer help to shelters for battered women. She ended her actuating speech with an appeal and a simple but powerful statistic. The speaker was careful not to bombard listeners with complicated numbers; she simply related the one statistic referring to the time it took her to deliver the speech. The statistic was a dramatic reminder of the extent of the problem.

## outlining the conclusion

You can outline the conclusion in almost the same way you outlined the introduction. Here are examples of outlines with one and two levels:

**ONE-LEVEL OUTLINE:**

Conclusion
(First sentence)      I. "But we often think, 'Well, there're so many problems in the world, and I'm just one person, what can I do?'"
(Strategy)      II. Story of an elderly lady

TWO-LEVEL OUTLINE:

Conclusion
(First sentence)      I.  "But we often think, 'Well, there're so many problems in the world, and I'm just one person, what can I do?"
                          A. Involvement in Meals on Wheels helps
                          B. Volunteers remember forgotten people
(Strategy)           II.  Story of an elderly lady
                          A. Woman given a flower
                          B. Woman expressed overwhelming appreciation
                          C. Woman offered volunteer mink stole

In both examples, numeral I is the first sentence of the conclusion. Also, numeral II describes the strategy that the speaker employs for the conclusion; that is, whether the entire conclusion is a quote, story, question, summary, challenge, combination of approaches, and so forth. The one-level outline is the abbreviated form that can be used if you really know your conclusion well. The two-level outline provides more detail to help you progress through each major idea in the conclusion. When you are outlining the introduction of your speech, use the approach that is most helpful to you.

# speaking notes for the introduction and conclusion

Here are some sample notecards for the introduction and conclusion of the speech, "Raising the *Monitor*." Both examples use a two-level outline and can be compared to the notecards of the body presented in Chapter 10. You can read the entire speech at the end of Chapter 15, "Speaking to Inform."

---

**INTRODUCTION**                    **(1)**

I.  "March 8, 1862, the confederate ship known as the *Virginia* virtually decimated a Union fleet of wooden warships off the coast of Newport News."

II. Example of historical battle scene image with PowerPoint slide to create suspense and interest.
   A. *Virginia*, 263-ft ship, formerly Union *Merrimack*, salvaged from Norfolk navy yard, destroyed *Cumberland*, 50-gun *Congress*, and forced *Minnesota* to shore
   B. *Monitor* ironclad, 172 ft long, with revolving gun turret appeared
   C. Two ships passed back and forth for two hours

---

**Intro continued**                    **(2)**

   D. Crews lacked training, firing not effective
   E. *Monitor* faster, more maneuverable, but fired every 7 to 8 minutes
   F. *Monitor*'s pilothouse hit, ship sheer to shallow water
   G. *Virginia* assumed ship was disabled, fired again on *Minnesota*
   H. First historical battle between ironclads concluded
   I. Ingenuity creating *Monitor* altered modern naval warfare

   **Thesis: "The historical significance of the USS *Monitor* led scientists and engineers to overcome extreme challenges that resulted in the successful recovery of the vessel's turret."**

---

### CONCLUSION                    (12)

I. **"The USS *Monitor*'s turret will now join the collection of over 400 other *Monitor* artifacts."**
II. Summary, quotation from Robert Sheridan and President Bush, and a series of descriptive statements regarding *Monitor*'s significance
   A. Summary of main points of body
   B. Descriptive statements of *Monitor*'s significance: new information, innovation, impact on today's navies
   C. Quote from Geophysics Professor Robert Sheridan: **"History becomes so much more meaningful when you can see the things that made it."**
   D. Quote from President Bush: **"An important service in these challenging times."**

---

## SAMPLE OUTLINE: raising the *monitor*

*Here is a complete outline of an informative descriptive speech presented by Chaim Verschleisser.*[28]

**RAISING THE MONITOR**
*Chaim Verschleisser*

> **Topic:** The raising of the *Monitor*'s turret
> **General Purpose:** Informative speech to describe
> **Specific Purpose:** To describe the significance of the recovery of the USS *Monitor*'s turret
> **Thesis Statement:** "The historical significance of the USS *Monitor* led scientists and engineers to overcome extreme challenges that resulted in the successful recovery of the vessel's turret."

The title describes the subject matter.

The stated topic and the general purpose, indicating an informative descriptive speech that enlightens and educates listeners. The thesis previews the three main points in the body.

### INTRODUCTION

I. (slide 1) "March 8, 1862, the confederate ship known as the <u>Virginia</u> virtually decimated a Union fleet of wooden warships off the coast of Newport News."
II. Example of historical battle scene image with PowerPoint slide to create suspense and interest
   A. *Virginia*, 263-ft ship, formerly Union *Merrimack*, salvaged from Norfolk navy yard, destroyed *Cumberland*, 50-gun *Congress*, and forced *Minnesota* to shore
   B. *Monitor* ironclad, 172 ft long, with revolving gun turret appeared (slide 2)
   C. Two ships passed back and forth for two hours
   D. Crews lacked training, firing not effective
   E. *Monitor* faster, more maneuverable, but fired every 7 to 8 minutes
   F. *Monitor*'s pilothouse hit, ship sheered to shallow water
   G. *Virginia* assumed ship was disabled, fired again on *Minnesota*
   H. First historical battle between ironclads concluded
   I. Ingenuity creating *Monitor* altered modern naval warfare
III. To inform about the historical significance of raising the USS *Monitor*'s turret
IV. "The historical significance of the USS *Monitor* led scientists and engineers to overcome extreme challenges that resulted in the successful recovery of the vessel's turret."

The specific purpose points to the goal of the speech.

Each part of the speech is clearly labeled as introduction, body, or conclusion. Numeral I is the first sentence—the first line the speaker will say. Numeral II determines the introduction strategy—a historical example presented in a suspenseful manner and PowerPoint slides. Although the specific purpose in numeral III is not stated, quotation marks indicate that the thesis (numeral IV) is taken directly from the speech. The introduction is an informal outline: It includes both sentence and topic form.

BODY

I. History and importance of the *Monitor*
   A. Building and launching of *Monitor* (*slide 3*) (*New York Times*, Jul 30, '02, 1)
      1. Built Greenpoint, Brooklyn, and launched into East River, January 30, 1862
      2. Rotating turret, distinguishing feature, now standard on modern war ships
   B. Specifications (*Encyclopedia Britannica Online*, Aug 26, '02)
      1. 8-inch-thick iron-plated walls, 9 ft high, 21 ft across, 150 tons
      2. Dahlgren-manufactured guns, firing shells/cannonballs 2 miles
   C. Impact and effects (*New York Times*, Jul 30, '02, 1)
      1. Union started building a new class of *Monitor*-type vessels
      2. British Royal Navy canceled construction of wooden warships
   D. Sinking in a storm (*slides 4–5*) (*USA Today*, Jul 22, '02, D.06)
      1. Encountered violent storm off Cape Hatteras New Year's Eve
      2. 10:30 p.m. commander sent lantern distress signal to tow vessel
      3. Some men saved; after midnight, lantern disappeared
      4. Turret sunk to seafloor, 240 ft. down
      5. Missing were 12 crewmen, 4 officers, ship's mascot, black cat
   E. Discovery of wreck (*Newsday*, May 26, '87, 03)
      1. Duke University expedition found remains 16 miles from Hatteras in 1973
      2. Named nation's first marine sanctuary for protection from treasure hunters in 1975
      3. Hull plate and signal lantern recovered in 1977
      4. Anchor recovered in 1983
   F. Turret the prize, containing answers to 140-year-old questions (*Christian Science Monitor*, Aug 9, '02, 3)
      1. Turret only way crew could exit ship
      2. Turret contained answers to 140-year-old questions
      3. Human (and feline) remains, artifacts expected
      4. Federal officials made plans for extensive retrievals in 1997

**Transition:** "Although the recovery and preservation of the *Monitor*'s turret is such important testimony to our nation's history, the scientists and agencies involved in its retrieval faced very serious challenges in the process." (*slide 6* )

II. Challenges faced in retrieving the turret
   A. Money major issue
      1. Expedition costs were $14 million over past 5 years
      2. Teams of scientists tried to reverse artifact deterioration (*Atlanta Journal–Constitution*, May 27, '02, A1)
      3. Maintenance is delicate and expensive (*Atlanta Journal–Constitution*, May 27, '02, A1)
         a. $30 million slated to build USS *Monitor* Center in Newport News, Va.
         b. $20 million is cumulative cost to date
         c. Archaeologists worry about preserving artifacts already raised
   B. Time (*Atlanta Journal–Constitution*, May 27, '02, A1) (*slide 7* )
      1. Surveys in mid-90s indicate corrosion accelerating
      2. Race against time and elements created pressure to complete job
      3. Other issues worried scientists about recovered artifacts
         a. Continued exposure to temperature changes could accelerate decay

---

The body of the speech represents the formal outline. Unlike the introduction, the body does not mix topics and sentences. This outline contains topics except where quoted material is introduced. Parentheses provide abbreviated sources, verifying information.

The external transition connects numerals I and II.

This outline includes three levels: Roman numerals, capital letters, and numbers. The three points marked with Roman numerals carry out the thesis statement. In this outline, main points are arranged in a topical sequence.

b. John Broadwater, NOAA and *Monitor* Marine Sanctuary manager, quoted: "Instead of $30 million for a new center, I think we'd rather see $30,000 worth of conservation."

C. Massive undertaking
1. "One of heaviest artifacts ever lifted from such a depth," Broadwater quote
2. Operation conducted from 300-ft barge (used for oil operations)
3. Retrieval would take 100 navy divers 24/7 hours for four weeks
4. Currents, weather unpredictable
5. Mixed-gas deep diving tricky
6. Divers forced to cut away 40-ft section of armor belt
7. Lifting device, "spider and claw," cradled turret to keep from collapsing

**Transition:** "After months of working through all of these complex challenges (*slide 9*), Navy divers lifted the 200-ton turret (including its contents) of the USS *Monitor* from the graveyard of the Atlantic on Monday, August 5, 2002."

III. The recovery of the turret
A. 1862 flag replica *Monitor* flew during sinking hoisted first (*Atlanta Journal–Constitution*, Aug 6, '02, A1)
1. Quote from Naval Commander Bobbie Scholley: "For a bunch of pretty tough Navy divers, there was a lot of cheering and hugging going on . . . I'm glad I was wearing sunglasses so the men couldn't see me cry." (*Atlanta Journal–Constitution*, Aug 6, '02, A1)
2. Dr. Broadwater quote: "It's sitting on a barge, and we're looking at dents that the *Virginia* put on it March 9, 1862." (*Newsday*, Aug 6, '02, A06)
B. Important discoveries made
1. Bones from 3 human bodies recovered (no cat yet) (*New York Times*, Aug 9, '02, 10)
2. Actual ship differs from plans and drawings (*New York Times*, Jul 30, '02, 1)
a. Parts and braces were undocumented
b. Presumed gauge was large clock
3. Last positions of clock hands were near 1 and 3
a. Reported by survivor, Paymaster Keeler, who said ship sank at 1 a.m. (*New York Times*, Jul 30, '02, 1)
b. Broadwater quoted, "It turns out we didn't have the big picture."
4. Numerous mustard bottles discovered at wreck
a. Union sailors' covered food with mustard
b. John Hightower, president of Mariners' Museum said, "suspect the food needed all the help it could get." (*New York Times*, Jul 30, '02, 1)
5. Discovery of word *Monitor* etched across top
a. Discovered by removal of old engine gauge encrustations
b. Quote from Curtiss Peterson, chief conservator at Mariners' Museum, "I smiled ear to ear.... If it had said something like 'Toledo,' we would have been in deep trouble." (*New York Times*, Jul 30, '02, 1)

CONCLUSION

I. "The USS *Monitor*'s turret will now join the collection of over 400 other *Monitor* artifacts."
II. Summary, quotation from Robert Sheridan and President Bush, and a series of descriptive statements regarding *Monitor*'s significance.
A. Summary of main points of body
B. Descriptive statements of *Monitor*'s significance: new information, innovation, impact on today's navies

The transition connects numerals II and III.

Each level is linguistically parallel, all subordinate points clearly support their headings, every item contains only one basic thought, and each level contains a minimum of two items.

Notice that the body includes many different types of supporting materials such as statistics, examples, quotations, and PowerPoint visual aids.

Like the introduction, the conclusion is informally outlined. Numeral I identifies the first sentence of the conclusion. Numeral II states the strategy used — in this case, a summary followed by quotations and descriptive statements.

The speaker has used a wide range of supporting materials from a variety of sources.

C. Quote from Geophysics Professor Robert Sheridan: "History becomes so much more meaningful when you can see the things that made it."

D. Quote from President Bush: "An important service in these challenging times."

**BIBLIOGRAPHY**

*References are listed alphabetically, and each source is entered according to correct bibliographic form based on the Modern Language Association.*

"Battle of Monitor and Merrimack." *Encyclopedia Britannica Online.* 26 August 2002 <http://0search.eb.com.library.ccbcmd.edu/eb/print?eu=54701 INTERNET>.

Broad, William J. "Retrieval Efforts Aim to Bring Ironclad Monitor Back to Life." *New York Times* 30 July 2002: F1.

Broad, William J. "More Human Remains Found in the Monitor's Gun Turret." *New York Times* 9 August 2002: A10.

Friend, Tim. "Marathon to Raise Monitor." *USA Today* 22 July 2002: Life, D06.

"Historic Monitor Turret Recovered." *Newsday* 6 August 2002: News, A06.

Jonsson, Patrik. "Through Gun Turret, a Sight on the Civil War." *Christian Science Monitor* 9 August 2002: 3.

Lane, Earl. "Research Raising What's Left of the Monitor." *Newsday* 26 May 1987: Discovery, 03.

Tones, Mike. "Success at Last." *Atlanta Journal–Constitution* 6 August 2002: News, A1.

Tones, Mike. "USS Monitor's Turret to Be Lifted After 140 Years." *Atlanta Journal–Constitution* 27 May 2002: A1.

## summary »

The introduction gains the attention of the audience, creates interest and links the topic to the needs of listeners, and introduces the topic. There are a variety of ways to introduce a speech: example, story, or illustration; shocking statement or situation; statistic; question; quotation; suspense; personal reference; humor; a flexible introduction; and a combination of approaches. The conclusion gives finality to the speech and communicates that the topic has been resolved. Types of conclusions are summary; quotation; reference to the introduction; challenge and appeal; humor; question; story, illustration, and example; and statistics.

To outline your introduction, numeral I should be the first sentence, numeral II should identify the strategy you intend to use, numeral III should present the specific purpose, and numeral IV should identify the thesis statement. You can outline the conclusion in the same manner without numerals III and IV. As opposed to the speech body, the outlines of the introduction and conclusion are considered informal: They often combine sentences and topics.

## SKILL BUILDERS »

1. Read the introductions and conclusions to the sample speeches presented in this text (Chapter 2, 6, 9, 12, 15, 16, or 17). Describe the different strategies used to begin and end each speech.

2. Select one of the sample speeches presented in this text and outline two additional introductions and two conclusions using different strategies that would be appropriate to the topic of the speech.

# BUILDING A SPEECH ONLINE »

Now that you've read Chapter 11, use your online Resource Center for Building a Speech for quick access to the electronic study resources that accompany this text. You can access your Resource Center at http://academic.cengage.com/login, using the access code that came with your book or that you bought online at http://www.iChapters.com. Your Resource Center gives you access to Interactive Video Activities, the book's companion website, Speech Builder Express 3.0, InfoTrac College Edition, and study aids, including a digital glossary and review quizzes.

# unit four

# REFINING THE APPEARANCE

© KEVIN DIETSCH/UPI/Landov

# chapter 12

# USING AUDIOVISUAL AIDS

## chapter objectives »

After reading and studying this chapter, you should be able to

1. Describe the types of audiovisual aids
2. Identify six guidelines for using the PowerPoint program
3. Describe the guidelines for using audiovisuals effectively in a speech

Research indicates that visuals such as the following increase the ability of listeners to remember information:[1]

- General David Petraeus displays charts and graphs in his testimony before a Senate committee, indicating that the level of murders and violence in Iraq has declined as a result of the troop surge in 2007 and 2008.
- An NBC newscast airs a disturbing YouTube video that shows several high school students beating up a teacher in a classroom.
- A pastor uses PowerPoint slides to explain how church offerings have decreased over the past year.
- Your speech instructor uses streaming video to illustrate an effective example of a demonstration speech.

When you use a picture or an object to convey ideas, your audience will not only have a more concrete mental image, they will also recall your speech more completely.

In this first chapter of Unit Four "Refining the Appearance," we identify the principal types of audiovisuals and consider their effective use in a speech. Visual aids can be used in almost any type of speech to promote interest, clarity, and retention.

66 *If you use words to rebut a visual image, we know the visual image is dominant.* 99

—*Kathleen Hall Jamieson*

key terms »

AUDIOVISUAL AIDS
COMPUTER
  PROJECTOR
DIGITAL VIDEO
DOCUMENT
  CAMERA
MECHANICAL
  MEDIA
OVERHEAD
  PROJECTOR
POWERPOINT
SCANNER
TRANSPARENCIES

# types of audiovisual aids

There are many types of audiovisuals that can help you to communicate ideas more effectively. **Audiovisual aids** are devices that may appeal to sight and to other senses as well: mechanical media, graphs, drawings and photographs, posters or chalkboards, physical objects, or some aspect of the speaker.

## MECHANICAL MEDIA

In recent years there has been a virtual explosion in the use of media by public speakers. College professors use computers projected onto large screens to demonstrate how to navigate complex software programs or intricate websites. Army generals, ministers, elementary schoolchildren, and Harley-Davidson employees[2] use the popular Microsoft **PowerPoint** program to demonstrate dirty-bomb attacks, display sermon outlines, produce colorful book reports, or explain how to build better bikes. Speakers can also support their presentations by creating audio CDs or digital videos with computerized digital software.

The term **mechanical media** refers to any type of electrical device that can be used as an audiovisual aid. We'll consider the following mechanical media: (1) the computer projector and the PowerPoint software program that are helpful in creating audiovisual aids, (2) projection equipment, and (3) recording equipment.

### The Computer Projector

If your speech requires that you display an Internet site, a software program, or a slide presentation on a computer monitor, you can use a **computer projector**, a device that is connected to the computer and allows your audience to see an enlarged version of the computer monitor on a movie screen. This device is an excellent tool for projecting slides created with the PowerPoint program, websites, procedures, video, photographs, or any type of computer program. Like many media systems, computer projectors vary in complexity and operation. To fine-tune the enlarged projection, many projectors have digital controls for focus, color, contrast, and frame adjustment. A projector must also be connected properly to a standard or laptop computer in order to operate effectively. Older computer projection technology used a flat device known as a liquid crystal display, or LCD unit. The LCD was connected to a computer and placed on the surface of an overhead projector. Although more expensive, the newer computer projectors eliminate the need for overheads and can be operated by remote control. Projectors and computers may seem complicated to connect and adjust if you are inexperienced with these technologies. To avoid any problems or unforeseen complications, check with a media specialist for instructions and help before using a computer projector in your speech.

### Projection Equipment

An **overhead projector** is useful if your visuals require you to add information as you speak. One speaker used the overhead to demonstrate how to fill out a tax form. The overhead allowed the student to add and subtract numbers to show listeners the steps involved in tax preparation. Another speaker used a series of interesting "overlays" to demonstrate the progressive stages of a corneal transplant. When using the overhead, remember that you will need to transfer all of your information to acetate **transparencies**. Fortunately, computers and software such as PowerPoint, graphics packages, or even

© Stockbyte/Getty Images

Computer programs such as PowerPoint can help speakers develop visuals that enhance a speech and increase the ability of listeners to remember information. But in addition to understanding computer software, speakers need to know how to use computers and data projectors in order to incorporate these sophisticated visuals successfully into a speech.

simple word processing programs have simplified this process. You can design a visual on the computer and then place acetate transparencies in the paper cartridge of the printer and print a transparency that is neat and professional in appearance. Before the speech, it is a good idea to inspect the overhead and practice with the transparencies to be sure that everything is in working order.

A **document camera** is an electronic device that is connected to a computer and a projector and is used to project images onto a large screen. A document such as an illustration, graph, magazine, or book is placed on a flat surface, and an overhead camera can enlarge any portion of the page for the projection. Although it is similar in appearance to an overhead projector, the document camera does not require acetate transparencies. A speaker needs special training to use this sophisticated piece of equipment. Be sure to get assistance from a media specialist before you attempt to use it in a presentation.

Although computer projectors now often replace older visual aid technologies formerly used in speeches, there are still occasions when a slide projector can support a presentation if a speaker uses it with consideration for the audience. One speaker employed a slide projector to demonstrate how to bake chocolate chip cookies. The student spent a great deal of time preparing and photographing the various stages of the process, from mixing and baking to the finished product. The speech was interesting, well organized, and kept to the 5-minute time limit. The speaker made certain that she had allowed enough time to photograph the process and develop the film in order to adequately prepare for the scheduled speech.

There are pitfalls to using slide projectors as well. Slides can be inserted upside down or backwards, bulbs can burn out easily, automatic focusing devices can malfunction, or changing mechanisms can be jammed. Problems can also occur if a room does not have a screen or proper surface for projecting slides, or if the room can't be adequately darkened. Sometimes slide shows themselves are boring due to poor photography, needless repetition of scenes, or lengthy explanations. If you intend to use slides, rehearse your speech with the projector. Examine the equipment carefully, and test the projector in the room where you will present the speech. Choose slides with care, using enough to support your ideas but eliminating those that are unnecessary.

**Digital video** equipment projects photographs, video, or text onto a monitor or large screen from a small laser disc or DVD that is identical in appearance to an audio CD. Unlike VCRs, which require a time-consuming process of rewinding or fast-forwarding to reach appropriate segments, the DVD player provides almost immediate access because it does not need to be viewed in a linear manner. A speaker can access a media clip with a number or bar code at any time and in any sequence during a speech to present a concept or an issue. The speaker uses a light pen to scan a bar code for a particular sequence, and the clip is projected onto a screen in just a few seconds after a button is pressed. This instant access saves time and allows a speaker to reinforce ideas and work quickly from one set of projections to another. In addition, many DVD players are now capable of recording video and audio in addition to merely replaying media, and many computers contain software that allow users to design and create their own video and audio CDs. DVD players are easy to use and can be operated with remote control devices similar to VCRs. But you should get some instruction from a media specialist if you have never used this type of equipment before.

Film projectors aren't as popular as they once were, due to VCRs. Sometimes, however, a vintage film will not be available on videotape, and a speaker may need to use a portion of a film to support a speech. For example, one student used a 1945 film clip to illustrate the destruction the atomic bomb caused to the cities of Hiroshima and Nagasaki. A brief segment like this can be effective, but you can't substitute a film for an entire speech. Like other visuals, a film should only amplify portions of a presentation; you must develop the substance of the speech.

### Recording Equipment

Audiotape or video recording equipment can generate interest among audience members. One speaker, describing the history of jazz, used tape-recorded music as a background to her introduction. Another speaker showed a videotape of a diving experience to explain scuba gear, and a different speaker used a videotape to demonstrate how to change the oil in a car.

### Using Media

When you use recording equipment, your audio-, videotape, or DVD should be properly cued to each segment of your speech. If you want to play a tape or a video while you are speaking, be certain you turn the sound down so that the audience can hear you comfortably. If the tape or video is the focus of the presentation, adjust the volume to reach all areas of the room or auditorium. A well-chosen CD or video can add interest to a portion

# guidelines for using the powerpoint program »

The Microsoft PowerPoint program is used extensively in public speeches, classrooms, corporate boardrooms, institutions, and government. Speakers choose PowerPoint because the program is easy to learn, and users can create slides, lettering, and graphics that are visually appealing and professional in appearance. A good PowerPoint slide show, however, does not ensure that a presentation will be effective. Some speakers also incorrectly believe that a bad PowerPoint performance is better than having no visual aids at all. Unfortunately, there are a lot of mistaken notions about speeches with PowerPoint and numerous ineffective PowerPoint presentations that do nothing but detract from speeches. Although these guidelines do not teach you the details of the program itself, they offer some tips and sound advice to help you develop and present PowerPoint presentations that will be successful and enhance the quality of your speeches.

## 1. Know Your Options

The PowerPoint program gives you the flexibility to create numerous types and forms of slides and/or graphics to reinforce your presentation. If you are delivering a speech that requires statistical evidence, you can simply enter your data into a predesigned format that will display the numbers on professional-looking visuals such as line, pie, or bar graphs. You also have the flexibility of selecting different fonts, colors, backgrounds, and graphics to help lines of text or art stand out prominently. In addition, you can download art, photographs, video, and audio from the Internet; transfer files from digital cameras or from a personal computer; or copy pictures, drawings, and illustrations by using a scanner connected to the computer. The program allows you to design the colors and styles of your slides, or you can choose from numerous templates already designed for you. You may also want to customize the content of each slide and "fly in" various bulleted or numbered lines of text that you may wish to emphasize at a particular moment in your speech. You can add sound effects as you fly in different lines of text and even time the slides to run automatically in sequence as you speak. The program is easy to use and provides numerous choices for the development of outstanding visuals.

## 2. Keep Visuals Simple

A student once used more than thirty different PowerPoint slides in a 5- to 7-minute speech. Each slide contained numerous special effects as well as "whoosh" and "screeching tire" sounds when each line of text was introduced. In addition, the student used a different design or template for each slide. The result was a hodgepodge of competing designs, clashing colors, and distracting noises. It is helpful to remember that an effective PowerPoint presentation is simple, clear, and easy to understand. Avoid using numerous sentences or long paragraphs on PowerPoint slides. Listeners often feel overwhelmed if they are forced to view endless writing projected onto a screen. Audiences retain concise bulleted words or phrases, photographs, illustrations, and highlighted graphs more easily than they recall lengthy script. When designing lettering, keep fonts large with sharp color contrasts between the lettering and the background so that the text is easy to read. Be consistent with the style and content of slides. If you are unsure about your own design, select an eye-catching and appealing style from the predesigned templates. Be consistent when using effects such as custom animation, and use sound sparingly if at all. Use enough slides to clarify concepts and reinforce ideas, but not so many that listeners are distracted and overwhelmed. Remember that less is often better than more. Your visuals are there to support your speech—not to upstage the show.

### 3. Know How to Use the Program During the Speech

When you are delivering a speech that is supported with PowerPoint slides, make sure that you know how to operate the system smoothly and efficiently. Understand how to highlight the first slide, and know the icons or files to click in order to begin the slide show. Also know how to navigate forward and backward through the program by using the mouse and arrow keys or end the slide show with the escape key. Needless problems can occur when speakers fumble with the program, click on the wrong icon, or bring up an unwanted menu or file. One speaker started with the wrong slide of her presentation, and another began by clicking on a file used to construct a new slide. These embarrassing problems occurred in front of waiting listeners and were largely the result of insufficient knowledge, practice, and preparation. To avoid these difficulties, practice extensively with the PowerPoint program and make it work for you successfully.

### 4. Be Sure that the Technology Is Set Up and Working Properly

Before you present your speech, it is vital to make sure that all elements of the computer and projector system are working properly. If you are knowledgeable about computer technology, check the connections, disc drives, monitor, keyboard, mouse, projector controls, and projection screen to verify that everything is in working order. If you are uncomfortable with this technology, get a media specialist to help you. Many institutions have media departments with technology experts who can set up computer systems or deliver "smart carts" with laptop computers already connected to projectors. Whether the media is set up by the speaker or a specialist, it is still the speaker's responsibility to determine if the system works. Imagine how embarrassed you would feel if you pressed the mouse and nothing happened because the keyboard was not connected, or you inserted a disc that couldn't function because the PowerPoint program had never been installed on the computer. Check, double-check, then check again. Make sure a problem that can be easily corrected before the speech doesn't create an awkward moment during your speech in front of an audience.

### 5. Have a Backup Plan If the Media Fails

You may have checked the media thoroughly and are satisfied that the PowerPoint program is functioning smoothly as you begin your slide show. But as we all know, in the world of technology, malfunctions can occur that we are unable to control. The computer freezes up, a projector bulb burns out, or the program ceases to operate for some unknown reason. Instead of interrupting your speech and fumbling with keyboards and cables in front of your listeners, it is helpful to be prepared with a backup plan. One of the easiest ways to resolve computer malfunctions is to print out all of your PowerPoint slides onto acetate transparencies that can be used on an overhead projector. If there is a problem with the computer system, you can still keep the presentation running smoothly by simply placing a transparency of the next slide on the overhead projector. A backup plan takes forethought and preparation. Whether you use transparencies, videos, or posters as a substitute, you must prepare your speaking situation in advance to have the necessary equipment, such as overheads, VCRs, or easels, in place to accommodate your alternative. But a backup plan will salvage your presentation and still allow the audience to understand the concepts you are trying to communicate.

### 6. Consider the Audience at All Times

When you set up media for a PowerPoint presentation, consider where your listeners are seated in the room. Make sure that the monitor, computer, and projector do not block the speaker or the projection screen, and rearrange the seating if necessary before your speech so that every audience member will have a clear and unobstructed view. Also place the monitor facing the lectern or the area where you are speaking so that you can see the slide show without having to turn away from the audience to look at the screen. In addition, position the mouse and keyboard so that they are easy to use without forcing you to stretch or walk back and forth, causing a distraction. Examine the angles, lines of sight, and positions of seating relative to the screen to determine if every listener can see all of your slides easily. The more you plan and prepare your visuals in advance, the more likely it is that you will have a successful speech and your listeners will have a positive experience.

of your presentation, but media can also present problems. A speaker brought an extension cord that was too short to reach from the single outlet at the back of the classroom to the lectern at the front. Another student, who failed to inspect a DVD player, discovered later in the speech that he had trouble operating the complicated system supplied by the media department. A speaker who failed in his attempts to link to the web during his speech finally gave up, saying, "Well I can't understand why it won't connect. Your classroom computer isn't any good." One student placed a small photograph on the glass surface of an overhead projector only to find that nothing happened on the screen.

Most of these disasters can be avoided by careful planning. Practice the speech with your visuals. Check out your visuals in advance and know how electronic equipment operates. Examine the room for electrical outlets, projection screens, or tables for stationing equipment. If you use computer, audio, or video equipment, pay attention to setup procedures. Check out batteries or extension cords; allow extra time to carry in and to place heavy equipment. Try to anticipate problems like burned-out bulbs, unplugged connections or cords, or inadequately darkened rooms.

## GRAPHS

Suppose that you needed to show your audience how deaths from motorcycle accidents have increased over a 4-year period in the United States. You could simply relate the regrettable statistics: 2,483 deaths in 1999 increased to 3,244 in 2002.[3] The audience might listen to you, but they would also soon forget the information. Another way to present the information is by constructing a graph to display the data visually. Graphs are helpful in explaining trends, showing comparisons, or indicating portions of a whole. We will consider three basic types of graphs that can reinforce information in a speech: the bar, line, and pie graph.

### Bar Graph

A bar graph is helpful when you want to compare and contrast several causes or categories, such as the major causes of divorce or the main causes of heart disease. Bar graphs allow your audience to visualize similarities or differences among categories at a glance.

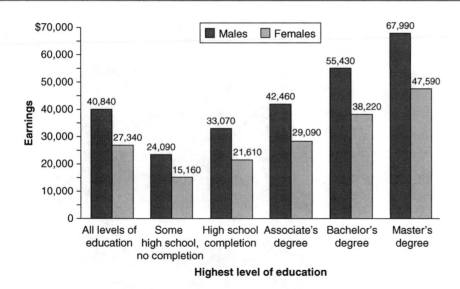

FIGURE 12.1  Median Annual Earnings of Persons 25 Years and Over, by Highest Education Level and Sex, 2006
*Note:* Excludes persons without earnings.
*Source:* Chart prepared by U.S. Department of Commerce, Census Bureau.

The bar graph in Figure 12.1 displays the annual earnings (by median, or middle, number) of people 25 or older according to education and sex. Just a quick glance tells you that the higher the degree, the higher the income. The graph also shows that men still earned more then women in 2006.

A bar graph like this one is relatively easy to construct and easy to read. You can use black on white with gray shading to indicate different categories, or you can highlight specific categories with color. Your bar graph must be clear and understandable so that listeners realize how it supports your point.

## Line Graph

The line graph displays upward or downward trends over a period of time. Speakers use these graphs to show an increase or decrease in topics such as crime, disease, teenage suicide, income, inflation, or interest rates.

The line graph in Figure 12.2 shows the total greenhouse gas emissions in million metric tons from the year 1990 to 2006. Even though listeners might not be able to calculate the intricacies of metric tons, they could easily conclude that greenhouse gas emissions have been steadily rising for the past sixteen years.

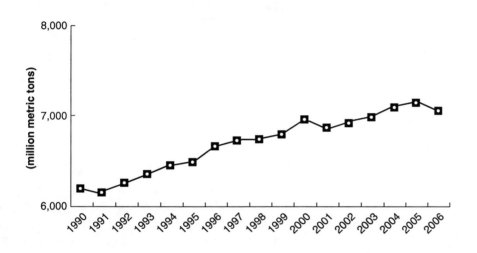

FIGURE 12.2  Greenhouse Gas Emissions Still Rising, 1990–2006
*Source:* Energy Information Administration.

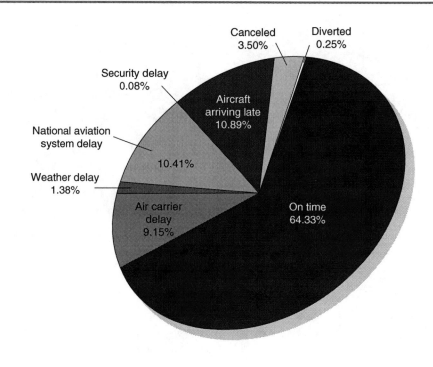

FIGURE 12.3 Arrival Performance of Domestic Flights, December 2007 *Note:* Percentages do not total 100 due to rounding. *Source:* Chart prepared by U.S. Department of Transportation, Bureau of Transportation Statistics.

### Pie Graph

The pie graph displays portions of a whole sum. Pie graphs are helpful to speakers who want to show numbers or percentages. Where our tax money goes, how individuals spend their income, or the racial makeup of the U.S. population are among the many subjects that lend themselves to pie graphs.

A speaker can use the pie graph in Figure 12.3 to indicate the causes of aircraft delays in the month of December 2007. A quick glance shows you that during that month almost 11 percent of all delays were caused by aircraft arriving late.

### Developing Graphs

Before constructing any of these graphs, make sure that you clearly understand the information and the statistics in order to report the data accurately. The *percentage* of crimes, for instance, is a far different concept from the *number* of crimes. Know what your data are saying so that you will choose a graph appropriate for displaying the information.

When you understand the data, construct graphs that are simple and easy to read. Don't make the charts busy by drawing too many lines or numbers that can confuse listeners. Use color to emphasize different categories and bold lettering to convey meaning. Label the graph with direct and uncomplicated wording. Keep in mind that many computer graphics programs such as PowerPoint, discussed previously, can help you design line, pie, or bar graphs that are of professional quality and can enhance your speaking presentation. Remember that the purpose of a graph is to help the audience understand concepts quickly.

## ILLUSTRATIONS, PHOTOGRAPHS, AND PICTURES

Imagine a speaker trying to explain how to use a computer keyboard without a diagram or attempting to describe the terrorist attacks of September 11 without a picture. Without visuals, the audience would not understand the impact of the speaker's message. Topics like these require communication in visual as well as verbal channels of communication.

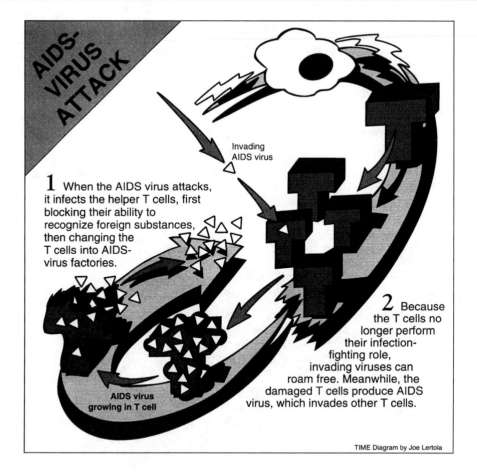

FIGURE 12.4 AIDS
Virus Attack
Copyright © 1985
Time, Inc. Reprinted by
permission.

Drawings, photographs, and pictures enable listeners to visually complete their understanding of events and procedures.

Illustrations can be used to explain complicated topics such as the AIDS virus or to portray elementary procedures like the basic tennis serve. Figure 12.4 describes in a simple diagram how the AIDS virus attacks the T cells of the body's immune system. The visual in Figure 12.5, showing how to give injections properly, was designed by a student who used a desktop publishing system. And in Figure 12.6, a speaker used very elementary sketches to demonstrate the seven basic body positions in the tennis serve.

You don't have to be an artist to draw effective illustrations like these. The principal ingredient that contributed to each drawing was not talent, but time. Whether you are an artist or simply know how to use the computer effectively, be willing to spend the time necessary to create similar visuals that are neat, simple, and clear.

Photographs and pictures also provide listeners with vivid images. A speaker who describes starvation can generate more sympathetic feedback by showing a photograph of a hungry child. One student who delivered a speech about sex in advertising displayed several magazine ads that used strong sexual images to sell products. And a student who described several types of drive-in businesses showed the audience a photograph (shown on page 201) of a drive-through funeral home.

### Using Pictures

Pictures and photographs promote curiosity and interest, but they must be large enough for the audience to see. Wallet-size pictures or tiny magazine photographs will not support

## Angle of Insertion for Parenteral Injections

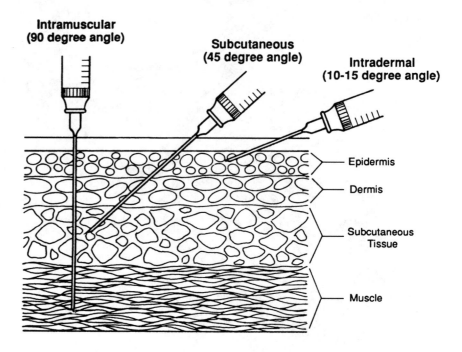

FIGURE 12.5 Proper Techniques for Giving Injections Used by permission of Sherry Blye.

a speech unless you make some adjustments. You can have the visuals professionally enlarged or photographed and made into slides—procedures that are often expensive. If you have a **scanner** connected to a computer, you can easily scan photographs into the PowerPoint program to create a slide show. Be willing to take the trouble to develop and present these important visuals effectively so that all members of your audience can view them without difficulty.

## POSTERS, FLIPCHARTS, AND CHALKBOARDS

Posters, flipcharts, and chalkboards are also useful tools to help you convey ideas. Posters can support the steps of a process, reinforce main headings of a speech, or explain unfamiliar concepts. The poster in Figure 12.7 identifies three symbols used in weather forecasting. This visual is simple, yet eye-catching because the speaker used different colors to coordinate symbols with the appropriate explanations.

Flipcharts can be prepared in advance or used in interactive speaker-audience situations where listeners are reporting on group tasks or accomplishments. The speaker can process and synthesize feedback from the audience, write down key points with a marker, and quickly move on to other items by turning over large connected sheets of paper positioned on an easel.

Unlike prepared posters, the chalkboard gives you a great deal of flexibility as you are speaking. You can quickly write down unfamiliar terms, list the principal steps of a process, or draw a simple explanatory sketch.

FIGURE 12.6 Seven
Positions of Tennis Serve
Illustration by George
Goebel.

### Using Posters, Flipcharts, and Chalkboards

If you decide to draw posters by hand, prepare them carefully. Lettering should be neat, large, and bold for easy reading. If you present the speech in a room that is 25 to 30 feet long, it is a good idea to use letters on your poster that are at least 1 inch high.[4] You also need to leave plenty of space next to words and between lines of print, so that listeners can see the entire poster in a glance. Know where you are going to place your posters—taped to an easel, tacked to a bulletin board, held by a volunteer—so they will be easy to use during the presentation.

A flipchart can be helpful if the speaker knows how to use it efficiently. If you need to write on the chart as you speak, stand beside the chart at an angle so you can see both the easel and the audience as you write. When you finish, turn around, facing the audience, and move away from the chart so your audience can see the visual easily. If your chart is

During an informative speech about drive-through businesses, a student used this photograph of a "convenience" funeral home to stimulate interest and curiosity among listeners.

© Bruce Dale/© National Geographic Society

already prepared, you can look toward the audience and flip each page as you move from one topic to another. Avoid problems such as tearing or fighting with pages as you turn the charts or fumbling with markers that are too dry or that lack contrast with the background. As always, practice thoroughly with flipcharts to ensure a smooth and successful presentation.

Even though you can be more spontaneous with a chalkboard, you still need to know how to employ it effectively. We've all suffered through the class where the teacher scrawls numerous concepts on the board with one hand and erases everything with the other asking, "Did you all get that?" Avoid this problem by practicing with a chalkboard. Don't scribble down random ideas; write phrases neatly. If you need to draw a diagram, make sure it is clear and precise. Take the necessary time to plan your visuals by placing information on the board *before* you speak, or writing ideas carefully *while* you are speaking. And allow the audience time to absorb the material before you erase it.

FIGURE 12.7 Weather Symbols
Used by permission of Michael E. Gerber.

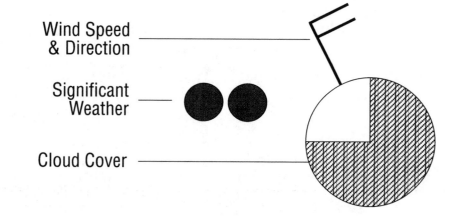

Displaying objects can help speakers to convey ideas quickly and motivate audiences to listen.

© A. Ramey/PhotoEdit

We've described the chalkboard in case you need it for brief or incidental use in a speech. Using a chalkboard is not recommended, however, in a presentation such as a demonstration or a descriptive speech that is primarily dependent upon visuals. Visuals in these speeches require a great deal of time to plan effectively. Don't use the chalkboard as a shortcut for preparation; be willing to spend the time needed to create worthwhile visual aids.

## MODELS AND OBJECTS

As a speaker, you can generate interest and stimulate curiosity with scale models, parts of objects, or the actual objects themselves.

### Scale Models

Scale models reduce large objects or complicated procedures for easy visualization. College instructors use models of the eye or the heart to help students understand vision or circulation. A student once used a model of a miniature volcano to explain how an actual eruption occurs.

Scale models create interest, but they must be large enough for the audience to see. A speaker attempted to demonstrate a new trash removal system that had been selected by several cities. Problems surfaced, however, when the speaker took out three tiny toy trucks from her handbag and pointed to the rear-end loader, the wheels, and the cab. Listeners leaned forward and squinted in an effort to follow the process, but they soon gave up because of the inadequate visuals. Don't use scale models that are too small or too intricate; make sure that objects are large and practical enough for the audience to see and to comprehend easily.

### Parts of Objects

When it is impractical to bring the actual object, you can use a sample or a cross section. A student demonstrated how to refinish furniture by displaying several pieces of wood in various stages of completion. Another student used a small cross section of a studded wall to inform listeners how to wire an electrical outlet. And another speaker used pieces of shrubbery and small fir branches to explain how to do professional landscaping. Since it was not possible to bring in a china cabinet, half a house, or a nursery, each speaker sensibly chose to use parts of the object that could be managed easily in a classroom.

### Actual Objects

When listeners see a life-size visual aid, they are quickly motivated to listen. One student explained the process involved in decorating a wedding cake. Toward the end of the speech, she revealed a perfect three-tiered cake complete with a miniature bride and groom on top. The cake was an aromatic visual, appealing to the sense of smell as well as to sight. A skydiver showed listeners his parachute to demonstrate how to fold it before a jump. An antique gun collector brought out several muskets to explain how American colonists used these firearms during the Revolutionary War.

# five guidelines for using audiovisual aids »

### 1. Talk to the Audience, Not to the Visual Aid

Some speakers become so involved with their visuals that they quickly forget to look at listeners. One classroom speaker turned her back and talked to her PowerPoint slides on the projection screen instead of facing the monitor and the audience. If you have practiced adequately, you shouldn't need to look at your visual. Remember that visuals reinforce main ideas; they won't speak for themselves, and they are not substitutes for communication. Your job as a speaker is to present visuals to your listeners and to help audience members understand them. Use a pointer, easel, table, or some other device that helps you to communicate your visuals effectively. Maintain frequent eye contact with listeners, and, above all, talk to your audience—not to the visual.

### 2. Don't Pass Objects Around During the Speech

A student who collected fossilized rocks described each specimen and then passed them to listeners during his presentation. The speaker had about twenty-five different examples, and listeners concentrated on looking at each rock and handing it to the next person. The problem, of course, was that the speaker lost listeners' attention because of the numerous interruptions. Develop other ways to convey visuals. The fossil collector, for instance, could have taken photographs of his examples and used a computer projector or a slide projector to describe the objects. Keep the attention of the audience focused on you, the speaker, and avoid circulating materials that could be distracting.

### 3. Be Sure that the Audience Can See Your Visuals

Although it may seem obvious that visual aids need to be large enough for everyone to see, well-intentioned speakers sometimes take audience members for granted and neglect this important rule. Unprepared speakers often use photographs, objects, or scale models that are too small, posters with thin or tiny lettering, or visuals that are obstructed. One speaker who explained how to make baklava, a Greek dessert, placed all the materials and ingredients directly in front of the mixing bowl, blocking the entire demonstration. The hard work that went into researching and structuring the speech was wasted because of the poorly executed visual aids.

In addition to these problems, listeners may not be able to see visuals due to the angles of the speaker's stand, the easel, TV monitor, computer projector, or the room arrangement. If even one or two people in the audience can't see comfortably, the speaker should have planned the presentation more carefully. Depending on the setting, the speaker may need to readjust the visual aid, rearrange the seating area, or ask listeners to move forward. It is the speaker's responsibility to prepare visuals and to plan an environment in which listeners can easily see everything a speaker wants to communicate.

## 4. Use Visuals at the Right Psychological Moment

If you have a lot of audiovisual aids, you may need to set them up before the speech so that you don't cause unnecessary disruptions during the presentation. But in some cases, you may want to wait and reveal your visuals at the right psychological moment, that is, when the audience will be most interested.

For example, if you have three different charts, you might decide to tape all of them to the chalkboard prior to the speech. The problem with this arrangement, however, is that the audience will read the visuals before you want them to, and they may not listen to your speech because of the visual distraction. It would be more effective to develop a flipchart that allows you to reveal each poster as you actually talk about it. This method generates curiosity and helps to control the attention of your audience. Speakers can apply the same principle to a single poster by covering all of the information and then removing one portion at a time. One of the advantages of computer graphics software such as PowerPoint is that the speaker can use custom animation to "fly in" lines of text or art and introduce slides at the precise moment that the speaker is presenting the concept.

What is important is that you carefully think through how and when to use posters, charts, slides, and objects during a speech. Talk about objects when you display them; and as a rule, don't reveal visuals before you verbally refer to them. Equally important, it is usually more effective to remove visuals when you have finished referring to them. If you keep projections on a screen or objects in front of listeners, you'll have a hard time directing their attention to other visuals or back to your speech.

## 5. Be Clear at All Times

Although audiovisual aids can support a presentation, they cannot speak for you. Be clear both verbally and nonverbally. Use clear explanations and precise descriptions to integrate visuals successfully into a speech. Explain the purpose of slides, posters, or charts: Point out relationships, show comparisons, or indicate contrasts in data. Use precise gestures when referring to objects or describing procedures. A laser pointer or the keyboard mouse can help you identify items on a photo, chart, or PowerPoint illustration. Draw conclusions from graphs or informational lists, and relate audiovisuals to your ideas. Describe objects precisely, and reinforce physical actions or motions with verbal clarifications. When you employ photographs and pictures, integrate them smoothly by emphasizing significant areas or details. If you use a computer projector, VCR, DVD player, or other mechanical media, introduce the audiovisual segment with the appropriate verbal descriptions. Provide brief explanations of slides and transparencies to amplify concepts and ideas. Your goal in using audiovisuals is to help listeners understand how they support your presentation.

Each of the speeches described was interesting. But the life-size visuals required a great deal of planning. The fragile wedding cake had to be transported to the classroom. The skydiver had to ask listeners to sit in a large semicircle to provide enough space to fold his parachute. And the collector had to use a special gun rack to display the large muskets effectively. If you want to use life-size objects, you must realize they will take some added effort in addition to the standard organization of a speech. Don't exhaust your energies on the visuals alone; research, structure, and delivery remain the focal point of a public speech.

## YOU AS A VISUAL AID

Your own body movements, gestures, and actions can serve as visual aids in a speech. Imagine how body movements could simulate aerobics or weight lifting and how gestures could illustrate sign language or skin care. One student demonstrated how actors apply theatrical makeup to enhance their appearance under intense stage lights. The speaker's face and hands were the visuals. He came prepared with a small mirror that allowed him to put on layers of makeup while he explained the steps of the process.

While gestures and movements may seem easier to convey than other visuals, they require preparation. If you are demonstrating a detailed process such as a golf swing or a karate move, your gestures and movements need to be precise and well defined. These actions should communicate so well that audience members could repeat them if necessary. Avoid sloppy gestures or vague actions that lack clarity and create confusion. Run through the speech several times to practice the movements you intend to use. Refine and improve these actions until you feel confident that they will communicate effectively to your audience.

In addition to the speaker, a volunteer from the audience can also be a visual aid. For example, administering the Heimlich maneuver, bandaging an arm, dancing an Irish jig, or throwing a curveball are procedures that could require another person's presence. When you work with an assistant, be sure that the volunteer knows exactly what to do. Rehearse the speech several times, so that both speaker and assistant are comfortable with planned actions and motions. Don't call on a volunteer from the audience unless you want a cold response. This uninformed assistant could actually be a detriment to you. Be sure that the "volunteer" really wants to help you, is adequately prepared, and will contribute positively to your speech.[5]

## SAMPLE SPEECH: how do airplane wings produce lift?

*The following demonstration speech was presented by a student in the basic speech course. Mark Yingling was a licensed private pilot and aviation student who wanted to share his passion for flight with the members of his audience. The speech not only represents effective research, organization, and delivery but also illustrates how a speaker used PowerPoint software to develop an effective slide show that was shown with a computer projector.*

### AN INFORMATIVE SPEECH TO DEMONSTRATE
*Mark Yingling*

1. The speaker begins his introduction. Because Mark's classroom audience already knows him, it is not necessary to begin with a personal

1.  (slide 1) Good afternoon. My name is Mark Yingling. Today I'd like to talk to you about airplane wings, but more specifically, how airplane wings produce lift. I'd like to begin with a quote from Leonardo da Vinci (slide 2): "For once you have tasted flight, you will walk the earth with your eyes turned skyward, for there you have been,

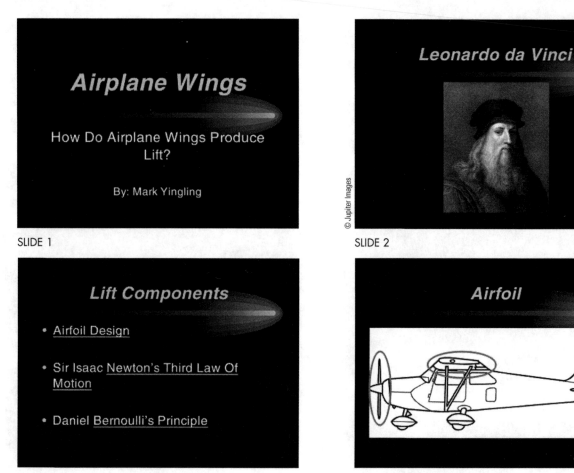

SLIDE 1

SLIDE 2

SLIDE 3

SLIDE 4

and there you long to return." Da Vinci was fascinated with flight five hundred years ago, and Jeppesen wrote a book called the *Private Pilot Manual,* and it describes him as having a manuscript with sketches and drawings of flying machines.

2. To fly, you need a force called "lift," and that's what I'm going to talk about today. (shows slide 3) We're going to talk about three components of lift: We're going to talk about airfoil design, we're going to talk about Sir Issac Newton's Third Law of Motion, and we're going to talk about Daniel Bernoulli's principle.

3. So let's begin and examine the airfoil. (slide 4) What is an airfoil? An airfoil is any surface that is designed to produce lift when it is interacting with air. On an airplane, a wing is an airfoil and a propeller is an airfoil. If you ever get a chance, look at a propeller: It looks very similar in shape and design to a wing. Now I brought my little model here (*displays a model airplane*). The parts of an airfoil: We have a leading edge, and we have a trailing edge, and this curvature here is called "camber." Now when the air is moving over the wings, it has to follow this camber, and it is directed downward to increase (slide 5) what we call downwash, and it is this downwash that helps to produce lift. The best analogy I can give you is to take a garden hose and hold it at an angle at the ground and let it go full blast, and you can feel that it wants to push up.

4. Okay, next let's talk about Sir Isaac Newton's Third Law of Motion. (slide 6)

greeting. It would be more effective to start with the quote, "For once you have tasted flight...."

2. The speaker presents his three-point thesis statement. It is not necessary to "announce" the thesis with "I'm going to talk about."

3. Mark introduces the first numeral of the body.

He uses a model airplane to demonstrate the different parts of the wing.

Mark uses an effective analogy to a garden hose.

4. The external transition is clear, if somewhat abrupt.

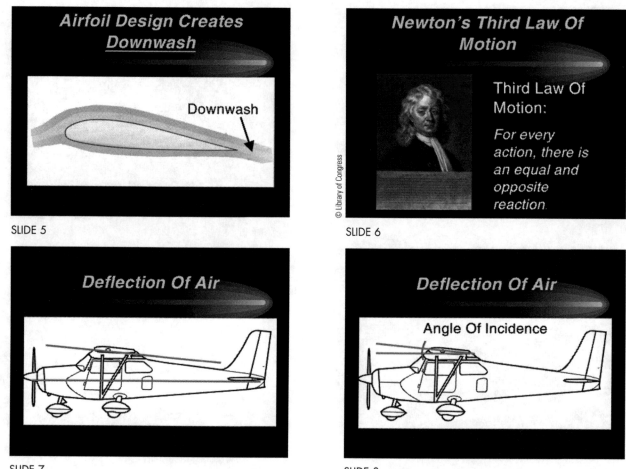

SLIDE 5

SLIDE 6

SLIDE 7

SLIDE 8

5. The speaker supports his speech with a credible source.

5. Isaac Newton was a seventeenth-century physicist-mathematician, and his Third Law states that for every action there is an equal and opposite reaction—everybody has heard of this one before. Irvin Gleim wrote a book called the *Pilot Handbook,* and he best describes this as the deflection of air. Now to understand this, let's see how the wing is attached to the plane (slide 7). Let's begin by drawing a line through the longitudinal axis of the plane and then let's draw a line through the leading edge and trailing edge of the wing. When you bring those lines together (slide 8), you can see that they are slightly different, and it forms a small angle; and this angle is called the "angle of incidence" and basically it is the way the wing is attached to the plane—it's got a slightly upward slant to it compared to the longitudinal axis of the plane. So as air is coming (slide 9), it hits underneath the wing and deflects downward. That is the action (slide 10). The reaction is the upward force. So you have action, deflection of air, and reaction, the lifting of the plane.

6. A better external transition might be, "Now that you know how Newton's Law applies to flight, let's consider Bernoulli's Principle."

6. Next, let's talk about Bernoulli's Principle (slide 11).

7. Now Daniel Bernoulli was an eighteenth-century Swiss mathematician, and he studied the movements of fluid. He also studied the pressure differences with velocity.

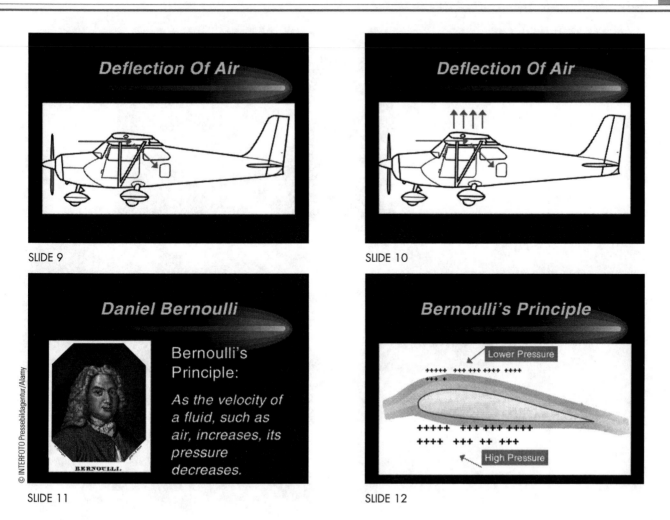

SLIDE 9

SLIDE 10

SLIDE 11

SLIDE 12

© INTERFOTO Pressebildagentur/Alamy

Bernoulli's Principle states that as the velocity of a fluid such as air increases, its pressure decreases. Now this is a little bit difficult to understand, but Jeppesen wrote a book called the *Instrument/Commercial Manual*, and it best describes how the wing takes advantage of Bernoulli's Principle by differences in pressure (slide 12). Now as air is moving over the wing as the velocity is increasing, it has to travel a longer distance to get over this camber so the velocity is increasing, which decreases the pressure. The pressure underneath the wing is increasing. So this high pressure underneath the wing wants to get on top of here because pressures are always trying to equalize, and the golden rule is, high pressure always goes to low pressure. So in essence this high pressure wants to get on top of here and pushes the plane.

7. The speaker cites another source to verify the credibility of his research.

8. So as a (slide 13) result of Newton's Third Law of Motion, we have the deflection of air, which is the action/reaction of the lifting of the airplane. We have Bernoulli's Principle, which is the difference in pressure. We have the high pressure underneath the wing, the lower pressure on top of the wing, and the higher pressure pushes the plane up and tries to get on top of this lower pressure. And we have the shape of the airfoil. The air, moving over the wing, has to follow the camber downwards creating that downwash, helping the airplane produce lift. So lift is accomplished, and flight is made possible by these three components. Now I'd like

8. Mark begins his conclusion with a summary of the three main numerals of his speech.

The speaker ends by referring briefly back to his introduction and making a personal comment about flying.

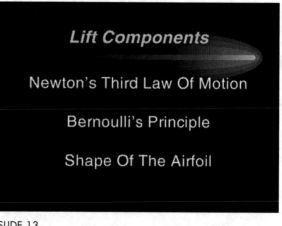

SLIDE 13

to conclude by saying that like da Vinci, I'm also fascinated with flight, and I long to return to the sky as soon as possible.[6]

## summary »

The term *audiovisual aid* refers to a device that may appeal to any of the senses: mechanical media (including the useful PowerPoint program); graphs (line, pie, and bar); drawings, photographs, and pictures; posters, flipcharts, and chalkboards; physical objects; and you, the speaker. The computer projector, often used with graphics software such as PowerPoint, is a popular visual aid.

Here are six guidelines to help you use the PowerPoint program successfully:

1. Know your options.
2. Keep visuals simple.
3. Know how to use the program during the speech.
4. Be sure that the technology is set up and working properly.
5. Have a backup plan if the media fails.
6. Consider your audience at all times.

Other mechanical media—such as digital, video, and audio; overhead, slide, or film projectors; and audio- and videotape-recording equipment—are useful in different situations. Posters, either hand-drawn or produced with a computer, can reinforce ideas effectively, and the chalkboard is useful for brief or incidental support of a speech. You can also include scale models, partial objects, or life-size objects in a speech. As a speaker, *you* are also a visual aid. You can incorporate your own body movements and actions into a speech, and you can ask someone to help you.

Observe five general guidelines to use visual aids effectively:

1. Talk to the audience, not to the visual.
2. Don't pass objects around during the speech.
3. Be sure listeners can see your visuals.
4. Use visuals at the right psychological moment.
5. Be clear at all times.

## SKILL BUILDERS»

1. List three different types of visual aids that you intend to use in your next speech. Describe how and when you intend to employ them in the speech, and discuss how you will avoid any potential difficulties presented by the visuals.
2. Read the sample speech in Chapter 6 titled "Practice, Practice, Practice. . ." by Thomas C. Stewart. Suggest at least two visual aids that the speaker could use to support his presentation effectively. When and how would you use them in the speech? Explain.

## BUILDING A
## SPEECH ONLINE »

Now that you've read Chapter 12, use your online Resource Center for Building a Speech for quick access to the electronic study resources that accompany this text. You can access your Resource Center at http://academic.cengage.com/login, using the access code that came with your book or that you bought online at http://www.iChapters.com. Your Resource Center gives you access to Interactive Video Activities, the book's companion website, Speech Builder Express 3.0, InfoTrac College Edition, and study aids, including a digital glossary and review quizzes.

© AP Photo

# chapter 13

# CONSIDERING LANGUAGE

## chapter objectives »

After reading and studying this chapter, you should be able to

1. Recognize language that is clear and concrete
2. Describe figures of speech and stylistic elements
3. Discuss the importance of appropriate language usage
4. Know how to make ideas meaningful and interrelated

Imagine that one of the most famous speeches in American history began like this:

> *Eighty-seven years ago our ancestors came to this land to build a new country dedicated to liberty and equality. But at the present time, we are in the process of a conflict which will prove if this new country or any new country founded on such principles can live on.*

This passage may sound simple and straightforward enough. But listen to the way it was actually written:

> *Fourscore and seven years ago our fathers brought forth, upon this continent, a new nation, conceived in liberty and dedicated to the proposition that all men are created equal. Now we are engaged in a great civil war, testing whether that nation, or any nation so conceived and so dedicated, can long endure.*

" *Eloquence is the power to translate a truth into language perfectly intelligible to the person to whom you speak.* "

—Ralph Waldo Emerson

Abraham Lincoln chose his words carefully and refrained from using commonplace language in the Gettysburg Address. He realized that the words "fourscore and seven years" were more effective than "eighty-seven

key terms »

ALLITERATION
AMPLIFICATION
ANTITHESIS
CONNOTATION
DENOTATION
EUPHEMISMS
METAPHOR
MNEMONIC
   PHRASES
REPETITION
SIMILE
TRANSITIONS

years ago." He also recognized that a metaphor could be effective in communicating the nation's origins. Instead of an impersonal reference to the nation's "ancestors," Lincoln humanized the reference to "our fathers" and continued the metaphor with the words "brought forth, conceived, and dedicated." Lincoln conveyed the image that our fathers "brought forth" or "gave birth" to a child, thereby implying struggle, labor, pain, and hardship. The words "conceived in liberty" extended the metaphor and revealed the sanctity of the new nation's purpose and ideals.

Lincoln's speeches demonstrate the power of language. In your own speeches your language can remain plain and ordinary, or it can elevate the mind, stimulate thought, and connect to the diverse members of your audience. In this chapter we consider language that conveys your ideas with clarity, concreteness, style, and appropriateness. We also briefly explore how language can make ideas more meaningful and interrelated. Choose language carefully to refine the appearance of your speech.

## developing clarity

One of the most important rules of language usage is to say what you mean. Use precise words to create mental pictures for your listeners, and use clear terminology that your audience will understand. Speeches that include obscure terms and flowery words may sound impressive, but they aren't effective if they don't communicate to the audience. Former Vice President Spiro Agnew referred to Nixon administration critics as "nattering nabobs of negativism," "an effete corps of impudent snobs," and "pusillanimous pussyfooters."[1] His idiosyncratic style attracted public attention for a while, but audiences soon tired of searching through the dictionary to find out what he meant.

Another speaker who enjoyed using large words and complicated syntax was the late conservative columnist William F. Buckley, editor of the *National Review*. He demonstrated these qualities in this excerpt from a speech to the Ethics and Public Policy Center in Washington, D.C.:

*There is much room left over for argument, even as there is room left over, under this roof, for divisions about the impermanent things. But I tender you, Dr. Lefever, and your distinguished board of directors, and associates this challenge. Deliberate the means of saying it in our public philosophy, saying that however much respect we owe to those who hold other ideas than those that are central to Judaeo-Christian postulates, we mustn't confuse any respect for the preternatural dignity for the fruit of their reason. How at once to do both these things—to respect a difference of opinion without undertaking a respect for different opinions? It is a searing challenge, in a world sensitive to cultural condescension, a world inflamed by the notion that one man, one vote presupposes one culture, any culture; one philosophy, any philosophy; one God, any God.[2]*

It is possible that Buckley's audience knew what he was talking about. But it is more probable that they would need a dictionary and an interpreter.

Contrast the Buckley speech with this example:

*Mr. Chief Justice, my dear friends, my fellow Americans. The oath that I have taken is the same oath that was taken by George Washington and by every president under the Constitution. But I assume the presidency under extreme circumstances never before experienced by Americans. This is an hour of history that troubles our minds and hurts our hearts.*

217

*Therefore, I feel it is my first duty to make an unprecedented compact with my countrymen. Not an inaugural address, not a fireside chat, not a campaign speech, just a little straight talk among friends. And I intend it to be the first of many. I am acutely aware that you have not elected me as your president by your ballots. So I ask you to confirm me as your president with your prayers. And I hope that such prayers will also be the first of many.*

When Gerald Ford assumed the presidency on August 9, 1974, he took the oath of office under the most difficult circumstances. For many months President Nixon and the Congress had been engaged in a Constitutional crisis because of the Watergate scandal. When the House Judiciary Committee voted articles of impeachment, President Nixon resigned and Gerald Ford, his appointed vice president, was sworn in as the thirty-eighth president of the United States.

President Ford used simple language to express his ideas. He touched the hurt feelings within Americans, acknowledged his appointment to high office, and appealed for the goodwill and prayers of his fellow citizens. Ford correctly realized it would be inappropriate to deliver an eloquent address filled with high-sounding phrases. He knew that after the Watergate cover-up, Americans were weary of speeches and simply wanted to hear the truth conveyed in a "little straight talk among friends." The introduction and the speech indicate that the president analyzed his audience accurately and used language effectively.

## AVOIDING EUPHEMISMS

Sometimes people avoid saying what they really mean by employing nonoffensive terms or phrases called **euphemisms**. We tend to think that these veiled terms and phrases will soften the blow of the underlying meaning. But often euphemisms are so vague that the essence is lost. Look at the following euphemistic words, phrases, or sentences used in a variety of occupational and social situations, and then read the "translation":

| **The Following Euphemism . . .** | **Really Means . . .** |
|---|---|
| The government was engaged in disseminating disinformation. | The government was spreading deceit and propaganda. |
| I misspoke. | I lied. |
| She has a great personality. | She's ugly. |
| He's intelligent. | He looks like a nerd. |
| What we need in the economic stimulus bill are revenue enhancements. | We need a tax increase. |
| I'm going to the Physical Development Center. | I'm going to the gym. |
| She experienced a cerebral infarction. | She had a blood clot in the brain. |
| I need to consult the custodial engineer. | I'll get the janitor. |
| Your child needs help learning to use his leadership abilities more democratically. | Your kid is a bully. |
| Let me help you select a fitting memorial for the beloved. | Do you want to pick out a tombstone?[3] |

The vague language seems ridiculous when matched with the intended meaning. Although many of these examples may seem humorous, they are realistic.

Language is degraded and misused when people don't say what they mean. Bureaucratese, verbal clutter, and nonsense jabber will probably never disappear, but public speakers should be careful in their choice of generalized expressions. Eloquence doesn't mean using elaborate words and obscure phrases; it is more often composed of simple and direct language.

Now read these excerpts from a speech delivered by Lieutenant Commander Drew Brown, an attack pilot with the United States Navy. Commander Brown visits inner-city schools plagued with drugs and gang violence. He represents a positive role model to young African American teenagers who must stand up to the daily pressures of their surroundings. In this emotional presentation to students in a Los Angeles high school patrolled by police, Brown made his points emphatically:

*Michael Jackson goes around here saying he's bad. Mike Tyson thinks he's bad. You've got these gangs called the Bloods and the Crips and they think they're bad. They ain't bad—I'm bad. I'm bad because I can fly 550 miles an hour 50 feet from the ground and I can carry twenty-eight 500-pound bombs under my wings. I have the expertise, the know-how, and the technology not to just take out this school, but to take out the whole neighborhood. But the point I'm trying to make is, you know what makes me bad? I'm bad because I have a college education! . . . You want to get high? You go to med school after college. You learn how to be a doctor, you save somebody's life. You watch the gleam in their eyes as they hand you a check for $48,000 when you can go and buy your big Mercedes that nobody can take from you—and you are toasted! . . . There is no Black and White. But the bottom line is, Black and White is in your mind, so if you blame your color on somebody else's color or somebody else's origin on your success or your failures, you are a loser!*[4]

Brown did not hide behind obscure language. His point was loud and clear; don't give in to your surroundings—get an education. The audience might not have listened to the speaker had he used imprecise words or complicated sentence patterns. Brown was successful because he understood the kind of direct language and clear examples that would communicate his message to his teenage audience. Your speaking will be far more successful if your words and phrases convey your feelings and objectives clearly. And you will be effective if you analyze your audience well enough to understand the kind of clear language that will motivate them to listen.

## using concrete language

When you use language, it's important to be concrete. If you've ever had a friend tell you to "Bring me the things when we get together tomorrow," you were probably puzzled if your friend didn't tell you what he or she meant by "things." Speakers who use vague language sound as if their vocabulary consists of no more than a few hundred words. Look at the wording used in the following demonstration speech:

*Okay. Like the first thing you want to do is to find out how much of this stuff you need. You measure the wall longways, and then this way, and then you come up with how much paper you need. Go behind the door or somewhere else where you can't see if you mess up. Take this baby here, and measure 20 inches from the edge like so. Then just mark a line up and down. Like with the same gizmo, go from the bottom to the top of the wall and add 4 inches onto everything so you can adjust it.*

If you read between the lines, you may have understood that the speaker was demonstrating how to paper a wall. It was the vague language and verbal clutter—"Like with," "stuff," "longways," "this baby," "like so," "gizmo"—that made the demonstration sloppy and ambiguous. The speaker needed concrete words to describe materials and actions.

Now read the more precise wording of the process:

> *You have to know how much paper you need. It's very simple. You measure the height of the wall by the length of the wall, and you multiply them together and that gives the square footage. Do this on all four walls, add this together, and divide by 60. That's the number of double rolls that you'll need. If this is your first job, I'd suggest that you get pre-pasted paper.*
>
> *Start with an inconspicuous corner, such as behind the door. With a metal ruler, measure 20 inches from the corner. The paper is 20½ inches. With the extra half inch, you will paper around the corner. Then take a pencil and a level, and at the 20 inch mark, draw a vertical line on the wall. Take the same metal ruler, measure from the floor to the ceiling, and add 4 inches. The extra inches give you 2 inches at the top and 2 inches at the bottom to allow for adjustment of the pattern.*[5]

## DENOTATION AND CONNOTATION

Knowing the difference between **denotation** and **connotation** can help to make your language more concrete and vivid. Denotative meanings are the dictionary definitions of words; connotative meanings are their more personal and subjective meanings. For instance, a speaker who wanted to present an objective informational report about a proposed handgun bill might want to use words that generate denotative meanings within audience members:

> *According to the Justice Department, 80 percent of the small handguns that are manufactured in the United States are produced in the Los Angeles area. A measure proposed by the members of the city council in West Hollywood, California, would ban the sales of these weapons.*

In this example, words like "small handguns," "ban," "manufactured," "sales," and "weapons," are general terms that can generate denotative meanings. It is possible, of course, that depending on the type of audience, the statistics could stimulate strong feelings.

But suppose this speaker strongly opposed the unregulated sale of handguns and wanted to persuade listeners to support a strict handgun law.

> *According to the Justice Department, 80 percent of the small handguns that are manufactured in the United States are produced in the Los Angeles area. These sinister little weapons, referred to as "Saturday night specials," are cheap, dangerously inaccurate, and easy to hide. Many thugs prefer these badly made guns because they can be concealed in the palm of the hand like a straight-edge razor. As a matter of fact, one mini-derringer is no longer than 4 inches and fits inside a carrying case that looks like the electronic paging beepers that people carry on their belts. Would you want these instruments of destruction in your community? Well they certainly don't want them in West Hollywood because all five members of the city council have endorsed a law that would ban them.*[6]

Words such as "sinister little weapons," "Saturday night specials," "thugs," and "instruments of destruction" are chosen to evoke strong subjective meanings within listeners. The speaker can then suggest that members of the audience who feel strongly about the issue can support a law prohibiting the sale of handguns.

Obviously the effect of these connotative meanings depends upon the audience. The above passage could be very effective with many audiences but could backfire with other groups. As in any speech setting, you must analyze your audience well enough to know the type of language that will best evoke your desired response.

Here are a few examples of how a speaker can transform denotative, or dictionary, meaning into more subjective, connotative meaning:

**Words from Their Most Denotative to Most Connotative Meanings**

| | | |
|---|---|---|
| tall building | steel skyscraper | towering deathtrap |
| runner | fleet-footed racer | Olympic-class sprinter |
| dog | puppy | adorable furball |
| homeless woman | bag lady | pitiful pauper |

As you move from left to right, the meanings become more connotative and precise. If you want listeners to respond to your speech with strong mental images, use connotative words that have the capacity to stimulate concrete feelings and specific pictures.

## building a unique style

Style refers to the distinctive manner in which a speaker uses language to convey ideas and feelings. A speaker develops style with unique phrases, memorable lines, and technical devices designed to make language colorful, forceful, and dramatic. You can build an expressive style by including figures of speech like similes and metaphors and devices such as alliteration, amplification, antithesis, repetition, and mnemonic phrases.

## SIMILES

A **simile** is a figure of speech in which the words *like* or *as* are used to show comparison. Here are some examples:

> Our current tax system is like an old inner tube that is covered with patches. We must replace it with a new, fair, simple tax system.
> —H. Ross Perot, from a televised political broadcast

> Thank you very much. Inviting a physician to talk about the United States Constitution is a little like inviting James Madison to do an appendectomy. However, only one of us is going to be guilty of malpractice tonight.
> —Harvey Sloame, from "Jefferson, Madison, and Franklin"

> The fat cells are in your body just waiting, like Mr. Pac Man, to start eating. . . .
> —Vickie Chester, student speaker

> As for annexing the island, I have about the same desire as a gorged boa constrictor might have to swallow a porcupine wrong-end-to.
> —Theodore Roosevelt, from a letter to a German diplomat

These speakers used similes to make comparisons that were colorful, vivid, and interesting.

## METAPHORS

In the introduction to this chapter, we identified the "birth" metaphor that Abraham Lincoln employed in the Gettysburg Address. Like a simile, a **metaphor** is a comparison, but without the use of the words *like* or *as*. Here are some other examples:

> Lift up your hearts
> Each new hour holds new chances
> For new beginnings.

*Do not be wedded forever*
*To fear, yoked eternally this fine day*
*You may have the courage*
*To look up and out and upon me, the Rock, the River, the Tree, your country.*
　　　　　　　—Maya Angelou, from "On the Pulse of Morning"

*In order for any type of plant to grow, it must first have a healthy root system. But then it must be continually maintained in water to blossom. The same theory of growth holds true for our major cities today. In order for them to grow, they too, need healthy root systems, and these roots lie in their downtown districts.*
　　　　　　　—Edward L. Bokman, student speaker

*You remember the story of Chicken Little. She ran around the barnyard proclaiming that the sky was falling, and for a while she had all the other animals in a state of alarm. Today, we have the Chicken Little theory of economics. This time it isn't the sky that's falling. Rather, America's middle class is disappearing; vanishing before our very eyes. And, guess whose fault it is? Yours, and everyone else engaged in a service business. Imagine that. You are performing magic tricks with the economy and don't even know it.*
　　　　　　　—Paul Laxalt, from "Chicken Little Is Wrong Again"

*Epilepsy is a thunderstorm in the brain.*
　　　　　　　—Brad Piern, student speaker

*The Student Government Organization is the sun, and the clubs, organizations, and committees are the planets that revolve around it.*
　　　　　　　—Bonnie J. McGrew, student speaker

Metaphors can add life to the language of your speech. Don't be afraid to experiment with comparisons, but be certain that the comparison you make is sensible and consistent. Avoid mixed metaphors that shift comparisons midway through a presentation. A speaker who says "The Ship of State is on the 5-yard line, ready to go in for the touchdown" ought to stick with either the nautical theme or the football comparison.

## ALLITERATION

**Alliteration** refers to the repetition of the same sounds to emphasize ideas in a speech. We've already referred to former Vice President Agnew's alliterative "nattering nabobs of negativism." Some speakers have the ability to use this device with great effect.

*Today when we debated, differed, deliberated, agreed to agree, agreed to disagree, when we had the good judgment to argue our case and then not self-destruct . . . .*
　　　　　　　—Jesse Jackson, from "Common Ground and Common Sense"

*We are here, not only to keep cool with Coolidge, but to do honor to Alexander Hamilton.*
　　　　　　　—Will Rogers, from "Wealth and Education"

*Provided that every effort is made, that nothing is kept back, that the whole man power, brain power, virility, valor and civic virtue of the English speaking world, . . . is bent unremittingly to the simple but supreme task . . . .*
　　　　　　　—Winston Churchill, from "Address Before United States Congress"

*A firm fruit is a friendly fruit.*
　　　　　　　—Carol Denise Manis, student speaker

Alliteration is a creative way to develop a vivid style, but it is wise to use it sparingly.

# AMPLIFICATION

A speaker who employs **amplification** arranges words or phrases in order of importance to emphasize an opening or closing statement. For example:

> *I am in earnest—I will not equivocate—I will not excuse—I will not retreat a single inch—and I will be heard.*
>
> —William Lloyd Garrison, from *The Liberator*

> *We shall not flag nor fail. We shall go on to the end. We shall fight in France, we shall fight on the seas and oceans; we shall fight with growing confidence and growing strength in the air. We shall defend our island whatever the cost may be; we shall fight on the beaches, we shall fight on the landing grounds, we shall fight in the fields and in the streets, we shall fight in the hills; we shall never surrender.*
>
> —Winston Churchill, from "Dunkirk"

In the first example, abolitionist editor William Lloyd Garrison used an ascending order of ideas to emphasize the final, most important line of his antislavery message: "I will be heard." Winston Churchill also used amplification (as well as alliteration) in a speech defending British withdrawal from the city of Dunkirk in World War II. Even though British troops had suffered a defeat by the Nazis, Churchill wanted to rally the nation by repeating ideas that emphasized British determination "not to flag nor fail" and ending with the strong, emotional phrase "We shall never surrender."

# ANTITHESIS

When using **antithesis**, a speaker combines contrasting ideas or qualities to convey a concept. Here are two examples:

> *The race of man, while sheep in credulity, are wolves for conformity.*
>
> —Carl Van Doren, from "Why I Am an Unbeliever"

> *Not often in the story of mankind does a man arrive on earth who is both steel and velvet, who is as hard as rock and soft as drifting fog, who holds in his heart and mind the paradox of terrible storm and peace unspeakable and perfect.*
>
> —Carl Sandburg, from "Address Before Congress on the 150th Birthday of Abraham Lincoln"

Carl Van Doren effectively combined opposite metaphors to describe the gullibility and like-mindedness of human beings. Carl Sandburg, speaking to Congress on the occasion of Abraham Lincoln's 150th birthday, used contrasting metaphors as well as similes to characterize the "paradoxes" of our sixteenth president.

# REPETITION

**Repetition** of words and phrases is an effective way to emphasize key ideas, to increase interest, and to convey vivid images. Speakers throughout history have employed this colorful literary device to strengthen emotion and to summon courage. Here are two excerpts from the well-known speeches of Martin Luther King, Jr. and Franklin D. Roosevelt, who employed repetition to intensify the feelings of their listeners.

> *Let freedom ring from the snowcapped Rockies of Colorado!*
> *Let freedom ring from the curvaceous slopes of California!*
> *But not only that; let freedom ring from Stone Mountain of Georgia!*

*Let freedom ring from Lookout Mountain of Tennessee!*
*Let freedom ring from every hill and molehill of Mississippi.*
*From every mountainside, let freedom ring.*
                                  —Martin Luther King, Jr., from "I Have a Dream"

*Last night Japanese forces attacked Hong Kong.*
*Last night Japanese forces attacked Guam.*
*Last night Japanese forces attacked the Philippine Islands.*
*Last night the Japanese attacked Wake Island.*
*And this morning the Japanese attacked Midway Island.*
                                  —Franklin D. Roosevelt, from "For a Declaration of
                                  War Against Japan"

In his famous "I Have a Dream" speech, delivered at the Lincoln Memorial during the 1963 March on Washington, King repeated the words "Let freedom ring" from the song "My Country, 'Tis of Thee." King used this repetition at the conclusion of the speech to summarize his dream that every part of America serve the cause of liberty and equal justice. Franklin D. Roosevelt used repetition to energize his audience to support a different cause. After the bombing of Pearl Harbor on December 7, 1941, the president asked members of Congress to declare war on the empire of Japan. The repeated instances of Japanese military aggression quickly made an overwhelming case for the declaration of war.

## MNEMONIC PHRASES

Speakers often develop ear-catching **mnemonic phrases** that summarize main ideas and help people to remember significant themes. We tend to remember phrases like "I have a dream" or "all we have to fear is fear itself." Some of the greatest speeches in history have contained phrases that summarized the speaker's philosophy:

*If the British Commonwealth and Empire last for a thousand years, men will still say, "This was their finest hour."*
                                  —Winston Churchill, from "Their Finest Hour"

*With malice toward none, with charity for all, with firmness in the right as God gives us to see the right.*
                                  —Abraham Lincoln, from "Second Inaugural Address"

*I know not what course others may take; but as for me, give me liberty, or give me death!*
                                  —Patrick Henry, from "Give Me Liberty, or Give Me Death!"

*When this is done, I will go to the king, even though it is against the law. And if I perish, I perish.*
                                  —Queen Esther, from Esther 5:16

*Let us never negotiate out of fear. But let us never fear to negotiate.*
                                  —John F. Kennedy, from "Inaugural Address"

*I have always been fond of the West African proverb: Speak softly and carry a big stick; you will go far.*
                                  —Theodore Roosevelt, from a letter to Henry L. Sprague

Each of these mnemonic phrases was effective because it captured the essence of the speaker's intention. In your own presentations, think of creative phrases that sum up your ideas. Recognize that memorable lines, if used sparingly in a speech, can stimulate thought and heighten audience feeling about your point of view.

# being appropriate

Speech students often ask, "What exactly is inappropriate language? Shouldn't that decision be left up to the individual speaker?" Certainly each of us uses a different standard to define inappropriateness. But a speaker cannot simply make decisions in a vacuum. A speaker who wishes to have an impact must make perceptive decisions about the language he or she uses based upon the diverse members of the audience. (See a complete discussion of audience analysis in Chapter 3.) Here are some suggestions that can help you to be more aware of your listeners and avoid words, terms, phrases, and expressions that listeners might consider ineffective or improper.

## BE AWARE OF CULTURAL DIFFERENCES

In most public speaking situations you encounter, there will probably be enormous differences in the cultural backgrounds of listeners. An audience of twenty people could include Hispanics, Caucasians, African Americans, Russians, Asians, southerners, westerners, or northeasterners. If you want to educate or influence individuals of such diversity, you need to understand the impact of culture upon language.

Consider these examples: The word *submarine* is used throughout many parts of the United States to describe a large, overstuffed sandwich on an Italian roll. But terminology changes based upon geography. Bostonians may call it a "grinder," New Yorkers may order a "hero," Philadelphians might ask for a "hoagie," and residents of New Orleans may want a "poor boy." Imagine the misunderstandings that can occur when individuals whose second language is English attempt to define *submarine, hero,* or *grinder* literally. An American asks, "Can I give you a lift?" but a British citizen defines the word *lift* as an "elevator." The Eskimo language contains numerous words to describe varieties of snow, such as "wet snow" or "fluffy snow," and in Brazil there are dozens of terms referring to the word *coffee*.[7] When several American car companies decided to use the phrase "Body by Fisher" as a selling point in overseas advertisements, they discovered in horror that in some foreign markets the term was translated as "Corpses by Fisher."[8] And General Motors learned

Speakers and audiences alike must be aware of the enormous impact of culture and ethnic background on language and speaking practices.

that one of the reasons its Chevrolet Nova models failed to sell in many Latin American countries was that *no va* means "does not go" in Spanish.[9]

If regional and ethnic differences can affect simple words and concepts, imagine how culture can influence more complicated language structures. In America, individuals with extensive knowledge about a topic tend to be direct and assertive, speaking in a straightforward manner. However, in a country such as Japan, where people are concerned with saving face, those with great knowledge tend to speak indirectly and avoid direct statements that would appear dictatorial.[10] Americans enjoy talking and initiating conversation, but many Chinese use more silences within their language patterns.[11] Some Hispanic, French, and Italian Americans complain that English does not allow them to express feelings as comprehensively as their own "romance" languages.[12] The native Hawaiian language includes only five vowels and seven consonants,[13] and some American Indian languages contain no past or future tenses.[14]

As you discover how profoundly culture influences language, you can develop speaking practices that convey greater sensitivity to the diverse members of your audience. We offer these suggestions:

- Use language that is inclusive.
- Avoid "in-group" terms, jargon, and shorthand speech that excludes another's background or experience.
- Be clear and carefully define terms that listeners may not understand.
- Recognize that accents are not "wrong" or "bad."
- Speak slowly and distinctly; be aware that people of diverse backgrounds may need to listen to your dialect or accent at a more comfortable speaking rate.
- Make an effort to understand the language of your audience; learn greetings or important words that help you link your topic to diverse listeners.
- Respect the diversity of your audience.
- Avoid patronizing, embarrassing statements or inappropriate humor poking fun at listeners' culture or language.
- Recognize that the differences in language and culture are a positive source for learning.
- Build bridges of understanding—not walls of separation.[15]

## RECOGNIZE DIFFERENCES DUE TO GENDER

Do women talk more than men? Are men more direct than women? Are there distinct men's and women's languages? The answers to these questions may surprise you. But before we begin examining differences in language, be aware that the concepts being considered here are based upon researched conclusions that have numerous exceptions. The language used by men and women can be influenced by family, education, or cultural socialization. Men and women can communicate differently or similarly based upon occupation, experiences, relationships, interests, needs, or social groupings. As men and women differ in size, color, age, shape, or interests, so can they vary in vocabulary, sentence structure, grammar, and language patterns.

First of all, it is a myth that women talk more than men do. Studies indicate that men not only talk more but control conversation and maintain their dominance by interrupting others more often.[16] Men seem to be less concerned with grammatical errors and tend to use vocalized pauses to occupy center stage. Men use competitive and task-oriented language to take charge and get things done. Men will frequently issue orders and directives, such as "You need to fax this report" or "Let's get to the bottom line." Men have greater technical vocabularies and tend to be more fact-oriented than women.

Men's language is more intense, and some men's language includes more curse words and profanity. Men like to talk about topics such as sports, business, or current events. While they enjoy conversations with other men to escape, to share interests, and to experience "freedom," men seldom call each other simply to talk.[17]

There are interesting differences in the language used by women. Women tend to speak with more qualifiers, such as "possibly" or "maybe," and more disclaimers, such as "this might be silly, but . . . ." Unlike men, women typically don't interrupt conversations, and they use more polite forms for giving orders: "If you don't mind . . ." or "If it isn't too much trouble . . . ." Women tend to use more "tag" questions, such as "That's the way it is, right?" and more descriptive words like *exceptionally, adorable, precious,* and *lovely.* Women use more complex sentence structures, prepositional phrases, and adverbs than men do, and they ask questions three times as often as men do. Women also use more words and convey more comprehensive details than do men. Women tend to use more tentative phrases, such as "I guess" or "I think"; employ language that is less assertive than that used by men; and make statements that express negations by describing what things are not. Unlike the more dominant males, women try to support conversation and help to keep it going. Women are more comfortable disclosing personal information and expressing emotional needs and psychological states. Women talk with other women to express empathy, to share feelings, or "just to talk."[18]

What can we learn from some of these conclusions, and what are the implications for the speaker and listener? We must remember that differences in language patterns can depend upon the situation, place, and environment. A businesswoman presenting a training lecture to new employees could use language that is direct, task-oriented, and to the point. At the same time, a man recounting a spectacular scuba-diving experience in the Caribbean could use numerous details and include descriptive adverbs. Much has been made of "the battle" of the sexes, and much has also been written about the dominance of one gender or the vengeful role reversal of another. But if we recognize that the rhetoric of confrontation is harmful, we can begin to listen honestly and genuinely learn from one another. We should enjoy the unique speaking patterns of women, who can convey the depth and richness of language with expressive shades and images. We can also appreciate the directness of men, who contribute power, intensity, and technical depth to language. If we avoid making judgments and understand that the language of one gender is not wrong and the other right, we can appreciate that our differences can actually complement each other. We can be more open when women or men need to alter their language patterns in response to different environments or roles. And we can also be more accepting of the unique perspectives that each gender offers.[19]

## AVOID OFFENSIVE TERMS

Chapter 3 on audience analysis mentions radio talk-show host Don Imus, actor Isaiah Washington, comedian Michael Richards, and actor/director Mel Gibson who used language that offended the race, religion, or sexual orientation of many Americans. Some other high-profile individuals have made comments that were equally insulting to individuals and groups of Americans. Former Governor Jesse Ventura of Minnesota upset many church members and religious leaders when he told a *Playboy* magazine interviewer that "organized religion is a sham and a crutch for weak-minded people who need strength in numbers."[20] Vicente Fox, former president of Mexico, made a statement that Mexican migrants to the United States are willing to take jobs that "not even blacks want to do." His controversial remarks were harshly criticized by American politicians, civil rights leaders, and African Americans.[21]

These speakers all had one thing in common: Each of them employed language that significantly offended large groups of Americans. Whenever a speaker uses racist or sexist language or words that attack an individual's religion, culture, or sexual orientation, the listener will react with hostility. As a speaker, you want to win listeners and open their minds to your ideas.

You should also avoid using obscene words and phrases that can offend some listeners. During the latter part of the 1960s and early 1970s, many younger Americans discovered that they could gain public attention to their causes by shouting obscenities during rallies and protest demonstrations. The demonstrators got attention, but their language also helped to polarize listeners. Commentators often referred to "the generation gap" or the "age gap." In your own speeches, it is good to remember that you are being evaluated by your audience. If you utter four-letter words for their shock value, you will probably get many listeners to take notice, but you will also discover that many will be offended. Those who are insulted will judge you negatively and switch you off mentally. You may find your credibility damaged and reduced.

The guideline is to refrain from using language that offends your audience. Analyze your listeners, understand their backgrounds, and respect their differences. Use positive language that wins them over to you, builds your credibility, and generates constructive feelings about you as a speaker.

## ELIMINATE IRRELEVANT LANGUAGE

It's a good idea to avoid the use of unnecessary verbiage or linguistic clutter. A speaker who constantly repeats words and phrases such as "like you know," "and so," and "well" or vocalized pauses like "um" creates external noise, thus interfering with communication and frustrating the listener. Dr. Nicholas Christenfeld, a psychologist at the University of California in San Diego, has studied what he calls the "um phenomenon." He reports that most people use several hundred vocalized pauses every hour, and some individuals use as many as nine hundred verbalized pauses in one day. From his research, Christenfeld concludes that speakers who use irrelevant vocalizations are trying to buy time in order to struggle for the next word or phrase. He observes that "people don't admire people who um."[22]

It's also a good idea to avoid including irrelevant details that are not important to the speech. In this example, a speaker attempts to explain the tools needed for professional painting but loses sight of the specific purpose:

> *First, you set up a flat table for your materials where you want to do the painting. I set mine up in the family room. You know, my wife and children spend a lot of time there—they enjoy watching TV, playing video games, or just reading. We find that the family room is a nice place to escape from it all. It's also a great place to have parties with friends.*

This speech began as a demonstration of the steps involved in painting a room but soon deteriorated into a trivial description of life in the family room. Listeners will lose interest in presentations that get sidetracked.

## AVOID TRITE EXPRESSIONS

Our vocabulary frequently suffers from underuse due to peer pressure, lack of knowledge, or just plain laziness. Imagine how disruptive it would be for a speaker to constantly repeat slang phrases, such as "Like, I don't know," "It's bad," "It's awesome," "She's outta sight," or "kewel." English Professor Patricia Skarda of Smith College in Northampton, Massachusetts, counted the use of the word *like* in a conversation between two students. She reported that one used the word forty-eight times and the other mentioned *like* thiry-seven times. Such trite language is referred to as "mallspeak" or "teenbonics," which former Smith College President Ruth Simmons characterized as "repetitive," "inarticulate," and "imprecise."[23] To counteract mallspeak, colleges such as Smith, Mt. Holyoke, the Massachusetts Institute of Technology, and Wesleyan University have instituted speaking-across-the-curriculum and speech-mentoring programs to help students organize logical arguments and express themselves with more verbal competence and confidence.[24]

Audiences also become tired of hearing trite expressions, such as "The moral of the story is," "To each his own," "The bottom line is," "TMI," or "And now, in conclusion I'd like to say. . . ." It is better for speakers to avoid using these phrases and include language indicating that they are capable of thinking creatively and independently.

We aren't suggesting that you must never use familiar expressions or slang in your presentations. The speech delivered by Lieutenant Commander Brown suggests that in some speaking situations the use of slang can appeal to specific audiences and reinforce important ideas. But it's usually much more effective for a speaker to use inventive wording than to rely on clichés.

## ELIMINATE GRAMMATICAL ERRORS

Mistakes in grammar disturb listeners and tend to raise questions about a speaker's credibility. Imagine that, after conducting a physical examination, your doctor said, "Your X-rays don't show nothin'. Everything come out fine." Or suppose your pilot in a cross-country flight radioed to passengers that "I seen some turbulence up here." Your confidence in the doctor or your pilot might deteriorate. The same principle can be applied to your own speaking situations. If in a job interview you claim to have a two- or a four-year college degree, your prospective employer will expect you to communicate without major grammatical flaws. Your instructor will no doubt insist on the same standard in your speeches.

It's always possible to make a slip in noun-verb agreement as you are moving rapidly through a complicated speech in front of an audience. But it is important to avoid any consistent grammatical problems when you are delivering a speech. If you are weak in grammar, use the opportunity provided in your speech course to improve your skills. You may not be able to change all of your speaking difficulties in one semester, but you can reduce your grammatical mistakes by attending writing labs, taking a backup course, or getting tutoring help.

You aren't expected to understand all the intricate details of the "King's English," but you should know enough about language to be aware of the difference between good and bad grammar. A basic knowledge of a few grammatical principles will enable you to use English that will build credibility with your listeners.

## BUILD VOCABULARY SKILLS

Do as much as you can to increase your vocabulary. Take the time to look up unfamiliar words in the dictionary. Good reference sources like *Roget's International Thesaurus* or the *Random House Thesaurus* can help you to choose effective wording for your presentation. The more varied your vocabulary, the more interesting and colorful the speech will sound to your audience.

## making ideas meaningful and interrelated

Speakers can use language to create a sense of participation within an audience and to help listeners connect ideas smoothly. To achieve these objectives, you can employ personal pronouns and transitions.

## PERSONAL PRONOUNS

Listeners are more interested in a speech when they feel involved with the topic. An effective way to include the audience is to use personal pronouns like you, your, us, our. In the following example, notice how the speaker has excluded listeners:

> *Not many people in this country can say that three generations ago their family was only American. Most people in this nation were originally from somewhere else. Whether it was Russia, France, Italy, or Ireland, immigrants came here seeking freedom—freedom of religion, freedom of speech, and freedom to contribute to this great country.*

"Many people" and "immigrants" are vague and impersonal. The speaker does not allow listeners to feel any sense of involvement.

Now read this altered example:

> *How many of you can say that three generations back your family was "only American?" Almost all of our ancestors were originally from somewhere else. Whether from Russia, France, Italy, or Ireland, they originally came here seeking freedom—freedom of religion, freedom of speech, and freedom to contribute to this great country of ours.*
>
> —Evan Feinberg, student speaker

With some minor changes, the speaker has made the same passage much more personal. The introductory question addresses the audience directly—"you" and "your family." Personal pronouns used in phrases such as "our ancestors" and "country of ours" allow listeners to feel like participants. When it is appropriate in your speech, use these personal pronouns to relate to your audience. Avoid vague, third-person references such as "people," "individuals," or "they." You want your listeners to feel they are a part of your topic whenever it is appropriate.

## TRANSITIONS

Suppose you have come to the end of the first of three main numeral headings in the body of your speech. One way to end is by saying, "I've finished my first point. Now for point two." This external transition tells the audience they are about to hear your second main idea, but the line is abrupt and jarring. Improved language would enable ideas to flow more smoothly from one point to another. **Transitions** are connectives between major or minor ideas in a speech. External transitions connect main points; internal transitions join subordinate ideas within a point.

Here are some examples of external transitions:

**Specific purpose:** The purpose is to inform the audience about circus clowns.[25]
**Thesis statement:** Clowning has a history, an educational process, and famous personalities.

Possible transitions to introduce main point I, history of circus clowns:

1. Let me first tell you about circus clowns and their history.
2. Circus clowns have an interesting history.
3. I found out some really interesting aspects of clown history.

Possible transitions to introduce main point II, college for clowns:

1. Now that I've told you about clowns and their history, I want you to know that they also have their own college.

2. Circus clowns not only have a history; they also have a college.
3. While I found that clown history was interesting, I soon discovered that clown college was unimaginable.

Possible transitions to introduce main point III, well-known clown personalities:

1. Since I've told you about clown college, I'd like you to hear about a few well-known clown personalities.
2. But clowns are not complete without personality, and I'd like to talk about some of the most famous clown personalities.
3. After I discovered clown college, I came across some fascinating clown personalities.

Possible transitions to introduce the conclusion:

1. Now that you've heard about clown history, education, and famous clown personalities, I hope you will have a little more appreciation of this art the next time you see a circus clown.
2. In every part of the world, people of all ages have laughed at these interesting creatures called clowns.
3. I hope you've enjoyed some of the discoveries I've made about clowns.

Each external transition is a sentence that acts as a bridge to link the previous thought with the next main idea. Notice that a transition line after the thesis helps to make a smooth connection between the introduction and main point I of the body. Similarly, an external transition after the last main point of the body helps to bond the last point to the conclusion. Research indicates that external transitions flag main ideas and increase listener comprehension.[26] Remember that members of your audience don't have copies of your manuscript or outline; they won't be able to distinguish major or minor points easily unless you clearly indicate them.

External transitions are complete sentences that separate main points in the body of the speech; internal transitions separate minor points under main points. Connectives such as *also, then,* and *next* can tell listeners that a subheading has several items that are linked together. Here are a few examples of internal transitions:

| | | |
|---|---|---|
| and | and so | in addition |
| then | finally | in addition to |
| next | first, second, third . . . | another |
| also | often | but |

Be sure not to mix external and internal transitions. If you were to use *also, and,* or *in addition* as your only connecting transition between two main points in the body, you would confuse your audience because they would not be easily able to separate the major elements of the speech. Your presentation would sound like one long main point rather than a series of headings with subordinate points. If you use complete sentences as your external transitions between main ideas, then one-word connectives will work effectively for internal transitions between supporting points.

## summary »

You can communicate more successfully if your language is clear and direct, rather than obscure or euphemistic.

Concrete language is also more effective than ambiguity. If you want to evoke subjective feelings within listeners, use connotative rather than denotative language. You can develop a colorful and forceful style by using figures of speech like similes and metaphors and devices such as alliteration, amplification, antithesis, repetition, and mnemonic phrases.

The language of a speech should always be appropriate to the diverse members of your audience. Understand how culture and gender affect the language of your listeners. Avoid offensive words and terminology, and eliminate unnecessary language and extraneous verbal clutter. Avoid using trite expressions, and eliminate grammatical mistakes. Work to build a comprehensive vocabulary that enables your language to be more vivid.

You can make a speech more meaningful through the use of personal pronouns. Link your ideas together more effectively by developing external transitions to bridge main points and using internal transitions to connect subordinate elements.

## SKILL BUILDERS »

1. Select a speech presented by one of the famous speakers identified in this chapter (Martin Luther King, Jr., John F. Kennedy, Abraham Lincoln, Maya Angelou, Jesse Jackson, Winston Churchill, Franklin D. Roosevelt, Theodore Roosevelt). As you read, find examples of several figures of speech that the speaker uses and present the findings to your class.
2. Choose an effective speech from the present or recent past that represents an example of clear, direct language with colorful figures of speech. The speech can be one presented by a prominent individual in politics, sports, education, medicine, or entertainment. (A database search of Vital Speeches of the Day is one source that could be helpful for this assignment.) Present a summary of the speech to your class and provide specific examples of colorful language as well as figures of speech.

## @ BUILDING A SPEECH ONLINE »

Now that you've read Chapter 13, use your online Resource Center for Building a Speech for quick access to the electronic study resources that accompany this text. You can access your Resource Center at http://academic.cengage.com/login, using the access code that came with your book or that you bought online at http://www.iChapters.com. Your Resource Center gives you access to Interactive Video Activities, the book's companion website, Speech Builder Express 3.0, InfoTrac College Edition, and study aids, including a digital glossary and review quizzes.

# chapter 14

# DEVELOPING THE DELIVERY

## chapter objectives »

After reading and studying this chapter, you should be able to

1. Discuss techniques for proper breathing
2. Describe the elements of vocal delivery
3. Describe the elements of visual, nonverbal delivery
4. Know how to combine vocal and visual elements
5. Recognize how to build a skillful delivery

During the hotly contested Democratic primary campaign between Barack Obama and Hillary Clinton in 2008, candidates and their families crisscrossed the country looking for votes. Michelle Obama, Senator Obama's wife, was introduced to an audience at a town hall meeting in Reno, Nevada, where she received a warm reception from the crowd. Mrs. Obama began her speech: "I'm really happy to be here in Nevada." Immediately, the warm welcome ended and the crowd began shouting at Mrs. Obama and some even started booing. What was the problem? Mrs. Obama had only stated the first line of her speech: What could she possibly have said that was so offensive? Well it happens that she mispronounced the name of the state. She said "Nah-VAH-da rather than the more nasal "Neh-VAAD-ah." Nevadans want their state's name to be pronounced accurately and audience reactions were meant to correct her mistake. Sufficiently embarrassed, Mrs. Obama quickly pronounced "Neh-VAAD-ah" several times correctly and went on to present a successful speech.[1]

> ❝To be an orator, you have to use your own words and be on fire with them. ❞
>
> —Fulton John Sheen

Correct pronunciation is just one of many aspects of delivery that are necessary for an effective speech. In this last chapter of Unit Four, we identify the skills you need for a successful delivery. We examine some of the important aspects of your vocal and visual delivery, and consider some brief suggestions to help you develop your delivery techniques. Additionally, at the end of this chapter you'll find a delivery checklist, which you can use to help ensure that your delivery will always be effective and appropriate. You can access this checklist online at the Building a Speech website under Chapter Resources for Chapter 14.

## delivering the speech

Students often ask public speaking instructors, "Is delivery or content more important in a speech?" The instructors' usual answer is "yes." The problem with this question is that it assumes delivery and content are somehow isolated and that a speech can successfully depend upon one or the other. An eloquent delivery is not helpful, however, if the message is disorganized or poorly researched. At the same time, well-researched and clear ideas can fail to communicate if the delivery is poor.

You need effective skills in both delivery and content to succeed in communicating your message. Martin Luther King, Jr.'s famous "I Have a Dream" speech would have been only moderately interesting had it been published in a book or magazine. It was the civil rights leader's ringing style of delivery that projected King's ideas forcefully to his audience.

A speaker's facial expressions, gestures, vocal inflections, and voice projection can convey energy and enthusiasm about a topic.

© Thomson Learning

There are two aspects of delivery—the vocal and the visual, or nonverbal. Imagine a speech that you hear over the radio. You listen to the speaker's increase and decrease in volume, quickening or slowing of the speaking rate, and emphasis on key words and phrases. Now picture a televised speech with no sound as the speaker gestures, smiles or frowns, and makes visual contact with the audience. The radio or the silent TV speech can have a degree of success, but unless the vocal and visual aspects of delivery are combined, meaning will not be fully projected over all the available channels of communication. For example, those who heard the 1960 presidential debates between Senator John F. Kennedy and Vice President Richard M. Nixon on radio thought Richard Nixon had been the most effective speaker. But most of those who watched the debates on television thought Kennedy was the clear winner. Richard Nixon's "five o'clock shadow" and sluggish performance contrasted poorly with John F. Kennedy's sharper image and energetic delivery. Vocal and visual delivery are equally important when you present a speech. If one channel is blocked, communication can be significantly altered.

## proper breathing for vocal delivery

You need a supply of air not only to survive but also to produce the sound needed for an effective vocal delivery. It is the diaphragm that is primarily involved in inhalation. The diaphragm is a dome-shaped muscle attached to the base and sides of the lower ribs separating the abdomen from the chest. When you inhale, the diaphragm contracts and moves downward, while the ribs move upward and out, increasing the size of the chest cavity. At the same time, air flows into the lungs and fills the vacuum. As you exhale, the diaphragm slowly begins to relax, and the abdominal muscles exert pressure upward to force air out of the lungs, through the trachea and into the larynx, where the air vibrates the vocal folds and produces sound.

If you gasp for air or raise your shoulders when you inhale, you are possibly using **clavicular breathing**, or respiration from the top of the lungs. Slouching or leaning over a lectern can interrupt the natural process of inhalation and contribute to improper breathing. Clavicular breathing causes unsteadiness in the air supply and creates tension in the neck and throat. If you place your hand over your abdomen and inhale, you should feel the stomach muscles move forward in **diaphragmatic breathing**. A good, steady breath from the diaphragm produces the constant supply of air needed to produce sound.[2] The following exercises can help you to breathe properly and to establish breath control.[3]

**Exercise 1:** Sit in a chair that is comfortable but firm and has good back support. Stretch your hands on your abdomen immediately below your ribs, with your thumbs pointing to the rear and fingers pointing forward. Sit erect but relaxed, with your feet firmly on the floor. Inhale slowly, then exhale. When you inhale, you should feel your stomach muscles push forward, and when you exhale, they should pull in. Now repeat this exercise, but this time take about 5 seconds to inhale. Then take 10 seconds to exhale. If you run out of breath before 10 seconds, try the exercise again and exhale much more slowly. Repeat this exercise several times.

**Exercise 2:** Stand up straight with both feet firmly on the floor. Inhale normally and then exhale on the sound *s*. Maintain the sound as evenly as possible for about 10 seconds. Repeat the exercise and exhale on the sounds *sh*, *th*, and *f*.

# vocal delivery

In this section we will examine the following elements of vocal delivery: volume, articulation, pitch and inflection, quality, rate, pronunciation, pausing, emphasis, and phrasing.[4]

## VOLUME

**Volume** is the intensity, or loudness and softness, of your voice. If you have ever been approached by a person who shouts a 10-minute sales pitch at you, or if you have ever strained to hear a speaker in a large auditorium, you are already aware of the importance of volume in speech delivery. Either of these situations is irritating, and listeners will block out a speaker who fails to adjust volume to meet the needs of a particular speech setting. If you present a speech in a gymnasium without a microphone, you'd better be prepared to project your voice so the individual in the last row can hear you comfortably. Conversely, you may need to speak more softly to a handful of people in a small conference room.

In speech classes, people rarely have the problem of projecting too much volume; more often, they aren't loud enough. It takes experience and training to develop vocal sensitivity. Experienced actors and actresses can project their voices, even in a whisper, without amplification in cavernous playhouses or in vast open-air amphitheaters. Unless there is a physical problem, most of us have the ability to develop good vocal projection. By doing some vocal exercises and practicing diaphragmatic breathing, you can control the intensity of your voice so that the audience can hear you comfortably.

Adjusting your volume can also be an effective way to emphasize significant portions of a speech. You can increase or lower your volume for dramatic emphasis when you convey startling information or emotional examples. The late Leo Buscaglia—an educator, author, and public speaker who toured the country lecturing on love and human emotions—told this story of a smiling girl "with kind eyeballs" who was formerly a student in one of his huge lecture classes at the University of California:

> And about five weeks into the semester this beautiful young girl was not in her seat and when Monday, Wednesday, Friday, Monday, Wednesday, Friday came, I became curious, and I went down and asked the people around her what had happened to her. And do you know that in something like six weeks of school, they didn't even know her name? . . . and so I went to the Dean of Women and I asked about her . . . [and she said] "Oh Leo, I'm sorry, haven't I told you? This girl went to Pacific Palisades (which is an area where many of you know where sheer cliffs fall into the sea), and there were people there having a picnic on the grass, and they saw her drive her car up and she left the ignition running and zombie-like, she walked across the grass and without a moment's hesitation, threw herself off onto the rocks below." She was 22.[5]

When he used this example, Buscaglia increased his volume on the words "they didn't even know her name" to show anger and disgust. Then he contrasted that emotion by softening his voice almost to a whisper on the line "and threw herself onto the rocks below" to reinforce the tragedy and shock of the story. Volume can be an effective device to shade meaning.

## ARTICULATION

Another aspect of delivery is **articulation**, which refers to the clarity and enunciation of words, phrases, and sentences in a speech. Americans often exhibit sloppy enunciation; we frequently eliminate vowels and consonants, run words together, and mumble sentences. The unfortunate result often sounds like some kind of verbal jumble that not even fellow

English-speaking citizens can easily understand. The following exchange could take place on almost any college campus in the country. See if you can decipher some of the garbled words and phrases.

**Man:** Haryadoin?
**Woman:** Fine. Whatchurnam?
**Man:** Laryowns—urz?
**Woman:** Molyilsn. Whouwerkfor?
**Man:** Blakndeckr. Wheryagodaskool?
**Woman:** Eescampus.
**Man:** O. Imonweseye. Wheryagoinow?
**Woman:** I dunno.
**Man:** Yasingl?
**Woman**: Yeh.
**Man:** Yawannagodamyplas?

Although the example may be humorous, it makes a serious point. To communicate effectively, a speaker must enunciate clearly. The audience must be able to understand words and phrases easily without having to guess at the meaning. When you speak, you should make the effort to open your mouth and use clear articulation. Remember that words have vowels and consonants, and some words must be distinctly separated in order to be understood. Try to pronounce each of the following words containing difficult sound combinations:[6]

| | | |
|---|---|---|
| fifths | grasped | asks |
| frisked | answer | fists |
| sixths | oaths | months |
| thousands | depths | twelfths |
| widths | lengths | hundredths |

Many problems of articulation are simply a result of bad habits caused by verbal laziness. But there are some serious problems, such as stuttering, cleft palate, or aphasia, that may have emotional or physical causes requiring extensive speech therapy. Individuals with these speaking disorders need patience, love, and understanding in addition to good speech therapy to build confidence in their communication abilities. Many articulation problems can be improved through simple vocal exercises and by opening the mouth and speaking more distinctly.

## PITCH AND INFLECTION

**Pitch** is the vocal element that refers to the highness or lowness of sound. If you spoke in a normal voice and struck a note on a piano corresponding to your vocal note, you would find your approximate pitch. Children have high-pitched voices, women have lower voices, and men's voices tend to be still lower. Changes in pitch, called **inflections**, are important in effective vocal delivery. A presentation in which a speaker uses a variety of inflections sounds interesting. If you have ever had to endure a speaker who delivered an entire speech using the same monotonous pitch, you know how bored and frustrated you felt. The most interesting written material can often seem tedious if a speaker uses a monotone. Here is an exercise underscoring the contrast between the two styles of delivery. Read the following lines to a children's story using only a monotone:

*Once upon a time, deep in the forest, there lived a talkative owl, a one-legged grasshopper, and a turtle who could climb trees. One day the owl swooped down near the ground and discovered the grasshopper hobbling along.*

*"Wholoo there," said the owl perched on the lower limb of a tree. "I've been very lonely lately because I've had no one to talk to. Why don't you jump up on this limb, climb on my feathers and we'll go for a ride?"*

*"I can't," said the grasshopper slowly and sadly. "I lost a leg in a fierce battle with a kitten, and now I can hardly do anything at all."*

*"Ha ha," said the talkative owl, "at least you're still alive!"*

*"Not funny," clicked the one-legged grasshopper. "Not funny at all. At least you can fly."*

*"Oh yes," said the owl, "and I can turn my head all the way around, and I have sharp, sharp claws, and I am very, very wise."*

*"I've heard enough from you," said the one-legged grasshopper, who began to limp away.*

*"Wait," yelled the owl. "You can do all sorts of things that I can't do. You can sneak under doors and get into people's houses, you can crouch into corners and not be seen, and best of all, you have a lovely, lovely voice to sing with. As a matter of fact, why don't you sing and entertain me right now?"*

Now do it again, this time using a lot of vocal variety and different voices for each character as if you were telling the story to an audience of preschoolers. If you let yourself go during the reading, your preschoolers would probably have been fascinated. Vocal variety helps you to emphasize meaning and to create interest in the material. You will get a similar result when you use vocal variety in your speeches. If you vary your inflection, your listeners will be much more interested and involved in your topic.

## QUALITY

Voice **quality** refers to the sound or timbre of the voice. It is the element that makes each speaker's voice unique. No doubt you have heard speakers whose voices sounded harsh, nasal, breathy, gravelly, melodious, seductive, or hollow. Think of the differences in vocal quality of Fran Drescher, Barack Obama, Sarah Palin, Will Smith, Rosie O'Donnell, Marilyn Monroe, Chris Rock, Maya Angelou, Jerry Seinfeld, Roseanne, James Earl Jones, Jay Leno, and David Letterman. We recognize each of these individuals by their unique trademark—the sound of their voices.

Vocal quality can add to or detract from an individual's speech. If you've ever picked up the telephone and heard a nasal "Hallow—Haw are yoooooo?" you probably had difficulty concentrating on the message because the nasal sound was so annoying. On the other hand, you probably listened actively to a speaker who greeted you in a rich, mellow voice.

The voice quality of most adults is usually established by long-term vocal habits. Frequently, however, some bad habits that are responsible for unpleasant voices can be altered through tension-reducing vocal exercises. A good voice and diction coach should be consulted for treatment.[7]

## RATE

The **rate** of speech refers to the number of words an individual speaks every minute. Your speaking rate can affect the audience's comprehension of your meaning. If you rush through your speech, listeners cannot grasp your ideas or keep up with you. One student who delivered a speech too rapidly told a joke and was surprised to discover the audience laughing several seconds later when he had moved on to more serious information. A speaker needs a comfortable rate of delivery that allows ideas to sink in. The most desirable speaking rate falls somewhere between 125 and 150 words per minute.[8] Anything significantly more or less than that is either too fast or too slow. Because of apprehension, many beginning speakers unconsciously speed up their rate. If this happens to you, try to make a conscious effort to slow down so that your listeners can absorb your ideas. Use dramatic pauses to break up important thought groups and to give listeners time to think about your ideas.

Rate can also be important in the interpretation of a speech. You can increase your rate when you want to create suspense and generate emotional feelings. You can slow down at the conclusion or during climactic points in the speech to demonstrate finality and resolution. Read the following dramatic incident aloud, and adjust your speaking rate to reinforce the meaning of the material:

> The woman escaped from her assailant and ran out of the house. She ran up the street and began yelling and pleading, "Will anyone help me? Please, please, protect me. Someone's trying to kill me!" She kept running and glancing over her shoulder to see if the assailant was coming after her. She ran around a corner and spotted a police car two blocks ahead. She ran the last two blocks waving her arms wildly. "Please, save me," she screamed. Finally, finally, she saw the beautiful car with the red and blue revolving light coming toward her. She slowed to a half run, half walk. Between her sobs and heavy breathing she whispered, "Thank God!"

If you followed the events in the narrative closely, your speaking rate was probably rapid at the beginning. As the pace of the story quickened, you may have increased your rate, and as the events concluded, your pace decreased. Your rate of speech is a valuable tool you can employ to emphasize as well as interpret meaning.

## PRONUNCIATION

**Pronunciation** describes the combinations of vowels, consonants, syllables, and accents a speaker chooses to emphasize in a specific word. As the introduction to this chapter indicates, it is important to know how to pronounce common English words as well as difficult terminology you employ in a speech. Stumbling over words or making frequent errors in pronunciation interrupts the flow of ideas and raises questions about a speaker's credibility. Michelle Obama discovered that listeners have difficulty getting past a glaring error that could have been avoided with proper research. Knowing how to pronounce a word means understanding the generally accepted pronunciation. While pronunciation can differ remarkably depending upon the region of the country, a good dictionary should be a helpful guide to the preferred pronunciation.

As part of your standard speech practice, you should check the pronunciation of any difficult words or terms unfamiliar to you. Here are some common words that are frequently mispronounced. Read the list carefully, and make sure that you are able to use the generally accepted pronunciation of each word.

| | | |
|---|---|---|
| adjective | gesture | picture |
| aluminum | harassment | potato |
| cavalry | mischievous | pumpkin |
| congratulate | neither | recognize |
| either | nuclear | statistics |
| escape | particularly | tomato |
| exits | pecan | veterinarian |

## PAUSES

**Pauses** are breaks or interruptions in speech that separate thoughts and ideas. **Dramatic pauses** are intentional breaks or silences between major ideas that can bring out the

First Lady Michelle Obama uses forceful gestures when she speaks about issues such as the family and American troops abroad.

© RICK WILKING/Reuters /Landov

meaning of a specific passage. Dramatic pauses can help a listener to focus on a startling fact or create a moment that allows a listener to experience an emotion. Notice how the following passage reads when you place dramatic pauses in strategic parts of the story:

> *Melanie was a bright, 17-year-old girl. She was a straight-A student, she had numerous friends, and she was extremely attractive. Everything seemed to be going well for Melanie. But Melanie had one problem that few people knew about. [pause] Melanie was an anorexic [pause] and it was killing her!*

You can use pauses effectively in a number of places to bring out the meaning of this passage. If you pause briefly at each punctuation mark and then use longer pauses at the brackets, the punch line to the story is dramatically emphasized. Read it several more times, and experiment with different combinations of pauses. Experiment in your speeches as well. Use pausing where it is most likely to enhance and emphasize emotional examples, startling statements, and colorful quotations.

**Vocalized pauses** are verbalizations, such as "uh" and "um," that cause distractions in speaking. Speakers sometimes use vocalized pauses because they are nervous or because they may be uncomfortable with silence. It was not helpful to Caroline Kennedy's failed attempt to seek appointment to Hillary Clinton's New York senate seat when she uttered the words "you know" numerous times in a brief televised interview. As he was giving impromptu remarks, former President George W. Bush often used the vocalization "um."

Try to eliminate this habit from your verbal delivery. Vocalized pauses are annoying and keep listeners from concentrating on your presentation.

Remember that you don't have to verbalize 100 percent of your speaking time. Use silences to your advantage when delivering your presentations. Dramatic pauses can help you to separate thoughts and can give the audience time to grasp your ideas.

## EMPHASIS AND PHRASING

You use **emphasis** in a speech when you alter your rate, volume, and pitch to highlight significant words and sentences. In **phrasing**, you group words and sentences into units of thought that make ideas easier to understand. Both emphasis and phrasing help to make a speech interesting and clear. In the following example, emphasize the italicized words by increasing your volume and slowing your rate. Use pauses wherever you see the caret ($_\wedge$).

> The U.S. national debt is eleven trillion dollars. $_\wedge$Think of it. $_\wedge$ Eleven $_\wedge$trillion $_\wedge$ dollars.

You can hear how emphasis verbally helps to underscore important words and thoughts and how phrasing helps to clarify the meaning by grouping sentences into smaller thought units. The markings reflect the emphasis and phrasing each individual used to deliver the following passages:

> And so, my fellow Americans: $_\wedge$ask not what your country can do for you—
> $_\wedge$ ask what you can do for your country.
>
> —John F. Kennedy

> I have a dream $_\wedge$ that my four children will one day live in a nation where they will not be judged by the color of their skin but by the content of their character. I have a dream today.
>
> —Martin Luther King, Jr.

> The only thing we have to fear is $_\wedge$ fear itself.
>
> —Franklin D. Roosevelt

The ideas are dynamic enough. But each speaker used his unique delivery to promote an even clearer understanding of his words. The results were powerful. If you reread each quotation using different emphasis and phrasing, the meaning is altered, and the overall effect is much less dramatic.

Your ideas can be emphasized in many ways, and your words can be grouped into a variety of patterns. Choose the emphasis and phrasing that most effectively reflect your intention and that will, in turn, contribute to the audience's understanding of your meaning.

## visual, nonverbal delivery

*Visual delivery* refers to the nonverbal aspect of communication. This aspect of speaking is important because we communicate so many of our thoughts and feelings spontaneously through facial expressions, eye contact, or body movements. One study, for example, indicates that 55 percent of meaning conveyed in conversation is expressed through the face.[9] In addition, a speaker's appearance or "physical attractiveness" can significantly enhance a speaker's persuasive influence.[10] So it is helpful to understand that your eye contact, appearance, gestures, facial expressions, body position, and movement, as well as characteristics related to your culture or gender, can have a significant impact on audience perceptions of your communication.

## EYE CONTACT

**Eye contact** is a very important aspect of your visual delivery. Through the eyes, you can reach the intellect and emotions of your audience and gauge their feedback to your ideas. Research indicates that poor eye contact may even have a negative impact on the amount of information an audience comprehends during a speech.[11] Any audience wants the speaker's recognition and awareness. A speaker who reads word for word, without ever looking up, will promote indifference and boredom.

> *The teacher arrived for every class period just 3 minutes late. She always sat down gingerly, pulling her chair up very slowly under the desk. She tugged three times at her skirt, making certain that it was stretched over her knees. She then began the lecture, without ever once looking at her students. "Today we are going to discuss the dangling participle," she droned in a monotone, ". . . an exciting lesson in rhetorical dysfunction."*
>
> *One student commented at the end of the semester, "She never looked at me any time during the whole course. I don't think she ever knew I was alive. The trouble is, I'm not sure that she was alive."*

Contrast this experience with one of your most interesting instructors. You'll find that the professor who is an effective communicator uses a great deal of eye contact. The good instructor is always aware of student reactions and knows when to repeat ideas, ask questions, or proceed to new information. This instructor combines good eye contact with many other techniques of effective delivery. The communicative professor walks around, gestures, uses facial expression, and shows interest in students who respond by becoming actively involved and interested in class discussions.

When delivering a speech, you must establish visual contact with your audience. You aren't expected to memorize the speech, but you should have rehearsed enough to free yourself from paying too much attention to notecards. It may take some practice and repeated experience to discover how often to glance at notes and how much visual contact to make with listeners. When you look at the audience, sustain eye contact long enough to let them know you see them and are following their reactions. Look at each area of the audience at some point in your speech. Avoid bobbing your head up and down between notecards and audience. This practice detracts from your speech and doesn't establish eye contact. If you feel insecure in front of people, find several friendly, attentive faces at the right, center, and left. Begin by looking at these supportive individuals and gradually expand your field of vision to other audience members. Practice your speech thoroughly so that you will feel confident enough to look away from your notecards and establish rapport with your audience.

## APPEARANCE

Your **appearance** can support or detract from the communication process. A student who worked as a school-crossing guard gave a speech informing the audience about the duties and responsibilities of her job. On the day of the speech she wore her school guard uniform, complete with hat, badge, and whistle. She spoke of her role as a protector and guardian of "her kids" and firmly reminded the audience that it is her job to stop traffic whenever it is in the children's best interests. The speaker's words and feelings conveyed commitment to the topic, while her appearance communicated authority and dedication on a nonverbal level.[12]

Politicians carefully analyze speaking situations when they make decisions about their appearance for important speeches. A governor eating chicken and politicking for votes at the local county fair may wear blue jeans and suspenders. But the same governor will probably choose a conservative suit with red, white, and blue accessories for the inaugural address at the state capitol.

At the beginning of the lengthy O. J. Simpson murder case, prosecuting attorney Marcia Clark appeared in court each day with a distinctive curly hairstyle. At the midpoint of the trial, however, Clark had a makeover, transforming her hairdo into a darker, straighter style. Some legal analysts suggested that it might have been unwise for the prosecutor to modify her appearance during the course of the trial because the change could have negatively affected the relationship between the attorney and the jurors.[13]

You create a positive impression when you dress appropriately for the audience, the occasion, and the topic. Avoid distracting styles: straps that fall down, skirts that ride up, jewelry that dangles noisily, hair that hides eyes or face, shoes that skid or squeak. An appropriate appearance—neat, clean, neither too formal nor too casual—lets the audience know that you care about the speech and that the occasion is important to you.

## GESTURES

Enhance your speeches by using **gestures** to emphasize words or phrases, to describe physical objects or events, and to point out directions or locations. In the early part of the twentieth century, there was an emphasis on elocutionary speaking, which involved the study of vocal production and gesturing in speech delivery. Speakers practiced complicated vocal exercises and studied manuals containing illustrations and definitions of gestures. From this analysis, speakers learned to project their voices in large assembly halls and to use gestures forcefully in their presentations. William Jennings Bryan, Teddy Roosevelt, and Robert Lafollette were prominent elocutionists of this time whose booming voices and animated delivery influenced millions of Americans. Although these speakers were effective in their era, their speeches would seem overdone today. Radio, television, and microphones have enabled speakers to be more conversational and to use more descriptive gestures in speech delivery. Modern speech educators feel gestures should be spontaneous and reflective of an individual's feelings and energies.

While it's not advisable to memorize gestures, as some of the elocutionists did, you can increase the effectiveness of your gestures through practice. Successful gestures are precise and punctuate your words and ideas clearly. Think of the varieties of gestures you might need to describe tying a shoelace or giving directions to your home. Beginning speakers are sometimes afraid to use gestures in their presentations. They often stand with their arms stiffly at their sides, hands clasped behind or in front of them or resting rigidly on the speaking lectern. If you make a conscious effort, you will find that gestures can help you work out some of your nervous energy in a speech. Don't let yourself be controlled by nervous mannerisms such as distracting hand, arm, or body movements. Show enthusiasm and project confidence to your audience by using gestures to punctuate ideas and to describe objects and concepts.

## FACIAL EXPRESSION

Our memories are imprinted with the stark images of the crumbling World Trade Center, the blazing Pentagon, and the smoking Pennsylvania crash site as a result of the September 11 terrorist attacks. But the heroic image that also remains in our memories is the photograph of three firefighters raising the American flag amidst the rubble of the Twin Towers. No words are needed to describe the picture; the image alone expresses the power, hope, and determination of the American spirit.

Each of us has an extraordinary set of muscles in our faces that can express a silent picture. We can smile, frown, show sadness and anger, or convey love and joy. Our **facial expressions** help to reinforce our words. If you were to say "I love you" and show anger in your expression, your listener would either be confused or interpret the message negatively. If you had a blank facial expression, your listener might wonder if you had any feelings of love at all. A student presenting a speech about the importance of seat belts smiled broadly as he said, "If you were involved in a traffic accident and you didn't wear your seat belt, you might die!" The audience didn't take the speaker seriously, because his facial expression wasn't appropriate.

Your facial expression should clearly support your verbal message. If you talk about parental kidnapping, your expression should reflect anger and concern; if your topic is space exploration, your face should convey adventure and curiosity; if you are speaking about chronic illness, your face should show empathy and hope. Your facial expressions cannot be mechanically planned in advance. Like gestures, they should be spontaneous and reflect your natural feelings. Practice your speech in front of a friend or, if possible, a video camera to get some clues about your expressions and determine if they support your verbal messages. A speaker who projects emotion about a topic through facial expression will tend to receive a similar emotional response from the audience.

## BODY POSITION AND MOVEMENT

Your stance, posture, poise, and **body movement** can also contribute to your communication. An individual who has good posture appears to be more prepared than does a speaker who slouches or leans on the lectern. Standing on both feet gives a speaker greater stability than shifting from one leg to another. Good posture also allows a speaker to breathe more effectively to produce sound.

A student was in the process of presenting an informative speech about learning disabilities. She had researched the topic well, and she had found a number of interesting examples, statistics, and testimonies to support her main points. During her speech, however, she often wrapped one leg around the other the way a contortionist does at the circus. The audience was fascinated as they watched her legs tangle and unwind. It's obvious that the awkward body movement was a distraction that kept the audience from hearing the speech.

It's good speech practice to develop posture that is both relaxed and erect. Practice using your stance and body position to your advantage. A tall speaker with good posture can use height as an added means of persuasion. A short speaker can stand beside the lectern and develop greater intimacy with the audience. Be sure that your stance and posture add to your presentation and do not interfere with the message.

When you become a confident public speaker, you can develop some variations in body movement to emphasize the transitions in your speech. Here are some suggestions:

**Specific purpose:** To inform the audience about dyslexia
**Thesis statement:** Dyslexia has several causes and effects that can be described in a case study.

BODY                                                            SUGGESTED MOVEMENT

I. Causes of dyslexia
   *Transition line 1:* "I've just told you                    Move to right of lectern
   about some of the major causes of
   dyslexia; now I want to go into some
   of its effects on children."
II. Effects of the learning disability                          o o o o
   *Transition line 2:* "Now that I've                          Move in front of lectern
   considered some of the effects, let
   me tell you a personal experience
   that happened to my family."
III. Case study of dyslexia                                     o o o o

Cultures teach individuals to use nonverbal "language" uniquely. A listener must remember to keep an open mind when encountering differences in a speaker's gestures, expressions, or other nonverbal symbols.

In this presentation, the speaker begins the introduction and main point I of the body while standing behind the speaker's lectern. When delivering transition line 1, the speaker moves to the right of the lectern, thus reinforcing the change in thoughts. Again, when delivering transition line 2, the speaker moves in front of the lectern, standing closer to the audience. This final action not only supports the change in ideas but also establishes greater intimacy with listeners during the presentation of the personal experience.

You may want to gain some confidence behind the speaker's lectern before trying some of these suggestions. Experiment with body movement when you have become comfortable with your audience.

## CULTURE AND NONVERBAL DELIVERY

You can see that the nonverbal aspects of delivery can enhance and support a speaker's message. But although gestures, eye contact, facial expression, appearance, and body movement are important elements in presenting public speeches, not everyone uses and interprets these symbols in the same way. Nonverbal messages can vary widely depending on our **culture** and background.

A Caucasian American might look directly into the eyes to establish solid visual contact with listeners. But a speaker from Japan, China, or India might find such directness inappropriate, preferring instead to use only brief, peripheral glances. Some Native American cultures interpret direct eye contact as rude or offensive.[14] A speaker from southern Europe, Africa, the Middle East, or Latin America might decide to make a point by moving extremely close to the audience, showering listeners with a liberal supply of mouth spray. To many Americans, however, this behavior would be considered intrusive and a violation of personal space. Americans use the rounded "O" formed with the thumb and index finger to signify that something is "OK." But a similar gesture made by a French speaker indicates that the object under discussion is worth a zero; and for many Latin Americans, the gesture is obscene. In the United States, nodding the head up and down conveys a "yes" response, but in Greece or Turkey the movement means "no." American women enjoy a great deal of flexibility in dress and appearance, but many women in the Middle East are expected to have the body, limbs, and head completely covered. And in Indonesia, a speaker would not show or point the soles of the shoes toward a listener, because the action would signal that the listener is beneath or inferior to the speaker.[15] When George W. Bush visited Iraq in the final weeks of his presidency, he encountered a furious Iraqi reporter who threw stones at the president during a news conference to show contempt and extreme disrespect.

Upon hearing this classroom discussion about cultural differences in nonverbal communication, one student commented humorously, "Does this mean that we should be careful not to point our shoes at listeners when we deliver our speeches?" Well, not exactly, but the discussion does imply that both speakers and audiences need to make significant efforts to understand the differences in culture and be more aware of how these differences influence the speaking message or audience response.

When you speak or listen to someone from another culture:

- Avoid making quick decisions about the individual's nonverbal "language."
- Take time to observe a speaker's stance and body movements.
- Determine if the speaker is from a culture where there is little need for personal space, and if the speaker has less concern about "being too close" than do members of the audience.
- Understand differences that occur in appearance: Does the speaker wear a sari, facial dots, or other markings to indicate a distinct tribe, caste, or family classification?
- Be aware of variations in eye contact and facial expressions: Does the speaker avoid direct eye contact and facial expressions, or is the speaker accustomed to showing animated facial expressions and looking at listeners in a straightforward manner?
- Notice how culture influences the speaker's gestures.

Fiorello La Guardia was New York City's colorful mayor from 1934 to 1945. As a fluent speaker of three languages, La Guardia was a skillful politician. When campaigning for office in his native Italian, La Guardia used a particular set of gestures. But when he spoke in English, the mayor employed other gestures, and when he spoke to Jewish audiences, he used another set of actions to support his speeches.[16] Recognize that cultures teach individuals to use gestures differently and employ codes or emblems uniquely. In some cultures, gestures may be animated and energetic; in others, physical actions may be much more restrained.

When you encounter different nonverbal languages, avoid making snap judgments that categorize the behavior as "right" or "wrong." Observe the behavior and make determined efforts to understand the cultural differences by keeping an open mind. If you are uncertain or confused about nonverbal symbols, don't be afraid to ask questions of the speaker and audience. Remember that your objective is to understand and interpret the differences in culture so that you can convey your thoughts, ideas, and feelings with clarity, sensitivity, and efficiency.

## GENDER AND NONVERBAL DELIVERY

In American society, the roles of men and women have undergone tremendous changes in recent decades. As we saw in Chapter 3, occupations that were once viewed as only men's or women's are now frequently assumed by the other **gender**. But even though occupational roles may have changed, women and men still exhibit more traditional differences in their nonverbal communication patterns. Consider the research findings in the following box.

| Research shows that women . . . | . . . and men |
|---|---|
| • tend to be more expressive in their gestures than men are. | • are not allowed to show as much sadness or fear as women can. |
| • are more touch-oriented than men are. | • are given more latitude than women in expressing hostility and aggression. |
| • show more emotion, such as sadness or fear, than men do in facial expression and in the eyes. | • often use anger to mask pain and sorrow. |
| • maintain more fixed eye contact and stand physically closer to each other than men do. | • are able to read facial expressions that indicate disgust or dislike. |
| • are given more permission, in American society, to touch or hug another woman than men are to hug another man. | • have difficulty perceiving more subtle emotions. |
| | • are considered "unmanly" if they cry. |
| • interpret nonverbal language cues more effectively than males do and can more quickly read facial expressions such as anger, sadness, and fear.[17] | • use restraint in facial expressions. |
| | • stand farther apart from each other than women do. |
| | • stand much closer to the opposite gender than women do. |
| • are often rewarded for showing positive emotions such as smiling. | • have much less physical contact with members of the same sex than women do. |
| • are not encouraged to display strong or forceful displeasure. | • display physical contact with other men through aggressive touch, like handshaking, playful jabbing, or backslapping, within well-defined boundaries such as sports, occupations, or partying. |
| • often mask their anger with tears. | |
| • are seen as appropriate if they cry. | |
| • are seen as "unladylike" if they display anger.[18] | • are still regarded as the initiators of touch in male-female relationships, and women are expected to be the responders. |
| • tend to use more powerful and forceful nonverbal cues. | |
| • make larger gestures and occupy more space and territory than women do. | |

So what can we learn about our differences? First of all, it is helpful if we don't overgeneralize about the nonverbal cues we perceive. Listeners should take time to observe patterns of behavior and interpret nonverbal expressions and gestures in context. The behavior we see may have nothing to do with gender. A woman presenting a speech with a constant smile could be experiencing speech anxiety, or a man who frequently pounds the lectern with his hand could simply have an annoying mannerism. Recognize that differences due to gender represent generalizations and should not be viewed as concrete conclusions, because there are always exceptions. A female speaker can show strong anger to support a message, and a male is capable of expressive gestures. Also remember that nonverbal speaking actions can be influenced by numerous elements, such as the audience-speaker relationship, the topic, or the situation. A man delivering a speech to a lifeless audience may need to use a wide variety of facial expressions, gestures, and body movements to energize listeners. A woman presenting a speech on a highly controversial issue may want to use restrained expressions for a more rational approach to the topic. A speaker delivering a presentation to a large audience may need to use more expansive gestures, and a speaker lecturing to a small group could be more subtle.

Remember that effective speakers, whether men or women, should adopt styles that are relevant to the needs and requirements of particular speaking situations. Try not to read too much into a speaker's every gesture, expression, or action, and avoid interpreting nonverbal cues in isolation. Recognize that men and women can complement each other's nonverbal behavior and offer different perspectives that enrich and enlighten the listener. Above all, learn to enjoy the subtleties and nuances of nonverbal behavior, and be cautious when making judgments and observations.[19]

## combining vocal and visual delivery

Vocal and visual delivery are combined in the enthusiasm and vitality that a speaker projects to an audience. An enthusiastic speaker uses vocal inflection, volume, pauses, eye contact, gestures, and facial expressions to convey a feeling of involvement in his or her topic. Audience members experience the speaker's energy visually and verbally and think, "This person really cares about the topic—I'd better listen."

In the second 1992 presidential debate between President George H. W. Bush and Governor Bill Clinton, a voter asked how the recession had personally affected the lives of each candidate. President Bush's stumbling response included the comment "I'm not sure I get it." This reaction demonstrated the president's difficulty in communicating his concern about the economic hardships suffered by many Americans. By contrast, Governor Clinton used facial expression, body movement, and gestures to convey his

Effective skills in vocal and visual delivery allow a speaker to project ideas with clarity, passion, and style.

© GoGo Images/Jupiter Images

emotional response: "In my state when people lose their jobs, there's a good chance that I'll know them by their names." An individual does not have to be a vibrant public speaker in order to be president, of course. America has had many presidents who have not been effective speakers, for example, Calvin Coolidge, Lyndon Johnson, Richard Nixon, and Jimmy Carter. But some of our strongest leaders have also been dynamic public speakers—among them are Teddy Roosevelt, Franklin Roosevelt, John F. Kennedy, and Ronald Reagan.

To be successful in a speech, show that you care about the topic. Employ good eye contact with the audience; use your facial muscles to show appropriate emotion; alter your pitch for vocal variety and adjust your volume, rate, and phrasing for emphasis; use gestures to reinforce your ideas; and reflect your commitment in your appearance. Combine all of the vocal and visual aspects of delivery into a speaking performance that is enthusiastic and energetic.

## building skills in delivery

Here are a few suggestions to help you develop your skills in speech delivery.

## KNOW YOUR MATERIAL

One of the first principles of an effective delivery is to be knowledgeable about your material. Your research should be thorough, your sources should be credible, and your understanding of the topic should be extensive. Know how to pronounce difficult names, terms, or concepts, and be familiar with your supporting materials. One key to a successful delivery is confidence in your material, which can free you to relay the topic to your audience.

## BE WELL ORGANIZED

You need a good outline, written on notecards, to deliver a speech effectively. (See Chapter 10 for discussions of outlining and creating notecards.) Make sure the outline is clear and complete. Know exactly how you are going to begin and end the speech. Be certain that your specific purpose is defined and that the main points of the body are identifiable. Check your notecards for ease in reading. Write large enough to see comfortably, and double-space between phrases and sentences. Number your notecards in the upper corner to keep them in the proper order.

## MARK YOUR NOTES

A high school instructor marked his lecture notes with phrases like "insert joke here," "use gesture now," or "show grimace." Although this type of preparation can be helpful, it might promote a memorized or mechanical delivery. You don't have to plan every detail of your delivery, but you will be wise to develop your own system of marking to indicate areas of verbal and visual emphasis. Use a simple system of underlines, brackets, arrows, and highlighter, similar to the example in Figure 14.1.

Here just a few lines, highlighted phrases, and brackets indicate emphasis, and some slanting lines and arrows show increasing rate and volume. You don't need complicated notations. You merely need to be consistent in order to translate your markings into effective gestures, expressions, and verbal emphasis.

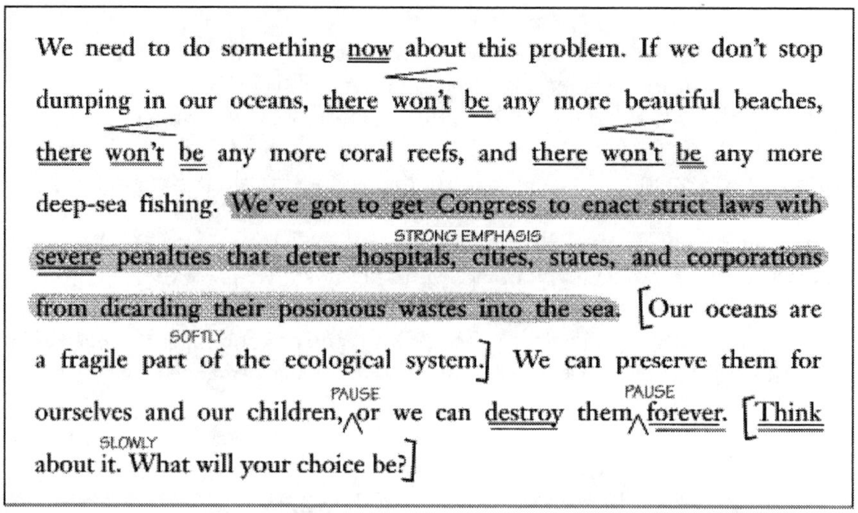

We need to do something <u>now</u> about this problem. If we don't stop
dumping in our oceans, <u>there</u> <u>won't</u> <u>be</u> any more beautiful beaches,
<u>there</u> <u>won't</u> <u>be</u> any more coral reefs, and <u>there</u> <u>won't</u> <u>be</u> any more
deep-sea fishing. We've got to get Congress to enact strict laws with
**STRONG EMPHASIS**
<u>severe</u> penalties that deter hospitals, cities, states, and corporations
from dicarding their posionous wastes into the sea. [Our oceans are
*SOFTLY*
a fragile part of the ecological system.] We can preserve them for
*PAUSE*                              *PAUSE*
ourselves and our children,ᴧor we can <u>destroy</u> themᴧforever. [Think
*SLOWLY*
about it. What will your choice be?]

FIGURE 14.1  Example of Marking Your Speech

## PRACTICE THE DELIVERY

When you have organized your material, and you know what you want to emphasize, practice the speech several times. (Review the delivery checklist in Figure 14.2.) Whenever possible, it is helpful to practice in an environment similar to your speech setting. Stand behind a speaker's lectern so that you can rest your notecards and practice some gestures. Rehearse the speech aloud and work on your vocal inflections, volume, articulation, and speaking rate. Rehearse your phrasing to develop pauses between the appropriate thought groupings. If you have an audio recorder or video camera, use it in your practice sessions. Replaying the speech can help you to evaluate your vocal delivery and detect vocalized pauses, improper pronunciation, and monotonous pitch.

It is also helpful if you can practice your speech in front of a friend or video camera. You can determine the success of your eye contact, facial expressions, gestures, and body movement as you deliver the presentation. Notice how often you need to look at your cards and how comfortably you manage your notes. Try to develop a visual delivery that reinforces every aspect of your material.

Situations frequently arise where speakers cannot engage in practice sessions. Executives, physicians, and business- or salespeople are often too busy with scheduled appointments to devote time for speech rehearsal. In such cases, it is helpful to have a "think-through" session on the plane or in the car on the way to the speech setting. In these brief sessions, the speaker can mentally review the main points of the presentation or jot down a few notes on a legal pad to organize the thought process.

Whether you have a think-through session or a formal rehearsal, work to project enthusiasm and confidence during the speech. Although it is appropriate to use your prepared notes, know your material well enough to maintain eye contact with your listeners without reading word for word. Concentrate on your ideas, and be natural and spontaneous. Your goal is to refine all the elements of your delivery into a smooth, unified presentation.

FIGURE 14.2 Delivery Checklist

## DELIVERY CHECKLIST

### Vocal Delivery

*Volume*—Is your voice loud enough for everyone to hear in the room where you are speaking?

*Articulation and Pronunciation*—Is your speaking clear, and do you know how to pronounce words and difficult terminology correctly?

*Pitch*—Do you avoid a monotone delivery and use a variety of vocal inflections, making your voice sound interesting and enthusiastic?

*Quality*—Do you know how your voice sounds to others, and have you done any vocal or breathing exercises to assist you?

*Rate*—Are you speaking at a moderate rate that allows listeners to hear and comprehend your ideas easily?

*Pauses*—Do you use silences as a tool to allow listeners to absorb meanings, and do you avoid vocalized pauses such as "um"?

*Emphasis and Phrasing*—Do you verbally stress specific words and phrases to highlight ideas and units of thoughts?

### Visual, Nonverbal Delivery

*Eye Contact*—Do you look at your listeners consistently, using brief glances at your notes but avoiding distracting head movements?

*Appearance*—Is your appearance appropriate to your topic, audience, and occasion? Are you careful to avoid any hair or clothing styles that distract?

*Gestures*—Do you show enthusiasm with spontaneous gestures that support your speech? Are you avoiding any mannerisms that take away from your presentation?

*Facial Expression*—Do your facial expressions show commitment to the topic and enthusiasm about sharing ideas with your listeners? Do you use the appropriate facial expressions to support emotions such as joy, sorrow, surprise, anger, happiness, humor, or concern?

*Body Position and Movement*—Do you have good posture as you are speaking? Do you use your position and movement to reinforce ideas, avoiding body motions that are distracting or unnecessary?

*Cultural Differences*—Are there any specific differences in culture between you and your audience that could affect your nonverbal delivery? How can you make alterations to bridge these differences?

*Gender Differences*—How could gender differences play a role in the delivery of your speech? What can you do to adjust to these differences?

## summary »

In this chapter we have examined proper breathing practices needed for an effective vocal delivery. We have also considered the aspects of vocal delivery: volume, articulation, pitch, quality, pronunciation, pauses (including dramatic pauses and vocalized pauses), emphasis, and phrasing. In addition to vocal aspects, we've focused on the importance of the visual or nonverbal aspects of delivery. A good speaker maintains eye contact with the audience, dresses appropriately for the audience, speech, and occasion, and uses gestures, facial expressions, and body movement. Listeners need to recognize that differences in culture and gender can influence the nonverbal behaviors of speakers. It is important to observe a speaker carefully and avoid making snap judgments about nonverbal delivery. When you combine all aspects of delivery, you should be projecting enthusiasm and vitality. Here are four simple guidelines to help you develop delivery skills: (1) Know your material, (2) be well organized, (3) mark your notes, and (4) practice the delivery. Perform a check of the verbal and nonverbal aspects of the speech to build a successful delivery.

## SKILL BUILDERS»

1. Working with your instructor, create a plan to improve your delivery in weak areas. For example, if you need to work on volume, rate, gestures, eye contact, or articulation, read portions of this chapter or a speech in front of a friend or classmate to achieve greater improvement in these areas of delivery.
2. Go to your library's website or media department and request a video of one of the famous speeches referenced in Chapters 13 and 14. Watch the speech and write down all of the effective aspects of vocal and visual delivery the speaker uses to convey his or her ideas.

## @ BUILDING A SPEECH ONLINE »

Now that you've read Chapter 14, use your online Resource Center for Building a Speech for quick access to the electronic study resources that accompany this text. You can access your Resource Center at http://academic.cengage.com/login, using the access code that came with your book or that you bought online at http://www. iChapters.com. Your Resource Center gives you access to Interactive Video Activities, the book's companion website, Speech Builder Express 3.0, InfoTrac College Edition, and study aids, including a digital glossary and review quizzes.

# five
unit

# CONSIDERING DIFFERENT TYPES OF STRUCTURES

# chapter 15

# SPEAKING TO INFORM

## chapter objectives »

After reading and studying this chapter, you should be able to

1. Recognize the difference between information and persuasion

2. Describe several types of informative speeches

3. Know how to build a descriptive speech

4. Be able to analyze and present an informative descriptive speech

5. Be able to analyze and present an informative demonstration speech

A CNN analyst explains the causes and effects of the subprime mortgage crisis in America. Astronauts orbiting the earth demonstrate how to repair the Space Shuttle on live television. A Red Cross worker describes the continuing genocide in Sudan. A neurosurgeon provides a comprehensive diagnosis to doctors in a distant hospital via a satellite downlink. A curator at an antiquities museum takes visitors through the ancient Egyptian art collection. A baseball commentator enumerates season averages for each player in the game. Even in an age of technology, it is still the responsibility of human beings to research, analyze, organize, and present information effectively.

Communicating in the information age isn't easy—there is an art to being clear, accurate, and concrete. This first chapter of Unit Five helps you develop your informative speaking skills. We'll examine the difference between information and persuasion, consider several categories of informative speeches, and explore some guidelines to help you build informative descriptive and demonstration speeches. Additionally, near the end of this chapter you'll find an analysis sheet (Figure 15.1) to help you evaluate an informative presentation.

> 66 *The best way to send information is to wrap it up in a person.* 99
>
> —*Robert Oppenheimer*

# key terms »
DEFINITION SPEECH
DEMONSTRATION
   SPEECH
DESCRIPTIVE
   SPEECH
INFORMATIVE
   SPEECH
LECTURE
PERSONAL
   EXPERIENCE
REPORT

# the difference between information and persuasion

As you begin to build your speech to inform, clearly recognize the difference between information and persuasion. Some rhetoricians agree with Aristotle that all speaking is persuasive; speeches differ only in the relative strength and weakness of the persuasion. This text, however, draws a distinction between communication that is informative and communication that is persuasive.[1]

Overall, an **informative speech** promotes understanding, enlightenment, and education about a topic; a persuasive speech seeks to influence and alter the beliefs, feelings, or behavior of listeners. Specifically, speeches to inform can be grouped into the following categories: description, demonstration or process, definition, personal experience, the report, and the lecture.

For the following three topics, consider how the specific purpose sentences would be phrased as informative and persuasive presentations:

| TOPICS TO INFORM | TOPICS TO PERSUADE |
| --- | --- |
| To define the al-Qaeda organization | To convince the audience that the U.S. government did not take strong enough action against the al-Qaeda terrorist network from the beginning |
| To provide a profile of a troubled teenage killer | To convince the audience that juveniles who commit violent acts in public schools should be tried as adults |
| To explain the process of interviewing sexually abused children for courtroom testimony | To actuate the audience to support efforts to change courtroom procedures for child witnesses |

The topics on the left generally provide information on an issue, while the topics at the right seek to influence the audience to agree with the speaker's point of view. In the list of informative topics, "al-Qaeda" would be considered a speech of definition, "profile of a troubled child" would be a descriptive speech, and "interviewing sexually abused children" would be considered a process speech.

Some communication specialists feel that informative speeches are "factual" while persuasive speeches are more "emotional."[2] We would like to caution you, however, about making this distinction. It is true that informative speeches can contain supporting materials such as statistics, surveys, or polls and visual materials such as graphs, maps, and charts. But informative speeches should also incorporate emotional elements such as personal experiences, illustrations, and examples that interest the audience. And although persuasive speeches should make use of strong emotional appeals, they should also be grounded in supporting evidence that incorporates sound logic and fact.

Recognize also that speeches are not always strictly informative or persuasive. Informative presentations often contain elements of persuasion that modify the thinking or behavior of listeners over a period of time. In persuasion, speakers often include large portions of informative material to educate and enlighten listeners before asking them to change attitudes or take action. Speeches frequently exist on an informative-persuasive continuum, with some presentations clustering around the informative end and others tending toward the persuasive.

Up to this point, we've been talking about defining informative speeches based on the topic. But sometimes it's the audience that will determine whether a topic is informative or persuasive. For example, after conducting careful research, you present an informative speech with the stated intention "to acquaint the audience with some interesting biographical data about Candidate X," a Libertarian. Your listeners, however, might have different ideas. If the audience members consisted of Republicans or Democrats who favored other candidates, they might feel that your speech was subtly persuasive rather than informative.

## types of informative speeches

In this chapter, we will consider four categories of information: (1) description; (2) demonstration; (3) definition; and (4) reports, lectures, and personal experiences.

## THE DESCRIPTIVE SPEECH

In **descriptive speeches**, speakers inform audiences about persons, places, objects, or events. (Note that an *object* includes both the animate and the inanimate, and an *event* is defined as an incident or an occurrence.) Here are several examples of specific purpose statements for descriptive speeches about these topics:

PERSON
    To describe the life of baseball legend Lou Gehrig
    To describe the feats of the tennis champions the Williams sisters
    To describe the culture of the Eskimo
    To describe the accomplishments of Susan B. Anthony

PLACE
    To describe the Baseball Hall of Fame
    To describe the American Indian Museum in Washington, D.C.
    To describe life in Japan

Informative speeches can educate and enlighten listeners about places, persons, objects, or events. Here, jubilant Navy divers raise the turret from the wreck of the USS *Monitor*, which remained on the ocean floor for 140 years. The history and the fascinating recovery expedition of the *Monitor* are described in the speech featured at the end of this chapter.

© AP Photo

To describe the largest mall in America

To describe the newly discovered planet in our solar system

OBJECT

To describe the destruction of the World Trade Center

To describe the relationship of color and personality

To describe the history of trademarks

To describe the wonderful, wily cat

To describe algae as an alternative fuel

EVENT

To inform an audience about the summer Olympics in Beijing, China

To describe the next generation of space vehicles after the Space Shuttle

To inform an audience about the causes of fires in California

To inform an audience of measures the government is taking to ease the recession

To describe the benefits of the Special Olympics

### An Example

In the following example, the speaker attempts to describe some of the highlights of Mexico City, with mediocre results:

*Mexico City is a huge city in the mountains inhabited by millions of people. The city contains artifacts dating back to the ancient Aztecs, buildings constructed by the Spaniards, and structures that reflect modern Mexico.*

## Building the Descriptive Speech »

Because a descriptive speech is one of the major types you will probably deliver in your speech course, here are some specific guidelines to help you build this presentation.

1. Choose an interesting topic.
    a. Choose an innovative topic providing new information.
    b. Select a topic that is interesting to you, the speaker.
    c. Examine your personal interests, experiences, and knowledge.
    d. Avoid repeating information the audience already knows.
    e. Choose a topic that is appropriate to listeners.
2. Conduct careful research.
    a. Review personal experience for primary source material.
    b. Use sources that are accurate, reliable, and up-to-date.
    c. Avoid sources lacking in credibility, such as *House and Garden* or condensed magazines for medical or scientific facts.
    d. Conduct interviews with experts.
    e. Build credibility with accurate examples, statistics, testimony, and audiovisual aids.
    f. Check details such as events, numbers, dates, and quotations for precision and accuracy.
3. Organize the speech in a logical sequence.
    a. Develop a creative introduction with a clear thesis identifying the main points in the body.

b. Choose an organizational plan appropriate to the topic.
   (1) Use external transitions to emphasize major headings.
   (2) Employ internal transitions to link supporting ideas.
c. Construct an interesting conclusion conveying finality.
   (1) Choose a poem, quotation, or example that resolves or summarizes the topic.
   (2) Avoid providing new information during the conclusion.
4. Employ vivid language.
   a. Use clear, colorful, connotative language.
   b. Employ images that evoke mental pictures and appeal to the senses.
   c. Avoid trite phrases or vague jargon such as "to each his own" or "stuff like that."
5. Use concrete supporting materials.
   a. Humanize the topic with realistic supporting materials such as examples, testimonies, and statistics.
   b. Round off statistics for easy comprehension.
   c. Employ colorful quotations.
   d. Avoid stringing together lists of statistics or hard facts.
   e. Use audiovisual aids for variety and interest.
6. Develop a clear, personal delivery.
   a. Pronounce difficult names and technical terms correctly.
   b. Define unfamiliar words or phrases.
   c. Avoid extensive technical terminology; use words and phrases that listeners understand.
   d. Maintain eye contact with the audience.
   e. Use personal pronouns such as *you, we,* and *us* to include listeners.
   f. Be conversational, use extemporaneous delivery, and avoid reading word for word.
   g. Make effective use of your eyes, face, hands, and voice.
   h. Stimulate feedback by using humor, asking rhetorical or open-ended questions, and employing emotion.
   i. Be sensitive to audience feedback, making minor adjustments to content or delivery based upon audience response.
   j. Practice the speech to gain confidence.

The terminology here is only denotative. Words such as *huge, artifacts, buildings,* or *structures* do not create mental images. The speaker employs vague generalities and uses no concrete supporting materials. This description will have little impact; the speaker has lost a wonderful opportunity to arouse interest.

Notice the improvement:

*In today's Mexico City, you can sample a tasty enchilada made with white cheese; feel the rough chisel marks of an ancient Aztec pyramid; take a leisurely stroll through the cool green palms and curving lakes of Chapultepec Park; experience the excitement of the clubs, cabarets, and outdoor cafes in the Zona Rosa; browse through shops filled with mounds of solid silver jewelry; contemplate the classic beauty of the oldest Spanish church in the Americas; navigate the flowered canals of the Xochimilco; and dance to the melodies of a hundred mariachi groups in Garibaldi Square.*

This description is effective because the words are connotative and the speaker uses numerous sensory examples as supporting materials. Vivid language such as "tasty enchilada," "rough chisel marks," "flowered canals" and action words such as "feel," "sample," "navigate," and "dance" invite listeners to participate with all their senses. Words that identify objects with their color ("white cheese," "green palms"), shape ("curving lakes"), and size ("mounds of ... silver") add to the visual imagery. Notice the foreign names that the speaker needs to pronounce correctly. The speaker has successfully created a variety of mental images.

### *Outlining the Descriptive Speech*

When developing the outline for the descriptive speech, you should follow the organizational principles suggested in Chapter 10. Remember that the main points of the body should be arranged according to chronology, space, cause-effect, topic, or a combination of sequences. Here are three examples that show how these sequences can be combined.

In the following descriptive topic, the speaker combines chronological with spatial order:

**Specific purpose:** To describe the Baseball Hall of Fame at Cooperstown, New York.
**Thesis statement:** The Baseball Hall of Fame has a unique history, and exhibits in the first, second, and third floors that preserve the legends of baseball for posterity.

BODY

   I. Brief history of museum
  II. First-floor Hall of Fame gallery
 III. Second-floor history sections
 IV. Third-floor rooms of memorabilia

Notice that subheadings under main point I would be arranged according to order of events and that main points II through IV are arranged spatially according to location of rooms in the museum.

In the next example, the speaker has organized main points using a combination of chronological and topic sequence.

**Specific purpose:** To describe the wonderful, wily cat
**Thesis statement:** Cats were respected in Egyptian times and feared in the Middle Ages; they are equipped for savage battle, yet make loving members of any family.

BODY

   I. Cats in Egyptian times
  II. Cats in the Middle Ages
 III. Cats as hunters
 IV. Cats as pets

The speaker uses chronology for the history in main points I and II, then incorporates a topical sequence for the last two headings.

In the next example, the speaker combines topic with cause-effect sequence.

**Specific purpose:** To inform you about the dangers of steroids
**Thesis statement:** I want to provide an explanation of steroids, describe their intended purpose, and identify their desired effects as well as their damaging consequences.

Cyclist Lance Armstrong overcame testicular cancer to win the Tour de France for seven consecutive years. As a public speaker, he is in great demand, lecturing across the country and raising awareness about cancer, the need for self-examination, early detection, and prompt medical treatment.

© JAMIE RECTOR/Bloomberg News/Landov

BODY

    I. General explanation of steroids
   II. Intended purpose of steroids
  III. Desired effects
  IV. Damaging consequences

Main points I and II are arranged in topic sequence, and points III and IV characterize the issue by describing its effects.

## THE DEMONSTRATION SPEECH

One important type of informative speech is the **demonstration**, which usually includes a variety of visual aids to show the steps of a process. In most businesses, institutions, and professional organizations, employees at all levels are required to present or participate in programs that explain procedures and processes. Seminars are conducted to teach workers how to use the Internet, new telephone systems, fax machines, or laser technologies; how to fill out purchase orders, insurance forms, or government documents; how to confront sexual harassment, use new sales techniques, or handle consumer complaints; how to treat new diseases, implement new manufacturing procedures, or conform to safety standards.

Venus and Serena Williams use visual aids to explain and demonstrate their tournament-winning tennis serves to school children.

These training sessions protect the company and employee, help to maintain a company's competitive edge, and improve workers' productivity or efficiency.

No matter what your career or profession, you will probably be required to explain how something works, how something is made, how something is done, or how something happens.

HOW SOMETHING WORKS

    To demonstrate how the eye works

    To demonstrate how a DVD system operates

    To demonstrate how a hybrid engine works

    To demonstrate how a Revolutionary War musket operates

HOW SOMETHING IS MADE

    To demonstrate how a guitar is constructed

    To demonstrate how the Chinese weave rugs

    To demonstrate how Greek moussaka is made

    To demonstrate the art of Japanese origami

HOW SOMETHING IS DONE

    To demonstrate how to tune a piano

    To demonstrate how to shear sheep

    To demonstrate how to mine rubies

    To explain how to rig a sailboat

HOW SOMETHING HAPPENS

    To explain how geysers develop

    To explain how dreams occur

    To explain how pearls form

    To explain how Parkinson's disease attacks the body

## An Example

Demonstrations are not simplistic show-and-tell speeches; they are sophisticated presentations that include carefully crafted visuals that support the process. For example, a student who was an avid mountain climber demonstrated how to do rappelling—descending a steep incline with a secured rope. He took the speech class outside to an 8-foot-high retaining wall on campus, where he described the necessary equipment and the proper procedure to descend the wall. Class members watched and listened intently as the speaker slowly lowered himself down the wall, carefully explaining each step of the process. Listeners commented that the speaker's creative approach made the speech important and "alive."

## Outlining the Demonstration Speech

Most process speeches incorporate numerous steps or phases that are often difficult for listeners to recall. For example, "Refinishing furniture" would include more than fifteen steps, and "Decorating a wedding cake" could incorporate more than twenty-three procedures. The body of a demonstration should never contain fifteen or twenty-three numeral headings. To keep the process simple, group the steps into categories.

> **Specific purpose:** To demonstrate how to refinish furniture
> **Thesis statement:** Refinishing furniture requires gathering the needed materials and following a structured procedure to create an attractive finished product.

### CHRONOLOGICAL ORDER

| Steps Grouped by Categories | Steps of the Complete Process |
|---|---|
| I. Selecting materials | A. Type of furniture for refinishing |
| | B. Sandpaper—coarse or fine |
| | C. Paintbrushes |
| | D. Stain |
| | E. Polyurethane varnish |
| | F. Cloths |
| II. Following a procedure | A. Clean surfaces with cloth |
| | B. Begin sanding |
| | C. Inspect sanded surface for missed spots |
| | D. Wipe surface |
| | E. Apply stain |
| | F. Allow to dry |
| | G. Apply polyurethane varnish |
| | H. Allow surface to dry |
| | I. Apply several more coats of varnish |
| | J. Let surface dry between coats |
| III. The finished product | A. Display results of refinished furniture |
| | B. Describe variations of refinishing process |

Notice at the right that there are at least eighteen separate steps in the process of refinishing furniture. Like any other 5- to 7-minute speech, process speeches should contain no fewer than two and no more than four main points in the body. On the left, you can see that the refinishing process can be grouped into three principal steps that incorporate all eighteen items. The three main points make the demonstration clear and easy to follow.

Notice that main points in the body of most demonstrations will be arranged according to some form of chronological sequence—by time or events. In the preceding example, main points are organized according to the order of occurrence. Some topics can be organized by combining chronological sequence with another arrangement. For example, Ann Foley combined topic sequence with chronology in the following demonstration of "fingerprinting."[3]

**Specific purpose:** To demonstrate the science of fingerprinting
**Thesis statement:** Fingerprinting, an important science that identifies individuals' fingerprint types, is an interesting process used in police work.

BODY

I. The importance of fingerprints
   A. Identify fugitives
   B. Identify victims
   C. Provide unmistakable verification
II. Different types of fingerprints
   A. Plain arch
   B. Fented arch
   C. The loop
   D. Plain whorl
   E. Central pocket loop
   F. Double loop
   G. Accidental (no set pattern)
III. The process of fingerprinting
   A. Insert fingerprint card in card holder
   B. Use small amount of ink on roller
   C. Apply thin ink coat with roller to glass inking plate
   D. Place subject approximately forearm away from fingerprint card
   E. For right hand, stand to left of subject
   F. Take right thumb and roll on inking plate
   G. Place inked thumb on fingerprint card
   H. Roll thumb from left to right for complete rounded print
   I. Continue with rolling process for other fingers
   J. Take prints of four fingers without rolling
   K. Repeat entire process with left hand

Ann chose a topic that could be demonstrated rather quickly. To give her speech more depth, she spent a few minutes explaining the importance of fingerprints and identifying the various types. Ann arranged her three main points in a simple topical sequence. Then in point III, "The process of fingerprinting," she used chronological order for the subdivisions. Because of her organization, Ann included enough material for an effective 6- to 7-minute process speech.

## THE SPEECH OF DEFINITION

In a speech of **definition**, you inform your audience about a philosophical concept such as a theory or idea or a more concrete subject like a science or art.

SCIENCE OR ART
   What is cryonics?
   What is impressionistic art?
   What is a phobia?
   What is vegetarianism?

# Building the Demonstration Speech »

Demonstrating a familiar process may sound easy, but when you are in front of an audience, many things can go wrong. Lack of preparation can cause misplacing or dropping a visual aid or displaying objects that are too small for the audience to see. To help you avoid these and other difficulties, here is a list of guidelines for building the demonstration or process speech.

1. Choose a topic from your experience or knowledge.
   a. Examine your professional expertise and life experience.
   b. Choose a topic that is demonstrative: how something works, happens, is made, or is done.
2. Investigate the location of the speech.
   a. Does the room or auditorium have everything necessary to support audiovisual aids?
   b. Do you need to bring extra equipment or supplies?
   c. Can the audience see your visuals easily?
3. Develop a logical outline.
   a. Include all required structural elements: an interesting introduction, a purpose statement, a well-organized body, and a clearly defined conclusion.
   b. Combine information in the body of the demonstration into overall categories like "gathering materials," "preparing for the process," or "finished product."
   c. Use chronological sequence to arrange events in order of occurrence.
   d. Employ any type of conclusion, using a summary to reinforce complicated or unfamiliar procedures.
4. Apply principles of effective delivery.
   a. Be clear.
      (1) Verbally emphasize important points and repeat steps, key ideas, or complicated material when necessary.
      (2) Use gestures to point out significant details.
      (3) Clarify main headings in the body with external transitions.
      (4) Use internal transitions—*then, next, finally*—to connect steps grouped beneath main headings.
      (5) Employ simple terms, defining unfamiliar words and pronouncing difficult terms correctly.
      (6) Speak slowly enough to allow listeners to follow the steps of the process.
      (7) Relate ideas to listeners with concrete examples.
   b. Keep the speech moving.
      (1) Keep talking as you demonstrate, avoiding awkward pauses or silences.
      (2) Be prepared with additional comments if the procedure takes longer than expected.
      (3) Keep to the time limit.
      (4) Include only essential elements of the process, eliminating unnecessary detail.
   c. Know how to use visuals.
      (1) Set up visuals in advance if possible.
      (2) Use enough visuals to support the process; avoid using too few or too many.

            (3) Reveal visuals at the right psychological moment.

            (4) Avoid distractions by not passing out objects while you speak.

            (5) Be sure that visuals are large enough for listeners to see.

            (6) Integrate visuals smoothly into the speech, eliminating awkwardness.

            (7) Remove visuals quickly if there are other speakers following your presentation.

        d. Be prepared.

            (1) Rehearse with all the visuals you intend to use.

            (2) Show enthusiasm and interest through vocal variety, facial expression, and gestures.

            (3) Maintain eye contact with the audience.

    5. Avoid the following problems:

        a. Long silences

        b. Lengthy, overly complex details or terms

        c. Visuals that are too small

        d. Too many audiovisuals

        e. Creating distractions with audiovisuals

        f. Disorganization

        g. Last-minute preparation

        h. Going over the time limit

## THEORIES OR IDEAS

    What is ethnic cleansing?

    What is Basque separatism?

    What is Shi'ite Islam?

    What is libertarianism?

With any of these topics, the thrust of your information would be to explain the meaning of an unknown term to your audience. When defining such terms, follow guidelines suggested for the descriptive speech. Be concrete and accurate, use plenty of supporting materials, and work to maintain the interest of your audience. Remember that definitional speeches are not simply intellectual explanations of dry theories or complex subject matter; these speeches must be just as creative and alive as any other informative presentation.

Here are two structural examples of speeches defining terms. The first example uses chronological sequence; the second employs topical order.

### EXAMPLE 1: CHRONOLOGICAL SEQUENCE

**Specific purpose:** To define Shi'ite Islam

**Thesis statement:** Shi'ite Islam is a religion originating in the Middle Ages and exhibiting specific characteristics today.

### BODY

  I. Shi'ite Islam in the Middle Ages

 II. Characteristics of the movement today

### EXAMPLE 2: TOPICAL SEQUENCE

**Specific purpose:** To define the term *vegetarian*

**Thesis statement:** Vegetarianism is a dietary practice that includes vegans as well as lacto-ovo vegetarians and that has clear advantages as well as disadvantages.

**BODY**

   I. Vegans—eliminating all animal foods
  II. Lacto-ovo vegetarians—using eggs and dairy products
 III. Advantages of the vegetarian diet
 IV. Disadvantages of the vegetarian diet

Notice that the Shi'ite Islam speech is organized according to chronology and that the one on vegetarianism is structured according to the natural headings reflected in the research.

For these topics, speakers can motivate listeners by using effective supporting materials. A presentation on Shi'ite Islam could incorporate visual aids and examples relating to current events taking place in Middle Eastern countries. A speech about vegetarianism could relate the topic to the physical health and welfare of listeners. In both topics, speakers can provide new, interesting, and helpful information to members of their audiences.

## OTHER INFORMATIVE TYPES: REPORTS, LECTURES, AND PERSONAL EXPERIENCE

The **report** is often required in business or industry. You may already have had to present reports to supervisors, committees, or clients. In this important speech, the quality of your presentation can improve or hinder your chances for success. Topics for reports are usually

Lectures are presented by experts in fields such as history and technology for instructional or educational purposes.

© AP Photo

based on limited issues, such as "the decrease in sales for the third quarter," "decisions of the search committee," or "marketing committee actions."

In many cases, your report will summarize the work of a committee or other employee unit. You need to be completely accurate, and your comments must reflect the collective decisions of the group. Even though your report is technical, it should still be interesting, clear, and well organized. Know your material thoroughly, maintain contact with your audience, interject humor when appropriate, and use concrete examples.

Business reports often incorporate visuals: PowerPoint slides, transparencies with overhead projectors, chalkboards, whiteboards with Magic Markers, and flipcharts on easels. Remember that effective use of visuals can create the perception among coworkers that you know what you're doing.

**Lectures** are presentations given by experts for instructional or educational purposes. Colleges and universities often receive grants to invite well-known authorities in science, humanities, and industry to speak on topics of national interest. Lecturers frequently read

---

**ANALYSIS SHEET FOR THE INFORMATIVE SPEECH**

**Introduction**

*Curiosity device*
Did the speech contain an effective device for building curiosity, such as a case study, question, or shocking statement?

Did the end of the introduction contain a clear specific purpose and/or thesis statement?

**Content**
*Topic*
Was the topic sufficiently limited and innovative?

Was the topic appropriate and interesting to the audience?

*Organization*
Were main headings and supporting points structured in a clear, logical, and interesting manner?

Were the main headings thoroughly developed?

*Accuracy*
Was the information accurate, up-to-date, and verified by credible sources?

*Supporting materials*
Did the speech contain a variety of clear, concrete, and creative supporting materials—examples, statistics, quotations, audiovisuals?

**Delivery**
*Language*
Did the speaker use connotative words and vivid language to create mental images?

Was the speaker's language appropriate to the topic?

Did the speaker's language reflect good English usage?

*Clarity*
Did the speaker use external transitions to flag main points and internal transitions to connect subordinate points?

**Delivery** *(continued)*
Did the speaker adhere to the topic and keep ideas moving in a logical sequence?

Were steps in demonstrations clear and understandable?

Did the speaker define and clarify unfamiliar terms?

*Vocal delivery*
Did the speaker enunciate words and phrases clearly?

Did the speaker pronounce difficult terms effectively?

Did the speaker's volume, rate, and vocal inflections enhance the speech?

*Visual aids*
Did the speaker spend time and effort developing audiovisual aids?

Did the speaker know how to use visual aids?

While using visuals, was the speaker able to keep the speech moving without awkward "dead space"?

*Enthusiasm*
Did the speaker's voice, eye contact, facial expression, gestures, and posture reflect enthusiasm for the topic?

*Emphasis*
Did the speaker employ verbal emphasis and/or repetition to highlight important areas?

Did the speaker support verbal emphasis with appropriate gestures, movement, and facial expression?

*Other*
Did the speaker display any other effective or ineffective techniques (pauses, mannerisms, movement, appearance) that would enhance or detract from the delivery?

**Conclusion**
*Method of ending*
Did the speech contain a clear device (quotation, summary, story, question) to provide closure to the topic?

---

FIGURE 15.1 Analysis Sheet for the Informative Speech

lengthy presentations from manuscripts and incorporate question-and-answer sessions at the end.

You already know from your own classroom listening experience that a 2-hour lecture can seem like either minutes or days, depending on the speaker's organization and enthusiasm. Some campus student groups publish evaluations rating faculty lectures according to interest, enthusiasm, and scholarship. There are also websites where students can rate their professors according to difficulty and interest level. Lectures don't have to be boring. They can be fascinating if the speaker is knowledgeable, structured, and communicates new or complicated information creatively. You will probably give a lecture, however, only if you are an expert in a particular field.

The **personal experience** speech provides information about an encounter or observation. Travelogues, harrowing adventures, or expeditions are good subject areas for personal experience speeches. These presentations are often exciting and interesting; they are also potentially boring. Use good judgment in developing the topic, and be sensitive to your listeners.

In your speech class, your instructor may ask you to present a brief personal experience speech. But remember not to substitute one lengthy personal experience for a major informative speech that requires a variety of research materials.[4] Figure 15.1 provides a checklist for you to use in evaluating informative speeches.

## SAMPLE SPEECH: raising the *monitor*

*This informative descriptive speech provides new information about an item of Civil War history that was once thought to be lost. Researched and presented by a public speaking student, "Raising the* Monitor*" includes remarkable supporting materials, such as narratives, statistics, quotations, and PowerPoint slides, to describe the historical significance of the USS* Monitor *and explain the complexities of recovering the vessel's bulky turret from the bottom of the ocean. The speaker has written an additional introduction and conclusion to show how different strategies can be developed to stimulate audience interest.[5] You can find more information about this amazing artifact at http://www.monitorcenter.org. (A complete outline of this speech is presented at the end of Chapter 11 on pages 187–190.)*

### INFORMATIVE DESCRIPTIVE SPEECH
*Chaim Verschleisser*

1. The speaker gains the attention of listeners with a historical narrative describing the famous battle between the *Virginia* (*Merrimack*) and the *Monitor*.

The PowerPoint slides showing the paintings of the battle provide the introduction with a sense of realism.

1.  March 8, 1862 (slide 1). The Confederate ship known as the *Virginia* virtually decimated a Union fleet of wooden warships off the coast of Newport News. She destroyed the *Cumberland* and the 50-gun frigate *Congress* and forced the *Minnesota* to run back to shore. The *Virginia* was originally a Northern-built steam frigate called the *Merrimack*, but the Confederates salvaged the ship from a Norfolk navy yard. They cut away the upper hull of the 263-foot ship, armored her with iron, and rechristened her the *Virginia*. The morning following the attack, the *Virginia* opened fire on the *Minnesota* just after 8:00 A.M. And that is when the *Monitor* appeared (slide 2). The Union's ironclad was 172 feet long and was equipped with an armored revolving gun turret. For hours, the two ships passed each other back and forth. Both crews lacked training, and firing was not very effective. The *Monitor* could fire only once in 7 or 8 minutes, but it was faster and more maneuverable than the *Virginia*. Eventually, the *Monitor*'s pilothouse was hit, and the ship sheered into shallow water. The *Virginia* assumed that the

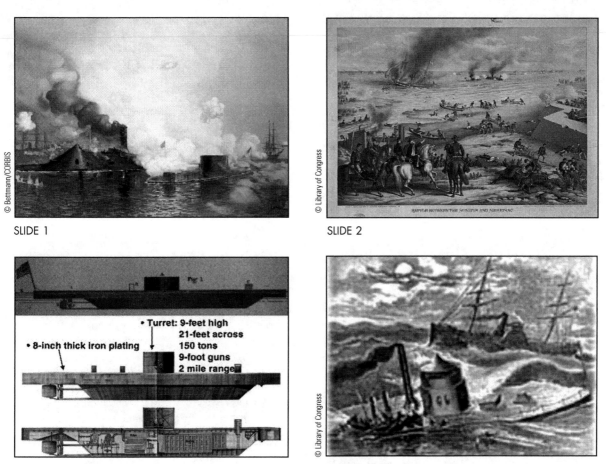

SLIDE 1

SLIDE 2

SLIDE 3

- 8-inch thick iron plating

- Turret: 9-feet high
  21-feet across
  150 tons
  9-foot guns
  2 mile range

SLIDE 4

© Bettmann/CORBIS

© Library of Congress

© Library of Congress

ship was disabled and turned to fire on the *Minnesota* again, but her officers reported low ammunition and damages, so instead she headed home. The Battle of Hampton Roads, history's first battle between ironclad warships, was over. Although the confrontation was inconclusive, it signaled the start of the age of armored battleships. The ingenuity that went into the creation of the *Monitor* altered the course of modern naval warfare.

2.   The historical significance of the *Monitor* led scientists and nautical engineers to overcome extreme challenges that resulted in the successful recovery of the vessel's turret.

2. A three-point thesis is presented at the end of the introduction.

3.   (slide 3) The *Monitor* was built in Greenpoint, Brooklyn, and launched into the East River on January 30, 1862. The distinguishing feature of the ship was her rotating turret, a technological first that is now standard on all modern warships. With 8-inch-thick walls of iron plating, the turret measured 9 feet high, 21 feet across, and weighed 150 tons. It housed two 9-foot, Dahlgren-manufactured guns that were capable of firing shells or cannonballs farther than 2 miles. After the historical battle, the Union began building a whole new class of *Monitor*-type vessels. According to a July 2002 *New York Times* article, when the British Royal Navy heard about the clash of the two ironclads, the world's preeminent naval force canceled all construction of wooden warships.

3. The speaker begins main point I of the body by describing the statistical dimensions of the *Monitor*. The slide gives visual support to the statistics.

The speaker uses a credible source to verify the vessel's significance in transforming the construction of warships.

4.   (slide 4) Nine months after the battle, the *Monitor* encountered a violent storm off the coast of Cape Hatteras on New Year's Eve. At 10:30 P.M. the commander sent a distress signal, via lantern, to a tow vessel. Some of the men were saved, but shortly

4. The speaker returns to the historical narrative and describes what happened to the *Monitor*.

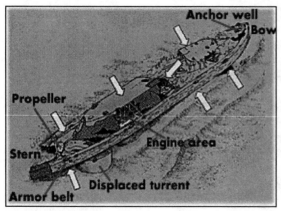

SLIDE 5

SLIDE 6

after midnight the lantern disappeared. The famous turret came to rest upside down on the seafloor at a depth of 240 feet (slide 5). Among the missing were twelve crew members, four officers, and the ship's mascot, a black cat. The ship was lost until 1973, when a Duke University expedition found the scattered remains 16 miles off Cape Hatteras.

In 1975, it was named the nation's first marine sanctuary to protect the wreck from treasure hunters. A hull plate and the signal lantern came up in 1977, and the anchor was recovered in 1983. The turret, however, was the prize they were aiming for. Aside from its historical significance, the turret may contain the answers to 140-year-old questions. The turret was the only way out of the ship, so scientists expected to find human (or even feline) remains as well as important artifacts that may have been dropped by crew members trying to escape. Federal officials laid plans in 1997 for more extensive retrievals.

**5. An external transition connects point I to point II.**

The slides showing actual photos from the Civil War provide realism and stimulate listener curiosity.

5.  Clearly, the *Monitor* and her famous turret (slide 6) are of tremendous significance to our nation's history, but the scientists and agencies involved in their retrieval were faced with very serious challenges in the process.

**6. The speaker uses statistics to describe many of the financial challenges of recovering the turret and preserving artifacts that had already been recovered.**

6.  For starters, money was a major issue all along. The effort to raise the turret over the last five years had cost over $14 million, and that was not the biggest bill. There are teams of scientists working on ways to reverse the deterioration of the artifacts. Once artifacts are recovered, maintaining them properly is a very delicate and expensive process. The Mariners' Museum in Newport News has plans to build a $30 million USS *Monitor* Center in which all of the *Monitor*'s remains will be conserved and publicly displayed. At one point the cumulative cost of recovery was approaching $20 million and archeologists began to worry more about funding for conservation of the relics they already had.

**7. The speaker uses a credible source to refer to surveys that showed the impact of corrosion.**

Chaim uses a quote from NOAA expert Dr. Broadwater to support the need for conservation. Notice that the speaker uses the *Atlanta Journal–Constitution* to verify the quotation.

7.  Then there was the issue of time (slide 7). The *Atlanta Journal–Constitution* reported in a May 2002 article that surveys in the mid-1990s showed that corrosion of the vessel was accelerating. These studies created additional pressure to complete the job. It had become a race against time and the elements. These issues also worried the scientists in charge of conserving the artifacts that had already been recovered. Those artifacts had continued to accumulate in outdoor tanks, and federal archaeologists grew increasingly concerned that the continued exposure and rapid fluctuations in temperature might accelerate the deterioration. John Broadwater, manager of the

© The Mariners' Museum/CORBIS

SLIDE 7

© Library of Congress

SLIDE 8

National Ocean and Atmospheric Administration's (NOAA) *Monitor* Marine Sanctuary, expressed his concern for funding the conservation process. He told the *Atlanta Journal–Constitution* that "instead of $30 million for a new center, I think we'd rather see $30,000 worth of conservation."

8. Aside from financial, time, and conservation concerns, the process of lifting the turret was a massive undertaking in itself (slide 8). According to Dr. Broadwater, it was "one of the heaviest artifacts ever lifted from such a depth." The operation was to be conducted from a 300-foot barge that was normally used for deep-water oil operations. It was predicted that the retrieval of the turret would take a crack team of Navy divers, working around the clock, seven days a week, at least four weeks. More than 100 divers and support staff were needed. To complicate things even more, there were swift currents on the ocean floor, the weather was unpredictable, and the depth of the operation required sophisticated mixed-gas diving. To reach the turret, divers had to cut away a 40-foot section of the ship's armor belt. Then they had to attach a lifting device, dubbed the "spider and claw," to cradle the treasure in hopes that it wouldn't collapse when they picked it up.

> 8. The speaker cites another quotation and presents a fascinating narrative of the process of lifting the heavy turret from the ocean floor.

9. After months of working through all of these complex challenges (slide 9), Navy divers lifted the 200-ton turret (including its contents) of the USS *Monitor* from the graveyard of the Atlantic on Monday, August 5, 2002.

> 9. The speaker states a transition between main points II and III of the body.

10. First to be hoisted into view was a flag that had been planted by Navy divers—a replica of the 1862 U.S. flag that the *Monitor* was flying when it sank. Navy Commander Bobbie Scholley reported that "for a bunch of pretty tough Navy divers, there was a lot of cheering and hugging going on [ … ] I'm glad I was wearing sunglasses so the men couldn't see me cry." An August 2002 *Newsday* article quoted Dr. Broadwater as saying, "It's fantastic [ … ] It's sitting on a barge, and we're looking at dents that the *Virginia* put on it March 9, 1862."

> 10. The narrative describes the first sight of *Monitor*'s turret above water since 1862.
>
> The two quotations provide the emotional reactions of the men who labored to retrieve this prized artifact.

11. The retrieval of the turret has already brought many new and important discoveries. Some bones from three different human bodies were found (but no cat yet). Experts resurrecting the ship are finding that the *Monitor*'s remains are actually quite different from plans, documents, and period drawings. There are many undocumented

> 11. The specific details of the discoveries inside the turret are fascinating: the human bones, the clock with hands pointing to the hour the

© Library of Congress

SLIDE 9

© Mary Evans Picture Library/The Image, PCL/Alamy, David Ball/ Alamy, 2001 Thomas E. Franklin, staff

SLIDE 10

*Monitor* sank, and the numerous mustard bottles.

The speaker uses another credible source to support his ideas.

The Peterson quotation provides some humor to the speech.

The speaker summarizes portions of the speech.

An example is provided to relate to the *Monitor's* broader historical significance.

The speaker uses a brief quotation as reinforcement.

12. The speaker begins his conclusion.

13. Beginning with a brief quotation from President Bush, the speaker

parts and braces. A presumed gauge turned out to be a large clock. Upon closer inspection, they found that the last positions of the hands were near the 1 and 3. William F. Keeler, a paymaster who had survived the sinking, wrote that the ship went down a little after 1 A.M. In response to the discoveries, Dr. Broadwater said, "it turns out we didn't have the big picture." In a more mundane discovery, it seems that the Union sailors used to cover their meals with mustard, judging by the many condiment bottles found at the wreck site. According to a July 2002 *New York Times* article, the president of the Mariners' Museum, John Hightower, explained that they "suspect the food needed all the help it could get." Curtiss Peterson, the chief conservator at the Mariners' Museum, was removing encrustations from an old engine gauge, and he uncovered the word "Monitor" etched across the top. He said, "I smiled ear to ear [ . . . ] If it had said something like 'Toledo' we would have been in deep trouble."

12. The USS *Monitor's* turret will now join the collection of over 400 other *Monitor* artifacts (slide 10). And just like all of the other artifacts, the turret is teaching scientists and historians a wealth of new information. The *Monitor* and its famous turret represent American innovation and bravery. The impact that this incredible ship made is still felt today by navies and shipbuilders throughout the world. The recovery of such an important artifact helps us to learn more about the brave men that fought in it.

The delicate paper scales found in hydrometers illustrate how fine-tuned the skills of these sailors had to be in order to keep the ship running at optimum performance. In the words of Robert Sheridan, a geophysics professor from Rutgers University, "history becomes so much more meaningful when you can see the things that made it." Perhaps that was what the hundreds of dedicated scientists, engineers, and divers were thinking. Perhaps that is what drove them to continue working at a goal that, at times, seemed unachievable.

13. In a recent letter, President Bush praised the museum for preserving the remains. He called the job "an important service in these challenging times." Indeed, these

times are challenging, and a recovery like this one is exactly what this country needs. It reminds us that we have been through rough times before, and that the innovation and ingenuity of our great nation persevered and pulled us out of the slump. It reminds us of our nation's powerful history and traditions. It reminds us that when we stand together as one and aim for a common goal, we can accomplish amazing things.

*reminds listeners of the challenges of "rough times"—an indirect reference to the events of September 11. But the last PowerPoint visual makes a powerful patriotic statement.*

## Alternative Introduction: Series of Questions

1. Do you remember learning about the *Monitor* and the *Merrimack* back in elementary school? Is there anyone in this room that was sitting in that history class thinking, "Wow, those ironclad ships were amazing!" Have any of you ever wished that, one day, you would have the opportunity to look at the actual *Monitor* itself? I suspect that most of the people here probably feel the way I felt about the *Monitor* before I read up on it: "It's a neat story and all, but what's the big deal? It's just an old boat, right?"

*1. The speaker poses a series of rhetorical questions to the audience.*

*The speaker connects his thoughts to listeners' perceptions in order to establish common ground and prepare listeners to take a different look at an old topic.*

2. What I did not realize was that the effects of that old boat are what we think of today when we think of battleships, aircraft carriers, submarines, and even cruise ships. The ironclad revolutionized the nautical world. The historical battle between the *Monitor* and the *Virginia*—formerly known as the *Merrimack*—was not only a battle between two new-age warships. It was a battle of technological advancement and status that had major social effects as well. The *Monitor* was *the* icon of Yankee ingenuity, bravery, and accomplishment.

*2. The speaker describes the significance of the vessel as a preparation for the thesis statement.*

3. The historical significance of the *Monitor* led scientists and nautical engineers to overcome extreme challenges that resulted in the successful recovery of portions of this priceless artifact.

*3. The thesis is stated.*

## Alternative Conclusion: Quotation

1. The executive officer of the USS *Monitor*, Lieutenant S. Dana Greene, wrote up a document titled "In the *Monitor* Turret," in which he recalls his experiences on the ship. After describing the battle in incredible detail and illustrating the astonishing heroism of the men onboard the *Monitor*, Lieutenant Greene concluded with words that give us a good understanding of the influence that the great ironclad had on Americans at that time: "No ship in the world's history has a more imperishable place in naval annals than the *Monitor*. Not only by her providential arrival at the right moment did she secure the safety of Hampton Roads and all that depended on it, but the idea which she embodied revolutionized the system of naval warfare which had existed from the earliest recorded history. The name of the *Monitor* became generic, representing a new type; and, crude and defective as was her construction in some of its details, she yet contained the idea of the turret, which is today the central idea of the most powerful armored vessels."

*1. The speaker acquaints listeners with the Monitor's executive officer, who wrote the ending quotation.*

2. In a world of wooden warships, the ironclad was not only an innovation, she was an inspiration. She inspired navies worldwide to follow in her footsteps. She inspired the citizens of a nation in the midst of civil war to regain the morale that they had lost. She was *the* icon of American ingenuity and accomplishment in her time. Now, as she rests in plain view once again, we can look to her with pride and patriotism, and we can recognize her testimony to the honor and bravery of our great nation.

*2. The speaker ends with an affectionate tribute to the Monitor and acknowledges its permanent place in history.*

## summary »

When you deliver speeches to inform, you seek to educate and enlighten your audience—not to influence their beliefs, feelings, or behavior. Four categories of informative speeches are description, demonstration, definition, and other informative types (reports, lectures, and personal experiences). The descriptive speech is related to a person, place, object, or event. The demonstration speech describes a process: how something works, how something is made, how something is done, or how something happens. A speech of definition identifies and explains a theory or subject area. Three other informational types are the report, which is used primarily in organizations and institutions; the lecture, which is presented by experts; and the personal experience.

## SKILL BUILDERS »

1. Following the guidelines presented in this chapter, develop four topics that would be suitable for a descriptive speech about a person, place, object, or event. After listing the topics, identify several credible sources where you can find effective supporting materials. Write a specific purpose and thesis statement for each topic.

2. From your own knowledge, interest, and/or research, select four topics for a demonstration speech in these categories: how something is done, works, is made, or happens. Write a specific purpose and thesis statement for each topic. Describe the types of visual aids you intend to use for your demonstration. (See Chapter 12).

## BUILDING A SPEECH ONLINE »

Now that you've read Chapter 15, use your online Resource Center for Building a Speech for quick access to the electronic study resources that accompany this text. You can access your Resource Center at http://academic.cengage.com/login, using the access code that came with your book or that you bought online at http://www.iChapters.com. Your Resource Center gives you access to Interactive Video Activities, the book's companion website, Speech Builder Express 3.0, InfoTrac College Edition, and study aids, including a digital glossary and review quizzes.

© AP Photo

chapter 16

# SPEAKING TO PERSUADE

## chapter objectives »

After reading and studying this chapter, you should be able to

1. Discuss the nature of persuasion
2. Describe three types of persuasive speeches
3. Develop propositions of fact, value, and policy
4. Describe the three means of persuasion
5. Describe unethical persuasive practices
6. Define and develop three types of logical arguments
7. Describe and define fallacious arguments
8. Analyze a persuasive convincing speech
9. Develop and present a persuasive convincing speech

> ❝ *The freedom to persuade and suggest is the essence of the democratic process.* ❞
>
> —Edward L. Bernays

Think of all the persuasive situations you encounter in a day or a week. A TV commercial tries to sell you a new breakfast cereal. A smiling politician shakes your hand requesting your vote. You text a friend to meet for lunch. Four-dollar-a-gallon gas persuades you to think more seriously about buying a hybrid or flex-fuel vehicle. A homeless person huddled at a street corner asks you for money. A coworker wants you to wear a pink ribbon and participate in the walk for cancer prevention. The loss of lives in Afghanistan influences you to favor immediate withdrawal of U.S. troops. Whether you are asking your boss for a raise, listening to a eulogy, or explaining a speeding ticket to a judge in traffic court, you are involved in a persuasive activity. Because persuasion is so important in your life and in our society, it is helpful to understand, acquire, and practice the skills that can increase your persuasive effectiveness.

In this chapter we consider persuasion in today's society, the nature of persuasion, and the different types of persuasive appeals. We also examine the elements of persuasive organization and look at some guidelines to help you construct the persuasive speech to convince.

## persuasion in today's society

We are bombarded with hundreds of persuasive messages each day. Television ads tempt us to buy "green" automobiles or switch our cell phones to more convenient and less expensive plans. Police officers solicit nationwide help in the search for a child kidnapped from her home. Jurors debate the verdict of a teen who is being tried as an adult for murdering his parents. A Fox news website asks Internet users to vote on whether or not they agree with attempts to solve illegal immigration. Commentators on a Sunday morning news program debate the pros and cons of a judicial nominee to the Supreme Court. Editorials in the media criticize judicial decisions that force reporters to reveal their sources in special circumstances. Organizations use television, e-mail, or direct mail to ask individuals to buy virus protection, donate to disaster victims, volunteer time in nursing homes, join religious groups, or become involved with twelve-step programs. Radio talk-show hosts rant and rave about contemporary issues, claiming to transmit truth.

The trouble is that after being subjected to so many persuasive messages, how are we to judge the value and content of ideas? How do we evaluate which argument is the most credible or logical? How are we to know if a speaker is genuinely concerned about the community or merely wants to exploit us? How do we know which course of action is the best for us to take? How can we decide if a message is good for us or potentially harmful? How do we know if a radio talk-show host is really stating facts or simply spouting forth his biased, unsubstantiated opinions? Here's what Don Trent Jacobs, a health psychology professional and writer of the book *Patient Communication* says about persuasion in our modern world:

> *An accomplished persuader knows how to use the tools of language to achieve his purpose. In particular, these tools include "persuasive words." Top salespeople, negotiators, and trial lawyers use them regularly. Most of us do not fully understand how or why their words wield such power, but university research shows that certain kinds of language can significantly diminish a listener's critical thinking.*[1]

Dr. Jacob clearly indicates that "persuasive words" can be used as tools to sway listeners who are unaware of manipulative or coercive strategies. Such manipulation is frightening and, if received uncritically and unchallenged by listeners, can cause great harm.

It is evident that in order for us to cope with the daily barrage of persuasion, we must become educated about the different kinds of persuasive messages and the various techniques speakers use to persuade us. Once we are equipped with the knowledge and awareness of persuasive strategies, we will be able to think more critically and logically about the values of a speaker and the merits of a persuasive message. When we are armed with the tools of critical analysis and alert thinking, we will be able to make judgments and take actions that are beneficial to our well-being.

Former National Security Advisor Condoleezza Rice presented numerous types of speeches to world leaders in her former role as secretary of state.

© AP Photo

## the nature of persuasion

Persuasion can be defined as communication that influences and changes the beliefs, feelings, or behavior of a listener. **Persuasive speeches** convince, stimulate, and actuate. To develop the correct speech for the appropriate persuasive situation, you must know how each of these types of presentation differs.

## SPEECHES TO CONVINCE

The goal of the speech to **convince** is to alter the beliefs and judgments of an audience. A prosecuting attorney tries to convince jurors that a defendant is guilty. A senator attempts to convince other legislators that laws should be enacted to help home owners who are facing foreclosure. A parent tries to convince the board of education to adopt stricter policies against school bullies. Although a convincing speech may lead an audience to take some future action, it is important to emphasize that the immediate goal of a speech to convince is to obtain mental agreement with the speaker's position. In a speech to convince, a speaker persuades an audience to believe that a problem exists, that a proposed solution is a better alternative, or that some future action may be required.

## SPEECHES TO STIMULATE

In a speech to **stimulate,** the speaker seeks to reinforce and intensify the beliefs or feelings of listeners. A coach gives the football team a pep talk at halftime to generate enthusiasm and a winning spirit. A religious leader reminds the congregation about basic beliefs to strengthen faith. A political leader makes a speech on September 11 to honor the memory of those killed in the terrorist attacks. Therapeutic groups come together for mutual reinforcement. Members of Alcoholics Anonymous, drug rehabilitation centers, or divorce recovery groups relate their personal experiences for empathy, encouragement, and positive change. As a rule, agreement already exists between speaker and audience about basic beliefs and goals. It is the purpose of the stimulating speech to focus on these sentiments and bring them to the surface.

## SPEECHES TO ACTUATE

Speeches to **actuate** motivate audiences to act. A salesperson selling a product, a candidate asking for votes, or a humanitarian appealing for donations to a worthy charity are all seeking to affect the behavior of the audience. Highly effective 30- to 60-second commercials motivate children, teenagers, young adults, or senior citizens to buy products designed "with you in mind." In a speech to actuate, a speaker generates curiosity, clarifies a problem, identifies a solution, and then persuades the audience to perform a specific action related to the solution. The action the speaker solicits is clear, direct, and observable.

## SELECTING THE PERSUASIVE TOPIC

When beginning to build your persuasive speech, you must first choose a topic with potential to influence your audience. Begin by analyzing some of your interests, concerns, and activities. You might have a concern about global warming. You might be an avid hunter who resents gun-control legislation. Or you might be upset about the high cost of energy. Hundreds of issues would make excellent topics for persuasive speeches. The key to your success, as in any speech, is your degree of commitment to the issue, your ability to select appropriate supporting materials, and your competence in organizing and delivering your thoughts.

## WORDING THE PROPOSITION STATEMENT

Once you have selected a topic, write a statement called a **proposition**: an arguable resolution phrased in a declarative sentence. The proposition acts as the focal point for your arguments and supporting materials. Like the specific purpose sentence, the proposition statement is made at the end of the introduction and relates the overall objective of the speech. But unlike the specific purpose, the proposition reveals a clear point of view on a controversial topic.

To convince your audience that a relationship exists between the Web and teenage violence you could state several propositions:

Websites such as YouTube contribute to violence among teens.
Teenage acts of violence that are posted on the Web contribute to greater violence among teens.
Videos showing acts of bullying or teen violence should be banned from the Web.

You would select one of these three statements and conduct research to find supporting evidence—statistics, testimonies, examples, and audiovisual aids. You would need to be certain that the evidence did indeed back up your proposition. If it did not, you would be faced with three choices: (1) Conduct a more extensive search for evidence until you found suitable data, (2) rephrase the proposition to correspond to existing evidence, or (3) look for another issue.

It is important to select a topic and word a proposition that seeks reasonable change within your listeners. For example, a speaker who attends an antiabortion meeting and attempts to deliver a speech supporting a proposition that "more pro-choice justices should be appointed to the Supreme Court" would be unrealistic in expectations. Listeners in direct opposition to such a topic are often fixed in their opinions and may be unwilling to change their viewpoints after hearing only a brief 5- or 7-minute speech. Carefully analyze your audience, and avoid extreme topics that are directly opposed to audience values or opinions. Select topics that give you a *realistic* opportunity to change your listeners' beliefs, feelings, or actions. (For more information on this issue, see "Audience Perception of the Topic" in Chapter 3, "Analyzing Your Audience.")

Once you have written your proposition and gathered your evidence, you would construct logical arguments to support your point of view. (We will consider logic and reasoning later in this chapter.) Thorough research and appropriate evidence are extremely important to your success as a persuasive speaker. Your speech will have a significant impact on your listeners if they feel your proposition is validated by careful research and good evidence.

## Propositions of Fact, Value, and Policy

You can select any of three proposition statements for a persuasive speech: propositions of fact, value, or policy.

**Propositions of Fact.** In a **proposition of fact**, you develop a statement you believe is true and must be verified by evidence. Here are some examples:

Terrorist attacks will continue on coalition countries that invaded Iraq.
Columbus did not discover America.
Victims of rape are treated as criminals by the judicial system.
There will be a major volcanic eruption on the West Coast of the United States within the next five years.
Global warming is a myth.
Pluto is a legitimate planet in our solar system.

These propositions are not actual facts, but facts as they are perceived by the persuasive speaker. If you took a survey in most audiences, you would probably find a variety of opinions about each statement. It is the speaker's job to gather evidence that persuades the audience that the perceived fact stated in the proposition is correct.

**Propositions of Value.** In a **proposition of value**, you are required to judge or evaluate an issue. You ask the audience to believe something is right or wrong, good or bad, effective or ineffective.

Home schools are beneficial to children.
The practice of "don't ask, don't tell" regarding the sexual preference of military personnel is discriminatory.
Fast food is dangerous to your health.
The Patriot Act violates the U.S. Constitution.
Excessive use of cell phones is physically harmful.
Billion-dollar bailouts of taxpayer money to falling corporations is wrong.

Notice that these propositions contain words like *beneficial, discriminatory, dangerous, violate, harmful,* or *wrong,* which contribute to judgment or evaluation of the issue. If you choose a proposition of value for your persuasive speech, you must support it with appropriate evidence.

**Propositions of Policy.**  If you were to select a **proposition of policy**, you would advocate the adoption of a future action or behavior.

Prices for prescription drugs should be strictly regulated.
Stem cell research should be funded by the federal government.
Botox parties should be prohibited.
The United States should place a 10 percent luxury tax on all SUVs.
America should not invade foreign countries without provocation.
The Internet should be strictly regulated and controlled.

Each proposition contains the word *should* and proposes an action or a change in the **status quo**. The status quo represents the existing condition or present state of affairs. For example, in each of these propositions, the status quo is the opposite of the statement: Prices for prescription drugs are not now regulated, SUVs are not subject to a luxury tax, and Botox parties occur openly. A speaker who selects any of these propositions wishes to change the status quo or current state of affairs. Each issue requires extensive evidence to persuade the audience to believe that the intended policy is the correct course of action.

Spend some time developing your proposition statement. Choose simple words and clear phrases so that the statement flows evenly and conveys your viewpoint on a debatable issue regarding a fact, value, or policy.

## ethos, pathos, and logos: the means of persuasion

The Greek rhetorician Aristotle wrote that there are three means of persuasion: "The first kind reside in the character [ethos] of the speaker; the second consist in producing a certain attitude [pathos] in the hearer; the third appertain to the argument proper [logos]."[2] In ancient Greece these three elements were considered as separate structures, but today we view them as interrelated. Think of ethos, pathos, and logos as a pyramid that is not complete without any one of its three sides. Persuasion without ethos has no credibility; a speech without pathos generates no feeling; and a speaker deficient in logos reasons without sound argument. Although we will consider each area separately, it is important to remember their interconnection.

### ETHOS: THE ETHICAL APPEAL

**Ethos** represents the dimension that causes us to trust and believe the individuals persuading us. We have confidence in speakers when they are sincere and knowledgeable about issues, show commitment to their persuasive goals, and demonstrate concern for the welfare of others. Ethos involves ethics, character, and credibility. To Aristotle, ethos was "the most potent of all the means to persuasion."[3]

A student remarked in class, "I believe that the most important thing in persuasion is the number of individuals the speaker is able to influence. If the speech changes the opinions or behavior of a lot of people, then it was successful, don't you think?" The problem with this idea is that it measures persuasion in terms of outcomes, without considering the means to the ends.

The success of a persuasive speech must not be measured entirely by outcomes, or civilization will continue to nurture terrorists like Osama bin Laden, Abu Nidal, Adolf

Hitler, Jim Jones, or David Koresh. A persuasive speech should be judged by the ethical means speakers use to influence listeners. When Osama bin Laden appears in a videotape, Americans react with intense anger because of the horrifying terrorist attacks of September 11. When former South African President Nelson Mandela presents a speech, however, we listen with interest because of his lifelong struggle against the practice of apartheid and his devotion to democratic reforms for the people of South Africa. Because of her unselfish service to humanity, people of all spiritual beliefs responded to the words and deeds of the late Mother Teresa. If a speaker advocates ideas that benefit others, demonstrates commitment to persuasive goals, and displays personal behavior consistent with stated beliefs, the persuader will be establishing a positive foundation for ethical appeals.

In a democratic society, citizens expect ethical persuasive techniques. To help you become more aware of **unethical practices**, here is a partial list, including some brief explanations and examples.

President Barack Obama is a gifted speaker who uses persuasion to urge Congress to enact legislation that stimulates the economy, improves health care, and withdraws America's troops from Iraq. (You can read President Obama's inaugural address in Appendix A.)

UNETHICAL PERSUASIVE PRACTICES

**Advocating harm:** Withholding information necessary for people's welfare; inciting people to violence; scapegoating, or isolating groups according to ethnicity, race, religion, or other characteristics for the purpose of assigning blame. Prior to World War II, Hitler blamed the Jewish people for all of Germany's economic problems. Scapegoating was just one sinister tactic Hitler used to prepare for the Holocaust. America also used scapegoating by placing many Japanese citizens in internment camps because of fear they would be disloyal.

**Name-calling:** The so-called ad hominem argument that attacks the character or personality of an individual; the use of loaded words to attack an individual or group. In the Democratic primary of 2008, one of Senator Obama's senior foreign policy advisors referred to Senator Hillary Clinton as "a monster." The advisor had to quit the Obama campaign as a result of the comment.[4] In the 1950s, Senator Joe McCarthy falsely accused many Americans of being "card-carrying Communists." The accusations led to congressional hearings, poisonous recriminations, and unjustified firings of many innocent people.

**Plagiarizing:** Intellectual stealing; quoting or paraphrasing words and phrases without identifying the source. Vice President Joseph Biden ran for president in

2008 and in 1987. In the earlier presidential primary, he was forced to withdraw from the race because he used phrases from the speeches of other politicians without giving them proper credit.

**Providing false information:** Any argument that is inaccurate, false, taken out of context, or deliberately distorts information to mislead the audience. This practice is often called "the big lie." In a 2007 speech at Columbia University Iranian President Mahmoud Ahmadinejad denied that the Holocaust ever existed by saying "there's nothing known as absolute." Also, in response to a question about the execution of homosexuals in Iran, he stated, "In Iran we don't have homosexuals like in your country."[5]

**Using offensive language:** Language that is vulgar, obscene, or insulting; language that is offensive or injurious to any person or group. Any public speaker who uses obscenities for shock value violates the ethical standards of the community and causes most audience members to stop listening.

**Card stacking:** Presenting arguments in a biased and unfair manner; arguments that unfairly stack the deck against an issue, deliberately ignoring opposite information. Here's an example of a "buy American" sales pitch: "Americans buy more American cars than any other models; American cars cost less than foreign models; American cars have increased fuel efficiency over the past decades, and American cars have better overall performance than foreign makes." This argument ignores the fact that hardly any cars are purely American, since many vehicle parts are made outside the U.S., foreign sales have skyrocketed in recent years to more than 30 percent of the market, Toyota has become the leader in auto sales, and both Honda and Toyota have vehicles that average over 40 miles per gallon.

## PATHOS: THE EMOTIONAL APPEAL

**Pathos** plays a very important part in persuasion. Speeches come alive when the speaker appeals to the heart as well as the intellect of the listener. Without emotion, persuasive speeches would contain a lifeless collage of intellectual quotations and statistics. Think of a speech about Parkinson's disease with no reference to Michael J. Fox, or a presentation about overcoming paralysis with no mention of an individual such as the late Christopher Reeve. It is emotion that helps to connect an audience to a topic and create sympathy for the speaker's point of view.

The emotions that are employed in a speech usually depend upon the topic, audience, speaker, and occasion. As you think about the use of emotion, ask yourself the following questions about the speech:

1. What emotions are appropriate to my topic?
2. What are the characteristics of my audience, and which emotions will be most persuasive to them?
3. What feelings do I have about the topic, and which emotions could I convey spontaneously and effectively?
4. What emotions are appropriate or inappropriate to the occasion of the speech?

### Identify Emotions

As you are preparing your speech, identify the specific emotions you want to reach within your listeners. Do you want them to experience a feeling of empathy, or should they be angry because of a problem or issue? Should they feel compassion or resentment due to an ongoing condition or situation? The following list presents several emotions, with sample issues, that you might use to influence your audience. Remember, however, that this is only a partial listing of all the emotions and combinations of feelings that are available for persuasive presentations.

EMOTIONS THAT CAN BE EMPLOYED IN A SPEECH

**Anger:** The terrorist attacks of September 11, 2001; treatment of rape victims; drug-related crimes; abuse of children by a religious sect or members of the clergy; female circumcision in Third World countries; airline delays; 4-dollar gas at the pump

**Despair:** Famine and starvation in Ethiopia or Somalia; public school beatings or shootings of teachers and students; continued worldwide terrorist attacks; destruction from a tornado; enslavement due to alcohol, heroin, or gambling addiction

**Fear:** Chemical and biological warfare; losing health insurance, Social Security, or Medicare; global warming; the lack of automotive or airline safety; identity theft; bankruptcy; violent crime; losing a job

**Hope:** Progress in the war against terrorism; the ability of people to work together to help people afflicted with muscular dystrophy, cystic fibrosis, multiple sclerosis, Alzheimer's disease, and autism

**Horror:** Witnessing the devastation from a tsunami; women being stoned as a punishment for committing adultery; a child kidnapped from a parking lot

**Joy:** Watching troops return home from a war; winning the World Series or Super Bowl; witnessing the nighttime eruption of a Hawaiian volcano; conquering cancer; surviving paralysis; overcoming addiction; losing weight

**Love:** A grandparent or parent; husband or wife; a child, friend, or pet

**Pride:** Work; physical appearance; saving lives; a hobby or interest; church, community, city, state, country, or flag

**Sorrow and compassion:** Families who lost loved ones in the massacre at Virginia Tech; an Alzheimer's patient and family; death of soldiers killed in battle; individuals losing worldly possessions because of a hurricane, war, flood, forest fire, earthquake, or volcano

After researching her topic, Pamela Rumber became concerned about disreputable online pharmacies and the ease with which many Internet users could bypass physicians and get prescriptions without a physical examination or adequate diagnosis. As you read this passage from her persuasive speech, notice how the speaker uses emotional appeals to convince listeners that Internet pharmacies should be banned.

*Disreputable online pharmacies don't care about your health and well-being. They only want your money and they will deceive you in order to get it. Do you know how these disreputable pharmacies operate? Well, they'll have you fill out an online questionnaire and may have the correct answers already filled in. For example, in a WebMD Medical News article I read that Texas Attorney General John Conran described a sting operation where two online dot-com Web sites had the question "Do you have high blood pressure?" and they already had the answer "No" checked off. They then proceeded to sell the medication. According to an article in the February 2000 issue of* Business Week, *some dot-coms go so far as to brag "no medication, no problem." And some make outrageous, untrue, and unsubstantiated medical claims that shark cartilage and cat's claw will cure cancer, arthritis, and AIDS.*

*Think about it. How many men with heart disease can resist the temptation of what Viagra can do for them even if they have to go against their doctors' orders? How many anorexics and bulimics can resist being able to buy Meridia to help them lose weight? What about all of the addicts out there? Can they resist being able to buy mind-altering drugs like Prozac, Valium, amphetamines, and morphine? What about that 15-year-old boy who decides to bulk up on steroids because he was too small to make the football team last year? And what about those of you who have small children at home? You love these children, you care for them, you protect them. I'm sure you would never allow a common drug dealer to come into your home and fraternize with your children. However, even though you don't mean to, that's what you're doing every time you allow them to log on to the Internet.*[6]

Pamela clearly understood the emotions she wanted to reach. She made listeners angry by asserting that disreputable prescription websites don't care about the health of consumers. After substantiating her claim with effective supporting materials, she asked the audience a series of direct questions, making them feel uneasy about the types of people who could purchase medications online. The final question about their "small children at home" was a direct threat to the safety and security of listeners, designed to make them feel fearful and threatened by unscrupulous Web-based pharmacies. Notice that the speaker documents her speech with credible research sources.

### Understand Audience Emotions

As you think about developing emotional appeals, you need to analyze your audience thoroughly in order to discover what emotional buttons to push.

1. Are listeners college students who are angry at rising tuition costs and supplemental "user fees" such as parking permits, library cards, laboratory charges, and technology fees?
2. Are they minorities who have experienced feelings of hurt and anger as a result of prejudice and discrimination?
3. Are your listeners new parents who have experienced the joy and pain of childbirth, yet face the future with insecurity and uncertainty?

If you know the motivations and needs of your audience, you will be able to develop appeals that connect to their interests and gain sympathy for your cause.

This speaker carefully analyzed the emotions of his audience. He knew that many of his listeners were parents with school-age children, and he also knew that they had computers at home. Notice how the speaker combined vivid examples with concrete language to create emotional appeals that frightened the parents in his audience.

*Imagine that a child you know well is lured away from home by a pervert that he met online. Imagine that another child has a new friend that he spends countless hours with online, and that this "new friend" is not a peer, but turns out to be a pedophile. Imagine that a young girl has nude pictures of adults engaged in acts of bondage and sodomy that she has obtained online. These online services should be banned until they are childproof because our children are being lured away from their homes and abused, our children are being exposed to explicit photos and texts, and pedophiles are cloaking their real identities.*

*Right now, a 51-year-old man is serving six years in a California prison for raping a 16-year-old boy. They met online. According to an article in a June 27, 1993, issue of the* Baltimore Sun, *he lured the boy to his home by pretending to have some brand-new computer software. This boy later attempted suicide. These Internet, online services provide the perfect cover for people who would victimize our children. People pose as sisterly or brother figures, motherly or fatherly figures, they masquerade as other children, and they pretend to be devoted to hobbies or subjects that interest our kids. One man went so far as to set up his own Star Trek bulletin board to attract children that he later abused.[7]*

Kenneth Ruffin openly appealed to fear and anger. The speaker used the words "our children," "victimize," and "online" as tools to underscore the intensity of parental emotions and get to the heart of the issue. Following the speech, a spirited discussion took place. Audience members said they often felt "violated" by the Internet and "helpless" when attempting to control these online services coming into their homes. One parent also expressed frustration at her inability to closely monitor her children's computer activities outside the home. Ken's study of the audience paid off. His research enabled him to select an issue that was vitally important to listeners.

## Express Your Own Feelings

A personal commitment to a topic is extremely helpful when a speaker wants to convey the emotional aspects of a presentation. Topics that are linked to your interests, experiences, and/or knowledge can provide the stimulus for expressing your feelings spontaneously to listeners. You can share your feelings more deeply if you have a personal involvement or interest in the issue.

Emotions can seldom be mechanically rehearsed or artificially staged; they are expressed more effectively when the speaker allows feelings to surface naturally during the course of a speech. A successful speaker conveys the degree and intensity of these natural emotions through the delivery of the presentation. Increased or decreased volume can communicate strength of feeling. Verbal emphasis, facial expression, movement, and gesture can reinforce important emotional segments such as stories or examples. Dramatic pauses or silences can allow time for feelings to sink in. A speaker cannot influence listeners effectively without knowing how to deliver the emotional elements needed for persuasion.

This speaker selected a topic from her own painful experience with an alcoholic parent. Notice how she combined logical appeals with emotions in this brief narrative.

*Of 28 million children of alcoholics in this country, the odds are that there are two within this class. Now I'm not going to survey and try to prove or disprove the odds. I will tell you that there is definitely one. Like Suzanne Somers, I too am an adult child of an alcoholic. I am in the process of learning how to talk about it, how to trust, and how to feel and own all my emotions. Suzanne's story is incredible because her entire family recovered, including those who were alcoholic. In my family there were four children. I too, like Suzanne, escaped alcoholism. But two of my siblings did not. It is my hope that, one day, my entire family will recover.*

The statistic, example, and testimony comprise the logical, factual evidence. But the evidence becomes deeply emotional when the speaker reveals her personal experience. The emotion genuinely moved the audience because the speaker used effective facial expressions, vocal inflections, and eye contact to communicate strong personal feelings. As Aristotle said about pathos, "we give very different decisions under the sway of pain or joy, and liking or hatred."[8]

### Connect Emotions to the Occasion

Numerous speeches are presented to celebrate or pay tribute to individuals, groups, symbols, or events on important occasions. Speakers who want to be well prepared seek to understand and acknowledge the emotions that are significant on these occasions. A supervisor might pay tribute to the loyalty of a worker who is retiring after 35 years of service. A religious official might refer to shared spiritual values when dedicating a new church, mosque, or synagogue. A family friend could reminisce about a couple's courtship at a fiftieth wedding anniversary. And a governor might acknowledge the shared pain of citizens on the anniversary of a bombing, a natural disaster, or an assassination. No matter what the event, the speaker must understand the occasion completely in order to develop language and create images that will elicit the appropriate feelings and response.

On August 31, 1997, Princess Diana of Great Britain was involved in a tragic automobile accident in Paris, France. In just a few hours, the shocking news spread throughout the world of the car crash that killed the princess, her companion (Dodi Al Fayed), and a driver and seriously injured a bodyguard. The world community reacted with disbelief as the details of the accident investigation revealed facts about an intoxicated driver operating the Mercedes at excessive speeds to escape the ever-present media or paparazzi. Several days later, a memorial service was held in London's Westminster Abbey to honor the life of the beloved princess. It became the task of Diana's brother, Earl Spencer, to eulogize his sister in an emotional tribute witnessed by Diana's two teenage sons, her ex-husband Prince Charles, the British Royal Family, and an immense worldwide audience:

> I stand before you today the representative of a family in grief, in a country in mourning before a world in shock. We are all united not only in our desire to pay our respects to Diana but rather in our need to do so. For such was her extraordinary appeal that the tens of millions of people taking part in this service all over the world via television and radio who never actually met her, feel that they, too, lost someone close to them in the early hours of Sunday morning. It is a more remarkable tribute to Diana than I can ever hope to offer her today.
>
> Diana was the very essence of compassion, of duty, of style, of beauty. All over the world she was a symbol of selfless humanity, a standard-bearer for the rights of the truly downtrodden, a truly British girl who transcended nationality, someone with a natural nobility who was classless, who proved in the last year that she needed no royal title to continue to generate her particular brand of magic. . . .
>
> Without her God-given sensitivity, we would be immersed in greater ignorance at the anguish of AIDS and HIV sufferers, the plight of the homeless, the isolation of lepers, the random destruction of land mines. Diana explained to me once that it was her innermost feelings of suffering that made it possible for her to connect with her constituency of the rejected.[9]

Spencer clearly understood the intense emotions of the occasion. He acknowledged the feelings of millions who felt an emotional link to the princess, and he was candid about Diana's deep insecurities that led to eating disorders and other difficulties. Although the speech was not without controversy in its remarks aimed at the Royal Family, it honored Diana's memory and her earnest dedication to humanity.

**Charisma.**   Some speakers possess special magnetic qualities, called **charisma**, that attract audiences and inspire confidence. Franklin D. Roosevelt, John F. Kennedy, Martin Luther King, Jr., Ronald Reagan, Maya Angelou, and Barack Obama are speakers who have influenced audiences because of these unique abilities. No one expects you to have the charisma of these effective leaders. But every speaker has a unique personal style that can be developed with speaking experience. Whether you use dramatic pausing, effective gestures, or vivid mental images, you can refine your personal style to communicate emotion successfully.

**A Word of Caution.** Emotion is a powerful motivator, and audiences are often captivated when charismatic speakers employ passionate examples. Emotion can be inappropriate, however, if speakers use a long string of emotional examples without appealing to the listener's intellect. Although emotion can arouse curiosity and maintain audience interest for a while, strong emotion tends to fade, resulting in a shallow basis for persuasion.

Emotion and charisma can also be dangerously exploitive. In Chapter 6 we discussed how a strong emotional appeal and a magnetic personality may often conceal hidden agendas of greed. Numerous charlatans have successfully contrived emotional appeals to religious feelings, humanitarian causes, or consumer needs to reap huge personal benefits. Be wary of the individual who uses only strong appeals to personal feelings. Remember that the effective persuader must appeal to ethics and logic and use emotion judiciously.

# logos: the appeal to reason

Your ultimate goal in a persuasive speech is to influence the audience to consider, and ultimately to accept, your point of view through **logos**. Your task is similar to that of a trial attorney who builds a case based upon solid evidence and draws conclusions to persuade jurors of a defendant's guilt or innocence.

One way to achieve your persuasive objective is to follow a process called **reasoning**, in which you present logical arguments to your audience. Most people are familiar with arguments or disputes in which we express our feelings and personal opinions about relationships, current events, movies, or fashion. Logical **arguments** in a persuasive speech, however, must be grounded in clear and correct facts, complete evidence, and accurate reasoning. A common way for persuasive speakers to develop arguments is by presenting relevant supporting materials such as statistics, testimonies, and examples and by drawing conclusions from the data to back up a point of view.[10]

A speaker wanting to support a claim that a campus parking problem exists could phrase an argument like this:

> I'm sure many of you already know that we have a severe parking problem on our campus. Statistics from the Dean of Student's office indicate that there are 2,000 more commuter students than there are parking spaces. I did an informal survey of fifty students and asked them if they thought there were parking problems on campus. Thirty-nine of them said yes, six who used the bus said no, and five didn't have an opinion. The majority of the students in this survey—78 percent—felt that a parking problem exists. I also interviewed the Director of Student Activities who told me that [quote] "We have a campus parking crisis." And I want you all to know that I was 10 minutes late for this class, and almost missed my speech today, because I had to "hawk" a parking place way over on the other side of campus next to the stadium. You can see that the evidence indicates that we have a severe problem—a problem that we've got to solve.

The speaker has provided a list of supporting materials that include two statistical cases, one testimony of authority, and a personal experience. The speaker cites a clear conclusion to summarize the data and to support the claim. The logical argument can be written in the form of a diagram.

**Claim:** There is a parking problem on campus.
**Supporting evidence:**   A.   There are 2,000 more commuter students than parking spaces.
B.   Seventy-eight percent of students in informal survey said there was a parking problem.

C.  Director of Student Activities says there is a parking "crisis."

D.  I was late for class because of parking problem.

**Conclusion:**  Evidence indicates that there is a parking problem on campus.

When constructing arguments, be very careful how you draw conclusions from your data. Notice how this speaker states that the evidence "indicates"—the speaker does not say that it "proves" the conclusion. Evidence does not offer conclusive proof, but rather points to a conclusion. Your audience will be more open to persuasion if you use terms such as *imply*, *signify*, *suggest*, *indicate*, or *reveal* and stay away from terms that express absolute statements of proof.

When you use a logical argument, you must avoid fallacious reasoning. A **fallacy** occurs whenever a speaker uses unclear or incorrect facts, incomplete evidence, and/or erroneous reasoning.

*Biased sampling* is a fallacy occurring when statistics or examples are not representative of the entire population. For instance, were students in the informal parking survey selected by random sample, or were they deliberately chosen because they already agreed with the speaker's point of view?

A *hasty generalization* is another fallacy that occurs when a speaker draws a faulty conclusion from extreme exceptions or from limited evidence. Are there other university officials who agree with the student activity director's viewpoint, or is the director an exception? Were the parking difficulties experienced by the speaker a normal occurrence, or were they due to a special event such as a conference or a basketball game? We've all been guilty of making hasty generalizations. The victim whose home has been burglarized declares, "I came home and discovered I was robbed. I called the 911 emergency number, and it took 25 minutes for the police to respond. The cops are never around when you need them." The victim is obviously frustrated, but the one example could have been an isolated case. Much more statistical and testimonial evidence must be presented before a speaker should draw such a conclusion. Some arguments are so frequently used that they have been classified and labeled. These arguments can help you apply general models of reasoning to your persuasive speeches. We will consider arguments based upon enumeration, analogy, and causation.[11]

## ARGUMENTS BASED ON ENUMERATION

When you employ **enumeration** in a speech, you cite a series of specific cases to support a generalization. If you wanted to support a claim that most large cities have a drug problem, you could develop the following argument of enumeration:

**Claim:**  Most large cities have a drug problem.

**Supporting evidence:**  A.  Los Angeles, in the top twenty largest cities, has a drug problem.

B.  New York, in the top twenty largest cities, has a drug problem.

C.  Chicago, in the top twenty largest cities, has a drug problem.

D.  Houston, in the top twenty largest cities, has a drug problem.

**Conclusion:**  Most of the top twenty largest cities have drug problems.

In this argument, the speaker cites four different examples of large cities with drug problems and states a conclusion that accurately reflects supporting evidence. The speaker uses the word <u>most</u> in the conclusion to indicate that "a great majority" of the largest cities have drug problems. The speaker could present a stronger argument by stating "All of the twenty largest cities have a drug problem." The word _all_ cannot be used, of course, unless each of the twenty largest cities has been researched and found to have these difficulties. The weakest arguments are those where the word(s) _some_ or _a few_ are used. If supporting evidence were to force a speaker to draw the conclusion that only "some cities have a drug problem," then the argument would lack strength and influence.

Determine the amount of evidence you need for a particular conclusion. If your conclusion is highly controversial—such as for or against Internet regulation, surrogate parenthood, or the right to die—you will need many more statistics, examples, and testimonies to construct coherent arguments and draw logical conclusions.

## ARGUMENTS BASED ON ANALOGY

When you reason from **analogy**, you are comparing two or more similar cases to show that, because of their similarity, what applies to one case can also apply to the other.[12] For example:

**Claim:** Detroit is similar to other cities with urban revitalization programs.
**Supporting evidence:**    A.  Jacksonville, Baltimore, and Cleveland have populations of 500,000 or more.
B.  These cities have had similar economic and urban decline.
C.  Jacksonville, Baltimore, and Cleveland all have allocated considerable funds to rehabilitate downtown areas.
D.  Further, we know that Jacksonville, Baltimore, and Cleveland have been successful with their inner-city development programs.
**Conclusion:** Because Detroit is similar in important ways to other cities that have been successful with inner-city revitalization, it is likely that Detroit will be successful as well.

In this analogy, the speaker has cited examples to illustrate the similarity of other cities to Detroit. The conclusion then seeks to persuade listeners that because conditions in Detroit are similar to conditions in other cities, Detroit will obtain a similar result.

Arguments based on analogies can be effective if the examples being compared share a number of characteristics. _Faulty analogies_ occur, however, when examples are dissimilar. A speaker in New Jersey who wants to raise the speed limit to 70 on state highways and compares New Jersey to Wyoming and Kansas is guilty of a faulty analogy. New Jersey is an urban state with high population density, while Wyoming and Kansas are not. For an effective analogy, your examples must have a variety of similar principles or characteristics. Your audience will be persuaded if your analogy is valid in several areas.

## ARGUMENTS BASED ON CAUSATION

When you use logical arguments based upon **causation**, you identify known causes to determine unknown effects (cause-to-effect reasoning) or you identify known effects to determine the unknown cause (effect-to-cause reasoning). Here is an example of cause-to-effect reasoning:

**Claim:** The current severe drought in the Midwest will contribute to higher food prices in the fall.
**Supporting evidence:**    A.  People continue to buy food during droughts.
B.  Severe droughts contribute to food shortages.
C.  In the past, severe droughts have created higher food prices.

Secretary of State Hillary Clinton travels the world persuading America's allies to support changes in U.S. foreign policy.

**Conclusion:** The current drought will create a shortage that will cause food prices to rise in the fall.

In this argument, the speaker has used the known cause—the current drought—as well as evidence of past droughts to predict the unknown effect: that prices will rise in the fall. So the speaker's claim that food prices will rise during the harvest is persuasive because it is based upon good evidence and sound reasoning.

Fallacies, known as *faulty causes* or *faulty effects*, can sometimes occur in causative reasoning. Effects often have more than one cause. For instance, the food shortage could have other causes, such as fewer farms producing wheat due to the grain-subsidy program and/or massive government exports that depleted grain reserves. Also, some causes are not capable of producing the assumed effects. For example, erratic weather conditions in the United States are often said to be caused by a phenomenon known as El Niño, which refers to a gradual warming of the oceans. Although this natural occurrence is a legitimate scientific explanation for many irregular weather patterns, El Niño often takes the blame for anything unpleasant, such as an earthquake, a downturn in the stock market, or rising food prices.

Make certain that your evidence clearly supports a single cause of the effect and that the cause is capable of producing the identified effect. Here is an example of reasoning based upon effect to cause:

**Claim:** High cholesterol contributed to Jack's heart attack.
**Supporting evidence:**  A.  Jack's doctor repeatedly warned Jack to lower his intake of cholesterol.
 B.  Diets containing high cholesterol can increase blockage of arteries, which according to the American Medical Association contributes to heart attacks.
 C.  Jack's cholesterol level was checked a week before his heart attack and found to be high.
**Conclusion:** Jack's diet of high cholesterol contributed to his heart attack.

In this example, the speaker has observed the known effect, Jack's heart attack, and drawn a speculative conclusion about the unknown cause from supporting data provided about Jack. Although it is highly probable that Jack's diet of high cholesterol contributed to his heart attack, this may be a faulty cause. Were there other possible causes of the heart attack such as Jack's weight, his lack of exercise, or his stressful lifestyle? Was his diet of high cholesterol merely a coincidental contributing factor? If Jack had lost weight, exercised, and reduced tension, would his diet have contributed to a heart attack?

Use caution when you reason from effect to cause. A woman with a black eye may not have been beaten by her husband but might have been in a car accident. The recession of 2008 may have been caused not only by high oil prices; there could have been a variety of reasons, including the subprime mortgage crisis and a downturn in global economy.

Keep in mind that arguments of enumeration, analogy, and causation are often used interchangeably throughout most types of persuasive speeches. They are also used to support various methods of persuasive organization. Some arguments are more logically applicable to particular organizational methods than others are; we will consider these arguments in the section "Methods of Organizing Persuasive Speeches."

## OTHER LOGICAL FALLACIES

In the previous logical arguments, we have considered several fallacies—biased sampling, hasty generalizations, faulty analogies, and faulty causes or effects. Here is a chart listing some additional fallacies that you should avoid when building your persuasive speeches.

| Fallacy | Example | Explanation |
| --- | --- | --- |
| Loaded Question | "Are you still using drugs?" | The question forms a no-win trap. Answering "yes" is an admission of guilt; responding "no" still admits to former drug use. |
| Either/Or Question | "We can continue the high deficits and corruption of this administration, or we can elect a new, competent, honest government." | The "choice" presents two extremes: one evil, one good. Alternatives are seldom this simplistic. |
| Begging the Question | Mr. A: "The U.S. must reduce defense commitment and spend more on social programs." Ms. B: "Why?" Mr. A: "Because it's imperative that our defense spending be reduced and our social programs be increased." | The reasoning is circular. Debater A "begs the question" by restating the issue and offering the claim as evidence. The claim remains unsubstantiated. |
| Complex Question | "America's strong foreign policy has contributed to stability in Afghanistan." | Several complicated issues are combined into one claim, making it difficult to sort through. |
| False Authority | "I've taught myself the art of massage, and in my experience I have seen the healing power of this art. In my intensive study of this science, I have found, over and over, that people can be healed in mind, body, and spirit, if they are willing to begin a course of therapeutic treatment." | The speaker offers no credible evidence of schooling, certification, or other documentation to support claims of knowledge. Manipulative words such as *self-taught, my experience, intensive study,* and *over and over* are used to justify expertise. The authority is illegitimate. |

| Fallacy | Example | Explanation |
|---|---|---|
| Irrelevant Evidence | "Joe Smith should be elected attorney general: He is a true American, a good family man, a church member, and a friend of the poor." | The information does not support the claim. To evaluate Joe, we need to know about his experience, his skill at handling cases, and opinions of Joe from other attorneys. The "evidence" has little to do with the job of an attorney general. |

## DEVELOPING REBUTTAL ARGUMENTS

Some persuasive issues are so controversial that audiences will listen with skepticism and doubt about the wisdom of the speaker's proposition. A speaker who ignores this resistance will not be taken seriously. It is crucial for a persuasive speaker to acknowledge the viewpoint of listeners who strongly disagree with the speaker's proposition and use powerful counterarguments to undermine the opposing idea. The argument that is held by audience members who strongly disagree with a speaker's proposition is called an **opposition argument**. The counterargument that the speaker uses to weaken the opposition is known as the **rebuttal argument**.

For example, imagine a speaker who believed that nuclear power was the answer to America's energy problems developed a proposition of policy, stating that more nuclear power plants should be built in this country. After an effective introduction, the speaker presented a thesis declaring that nuclear power plants are safe, efficient, and cost-effective. Upon hearing the speaker assert that nuclear plants are safe, many listeners would immediately recall the nuclear meltdown in Chernobyl and/or the disaster at Three Mile Island, which would raise serious disagreements with the speaker's proposition. The speaker cannot press on without ever acknowledging or answering the strong objections of the opposition; to do so would be persuasive suicide. Audience members would question the speaker's concern for their welfare, awareness of the facts, and understanding of the problem. One way for the speaker to meet this challenge would be to meet the opposition argument head-on.

The speaker could say, "When you hear that nuclear power plants are safe, I'm sure many of you may think about the disasters at Three Mile Island and Chernobyl. I understand your concerns, and I want to assure you that such tragedies must be prevented." After establishing and developing the opposition argument further, the speaker would then begin to form a rebuttal argument to undermine the opposition and provide evidence that the opposing view was flawed or inaccurate. The speaker could begin the rebuttal in this manner: "These disasters are well-publicized failures from past history that do not fairly represent the more stringent policies and guidelines now regulating nuclear reactors." The speaker could provide additional rebuttal information about the flawed structure and regulation of the Soviet reactor or improper management and safety inspection of the Three Mile Island plant.

It is important for a persuasive speaker to carefully craft opposition and rebuttal arguments to gain the confidence of listeners and demonstrate a thorough understanding of both sides of the issue.

## methods of organizing persuasive speeches

Because there are different goals in persuasion, there are different methods of structuring persuasive messages. In an actuating speech, for instance, the speaker must organize the message to identify a problem that requires solution and action. In a speech to convince, the speaker uses reasons to develop a positive case in support of the proposition. To build a successful persuasive speech, you need to understand and be able to apply the best methods of organization for your particular assignment. You can structure persuasive messages according to reasons, problem-solution, comparative advantages, and the motivated sequence.

# REASONS

Using the method of citing **reasons** is a clear and straightforward organizational approach, especially in a speech to convince. With this method, a speaker uses the three or four convincing reasons as main headings in the body of the outline. If you use this technique, be certain that your reasons are the strongest possible, that they support the specific purpose or proposition, and that they themselves can be supported with concrete evidence.[13]

The reasons organizational sequence is often combined with arguments of enumeration. Each reason that supports a proposition lists or "enumerates" the evidence that backs up the reason. For example, the following speaker, Anna D'Archangelis, wanted to convince her audience that computer-enhanced advertisements should be labeled. After researching her proposition of policy, Anna found three strong reasons that she felt would persuade the audience to agree with her. She then supported each reason with an argument of enumeration that listed supporting evidence—statistics, testimonies, examples, visual aids—to validate the reason.

> **Specific purpose (proposition of policy):** Computer-generated or airbrushed advertisements should legally be labeled as such.
>
> **Thesis statement:** Computer-enhanced advertising misrepresents products, portrays women unrealistically, and induces unhealthy behaviors.

BODY

*Reason 1*
 I. Misrepresents products
   A. Use of products creates happiness (quote from former model, PowerPoint examples)
   B. Both men and women targeted (testimony, PowerPoint examples)
   C. 3,000 marketing messages sent daily (statistics)

*Reason 2*
 II. Portrays women unrealistically
   A. Blurs line between fantasy and reality (magazine cover example, humorous example)
   B. Promotes dissatisfaction, unhappiness with body (statistics)
   C. Shows severely underweight "ideal models" according to Body Mass Indexing (stats)

*Reason 3*
 III. Induces unhealthy behaviors
   A. Eating disorders (statistics)
   B. Obsession with appearance (quotation)
   C. Low self-esteem (quotation, example of former model)

The speaker, Anna, was successful in choosing three equally strong reasons to support the proposition. Notice that she supports each reason with an argument of enumeration that lists a combination of statistics, examples, quotations, and visual aids to draw a conclusion and validate the reason. You can read the entire persuasive speech at the end of this chapter.

Students sometimes have difficulty coordinating their reasons smoothly with the proposition. To phrase each heading of the body more clearly, place a mental "because" in front of each reason. This method is an effective organizational tool for both speaker and listener: It helps a speaker to be logical and clear in supporting the proposition, and it enables the listener to follow the speaker's principal arguments.

## PROBLEM-SOLUTION

The **problem-solution** method is also useful in structuring a speech to convince. This method reflects the problem-solving techniques developed many years ago by educator John Dewey in his book *How We Think*.[14] (Read "Developing a Problem-Solving Agenda" in Chapter 19, "Speaking in Groups," for a discussion of John Dewey's problem-solving techniques.) The problem-solution method is most often used for propositions of policy, and it is easy to incorporate into a speech outline. Problem-solution organization can be combined with arguments of enumeration and causation. In the following outline about the automotive repair industry, Karen Anderson made effective use of the problem-solution structure by employing arguments of enumeration to support the problem and solutions.

> **Specific purpose (proposition of policy):** To convince the audience that the auto repair industry should be strictly regulated
>
> **Thesis statement:** Incompetent and unnecessary repairs must be corrected by strict regulations.

BODY

*Problem*
  I. Americans are taken advantage of
     A. Forty percent of consumer auto repair spending wasted on unnecessary repairs
     B. Sears scandal demonstrates company fraud
     C. "Gypsy" parts are purposely inferior
     D. Small, everyday scams rip off public
     E. Incompetent service affects consumer

*Alternative solutions*
  II. Several means exist to rectify problem
     A. Voluntary certification
     B. Industry-wide control
     C. Consumer awareness

*Selected solution*
  III. Regulation can help consumer
     A. Mediate disputes
     B. Detect fraud
     C. Protect consumer

## developing a controversial issue: an example »

We will examine a topic selected from the *Opposing Viewpoints*[15] database to see how a controversial issue can be developed into two opposing persuasive speeches. You will notice a clearly worded proposition, a two-point thesis on opposite sides of the issue, and supporting materials that validate each position. Recognize that these arguments represent an early stage of speech planning. More research and preparation will be necessary to develop 6- to 7-minute speeches that are satisfactory for classroom presentation.

**Proposition of policy:** Illegal immigrants should be allowed to receive U.S. health care benefits

| Favor | Opposed |
|---|---|
| **Thesis statement:** The U.S. has an ethical obligation to treat illegal immigrants and a national responsibility to protect the health of American citizens. | **Thesis statement:** Granting health care to illegal immigrants damages America's health care system and puts Americans at risk for serious diseases. |
| I. Required to treat illegal immigrants | I. Damages the health care system |
| In the *New England Journal of Medicine*, Bernard Lo, a medical doctor, states that denying illegal immigrants health care would violate physicians' "ethical responsibilities to protect the public health, care for persons in need, and respect patient confidentiality." | According to an article in a 2005 issue of *Journal of American Physicians and Surgeons*, there are more than 43 million people who are uninsured in America and it is estimated that 12 million, or more than 25 percent, are illegal immigrants. These illegal immigrants have cost the U.S. health care system dearly. For example, the EMTALA Law has caused 84 California hospitals to close their doors due to bankruptcy. |
| Furthermore, a federal law titled the Emergency Medical Treatment and Active Labor Act of 1985 (EMTALA) already mandates that hospitals treat uninsured patients or pay a fine if they refuse treatment to any individual. | |
| II. Protects public health from contagious diseases | II. Puts Americans at risk for contagious disease |
| Denying health care to undocumented workers would leave untreated any contagious diseases that they might carry. According to an article in a 2006 issue of *Opposing Viewpoints*, tuberculosis and other rare diseases have been detected and treated because uninsured Americans and illegal immigrants are allowed to receive emergency room care. If these individuals are denied treatment, their diseases will be a threat to public health. Which is better: to deny health care to undocumented workers and create a risk to every American, or treat their health issues and reduce or eliminate the threat to public health? | Because of the increase in immigration, both legal and illegal, diseases that were once eradicated or unheard of in the U.S. are now making a resurgence. For example, tuberculosis was virtually eliminated in Virginia, but in 2002 there was an increase of 17 percent in northern Virginia. Polio was wiped out but is now carried into the U.S. by some illegal immigrants, as well as hepatitis A, B, and C. And leprosy, which was rare or nonexistent in America, has been found in more than 7000 people in the U.S. since 2002. An article in a 2006 issue of *Opposing Viewpoints* states that the increase and resurgence of these and other diseases, like malaria, are caused by illegal immigrants. |

The body of the speech contains three main headings that identify the problem, explore alternative solutions, and present the desired solution. The speaker uses an argument of enumeration to list a combination of statistics and examples as evidence to support her three headings.

One variation of this method is the "problem-cause-solution" sequence, in which the speaker incorporates an argument of causation to include a section identifying principal causes of, or reasons for, the problem. Here's how the preceding outline can be adapted to this method:

> **Thesis statement:** Incompetent and unnecessary repairs, caused by lack of control, must be corrected by strict regulations.

**BODY**

*Problem*
I. Americans are taken advantage of

*Cause of problem*
II. Lack of control contributes to negligence
   A  Anyone can claim automotive expertise
   B.  ASE sets only voluntary standards
   C.  Consumers are uneducated
   D.  Most states don't regulate

*Alternative solutions*
III. Several means exist to rectify problem

*Selected solution*
IV. Regulation can help consumer

In this outline, numerals I, III, and IV were organized using arguments of enumeration. Numeral II, however, uses a causal argument to list the principal causes of the problem, or the reasons that Americans are exploited. You can see that the problem-solution method is adaptable to a variety of arrangements. You don't need to let any of these methods constrict your topic; adjust the approach to the unique demands of the topic, developing your speech in logical sequence.

## COMPARATIVE ADVANTAGES

The **comparative advantages** method is helpful in organizing convincing or actuating speeches that pose problems with many solutions. When using this organizational tool, speakers usually assume their listeners already agree that something must be done, although they may disagree about the solution. The speaker then tries to persuade the audience that the selected solution is superior to all others. The comparative advantages structure is often used with propositions of polices and supported by evidence that provides comparisons and contrasts.

> **Specific purpose (proposition of policy):** To persuade the audience that Ms. Juanita Hernandez should be elected president of the United States
> **Thesis statement:** Ms. Hernandez is more sensitive to health care issues, more experienced in foreign policy, and has a better economic plan.

**BODY**

I. Ms. Hernandez is more sensitive to health care issues.
   A.  She overhauled the health care system as governor of State X.
   B.  As a Hispanic, she is sensitive to minority workers without health care.
   C.  As a wife and mother, she is sensitive to family health issues.

II. Ms. Hernandez has more experience in foreign policy.
   A. She was U.S. Secretary of State.
   B. She was the president's national security advisor.
III. Ms. Hernandez' economic plan will provide more jobs.
   A. As governor of State X, her economic plan lowered jobless rate.
   B. Her plan provides more incentives to business and industry to hire and train new workers.

With this topic, the speaker can assume that most listeners are voters who are interested in selecting a new president. But the speaker has chosen a candidate and provided three comparative advantages to show that Ms. Hernandez is more qualified than all other presidential candidates. Each numeral is then supported by evidence that uses comparative examples to show that the selection of Ms. Hernandez would be the superior choice. With this organizational tool, speakers often use arguments of analogy as well as enumeration. For example, in numeral IIIA, the speaker might say, "As governor of State X, Ms. Hernandez lowered unemployment to 3.5 percent. As president, Ms. Hernandez will carry out an economic plan to do the same." In addition, each numeral uses an argument of enumeration to list evidence to show how Hernandez is qualified.

## MOTIVATED SEQUENCE

The motivated sequence is an organizational method that is used in speeches to actuate. This strategy is composed of five steps: attention, need, satisfaction, visualization, and action. In Chapter 17, we will examine this important technique in detail.

## Building the Persuasive Speech to Convince »

We've discussed the nature, means, and organization of several persuasive speeches. Here is a list of guidelines to help you build your persuasive speech to convince.

1. Choose a controversial topic.
   a. Examine your attitudes and the opinions of others.
   b. Select a topic that is appropriate to listeners.
   c. Explore current events topics.
   d. Avoid overworked issues.
   e. Provide new insights into familiar topics.
2. Conduct extensive research.
   a. Examine library sources for testimonies, statistics, and examples to build your case.
   b. Be certain that sources are accurate and up-to-date.
   c. Interview experts on the topic.
   d. Research specialized institutions and organizations.
   e. Develop visual aids for variety.
   f. Be willing to change or modify the topic if evidence does not support your viewpoint.
3. Phrase a clear proposition.
   a. Know the difference between fact, value, and policy propositions.
   b. Make sure that the proposition is controversial.
4. Analyze the audience.
   a. Determine prior attitudes about a topic through interviews, surveys, or questionnaires.

(1) Agreement implies the opportunity of using evidence as reinforcement of audience attitudes.

(2) Neutrality indicates the necessity of employing strong evidence to influence listeners.

(3) Opposition to the topic suggests the need to present extensive supporting evidence.

b. Develop persuasive appeals linking your topic to audience interests and motivations.

c. Make the audience the central focus of speech development.

5. Develop sound arguments and coherent organization.

a. Present well-defined claims supported by good evidence and sound reasoning.

(1) Use evidence in the context of its intended meaning.

(2) Include materials that are relevant and up-to-date.

b. Avoid using subjective phrases such as "I think" or "in my opinion."

c. Identify research sources to build credibility.

d. Avoid unethical practices.

e. Use a balance of logic and emotion.

f. Choose an appropriate organizational method for the topic.

g. Use external transitions to emphasize major arguments.

6. Construct a sophisticated introduction.

a. Choose a strategy to generate curiosity and establish rapport.

b. Present the proposition and thesis statements at the end of the introduction.

(1) Avoid opinionated statements such as "I'm going to convince" or "prove," which alienate the audience.

(2) State the proposition in a straightforward manner.

(3) State the thesis clearly, creating receptiveness among listeners.

7. Develop a forceful conclusion.

a. Use a challenge in the convincing speech to stimulate thought or ask listeners to change their minds.

b. Use the challenge in combination with most types of conclusions.

c. Avoid summary conclusions in convincing speeches.

8. Build an effective delivery.

a. Maintain eye contact with listeners when conveying emotional examples.

b. Report statistics accurately without stumbling.

c. Use gestures to emphasize arguments and facial expressions to express emotion.

d. Express feelings through enthusiasm, verbal emphasis, and vocal inflections.

e. Practice the speech in order to project confidence in the topic.

 SAMPLE SPEECH: computer-enhanced advertising should be clearly labeled

*Anna D'Archangelis, a speech communication student, was concerned about computer-enhanced advertising that affected the image of women (and men) in the media. Through her research, she discovered that computer-altered photos and ads portrayed women as unrealistically perfect and even dangerously thin. To underscore her persuasive viewpoint,*

*Anna assembled an impressive collection of PowerPoint slides that reinforced her conclu-sions and maintained the interest of her listeners. As you read this engaging and conver-sational speech to convince, notice how Anna draws the audience into the topic and uses Aristotle's three means of persuasion to influence listeners to accept her proposition. Con-vincing speeches can be organized by using a reasons, problem-solution, or comparative advantages sequence. This speech is arranged according to the reasons organizational sequence.*

## PERSUASIVE SPEECH TO CONVINCE
*Anna D'Archangelis*

1.  When you look at any women's magazine or picture, what do you normally see? (slide 1) You see beautiful women with clear, flawless skin, great hair, (slide 2) trim waists, perfect makeup, and cool clothes, right? (slide 3) Many women see these models as idols, or what Don Oldenburg in a June 1998 article in the *Washington Post* likes to call, "the ideal of feminine attractiveness." In all reality, yes, these are real women posing in front of the cameras, but also computer-generated and airbrushed before being put on the cover. Let me show you a couple examples. (slide 4) Here is a photo of a thirteen-year-old girl. She's a good-looking teenager, right? OK, she has a few wild strands of hair, some facial blemishes, and uneven eyebrows, but so what. But wait. Let's make some improvements. We'll give her rosy cheeks, a better hair day, some whitened teeth, and even up the eyebrows a little. We'll even take the lines out of her face—and ta da! There she is on the right. We've just digitally altered her appearance. Here's another. (slide 5) The same girl on the left looks good, but let's make her taller, slimmer, and less real, like the girl on the right. There you go! You saw it. Computer magic!

    *1. In her introduction, the speaker uses a series of carefully crafted PowerPoint slides to demonstrate the differences between the natural flaws of posed models and the more "perfect" images created through computer enhancement.*

2.  Computer-generated or airbrushed pictures and ads should legally be labeled as such because they misrepresent the product, portray women unrealistically, and induce unhealthy behaviors.

    *2. The speaker states the proposi-tion of policy, followed by her three reasons.*

3.  The misrepresentation of products is seen all over the place. A lot of times these pic-tures show thin, sexy women endorsing their products, putting into women's minds that if you buy their products, you too will be happy, beautiful—just like them. The advertisers will tell you that their ads are intended to help women focus on exterior problems and offer products in slick, glossy images to reduce weight, become more physically beautiful, and look more fashionable. But former model Jane Kilbourne writes in her book titled *Deadly Persuasion: Why Women and Girls Must Fight the Addictive Power of Advertising* that "the problem with advertising isn't that it creates artificial longings and needs, but it exploits our very real and human desires." Kil-bourne says that while these ads appear to focus on exterior problems, "the products themselves claim to satisfy internal needs for connection, self-worth, and love." A lot of times these ads show very happy, beautiful people, but they are really just giving you a substitute for something you are not getting anywhere else.

    *3. The speaker begins reason 1 by stating the opposing argument offered by advertisers. She then uses quotations from a verifiable primary source—a book written by a former model—for the rebuttal argument.*

4.  Not only women are affected by these ads, but men too. (slide 6) As you can see, this guy—he looks charming, handsome, cool, right? Any guy wants to be like that. (slide 7) Same thing with these guys. Who knows? Do their bodies really look like that? I don't think so. Airbrushed and computer-generated images are used to sell anything from per-fume (slide 8), to hip clothes (slide 9), underwear (slide 10), and even alcohol (slide 11).

    *4. As in the introduction, Anna appeals to men in the audience by using examples showing slides of male models in addition to the slides showing "ideal" women.*

© Business Wire/Getty Images

SLIDE 1

© Splash News/NewsCom

SLIDE 2

© Patrick Demarchelier/COSMO/NewsCom

SLIDE 3

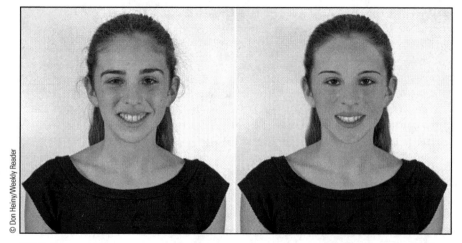

© Don Heiny/Weekly Reader

SLIDE 4

© Don Heiny/Weekly Reader

SLIDE 5

© The Advertising Archives

SLIDE 6

SLIDE 7

SLIDE 8

SLIDE 9

SLIDE 10

SLIDE 11

SLIDE 12

The speaker uses a statistic as support for her reason.

Just looking around the room, what does this image say to you? Women and men are influenced all the time during the course of the day. Kilbourne points out again that an average American is exposed to 3,000 marketing messages every day without even realizing it.

5. The external transition clearly ends reason 1 and begins reason 2.

5. If there is anything that misrepresentation can do, it makes us perceive women unrealistically.

6. Throughout the speech, Anna uses arguments of enumeration to support her reasons. Here, she uses a humorous analogy to show how unrealistic computer advertising can be.

Next, she cites a quotation from a credible source.

The speaker also cites a statistic from the *Post*.

The speaker continues by reporting a study from a psychology professor.

Interesting statistics are cited about the BMI that were reported in the *Post*.

6. (slide 12) Just take a look at this cover featuring Gwen Stefani. How skinny can she possibly get? Seeing these pictures of unrealistic women is kind of the same as the Barbie doll rumor we've all heard, right? Wait a minute—you don't know? OK. Let me tell you. Barbie's breasts are so big and her legs are so long that if indeed she could possibly stand up, she would immediately fall over forward and have to walk on all fours. Anyway, Jane Brody, from a November 19th, 2002, article in the *New York Times*, states that "photographic editing, soft-focus photography techniques and airbrushing have blurred the line between fantasy and reality, making ideals seem more attainable and to me, way too unrealistic to ask of any woman." Many women strive to be what they see on these magazine covers—to conform to an ideal, slender body, to have definition, and bigger breasts. A study reported in the *Washington Post* (previously mentioned) has shown that about 80 percent of American women are dissatisfied with their bodies and when they fail, they suffer unhappiness and disappointment. Many people who used to be considered healthy are now considered overweight, whereas many years ago being full-bodied, maybe a little overweight, was considered attractive. It showed fertility. It showed wealth. What does it show now? It shows that you eat too much, right? The *Washington Post* article says that the Federal government's new guidelines have been lowered for the body mass index or what we like to call BMI and separates normal weight from overweight. Patricia Owens, a professor of psychology at St. Mary's University in San Antonio, found in a case study called "Weight and Shape Ideals" that almost half of the *Playboy* centerfolds and a little more than a third of the Internet models met malnutrition criteria for being severely underweight. As we all know, we see *Playboy* models as being sleek and sexy but not really knowing that most of them are underweight. A person's BMI should fit together with their height and their weight. At a height 5' 6-1/2", a one-hundred-pound model scores a BMI of 15.6. This is twenty-eight pounds under the weight criteria needed to score on a healthy guideline. A healthy range would be anywhere between 20 to 25. Many women strive to be these ideal weights not knowing that these women are unrealistic and under a healthy weight range.

7. The external transition connects reasons 2 and 3.

7. Now seeing how magazines and advertisers have represented women unrealistically, you can only imagine the unhealthy behaviors that are induced from these images.

8. The speaker cites a survey from the *New York Times*.

Anna uses an appeal to relate the topic to her college audience and to herself.

She uses a quote as supporting material.

8. Did you know that because of our media today an estimated 3 percent of young American women suffer from eating disorders? The *New York Times* reported a survey from the National Institutes of Mental Health that says this percentage may be five or six times as high among college women my age. This is what I look at every day. It was also reported that there is a growing dissatisfaction with appearance which is directly linked to the parade of thin bodies in movies and sitcoms. But we all know that these magazines like to keep us depressed and keep our self-esteem nice and low. How else would they keep selling their magazines? Many women are obsessed with their bodies. They love reading fifty-three ways to a brighter smile or how to lose those saddlebags and keep them off. Patricia Owen says that "if these models

were exemplars of ideal beauty, then the measure for women is that to be beautiful, starvation-level fitness is required." A lot of these beautiful images cause self-loathing among women. They think, "I'm not thin enough, my boobs aren't big enough." This thinking sometimes brings on eating disorders and plastic surgery—all this to get out of their poor body image. Previously, I mentioned a book written by former model Jean Kilbourne. Well, she writes not only from her modeling experience but also because she was once addicted to drugs and alcohol. Unfortunately, Jane Brody of the *New York Times* says in a 2002 article that "the poor body image is more likely to lack in self-esteem"—true—"confidence"—true again— "which in turn can impede social, academic, and vocational pursuits." You can see that many women obsess over their bodies day after day and become malnourished and only worry about what they look like on the outside and constantly judge one another.

*Anna uses an effective example about self-destructive behavior by the author and former model mentioned previously.*

*Notice the conversational delivery Anna uses to state the Brody quote from the* New York Times.

9. On advertisements and catalogs that have sleek, sexy models, does there need to be a warning that says: "Health hazard: models appear thinner than physically advisable?" Maybe then women would take into account their own health. Making a label on advertisements and pictures that are computer-generated or airbrushed would be an effective way to help women realize that we don't have to live in a fantasy world. As Dr. James Claiborn, a psychologist in Manchester, New Hampshire, and Cherry Pedrick, a registered nurse, once wrote in their book on body image disorders: "It's time to accept and embrace the many variations of our bodies rather than strive to conform to unrealistic ideals determined by the cosmetic, fashion, and diet industries. We are more valuable than our outer packaging."

*9. The speaker begins her conclusion by paraphrasing her proposition.*

*At the end, Anna uses a quotation from a reputable psychologist and a nurse to challenge listeners to accept her point of view.*

## summary »

Persuasive speakers influence audiences by altering beliefs, reinforcing feelings, or generating action. Speakers phrase persuasive topics into arguable propositions of fact, value, or policy. To persuade an audience, a speaker must construct ethical appeals to build trust and confidence; emotional appeals to deepen feeling; and logical arguments based upon correct facts, complete evidence, and accurate reasoning. At the same time, a speaker must avoid unethical practices, extreme emotionalism, and fallacious reasoning.

Persuasive speeches can be structured according to reasons, problem-solution, comparative advantages, and the motivated sequence.[16]

## SKILL BUILDERS »

1. Choose two controversial topics for a persuasive convincing speech. Investigate your library databases to gather credible resources to find appropriate examples, quotations, and statistics to support your topic. Write propositions and thesis statements for each topic following the guidelines presented in this chapter.
2. Using your library databases, find a persuasive speech from current events or from history that demonstrates Aristotle's three means of persuasion. As you read the speech, write down the appeals to ethos, pathos, and logos. Be specific with your examples from the speech and present your findings to your class.

## BUILDING A
## SPEECH ONLINE »

Now that you've read Chapter 16, use your online Resource Center for Building a Speech for quick access to the electronic study resources that accompany this text. You can access your Resource Center at http://academic.cengage.com/login, using the access code that came with your book or that you bought online at http://www.iChapters.com. Your Resource Center gives you access to Interactive Video Activities, the book's companion website, Speech Builder Express 3.0, InfoTrac College Edition, and study aids, including a digital glossary and review quizzes.

© Mark Mainz/Getty Images

# chapter 17

# SPEAKING TO PERSUADE: MOTIVATING AUDIENCES

## chapter objectives »

After reading and studying this chapter, you should be able to

1. Develop strategies for motivating listeners

2. Describe the motivated sequence

3. Analyze a persuasive actuating speech

4. Develop and outline a persuasive actuating speech using the motivated sequence

If you remember any of the following wacky advertisements, you are one of more than 90 million people who watch about fifty TV commercials during the Super Bowl.

- A Dalmatian becomes a personal trainer for a horse who wants to be a famous Clydesdale pulling the Budweiser wagon.

- A giant Dorito rat attacks a man eating a potato chip.

- A store security camera reveals a Coke delivery man trying to steal a Pepsi from a cooler while background music plays "Your Cheatin' Heart."

- A husky tow truck driver gulps down an energy drink and connects jumper cables to his nipples to charge a car battery.

- A talkative baby ends a monologue about making investments and trading stocks by throwing up.

> " To know what has to be done, then do it, comprises the whole philosophy of practical life. "
>
> —Sir William Asner

Although these ads are funny and entertaining, the business behind them is very serious. In 2008 alone, advertisers paid $324,000 per second or $2.7 million for a half-minute of TV time to promote their products during the Super Bowl. Over the past two decades, Anheuser-Busch has spent $275 million on Super Bowl ad time and Pepsi has bought $193 million. Why? Because these companies know that good advertisements are successful selling their products to a huge captive audience.[1] A Super Bowl ad is one type of a motivational presentation, similar to a persuasive actuating speech. If someone asks you to buy a product, donate to a cause, or volunteer in your community you are listening to a persuasive speech to actuate.

This chapter helps you understand how people are moved to action. We will consider strategies for motivating audiences, Monroe's motivated sequence, and guidelines for constructing the persuasive actuating speech.

## strategies for motivating listeners

As a persuasive speaker, you can influence listeners to believe in your message, feel more deeply about an issue, or act upon a proposal. It is difficult to be effective, however, unless you find specific ways of motivating your audience. Here we examine several strategies: appealing to needs, appealing to beliefs and values, providing incentives, and involving emotions.

### APPEAL TO THE NEEDS OF THE AUDIENCE

In Chapter 3 we considered some of the basic needs that all human beings have in common, and we looked briefly at how one psychologist, Abraham H. Maslow, organized these drives into five levels called a **hierarchy of needs**. If you connect your topic to one or two of these strong drives, your persuasive speech will have more impact upon listeners. For example, if you wanted to persuade your audience to plant trees to improve the environment, you could conceivably develop persuasive appeals for each level of Maslow's hierarchy. Here are some examples:

#### Physical

> Trees remove the carbon dioxide from our air and give us oxygen. One acre of trees can keep fifteen people breathing for one year. Unfortunately, we are losing this valuable resource at the rate of 3,000 acres per hour.

#### Safety and Security

> Trees keep us warm in the winter, and they cool us with their shade in summer. Trees hold large amounts of soil that help to control erosion and filter out nitrogen and phosphorous contained in runoff. When trees are cut down, a chain reaction is started that not only harms the ecology but affects us as well. When too much nitrogen and phosphorous enter the water system, algae grows and shades aquatic grasses, which are nurseries for fish. When aquatic grasses are shaded they die, and there is no food for fish. When the fish die, our food supply is depleted, the fishing industry is affected, and the economy is damaged.

#### Love

> Trees provide wildlife with habitat, from the tiniest little microorganism to the largest elk. Trees are the oldest living things: There's a bristlecone pine tree in California that is more than 4,600 years old.

### Esteem

*The governor has officially declared this month to be "Tree-mendous" month. So why don't we all pitch in and help plant a tree to make our community better? If you plant a tree, you can return this application to the agricultural department, and you will receive a certificate identifying you as a "Tree-mendous Marylander."*

### Self-Actualization

*Teddy Roosevelt established the national park system in order to preserve the beauty and wonders of nature for future generations. Today, there are over 200 million acres of forests in these national parks for all of us to enjoy.*

The speaker reminds listeners that trees provide the oxygen necessary to physical survival. She also describes how the lack of trees can lead to a chain reaction that is harmful to the safety and economic security of the audience. Next the speaker uses the elk and the bristlecone pine to appeal to her listeners' love of wildlife and respect for antiquity. She introduces esteem by referring to the governor's program and awarding certificates to those who plant trees. In a final appeal to self-actualization, the speaker asks listeners to "enjoy" and "preserve" the wonder and beauty of these forests.[2]

Many persuasive topics cannot be linked so comprehensively to audience needs. You can be successful if you select one or two levels of Maslow's hierarchy and develop strong persuasive appeals that connect the topic to your listeners' needs.

Although Senetor John McCain was unsuccessful in his bid to become president of the United States in the election of 2008. He is respected and admired by millions for his sacrifice and service to America.

## APPEAL TO LISTENERS' BELIEFS AND VALUES

As you develop motivational appeals, it is important that you understand the specific beliefs and values of your audience. What beliefs do listeners have in common? What goals are important to audience members? What characteristics or qualities do your listeners most admire? You can influence listeners by explaining how your proposal is in harmony with their beliefs and value systems.

As the introduction indicates, some of the most common examples of appeals to values and beliefs are found in media advertising campaigns. An ad showing a smiling sun, a damp cloud, and a colorless rainbow markets ready-made Jimmy Dean breakfasts to families in a hurry. General Motors used a religious appeal—"What would Jesus drive?"—to sell

Chevys in its ad campaign against SUVs. And a previous Super Bowl ad for CareerBuilder
.com, a web-based employment site targeting job seekers, pictured an unsuccessful man
working in a dead-end job and surrounded with chimpanzee workers—one of which literally kissed the rear of the chimpanzee boss.[3]

Appeals to beliefs and values can also be successful in a negative sense. The R. J.
Reynolds Tobacco Company created a magazine ad picturing a hip cartoon character
named Joe Camel enjoying a cigarette. The ad attracted the attention of numerous children, who are fascinated by cartoons and caricatures. Armed with studies from the *Journal
of the American Medical Association,* health groups protested the ad campaign and accused
Camel of devising strategies that persuaded children as young as 12 to smoke cigarettes.[4]
The tobacco company denied the allegations and continued the ad campaign using the
Joe Camel character until a lawsuit filed by forty states forced tobacco companies to stop
these types of cartoon and billboard ads.[5]

These strategies were effective because the advertisements connected products to the
values of listeners. If you are interviewing for a job, you can sell yourself by linking your
qualifications to the goals of your prospective employer. If you are presenting a classroom
speech, you can relate many topics to the specific interests and values of your listeners. If
you are required to promote your company's products at a trade convention, you can look
for creative ways of appealing to the beliefs and values of prospective customers. Remember that it is the speaker's responsibility to analyze and understand the values of a specific
audience in order to develop appeals that are successful.

## PROVIDE LISTENERS WITH INCENTIVES

When you are presenting a persuasive speech, you need to be aware that listeners will
silently ask themselves how they will benefit from your proposals. An effective persuasive
speaker clearly communicates the advantages of a proposal by providing long- and short-
term incentives for the audience.

**Long-term incentives** are benefits that listeners gain over a period of time after agreeing to a speaker's proposal. One speaker advocated a tax deduction for responsible pet
owners. She provided statistics showing that county governments are spending significant
tax funds to maintain animal shelters for stray pets. The speaker provided two long-term
incentives for those who agreed with her plan: (1) Deductions would provide financial
assistance to individuals who adopted stray animals; and (2) increased pet adoptions
would save taxes by reducing the number of strays in animal shelters.[6] Another speaker
who urged listeners to research their family genealogy identified these specific incentives:
(1) Researching family history can help individuals discover genetic illness; (2) understanding genealogy can encourage people to alter previous family lifestyles and prolong
life; and (3) understanding our heritage can lead to actions that improve the health of
future generations in families.[7]

In these examples, speakers explained that listeners would benefit by saving money or
improving their health. If audience members are told that a proposal will help them to look
or feel better, protect their families, save money, improve their safety, be wiser consumers,
or live more successfully, they will see the long-term advantages of supporting the plan.

Speakers can also include **short-term incentives** to motivate listeners and provide
immediate reinforcement of ideas. A speaker who advocated courteous driving practices
handed out buttons with the slogan "Please be patient: God isn't finished with me yet."[8]
Another student who suggested that listeners improve their nutrition passed out carrot
sticks at the end of a speech. A speaker who urged audience members to bring toys for
tots at Christmas presented a carnation with a friendly reminder to each listener. Bum-
per stickers saying "I brake for animals" were given out to support a speech on animal

rights. Speakers have used pamphlets, seeds, T-shirts, pens, sugarless cookies, refrigerator magnets, and pins as short-term incentives to reinforce messages. Remember that these items should not detract from the speech and should be handled in a manner that enhances the presentation.

Present listeners with long- and short-term incentives. Let members of your audience know how their lives will be improved by agreeing to your proposal, and provide immediate incentives to encourage them.

## INVOLVE THE AUDIENCE EMOTIONALLY

A persuasive speaker cannot be completely successful unless listeners experience an emotional connection to the topic. Speakers make these connections by using colorful language, stirring examples, and an expressive delivery.

Pat Masimore, a speaker of Native American descent, believed that professional teams should not adopt Indian names because the practice is insulting and disrespectful. She described how sports fans who wear costumes made from chicken feathers unknowingly ridicule the Native American ceremonial headdress of eagle feathers. She used this quotation from an editorial in *Sports Illustrated*[9] to express her strong emotional feelings about Indians:

> An anthropologist was studying Indians in the mid-1800s when he came across an old, old tribal chief. He asked the chief what America was called before the white man came. The old Indian looked at him and said, "Ours."

The speaker used vocal emphasis and a dramatic pause to stress the emotion in the line containing the Indian's response. Audience members got the message.

Another speaker conveyed sympathy for the homeless by asking listeners to hold small plastic bags filled with ice cubes during a portion of a speech. When audience members became uncomfortable with the subfreezing temperatures, Becky Meyers asked listeners to briefly express how they felt. One listener commented, "My fingers were so numb that I could hardly concentrate on what you were saying." Another observed, "If I had difficulty holding ice cubes for 2 minutes, imagine how a homeless person feels, existing in these temperatures for an entire winter." Becky had succeeded in using emotion to link the audience members to her topic.[10]

Ashley Pettis wanted listeners to volunteer for Movable Feast, an organization that distributes one meal a day to AIDS sufferers. At one point in the presentation, the speaker played a videotape of her interview with a patient who had benefited from the program. In simple but emotional words, the AIDS victim appealed to Ashley's audience: "I don't know what to say, but I know it's a great organization, and I certainly couldn't have done without it. I didn't realize it existed until I needed it. They're beautiful people."[11]

These speakers understood the importance of relating their topics to the emotions of audience members. Similarly, you can employ emotional examples, vivid language, and expression in your persuasive speeches. Recognize that listeners will be more likely to accept your ideas if you touch their emotions.[12]

## the speech to actuate

The persuasive speech to actuate is an excellent presentation to build if you want to motivate listeners to perform a specific action. This speech often incorporates an organizational method known as the **motivated sequence**, which was developed by **Alan Monroe**,

Actuating speakers must connect to beliefs, motivations, and emotions in order to persuade listeners to "buy into" recommended actions to solve problems.

© Joel Gordon

a professor of speech at Purdue University in the 1930s. Monroe used this method successfully to train sales personnel by combining problem-solution techniques with motivational approaches.[13] The motivated sequence consists of five steps: attention, need, satisfaction, visualization, and action.

## ATTENTION STEP

The **attention step** is the introductory phase of the speech that arouses the curiosity and stimulates the interest of the listener. Any of the types of introductions we discussed in Chapter 11 (including shocking statement, quotation, and narrative) would be appropriate techniques to get the attention of your audience in a speech to actuate.

## NEED STEP

Next, in the **need step**, a speaker must persuade the audience that there is a need or problem that remains unsolved. Issues such as "Our oceans and beaches are being polluted," "We must become less dependent on oil imports," or "The government should not provide billions to bail out the auto industry" can be appropriate choices for actuating speeches. When identifying a problem, you can use statistics, testimony, and examples to persuade the audience that there is a real problem and that the problem affects them. For example, if you show pictures of polluted beaches and cite instances of ocean dumping, you are providing supporting evidence for the problem. If you tell your audience about unpleasant vacations at the ocean, where hospital waste has washed ashore, your listeners will begin to see that the problem affects them directly.

## SATISFACTION STEP

After identifying and developing the problem, you must provide a solution, or **satisfaction step**. It is helpful if you have evidence to indicate that the solution has worked in similar situations and that a number of authorities and experts have supported it. If you advocate that "the United States must allocate more resources to combat terrorism in subway, bus, and railway systems," you need to supply statistics, testimonies, and/or examples to persuade the audience that this solution is sensible and workable.

## VISUALIZATION STEP

In the **visualization step**, you must use vivid words and examples to help your audience form a mental picture of what will happen in the future if they adopt your proposed solution—and the negative results if they do not. A speaker tells the audience, "We can continue to watch gas prices increase from $3.00 to $5.00 per gallon or we can support a new energy bill in Congress that explores alternative methods of producing energy and reduces our dependence on foreign oil." Although this statement must be supported with specific evidence, it is an effective visualization because it portrays both positive and negative results. Visualization is a crucial step in the actuating speech: Audience members learn how supporting the solution will benefit their future.

## ACTION STEP

The **action step** is the *who, what, when, where, why,* and *how* of the motivated sequence. The speaker tells audience members exactly what they are to do if they support the solution. The action should be as specific as possible—"Give blood next Wednesday," "Register to vote," "Join a health club"—so that listeners can take an active part. The action step is placed near or in the conclusion and can be combined with an appeal, personal testimony, or experience. If your action is clear and specific, your audience will be able to demonstrate their agreement with your solution by performing the action you advocate.

## PHRASING THE THESIS

In a persuasive actuating speech that uses the motivated sequence, a speaker should develop a thesis that briefly summarizes the three steps in the body of the speech. The thesis should *not* include the action step, because the speaker wants the audience to listen to all aspects of the need, satisfaction, and visualization of a topic before asking them to perform a specific activity. The action is best stated near or in the conclusion of the speech.

When phrasing the thesis, you can follow or paraphrase a simple template that includes the need, satisfaction, and visualization steps. For example:

**Actuating thesis template:** _____ is a problem that must be solved by _____ in order to _____.

Here is how the template can be applied to an actuating topic:

**Specific purpose:** To actuate the audience to donate cans of food for the homeless
**Thesis statement:** The lack of food for the homeless is a problem that must be solved by our participation in order to restore hope to deserving Americans.

### BODY

| | |
|---|---|
| Need step | I. Lack of food for the homeless |
| Satisfaction step | II. How we can participate |
| Visualization step | III. Restoring hope |

In this thesis, "the lack of food for the homeless" represents the need step or numeral I of the body, "our participation" presents the satisfaction step or numeral II, and "restore hope to deserving Americans" covers the visualization step in numeral III. Although the specific purpose clearly indicates what action the speaker wishes the audience to perform, the specific purpose is not stated in the introduction, and the action is not included in the thesis statement.

## applying the motivated sequence

In this section we consider some examples from a speech that applies the motivated sequence to persuade and actuate the audience. We also examine how to incorporate the five steps of the motivated sequence into your speech outline.

Here are five excerpts from a speech to actuate—"Feeding the Hungry Here at Home," by Kara Jenkins.[14] Notice how the speaker develops each phase of the motivated sequence to reach her ultimate goal of action.

> **Specific purpose:** To actuate the audience to bring cans of food for the hungry
> **Thesis statement:** The lack of food for the homeless is a problem that must be solved by our participation in order to restore hope to deserving Americans.

### Attention Step

In her introduction, Kara gets attention by combining her personal testimony with a series of brief examples. She uses repetition of the words "A place where I saw" for emphasis and dramatic effect:

> *Not long ago, my older brother took me to a place that I will never forget. A place where I saw people who were homeless and poor and hungry. A place where I saw old women who carried trash bags with everything they owned in them. A place where a man begged me for one more piece of bread. A place where I saw a mother sit down with her four tiny children. This place is not on TV or in the movies—this place is not in Ethiopia. This place is Our Daily Bread—a soup kitchen right here in Baltimore.*

The examples were short but powerful. Kara conveyed strong emotion as she related her personal testimony. The "I was there" approach achieved the purpose of the introduction and aroused the attention of her audience.

### Need Step

Kara uses testimony from two experts and her own observation to develop the problem:

> *I talked to Mrs. Johnson, a food coordinator for Social Services, and she told me that there are about thirty-one soup kitchens in Baltimore. I also talked to one of the workers at the soup kitchen, Raleigh Lemon, who said that anywhere from 350 to 500 people eat at Our Daily Bread in one day. The center is run by Catholic Charities and serves one meal between 11:00 A.M. and 1:00 P.M. Since this center is a private, nonprofit organization, it depends on volunteers and donations to keep it running. I remember when I was there they were having a shortage of rye bread, so we could only give one slice to each person. I remember one very shy old man whispering to me, "Please Hon, could you just get me one more slice of bread?" More food is needed so people don't have to beg for another slice of bread. We need to develop some solutions to this problem.*

The speaker used statistics as a logical appeal to help listeners understand how many people must be fed at the soup kitchen every day. She then quoted the old man to appeal to each listener's emotions and to convey the human dimension of the problem. Kara's use of logic and emotion was successful; listeners were deeply touched as they heard about the tragic consequences of hunger in their city.

## Satisfaction Step

The speaker tells the audience what other people are doing to help the homeless. The variety of solutions allows the audience to choose their degree of commitment to the issue:

*Let me tell you what others are doing to help. Sue Thompson, an assistant director of Our Daily Bread, said that business groups sponsor breakfasts on Monday, Wednesday, and Friday mornings. Church groups, private organizations, and concerned individuals sponsor one main meal a month for the 350 to 500 hungry people. If that is too much for a small organization, they can sponsor just the juice, salad, or dessert portion of the meal. There are also many volunteers who donate their time to serve the food and help with the cleanup afterwards. And some who can't donate a meal or their time donate canned goods, clothes, socks, or toothpaste—anything that a homeless person could use. So while we may not be able to take 500 people into our own warm homes, the least that we can do is make sure that these people have some nourishing food.*

Even though she lists a variety of solutions, notice that the speaker's easiest alternative—"some who can't donate their time can donate canned goods"—is the last in the list. It is this solution that will be the requested action. Notice that the testimony from the assistant director provides valid evidence that businesses, churches, and "concerned individuals" are an important part of the solution.

## Visualization Step

The speaker provides both negative and positive visualization. She tells the audience what will happen if we "just sit back and do nothing," and she explains how adopting her solution will answer the immediate need.

*We've all driven past a bum or a bag lady, and most of us feel sorry for them and wish that we could do something. Today, I'm giving you all a chance to make a difference in their lives. We can just sit back and do nothing and that bag lady will miss another meal, and those children I mentioned earlier won't get a second helping to fill their stomachs. Or we can provide more food so that all of these people can have nourishing and fulfilling meals. We can tell our friends, relatives, and neighbors about the ongoing need for food and keep providing these lifesaving meals.*

Notice how skillfully Kara connects the solution to her listeners' motivation or wish to help the hungry. Also notice the effective use of language ("filling their stomachs" and "fulfilling meals") to visualize the results of supporting or of not supporting the solution.

## Action Step

In the conclusion, the speaker requests a clear, direct, easy-to-follow action:

*I hope that you all care about this problem and really want to help. I'm not going to ask for a big portion of your time or your money. All I want you to do is to reach into your pantry and pull out a couple cans of corn or green beans and bring them to class on Tuesday, May 17th, and I will take them down to Our Daily Bread.*

*Remember when your mother said, "Eat all your food—there are starving people in Ethiopia?" I think she forgot that we don't need to go as far as Ethiopia—there are people starving right here in Baltimore. I know that the people who eat your canned food may not know your name or who you are, but they will know that there is a light at the end of the tunnel—there is someone out there who cares. Please, won't you take a few minutes of your time and be that light for these people?*

In one brief sentence, the speaker has told audience members the what, where, and when of the action step: "Bring cans to class Tuesday, May 17th." She has also taken the familiar motherly admonition of "Eat your food because of the starving in Ethiopia" and related it to the solution and action she advocates. Kara ends the speech with an earnest appeal to "take a few minutes of your time."

## Building the Persuasive Actuating Speech »

We've considered several strategies for motivating audiences and examined the organization of the speech to actuate. Here is a list of guidelines to help you build this important persuasive message.

1. Choose a topic requiring audience commitment.
   a. Examine your attitudes and the opinions of others.
   b. Explore topics from current events.
   c. Avoid overworked issues.
   d. Provide new insights into familiar topics.
   e. Choose a topic that allows listeners to perform a specific action.
   f. Be certain the topic is appropriate.
2. Conduct extensive research.
   a. Examine library sources for testimonies, statistics, and examples.
   b. Interview experts on the topic.
   c. Research specialized institutions and organizations.
   d. Be certain that sources are accurate and up-to-date.
   e. Select audiovisual aids for variety.
   f. Be willing to change or modify the topic if evidence does not support your viewpoint.
3. Phrase a clear, specific purpose and thesis.
   a. The specific purpose contains the specified action but is not stated in the introduction.
   b. The thesis includes the need, satisfaction, and visualization steps of the body and is stated at the end of the introduction.
   c. Avoid including the action in the thesis statement.
4. Analyze the audience.
   a. Make the audience central to speech development.
   b. Determine prior attitudes about a topic through interviews, surveys, or questionnaires.
   c. Develop persuasive appeals linking your topic to audience interests and motivations.
   d. Plan alternative strategies if the audience resists solutions or suggested actions.

5. Develop sound arguments and coherent organization.
   a. Present well-defined claims supported by good evidence and sound reasoning.
      (1) Use evidence in the context of its intended meaning.
      (2) Include materials that are relevant and up-to-date.
   b. Avoid subjective phrases such as "I think" or "in my opinion."
   c. Identify research sources to build credibility.
   d. Avoid unethical practices.
   e. Use a balance of logic and emotion.
   f. Be able to apply the five steps of the motivated sequence.
   g. Use external transitions to emphasize major arguments.
6. Construct a sophisticated introduction.
   a. Employ a creative strategy for gaining audience attention.
   b. State a clear thesis at the end of the introduction.
      (1) Avoid stating the specific purpose containing the specified action.
      (2) Avoid opinionated statements such as "I'm going to actuate" or "prove," thus alienating the audience.
      (3) State the thesis in a straightforward manner, creating receptiveness among listeners.
7. Develop a forceful conclusion.
   a. Employ an appeal in the actuating speech to seek a specific commitment from the audience.
      (1) State the action clearly.
      (2) Provide listeners with all necessary details of the action.
   b. Use the appeal in combination with most types of conclusions.
   c. Avoid summary conclusions in actuating speeches.
8. Build an effective delivery.
   a. Maintain eye contact with listeners when conveying emotional examples.
   b. Report statistics accurately without stumbling.
   c. Use gestures to emphasize arguments and facial expressions to convey emotion.
   d. Express feelings through enthusiasm, verbal emphasis, and vocal inflections.
   e. Practice the speech in order to project confidence in the topic.

## OUTLINING THE MOTIVATED SEQUENCE

It is easy to incorporate the motivated sequence into the traditional speech outline. This brief outline of the following speech, "Genocide in Sudan," can help you structure the introduction, body, and conclusion of the speech to actuate.

**Specific purpose:** To actuate the audience to sign a letter requesting Congress to pass legislation that stops the killings in Sudan

**Thesis statement:** The genocide in Sudan is not only a crime against the citizens in Darfur but also a crime against humanity that is in desperate need of international intervention in order to prevent a greater number of atrocities from occurring.

## INTRODUCTION

*Attention Step*

    I. "During the last hour we have been sitting in this classroom, more than 13 people have died in Sudan."

    II. Startling statistics and examples followed by shocking PowerPoint photos showing atrocities.

## BODY

*Need Step*

    I. Genocide is occurring in Sudan.

      A. Janjaweed (devils on horseback) kills women, men, elderly, infants, children.

      B. Over 180,000 are dead and climbing.

      C. Two million are short of food and water.

      D. World fails to classify atrocities as "genocide."

*Satisfaction Step*

    II. Failed attempts made to stop genocide.

      A. African Union only monitors and reports killings.

      B. International Criminal Court could help but U.S. fails to join.

      C. U.N. resolutions blocked by some countries supporting Sudanese government for selfish reasons.

      D. Talks of travel bans, asset freezes, oil embargoes produce little action.

*Visualization Step*

    III. Further atrocities will occur if problem is not stopped.

      A. Darfur could become worse than Rwanda, where 800,000 were slaughtered.

      B. Holocaust similar to Nazi crimes could occur.

## CONCLUSION

*Action Step*

    I. "Today is Holocaust Remembrance Day and I ask that you take just a moment to consider what happened seventy years ago and take into account what is happening now and try to pull together to do something."

    II. An appeal

      A. Educate the public.

      B. Call killings in Darfur "genocide."

      C. Sign letter addressed to members of Congress.

      D. Think about it.

## SAMPLE SPEECH: genocide in sudan

*Omolola Otukoya is a Nigerian American who is deeply concerned about the atrocities in Sudan and the indifference of the world community to the catastrophe. In her speech she used graphic visual examples, compelling statistics, and powerful quotations to persuade the audience that the problem needed immediate solution. As you read this effective persuasive speech, notice how the speaker blends forceful motivational appeals throughout the motivated sequence to move her listeners to action.[15] Because the photos are very graphic in nature, they are not included with this text of the speech. If you wish to view the images, you can access the article—Kristof, Nicholas D. "The Secret Genocide Archive," New York Times, 23 Feb 2005: A19—through most library databases.*

## A PERSUASIVE SPEECH TO ACTUATE
*Omolola Otukoya*

1. During the last hour we have been sitting in this classroom, more than 13 people have died in Sudan. (slide 1) By the time this day is over, 330 more people will have been senselessly murdered or raped in the name of racial cleansing. (slide 2) These are the victims of our indifference. The picture in the upper left is of a little boy. The picture does not show his five-year-old older brother who lay beside him because his face was so badly beaten that he was not recognizable. The picture also fails to show the corpse of his mother who had been shot and lay beside both of the boys. The picture at the upper-right corner shows a man who has obviously been shot and who could not make it out of the village when raiding Arab militiamen known as janjaweed terrorized their village. The picture at the lower left-hand corner shows the corpse of a man who fled barefoot and was unable to leave when the raiding militiamen entered the village. The picture in the lower-right corner shows a corpse that is still bound at the wrist. The pants are pulled down so that the militiamen could sexually abuse the victim before death. If it was a man, they would castrate him. If it was a woman, she was probably raped several different times by several men before she was shot and killed. These sickening images from a February 2005 issue of the *New York Times* are dramatic evidence that we are living in a time of a holocaust and we are witnessing what our grandparents and great-grandparents witnessed sixty and seventy years ago during the Holocaust in Europe.

2. The genocide in Sudan is not only a crime against the citizens in Darfur but also a crime against humanity that is in desperate need of international intervention in order to prevent a greater number of atrocities from occurring.

3. (slide 3) This picture here is the country of Sudan and this is Darfur, the region of Sudan where the social repercussions are occurring. According to an article in an October 2004 issue of *Time* magazine, the genocide began in 2003. The most recent attacks have involved raping and murder. Men, women, children, and the elderly are targets. The raiding militiamen are known as "janjaweed," which means devils on horseback. They come into the villages. They take the water supply. They kill infants and children, 3, 4, and 5 years old, as well as middle-aged and elderly women.

   An April 13, 2005, issue of the *Christian Science Monitor* says that the death and poverty rate is now numbered at over 180,000 dead and climbing. Two million are short of food and water and refugees have left and entered bordering countries like [points to map of Sudan] Chad, Eritrea here, and also this portion of Ethiopia. According to a March 2005 article in the *New York Times* entitled "The American Witness," U.N. Undersecretary for Humanitarian Affairs Jan Egeland commented on the global inaction by stating, "The world is failing Darfur. We're only playing the humanitarian card, and we're just witnessing the massacres."

4. A major problem is the world community's apprehension in calling the atrocities in Sudan "genocide." By labeling the problem as genocide, we give it power and recognize that there is a widespread problem occurring. In 1948 the U.S. among other countries signed a genocide treaty that was created by a man who left Poland during the Nazi invasion. The genocide treaty commits all signers to intervene at any time there is genocide occurring in the world. By not officially recognizing the problem in Darfur as genocide, the United States does not have to intervene and neither do the other countries or the U.N.

1. In her introduction, Omolola gets the attention of her audience through startling statistics and shocking photographs of the atrocities in Sudan.

The speaker verifies the credibility of her visual aids.

2. Omolola presents the thesis statement that includes the need, satisfaction, and visualization steps of the motivated sequence. Notice that the action is not stated in the thesis.

3. In numeral I, the need or problem is clearly developed by using a map of Sudan, a definition, statistics, and a quotation.

Notice that the supporting materials are well documented with verifiable research.

4. Omolola describes the indifference of the world community, which resists classifying the atrocities as genocide under the 1948 Genocide Convention.

**5.** The speaker states a clear transition between the problem in numeral I and the solution in numeral II.

**6.** The speaker begins the satisfaction or solution step by describing the African Union and its inability to stop the killings. A quotation from an eyewitness reported in a credible source strengthens her argument.

**7.** Omolola presents another solution that is weakened and rejected by the United States.

**8.** She also describes the shortage of food supplies.

**9.** Omolola provides examples indicating how some nations are blocking attempts to stop the killings. Again, she cites a credible source.

**11.** A clear transition connects numeral II with numeral III—the visualization step.
**12.** The speaker cites a powerful quote from President Kennedy to begin numeral III.

Omolola paints a horrifying picture of the future and uses an analogy that compares the past genocide in Rwanda to the present atrocities in Sudan.

5. It is clearly evident that the genocide in the Sudan is definitely a problem that needs to be solved immediately.

6. (slide 4) The world community has made attempts to halt the genocide in Sudan. There is a group called the African Union. The pros of the African Union are that international workers come together to oppose what is going on in Sudan. However, they are limited and can't really fight against the militia in the Sudan—they can only monitor it. So they basically witness what is going on and they write reports about it and report it to local news media groups. Another problem with the African Union is that they are not fully equipped with the right amount of troops and they are also limited to weapons that can only protect themselves. They do, however, feed and clothe some of the refugees and fleeing persons in Darfur. The March 2005 *New York Times* article quoted former Marine captain Brian Steidle, who was one of three U.S. military advisors to the African Union's monitoring team in Sudan. Captain Steidle said that "it was extremely frustrating seeing the villages burn, hearing gunshots and not being able to do anything."

7. There is also the International Criminal Court, otherwise known as the ICC. The ICC's basic job is to pinpoint problems of genocide and widespread problems in other countries and prosecute leaders of these countries once these crimes have been committed. However, the United States refuses to join and follow the ICC because the Bush Administration feels that the ICC could prosecute American troops for wrongdoing in other countries.

8. There is also international aid seen in the Darfur region. You have the U.N. coming in and providing food. However, food is running low and there is not enough food because of a shortage of funds to support the supplies that are being sent to Darfur.

9. We also have other countries that are coming together and are supporting the government of Sudan for selfish reasons. Arab countries are sympathetic to Sudan, and Pakistan and China are deeply involved in Sudan's oil industry. Mainly China, which gets 10 percent of its oil from Sudan, has invested heavily in Sudan's oil industry. The article I cited in the *Christian Science Monitor* reports that China has consistently blocked U.N. sanctions against Sudan to gain more influence and tap into more of Sudan's oil reserves.

10. There are talks of oil embargoes, travel bans, asset freezes; however, amidst these talks neither former Secretary of State Colin Powell nor U.N. Secretary General Kofi Annan have done anything to arm the African Union or other troops within Sudan.

11. Furthermore, these steps have not been successful on a wide scale and if the problem in Sudan is not stopped immediately, further atrocities will occur.

12. (slide 5) President John F. Kennedy once said, "The hottest places in hell are reserved for those who in a moment of moral crisis maintain their neutrality." So I ask you today, where do you stand? Right now if nothing is done in Sudan, there will be a higher death rate. According to an October 2004 article in *Time* magazine entitled "Tragedy in Sudan," if something isn't done now, Darfur could become worse than Rwanda where 800,000 people died as a result of genocide in 1994. Also, there's not enough food right now being sent by U.N. workers and Christian groups to feed the refugees that have fled to Chad and other bordering countries.

13. If we do not do anything to stop what is going on, we could see a full-scale holocaust in Sudan. There are a lot of similarities between what is happening in Sudan today and what happened in Europe seventy years ago when Adolf Hitler took command and the Nazis took over Germany and invaded other countries. We are appeasing Sudan. By not going in and just giving them warnings we are doing nothing—just as we did with Adolf Hitler seventy years ago.

13. Omolola uses another analogy when comparing the Sudan with the Nazi-driven Holocaust.

14. Today is Holocaust Remembrance Day and I ask that you take just a moment to consider what happened seventy years ago and take into account what is happening now and try to pull together to do something. (slide 6) First, we can educate the public. We must spread the message and tell people what is going on in Sudan. Then we can call what is happening in Sudan by its rightful name: genocide. Then we can act collectively and individually. On Tuesday at our next class period, I'm going to bring in a letter addressed to our two Maryland senators and our entire congressional delegation, urging them to pass legislation to end the genocide in Sudan. I ask that everyone sign this letter in the hopes of stopping what is going on. (slide 7) Finally, I want you to listen to this quote written by a well-known Protestant minister during the Holocaust: "First they came for the Communists, but I was not a Communist so I did not speak out. Then they came for the Jews, but I was not a Jew so I did not speak out. And when they came for me, there was no one left to speak out for me." Think about it.

14. The speaker begins her conclusion by relating her topic to the occasion of her speech.

Omolola describes a long-term action: Call the killings genocide. Next she provides a short-term action: Sign a letter in next Tuesday's class, urging Congress to stop the killings in Sudan. Finally, she ends her conclusion with a powerful quotation symbolizing the indifference of the world to the Holocaust.

## summary »

A persuasive speaker must find ways of motivating audiences. Strategies of involving listeners include appealing to needs, values, and beliefs; providing incentives; and involving emotions.

The persuasive speech to actuate is an excellent motivational presentation. It is organized using Monroe's motivated sequence, which includes five steps: attention, need, satisfaction, visualization, and action.

## SKILL BUILDERS »

1. Find examples of an Internet, magazine, newspaper, and/or recorded TV advertisement that uses questionable ethics. Develop a classroom presentation that describes the success of the ads, the targeted audience, and the unethical practices used. Support your ideas with visual aids showing the advertisements.
2. Review the speech in this chapter titled "Genocide in Sudan," by Omolola Otukoya, and answer the following:
   a. Describe the effectiveness of the speaker's persuasive message.
   b. Explain how closely the speaker follows the motivated sequence.
   c. Describe the appeals that the speaker uses to connect to the audience.
   d. Discuss the effectiveness of the action the speaker suggests. Are there other actions that she might have suggested for her listeners to consider?

## BUILDING A SPEECH ONLINE »

Now that you've read Chapter 17, use your online Resource Center for Building a Speech for quick access to the electronic study resources that accompany this text. You can access your Resource Center at http://academic.cengage.com/login, using the access code that came with your book or that you bought online at http://www.iChapters.com. Your Resource Center gives you access to Interactive Video Activities, the book's companion website, Speech Builder Express 3.0, InfoTrac College Edition, and study aids, including a digital glossary and review quizzes.

# chapter

# 18

# SPEAKING FOR SPECIAL OCCASIONS

## chapter objectives »

After reading and studying this chapter, you should be able to

1. Identify twelve types of speeches for special occasions
2. Describe the purpose of each special-occasion speech
3. Develop speeches for special occasions

They stood in deadly silence as the honor guard filed into Cassell Coliseum on the campus of Virginia Tech. Two days before, on April 16, 2007, a mentally disturbed student burst into classrooms in Norris Hall and shot 30 students and faculty and wounded 24 others. Altogether, 32 people were murdered before the killer took his own life on the campus of Virginia Polytechnic Institute in Blacksburg, Virginia. Dressed in orange and maroon, thousands of shocked students gathered with faculty and grieving families to mourn their heartbreaking loss.[1] Attending the convocation were the President, Virginia's governor, the University president, and poet Nikki Giovanni, who offered these consoling thoughts:

> *We are sad today, and we will be sad for quite a while.*
>
> *We are not moving on, we are embracing our mourning.*
>
> *We are Virginia Tech.*
>
> *We are strong enough to stand tall tearlessly, we are brave enough to bend to cry, and we are sad enough to know that we must laugh again.*
>
> *We are Virginia Tech. . . .*

**"** *Prose on certain occasions can bear a great deal of poetry.* **"**

—*Walter Savage Lander*

321

Giovanni ended her poem with "We will prevail," and "We are the Hokies," as the crowd jumped to its feet and chanted the team cheer, "Let's go Hokies. Let's go Hokies." With these sad but stirring words, Ms. Giovanni illustrated one of the ways we honor those we have lost.[2]

The tribute is one of many speeches for special occasions that you may be called upon to deliver during your lifetime. In this chapter we will examine the tools that are necessary to build tributes, as well as speeches that are appropriate to a variety of other occasions.

## types of special-occasion speeches

## THE SPEECH OF TRIBUTE

Speeches of tribute recognize distinguished careers and contributions of either the living or the dead. The tribute may be a **testimonial** presented at a retirement or other going-away ceremony or a **eulogy** delivered at a memorial service or funeral. The speech of tribute seeks to stimulate and reinforce feelings people share about a person (or group) admired within a community. In this presentation, the speaker's goals are to acquaint the audience with the individual's life, remind listeners of the person's significant contributions and virtues, and leave people feeling positive and hopeful for the future.

### Construct a Brief Biographical Sketch

Clearly identify the individual who is the subject of your tribute. Conduct accurate research to collect interesting anecdotes and incidents amplifying the individual's character and personality. Present a biography or life sketch providing insights into the individual's family background, role models, education, and occupation. Be brief; include information that promotes understanding, and avoid insignificant details that interrupt the flow of the speech. Be sensitive to the setting of the presentation. If you are delivering a eulogy, recognize that your audience will be grieving at the loss of a family member, friend, or business associate. Choose examples and quotations that contribute to the healing process. For instance, Nikki Giovanni realized that language was a powerful tool for capturing the feelings of her grieving listeners at Virginia Tech. If your speech celebrates the current life of a distinguished person, you may have greater latitude in the use of supporting materials, such as colorful vignettes and humorous anecdotes. In both cases, however, choose materials honoring individuals, and avoid negative incidents or hostile satire revealing unsavory qualities. Construct a positive and hopeful tribute celebrating a unique personality.

### Acknowledge Significant Achievements and Virtues

Speeches of tribute focus upon achievements and virtues. Speakers recount examples of heroism in battle, contributions in science, religion, or sports; or charitable service to humanity. These examples often identify and praise high moral values—qualities that serve as models for others. Speakers presenting tributes frequently include comments such as "She was the best athlete in her category," "He worked tirelessly in the cause of equality," or "He kept going in spite of extreme adversity." The intention is to remind the audience of the qualities that contributed to the significance or greatness of the individual.

### Convey Hope and Encouragement

Effective tributes link past virtues and achievements to present times by encouraging listeners to continue similar struggles or to embrace the values of those they admire.

Audiences experiencing separation from loved ones as a result of retirement, relocation, or death should not be left with a sense of despair or futility. It is appropriate to use biblical quotations, citations of individuals being honored, or testimonies from others to reinforce feelings and to inspire listeners to grow from difficult experiences.

In a tribute presented at the funeral of Robert F. Kennedy in 1968, Edward M. Kennedy praised his brother's values and quoted one of his brother's speeches to encourage listeners to "shape" America with reason and principle:[3]

> "Our future may lie beyond our vision, but it is not completely beyond our control. It is the shaping impulse of America that neither faith, nor nature, nor the irresistible tides of history, but the work of our own hands, matched to reason and principle, will determine our destiny."
>
> There is pride in that, even arrogance, but there is also experience and truth, and, in any event, it is the only way we can live. That is the way he lived. That is what he leaves us.
>
> My brother need not be idealized or enlarged in death beyond what he was in life. He should be remembered simply as a good and decent man who saw wrong and tried to right it, saw suffering and tried to heal it, saw war and tried to stop it.
>
> Those of us who loved him and who take him to his rest today pray that what he was to us, and what he wished for others, will some day come to pass for all the world . . .
>
> As he said many times, in many parts of this nation, to those he touched and who sought to touch him: "Some men see things as they are and say why. I dream things that never were and say, why not."

## THE PRESENTATION SPEECH

Speeches of presentation are given to honor specific achievements of individuals in institutions, occupations, or community organizations. The president awards the Medal of Freedom to distinguished Americans; the Pro Football Hall of Fame inducts sports personalities into membership; the Academy of Motion Picture Arts and Sciences annually selects a best actor, actress, director, and best picture; public school systems award certificates to outstanding teachers, and universities award scholarships to deserving students; businesses give away trips and prizes to employees with distinguished service records.

Because these speeches often take place in public ceremonies, they must be carefully crafted. The speech of presentation must be brief, accurate, and clear. It should identify the nature or type of award, provide brief information about the recipient's life or career, and acquaint the audience with the individual's specific achievement or service. The speech often includes adjectives like *most*, *best*, *first*, *last*, and *greatest* to describe the individual's merits and accomplishments. The speaker usually ends the speech by formally presenting the award to the recipient.

The speech of presentation should exhibit polish and show evidence of rehearsal. The speaker must know how to pronounce the recipient's name correctly and deliver phrases smoothly. During the presentation, the speaker should avoid embarrassing actions such as dropping framed certificates or handing out plaques upside down. The award should be presented carefully, without unnecessary fumbling. A speaker will often follow the presentation with a handshake or hug (if appropriate) and then step aside to allow the recipient to deliver the acceptance speech.

During the July 3, 1986, celebration marking the 100th anniversary of the Statue of Liberty, President Reagan awarded the Medal of Liberty to twelve distinguished

American immigrants—among them comedian Bob Hope and songwriter Irving Berlin. ABC newsman Ted Koppel narrated the televised ceremony and made the twelve speeches of presentation. Here are two of these speeches—one honoring educator Hannah Holborn Gray and another saluting author Elie Wiesel.[4] Because of the number of awards, each presentation had to be brief, yet each speech effectively acquainted listeners with the recipient, describing the individual's contribution to American life.

> When Hannah Holborn Gray was 4 years old, her father was dismissed from his teaching position in Heidelberg for opposing the Nazi party. He moved to New Haven, Connecticut, where Hannah pursued her education, becoming the first female provost at Yale University and eventually being chosen in 1979 to be the first woman president of the University of Chicago. The Medal of Liberty is awarded to this outstanding educator, Hannah Holborn Gray.
>
> Elie Wiesel was born in Rumania, and as a boy he lost both parents and a sister in the concentration camps. When the Americans liberated Buchenwald in 1945, they found the 14-year-old boy who had cheated death. He vowed to dedicate himself to bearing witness to what had happened during the Holocaust in the hope of preventing that dark history from ever being repeated. He has become, through his writings and teachings, the foremost voice of warning and remembrance. The Medal of Liberty is awarded to Elie Wiesel.

## THE ACCEPTANCE SPEECH

The acceptance speech is the response to the presentation. The recipient gratefully acknowledges an award, gives proper credit to those who have assisted in or been part of the achievement, and states personal values and convictions that led to the accomplishment.

The speech should be well prepared. In many ceremonies, individuals know in advance if they will receive awards; in others, individuals may know only that they have been nominated. In either case, potential recipients should have acceptance speeches prepared to deliver if called upon.

The speech should be brief. The recipient should thank the presenter and organization for the honor and identify colleagues who have contributed to the achievement, as well as personal friends or associates who have given emotional support.

The speaker should exercise care, however, with the number of acknowledgments given. If you've ever watched the televised Academy Awards ceremony, you have seen embarrassing speeches where Oscar winners have thanked everyone from the obstetrician to the usher opening the theater door. Such problems can occur when recipients attempt to deliver impromptu speeches or ramble on without considering the needs of their audiences.

The recipient should exhibit poise in delivery. The speaker should receive the award graciously, possibly holding up the plaque, statue, or certificate to allow the audience to see it easily. The speaker can then place the award on the lectern (if available) to allow freedom of gesture and movement. The recipient should try to avoid distractions such as wiping the forehead or clearing the throat. Although agitated mannerisms or brief references to human feelings ("I'm really nervous tonight") might generate some empathy from the audience, listeners expect a speaker to show competence and demonstrate the qualities being honored.[5]

At the 2007 Academy Awards ceremony in Los Angeles, Forest Whitaker won Best Actor for playing the role of Ugandan dictator Idi Amin in *The Last King of Scotland*. After receiving the Oscar, Whitaker delivered his acceptance:

> When I was a kid, the only way that I saw movies was from the backseat of my family's car, at the drive-in. And it wasn't my reality to think I would be acting in movies,

*so receiving this honor tonight tells me that it's possible. It is possible for a kid from east Texas, raised in South Central L.A. in Carson, who believes in his dreams, commits himself to them with his heart, to touch them, and to have them happen.*[6]

Whitaker referred to his humble beginnings, showed appreciation for the honor, and celebrated the achievement of his dreams.

## THE SPEECH OF DEDICATION

The speech of dedication is presented to commemorate the completion of projects such as national monuments, museums, churches, ships, or hospitals. The speaker refers to the sacrifice and service of individuals who fostered the project and moved it to completion. Effective dedication speeches acknowledge the symbolism of the venture and convey its meaning to the community. Speakers often remind listeners of their values and emphasize the way the finished project will meet individual or collective needs. Dedication speeches usually include phrases revealing the purpose of the project: "This is a place where families can receive help" or "This building will be a house of culture and creative thought." Dedication speeches can bring the members of a community together by reacquainting listeners with their shared interests and common goals.[7]

On November 11, 1984, the Vietnam Veterans Memorial was presented to the U.S. government at a special dedication ceremony in Washington, D.C. Among the principal speakers at the event was Jan C. Scruggs, a Vietnam veteran whose commitment to the memory of his colleagues moved him to raise the $8 million needed for the monument. In his dedication speech, Scruggs acknowledged the bitter dissension caused by the war. But he also described the memorial as a symbol of national reconciliation: a "sacred" site where the sacrifices of young soldiers could be remembered and where national healing could take place.

> *But before we give the Vietnam Memorial away to the government, I have a few things to say. At age 18 I was among the thousands who volunteered for combat in Vietnam. We returned home scorned as the nation was too divided over that war to honor those who served and only wanted to forget those who died. In 1979 I decided to remind America of our patriotic service and to make certain that the names of the 58,000 who died would never be forgotten.*
>
> *So today the memorial is to be given to the United States government. Vietnam veterans are giving this beautiful statue and the wall of names to America. It seems ironic. Indeed, it seems that rather than Vietnam veterans building a memorial for the government, that the government should have built the memorial for the veterans. But Vietnam was that kind of war.*
>
> *My fellow veterans, because of this memorial, we now have our recognition. And we can now say that we have honored our dead. All of this has been a long time in coming and is a time for America to be proud again.*
>
> *Yet this memorial has given America far more than that. Out of the bitter divisiveness of Vietnam has come a symbol of national unity. This is a memorial to heal the wounds of the veterans and to heal the wounds of a nation.*
>
> *People will always debate that war—and let them. But this site is sacred ground where Americans have shown their honor and their respect for the sacrifices made by a generation of young soldiers who answered the call to duty . . . .*
>
> *Today we also thank those who gave the funds for the memorial: locals from the AFL-CIO, schoolchildren, veterans' posts, antiwar protesters, conservative businessmen, retired people. From across America, compassionate people responded to the need for funds. Thank you, America.*[8]

## THE SPEECH OF WELCOME

Welcoming speeches extend greetings to new or returning members of organizations. University officials welcome incoming students, company representatives say hello to new employees, elected officials welcome new citizens, religious leaders greet new converts, and convention organizers extend warm regards to delegates. The speaker giving the welcome should express pleasure at seeing new as well as familiar faces, mention the goals of the group or organization, briefly identify problems to be solved, and convey best wishes to the audience members for success. The speech of welcome should be concise, communicate warmth in its tone and message, build trust and support, and establish common ground.

This welcome, presented to a group of public speaking students on the first day of class, uses questions to build a sense of community, identifies general course goals, and emphasizes positive achievement:

> I want to give all of you a special welcome to this class. First, I'd like to ask a couple of questions. How many of you have ever had any type of speech or communications course before, either in high school or in some other college class? A few of you—fine. Now for another question. How many of you have ever participated in a theatrical production or in a debate, given a report in a class, or been asked to deliver a talk in church or at your job? Well that's almost all of you. You can see that almost every one of you has had some experience with public speaking in your lifetime. And certainly all of you had to present a series of mini-speeches to sign up officially for the course.
>
> No matter what your background, your experience, or your knowledge, this course will help you. You'll get to know people you've never met before, you'll be confronted with a variety of ideas—some unfamiliar, some unconventional—and you'll participate in a number of learning situations that will contribute to your growth. If you're willing to work, listen, and participate, you should succeed.

## THE SPEECH OF INTRODUCTION

The speech of introduction acquaints the audience with a speaker or lecturer. The introduction should help to establish speaker credibility by relating the speaker's occupation, experience, and expertise regarding the topic. The introduction might include descriptions of personal qualities—"He is a family man" or "She is an avid gardener"—and brief anecdotes providing insights into the speaker's personal life. The speech of introduction also describes values the speaker has in common with the audience.

The introduction should be concise and well organized. Lengthy or flowery introductions can exhaust audiences and defeat speakers before they are able to establish credibility on their own. The goal of the introductory speech is to enlighten the audience about a speaker and to prepare them positively for the speaker's remarks.

Dr. Paul Hardin, president of Drew University, gave the following introduction of actor Alan Alda, who delivered the commencement address at this small Methodist-affiliated institution in Madison, New Jersey. The university had originally invited Jesse L. Jackson to be the commencement speaker, but because of illness, he was replaced by Mr. Alda. This excerpt from Dr. Hardin's speech demonstrates an effective verbal transition from Jackson to Alda, conveys familiar as well as unknown information about the speaker, and describes some of Alda's important qualities and virtues:

> We are, of course, very sorry that Mr. Jackson became ill and most regretful that he cannot be with us today. We wish him a speedy recovery. I would have been proud indeed to present him to you.

*I am equally proud, I assure you, to present to you the man who on just 36 hours notice, gracefully and unselfishly agreed to rescue us from a terrible predicament and to speak from this platform today. Oh, I might say, Hawkeye to the rescue!*

*MASH is an acronym. MASH stands for Mobile Army Surgical Hospital. It also is the title of what has been called the most literate comedy series in the history of television. Probably everyone in this audience knows the series and loves its leading character, Captain Benjamin Franklin Pierce, better known as "Hawkeye." Hawkeye and his fellows are constantly fighting the insanity of war, even as they fight to save the wounded victims of war. They instruct as they entertain.*

*The talented actor who plays Hawkeye was a hard-working and much traveled and successful veteran of stage, screen, and television, long before he made the role famous. This distinguished actor is the son of another distinguished actor, Robert Alda, who taught him much of what he knows. He is also a graduate of Fordham, an army veteran, a writer, producer, at times a television critic, an impassioned supporter of good causes, including the Equal Rights Amendment; and our speaker is justly respected as one of our nation's foremost family men. Happily for Drew on this occasion, our speaker, his wife Arlene, and their three daughters love their small town in New Jersey.*

*Will you please give a very generous welcome to Hawkeye, to the very distinguished and humane actor and writer, Mr. Alan Alda!*[9]

## THE KEYNOTE SPEECH

The **keynote speech** is a presentation given at the beginning of a major conference or convention. Democrats and Republicans invite nationally known speakers to address their conventions every four years. Teachers, lawyers, physicians, auto makers, and chefs are among the many groups who ask experts to focus on specific issues at regional or national conferences.

Keynote speeches can be lengthy, sometimes as long as 45 minutes to an hour. Keynote speakers highlight challenges and obstacles to goals such as divisiveness, inferior working conditions, unknown cures, or inequality. To help members face these challenges together, speakers remind listeners of unifying principles and values within party platforms, bylaws, or creeds. Portions of keynote speeches identify solutions the group must accomplish—overturning Supreme Court decisions on abortion, defeating opposing candidates, or building better cars. Keynote speeches should convey emotion, reinforce feelings about organizational values, and inspire commitment to group goals.

On July 12, 1976, Barbara Jordan became the first African American woman to deliver a keynote address to the Democratic National Convention. In her remarks, the congresswoman from Texas called for strong ethics in government, asked party faithful to provide America with a "vision for the future," and appealed for a sense of community and participation. As this excerpt reveals, Jordan's ideas are as applicable today as they were in the 1970s:

*And now, what are those of us who are elected public officials supposed to do? We call ourselves public servants, but I'll tell you this: We as public servants must set an example for the rest of the nation. It is hypocritical for the public official to admonish and exhort the people to uphold the common good if we are derelict in upholding the common good. More is required of public officials than slogans and handshakes and press releases. More is required. We must hold ourselves strictly accountable. We must provide the people with a vision of the future.*

*Now, I began this speech by commenting to you on the uniqueness of a Barbara Jordan making the keynote address. Well I am going to close my speech by quoting a Republican president, and I ask you that as you listen to these words of Abraham Lincoln, relate them to the concept of a national community in which every last one of us participates: As I would not be a slave, so I would not be a master. This expresses my idea of democracy. Whatever differs from this, to the extent of the difference, is no democracy.*[10]

## THE NOMINATING SPEECH

Nominating speeches present the names of individuals for consideration to elective office before a group. The nomination should identify the qualifications necessary for the job, state the values and achievements of the nominee, and discuss how the group will succeed under the nominee's leadership.[11]

An effective nominating speech is accurate, brief, and optimistic. The speaker should have carefully researched the nominee's background to avoid embarrassing misstatements or factual errors. The speaker should mention the nominee's experience and qualifications but eliminate biographical details having little significance to the position sought. A nominating speech should be short: A lengthy speech can affect listeners negatively, even damaging the nominee's chances of election. The nomination can include statements of the individual's virtues, quotations from speeches, or brief anecdotes and testimonials. The speech should end positively, conveying inspiration and promise.

In this speech nominating General Dwight D. Eisenhower for the presidency at the 1952 Republican National Convention, Governor Theodore McKeldin of Maryland reminded delegates of Eisenhower's heroism as Supreme Allied Commander during World War II. He also portrayed Eisenhower as a simple man, "rooted in the soil" of the Midwest, who could unite the nation and its allies:[12]

*The man whose name I shall present . . . has been summoned successively from one gigantic task to another in freedom's cause. His whole career as a soldier, statesman, administrator has prepared him uniquely for the greatest office in the realm of our people's sovereignty—the presidency of the United States . . . . Here is the man to unite our party; here is the man to unite our nation; here is a man to unite our productive forces—labor and capital—in the teamwork that is essential to the times, fully recognizing the dignity and the rights of each; here is the man to unite our allies and potential allies against communism and all threats of aggression and oppression.*

*. . . While some of us kept interparty competition alive and active in our states, the candidate whose name I shall give you was engaged in leading America's brave sons in the great, successful invasion of Normandy on D-Day . . . . This man is a true son of America's frontier. His beginnings are rooted in the soil of our great Middle West and in the deep religious convictions of his devout, Bible-reading parents . . . . He was appointed to West Point during the Administration of President William Howard Taft . . . . It is with pride that I place before this convention for president of the United States the name of Dwight David Eisenhower.*

## THE FAREWELL SPEECH

Farewell speeches are given on the occasion of retirements, resignations, or some other change in status and position. The speaker thanks listeners for their association and friendship, conveys appreciation for their help and/or support, and expresses hope and best wishes for the future. These speeches are often emotional and moving, especially if speakers are saying goodbye after many years of association with listeners.

Some of the most celebrated farewells in history were presented by leaders such as George Washington, who advised the new nation to "steer clear of permanent alliances with any portion of the foreign world"; General Douglas MacArthur, who identified himself with "old soldiers [who] never die; they just fade away"; and Abraham Lincoln, who told friends in Springfield, Illinois, that he owed them "everything."[13] In Lincoln's brief Farewell Address at Springfield in 1861, he acknowledged his friends and family origins, invoked God's blessing, and expressed almost prophetic uncertainty about the future.

> No one, not in my situation, can appreciate my feeling of sadness at this parting. To this place, and the kindness of these people, I owe everything. Here I have lived a quarter of a century, and have passed from a young to an old man. Here my children have been born, and one is buried. I now leave, not knowing when or whether ever I may return, with a task before me greater than that which rested upon Washington. Without the assistance of the Divine Being who ever attended him, I cannot succeed. With that assistance, I cannot fail. Trusting in Him who can go with me, and remain with you, and be everywhere for good, let us confidently hope that all will yet be well. To His care commending you, as I hope in your prayers you will commend me, I bid you an affectionate farewell.[14]

## THE VICTORY SPEECH

Victory speeches are presented by individuals who have won significant contests in sports, politics, the military, or business. They often occur after hard-fought battles or competitions that require physical and psychological endurance as well as support from others. For example, an athlete winning a gold medal at the Olympics, a winning coach of a Super Bowl team, a military general who has defeated a foe, a real estate salesperson selling the most houses in a year, or a politician who has won election to public office would present a victory speech. These speeches can be as informal as a media interview or as formal as a carefully scripted speech delivered to a large audience. Victory speeches generally celebrate the winning accomplishment, thank those who encouraged and supported the winner, and offer conciliatory remarks for the valiant efforts of the opponent.

After becoming the first African American to win the race for the White House on election night, November 4, 2008, President-elect Barack Obama presented this introduction to his victory speech before the world media and a huge audience assembled at Grant Park, in Chicago, Illinois,

> Hello Chicago.
>
> If there is anyone out there who still doubts that America is a place where all things are possible, who still wonders if the dream of our founders is alive in our time, who still questions the power of our democracy, tonight is your answer.
>
> It's the answer told by lines that stretched around schools and churches in numbers this nation has never seen, by people who waited three hours and four hours, many for the first time in their lives, because they believed that this time must be different, that their voices could be that difference.
>
> It's the answer spoken by young and old, rich and poor, Democrat and Republican, black, white, Hispanic, Asian, Native American, gay, straight, disabled and not disabled. Americans who sent a message to the world that we have never been just a collection of individuals or a collection of red states and blue states.
>
> We are, and always will be, the United States of America.[15]

During the speech, President-elect Obama celebrated his historic victory, thanked his family and supporters, offered appreciation to his opponent, Senator McCain, and outlined a vision for America's future. You can read a transcript of the entire speech at http://edition.cnn.com/2008/POLITICS/11/04/obama.transcript/.

## THE COMMENCEMENT SPEECH

Commencement speeches are given to honor the graduates of an institution, seminar, or field of study. Speakers congratulate listeners for their achievements, identify problems they will encounter throughout life, and refer to values that should guide their thinking.[16] Too often, when well-intentioned speakers become too self-absorbed or try too hard to sound eloquent and intellectual, graduation speeches become tiresome affairs, with speakers proclaiming platitudes having little meaning or interest to graduates.

Since the circumstances require the announcement of hundreds, and sometimes thousands, of graduates, successful commencement speeches should be brief. The speaker should remember that the focus of the ceremony is the awarding of diplomas—not the speech. A commencement speech should contain clear ideas and meaningful examples. The down-to-earth speaker will often be received more favorably than the individual who attempts to create high-sounding phrases.

© Tim Boyle/Getty Images

Oprah Winfrey is often considered to be one of the most influential women in America. Through her television show and magazine, she has focused national attention on child abuse, AIDS, women's issues, and ethics in government and the media.

## THE AFTER-DINNER SPEECH

The after-dinner speech is usually a light, humorous presentation designed to entertain or amuse an audience. This type of speech would be appropriate on many occasions: an "over-the-hill" party satirizing a friend's fortieth birthday, a football victory celebration poking good-natured fun at the coach, a business luncheon "roasting" the boss, a graduation party lampooning teachers, or an end-of-speech-class party reviewing the memorable blunders and bloopers of the semester.

The objective of the after-dinner speech is usually to entertain, but it should not consist of a series of unconnected jokes and disjointed stories. After-dinner speakers should observe the same principles of development needed for any other speech occasion. An after-dinner speech requires a unifying theme—a topic that generates interest and captures the imagination of the audience. Topics such as "Mind-Expanding Courses to Get You Through College," "Doing Spain on One Foreign Word a Day," or "Renaming Vegetables" could be developed into successful entertaining speeches. After-dinner speeches can be lighthearted, satiric, or subtly serious.

Although research for entertaining speeches often involves exploring your own imagination and creativity, these presentations require specific supporting materials such as quotations and examples to clarify ideas. The introduction should generate curiosity and include a clear thesis statement identifying the main points of the speech. The body should contain proper transitions and references to sources where necessary. The speech should conclude with a suitable quote, reference to the introduction, or interesting narrative.

In a wedding toast, a speaker may acknowledge past relationships, relate a humorous incident, and express best wishes for the future.

One way after-dinner speeches differ from other types is in the use of humor. Your speech may deal with a light topic designed to amuse an audience, but you should not try to become a stand-up comic or a professional entertainer. Develop your own natural and spontaneous style. It is more important to elicit a few genuine smiles from the audience than to force raucous laughter. Humor depends upon timing and smooth delivery. If you've ever heard a comedian stumble over a punch line, you know how verbal blunders can destroy humor. Practice the after-dinner presentation as you would any other speech. Deliver anecdotes and punch lines clearly, and wait for laughter to subside before you continue. If you feel uncomfortable with humor, evaluate some of your strengths to determine what to include in the speech. Are you a good mimic? Can you tell a good story? Are you good at facial expressions or bizarre voices? Can you write clever rhymes or catchy poems?

## TOASTS

Toasts are presented to honor individuals at ceremonial occasions such as birthdays, bar mitzvahs, weddings, graduations, or the conclusion of negotiated agreements and business transactions. An effective toast acknowledges past relationships, salutes the events surrounding the present ceremony, and expresses best wishes and hope for the future.

Depending on the occasion, toasts can be serious or humorous. A U.S. president welcoming a foreign head of state will often use a toast to define areas of unity or disagreement between countries, demonstrate commitment to continuing association, and convey interest in solving problems. At a birthday or wedding party, a speaker can be more humorous. The toast can relate colorful incidents from past relationships to enliven the speech and to entertain the audience. The speaker usually concludes the toast by expressing sincere wishes for the happiness and future success of the individuals being saluted.

Robert Dole, former majority leader of the U.S. Senate, was wounded in World War II and was chairman of the National World War II Memorial, which successfully raised $197 million in donations to pay for the structure. Senator Dole's speech at the dedication of the memorial appears at the end of this chapter.

In the following wedding toast, the speaker summarizes listeners' mutual feelings, relates one humorous incident, and wishes the couple success and happiness for the future:

*Good friends, I'd like to propose this toast to Jamal and Ayanna—the reason we're all here today. I remember when Jamal came over to our house after proposing to Ayanna, he said, "She didn't say yes, and she didn't say no," and he asked me, "What should I do?" Now I don't usually give advice in these situations, but I said to Jamal, "Why don't you just wait and call her tomorrow. Maybe Ayanna is testing you, and she'll give you an answer in a day or two." Well, the "test" lasted for about six weeks (you can see why I don't give advice). But we're all glad that you both came to terms and decided to make the arrangement official.*

*Will you all raise your glasses with me in wishing the best possible for Jamal and Ayanna—happiness in life's joys, mutual comfort in life's sorrows, and most important, a lifelong respect and love for each other. Here's to the bride and groom.*

## SAMPLE SPEECH: dedication of the world war II memorial

*Almost 60 years after the end of World War II, the United States dedicated a national memorial to the courageous soldiers who fought with American allies in Europe and the Pacific. The memorial honors the 16 million citizens who served and the 400,000 Americans who died in the war. Robert Dole, a former majority leader of the U.S. Senate and unsuccessful candidate for president, was severely wounded on the battlefield and was twice decorated with the Bronze Star and the Purple Heart. He was the national chairman of the National World War II Memorial, which successfully raised $197 million in donations to pay for the structure. On Saturday, May 29, 2004, Senator Dole delivered these remarks at the dedication ceremony, which was attended by former Presidents Bill Clinton, George H. W. Bush, and George W. Bush, and more than 150,000 people, many of them aging veterans in their seventies and eighties.*

## A SPEECH OF DEDICATION
*Bob Dole*

1. Thank you very much. Never had a crowd like this when I was running. Well it's a real honor and privilege to be here and I won't even start to begin to say thank you because where do you stop?

2. But Fred Smith who so kindly introduced me was my mainstay and opened a lot of doors along with General (John) Herrling and Jim Aylward and others on our commission and P. X. Kelley has done a splendid job and has a great staff and when our fund-raising was sort of ebbing, President Clinton, you recall, you took us down to the White House and brought in some potential contributors and a little spark.

3. I want to thank both President Clinton and President Bush 41 (George H. W. Bush), for their generous contributions to the World War II Memorial.

4. In the first week of January 1945, a hungry and lonesome second lieutenant from small-town Kansas dispatched a message to his folks back home: "You can send me something to eat whenever you're ready," he wrote, "send candy, gum, cookies, cheese, grape jelly, popcorn, nuts, peanut cluster, Vicks Vapor rub, wool socks, wool scarf, fudge cookies, ice cream, liver 'n onions, fried chicken, banana cake, milk, fruit cocktail, Swiss steak, crackers, more candy, Life Savers, peanuts, the piano, the radio, the living room, the suite, and the record player and Frank Sinatra."

5. "I guess you might as well send the whole house if you can get it into a five-pound box. P.S. Keep your fingers crossed." In authoring that only slightly exaggerated wish list I merely echoed the longing of 16 million Americans whose greatest wish was for an end to the fighting.

6. And 60 years on our ranks have dwindled. To the thousands assembled here on the Mall to the millions more watching all across America in living rooms and hospitals and wherever it may be. And overseas, our men and women overseas and our friends in Great Britain and our allies all around the world. Our final reunion cannot long be delayed.

7. If we gather in the twilight, it is brightened by the knowledge that we have kept faith with our comrades from a distant youth. Sustained by over 600,000 individual contributions—600,000—we have raised this memorial to commemorate the service and sacrifice of an entire generation.

8. What we dedicate today is not a memorial to war, rather it is a tribute to the physical and moral courage that makes heroes out of farm and city boys and inspires Americans in every generation to lay down their lives for people they will never meet, for ideals that make life itself worth living.

9. This is also a memorial to the American people, who in the crucible of war forged a unity that became our ultimate weapon. Just as we pulled together in the course of a common threat 60 years ago, so today's Americans united to build this memorial. Small children held their grandfather's hand while dropping pennies in a collection box. Entire families contributed in memory of loved ones who could win every battle, except the battle against time.

10. I think of my brother Kenny and my brothers-in-law Larry Nelson and Allen Steele— just three among the millions of ghosts in navy blue and olive drab we honor with this memorial.

---

*Side annotations:*

1. Senator Dole begins with humor directed at his failed bid for the presidency in 1996.

2–3. The senator acknowledges those who helped to raise funds for the memorial.

4–5. Senator Dole begins his speech by quoting a humorous letter he wrote home to his parents from the war front.

6. The speaker acknowledges the assembled listeners and the vast audience watching around the world.

7. The senator pays tribute to the individuals who have contributed to the memorial.

8. Dole refers to the ideals that the memorial represents.

9. The speaker refers to the memorial as a symbol of American unity.

10. The senator uses personal examples to represent the "millions" that are memorialized.

11. The mention of comedian Bob Hope and actress Betty Grable, whose shapely swimsuit photo was pinned on the lockers in many GI barracks, brings humor to the occasion.

12–13. Senator Dole refers to two former presidents who served in the war: John F. Kennedy, a PT boat commander, and General Dwight D. Eisenhower, supreme allied commander.

14. The speaker makes a reference to the war in Iraq and the "chain of sacrifice" to meet the "test of our times."

15–16. Dole refers to the "chains" reflected in the giants of history who were "soldiers of freedom."

16. The speaker describes the symbolism of the memorial — the struggle for liberty and justice for the enslaved.

17. The senator describes "painful lessons" learned about injustices to many of our own minority American soldiers.

19. The speaker describes America as a "work in progress."

20. As is customary in a speech of dedication, the speaker refers to the memorial in lofty terms, such as "sacred ground."

21. Dole again refers to the sacrifice represented by the 4,000 gold stars that symbolize the 400,000 who gave their lives in the war.

11. And of course not every warrior wore a uniform. As it happens, today is the 101st birthday of Bob Hope—the GIs' favorite entertainer who did more to boost our morale than anyone, next to Betty Grable.

    I can already hear Bob, "But I was next to Betty Grable!"

12. And it's hard to believe today is also the 87th birthday of John F. Kennedy. A hero of the South Pacific who, a generation after the surrender documents were signed on board the USS *Missouri*, spoke of a generation of Americans tempered by war that was never less willing to "pay any price, to bear any burden, to meet any hardships, support any friend, oppose any foe to assure the survival and the success of liberty."

13. And we will always honor the memory of our great leader and our American hero General Eisenhower, who led us to victory all across the world.

14. As we meet here today, young Americans are risking their lives in liberty's defense. They are the latest link in a chain of sacrifice older than America itself. After all, if we meet the test of our times, it is because we drew inspiration from those who had gone before—including the giants of history who are enshrined on this Mall.

15. From Washington, who fathered America with his sword and ennobled it with his character, from Jefferson whose pen gave eloquent voice to our noblest aspirations, from Lincoln who preserved the union and struck the chains from our countrymen, and from Franklin Roosevelt who presided over a global coalition to rescue humanity from those who had put the soul itself in bondage.

16. Each of these presidents was a soldier of freedom. In the defining event of the 20th century, their cause became our cause. On distant fields and fathomless oceans, the skies over half the planet and in ten thousand communities on the home front we did far more than avenge Pearl Harbor. The citizen soldiers who answered liberty's call fought not for territory, but for justice. Not for plunder, but to liberate enslaved peoples around the world.

17. In contending for democracy abroad, we learned painful lessons about our own democracy. For us, the Second World War was in effect a second American revolution. The war invited women into the workforce; it exposed the injustices to African-Americans, Hispanics, Japanese-Americans, and others who demonstrated yet again that war is an equal opportunity employer.

18. What we learned in foreign fields of battle we applied in postwar America. As a result our democracy, though imperfect, is more nearly perfect than in the days of Washington, Lincoln, Roosevelt.

19. That's what makes America forever a work in progress. A land that has never become, but is always in the act of becoming.

20. And that's why the armies of democracy have earned a permanent place on this sacred ground.

    It is only fitting when this memorial was opened to the public about a month ago the very first visitors were school children.

21. For them, our war is ancient history and those who fought it are slightly ancient themselves, yet in the end they are the ones for whom we built this shrine. And to whom we now hand the baton in the unending relay of human possibility. Certainly the heroes represented by the 4,000 gold stars on the freedom wall need no monument to

commemorate their sacrifice. They are known to God and to their fellow soldiers who will mourn their passing until the day of our own.

22. In their name we dedicate this place of meditation. And it is in their memory that I ask you to stand, if possible, and join me in a moment of silent tribute to remind us all that in some time in our life we have or may be called upon to make a sacrifice for our country to preserve liberty and freedom. God bless America.

22. Senator Dole again uses another lofty metaphor to describe the memorial as a "place of meditation."

## summary »

In this chapter we have considered speeches for special occasions. The tribute recognizes distinguished careers and contributions of people either living or dead. Speeches of presentation honor the accomplishments of individuals, and acceptance speeches are given by individuals who receive honors and awards.

Dedication speeches memorialize the completion of national or community projects, welcoming speeches extend greetings to new or returning members of organizations, and speeches of introduction acquaint audiences with speakers or lecturers.

Keynote speeches are thematic presentations given at the beginning of major conferences or conventions; nominating speeches present the names of individuals for possible election to an office; farewell speeches are given on the occasion of retirements, resignations, or other changes in status and position; victory speeches are presented by individuals who have won significant contests after hard-fought battles or competitions; and commencement speeches honor candidates for attaining degrees.

The after-dinner speech is designed to entertain, and toasts are presented to honor individuals at ceremonial occasions.

## SKILL BUILDERS »

1. Using InfoTrac College Edition or your library database, search in Vital Speeches of the Day or in another credible source to find a special-occasion speech. Present a report describing the following:
   a. Who was the speaker and what type of special-occasion speech did the speaker present?
   b. Describe the date, purpose, and setting of the occasion.
   c. Describe how closely the speaker followed the guidelines presented in this chapter.
   d. View a copy of the speech on DVD streaming video or videotape (if available) and describe the positive aspects of the speech and areas you think could be improved.
2. Divide into teams of two in your speech class and create presentation and acceptance speeches using the guidelines discussed in this chapter.
   a. State the purpose, setting, and occasion of the speech.
   b. Team member A delivers a 2- to 3-minute speech of presentation and team member B makes a 2- to 3-minute acceptance speech.
   c. Do the assignment again, switching roles and delivering speeches for another occasion.

# BUILDING A
# SPEECH ONLINE »

Now that you've read Chapter 18, use your online Resource Center for Building a Speech for quick access to the electronic study resources that accompany this text. You can access your Resource Center at http://academic.cengage.com/login, using the access code that came with your book or that you bought online at http://www. iChapters.com. Your Resource Center gives you access to Interactive Video Activities, the book's companion website, Speech Builder Express 3.0, InfoTrac College Edition, and study aids, including a digital glossary and review quizzes.

© Purestock/Jupiter Images

# 19

# chapter

# SPEAKING IN GROUPS

After reading and studying this chapter, you should be able to

1. Define and describe the characteristics of small groups
2. Describe the development of a small group
3. Explain how small groups solve problems
4. Identify and develop three types of discussion questions
5. Identify group-centered behavior
6. Describe negative, self-centered behaviors
7. Recognize and describe positive leadership behavior
8. Understand special discussion formats

*We have to face the fact that either all of us are going to die together or we are going to learn to live together, and if we are to live together we have to talk.*

—Eleanor Roosevelt

Joanne was frustrated at work. Her management team never seemed to accomplish their goals and they always fell behind schedule. There was one problem after another. Some workers would show up late or call in sick. Others would spend time making personal phone calls. Some employees would take long lunch breaks or spend too much time at the company gym. Tasks were often sent back for revision or overhaul. Joanne would complain to her boss, who was friendly and understanding but never seemed to take any action. She would speak to some of her coworkers about the problem but they would often shrug their shoulders and walk away. Joanne was so discouraged at times she thought about quitting, but as a single parent, she needed the paycheck.

Have you ever been a part of a group like this? It could be a job, a church committee, or a Little League board of directors. The frustrations that are associated with membership in unproductive groups are sometimes inevitable. These situations don't need to occur, however. When you know how a group develops, operates, and solves problems you can avoid some of the difficulties that Joanne encountered.

This chapter describes the characteristics and development of small groups, types of discussion questions, and ways to solve problems. It also includes guidelines for successful group participation and leadership. In addition, the chapter presents information concerning special discussion formats.

## characteristics of small groups

Think of the number of small groups to which you belong. You may be a participant in a campus club or association, a leader of an advertising committee at work, or a member of a bowling league. You may have joined these diverse groups for different reasons: to develop friendships, to get a job accomplished quickly, or simply to relax. The groups may differ, but they have several similar characteristics: Each has a shared goal, group interactions, a number of members meeting over a specified period of time, and a leader.[1]

### SHARED GOALS

Groups have goals that bring individuals together. Researchers refer to this quality as **cohesiveness**—that is, the unifying element, common purpose, or mutual feelings of members. Individuals belonging to a church have similar beliefs; employees in an assembly plant share production quotas. Small groups can be classified into types based upon general goals.[2]

**Task groups** emphasize the completion of objectives or implementation of solutions. Employers form search committees to review applicants, conduct interviews, and recommend candidates for positions. Baseball teams develop athletes to play specialized positions in the effort to win games. Civic groups organize membership, nominating, entertainment, or fund-raising committees, each with a different objective. As a member of a college class, you have the task of completing certain specific course requirements for a number of credit hours.

**Encounter groups** contribute to interpersonal learning and to insight. Couples go away for weekend encounters to develop greater sensitivity and to improve communication. Companies sponsor retreats for employees, managers, or executives to increase self-understanding and awareness of others. Support and therapy groups such as Parents Without Partners, Victims of Child Abuse, or Alcoholics Anonymous provide a caring environment for individuals with similar experiences. Colleges and universities sponsor retreats for student leaders to identify leadership strengths and weaknesses.

**Social groups** help members to establish friendships and personal relationships. If you go to the park for a picnic with a few friends or invite a roommate to a party, you are participating in a group to fulfill social needs. A social group can be an informal gathering like the "lunch bunch" at work or a more structured arrangement like the Tuesday night poker game.

338

In a successful group, members share tasks, maintain dynamic interactions, and work together to achieve common goals.

## GROUP INTERACTION

Groups usually require interaction among members to accomplish goals. Imagine construction workers trying to complete a building without speaking or a football team attempting a touchdown without using signals or physical contact. Communication in groups is dynamic: It is continually active, steadily growing, and constantly changing. To maintain the dynamic energy of a group, members need personal contact with one another.

## SIZE

A small group consists of from three to fifteen members. Six to eight individuals often make an effective discussion—there are enough members for lively interaction, yet communication does not require limitation because of too many participants. Large groups are frequently divided into smaller work units of five or more members so that business can be conducted more easily and efficiently. The 535-member U.S. Congress, for example, conducts most of its business in small committees and subcommittees.

## TIME PERIOD

To make progress toward an objective, a group must meet over a period of time. A schedule allows a group to develop cohesiveness and to explore issues systematically. Intervals between meetings are sometimes as valuable as the meetings themselves. Members have time to process ideas and to bring fresh insights to the next discussion. An education committee, for example, would need to schedule a variety of meetings in order to design a new computer graphics curriculum. Members would come together to share preliminary ideas and to assign tasks; the group would then schedule future meetings to assess data, to formulate alternatives, and finally to write the curriculum.

## LEADERSHIP

Small groups usually require leaders to manage or to regulate discussion. In business, industry, or government, formal leaders with specific responsibilities are appointed or elected by organization members. A building foreman, a school principal, a club president, or a union negotiator are good examples of officially appointed or elected formal leaders. In groups without designated leaders, individuals with strong personality characteristics or competent management skills often become informal leaders. Leaderless gatherings such as protests, support groups, ad hoc committees, or social groups are often influenced by powerful individuals who gradually emerge as leaders during the course of group discussions.

# development of small groups

Imagine that you were elected for a 1-year term as a sophomore delegate to the student government association (SGA) at your university. You begin meeting in September, and you must get to know SGA officers and delegates from all the other classes and organizations for the first time. You convene in September and continue meeting once or twice a month for 9 months of the school year. Your group members will have ups and downs as they meet together, make decisions, and attempt to implement actions over a period of months.

Small groups like your student government organization actually have life cycles as they begin to work, attempt to solve problems, and conclude. Researchers have discovered that when small groups begin to meet, they go through several stages of development and change. Bruce W. Tuckman, a professor in the College of Education at Ohio State University, studied groups extensively and determined that small groups go through four stages of development. Tuckman coined the following terms for these stages: forming, storming, norming, and performing.[3]

## FORMING

The **forming** stage of development identifies the early phases of group meetings, when group members are in the process of orienting themselves to each other and to the task at hand. Group members are unsure of each other and try to determine what behavior is acceptable. In this stage of development, you might hear members use tentative language, including questions such as "Can you help me?" "Is this OK?" or "What are we supposed to do?" The group looks for guidance, support, and reinforcement. They are new to each other and the task, and they need to set ground rules.

## STORMING

The **storming** stage is characterized by interpersonal conflict. The group has been meeting for awhile, and the gloves are now off. There is often infighting, emotional reactions among members, lack of cohesiveness, and resistance to authority. Some members who dislike the idiosyncrasies of fellow participants even settle into subgroups or cliques. You might hear statements such as "I don't agree with you at all," "I didn't come here to do that," or "I think this whole thing has been a waste of time." Language usage is focused around the words *I* and *me,* and expressions of individuality are common. It is an uncomfortable, confrontational stage of group development.

## NORMING

In the **norming** stage, the group has worked through many of the conflicts of the storming phase and has now become more cohesive. Members are more open and willing to accept each other's peculiarities. The group avoids interpersonal conflicts and begins to act on ideas proposed by group members. You might hear "How do you feel about that?" or

"Let's take a look at your solution." Members tend to be in harmony and are now able to function as a group.

## PERFORMING

The fourth stage, **performing,** is characterized by insight and action. Members wish to complete tasks they were given and adopt constructive behavior to implement them. In this stage you might hear statements such as "Here are the solutions we need to address," "Let's go with this solution," or "Let's form subcommittees to come up with a plan." Notice that the statements use *we* and *us* language rather than *I* and *me* words. The various factions and diverse personalities of the group actually come together in order to get the task accomplished.

## solving problems in groups

It is helpful for a group to select a specific issue in order to clearly identify a problem. Once the issue has been chosen, the process of problem solving can begin.

## QUESTIONS FOR DISCUSSION

Issues for group discussions are usually phrased as **discussion questions.** Open-ended questions tend to promote better discussions than do yes-no alternatives. For example, the issue "Should we increase tuition to solve financial problems at the university?" limits discussion because it offers only two alternatives. The question does not give members the freedom to analyze the complexities of the problem or to explore a wide range of solutions. A more effective question would be "What can be done to solve the financial problems at the university?" Discussion issues can be phrased as questions of fact, value, or policy.

### Questions of Fact

Questions of *fact* explore issues where information is either unknown or disputed. For instance, the purpose of the 9/11 Commission was to determine "What could have been done to prevent the terrorist attacks of September 11?" When President John F. Kennedy was assassinated, the Warren Commission was established to search for answers to the question "Who was responsible for the assassination of the president?" Questions of fact require group members to research and analyze evidence in the effort to draw conclusions.

### Questions of Value

Questions of *value* require discussion members to use personal judgments or feelings to evaluate issues. Words such as *effective, fair, harmful,* or *beneficial* are often used in the phrasing of value questions. A group might discuss the issue "Have government bailouts of large corporations been effective?" or "Would pass-fail grading be more equitable than the current system?" The difficulty with these issues is that they often depend on personal opinions more than on evidence and research. Although questions of value may be useful topics for encounter groups, where personal feelings are important, these issues often have no real solution and simply generate circular discussions of members' views. Groups that want to gather facts to form conclusions or develop specific solutions to problems should avoid questions of value.

### Questions of Policy

Questions of *policy* stimulate discussion about solutions or future actions. Issues such as "How should America respond to nations and dictators it dislikes in a world filled with terrorism?" or "What should be done to reduce America's dependence on foreign oil?" would be effective problems for policy discussions. Questions of policy require research, analysis of facts, and discussion of possible solutions for implementation. The word *should* is frequently included in the phrasing of policy issues.

## DEVELOPING A PROBLEM-SOLVING AGENDA

To discuss a problem, a group must have an **agenda,** or an orderly list of topics the meeting will cover. One of the most effective ways to organize an agenda is to use a process known as "reflective thinking," developed in 1910 by educator John Dewey in *How We Think.*[4] Through the years, several researchers have adapted Dewey's ideas more comprehensively to the discussion process.[5] As an example of how to develop a systematic approach in a group discussion, we will consider an eight-point problem-solving plan similar to that described by Larry L. Barker and others in *Groups in Process.*[6] We'll use your student government association as the example.

### Define the Problem

Groups should clearly understand all elements of an issue under consideration. Members may need to define ambiguous terms and provide explanations of key phrases found in the discussion question. For example, because of the rapid deterioration of the student center building on your campus, your SGA group identifies the problem with this question: "What can be done to improve the appearance of the campus student center building?" The words "improve the appearance" then need to be more specifically defined. Definitions could range from "cosmetic change" and "space reorganization and redistribution" to "substantive change."

### Narrow the Problem

As is the case with speech topics, problems for discussion must be sufficiently limited. In narrowing topics, members should consider the needs of the group as well as the length of time available for discussion. The topic "What can be done to improve the appearance of the campus student center building?" is a broad one that might require discussion for a period of several months. Depending on how phrases are defined, the issue could involve enormous expenditures of money and amounts of time that the SGA does not have. One way to limit the problem would be to develop subcategories that could be managed more efficiently:

- Cafeteria and eateries need new tables and chairs.
- Cafeteria needs new appliances.
- Student lounges need new furniture and carpeting.
- Sidewalks and steps need renovation and repair.
- Outside of building needs beautification.

The group could select the subtopics that were most important to their analysis, and gauge their discussion according to time and financial limitations. Because your SGA members meet once a month for only two semesters of the academic year, they may not be able to solve all five areas of their identified problem. They may need to select one or two areas that can be resolved during the time of their 1-year elected terms. Other organizations, such as business or governmental groups that meet more often, might be able to handle many more subcategories of an issue.

## Analyze the Issue

The next step in problem solving is to research and analyze the issue. Let's say that the SGA has decided to address the needs of the cafeteria as the subtopic of their question "What can be done to improve the appearance of the campus student center building?" Members could divide the research responsibilities according to expertise or personal interest. A business major could research the cost of new appliances and cafeteria furniture. A sociology major might explore the types of tables and chairs available for people with differing needs of height, weight, and disability. An international student might research the specific eating requirements of a diverse student population. A nursing major might investigate the types of appliances and furniture that meet health and sanitation standards. A law student could analyze the legal requirements, permits, and guidelines with which cafeteria appliances must comply. If members conduct thorough research into the problem, they will have the tools necessary to discuss the complexities of the issue and to develop workable solutions.

## Set Up Criteria

Once the problem has been analyzed, the group should develop criteria or guidelines for a workable solution. This phase of problem solving keeps a discussion on track and helps a group to focus on successful results. When analyzing the narrowed topic of improvements to the cafeteria, the SGA might set up the following criteria:

1. Equipment should be cost-effective.
2. Equipment should meet needs of a diverse student body.
3. Equipment should meet all health, legal, and permit requirements.
4. Equipment acquisition, purchase, and installation should be completed 1 month before the academic year ends.

## Suggest Solutions

Next, the group develops various potential solutions from individual research, through spontaneous discussion, and/or as a result of brainstorming techniques. SGA members discussing the purchase of new cafeteria equipment might have obtained bids from several companies estimating costs. Some members might have contributed new suggestions during the discussion process or thought of different alternatives as members jotted down ideas that came to mind.

## Apply Criteria to Solutions

Once a group has selected alternatives, members can apply the predetermined criteria to identify the most desirable solution. This step in problem solving enables a group to eliminate solutions that are not workable. Notice how the four criteria listed earlier can be applied to select a company to supply cafeteria equipment.

| | **Alternative Solutions** | **Application of Criteria** |
|---|---|---|
| Company A | Supplies standard kitchen and furniture package | *Violates 2:* <br> Does not supply wok or other diverse kitchen equipment; furniture does not meet diverse student needs. |
| Company B | Supplies custom-made furniture and appliances | *Violates 1 and 4:* <br> Equipment is too expensive; timeline is too long. |

*(continued)*

| | Alternative Solutions | Application of Criteria |
|---|---|---|
| Company C | Supplies standard industrial restaurant equipment | *Violates 2 and 3:* Equipment does not meet diverse student needs; exceeds space requirements of the permit. |
| Company D | Well-known college and university appliance and furniture supplier | *Meets criteria 1–4:* Costs, diversity, permits, and timelines are satisfactory. |

### Implement the Selected Solution

When group members make a final choice, their job is not complete until they actually implement the solution. In well-organized groups, members develop a plan of action and divide the responsibilities. To implement the plan for cafeteria equipment, for instance, some SGA members might contact the company to sign contracts, others might form a subcommittee to select furniture colors, and some could form another subcommittee to raise funds.

### Monitor the Success of the Solution

A solution needs to be monitored to determine its degree of success. Is the solution working as intended? Are there problems with any aspect of the plan? Does the group need to modify the solution or reevaluate its decision in view of new information? A group might need to conduct interviews or circulate questionnaires to examine how well the solution is working. After initial observations, for example, SGA members might discover that some of the tables and chairs were unstable. The group could either withhold payment until satisfactory modifications were made or reject the contract entirely and choose another company. Group members might also decide to evaluate the decision by circulating a survey asking students about the comfort, quality, and durability of the furniture and the quality of the food.

### A Sample Agenda

Here is a sample agenda to demonstrate how problem solving is applied in a group meeting. Notice that the agenda clearly identifies the time, date, and place of the meeting as well as the supporting documents included.

**Special Business Meeting of the Student Government Association**
Monday, September 28, 2009
Room 201, Student Center Building
2:00–4:00 p.m.

**Topic:** To discuss the need for physical improvements to the Student Center Building

I. Introduce new members
II. Approve minutes of 9/14/09
III. Introduce topics
    A. Decision-making process
    B. Scope of SGA responsibility
    C. Concerns of SGA delegates
IV. Discuss scope of problem
    A. Areas of building needing improvement—physical plant superintendent
    B. Budget available to cover costs—treasurer's report

C. Deadlines for decisions, implementation—dean of administration
D. Other related issues
V. Identify SGA decisions and recommendations
VI. Make committee and subcommittee assignments
   A. Subcommittee researching student needs
   B. Subcommittee researching comparative costs of projects
   C. Subcommittee determining feasibility of meeting deadlines
VII. Schedule next meeting and adjourn

Documents enclosed:

1. Agenda
2. Minutes of 9/14/2009

Keep in mind that the committee discussions are an ongoing process: Group members have made a preliminary decision to set up three subcommittees to conduct further research. But the SGA will need to conduct further research and to meet again in order to make future decisions. SGA members cannot select or even monitor a solution at this stage, because they are in the early stages of problem solving.

## participating in groups

Effective participation is vitally important to the success of a discussion and to the efficient completion of a task. Group members sometimes believe that they possess little power within an organization and that most of the authority remains with the leader. Such a view is usually mistaken. Although leaders can exercise influence, success within a group is often determined by the participants' skill and expertise. One individual can exert a powerful influence to move a group toward the completion of a task or to inhibit the decision-making process.

## GROUP-CENTERED BEHAVIOR

An effective discussion requires group-centered behavior: Members need to cooperate with one another and share responsibility to help the group work efficiently toward solution. Here are six group-centered behaviors that can contribute to positive decision making.[7]

### Be an Active Observer

An effective participant carefully observes a group by listening attentively and watching intently. When you are in a group situation, observe how members approach problems, how frequently they contribute to the discussion, or how effectively they perform tasks. Ask yourself these questions: Is there a difference between what members say and do? Is the group analyzing all aspects of the problem? Is the group making progress toward stated goals? Are there any contributions I can make that can move the group more effectively toward solutions? Active observation can help you to sense the right moment to make an appropriate contribution. For example, if you were to see a heated conflict developing between two group members, you might cool the argument with the suggestion "We can't solve all these problems at once." When discussion is at an impasse, you might recommend that members return to the issue later or introduce a new idea to rekindle discussion. If you have listened actively, you might have the opportunity to remind participants of previous decisions that have been forgotten.

### Support Group Procedure

Discussion groups usually have a wide variety of tasks for members to perform. As an active participant, you should be willing to take on your fair share of assignments. You might be asked to chair a subcommittee; you might be placed in charge of duplicating and circulating committee pamphlets, questionnaires, or supporting materials; the group leader might even request your assistance in preparing the agenda or contacting fellow members. One job participants frequently dislike is recording minutes of committee conversations and decisions. Keeping accurate records is important, however, especially in formal organizations where documentation of past committee actions is required. If a group has no assigned secretary, it is helpful to rotate this important responsibility among group members. As a participant, you should view tasks as opportunities to help the group complete its goals.

### Be Reliable

If groups are to function smoothly, members must perform tasks efficiently and on time. Groups are easily sabotaged by irresponsible members who are chronically late, who fail to complete assigned tasks, or who manage assignments carelessly. As a group member, take your responsibilities seriously. Be on time for group meetings, and complete duties conscientiously. Take care of any arrangements that may be required for your portion of a meeting: Do necessary research, notify invited guests of the time and place of the meeting, and have all handouts or other paperwork ready for circulation. Recognize that irresponsibility wastes everyone's time and energy within a group.

### Be Willing to Compromise

Group participation is not a game of winners and losers; an effective group experience should exhibit a healthy give-and-take among members. When you are a part of a discussion, you must be willing to hear other points of view and accept changes to some of your ideas and proposals. You are not expected to compromise your personal beliefs or values, but you should be able to alter your thinking if other suggestions prove to be more workable. Compromising is often viewed as watered-down or weak-willed decision making. But if a group is open to all the facts and genuinely seeks the best alternative, group members will often need to make compromises and modifications before coming to final decisions.

### Be Courteous and Respectful

Groups cannot function effectively when members are at odds. Participants who constantly interrupt one another, launch personal attacks, or exhibit insensitivity are engaging in disrespectful behavior that could eventually lead to the destruction of the group. Although members don't need to like one another in order to accomplish group objectives, they must demonstrate respect and common courtesy. When another member is talking, give your full attention. Wait until the individual is finished before you contribute an idea or make a suggestion. Respect the background, experience, and expertise of others, and recognize that everyone does not have the same perspective as yours. Be sensitive to those group members who speak English as a second language; they may need help in understanding difficult terms or colloquial expressions. Respect individual differences, and do not discriminate on the basis of appearance, sexual orientation, gender, race, or religion. Women should not be required to bring coffee or perform secretarial duties because they are female any more than men should be assigned leadership roles or asked to empty the trash simply because they are male. Individuals should not separate or isolate themselves according to race or gender, but place themselves in seating arrangements that will assist and facilitate group procedures and tasks. Recognize that members with special needs, including individuals in wheelchairs or those who are hearing impaired, may require specific arrangements such as accessibility to ramps or proximity to interpreters. Be patient with irrelevancies or inappropriate remarks. Avoid using tactics such as personal attacks or name-calling, which can stimulate anger. Don't ridicule the ideas of members or jump to conclusions about their decision-making abilities. Know when to exercise silence, and let the leader handle difficulties.

### Encourage and Energize Members

Groups must work together to solve problems. If an outfielder drops a fly ball, the second baseman doesn't laugh at the error; instead, the player tries to help the team by making a face-saving play. When members must complete difficult tasks, give your assistance or make helpful suggestions. Show encouragement to participants who perform competently. Compliment a member by saying, "Your idea is a good one—maybe we can use it as a basis for the solution." This type of support builds group cohesiveness and cooperation and helps to energize members to complete assignments. Participation is not a contest of wills: Individuals must be able to subordinate personal egos for the overall benefit of the group.

## SELF-CENTERED BEHAVIOR

Behavior that inhibits discussion in a group is often self-centered. A *self-centered* member uses the group to achieve personal goals and demonstrates a lack of interest in group needs or objectives. Self-centered conduct reroutes discussion and often stops problem solving. In 1948, Kenneth D. Benne and Paul Sheats studied groups extensively to determine some of the positive and negative characteristics exhibited by members within small groups. Here is a list of eight negative group behaviors, based on research by Benne and Sheats:[8]

| Negative Self-Centered Behaviors | | Example |
|---|---|---|
| Attacking | Displaying aggressive behavior toward group members by making hostile comments (telling nasty jokes or putting down individuals), showing envy, or expressing disapproval. | "You're dead wrong—you're *dead* wrong. Where did you go to school, anyway?" |
| Blocking | Behavior that delays the decision-making process, such as being unreasonable or negative, taking positions in opposition to the group (bringing up issues already decided or postponing issues members want to discuss), or generally failing to cooperate. | "I think we should table the motion—we've got a lot more important things to do than to spend our time talking about trivia like this." |
| Boasting | Attempting to impress group members and to maintain a central position in the group by bragging about professional expertise, personal qualifications, or past accomplishments. | "The company president always calls upon me when he needs a creative idea. . . . In fact, I had lunch with him yesterday and he thought my proposal was an excellent solution." |

*(continued)*

| Negative Self-Centered Behaviors | | Example |
|---|---|---|
| Clowning | Exhibiting a lack of involvement in the group by telling inappropriate jokes, expressing cynicism, advocating recreational objectives, or simply "goofing off." | "Why don't we have our next meeting in a bar?" |
| Confessing | Using the group as an encounter or therapy session to fulfill personal needs by relating irrelevant stories, inappropriate personal examples, or boring anecdotes. | "That reminds me of the time my husband and I were having communication problems, and we tried to work them out but. . . ." |
| Dominating | Attempting to display self-importance and superiority by monopolizing or manipulating group discussions. | "This problem should be no surprise to anyone who has listened carefully to my past statements—I have repeatedly predicted this situation." |
| Pleading | Trying to gain constant sympathy for help or support from group members by expressing insecurity or inadequacy. | "I've never been in charge of a subcommittee before—it seems almost overwhelming. Why don't you ask Tomika?—she's more experienced." |
| Promoting special interests | Behavior that seeks to manipulate a group based upon the needs, prejudices, or interests of one member. | "I never function before 11 a.m. and I can't meet after 2:30 because of a dentist appointment. Could we plan a lunch meeting instead?" |

## leadership in small groups

In order to be an effective leader, one needs to understand some of the theories of small group management and adopt positive leadership behaviors.

## LEADERSHIP THEORIES

There are many theories concerning group leadership. Some researchers believe that leaders possess certain powerful **traits** such as physical appearance, speaking ability, or behavior that determine leadership.[9] The trait approach suggests that leaders do not learn or acquire these skills, but are born with natural abilities. It can be argued, for example, that Abraham Lincoln, Winston Churchill, Franklin Roosevelt, Martin Luther King, and Mother Teresa possessed natural leadership abilities.

Another theory suggests that power and authority are significant factors in leadership.[10] Members of a group will respond to a leader's position, expertise, or job title—"chief executive officer," "lieutenant," "heart specialist," "committee chair," "florist," "builder," or "tax accountant." According to this theory, members opposing a decision might be persuaded to comply with an argument such as "You may not agree, but this proposal is what the president wants."

In the 1930s, Kurt Lewin, Ronald Lippitt, and Ralph K. White studied the reactions of 10-year-old boys to three different leadership behaviors over a 3-month period. This research, now classic in the field, identified three leadership styles: autocratic, democratic, and laissez-faire.[11] The **autocratic** leader acted as the chief decision maker of the group, giving orders and commands to group members. **Democratic** leaders functioned more as coordinators, promoting discussion and stimulating group decision making. The **laissez-faire** style was a leaderless group where members themselves took care of managerial or administrative responsibilities. In this study, researchers found that members of democratic groups experienced the greatest degree of satisfaction with leaders and group outcomes, while autocratic group members were least satisfied with leadership and group achievements. Members of leaderless groups were pleased with mutual associations and friendships acquired within groups, but participants felt that little was accomplished.

Research updating the Lewin study combines leadership style and personality. Investigators suggest that authoritarian personalities are more "object oriented," while democratic personalities tend to be more "people oriented."[12]

Today, some researchers view effective leadership in terms of adaptability. Arbitrary leadership styles or predetermined traits may not be appropriate in many group situations. Leaders may need to adopt a variety of approaches to meet group needs and to help members accomplish organizational tasks.[13]

## POSITIVE LEADERSHIP BEHAVIORS

Most of us will be leaders at some time in our lives, either by choice or by necessity. Whether you are a PTA president, a manager, a self-employed professional, a committee chair, or an executor of a will, you need to know some of the skills that contribute to effective leadership. In this section, we examine four positive leadership behaviors that are necessary for successful group management.

### Be Prepared

A leader cannot simply appear and improvise an agenda for a group meeting; effective leadership requires careful advance planning. A leader must choose an appropriate location, prepare an agenda, and anticipate potential problems.

**Choose an Appropriate Location.** Know the size of the meeting area; don't try to fit a large group into a tiny cubicle or a small group into a huge auditorium. Understand the characteristics of the room, and ask yourself these questions: Are there tables for discussion, are there enough chairs for participants, and can all members see one another easily? Will participants need small tables, whiteboards, or flipcharts? Are screens, electrical outlets, data projectors, connecting cables, and other equipment available to support laptop computers for PowerPoint or other software presentations? Do invited guests have any special room requirements? Is the meeting located near noisy traffic areas, or can the room be closed for privacy? Is the area flexible enough to accommodate any rearrangement that may be necessary during the meeting? Do you have a telephone or Blackberry for messages, and is a fax machine, computer, or DVD/CD recorder available to document or transmit committee discussions and actions? Make any arrangements required for scheduling the room. Be sure that the room will be unlocked and set up for the discussion on the day of the meeting.

**Circulate an Agenda.** As a leader you will need to prepare an agenda of the major topics to be covered during a meeting. Contact group participants to determine topics included in their presentations, and remind invited experts of their meeting obligations. Have the agenda and all supporting documents duplicated and circulated to the group well in advance of the meeting, so that participants are prepared for the discussion and can notify you if changes are necessary. Be certain that the agenda clearly identifies the date, time, and place of the meeting. If any guests may be unfamiliar with the location, include clear directions to the meeting place.

**Anticipate Potential Problems.** If you have smokers as well as nonsmokers in the group, be sure that everyone understands the policies governing smoking in the building where meetings are conducted. If there are no policies or regulations, establish clear guidelines to alleviate conflicts. To stimulate a positive discussion, it may be helpful to place shy members near more talkative participants or to separate members who constantly argue. Members with disabilities or special needs may require assistance with wheelchairs, interpreters, or readers. You may also need to handle potentially disruptive members by assigning specific tasks to keep them occupied. As a leader, you should be in contact with members a day or two before the meeting to determine if there are significant problems that could affect discussion and alter planning: Members with schedule conflicts might need to arrive late or leave early; members with extreme personal emergencies may ask to be excused or replaced; members having complicated group assignments may need extended deadlines; members discovering additional information may request further group discussion. Knowledge of potential problems and awareness of special circumstances can help you manage a discussion smoothly.

### Keep to Time Limits

Meetings should start and end on schedule. Tardiness not only wastes everyone's time but also conveys disorganization and contributes to member hostility. Individuals who are angry because a meeting began 25 minutes late will not be in a constructive mood for decision making. Leaders should be prompt and expect members to be on time. If a meeting is scheduled to end at a specific time, the leader should do everything possible to close off discussion. When a meeting drags beyond the closing time, members convey negative feedback by stacking papers into neat piles, watching the clock, or squirming uncomfortably. A leader should be sensitive enough to realize that little will be accomplished by keeping participants overtime. Keeping to schedules can increase the satisfaction of group members and contribute to efficient problem solving.

### Be Organized

Begin the meeting by announcing any changes in the published agenda. Remember that agendas are not fixed in stone; they contain topic outlines designed to serve group needs. A leader who is willing to be flexible and make a few changes builds cohesiveness and improves the climate for decision making. A brief procedural comment can convey sensitivity to individuals: "We'll consider item 3 on the agenda first—Julie is here from the daycare center. Because she has to leave to supervise the children, it would help her if we could deal with daycare issues first. Do you have any objections?"

Guide group members skillfully through the agenda. If the agenda is long, set time limits for specific items so that the group will cover all topics efficiently. If issues remain unresolved, establish additional subcommittees or work units to complete analysis and problem solving.

Help members seek information and analyze problems. Promote decision making by asking questions or interjecting thoughts, such as "Has that problem occurred before?" or "Maybe we need to distribute a questionnaire." Move members toward solution of issues by asking for alternatives and requesting data to verify solutions—"Has this solution been successful in other places?" Work for consensus on issues. Groups don't need to vote on everything; constant hand-raising or balloting can disrupt the flow of discussion. Reserve formal votes for final decisions or solutions.

Communicate effectively when you manage a discussion. Identify agenda topics clearly. Refer to exhibits, page numbers, or supporting documents distinctly so that members can easily follow what is being discussed. Be open to procedural questions or comments from members; let participants know that you want them to move forward toward solutions.

At the end of the meeting, clarify group tasks, summarize individual goals, and define future objectives. Set the time and place of the next meeting. Make sure the group feels a sense of accomplishment with the discussion, commitment to goals, and awareness of future responsibilities.

### Know When to Intervene

No theory or rule can tell you the exact moment you should do or say something as a leader of a group. It often takes many leadership experiences for an individual to develop a group "sense" or intuition regarding appropriate leadership behavior. There are, however, several ways a leader can intervene constructively during a group discussion. A good leader can resolve conflicts, provide emotional support, clarify and summarize, and demonstrate flexibility.

**Resolve Conflicts.** Conflicts are inevitable when group members are involved in the decision-making process. Participants can become fixed in their attitudes or take positions they feel the group must adopt. While disagreement can stimulate debate among participants, serious conflict can damage the survival and success of a group. The leader must handle major conflicts carefully to allow the group to complete its objectives. If a serious argument develops between two members or opposing forces, the leader should identify areas of common ground. If none exist, the leader can then restate each argument, identifying its relative strengths and weaknesses. When reviewing the conflicting positions, a leader should give equal time to each argument and avoid taking sides. Being fair will strengthen the leader's position; showing partiality will compromise and undermine the leader's effectiveness. If no agreement can be reached, the leader should define areas of progress, honestly acknowledge unresolved conflict, and move the discussion to other topics. Disputes can often be settled at a later time when emotions have cooled.[14]

**Provide Emotional Support.** There are occasions in a discussion when a leader must provide members with emotional support in order to maintain a positive climate for decision making. New members who are meeting with a well-established group for the first time may need reassurance and special courtesy to feel secure, comfortable, and less isolated. Group members may experience hurt feelings after engaging in disputes, suffer humiliation after losing arguments, or need encouragement when not participating. A comment such as "That's an excellent idea—but it may work better in a different situation" might help a member to save face in a discussion, or a statement like "That's a great idea—why don't you expand on it?" might encourage a member to participate more actively.

**Clarify and Summarize.** A good discussion is dynamic—there is a great deal of give-and-take. Although dynamism is a positive force in a discussion, a leader must occasionally summarize the comments of group members who relate incomplete information, make disjointed remarks, or draw vague conclusions. Summaries help members follow the discussion easily, keep the discussion from backtracking, and clarify group decisions. A good summary is brief and clear, providing an accurate synopsis of a participant's contribution or a group's decision. A leader who comments, "Devon, I think you're asking us to compare the data, is that right?" is diplomatically summing up Devon's remarks, while at the same time checking the accuracy of the comment with the member. If the leader is unable to comprehend the content of a member's remarks due to language, accent, or other cultural barrier, the leader should be careful not to embarrass or humiliate the individual. A considerate leader finds creative ways of clarifying a difficult contribution, such as obtaining a written outline, talking privately with the member during a meeting break, or asking for help from other members who are able to translate or summarize more easily.

**Demonstrate Flexibility.** A flexible and observant leader knows when to intervene and when to be silent. If a conversation gets offtrack, the leader should step in to check the irrelevancies. When a participant monopolizes the conversation, the leader should guide the discussion to other members. The leader needs to quiet the group clown who constantly engages in inappropriate humor or to gently reprimand the member who frequently interrupts others. Uncomfortable group silence may require the leader to activate discussion, while a hostile exchange may necessitate leader mediation. Not all situations, however, require intervention by the leader. A participant raising a point that seems irrelevant may, if allowed to continue, contribute important insights into an issue. A spontaneous joke related at the right moment can reduce tension and move an immobile conversation forward. Group silences can be necessary to help members think through ideas. A lively argument can be a productive force in solving a problem.

The style a leader adopts is often determined by the needs of the group as well as the requirements of the moment. Well-motivated participants who are experienced at discussion may require less intervention by the leader, while inexperienced members may require more guidance. A discussion that is moving along effectively may actually be impeded by an autocratic leader who tries to interject ideas or impose solutions. At the same time, members who are floundering may be frustrated with a democratic leader who provides little direction. During the life of a group, a combination of democratic, autocratic, and laissez-faire leadership styles may be necessary.

## THE DYSFUNCTIONAL GROUP

**Task:** Members of the personnel department are to write specifications for new offices in a new building complex.
**Leader:** Ana
**Group Members:** Juan, Lakesha, Min, Sarah
**Meeting Time:** 1:30 p.m.
**Place:** Conference Room 1

Members started drifting toward the conference room at about 1:40 p.m. Juan was the first to arrive; then came Ana, several minutes later. The members found the conference room already occupied with five people from graphics who were having a departmental meeting. Juan and Ana argued as they stood in the hall outside:

**Ana:** These people have stolen our meeting room. We'll just have to tell them to leave.

**Juan:** I already tried that, but they said they'd requested the room four weeks ago. They showed me the signed approval form. Did you screw up again, Ana?

**Ana:** Don't tell me I screwed up. You were the one who was supposed to take care of the form, weren't you?

**Juan:** I beg your pardon. That's never been my responsibility. I don't do forms, remember?

*(Lakesha enters)*

**Ana:** Hi, Lakesha. You're late again.

**Lakesha:** I'm really sorry. I had lunch downtown with a friend, and there was just too much traffic, and I couldn't make it back in time. I'm so very sorry. Why's everybody out in the hall?

**Juan:** Min or somebody messed up and forgot the sacred yellow form.

**Lakesha:** Well, why don't we meet in my office?

**Ana:** Oh gosh, your office is so teeny, there's only room for two people. Mine's so much more spacious and has a better view.

**Juan:** Yeah, the dumpster looks great when the sun is shining.

**Lakesha:** *(Ignoring Juan and insisting)* No, really, why don't we meet in my office? We can all crowd in. It's kinda cozy, I've got a coffee pot, and anyway I could use some company—I've had such a bad day. Please? *Please?*

**Ana:** Oh, all right. But there's only room for three chairs in Lakesha's office. What'll we do if Min and Sarah show up?

**Juan:** Don't worry, they won't show up. And if they do, they'll just have to stand. Serves 'em right for being late.

**Ana:** OK, let's go.

**Lakesha:** Shouldn't we leave a note or something on the door for Sarah and Min to let them know where we are?

**Ana:** Naw. We've waited long enough for them. They're late anyway so let them have to hunt a little to find us!

**Juan:** You're learning, Ana.

# THE FUNCTIONAL GROUP

**Task:** Members are to write specifications for their new graphics departmental offices in the new building complex.

**Leader:** Damian

**Group Members:** Suresh, Eduardo, Kyle, Tanya

**Meeting Time:** 1:30 p.m.

**Place:** Conference Room 1

Damian arrived about 1:15 p.m. to make sure the conference room was set up properly with enough chairs and work tables to accommodate group tasks. He placed folders at each member's table containing additional information needed for the meeting. Suresh and Eduardo arrived at 1:25. Tanya came in a couple minutes later and told Damian that she had received an e-mail from Kyle who said that he would be a few minutes late because of a child-care problem. The meeting began at 1:32 p.m.

**Damian:** Well, I'm glad everyone's going to be here today. Suresh, why don't we start with you, since you're the first item on the agenda. By the way, since it's after lunch, I brought dessert for everyone; so please, help yourself to the cookies in the middle of the table.

**Suresh:** Thanks. Gee, more calories. Everybody keeps bringing food. I'm going to have to go on a diet after these meetings are over! OK, I've got a lot of information that I want to pass around to each of you.

**Eduardo:** Do you need some help?

**Suresh:** Sure. That would be great. Thanks.

**Damian:** If you and maybe Tanya could distribute these spec sheets, then I'll circulate the rest of the documents. (*Kyle enters*) Hi, Kyle. Thanks for the message. We're just getting started. Suresh is passing around some documents from her research. Take some cookies.

**Kyle:** Thanks.

(*There is a knock on the door*)

**Tanya:** I'll get it. (*Answers the door to the conference room*) It's Juan from Personnel. He claims that their department has reserved this room for their meeting, and they want us to leave.

**Damian:** (*To Tanya*) Show Juan this yellow room confirmation form I have here in my folder. I reserved this room a month ago. Tell Juan that his group needs to send in a written request for the conference room in advance of the requested day. (*To Suresh*) Are you ready, Suresh?

**Suresh:** Yes. Does everyone have five spec sheets? All right, let's start with the first recommendation from our subcommittee.

# special discussion formats

There are a variety of special discussion groups, each with a different format and function. In this section we will consider focus groups, forums, panels, and symposiums as well as buzz groups and role-playing groups.[15]

## FOCUS GROUPS

**Focus groups** represent target populations that are assembled to test arguments, ideas, and products. Focus groups do not usually make formal presentations, but their members are brought together and often paid for their informal discussions and participation. Lawyers employ focus groups to test the strength of possible arguments they want to use to persuade jurors. They assemble a cross-section of four to six people who represent potential jurors and then listen to their discussions and reactions to "practice" arguments. Advertisers try out potential TV sales pitches to small groups of consumers to determine how effective their ad campaigns might be. TV news media such as CNN or ABC bring groups of voters together to listen and react to presidential debates or major presidential speeches. Comedians test jokes on invited audiences to find out if their humor is really funny. And businesses test new products on selected groups to determine if consumers would buy their products.

## THE SYMPOSIUM

The **symposium** is a highly structured group of about two to six experts who reveal their views and perspectives on some aspect of a problem. Participants deliver prepared speeches to an audience but do not discuss issues informally. A chairperson usually identifies the question, introduces each member, and explains how the meeting will proceed. Participants are usually seated at a table facing the audience while one member speaks from a lectern. An example of a symposium would be a convention program in which three renowned scientists report differing results from similar fusion experiments.

## THE PANEL

A **panel** is an informal discussion conducted by three to six individuals in front of an audience. One person acts as moderator, regulating participation and guiding the discussion through the problem-solving sequence. Panel members are often experts who speak from their own experience and knowledge. Participants do not deliver prepared speeches in a panel discussion; members make one point at a time, frequently interrupting each other and commenting upon ideas presented by other individuals. Panelists are often seated in a semicircle or a similar arrangement so that members can see one another during the discussion. Panels present issues and examine problems to inform and educate the audience. An example of a panel would be the nation's chief law enforcement officers considering America's war on terrorism.

## THE FORUM

A **forum** is a public discussion in which all members of an audience have the opportunity to ask questions, make statements, or deliver speeches about issues. Because so many individuals are involved, a leader is needed to set the ground rules for the discussion and

In a panel discussion, participants exchange ideas, analyze issues, and explore solutions to problems with the guidance of a leader or moderator.

© AP Photo

to regulate participation. The seating should be arranged so that all audience members can see everyone easily. The Senate and House of Representatives function as forums. In legislative forums, participation is guided by a speaker or president who operates according to strict rules of parliamentary procedure. In more informal town meetings or council hearings, moderators might allocate specific time limits for individual contributions. Forums are often used in combination with other formats such as symposium-forums or panel-forums. When panelists have completed discussion or symposium participants have presented speeches, the audience becomes involved in the discussion.

## BUZZ GROUPS

**Buzz groups** are often used in large organizations to involve many people in the decision-making process. Individuals are divided into small units or "buzz groups" of three to eight members. These smaller groups are then given specific tasks to accomplish or issues to examine within a time limit. Groups then report the results of their discussions to the larger organization through elected or appointed leaders. For example, a company could ask its 200 employees to discuss the topic "What can be done to improve productivity?" and divide into 25 groups of 8 individuals each. Using this method, a large number of ideas could be generated by many people in a short time.

## ROLE-PLAYING GROUPS

In **role-playing**, group members assume characters or personalities to portray relationships and interactions among individuals. Members act out conflicts between parents and children, criminals and victims, or supervisors and employees to reveal dilemmas and to portray inner turmoil. Role-playing experiences are used effectively in encounter groups to stimulate discussion and to help members with decision making and problem solving.

## summary »

Small groups are characterized by shared goals, several individuals engaged in face-to-face interactions over a period of time, and a leader. Types of groups include task, encounter, and social groups. Issues for discussion are phrased as questions of fact, value, or policy. Groups go through different stages of change and development during the life of the group. Problem solving involves choosing a systematic agenda based upon John Dewey's method of "reflective thinking." When involved in group discussions, members should adopt group-centered behavior and avoid negative, self-centered conduct. Although there are many leadership theories, recent research emphasizes the need for leaders to demonstrate flexibility in managing a group. Special discussion formats include the focus group, panel, symposium, forum, buzz groups, and role-playing grous.[16]

## SKILL BUILDERS »

1. Divide into a small group of at least four members in your speech class. Choose a topic from current events or contemporary issues (see the suggested topics in the back of the text). Meet and communicate with your group several times outside of class to complete the following assignment:
   a. Phrase the issue as one of the three discussion questions.
   b. Follow the eight steps of the problem-solving process presented in this chapter.
   c. Present the issue to your class.
2. Keep a journal describing the process of decision making in the preceding group assignment. Write daily entries of your perceptions in the following areas:
   a. Describe the problems that occurred in your group
      (1) Interpersonal conflict
      (2) Unreliable or irresponsible behavior
      (3) Inability to keep to tasks
      (4) Ineffective leadership or membership
   b. Explain how Tuckman's four stages of group development impacted your group.
   c. Describe your contributions toward solving the group issue and resolving any difficulties that occurred.
   d. Discuss your overall satisfaction with group process, leadership, and outcomes.

# BUILDING A
# SPEECH ONLINE »

Now that you've read Chapter 19, use your online Resource Center for Building a Speech for quick access to the electronic study resources that accompany this text. You can access your Resource Center at http://academic.cengage.com/login, using the access code that came with your book or that you bought online at http://www.iChapters.com. Your Resource Center gives you access to Interactive Video Activities, the book's companion website, Speech Builder Express 3.0, InfoTrac College Edition, and study aids, including a digital glossary and review quizzes.

# appendix

President Barack Obama's Inaugural Address

*History was made on January 20, 2009, when Barack Obama became the first African American to be sworn in as the forty-fourth President of the United States. There was not much time to savor the moment, however. Amid an economic meltdown that included massive layoffs and home foreclosures, wars in Iraq and Afghanistan, recurrent threats of terrorism, and continuing hostilities in the Middle East, President Obama faced some of the most serious issues in modern America. As millions watched on television and more than 1.5 million witnessed the ceremony in 11- degree wind chills on the national mall, the new President delivered this inaugural address[1] that charted his course to meet America's challenges.*

Thank you. Thank you.

My fellow citizens: I stand here today humbled by the task before us, grateful for the trust you have bestowed, mindful of the sacrifices borne by our ancestors.

I thank President Bush for his service to our nation . . .

. . . . as well as the generosity and cooperation he has shown throughout this transition.

Forty-four Americans have now taken the presidential oath.

The words have been spoken during rising tides of prosperity and the still waters of peace. Yet, every so often the oath is taken amidst gathering clouds and raging storms. At these moments, America has carried on not simply because of the skill or vision of those in high office, but because We the People have remained faithful to the ideals of our forebears, and true to our founding documents.

So it has been. So it must be with this generation of Americans.

That we are in the midst of crisis is now well understood. Our nation is at war against a far-reaching network of violence and hatred. Our economy is badly weakened, a consequence of greed and irresponsibility on the part of some but also our collective failure to make hard choices and prepare the nation for a new age.

Homes have been lost, jobs shed, businesses shuttered. Our health care is too costly, our schools fail too many, and each day brings further evidence that the ways we use energy strengthen our adversaries and threaten our planet.

Today I say to you that the challenges we face are real, they are serious and they are many. They will not be met easily or in a short span of time. But know this America: They will be met.

On this day, we gather because we have chosen hope over fear, unity of purpose over conflict and discord.

On this day, we come to proclaim an end to the petty grievances and false promises, the recriminations and worn-out dogmas that for far too long have strangled our politics.

We remain a young nation but in the words of Scripture, the time has come to set aside childish things. The time has come to reaffirm our enduring spirit; to choose our better history; to carry forward that precious gift, that noble idea, passed on from generation to generation: the God-given promise that all are equal, all are free, and all deserve a chance to pursue their full measure of happiness.

In reaffirming the greatness of our nation, we understand that greatness is never a given. It must be earned. Our journey has never been one of shortcuts or settling for less.

It has not been the path for the faint-hearted, for those who prefer leisure over work, or seek only the pleasures of riches and fame.

Rather, it has been the risk-takers, the doers, the makers of things—some celebrated, but more often men and women obscure in their labor—who have carried us up the long, rugged path towards prosperity and freedom.

For us, they packed up their few worldly possessions and traveled across oceans in search of a new life. For us, they toiled in sweatshops and settled the West, endured the lash of the whip and plowed the hard earth.

For us, they fought and died in places like Concord and Gettysburg; Normandy and Khe Sahn.

Time and again these men and women struggled and sacrificed and worked till their hands were raw so that we might live a better life. They saw America as bigger than the sum of our individual ambitions; greater than all the differences of birth or wealth or faction. This is the journey we continue today. We remain the most prosperous, powerful nation on earth. Our workers are no less productive than when this crisis began. Our minds are no less inventive, our goods and services no less needed than they were last week or last month or last year. Our capacity remains undiminished. But our time of standing pat, of protecting narrow interests and putting off unpleasant decision—that time has surely passed.

Starting today, we must pick ourselves up, dust ourselves off, and begin again the work of remaking America.

For everywhere we look, there is work to be done.

The state of our economy calls for action: bold and swift. And we will act not only to create new jobs but to lay a new foundation for growth.

We will build the roads and bridges, the electric grids and digital lines that feed our commerce and bind us together.

We will restore science to its rightful place and wield technology's wonders to raise health care's quality and lower its costs.

We will harness the sun and the winds and the soil to fuel our cars and run our factories. And we will transform our schools and colleges and universities to meet the demands of a new age.

All this we can do. All this we will do.

Now, there are some who question the scale of our ambitions, who suggest that our system cannot tolerate too many big plans. Their memories are short, for they have forgotten what this country has already done, what free men and women can achieve when imagination is joined to common purpose and necessity to courage.

What the cynics fail to understand is that the ground has shifted beneath them, that the stale political arguments that have consumed us for so long, no longer apply.

The question we ask today is not whether our government is too big or too small, but whether it works, whether it helps families find jobs at a decent wage, care they can afford, a retirement that is dignified.

Where the answer is yes, we intend to move forward. Where the answer is no, programs will end.

And those of us who manage the public's dollars will be held to account, to spend wisely, reform bad habits, and do our business in the light of day, because only then can we restore the vital trust between a people and their government.

Nor is the question before us whether the market is a force for good or ill. Its power to generate wealth and expand freedom is unmatched.

But this crisis has reminded us that without a watchful eye, the market can spin out of control. The nation cannot prosper long when it favors only the prosperous.

The success of our economy has always depended not just on the size of our gross domestic product, but on the reach of our prosperity; on the ability to extend opportunity to every willing heart—not out of charity, but because it is the surest route to our common good.

As for our common defense, we reject as false the choice between our safety and our ideals.

Our founding fathers faced with perils that we can scarcely imagine, drafted a charter to assure the rule of law and the rights of man, a charter expanded by the blood of generations.

Those ideals still light the world, and we will not give them up for expedience's sake.

And so, to all other peoples and governments who are watching today, from the grandest capitals to the small village where my father was born: know that America is a friend of each nation and every man, woman and child who seeks a future of peace and dignity, and we are ready to lead once more.

Recall that earlier generations faced down fascism and communism not just with missiles and tanks, but with the sturdy alliances and enduring convictions.

They understood that our power alone cannon protect us, nor does it entitle us to do as we please. Instead, they knew that our power grows through its prudent use. Our security emanates from the justness of our cause; the force of our example; the tempering qualities of humility and restraint.

We are the keepers of this legacy; guided by these principles once more, we can meet those new threats that demand even greater effort, even greater cooperation and understanding between nations. We'll begin to responsibly leave Iraq to its people and forge a hard-earned peace in Afghanistan.

With old friends and former foes, we'll work tirelessly to lessen the nuclear threat and roll back the specter of a warming planet.

We will not apologize for our way of life nor will we waver in its defense.

And for those who seek to advance their aims by inducing terror and slaughtering innocents, we say to you now that, "Our spirit is stronger and cannot be broken. You cannot outlast us, and we will defeat you."

For we know that our patchwork heritage is a strength, not a weakness.

We are a nation of Christians and Muslims, Jews and Hindus, and nonbelievers. We are shaped by every language and culture, drawn from every end of this earth.

And because we have tasted the bitter swill of civil war and segregation and emerged from that dark chapter stronger and more united, we cannot help but believe that the old hatreds shall someday pass; that the lines of tribe shall soon dissolve; that as the world grows smaller, our common humanity shall reveal itself; and that America must play its role in ushering in a new era of peace.

To the Muslim world, we seek a new way forward, based on mutual interest and mutual respect.

To those leaders around the globe who seek to sow conflict or blame their society's ills on the West, know that your people will judge you on what you can build, not what you destroy.

To those. . . .

To those who cling to power through corruption and deceit and the silencing of dissent, know that you are on the wrong side of history, but that we will extend a hand if you are willing to unclench your fist.

To the people of poor nations, we pledge to work alongside you to make your farms flourish and let clean water flow; to nourish starved bodies and feed hungry minds.

And to those nations like ours that enjoy relative plenty, we say we can no longer afford indifference to the suffering outside our borders, nor can we consume the world's resources without regard to effect. For the world has changed, and we must change with it.

As we consider the road that unfolds before us, we remember with humble gratitude those brave Americans who, at this very hour, patrol far-off deserts and distant mountains. They have something to tell us, just as the fallen heroes who lie in Arlington whisper through the ages.

We honor them not only because they are guardians of our liberty, but because they embody the spirit of service: a willingness to find meaning in something greater than themselves.

And yet, at this moment, a moment that will define a generation, it is precisely this spirit that must inhabit us all.

For as much as government can do and must do, it is ultimately the faith and determination of the American people upon which this nation relies.

It is the kindness to take in a stranger when the levees break; the selflessness of workers who would rather cut their hours than see a friend lose their job which sees us through our darkest hours.

It is the firefighter's courage to storm a stairway filled with smoke, but also a parent's willingness to nurture a child, that finally decides our fate.

Our challenges may be new, the instruments with which we meet them may be new, but those values upon which our success depends, honesty and hard work, courage and fair play, tolerance and curiosity, loyalty and patriotism—these things are old.

These things are true. They have been the quiet force of progress throughout our history. What is demanded then is a return to these truths. What is required of us now is a new era of responsibility—a recognition, on the part of every American, that we have duties to ourselves, our nation and the world, duties that we do not grudgingly accept but rather seize gladly, firm in the knowledge that there is nothing so satisfying to the spirit, so defining of our character than giving our all to a difficult task.

This is the price and the promise of citizenship.

This is the source of our confidence: the knowledge that God calls on us to shape an uncertain destiny.

This is the meaning of our liberty and our creed, why men and women and children of every race and every faith can join in celebration across this magnificent mall. And why a man whose father less than 60 years ago might not have been served at a local restaurant can now stand before you to take a most sacred oath.

So let us mark this day in remembrance of who we are and how far we have traveled.

In the year of America's birth, in the coldest of months, a small band of patriots huddled by dying campfires on the shores of an icy river.

The capital was abandoned. The enemy was advancing. The snow was stained with blood.

At a moment when the outcome of our revolution was most in doubt, the father of our nation ordered these words be read to the people:

"Let it be told to the future world that in the depth of winter, when nothing but hope and virtue could survive, that the city and the country, alarmed at one common danger, came forth to meet it."

America, in the face of our common dangers, in this winter of our hardship, let us remember these timeless words: with hope and virtue, let us brave once more the icy currents, and endure what storms may come; let it be said by our children's children that when we were tested we refused to let this journey end, that we did not run back nor did we falter; and with eyes fixed on the horizon and God's grace upon us, we carried forth that great gift of freedom and delivered it safely to future generations.

Thank you. God bless you.

And God bless the United States of America.

# notes

## chapter 1

1. Shannon, Claude E, and Warren Weaver. *The Mathematical Theory of Communication*. Urbana: University of Illinois Press, 1949.
2. Mortensen, C. David. *Communication: The Study of Human Interaction*. New York: McGraw-Hill, 1972; p. 14.
3. See Bucher, Marcel. "No Holy War." *Swiss News* Dec. 2001: 29; and Dergham, Raghida. "You Won't Win with Words Alone." *Washington Post* 14 Oct. 2001: B1.
4. Corbett, Edward P. J. *Classical Rhetoric for the Modern Student*. New York: Oxford University Press, 1971; p. 31.
5. Thonssen, Lester, ed. *Selected Readings in Rhetoric and Public Speaking*. New York: H. W. Wilson, 1952; p. 65.
6. Thonssen, p. 156.
7. Thonssen, p. 102.

## chapter 2

1. Interview with Candita Chapman. Community College of Baltimore County, Catonsville Campus, Catonsville, MD, 12 May 2005.
2. Bureau of Labor Statistics, U.S. Department of Labor. "Number of Jobs Held, Labor Market Activity, and Earnings Growth Among Younger Baby Boomers: Results From More Than Two Decades of a Longitudinal Survey." 27 Aug. 2002. 6 May 2008. <http://www.bls.gov/nls/>.
3. Garonzik, Jamie. "A Career in Anthropology." Informative descriptive speech presented in speech class, Community College of Batter more County, Catonsville, MD, 2008. Used by permission.

## chapter 3

1. See Poniewozik, James. "Who Can Say What?" *Time* 23 Apr. 2007: 32; Stuever, Hank. "Question Celebrity." *Washington Post* 17 Dec. 2006: W5; and Padget, Jonathan. "The Bionic Woman's Toughest Mission; Can She Get Her Gay Fan Base to Overlook Isaiah Washington? Stay Tuned. . . ." *Washington Post* 9 Sept. 2007: M5.
2. Baster, Roy P., ed. *Collected Works of Abraham Lincoln*, Vol. I. New Brunswick: Rutgers University Press, 1953, p. 273.
3. Stanton, William J. *Fundamentals of Marketing*. New York: McGraw-Hill, 1981, pp. 35–55, 155–156.
4. This definition is partially based on a contribution from E. Joseph Lamp, professor of speech, Anne Arundel Community College, Arnold, MD.
5. See Lipton, Eric. "Giuliani Will Return Diminished, But Not Finished, Associates Say." *New York Times* 1 Feb. 2008: B1, and Browne, J. Zamgba. "Kerik's Nomination Withdrawal Sparks Support and Criticism." *New York Amsterdam News* 16 Dec. 2004: 4.
6. See "The Audacity of Rev. Wright; A Tale of a Candidate, a Pastor, and Some Repugnant Remarks." *The Washington Post* 29 Apr. 2008. *ProQuest Newspapers*. ProQuest. CCBC-Catonsville Library, Baltimore. 30 Apr. 2008; Gerson, Michael. "Better Than the Bitter." *The Washington Post* 16 Apr. 2008. *ProQuest Newspapers*. ProQuest. CCBC-Catonsville, Baltimore, 12 May 2008; "Senator Hillary Clinton Lied About Dodging Sniper Bullets on Bosnia Visit." *New York Beacon* 27 Mar.–2 Apr. 2008.

*ProQuest Newspapers*. ProQuest. CCBC-Catonsville Library, Baltimore. 30 Apr. 2008; http://o-proquest.uml.com/library/ccbcmd.edu/pqdweb?index=5did=1462018031&srch . . . > and Baram, Marcus. "Will Obama's Move Win Over Whites, Anger Blacks?" *ABCNews* 30 Apr. 2008. <http://www.Abcnews.go.com/Politics/Vote2008/story?id=4752928&page=1>.

7. Littlejohn, Stephen W., and David M. Jabusch. *Persuasive Transactions*. Glenview, IL: Scott, Foresman, 1987, p. 54.
8. Hugenberg, Lawrence W., and Donald D. Yoder. *Speaking in the Modern Organization*. Glenview, IL: Scott, Foresman, 1985, p. 182.
9. Littlejohn and Jabusch, p. 46.
10. Littlejohn and Jabusch, p. 56.
11. Maslow, Abraham H. *Motivation and Personality*. New York: Harper & Row, 1970, pp. 15–22.
12. This section on audience needs and motivations uses the work of Holtzman, Paul D. *The Psychology of Speakers' Audiences*. Glenview, IL: Scott, Foresman, 1970, pp. 50–63; and Maslow, Abraham H. *Motivation and Personality*. New York: Harper & Row, 1970, pp. 46–47. Both authors identify specific needs, and both discuss hierarchies of needs or values. The authors differ in their approaches, however. Holtzman examines multiple values, whereas Maslow uses a five-level hierarchy of needs. Holtzman believes that audiences set priorities based on their goals; Maslow believes that people cannot achieve higher needs until they have fulfilled lower levels of needs.
13. I am grateful to the following students who gave permission to use their motivational appeals as examples in this section: Evan Feinberg, Colleen V. Deitrich, Heather Hay, Kristine Ozgar, and J. Luke Snow.
14. Deitrich, Colleen V. "Mandatory Retirement Should Be Illegal." Speech to convince presented in speech class, Carroll Community College, Westminster, MD, 1991. Used by permission.
15. This chart is synthesized from a larger table in Samovar, Larry A., Richard E. Porter, and Edwin R. McDaniel. *Intercultural Communication*, 11th ed. Belmont, CA: Thomson-Wadsworth, 2006, p. 181.
16. Bosley, Debbie. "More Lenient Sentences for Postpartum Moms." Speech to convince presented in speech class, Carroll Community College, Westminster, MD, 1992. Used by permission.
17. Kilduff, James. "Vegetarianism Is a Healthier Lifestyle." Speech to convince presented in speech class, Carroll Community College, Westminster, MD, 1989. Used by permission.
18. Dodd, Carley H. *Dynamics of Intercultural Communication*, 4th ed. Madison, WI: Brown & Benchmark, 1995, p. 69.
19. Riche, Martha Farnsworth. "We're All Minorities Now." *American Demographics*. Oct. 1991: 26–33; and Edmondson, Brad. "American Diversity." *American Demographics Desk Reference* July 1991: 20–1.
20. Ricks, D. *Big Business Blunders: Mistakes in International Marketing*. Homewood, IL: Dow Jones-Irwin, 1983, p. 41, cited by Adler, Ronald B. and Neil Towne. *Looking Out/Looking In*, 9th ed. Ft. Worth: Harcourt Brace, 1999, p. 219.
21. Alexander, Benjamin H. "The Uncritical Acceptance Today." *Vital Speeches* 15 July 1992: 605.

22. Adapted from *Dorland's Illustrated Medical Dictionary*, 25th ed., s.v. "Pancreas," W. B. Saunders Co., 1994.

23. Nicholas N. J., Jr. "The Boob Tube Gets Smart." *Vital Speeches* 15 June 1991: 535.

24. Iacocca, L. A. "In Order To." *Vital Speeches* 1 Oct. 1987: 745.

25. Callahan, Daniel. "Thomas Jefferson." Speech to inform presented in speech class, Catonsville Community College, Catonsville, MD, 1990. Used by permission.

26. Scheb, John M. "The American Patriot." *Vital Speeches* 1 April 1991: 377.

27. The Carter "cardigan speech" received much favorable reaction, although there were news accounts that reported some negative feedback to the sweater. Compare "Warm Words from Jimmy Cardigan." *Time* 14 Feb. 1977: 18 to "Pleasures and Perils of Populism." *Time* 21 March 1977: 25.

28. Stanton, p. 45.

29. I wish to thank Marie Skane, associate professor of mathematics at Catonsville Community College, who provided me with information about the SPSS computer program.

## chapter 4

1. "Asleep In The Cockpit?" 20 Feb. 2008 *CBSNews Online* 21 Feb. 2008 <http://www.cbsnews.com/stories/2008/02/20/eveningnews/main385475.shtml>.

2. *International Listening Association*. "Listening Factoids." 26 August 2002. <http://www.listen.org/pages/factoids.html.

3. Barker, Larry, Karen Gladney, Renee Edwards, Frances Holley, and Connie Gaines. "An Investigation of Proportional Time Spent in Various Communication Activities by College Students." *Journal of Applied Communication Research* 8 (1980):101–109.

4. De Chello, Christine. "The Art of Listening: As Important as the Power of Persuasion in Effective Telecommunications." *Telemarketing & Call Center Solutions* March 1997:74.

5. See Johnston, David, and Jim Dwyer. "Files Show Warnings Were More Dire and Persistent." *New York Times* 18 April 2004: 1.1; and Duffy, Michael, et al. "How to Fix Our Intelligence." *Time* 26 April, 2004: 26.

6. See Jordan, Mary, and Sue Anne Pressley. "Gruesome Contest to Raise Dead Led to Koresh's Takeover of Cult." *Washington Post* 7 March 1993: A3; and Gotschall, Mary G. "A Marriage Made in Hell." *National Review* 4 April 1994: 57.

7. Koehler, Carol. "Mending the Body By Lending An Ear: The Healing Power of Listening." *Vital Speeches of the Day* 15 June 1998: 543–544.

8. As reported in O'Neil, John. "When Patients Have Their Say." *New York Times*. 1 October 2002: F6.

9. As reported in Rosenbaum, Bernard L. "Rx for Better Doctors." *Training & Development Journal* August 1989:77–80.

10. Rosenbaum.

11. Wolvin, Andrew D. and Carolyn Gwynn Coakley. *Listening*, 5th ed. New York: McGraw Hill, 1996, pp. 69–96.

12. Wolvin and Coakley, p. 69.

13. Two sources were used as the basis for this section: Wolf, Florence I. and Nadine C. Marsnik. *Perceptive Listening*, 2nd ed. New York: Holt, Rinehart and Winston, 1992, pp. 88–103; and Wolvin, Andrew D., and Carolyn Gwynn Coakley. *Listening*, 5th ed. New York: McGraw-Hill, 1996, Part II, pp. 151–380. The authors of *Perceptive Listening* present five kinds of listening that include "self-listening." In *Listening*, the writers identify five areas but include a different type they call "comprehensive listening." The four listening types

presented in this chapter are those most commonly identified throughout the literature.

14. This list of common barriers to listening is synthesized from two sources: Hirsch, Robert O. *Listening: A Way to Process Information Aurally*. Dubuque, IA: Gorsuch Scarisbrick, 1979, pp. 36–41; and Nichols, Ralph G. *Are You Listening?* New York: McGraw-Hill, 1957, pp. 104–112.

15. Conrad, Peter. *Television, the Medium and Its Manners*. Boston: Routledge & Kegan Paul, 1982. Conrad makes some devastating and thought-provoking attacks on the invasion of television into our lives. "Talk on television isn't meant to be listened to. The words merely gain for us the time to look at the talker. The talk shows are theatres of behavior, not dialogues" (p. 48).

16. CNN.com/US. "'Bring it down' was about car, students' lawyer says." 15 Sept. 2002. <http://www.cnn.com/2002/US/09/15/fla.terror.students/> [2 April 2003].

17. Used by permission of the Mathematics Department, Toronto Board of Education.

18. Kelley, Charles M. "Empathic Listening," in Trent, Jimmie D., Judith S. Trent, and Daniel J. O'Neill. *Concepts in Communication*. Boston: Allyn & Bacon, 1973, p. 270.

19. Norton, Robert W. and Loyd S. Pettegrew. "Attentiveness as a Style of Communication: A Structural Analysis." *Communication Monographs* 46 March 1979: 13–16.

20. Nichols, p. 105.

## chapter 5

1. "Fears." Conducted by Bruskin Associates for Whittle Communications, Inc., 1986.

2. Jones, W. H. "Situations Causing the Most Anxiety." *New York Times* [New York] 18 Dec. 1984: C1. "Situational Factors in Shyness." American Psychological Association, Toronto. Used by permission.

3. See Radcliffe, Donnie. *Simply Barbara Bush*. New York: Warner Books, 1989, pp. 157–158; and Seligmann, Jean, Tessa Namuth, and Mark Miller. "Drowning on Dry Land." *Newsweek* 23 May 1994: 64.

4. Manchester, William. *The Death of a President, November 20–November 25*. New York: Harper & Row, 1967, p. 85.

5. Selye, S. Hans. *Stress Without Distress*. Philadelphia: Lippincott, 1974, p. 38.

6. McCroskey, James C. "Oral Communication Apprehension: A Summary of Recent Theory and Research." *Human Communication Research* 4 (Fall 1977): 78–96.

7. McCroskey, James C. "The Implementation of a Large-Scale Program of Systematic Desensitization for Communication Apprehension." *The Speech Teacher* 21 (1972): 255–264. This article provides a detailed description of the process that McCroskey followed to help people who experienced high levels of communication apprehension.

8. Ellis, Albert, and Robert Harper. *A New Guide to Rational Living*. Englewood Cliffs, NJ: Prentice Hall, 1975, pp. 102–112.

9. Glaser, Susan R. "Oral Communication Apprehension and Avoidance: The Current Status of Treatment Research." *Communication Education* 30 (October 1981): 330.

10. Maultsby Maxie C., Jr. "Emotional Reeducation." *Handbook of Rational-Emotive Therapy*, Albert Ellis and Russell Grieger, eds. New York: Springer, 1977, pp. 231–247.

11. Elliot, James. From speaking notes used in speech class, Carroll Community College, 1989. Used by permission.

12. Weekes, Claire. *Peace from Nervous Suffering*. New York: Hawthorne Books, 1972, pp. 69–73.

13. Seligmann, Namuth, and Miller, p. 64.

14. Dusek-Girdano, Dorothy. "Stress Reduction Through Physical Activity." *Controlling Stress and Tension*, Daniel A. Girdano and George S. Everly Jr., eds. Englewood Cliffs, NJ: Prentice Hall, 1979, pp. 220–231.

## chapter 6

1. See Schmidt, Michael S. "Jones Hands Over Her Olympic Medals." *New York Times* 9 Oct. 2007: D4, and "Jones Pleads Guilty, Admits Lying About Steroids." MSNBC 5 Oct. 2007. 9 Feb. 2008 <http://www.msnbc.msn.com/id/21138883/>.

2. See Pennington, Bill, Thayer Evans, and Michael S. Schmidt. "Steroid Report Depicts a Two-Player Domino Effect." *New York Times* 16 Dec. 2007: 1.1, and "Baseball Blues." *Scholastic News* 7 Jan. 2008: 2.

3. McCoy, Brian. "You Must Work Really Hard." *Vital Speeches* July 2007: 321–322.

4. Cooper, Lane, ed. *The Rhetoric of Aristotle*. New York: Appleton-Century-Crofts, 1960, p. 9.

5. Cooper, p. 47.

6. As cited in Colson, Charles W. "Right or Wrong in Today's Society." *Vital Speeches* 1 July 1991: 561.

7. I thank Paul S. Cunningham, professor emeritus of history and geography at Catonsville Community College, who provided valuable assistance for this section on history and ethics.

8. Slevin, Peter. "Bishops Extend Policy of 1 Strike for Sex Offenders." *Washington Post* 18 June 2005: A3.

9. Macur Juliet. "Landis Exercises Last Shot At Appeal." *New York Times* 11 Oct. 2007: D6.

10. See Cohen, Richard. "Oprah's Grand Delusion." *Washington Post* 17 Jan. 2006: A17, and Kurtz, Howard. "Oprah Throws the Book at Herself." *Washington Post* 27 Jan. 2006: A1.

11. MacDonald, G. Jeffrey. "'It's All Good, Boss!' Ethical Lapses in High Places Stem in Part from Lack of Honest Feedback." *Christian Science Monitor* 6 July 2005: 15.

12. Braden, Waldo W., ed. *Representative American Speeches, 1974–1975*. New York: H. W. Wilson Co., 1975, p. 52.

13. Lacayo, Richard, and Amanda Ripley. "Persons of the Year." *Time* 30 Dec. 2002/6 Jan. 2003: 32–33.

14. "Anti-War YouTube 'Vet' Admits He Is Faker." Report by Brian Ross and Vic Walter. *ABC News*. New York. 21 Sept. 2007.

15. Goldman, Russell. "9/11 Yarn A Web of Lies." *ABCNews* 27 Sept. 2007. 15 Feb. 2008 <http://www.abcnews.go.com/US/story?id=3662119&page=1>.

16. Saltzman, Joe. "Lying As America's Pastime." *USA Today* July 2006. *ProQuest Newspapers*. ProQuest. CCBC-Catonsville Library, Baltimore. 10 Feb. 2008.

17. Harvis, John F., and Dan Balz. "Clinton More Forcefully Denies Having Had Affair or Urging Lies." *Washington Post* 27 Jan. 1998: A1.

18. Zernike, Kate. "Macaca." *New York Times* 24 Dec. 2006: 4.

19. Terhune, Chad, and Carrick Mottenkamp. "Cleaning Up: for Some Workers, Storms in Florida Rain Opportunity; A $1 Billion Job Attracts Men with Trucks and Tricks; Feds Try to Prevent Fraud; A Hauler Protests His Score." *Wall Street Journal* 15 Sept. 2004: A1.

20. "Nifong Surrenders License; Prosecutor of Duke Lacrosse Rape Case Disbarred for Conduct." *The Sun* (Baltimore) 17 June 2003: 3A.

21. Thomas, Jo. "'No Sympathy' for Dead Children, McVeigh Says." *New York Times* 29 March 2001: A12.

22. Gatehouse, Jonathon. "All We Hoped For." *Maclean's* 24 Dec. 2001: 48–50.

23. Toosi, Nahai. "Iranian President Ahmadinejad Questions 9/11, Holocaust." *Chicago Citizen* 26 Sept. 2007: 9.

24. "Jarvik May Have Used Body Double in Ads." 7 Feb. 2008. 15 Feb. 2008 <http://www.abcnews.go.com/GMA/OnCall/story?id=4254997&page=1.

25. Mydans, Seth. "Four Held in Attack at Riots, Outset." *New York Times* 13 May 1992: A20.

26. Townley, Preston. "Business Ethics." *Vital Speeches* 15 Jan. 1992: 209.

27. These guidelines are quoted, in abridged form, from Capen's speech to the Conference Board Conference on Business Ethics in *Vital Speeches* 1 Sept. 1990: 686–687.

28. Stewart, Thomas C. "Practice, Practice, Practice: Knowing, Is Not The Same Thing As Doing." *Vital Speeches* July 2007: 321–322.

## chapter 7

1. Marszalek, Maria. "The Art of Egg Decorating." Demonstration speech presented in the Fundamentals of Public Speaking Course, Catonsville Community College, 1989. Used by permission.

2. I am appreciative of the following students who gave me permission to use their topics and specific purposes as examples in this chapter: Linda Carey, Jo Ann Dickensheets, Patricia Farquhar, Dawn Gyory, Stephen King, Lou Ann Pfister, Dwayne Mitchell, Sandra Prusin, Richard Renehan, Susan Stephan, Sherri Webb, and Tracey Weise. I also gratefully acknowledge the late Professor Stephen S. Hiten, who coined the phrase "Be clear, concise, and unambiguous" in his public speaking courses at Columbia Union College.

3. Speeches in this section were presented in the Fundamentals of Public Speaking Course, Catonsville Community College, Catonsville, MD, 1987, 1988, 1989, and 1990; and in Fundamentals of Speech Communication, Community College of Baltimore County, Catonsville Campus, 2004. All used by permission.

## chapter 8

1. In preparing this section, I was assisted by these Internet sources: Henderson, John. "ICYouSee." <http://www.ithaca.edu/library/ Training/hott.html> [22 July 1999]; and Grassian, Esther. "Thinking Critically about Discipline-Based World Wide Web Resources." *UCLA College Library Instruction*. <http://www.library.ucla.edu/libraries/college/instruct/web/critical.htm> [10 Nov. 1998].

2. "About Wikipedia." *Wikipedia, the Free Encyclopedia*. 29 Jan. 2008. Wikipedia. 30 Jan. 2008 <http://www.en.wikipedia.org/wiki/Wikipedia:About>.

3. Hacker, Diana. *A Writer's Reference*. New York: Bedford/St. Martin's, 2007.

4. "Owner Satisfaction." *Consumer Reports* Jan. 2008: 47.

5. Based on a definition used in Chaffee, John. *Thinking Critically*, 3rd ed. Boston: Houghton Mifflin, 1990, p. 37. Much of this section on critical thinking is based on Chapter 2 of Chaffee's book and Chapter 1 of Rieke, Richard D., and Malcolm O. Sillars. *Argumentation and Critical Decision-Making*. New York: HarperCollins, 1993, pp. 1–16.

6. Chaffee, p. 55.

7. I want to thank Cassidy Chesnut, reference and instruction librarian at the Community College of Baltimore County—Catonsville Campus, for his guidance and advice regarding this chapter.

## chapter 9

1. Francis, Charles. "How to Stop Boring your Audience to Death: Databases, Anecdotes, and Humor." *Vital Speeches of the Day* 15 Feb. 1996: 283.

2. Mayerowitz, Scott. "Oil Execs Grilled Over High Prices." *ABCNews* 1 April 2008. 1 April 2008. <http:://www.abcnews.go.com/Business/Economy/story?id=4566283&page=1>.

3. Zebraski, David. "Recycling Our Throwaways." Persuasive speech to convince presented in speech class, Catonsville Community College, Catonsville, MD, 1989. Used by permission.

4. Eitzen, Stanley. "Ethical Dilemmas in American Sport." *Vital Speeches* 1 Jan. 1996: 183.

5. Illustration created by the author.

6. Badshah, Neha. "The Indian Wedding Ceremony." Informative descriptive speech presented in speech class, Catonsville Community College, Catonsville, MD, 1992. Used by permission.

7. Hoguet, Andrea. "Parents Should Be Responsible for Their Children's Actions." Persuasive speech to convince presented in speech class, Carroll Community College, Westminster, MD, 1989. Used by permission.

8. Lamm, Richard D. "Time to Change Course." *Vital Speeches* 15 Oct. 1985: 4.

9. Birckhead, Kathy. "Buy American-Made Products." Persuasive speech to actuate presented in speech class, Carroll Community College, Westminster, MD, 1990. Used by permission.

10. "A Champ In, And Out Of, The Ring." Reported by Steve Hartman. *CBSEvening News* 7 March 2008. CBS News. 14 March 2008. <http://www.cbsnews.com/stories/2008/03/07/assignment_america/main3919119.shtml>.
Example quoted by the author.

11. *The Brady Law* 2008. The Brady Campaign. 14 March 2008. <http://www.bradycampaign.org>.

12. Kurian, George T. *The New Book of World Rankings*. New York: Facts on File Publications, 1984, p. 386.

13. Norko, Olga. "Differences Between the Russian and American People." Speech to inform presented in speech class, Catonsville Community College, Catonsville, MD, 1992. Used by permission.

14. Wishard, William Van Dusen. "Between Two Ages." *Vital Speeches* 15 Jan. 2002: 203.

15. Kammerzell, Robert. "Same-Sex Civil Unions Should Be Supported." Persuasive speech to activate presented in speech class, Community College of Baltimore County, Catonsville Campus, 2005. Used by permission.

16. Sajak, Pat. "The Disconnect Between Hollywood and America." *Vital Speeches* 15 Aug. 2002: 701.

17. Schwarzkopf, Norman. "Leaders for the 21st Century." *Vital Speeches* 15 June 1999: 519.

18. Trudeau, Garry. "The Impertinent Questions." *Vital Speeches* August 1986: 619–620.

19. Trudeau, p. 620.

20. Alexander, Gina. "Effective Interviewing Techniques." Speech to demonstrate presented in speech class, Carroll Community College, Westminster, MD, 1990. Used by permission.

21. Hollands, Peter. "The Flag Raisings at Iwo Jima." Informative descriptive speech presented in speech class, CCBC-Catonsville,

MD, 2008. Used by permission. My thanks to Jennifer Kafka Smith, assistant professor of speech communication, who provided valuable assistance with this speech.

## chapter 10

1. Humphrey, Judith. "Executive Eloquence." *Vital Speeches* 15 May 1998: 468–469.

2. I am grateful to the following students, who gave me permission to use their topics and to modify their outlines for this chapter: Lisa Hilton, "Ancient Egyptian Funeral Customs"; Steve Hogue, "The American Muscle Car"; Joe A. Lloyd Jr., "Colon Cancer"; Erin Ellis, "Major Causes of Child Abuse"; Mary Holmes, "Life in Dunoon, Scotland"; Richard Renehan, "HMOs and Quality Health Care"; Olivia J. Ellis, "The Process of Preparing an Ointment"; Ralph Thompson, "Understanding Mental Retardation"; Richard Watson, "The Art of Juggling"; Tina Cerrato, "Teenage Suicide"; Stephen Friedman, "The Art of Tattooing"; Susan Stephan, "Sex in Advertising"; Tara Baker, "Four Types of Masks," courtesy of Mary Anne Rhoades, associate professor of speech; Della Leister, "Chocolate—One of America's Passions"; Steven Sapp, "No Limits on Immigration"; and Dawn Anderson, "Discrimination Against Divorced Fathers."

3. I would also like to acknowledge the late Leroy Giles, professor emeritus of English at Catonsville Community College, for his helpful suggestions as I prepared this chapter.

## chapter 11

1. Plavetich, Richard G., and Brian H. Kleiner. "How to Be an Effective Public Speaker." *Training & Development* November 1992: 17+.

2. Anderson, Gary. "A Lesson in Modern Terrorism: In Memory of Juliana McCourt." *Vital Speeches* 1 Dec. 2001: 117.

3. Alexander, Gina. "Sexual Harassment." Speech to actuate presented in speech class, Carroll Community College, Westminster, MD, 1990. Used by permission.

4. Gerber, Michael. "Tornados—The Deadliest Wind of All." Speech to inform presented in speech class, Catonsville Community College, Catonsville, MD, 1989. Used by permission.

5. King, Stephen M. "The Right to Privacy." Speech to convince delivered in speech class, Catonsville Community College, Catonsville, MD, 1987. Used by permission.

6. Birckhead, Kathy. "Child Sexual Abuse." Speech to inform presented in speech class, Carroll Community College, Westminster, MD, 1990. Used by permission.

7. Schultz, George P. "The Changed World." *Vital Speeches of the Day* 1 July 2004: 546.

8. Allred, Michelle. "The Anti-Mormon Campaign." Speech to inform presented in speech class, Carroll Community College, Westminster, MD, 1990. Used by permission.

9. Perot, H. Ross. Paid political broadcast. 17 Oct. 1992.

10. "To Santa Claus and Little Sisters" from *A Cry for Help*, by Mary Giffin and Carol Felsenthal. Copyright © 1983 by Mary Giffin, M.D., and Carol Felsenthal. Reprinted by permission of Doubleday, a division of Random House, Inc.

11. Cerrato, Tina. "Detecting Warning Signs of Teenage Suicide." Informative speech delivered in speech class, Catonsville Community College, Catonsville, MD, 1987. Used by permission.

12. Leonard, Karen. "Roller Coasters." Informative speech presented in speech class, Carroll Community College, Westminster, MD, 1990. Used by permission.

13. Archambault, David. "Columbus Plus 500 Years." *Vital Speeches* 1 June 1992: 491.

14. Clinton, Hillary Rodham. "Remarks of Senator Hillary Clinton at the Opening of September 11th: Bearing Witness to History." 10 Sept. 2002. <http://clinton.senate.gov/speeches/020910.html INTERNET> [19 September 2002].

15. Alexander, Benjamin H. "Before You Lambast This Generation." *Vital Speeches* 15 Nov. 1987: 70.

16. Trader, Rick. "Participating in the Nationwide Movement Toward Recycling." Speech to actuate presented in speech class, Carroll Community College, Westminster, MD, 1989. Used by permission.

17. Koeppen, Chris. "The Intrigue of the Great Pyramid." Speech to inform presented in speech class, Carroll Community College, Westminster, MD, 1991. Used by permission.

18. Kreczmer, Meredith M. "How to Take Interesting Pictures." Speech to demonstrate delivered in speech class, Carroll Community College, Westminster, MD, 1990. Used by permission.

19. Jones, Kim. "Sojourner Truth." Speech to inform presented in speech class, Carroll Community College, Westminster, MD, 1992. Used by permission.

20. Anderson, Gary. "A Lesson in Modern Terrorism: In Memory of Juliana McCourt." *Vital Speeches*. 1 Dec. 2001: 125.

21. King, "The Right to Privacy."

22. Shields, Jacquelyn V. "Increasing the Length of the School Year." Speech to convince delivered in speech class, Carroll Community College, Westminster, MD, 1990. Used by permission.

23. Snyder, Shelley Y. "Let's Take a Stand Against Racism." Speech to actuate delivered in speech class, Carroll Community College, Westminster, MD, 1992. Used by permission.

24. Kittle, Kimberly L. "Helpful Ways to Use Everyday Products." Speech to inform presented in speech class, Carroll Community College, Westminster, MD, 1992. Used by permission.

25. Cooper, Ernestine D. "Aerobic Exercise Can Be Harmful." Speech to convince presented in speech class, Catonsville Community College, Catonsville, MD, 1989. Used by permission.

26. Ferris, Norma. "You Can Make a Difference." Speech to actuate delivered in speech class, Catonsville Community College, Catonsville, MD, 1987. Used by permission.

27. Bailey, Tresse. "Helping Battered Women." Speech to actuate presented in speech class, Catonsville Community College, Catonsville, MD, 1989. Used by permission.

28. Verschleisser, Chaim. "Raising the *Monitor*." Speech to inform presented at the Community College of Baltimore County, Catonsville Campus, MD, 2002. Used by permission.

## chapter 12

1. Petrie Charles R. Jr. "Informative Speaking: A Summary and Bibliography of Related Research." *Speech Monographs* 30 (June 1963): 82.

2. McLaughlin, Abraham. "The Radical Road That Harley Took." *Christian Science Monitor* 19 November 1999: 1.

3. Statistics regarding the increase in motorcycle deaths were obtained from *Statistical Abstracts of the United States, 2004*.

4. Kirkley, Donna. "Visuals Help Communicate." videotape. 1975.

5. I want to thank Hal Rummel, professor of computer graphics and visual communication at the Community College of Baltimore County, Catonsville Campus, who provided valuable information about the use of computers in developing visuals.

6. Yingling, Mark. "How Do Airplane Wings Produce Lift?" Demonstration speech, presented in Fundamentals of Speech Communication, the Community College of Baltimore County, Catonsville Campus, MD, 2002. Courtesy of Jennifer Kafka Smith, assistant professor of speech communication. Used by permission.

## chapter 13

1. "Leaves from a Lurid Lexicon." *Newsweek* 28 Sep. 1970: 24.

2. "Buckley's Remarks at Gala." *The National Review* 31 Dec. 1986: 24.

3. Moran, Terence P. "Public Doublespeak: On Beholding and Becoming." *Language Awareness*, 2nd ed. Paul Eschholz, Alfred Rosa, and Virginia Clark, eds. New York: St. Martin's Press, 1978, p. 54.

4. ABC. "Incredible Sunday." 30 Oct. 1988.

5. Ferris, Norma. "Papering a Wall." Speech to demonstrate presented in speech class, Catonsville Community College, Catonsville, MD, 1987. Used by permission.

6. The statistics and examples used in this passage were based on two articles: "First U.S. City Nears Ban on Saturday Night Specials." *Baltimore Sun* 24 Nov. 1995: A10; and "The Gun Law: Maryland's High-Powered Issue." *Baltimore Sun* 30 Oct. 1988: A1.

7. Dodd, Carley H. *Dynamics of Intercultural Communication*, 4th ed. Dubuque; IA: Wm. C. Brown, 1995, pp. 133–134.

8. Dodd, p. 136.

9. Armao, R. "Worst Blunders; Firms Laugh Through Tears." *American Business* Jan. 1981:11, cited by Adler, Ronald B and Neil Towne in *Looking Out Looking In*, 8th ed. Fort Worth: Harcourt Brace College, 1996, p. 101.

10. Dodd, p. 150.

11. Dodd, p. 149.

12. Dodd, p. 148.

13. Riegert, Ray. *Hidden Hawaii*. Berkeley: Ulysses Press, 1989, p. 25.

14. Dodd, p. 134.

15. Some of the suggestions used here are taken from the eleven-point plan for "Developing Skills in Language and Culture" in Dodd, pp. 149–150.

16. Trenholm, Sarah and Arthur Jensen. *Interpersonal Communication*, 3rd ed. New York: Wadsworth, 1996, p. 193.

17. Much of the information about gender differences in language was drawn from the following sources: Adler and Towne, pp. 214–219; Berko, Roy M., Andrew D. Wolvin, and Darlyn R. Wolvin. *Communicating: A Social and Career Focus*, 6th ed. Boston: Houghton Mifflin, 1995), pp. 208–212; Trenholm and Jensen, pp.193–195; and Weaver, Richard L. *Understanding Interpersonal Communication*, 5th ed. Glenview, IL: Scott, Foresman/Little, Brown Higher Education, 1990, pp. 173–178.

18. Adler and Towne, p. 216.

19. Weaver, pp. 175, 177.

20. "Ventura Says Religion Is for 'Weak.'" *New York Times* 1 Oct. 1999: A2.

21. Watson, Diane E. "Insensitivity Conflicts with Heritage." *Baltimore Sun* 29 July 2005: 13A.

22. Zamichow, Norma. "California Psychologist Follows the 'Ums' in Speech." *Baltimore Sun* 3 May 1992: 2A.

23. "Like, Wow, Colleges Include Speaking Class." *Baltimore Sun* 23 March 1999: 3A.

24. "Like, Wow, . . ."

25. Balick, Julie. "Circus Clowns." Informative speech presented in speech class, Catonsville Community College, Catonsville, MD, 1988. Used by permission.

26. Petrie, Charles R. Jr. "Informative Speaking: A Summary and Bibliography of Related Research." *Speech Monographs* 30 (June 1963): 81.

## chapter 14

1. Anburajan, Aswini. "Michelle Obama Booed Over 'Nevada.'" *MSNBC* 18 Jan. 2008. 4 April 2008. <http://www.firstread.msnbc.msn.com/archive/2008/01/18/589216.aspx>.

2. This section on the production of sound is based on five sources that you can consult for more detailed information: (1) Anderson, Virgil A. *Training the Speaking Voice.* New York: Oxford University Press, 1961, pp. 21–54; (2) Eisenson, Jon. *Improvement of Voice and Diction,* 2nd ed. New York: Macmillan, 1965, pp. 15–41; (3) Fisher, Hilda B. *Improving Voice and Articulation,* 2nd ed. Boston: Houghton Mifflin, 1975, pp. 3–23, 87–104; (4) Gray, Giles Wilkeson, and Claude Merton Wise. *The Bases of Speech,* 3rd ed. New York: Harper & Row, 1959, pp. 135–199; and (5) Lessac, Arthur. *The Use and Training of the Human Voice,* 2nd ed. New York: Drama Book Specialists, 1967, pp. 9–16.

3. These exercises were selected from Eisenson, 45–47.

4. Fisher, pp. 3–35. Definitions of vocal delivery are based on those of Hilda Fisher, which she provides in Chapter 1 of her text.

5. "The Art of Being Fully Human." Public Broadcasting Company Video. Washington, DC, 1980.

6. This exercise is drawn from a longer list of words provided in Anderson, p. 405.

7. Fisher, p. 67. Fisher recommends exercises that help the muscles of the larynx to relax. If you have some concerns about the quality of your voice, try some of the exercises she suggests on pages 64 to 72.

8. Petrie, Charles R. Jr. "Informative Speaking: A Summary and Bibliography of Related Research." *Speech Monographs* 30 (June 1963): 81.

9. Dodd, Carley H. *Dynamics of Intercultural Communication,* 4th ed. Dubuque, IA: Wm. C. Brown, 1995, p. 199.

10. Chaiken, Shelly. "Communicator Physical Attractiveness and Persuasion." *Journal of Personality and Social Psychology* 37 (25 Aug. 1978): 1387–1397. This article contains some interesting research about the impact of physical attractiveness on persuasion. The author concludes that "the present research indicates that physical attractiveness can significantly enhance communicator persuasiveness" (p. 1394).

11. Chaiken, p. 82.

12. Example based upon a speech delivered by Marie E. Miller, Catonsville Community College, Catonsville, MD, 1988. Used by permission.

13. See Adams, Lorraine. "The Fight of Her Life; Marcia Clark—Working Mother and O. J. Simpson's Lead Prosecutor—Takes Her Place Among Other Maligned, Adored and Misunderstood Modern Women." *Washington Post* 20 August 1995: F1.

14. Adler, Ronald B., Lawrence B. Rosenfeld, Neil Towne, and Russell F. Proctor II. *Interplay: The Process of Interpersonal Communication,* 7th ed. Fort Worth, TX: Harcourt Brace College, 1998, p. 58.

15. Examples used in this discussion were selected from these sources: Berko, Roy M. Andrew D. Wolvin, and Darlyn R. Wolvin. *Communicating: A Social and Career Focus,* 3rd ed. Boston: Houghton Mifflin, 1995, p. 158; Dodd, pp. 156, 175; and DeVito, Joseph A. *Messages: Building Interpersonal Communication Skills,* 2nd ed. New York: HarperCollins College, 1993, p. 143.

16. Berko et al., p. 156.

17. McLoughlin, Merrill, Tracy L. Shryer, Erica E. Goode, and Kathleen McAuliffe. "Attitude: In Politics and Management, the 'Gender Gap' Is Real." *U.S. News & World Report* 8 Aug. 1988: 56.

18. This comparison and contrast of gender differences in non-verbal behavior uses these sources: Arliss, Laurie P. *Gender Communication.* Englewood Cliffs, NJ: Prentice Hall, 1991, pp. 75–90; Trenholm, Sarah, and Arthur Jensen. *Interpersonal Communication,* 3rd ed. Belmont, CA: Wadsworth, 1996, pp. 195–196; and Weaver, Richard L. *Understanding Interpersonal Communication,* 5th ed. Glenview, IL: Scott, Foresman, 1990, p. 219.

19. Weaver, pp. 175, 219–220.

## chapter 15

1. Olbricht, Thomas H. *Informative Speaking.* Glenview, IL: Scott, Foresman, 1968, pp. 15–16. This chapter's discussion of the difference between information and persuasion coincides with Olbricht's analysis of the "traditional means of distinguishing informing from persuading" in his second chapter.

2. Olbricht, p. 15.

3. Foley, Ann. "Fingerprint Identification." Demonstration speech presented in Fundamentals of Public Speaking, Catonsville Community College, Catonsville, MD, 1988. Used by permission.

4. I wish to thank Kara Jenkins and Tom Pfeffer for permission to use portions of their outlines and Kelly O'Connor, Joan Stark, and Tresse Bailey for topic ideas.

5. Verschleisser, Chaim. "Raising the *Monitor.*" Speech to inform presented at the Community College of Baltimore County, Catonsville Campus, MD, 2002. Used by permission.

## chapter 16

1. Jacobs, Don Trent. "The Red Flags of Persuasion." *ETC.: A Review of General Semantics* Winter 1995: 375.

2. Cooper, Lane. *The Rhetoric of Aristotle.* New York: Appleton-Century-Crofts, 1932, p. 8. [I added the second and third bracketed comments.]

3. Cooper, p. 9.

4. Herbert, Bob. "Confronting the Kitchen Sink." *New York Times* 8 Mar. 2008. *ProQuest Newspapers.* ProQuest. CCBC Catonsville Library, Baltimore. 15 Apr. 2008. <http://o-proquest.gmi.com/librarry/ccbcmd.edu/pqdweb?index=1&did=1442216711&srch . . . >

5. Toosi, Hahal. "Iranian President Ahmadinejad Questions 9/11, Holocaust." *Chicago Citizen* 26 Sept. 2007: 9. *ProQuest Newspapers.* ProQuest. CCBC Catonsville Library, Baltimore. 18 Feb. 2008.

6. Rumber, Pamela. "The Sale of Prescription Drugs over the Internet Should Be Outlawed." Speech to convince presented in speech class, the Community College of Baltimore County, Catonsville Campus, MD, 2000. Used by permission.

7. Ruffin, Kenneth. "Online Services Should Be Banned." Speech to convince delivered in speech class, Catonsville Community College, Catonsville, MD, 1996. Used by permission.

8. Cooper, p. 9.

9. These excerpts are taken from the complete speech. See "Earl Spencer's Eulogy: Farewell to a Princess." *Baltimore Sun* 7 Sept. 1997: 27A.

10. Littlejohn, Stephen W., and David M. Jabusch. *Persuasive Transactions.* Glenview, IL: Scott, Foresman, 1987, p. 54. I want to thank James L. Koury, professor of philosophy at Catonsville Community College, who gave me valuable help and advice in the logic section of this chapter.

11. In this section on the appeal to reason, I used a system of argumentation similar to Hugenberg and Yoder's section entitled

"Use Logical Proof: Appeal to Logic and Reason," pp. 188–191 in *Speaking in the Modern Organization* (see note 12). However, I have altered the terminology, examples, and numbers of logical proofs. For a more traditional approach, see Ross, Raymond S, and Mark G. Ross. *Understanding Persuasion*. Englewood Cliffs, NJ: Prentice Hall, 1981, pp. 155–168.

12. Hugenberg, Lawrence W., and Donald D. Yoder. *Speaking in the Modern Organization*. Glenview, IL: Scott, Foresman, 1985, p. 190.

13. The following speeches used in this chapter were presented in the Fundamentals of Speech Communication class, the Community College of Baltimore County, Catonsville Campus: a speech where the name was withheld to protect privacy; and D'Archangelis, Anna. "Computer-Enhanced Advertising Should Be Clearly Labeled," 2004. Used by permission.

14. Dewey, John. *How We Think*. Boston: D. C. Heath, 1933, pp. 102–118. Read Chapter 6 of Dewey's book to understand the five phases of "reflective thinking." You will discover a great similarity to some of the problem-solution models presented in this persuasive speaking chapter.

15. Supporting materials and references used for the topic "Illegal Immigrants Should Be Granted Health Care Benefits" were paraphrased or quoted from two articles in the Opposing Viewpoints Resource Center, Greenhaven Press, 2006. See Dwyer, James. "Illegal Immigrants Have the Right to Receive U.S. Health Care." *At Issue: What Rights Should Illegal Immigrants Have?* Lori Newman, ed. Detroit: Greenhaven Press, 2006. *Opposing Viewpoints Resource Center*. Gale. Community College Of Baltimore County. 10 April 2008. Gale Document Number: EJ3010419202, and Cosman, Madeline Pelner. "Illegal Immigrants Threaten U.S. Health Care." *At Issue: What Rights Should Illegal Immigrants Have?* Lori Newman, ed. Detroit: Greenhaven Press, 2006. *Opposing Viewpoints Resource Center*. Gale. Community College Of Baltimore County. 10 April 2008. Gale Document Number: EJ301049203.

16. I want to thank the following students who provided topic ideas for this chapter: Michael Becker, Candy Chancellor, Evan Feinberg, Colleen Hamilton, Deborah E. Hensley, Lisa Hilton, Ken Kuzo, Marie Miller, Jeff Ritter, Pamela Rumber, Grover Sauter, Michelle M. Tawes, and Cheryl Zuretti.

## chapter 17

1. See Brown, Jenny, et al. "To Viewers, Happiness Is A Warm Puppy." *USA Today* 4 Feb. 2008 *Academic Search Premier*. Ebsco Host. CCBC Catonsville Library <http://web.ebscohost.com/ehost/detail?vid=6&hid=6&sid=834689fc-e7a9-4d43-9b35-2ebd . . . > Baltimore. 15 Apr. 2008: and Petrecca, Laura. "Best of the Past: Pepsi's Cheatin' Heart." .*USA Today* 4 Feb. 2008 *Academic Search Premier*. Ebsco Host. CCBC Catonsville Library, Baltimore. 15 Apr. 2008. <http://web.ebscohost.com/ehost/detail?vid=7&hid=8&sid=834689fc-e7a9-4d43-9d43-9b35-2ebd . . . >.

2. Examples used for the five stages of Maslow's hierarchy were taken from two speeches: Broos, Cecelia. "Deforestation," and Warhime, Kimberly. "Chesapeake Bay Pollution." Persuasive speeches to actuate, Carroll Community College, Westminster, MD, 1991 and 1992. Used by permission.

3. Information for this section is from Merrick, Amy. "Kmart Tries Pitch for Family Values in New TV Spots." *Wall Street Journal* 25 Feb. 2002: B16; Cobb, James G. "Ghost of Portholes Past." *New York Times* 29 Dec. 2002: 12.1; and Horovitz, Bruce. "You Just Can't Go Wrong with a Chimp." *USA Today* 8 Feb. 2005: 3B.

4. "Old Joe Must Go." *Advertising Age* 13 Jan. 1992: 16.

5. See Schofield interview and Shane, Scott. "Maryland to Join Tobacco Settlement." *Baltimore Sun*, 21 Nov. 1998: 1A.

6. Alexander, Gina. "Pet Owners Should Receive a Tax Deduction." Persuasive speech to convince, Carroll Community College, Westminster, MD, 1990. Used by permission.

7. Mundell, Karen. "Research Your Family Genealogy." Persuasive speech to actuate, Carroll Community College, Westminster, MD, 1990. Used by permission.

8. Manzer, Cathy. "Highway Etiquette." Persuasive speech to actuate, Carroll Community College, Westminster, MD, 1990. Used by permission.

9. Reilly, Rick. "Let's Bust Those Chops." *Sports Illustrated* 28 Oct. 1991: 11, as cited by Masimore, Patricia. "Sports Teams and Racism." Persuasive speech to convince, Carroll Community College, Westminster, MD, 1991. Used by permission.

10. Meyers, Becky. "People in Need in Carroll County." Persuasive speech to actuate, Carroll Community College, Westminster, MD, 1990. Used by permission.

11. Pettis, Ashley V. "Have a Moving Experience." Persuasive speech to actuate, Catonsville Community College, Catonsville, MD, 1992. Used by permission.

12. Suggestions for incentives and appeals to emotions are based on Verderber, Rudolph F. *Essentials of Persuasive Speaking*. Belmont, CA: Wadsworth, 1991, pp. 114, 116–119.

13. Gronbeck, Bruce E., Douglas Ehninger, and Alan H. Monroe. *Principles of Speech Communication*, 10th ed. Glenview, IL: Scott, Foresman, 1988, pp. 272–285.

14. Jenkins, Kara. "Feeding the Hungry Here at Home." Persuasive speech to actuate, Catonsville Community College, Catonsville, MD, 1988. Used by permission.

15. Otukoya, Omolola. "Genocide in Sudan." Persuasive speech to actuate, Community College of Baltimore County, Catonsville, MD, 2005. Used by permission.

## chapter 18

1. Fetterman, Mindy. "We Are the Hokies! We Will Prevail!" *USA Today* 18 June 2007.*Academic Search Premier*. Ebsco Host. CCBC Catonsville Library, Baltimore. 22 April 2008. <http://web.ebscohost.com/ehost/detail?vid=4&hid=116&sid=e1e8bacf-3ed8-4c77-8ce7-cf2 . . . >.

2. Giovanni, Nikki. "We Are Virginia Tech." *Vital Speeches of the Day* June 2007: 73 *Academic Search Premier*. Ebsco Host. CCBC Catonsville Library, Baltimore. 10 April 2008. <http://web.ebscohost.com/ehost/detail?vid=7&hid=6&sid=47b58e60-89d2-49e7-9616-713>.

3. Kennedy, Edward M. "A Tribute to His Brother." *Vital Speeches of the Day* 1 July 1968: 547.

4. "Liberty Weekend," ABC, July 3, 1986.

5. Johannesen, Richard L., R. R. Allen, and W. A. Linkugel. *Contemporary American Speeches*. Dubuque, IA: Kendell/Hunt Publishing Co., 1992, p. 343.

6. "Oscar's King and Queen." *ABCNews* 26 Feb. 2007 ABCNews. 24 Apr. 2008 <http://www.abcnews.go.com/search?searchtext=forest%whitaker%20oscar%20speech&type=>.

7. Johannesen et al., p. 342.

8. This excerpt was supplied courtesy of Jan C. Scruggs, who gave permission for its use.

9. Hardin, Paul, former president of Drew University. Speech delivered at the 111th Commencement of Drew University 19 May 1979. Used by permission of Paul Hardin, Chancellor, University of North Carolina.

10. Jordan, Barbara. "Keynote Address." *Vital Speeches of the Day*, 1976: 646.

11. Johannesen et al., p. 343.

12. "Excerpts from Texts of the Nominating Speeches." *New York Times* 11 July 1952: 9.

13. Bauer, Andrew. ed. *A Treasury of Great American Speeches*. New York: Hawthorn Books, 1970, pp. 47 and 296.

14. Basler, Roy P., ed. *Abraham Lincoln: His Speeches and Writings*. New York: Grosset and Dunlap, 1962, p. 568.

15. Johannesen et al., p. 343.

## chapter 19

1. Compare the definition and characteristics of a group discussion found in Barker, Larry L. et al. *Groups in Process*, 4th ed. Englewood Cliffs, NJ: Prentice Hall, 1991, pp. 7–10, with descriptions provided by Bormann, Ernest G. *Discussion and Group Methods*. New York: Harper & Row, 1969, pp. 3–6.

2. Compare Cragan John F., and David W. Wright. *Communication in Small Group Discussions*. New York: West, 1980, pp. 46–48, with Goodall, H. Lloyd Jr. *Small Group Communication in Organizations*. Dubuque, IA: Wm. C. Brown, 1985, p. 94. Cragan and Wright list three "generic" types of groups: task, encounter, and consciousness-raising groups, while Goodall uses Julia Wood's typology of task, social, and dually oriented groups (a combination of task and social groups). Because I believe that encounter and consciousness-raising groups can be combined into one category, I have used the labels—task, encounter, and social—as the classifications for study in this section.

3. Tuckman, Bruce W., and Mary Ann C. Jensen. "Stages of Small Group Development Revisited." *Group and Organization Studies*. December 1977: 419–427.

4. Dewey, John. *How We Think*. Boston: D. C. Heath and Company, 1933, pp. 102–118.

5. See McBurney, James H., and Kenneth G. Hance. *Discussion in Human Affairs*. New York: Harper and Brothers, 1950, pp. 3–15.

6. Barker et al., pp. 110–116.

7. Benne, Kenneth D., and Paul Sheats. "Functional Roles of Group Members." *Journal of Social Issues* 4 (Spring 1948): 45–46. Also see Cragan and Wright, pp. 116–117; Barker et al., pp. 46–47.

8. This discussion combines recommendations appearing in Cragan and Wright, pp. 114–116, as well as in Benne and Sheats, pp. 44–45, with some of my own suggestions.

9. Goodall, p. 122.

10. Cragan and Wright, pp. 75–76.

11. Lewin, Kurt, Ronald Lippitt, and Ralph K. White. "Patterns of Aggressive Behavior in Experimentally Created 'Social Climates.'" *Journal of Social Psychology* 10 (1939): 271–299.

12. Rosenfeld, Lawrence B., and Timothy G. Plax. "Personality Determinants of Autocratic and Democratic Leadership." *Speech Monographs* 42 (August 1975): 203–208.

13. Wood, Julia T. "Leading in Purposive Discussions: A Study of Adaptive Behavior." *Communication Monographs* 44 (June 1977): 152–165.

14. Goodall, p. 145.

15. Barker et al., pp. 193–219.

16. I want to thank Jennifer Kafka Smith, assistant professor of speech communication at Community College of Baltimore County, Catonsville Campus, who provided valuable assistance with this chapter.

# glossary

## a

**abbreviated sources** Partial references that are included in parentheses within the body of a written outline. They usually include only the author's last name, title of the book or periodical, and page number.

**abstract** A brief summary of an article, study, or narrative.

**action step** The fifth part of Monroe's motivated sequence that requires the persuasive actuating speaker to provide listeners with a specific behavior to perform in order to solve a problem.

**active listening** Attentive, involved behavior that represents a complete mental commitment on the part of the hearer.

**active listening behaviors** Becoming a better listener by withholding judgment about a speaker, providing honest attentive feedback, eliminating distractions, and evaluating the speech when it is finished.

**actuate** To present a persuasive speech that motivates listeners to action.

**agenda** An orderly list of topics a meeting or discussion group will cover.

**alliteration** Speech that employs the repetition of the same sounds.

**amplification** An arrangement of words or phrases in order of importance to emphasize an opening or closing statement.

**analogy** A logical argument comparing two or more similar cases to show that, because of their similarity, what applies to one case can also apply to the other.

**anecdote** A brief humorous story used to demonstrate a point.

**antithesis** A contrasting of ideas or qualities to convey a concept.

**appeal** A specific call to an audience to act on an issue such as a vote, donation of money, or volunteering for a cause. This strategy is often used in persuasive actuating speeches. See *challenge*.

**appearance** Dress that is appropriate for the audience, occasion, and speech topic.

**appreciative listening** Listening to hear the power and beauty of words, images, music, or the environment.

**argument** A logical, organized method of supporting a claim by presenting clear, correct, and complete facts and by drawing conclusions from the data to support the claim.

**Aristotle** (384–322 B.C.) Plato's famous student; wrote *The Rhetoric*, challenging many of Plato's negative opinions about oratory. He helped to gain respect for the study and practice of public speaking as an art and a discipline.

**articulation** The clarity and enunciation of words, phrases, and sentences.

**attention step** The first part of Monroe's motivated sequence that generates audience interest and curiosity in the persuasive actuating speech.

**attitudes** Prior inclinations people have about issues; a spectrum of audience perception from disagreement or neutrality to agreement.

**audiovisual aids** Devices that may appeal to any of the senses: graphs, drawings, photographs, posters, chalkboards, mechanical media, models, and objects.

**autocratic** A leadership style in which the leader is the chief decision maker and gives orders and commands to group members.

**awfullizing** A term coined by two psychotherapists, Albert Ellis and Robert Harper, referring to an irrational dread of the future.

## b

**barriers to listening** Poor listening behaviors such as blocking, selective listening, yielding to distractions, and avoidance. See *listening barriers*.

**beliefs** Conclusions people have about the world based upon observations, knowledge, and experiences.

**bibliography** The complete alphabetical listing in an outline of sources that are used as research for a speech.

**body** The longest part of a speech containing the main headings that were identified in the thesis statement.

**body movement** Stance, posture, and poise, which can support the ideas of a speech.

**brainstorming** The technique of rapidly and uncritically listing ideas to generate topics for a speech.

**buzz groups** Technique often used in large organizations of dividing the larger group into small units of three to eight members and reporting to the larger organization through designated leaders.

## c

**case study** An in-depth account of a situation or a set of circumstances.

**causation** A logical argument identifying known causes to determine unknown effects (cause-to-effect reasoning) or identifying known effects to determine the unknown cause (effect-to-cause reasoning).

**cause-effect sequence** The arrangement of main points of the body of a speech according to causes and/or effects.

**CD (compact disc)** An audio CD that is used for listening to music.

**CD-ROM (compact disc read-only memory)** A small laser disc containing video and audio that is used with a computer for education, information, and entertainment.

**challenge** A broad, generalized summons to an audience to support a topic. This strategy is often used to conclude a persuasive convincing speech. See *appeal.*

**channel** The means of transmitting a message through our senses of sight, sound, smell, taste, and touch.

**charisma** A special magnetic quality, possessed by some speakers, that attracts audiences and inspires confidence.

**Chicago Manual (CM)** *The Chicago Manual of Style* is a source that provides guidelines for annotating research sources in proper form. CM bibliographic form is often used in the humanities.

**chronological sequence** The arrangement of the main points of the body of an informative speech according to time or order of events.

**Cicero** (106–43 B.C.) A Roman orator, statesman, and respected teacher; in his book *De Oratore*, he discusses writing, audience analysis, anxiety, evidence, and argument.

**clavicular breathing** Incorrect respiration, from the top of the lungs.

**code of ethics** Standards of right and wrong that act as guides for ethical behavior and speaking practices.

**cohesiveness** One of the characteristics of a small group; represents a unifying element, common purpose, or mutual feelings of members.

**communication apprehension** Coined by university speech instructor James C. McCroskey to describe an individual's anxiety about speaking to another person or group.

**communication model** A system or plan that helps us understand the dynamic process of communication.

**comparative advantages** A method of organizing the main points of the body of a persuasive convincing speech by comparing the advantages of a proposed solution with the advantages and disadvantages of other solutions.

**comparisons** Similarities in situations or events.

**compliment** An introductory strategy in which the speaker praises elements of the audience or speaking occasion to build a relationship with an unknown speaker or unfamiliar audience.

**computer (or data) projector** A device that is connected to the computer, allowing your audience to see an enlarged version of the computer monitor on a movie screen.

**conclusion** The ending of a speech that resolves the ideas presented in the body.

**connotation** Personal, specific, and subjective meanings of words.

**content** The research, organization, and logical development of a speech topic.

**contrasts** Differences in situations or events.

**convince** To present a persuasive speech that seeks to alter the beliefs and judgments of an audience.

**coordination** Refers to the placement of equal ideas within the same level of an outline.

**Corax** (fifth century B.C.) One of the founders of Greek rhetoric; he influenced judicial oratory and developed methods that helped common people to argue cases successfully in court.

**credibility** Confidence that listeners place in a speaker due to the speaker's use of verifiable research and reliable sources.

**critical thinking** The ability to test information, be organized, listen to different perspectives, think independently, and use self-discipline.

**culture** An individual's background, origin, geography, and characteristic features of everyday existence that influence verbal and nonverbal messages.

## d

**database** A computer software system such as Academic Search Elite, InfoTrac College Edition, or ProQuest Direct that indexes periodicals, journals, and books and helps speakers to locate relevant research quickly.

**decoding** The thought process within the receiver that changes symbols into meaningful ideas, thoughts, or feelings.

**definition speech** An informative speech about a philosophical concept such as a theory or idea, or a concrete subject like science or art.

**delivery** The style or presentation of the speech.

**democratic** A leadership style in which the leader functions as a coordinator, promoting discussion and stimulating group decision making.

**demographic analysis** Collecting social and statistical information about listeners through surveys or interviews that will help the speech to receive a favorable hearing.

**demonstration speech** An informative presentation that includes a variety of audiovisual aids to show the steps of a process: how something works, is made, or is done; or how something happens.

**denotation** Dictionary definitions of words.

**descriptive speech** An informative speech related to persons, places, objects, or events.

**diaphragmatic breathing** Steady breathing from the diaphragm that produces a constant supply of air needed to produce sound.

**discriminative listening** Listening to learn, to be instructed, and to test theories.

**discussion questions** Open-ended issues that are phrased as questions and become the subject of a group discussion. Questions of *fact* explore issues where information is either unknown or disputed; questions of *value* require discussion members to use personal judgments to evaluate issues; questions of *policy* stimulate discussion about solutions or future actions.

**document camera** An electronic device that is connected to a computer and a projector and is used to project images onto a large screen.

**dramatic pauses** Intentional breaks or silences between major ideas that can bring out the meaning of a specific passage. See *pauses* and *vocalized pauses*.

**DVD (digital videodisc) player** Electronic system that uses a small laser disc similar to an audio CD and allows a speaker to project video onto a larger screen or monitor and switch quickly among clips with the press of a button.

**e**

**elements of virtue** In his book *The Rhetoric,* Aristotle identified these values of *ethics* as justice, courage, temperance, magnificence, magnanimity, liberality, gentleness, prudence, and wisdom.

**e-mail** Electronic messages that are sent via the Internet.

**empathic listening** Listening to understand and facilitate the needs and feelings of someone else, as in therapeutic listening.

**emphasis** Alterations in rate of speech, volume, and pitch to highlight significant words and sentences.

**encoding** The thought process within the sender that changes ideas, thoughts, or feelings into understandable symbols.

**encounter groups** A type of discussion that contributes to interpersonal learning and insight.

**entertaining speech** A type of speech that pokes fun at people, places, or events to gain a humorous response.

**enumeration** A logical argument in which the speaker cites a series of specific cases to support a generalization.

**ethics** Earning the respect and trust of listeners by avoiding deceptive practices and by being reliable, fair, and honest.

**ethnocentrism** The belief that one culture or environment is superior to another.

**ethos** One of Aristotle's three proofs; refers to the ethical appeal and the speaker's ability to gain the confidence and trust of listeners.

**eulogy** A speech of tribute delivered at a memorial service or funeral.

**euphemism** A vague, inoffensive term that conceals what an individual really means.

**evaluative listening** Listening as a response to a persuasive message.

**example** A brief, factual instance that demonstrates a point. It can serve as an introductory or concluding strategy or can be used as supporting material in a speech. See *illustration* or *story*.

**extemporaneous** Approaching speech development with research, a prepared outline, speaking notes, and effective eye contact. The style of speech delivery presented in a public speaking course.

**external transitions** Complete sentences or phrases that connect the major sections or main points of a speech.

**eye contact** Communicating visually to reach the intellect and emotions of the audience and gauge feedback to ideas.

**f**

**facial expression** Nonverbal signals such as smiles or frowns expressing feelings like anger, love, or joy, which can express silent messages and support the emotions of a speech.

**fallacies** Illogical arguments that employ unclear or incorrect facts, incomplete evidence, and/or erroneous reasoning.

**fax** A computer or machine that allows letters and messages to be sent electronically over a telephone line.

**feedback** A verbal or nonverbal response from the receiver to the sender. It can indicate whether communication has occurred, how it has been received, and whether it has been understood.

**focus groups** A type of group formed to represent target populations that are assembled to test arguments, ideas, and products.

**formal outline** The formal written structure that refers to the speech body. It includes the main points, subordinate elements, abbreviated sources, and written transitions.

**forming** The early phases of small-group meetings (theorized by Bruce Tuckman) in which group members are in the process of orienting themselves to each other and to the task at hand.

**forum** A public discussion in which all members of an audience have the opportunity for asking questions, making statements, or delivering speeches about issues.

**g**

**gender** Characteristics that are related to one sex. Women and men exhibit some traditional differences in their verbal and nonverbal communication patterns.

**general adaptation syndrome** Refers to Hans Selye's classic research in the field of stress reduction. He concluded that the body reacts to stress in stages through an *alarm reaction*, a *resistance stage*, and finally a *phase of exhaustion*.

**general purpose** The direction of the material presented in a speech: to inform, persuade, or entertain.

**general references** Library research tools such as the catalog and periodical indexes that help speakers locate books, publications, or other relevant research sources for speech topics.

**gestures** Physical movements of the hands and arms to emphasize words, describe physical objects, or point out locations.

**Gorgias** (483–376 B.C.) A brilliant Athenian speechmaker and teacher; he emphasized an ornate style, figures of speech, and emotionalism in speaking.

**graphs** Three types of graphs are the bar, line, and pie graphs, which are helpful visuals for explaining trends, showing comparisons, or indicating portions of a whole.

## h

**hidden agenda** An unstated, often deceptive speaking goal that a speaker uses to manipulate an audience.

**hierarchy of needs** Basic needs of all human beings; psychologist Abraham H. Maslow organized these needs based on five levels: physiological, safety and security, love, esteem, and self-actualization.

**home page** A website developed by an institution, business, or individual and placed on the Internet for information, publicity, commerce, or entertainment.

**humor** A joke or humorous anecdote that is used as a strategy to introduce or conclude a speech.

**hypothetical example** A fictitious situation or scenario that has a realistic application.

## i

**illustration** A long example that clarifies and amplifies an idea. It can be used as a strategy for the introduction and conclusion or provided as supporting material in the body of the speech.

**impromptu** A speech presented without prior notice or preparation; a "surprise" speech.

**incentives** Benefits or rewards people gain by agreeing with and adopting the goals of a persuasive speaker. *Long-term incentives* are benefits that listeners gain over a sustained period of time. *Short-term incentives* are devices that provide immediate reinforcement of ideas.

**indentation** Each level of supporting elements in an outline is indented under main points so that the outline clearly indicates the relationship between the heading and the subdivision.

**inflection** Changes in pitch that make a speech sound interesting and avoid monotony.

**informal outline** The portion of the written outline that refers to the introduction, conclusion, bibliography, and other outline preliminaries.

**informative speech** A type of speech that promotes enlightenment and education about a topic.

**internal transitions** Brief words and phrases such as *also*, *then*, *next*, *in addition to*, or *finally* that link the supporting materials *within* a subdivision of a speech.

**Internet** Computerized cyber system connecting offices, businesses, institutions, and homes to the World Wide Web.

**interview** A meeting in which the purpose is to obtain information from a person.

**introduction** The beginning of a speech that generates curiosity and prepares the audience for the topic and thesis statement.

**Isocrates** (436–338 B.C.) Greek orator and teacher; in manuscripts and autobiographies, he wrote that a speaker should be well educated, of good moral character, and possess freedom and independence tempered with self-control.

## k

**keynote speech** Presentation given at the beginning of a major conference or convention.

**keyword** A term or group of words that is used to search for documents in an electronic database.

## l

**laissez-faire** A leadership style in which no leader exists, or the leader exerts little or no influence. Group members take care of managerial or administrative responsibilities.

**lecture** A type of informative speech presented by an expert for instructional or educational purposes.

**linguistically parallel** Refers to the similarity of sentence structure and wording in each level of an outline.

**listening barriers** Poor listening behaviors, such as blocking, selective listening, yielding to distractions, and avoidance.

**listening model** A process describing how we receive, attend to, and assign meaning to stimuli. A model developed by Andrew Wolvin and Carolyn Coakley graphically demonstrates this process.

**logos** One of Aristotle's three proofs; it involves the speaker's appeal to logic and reason.

**long-term incentives** See *incentives*.

## m

**manuscript** A style of speech delivery that is written out and read word-for-word.

**Maslow, Abraham H.** A psychology professor at Brandeis University. He identified five levels of basic drives that he felt influenced our thinking and behavior. See *hierarchy of needs*.

**mechanical media** Any type of electrical device that can be used as an audiovisual aid.

**memorized** A style of speech delivery that requires the speaker to commit the entire speech to memory and make the presentation without speaking notes.

**message** A set of organized, structured symbols for communication.

**metaphor** A figure of speech used to show comparison without the words *like* or *as*.

**MLA** Developed by the Modern Language Association, this system provides a format for annotating bibliographic sources. It is the system suggested in this text and is most often used in college research papers, theses, and dissertations.

**mnemonic phrase** A memory device used to help people remember main ideas or significant themes.

**modem** A device connecting a computer to a telephone.

**Monroe, Alan** A professor of speech at Purdue University in the 1930s. He combined problem-solution techniques with motivational approaches to train sales personnel. His technique, known as the motivated sequence, is a five-step system used in persuasive actuating speeches.

**motivated sequence** A five-step system used in persuasive actuating speeches, developed by Alan Monroe.

**movement** See *body movement*.

**narrative** An experience or story that is told by the speaker.

**need step** The second part of the motivated sequence that identifies and develops the existence of a problem in the persuasive actuating speech.

**negative self-talk** Thinking negatively about one's efforts at public performance; having a derogatory attitude about public speaking.

**noise** A distortion or distraction to the communication process. Noise can be *external*, *internal*, or *semantic*.

**norming** The third stage of Bruce Tuckman's small-group theory; in this phase, the group has worked through many of the conflicts of the storming phase and has now become more cohesive.

**observation** A judgment based on what an individual has seen.

**occasion** The impact of the environment of the speech. It includes the purpose and location of the speech as well as the expectations of the audience.

**opaque projector** A bulky device that can display a small drawing or picture from a book onto a large screen. It has become mostly obsolete.

**open-ended questions** A strategy that requires a clear response from the audience. It is often used in the introduction to a speech. See *questions*.

**opinions** The verbal expressions of attitudes; verbal inclinations or perceptions about topics and issues.

**opposition argument** A strong argument against a speaker's proposition or viewpoint.

**organizational sequence** The manner in which the main points of the body are organized. Informative speeches can be organized according to chronology, space, causation, or topic. Persuasive speeches can be structured by problem-solution, reasons, comparative advantages, or motivated sequence.

**overhead projector** A device that is used, with clear acetate transparencies, to enlarge images onto a screen.

**panel** An informal discussion during which one person acts as moderator, guiding three to six members through an interactive problem-solving process in front of an audience.

**passive listening** Listening that is relaxed or "easy," such as listening to an iPod or watching a movie.

**pathos** One of Aristotle's three proofs. It involves the speaker's appeal to the emotions of an audience.

**pauses** Breaks or interruptions in speech that separate thoughts and ideas. See *dramatic pauses* and *vocalized pauses*.

**performing** The fourth stage of Bruce Tuckman's small-group theory; this phase is characterized by insight and action. Members wish to complete tasks they were given and adopt constructive behavior to implement them.

**personal experience** Direct, firsthand knowledge of a situation that can be valuable supporting material in a speech. Also a type of informative presentation that provides information about an event, such as a travelogue, adventure, or expedition.

**personal reference** An introductory strategy in which a speaker includes autobiographical facts to help listeners learn more about the speaker. This strategy is used when an audience is unfamiliar with the speaker.

**persuasive speech** A speech that influences a listener's beliefs, feelings, or behavior.

**phrasing** A vocal technique of grouping words and sentences into units of thought that make ideas easier to understand.

**pitch** Vocal element that refers to the highness or lowness of sound.

**Plato** (428–348 B.C.) Greek philosopher who argued that rhetoric was not a "true art" and attacked the methods of sophists in stories known as "dialogues." He described rhetoricians as individuals who were more interested in dishonesty, style, and opinion than in truth.

**polls** Samplings of opinion on selected issues.

**positive self-talk** Developing positive attitudes and thoughts about one's abilities at public performance.

**PowerPoint** A computer graphics program created by Microsoft Corporation to assist in the development of computer-driven visual aids such as tables, graphs, and images that provide support for a speech. The program is used with a computer and a data projector that displays images on a large screen.

**primary evidence** Original firsthand fact or experience such as an autobiography.

**problem-solution** An organizational sequence used to structure the main points of persuasive speeches by developing a problem and then proposing solutions.

**pronunciation** Describes the combinations of vowels, consonants, syllables, and accents a speaker uses to emphasize a specific word.

**proposition** An arguable, debatable statement that acts as the focal point for a persuasive convincing speech. *Propositions of fact* create a controversy out of commonly held beliefs; *propositions of value* seek judgment as to whether an issue is right or wrong, good or bad; and *propositions of policy* advocate the adoption of a future action or behavior that proposes a change in the *status quo*.

**q**

**quality** Refers to the unique sound or timbre of the voice.

**questions** Can be used as attention-getting devices in speech introductions or to stimulate serious thought among listeners in speech conclusions. *Rhetorical questions* are self-answered, and *open-ended questions* require a verbal response from the audience. See *rhetorical questions* and *open-ended questions*.

**Quintilian** (A.D. 35 to 95) A skillful Roman lawyer who wrote *The Institutes of Oratory*, which stresses that the orator must be "a good man . . . skilled in speaking."

**quotation** The exact restatement of a person's words. Quotations can be valuable supporting materials in the body of the speech or can be used as a strategy for the speech introduction or conclusion.

**r**

**rate** Refers to the number of words an individual speaks every minute.

*Readers' Guide* A general reference to articles in more than 200 popular magazines; often called the "average person index."

**reasoning** The process of presenting logical arguments to draw conclusions or inferences.

**reasons** A method of organizing the main points of a persuasive convincing speech by building a case using the strongest reasons from thorough research.

**rebuttal argument** Diffusing possible disagreement in a persuasive speech by providing evidence that opposing viewpoints are flawed or inaccurate.

**receiver** The destination or recipient of communication.

**reference to the introduction** A strategy used in the conclusion to remind listeners of a point, story, or issue mentioned at the beginning of the speech. This strategy promotes unity in the speech.

**reference to the occasion** A strategy used in an introduction to refer to a familiar event that is connected to the topic of a speech.

**repetition** The reiteration by a speaker of words or phrases to emphasize key ideas and convey vivid images.

**report** A type of informative speaking that is required in business or industry.

**rhetoric** In ancient times, referred to as "the art of the orator." Classical rhetoric dealt with the ability to persuade and move an audience to a specific viewpoint.

**rhetorical questions** Questions posed by a speaker that are self-answered. The audience does not respond verbally. A rhetorical question is often used as a strategy to introduce a speech. See *questions*.

**role-playing** A technique using an individual(s) to act out a brief skit, assume a character, or simulate a conflict. Also a type of group wherein members assume characters or personalities in order to portray relationships and interactions among individuals, act out family conflicts, or reveal inner dilemmas.

**s**

**satisfaction step** The third part of the motivated sequence that identifies and develops solutions to a problem in the persuasive actuating speech.

**scanning** The process of copying visual aids or written documents into a computer by using a scanner.

**search engines** Computer software programs designed to locate topics on the Internet. Major search engines are Lycos, Yahoo!, Alta Vista, and Google.

**secondary evidence** Information reported secondhand by an intermediary standing between the researcher and the original source.

**sender** The individual who originates communication with thoughts, ideas, or feelings.

**sentence outline** Refers to a format that includes complete sentences throughout main and subordinate elements of an outline.

**setting** The physical and psychological factors of the communication process that include occasion, environment, space, and time.

**Shannon and Weaver** In the 1940s, Claude Shannon and Warren Weaver wrote *The Mathematical Theory of Communication*, describing a classic communication model as a flat line with a source, message, channel, and receiver.

**shocking statement** A situation, experience, or phrase that the speaker uses in the introduction to get the audience's attention.

**short-term incentives** See *incentives*.

**similes** A figure of speech in which *like* or *as* is used to show comparison.

**social group** A type of group that helps members to establish friendships and maintain personal relationships.

**sophistry** In ancient Greece, *sophistry* referred to the practice of using deceitful methods and faulty methods of reasoning.

**sophists** Teachers in ancient Greece who taught oratory for a fee. At first they were respected, but later they were identified as con artists who exploited students for financial profit.

**source** A term relating to the origin of communication. It is used extensively in the Shannon and Weaver communication model.

**spatial sequence** The arrangement of main points of an informative speech according to geography or location.

**speaking notes** A brief outline written on 4-by-6-inch or 6-by-9-inch notecards that contain a brief written outline of the entire speech.

**specific purpose** Includes the general purpose and one topic idea, stated in clear and concise language.

**statistics** A collection of facts in numerical form. They can be used as credible supporting materials in the body of the speech, to gain the attention of listeners in the introduction, or to get the audience to think seriously about an issue in the conclusion. See *surveys*.

**status quo** Represents the existing condition or present state of affairs. Propositions of policy seek to change the status quo.

**stereotyping** An oversimplified perception and often a prejudicial opinion that all people in a group, culture, or region have the same rigid characteristics or qualities without much exception.

**stimulate** To present a persuasive speech in which the speaker seeks to reinforce and intensify the beliefs or feelings of listeners.

**storming** The second stage of Bruce Tuckman's theory. This stage is characterized by interpersonal conflict, infighting, emotional reactions to members, and resistance to authority.

**story** A short narrative that can be used as an attention-getting strategy for the introduction or as a final narrative in the conclusion. See *illustration* and *example*.

**subdivision** Refers to the subordinate points under a heading of an outline. The elements in a subdivision should be divided into separate and equal categories. See also *subtopic*.

**subject** A broad, general area or issue identified before narrowing to a limited topic for a speech.

**subordination** Refers to the placement of secondary, or lower-ranking, ideas beneath higher-order topics in an outline.

**substantive references** Sources such as biographies, encyclopedias, almanacs, books, and magazines that help the speaker locate specific information for a speech topic.

**subtopic** Refers to the lower-ranking ideas in an outline. See *subdivision*.

**summary** A strategy used in the conclusion to recap the main points or thesis statement of the speech. It is especially effective when the topic involves complicated subject matter.

**surveys** Studies that draw conclusions from research.

**suspense** A strategy used in the introduction to stimulate interest or make listeners curious about a topic.

**symbol** A verbal or nonverbal expression or action that has meaning.

**symposium** A type of highly structured group in which two to six experts reveal their views on some aspect of a problem and deliver prepared speeches to an audience without informal discussion.

**systematic desensitization** A process developed by James C. McCroskey for treating and reducing high levels of communication anxiety through relaxation tapes, visualization, and follow-up exercises.

**t**

**targeting** The process of identifying selected groups of listeners and designing specific appeals to motivate them.

**task groups** A type of group in which the completion of objectives or implementation of solutions is emphasized.

**teleconference** To gather research by interviewing an expert on a topic by telephone.

**testimonial** A speech of tribute presented at a retirement or other going-away ceremony.

**testimony** A statement or endorsement given by an expert or an individual with a logical connection to the topic.

**thesis statement** Often called the central idea or central objective, it is the sentence at the end of the introduction that expands the specific purpose and tells the audience exactly what main points the speech will cover.

**tiling** A computer-generated process of creating large posters with a graphics program.

**topic** An interesting, well-defined, and limited area that a speaker selects for speech development and delivery.

**topic outline** A format that includes brief phrases throughout the main and subordinate elements of an outline.

**topical sequence** Structuring the main points of the body of an informative speech by a logical or natural sequence; finding research that clusters around natural topics that can be earmarked as the main points of the outline.

**trait** A leadership philosophy suggesting that leaders possess certain powerful characteristics such as physical appearance, speaking ability, or behavior.

**transitions** Connectives or listening cues between major or minor ideas in a speech. See *external transitions* and *internal transitions*.

**transparencies** Clear acetate sheets of plastic used with an overhead projector to enlarge photographs or other documents onto a large screen for easy viewing.

## U

**unethical practices** Untrustworthy behaviors through which a speaker advocates harm, provides false information, uses offensive language or name-calling, plagiarizes, or stacks the deck to manipulate or exploit members of an audience.

**URL** Uniform Resource Locator or web address of a specific Internet site.

## V

**values** A set of principles or standards that people consider to be important and that cause individuals to achieve goals or states of mind and behave in certain ways.

**visualization step** The fourth part of the motivated sequence in the persuasive speech to actuate that pictures the future if a problem is or is not solved.

**vocalized pauses** Verbalizations, such as "uh" and "um," that cause distractions in speaking. See *pauses* and *dramatic pauses*.

**volume** The intensity or loudness and softness of the voice.

# suggested topic areas

The following lists contain suggested topics for speeches. Some issues are general and include a wide range of ideas, while others are more specific. Topic areas can be altered easily to fit the interests of a speaker, the general purpose of the speech, the needs of an audience, or the requirements of an occasion. We include these suggestions to stimulate creative thinking and productive investigation.

## art, crafts, and humanities

Classic movies

Collecting: airplanes, art glass, baseball cards, bottles, buttons, cars, Civil War memorabilia, clocks, coins, comics, dolls, fossils, guns, hats, juke boxes, linens, minerals, model trains, campaign buttons, phonograph records, porcelain, quilts, slot machines, stamps, teddy bears

Costs of maintaining museums

Creating: batik, designer cowboy boots, Greek moussaka, ice sculptures, perfect diamonds, stained-glass art

Designing: a home, clothing, flower arrangements, a landscaped garden, a mall, a wedding cake, a high-rise condominium, a city, a solar-powered car, a golf course, an Olympic-standard racing bicycle, a surf board, a jet ski, a tunnel, a stadium, an airplane, a race track, a submarine, a nuclear power plant, a suspension bridge, a guitar

Famous objects: Broadway theatres, cathedrals, jewels, lighthouses, museums, opera houses, palaces, prisons, ships, stadiums, streets, cities, ruins, mountains, forests, parks, trees, weapons, rivers, monuments, graves

Famous people: composers, musicians, painters, sculptors, actors, actresses, dancers, singers, authors, poets, presidents, first ladies, hall of fame personalities, Nobel Prize winners, world leaders

Fashion design and the consumer

Government funding of controversial art projects

Learning to make clay pottery

Life in a symphony orchestra

Looking for treasures at antique stores and flea markets

Major contemporary architectural styles

Manufacturing musical instruments

Re-enacting battles from the War of Independence or the Civil War

Science of restoring artworks

Understanding: Japanese origami, cubism, impressionism, Cajun cooking, the Amish, the game of cricket, soccer, lacrosse, Mexican history, Islam, Sioux tribal festivals, the festival of Kwanza, the celebration of Christmas in different countries, the feast of Ramadan, Hanukah, the Chinese New Year

Understanding ethnic food, music, or dance

## business and industry

Analyzing employee-owned companies

Bailouts of auto companies

Bar owners' responsibilities to their intoxicated customers

Cleaning up industrial pollution from major waterways

Change in the United States from an industrial to a service economy

Corporate scandals

Creative packaging for increased sales

Enforcing food-industry health standards

Government bailouts of Wall Street

Increasing the minimum wage

Rise, decline, and fall of the stock market

Making U.S. products more competitive with foreign goods

Maintaining business and industrial health and safety standards

Maintaining ethical practices in business

Manufacturing American goods in foreign "sweat shops"

Multitrillion-dollar national debt

Overcoming the groupthink mentality in large corporations

Positive and negative impact of labor unions on U.S. business

The profitability of legalized gambling

Rating airlines' service and safety

Reducing America's trade imbalance

Regulating the U.S. auto industry

Regulating the insurance industry after natural disasters

Regulating banks and mortgage companies

Subprime mortgage crisis

Women and minorities in management positions

## contemporary issues

Banning cigarette farming, production, and sales

Biological and chemical terrorism

Botox parties

Destructive nature of "designer drugs"

DNA testing, justice, and criminals

Effective prison rehabilitation programs

Eliminating street gangs

Eliminating inner city slums

Endangered species

"Going green"

Government bailouts of Wall Street

Government-supported day-care centers

Home testing kits for genetics, HIV, cancer

Improving relations among races

Investing portions of Social Security in stocks or bonds

Jury consulting as "legalized" jury tampering

Homeland security

Legality of car radar detectors

Mandating energy-efficient appliances and lighting

Most wanted criminals in the United States

The need for judicial reform

Police roadblocks as a deterrent to drunk driving

Preventing crime and violence in public schools

Red light cameras

Regulating auto insurance rates

Regulating health maintenance organizations

Reliability of child witnesses in sexual-abuse trials

Solutions to homelessness

Solutions to prison overcrowding

Stopping frivolous lawsuits

Universal health care

Victims' rights

## current events

Achieving energy independence

Airline regulation and safety since September 11

Airline ontime performance

Air passengers bill of rights

Apprehending: serial killers, child molesters, terrorists

Children sold into slavery and/or prostitution

The Brady Law: pro- and anti-gun legislation

Decline of the American dollar

Dominating role of the United States in world affairs

Detecting auto-sales fraud

Effectiveness or ineffectiveness of affirmative action

Eliminating the Internal Revenue Service

Eliminating nuclear weapons

Government effectiveness in responding to disasters

Hybrid, flex-fuel, hydrogen-fueled vehicles

Identity theft

Illegal immigration

Illegal tampering with foods and medicines

Iran and destabilization of Iraq

Legalized gay marriages

Mandating English as the national language

Middle East peace

Negotiating with American's enemies

Publishing ex-convicts' names and addresses in community newspapers

Repairing the interstate highway system

Raising vs. cutting taxes

Reducing the federal deficit and balancing the budget

Relevance or irrelevance of the vice-presidency

Selling organs for transplant

September 11: the Patriot Act, loss of freedoms, anthrax, smallpox, suitcase nuclear weapons, limits of American power, guns in airplane cockpits, limiting immigration, fighting terrorist nations

Skyrocketing price of gas

Success or failure of the president's economic program

Supreme Court decisions regarding: search and seizure, freedom of the press, freedom of expression, surrogate parenting, three strikes and you're out, Pledge of Allegiance, executive privilege, separation of church and state, affirmative action, lethal injections for capital punishment, illegal immigrants and social services, school prayer, cruel and unusual punishment, suing HMO insurance companies

Term limits for members of Congress

The "don't ask, don't tell policy" in the military

U.S. foreign policy (pro and con): aid to Russia, granting China favored-nation trade status, the United States as "the world's policeman," accepting immigrants from third-world countries, Iraq, Afghanistan, support of Israel, establishing a Palestinian state, outsourcing of U.S. companies to other countries for cheap labor, responsibility in feeding the world's hungry, responsibility for eliminating AIDS, free-trade agreements

Unemployment

Labor unions and auto companies

Violence on YouTube

Wasting tax money on beach replenishment

Welfare reform

Withdrawal of troops from Iraq and the Middle East

### education

Bullying in public schools

Cheerleading as a dangerous sport

Creative financing for a college education

Decline of the U.S. educational system

Defining and eliminating illiteracy

Differences between U.S. and Japanese educational systems

Eliminating the factory model of education

Eliminating same-sex public military education (such as the Citadel and Virginia Military Institute)

Eliminating sports programs vs. removing music, art, and dance curricula in public schools

Establishing tax vouchers for parents who choose to send their children to private schools

Future of fraternity and sorority systems

Internet degrees

"No child left behind" effectiveness

Public school issues (pro and con): mainstreaming students with special needs, mandating the learning of a foreign language, mandating year-around education, requiring high school students to perform community service

Performance stress among preschoolers

Prescriptive vs. non-prescriptive approaches to general education requirements for college

Privatization of public school systems

Reforming America's public schools

Sex education programs in public schools

Teaching "intelligent design" in public school science curricula

Teaching values in public schools

The effectiveness or ineffectiveness of home schooling

Impact of magnet schools on school districts

Television or the Internet as a positive or negative force in education

The harmful effects of fraternity hazing practices

The impact of budget-cutting on public schools

Understanding learning disabilities

Violence and security in America's schools

### family issues

Adoption: alternative methods, single parent, gay parent, adopting foreign children, buying and selling babies, bureaucratic difficulties, foster care, adoption scams, cross-racial adoptions, adoption rights of parents and children

Children abusing parents

Children divorcing parents or children suing parents

Children as murderers of peers or parents

Children's choice in choosing either of the divorced parents

Children and kidnapping by one parent

Coping with the sudden death of a family member

Donating the organs or tissues of deceased babies for transplants

Family problems: abuse, incest, alcoholism, dysfunctional family members, gay family members, sibling rivalry, in-laws, parent-child jealousy

Famous and infamous families

Effects of touch deprivation

Helping a family member with special needs

Having quintuplets

Making a will

No-fault divorce

Nursing homes, assisted living, or hospice care for family members

Parental responsibility for obese children

Parental responsibility for actions of underage children

Parents murdering children

Parents without partners

Positive and negative effects of a permissive upbringing

Pre-nuptial agreements

Preparing for a: family vacation, wedding, baby, birthday, anniversary, formal dinner party, funeral, bar mitzvah

Prison marriages

Psychological bonding of twins

Regulating the Internet to protect underage children

Removing driving privileges from an aging family member

Runaway children

"Tough-love" programs

Unusual wedding ceremonies

The "v" chip as an effective or ineffective device for controlling the TV viewing habits of children

## health

Advances in artificial-limb technology

Advantages, dangers, and disadvantages of cosmetic surgery

The benefits and risks of alternative medicine

Choosing a competent doctor or specialist

Comparative quality of health care in the United States

Cosmetic surgery

Cross-species organ transplants

Curing: Alzheimers, autism, infertility, cancer, diabetes, glaucoma, AIDS, multiple sclerosis, muscular dystrophy, heart disease, Gulf War syndrome, spinal cord injury

Detecting and prosecuting incompetent health practitioners

Doctors who make house calls

Doctors' perspectives on universal health insurance

Mandating HP vaccine to teenagers

The effectiveness and efficiency of Medicare

Effectiveness of transplant procedures

Excessive exercise

Family therapy as a treatment for abuse or other problems

Health insurance for pets

Home testing for HIV, genetics, cancer

Improper diets

In-home hospice care

Limiting financial awards for malpractice

Low-cholesterol cooking

Malpractice insurance costs

Medical insurance coverage for birth control and male impotence drugs

New treatments for mental illness

National crisis of nurse shortages

Programs to reduce prescription drug costs

Pro or con: regulating caps on doctor and hospital fees

Research using aborted fetal tissue

Risky medical procedures

Stem cell research

Tips for choosing a veterinarian

Tissue regeneration

Transsexual surgery

Treatments for sexual dysfunctions

## careers and occupations

Becoming: a jockey, a TV game show host, a casino manager, an Alaskan crab boat captain, a stand-up comic, an auctioneer, a roller-coaster designer, an air traffic controller, a navy radar specialist, a bombardier, a day-care supervisor, a lawyer, a sculptor, a weapons designer or manufacturer

Coaching a football team

Creating cartoons

Constructing neon signs

Jobs generated by the high-technology revolution

Making movies

Managing stocks and bonds

Protecting the Alaskan wilderness

SCUBA diving for fun, work, or national security

The history of: skywriting, pro bowling, chimney sweeping, jousting, polo, windsurfing, the Olympics, bungee-jumping, tennis, submarines

Unusual careers for women and men

Weather forecasting

Working as a park warden in Hawaii's Volcano National Park

## personal experience

Becoming a(n): chef, skydiver, gymnast, cruise director, clogger, bagpiper, parasailing expert, actress, ballet dancer, female impersonator, explorer of sunken ships, mountain climber, test pilot, circus-animal trainer, woman priest, zookeeper

Forgettable and unforgettable characters

Surviving: isolation, loneliness, death of a loved one, illness, hunger, poverty, children, parents, addiction, crime, Nazi death camps, divorce, the military, stress, mothers-in-law, the family vacation, college, the wilderness, rafting, terrorist attacks

## people

Famous: felons, presidents, scientists, inventors, doctors, lawyers, actors, musicians, artists, athletes, politicians, revolutionaries, journalists, activists, celebrities, religious figures, business people, engineers, Nobel Prize winners, Pulitzer Prize winners.

## science and technology

Availability of alternative low-cost fuels

Availability of alternative fueling stations in the U.S.

Bluetooth technology

Carbon dating

Cyber bullying

Development of space exploration plans

Driverless cars

Electric-powered vehicles

Flex-fuel vehicles

Gene manipulation and selection

Impact of fiber-optic technology on the consumer

How radio telescopes help astronomers

High-definition television

Human cloning

Hydroponic gardening as a solution to world hunger

Hydrogen-powered vehicles

Laser technology in medical science

NASA's space plane

New computer and micro-computer technologies

Positive and negative impacts of robotics

The possibility of cryogenics

Possibility of developing "designer" genes

Potential benefits from superconductor technology

Recent Mars exploration

Reclaiming oceans for human habitation

Status of research into fusion

Undersea exploration and colonization

Understanding the patterns of individual biorhythms

U.S. plans for a space station

Wind farms to manufacture energy

# index